Against Epistemic Apartheid

Against Epistemic Apartheid

W. E. B. Du Bois and the Disciplinary Decadence of Sociology

Reiland Rabaka

LEXINGTON BOOKS
A division of
ROWMAN & LITTLEFIELD PUBLISHERS, INC.
Lanham • Boulder • New York • Toronto • Plymouth, UK

Published by Lexington Books
A division of Rowman & Littlefield Publishers, Inc.
A wholly owned subsidiary of The Rowman & Littlefield Publishing Group, Inc.
4501 Forbes Boulevard, Suite 200, Lanham, Maryland 20706
http://www.lexingtonbooks.com

Estover Road, Plymouth PL6 7PY, United Kingdom

Copyright © 2010 by Lexington Books

All rights reserved. No part of this book may be reproduced in any form or by any electronic or mechanical means, including information storage and retrieval systems, without written permission from the publisher, except by a reviewer who may quote passages in a review.

British Library Cataloguing in Publication Information Available

Library of Congress Cataloging-in-Publication Data
Rabaka, Reiland, 1972–
  Against epistemic apartheid : W. E. B. Du Bois and the disciplinary decadence of sociology / Reiland Rabaka.
    p. cm.
  Includes bibliographical references and index.
  ISBN 978-0-7391-4597-5 (cloth : alk. paper) — ISBN 978-0-7391-4598-2 (pbk. : alk. paper) — ISBN 978-0-7391-4599-9 (electronic)
  1. Du Bois, W. E. B. (William Edward Burghardt), 1868–1963—Political and social views. 2. Sociology—Philosophy. 3. Sociology—United States—History. 4. Sociology—Political aspects—United States—History. 5. Degeneration—Social aspects—United States—History. 6. African Americans—Intellectual life. 7. African Americans—Segregation—History. 8. United States—Intellectual life—1865–1918. 9. United States—Race relations—History—19th century. 10. United States—Race relations—History—20th century. I. Title.
  E185.97.D73R322 2010
  303.48'4092—dc22   2010001799

∞™ The paper used in this publication meets the minimum requirements of American National Standard for Information Sciences—Permanence of Paper for Printed Library Materials, ANSI/NISO Z39.48-1992.

Printed in the United States of America

For my intellectual ancestor

W. E. B. Du Bois

For my mentors and intellectual elders

Lucius T. Outlaw Jr.
William M. King
Lewis R. Gordon

*And, as with all of my work,
for my mother, grandmothers, and great-aunt*

Marilyn Jean Giles
Lizzie Mae Davis
Elva Rita Warren
Arcressia Charlene Connor

Nkosi Sikelel' iAfrika

Contents

Acknowledgments	ix
INTRODUCTION On the Beginning(s) of Epistemic Apartheid: Du Bois, Intellectual Segregation, Conceptual Incarceration, and the Disciplinary Decadence of Sociology	1
1 Du Bois and the Early Development of Urban and Rural Sociology: *The Philadelphia Negro* and the Sociology of the Souls of Black Farming Folk	47
2 Du Bois and the Sociology of Race: The Sociology of the Souls of Black and White (Among Other) Folk	107
3 Du Bois and the Sociology of Gender: "The Damnation of Women," "The Freedom of Womanhood," and the Insurgent Intersectional Sociology of the Souls of Black (Among Other) Female Folk	175
4 Du Bois and the Sociology of Religion: The Sociology of the Souls of Religious Black (Among Other) Folk	223
5 Du Bois and the Sociology of Education: Critiquing the (Mis)Education of Black (Among Other) Folk	265
6 Du Bois and the Sociology of Crime: Critiquing the Criminalization of Black (Among Other) Folk	293

CONCLUSION On Ending Epistemic Apartheid: Continuing Du Bois's Transdisciplinary Transgressions	337
Bibliography	363
Index	407
About the Author	423

Acknowledgments

Against Epistemic Apartheid is not simply an intellectual exercise concerned with W. E. B. Du Bois's long-overlooked contributions to sociology. Much more, it also stands as a testament to what the many people who have contributed to my personal, professional, and radical political development have taught me. W. E. B. Du Bois, as I will repeat throughout the text, represents an intellectual-activist ancestor who provides me with several paradigms and points of departure to explore Africana studies' contributions to the deconstruction and reconstruction of both sociology and critical social theory. Although his thought and texts provide the primary points of departure here, the theories and praxes of many, many others have influenced and informed my conceptions of radical politics and critical social theory. Each chapter of this book bears the imprint of the diverse—although often disconnected—intellectual and political arenas and agendas I draw from and endeavor to establish critical dialogue with. As a consequence, the list of intellectuals, activists, archivists, institutions, and organizations to which I am indebted is, indeed, enormous. Such being the case, I hope I may be forgiven for deciding that the most appropriate way in which to acknowledge my sincere appreciation is simply to list them below without the protracted praise each has so solemnly earned. My deepest gratitude and most heartfelt *asante sana* (a thousand thanks) is offered, first and foremost, to my family: my mother, Marilyn Giles; my grandmothers, Lizzie Mae Davis (deceased) and Elva Rita Warren; my great-aunt, Arcressia Charlene Connor; my older brother and his wife, Robert Smith II and Karen Smith; my younger brother, Dwight Clewis; my nieces and nephews, Journée Clewis, Dominique Clewis, Kalyn Smith, Robert Smith III, Ryan Smith, and Remington Smith; my father, Robert Smith I; my grandfathers, Joseph Warren (deceased) and Jafari Jakuta Rabaka (deceased); and my innumerable aunts, uncles, and cousins throughout the Americas, the Caribbean, and Africa.

An undertaking as ambitious as *Against Epistemic Apartheid* would have been impossible without the assistance of colleagues and comrades, both far and wide. I express my earnest appreciation to the following fine folk, who each in their own special way contributed to the composition and completion of this book: Arthur McFarlane, W. E. B. Du Bois's great-grandson; Mireille Fanon Mendès-France, Frantz Fanon's daughter; Rhonda Tankerson; Lamya Al-Kharusi; Sara Bloom; Denise Lovett; Adam Clark; Elzie Billops; Sigmund Washington; Patrick DeWalt; Awon Atuire; Stacey Smith; Kimberly Marshall; Toroitich Chereno; De Reef Jamison; Anthony Lemelle; Troy Barnes; Zachary Epps; Ursula Lindqvist; Tiya Trent; La'Neice Littleton; Paget Henry; Deward Walker; Janette Klingner; Margaret LeCompte; James McGoodwin; Alan Sica; Vincent Harding; George Junne; Mpozi Tolbert (deceased); the National Association for Ethnic Studies (NAES); and the Association for the Study of African American Life and History (ASALH).

I cannot adequately convey the depth of my gratitude to the National Council for Black Studies (NCBS) for providing me with the critical feedback and fora to deepen and develop my relationship with W. E. B. Du Bois and the Africana tradition of critical theory. I have been presenting my research on Africana critical theory at NCBS's annual conferences for more than a decade. Along with saying *nashukuru sana* (very special thanks) to NCBS in general, I would be remiss not to single out several members whose key contributions and intellectual encouragement have made the present volume possible. I express my earnest appreciation to the following NCBS colleagues and comrades: Molefi Asante; Maulana Karenga; James Turner; Delores Aldridge; James Stewart; Martell Teasley; Ronald Stephens; James Conyers; Charles Jones; Sundiata Cha-Jua; Perry Hall; Shirley Weber; Barbara Wheeler; Alfred Young; Bill Little (deceased); Munasha Furusa; Akinyele Umoja; Fred Hord; Terry Kershaw; Jeffrey Ogbar; Scot Brown; Alan Colon; Abdul Nanji; Christel Temple; Patricia Reid-Merritt; Kevin Cokley; Salim Faraji; Cecil Gray; Ricky Jones; and Mark Christian.

The faculty, staff, and students in the Department of Ethnic Studies and the Center for Studies of Ethnicity and Race in America (CSERA) at the University of Colorado at Boulder deserve special thanks for their patience and critical support. *Nashukuru sana* to our steadfast staff, especially Sandra Lane, Jillian Mariani, and Tiya Trent, for always being there and lending a struggling brother a helping hand. I am also deeply indebted to my colleagues and comrades who selflessly serve on the faculty in the Department of Ethnic Studies, each of whom have patiently listened to me rant and rave about Du Bois's "sociological negation" over the last couple of years. I say *nashukuru sana*, therefore, to William King, Deward Walker, Elisa Facio, Daryl Maeda, Seema Sohi, Emma Perez, Arturo Aldama, Danika Medak-

Saltzman, Doreen Martinez, Bianca Williams, Stewart Lawler, and Vivian Delgado. Likewise, I express my gratitude to the National Science Foundation (NSF) and the Leadership Education for Advancement and Promotion (LEAP) Program in the Office of Faculty Affairs at University of Colorado at Boulder for providing me with much-needed research funds which facilitated the composition and completion of this book.

Over the last decade several libraries, research centers, special collections, and archives hosted and helped me transform this book from an inchoate idea into its fully realized form. I am indelibly indebted to the directors, research fellows, and staffs of the W. E. B. Du Bois Memorial Center for Pan-African Culture, Accra, Ghana; Africana Rare Books Room, Balme Library, University of Ghana, Legon; George Padmore Institute, London; Center for Ethnic Minority Studies, School of Oriental and African Studies, University of London; W. E. B. Du Bois Papers, Department of Special Collections and University Archives, W. E. B. Du Bois Library, University of Massachusetts at Amherst; W. E. B. Du Bois Department of African American Studies, University of Massachusetts at Amherst; W. E. B. Du Bois Institute for African and African American Research, Harvard University; Arthur A. Houghton Jr. Library, Harvard University; W. E. B. Du Bois Collection, Beinecke Rare Book and Manuscript Library, Yale University Library, Yale University; Schomburg Center for Research in Black Culture, New York Public Library; Nicholas Murray Butler Library, Columbia University; John Henrik Clarke Africana Library, Africana Studies and Research Center, Cornell University; Charles L. Blockson African American Collection, Temple University; Center for African American History and Culture, Temple University; Center for Africana Studies, University of Pennsylvania; Moorland-Spingarn Research Center, Howard University; John Hope Franklin Collection for African and African American Documentation, Rare Book, Manuscript, and Special Collections Library, Duke University; Carter G. Woodson Center for African American and African Studies, University of Virginia, Robert W. Woodruff Library, Atlanta University Center Archives; Manuscript Sources for African American History, Special Collections, Emory University; W. E. B. Du Bois Collection, Fisk University Library, Fisk University; Center for African and African American Studies, University of Texas at Austin; Center for African American Studies, University of Houston; African and African American Collection, University Library, University of California, Berkeley; Ralph J. Bunche Center for African American Studies, University of California, Los Angeles; Blair-Caldwell African American Research Library, Denver Public Library; Center for African American Policy, University of Denver; and African American Materials, Special Collections, Norlin Library, University of Colorado at Boulder.

Several publishers, estates, and archives graciously granted permission to use extended excerpts of various authors' work. My publisher and I would like to thank and openly acknowledge the curator, Danielle Kovacs, and the staff of the W. E. B. Du Bois Papers, Department of Special Collections and University Archives, W. E. B. Du Bois Library, University of Massachusetts at Amherst, who granted permission to use the cover photograph of W. E. B. Du Bois; International Publishers, who granted permission to reproduce copyrighted material from W. E. B. Du Bois's *The Autobiography of W. E. B. Du Bois: A Soliloquy on Viewing My Life from the Last Decade of Its First Century* (New York: International Publishers, 1968); and Henry Holt and Company, who granted permission to reproduce copyrighted material from David Levering Lewis's *W. E. B. Du Bois: Biography of a Race, 1868–1919* (New York: Henry Holt, 1993). I would also like to say *asante sana* to Sara Bloom for typing the bulk of the sprawling bibliography I compiled for *Against Epistemic Apartheid*. Her compassion, commitment to social justice, and solid support has been a very special source of inspiration for me during the research and writing of this book. It would not be too much to say that she served as a sort of sociological sounding board for me during the research and writing of *Against Epistemic Apartheid*.

Special mention must be made of the many aesthetic ancestors and elders whose lifework and legacies motivated me during the research and writing of this book. I began my collegiate years heeding the beckoning call of jazz. I was indefatigably determined to become a jazz drummer, following in the footsteps of Ed Blackwell, Art Blakey, Roy Brooks, Joe Chambers, Kenny Clarke, Jimmy Cobb, Alan Dawson, Jack DeJohnette, Ben Dixon, Al Foster, Al Harewood, Jabali Billy Hart, Louis Hayes, Roy Haynes, Albert Heath, Billy Higgins, Elvin Jones, Philly Joe Jones, Pete La Roca, Victor Lewis, Idris Muhammad, Dannie Richmond, Ben Riley, Max Roach, Mickey Roker, Art Taylor, Tony Williams, and so forth—perhaps my passion for the polyrhythmic jazz drumming tradition is palpable. Along with the work of jazz drummers from several different genres (e.g., big band, be-bop, hard bop, post-bop, modal, Afro-Cuban, and Latin jazz), the music of free, avant-garde, and modern creative jazz artists served as the soundtrack for *Against Epistemic Apartheid*. During the countless hours of research travel, reading, and writing, I was most especially inspired by the innovative music of the following: Muhal Richard Abrams; George Adams; the Art Ensemble of Chicago; the Association for the Advancement of Creative Musicians (AACM); Air; Geri Allen; Albert Ayler; Billy Bang; Bobby Bradford; Anthony Braxton; Ari Brown; Marion Brown; Jaki Byard; Don Byron; Roy Campbell; John Carter; James Carter; Don Cherry; Ornette Coleman; Steve Coleman; Alice Coltrane; John Coltrane; Olu Dara; Anthony Davis; Ernest Kabeer Dawkins; Bill Dixon; Eric Dolphy; Booker Ervin; Von Freeman; Charles Gayle; John Handy; Billy Harper; Andrew Hill; D. D. Jackson; Leroy Jenkins; Rahsaan Roland Kirk; Prince Lasha; Yusef Lateef; George Lewis; the Liberation Music Orchestra; Charles Lloyd; Joe Lovano; Frank Lowe; Jimmy Lyons; the

M-Base Collective; Makanda Ken McIntyre; Charles Mingus; Grachan Moncur III; Jason Moran; David Murray; Amina Claudine Myers; Herbie Nichols; Greg Osby; William Parker; Don Pullen; Sun Ra; Dewey Redman; Sam Rivers; Sonny Rollins; Pharaoh Sanders; Woody Shaw; Archie Shepp; Matthew Shipp; Sonny Simmons; Wadada Leo Smith; Horace Tapscott; Cecil Taylor; John Tchicai; Malachi Thompson; Henry Threadgill; David S. Ware; Edward Wilkerson; the World Saxophone Quartet; Larry Young; and Kahil El'Zabar. Each of these musicians or groups has incomparably contributed to the composition and completion of this book. Although I no longer perform professionally as a jazz musician, several interpreters and, on occasion, even some of the critics of my scholarship have noted a jostling "jazz aesthetic" at the heart of my work. Therefore, as with my previous books, my conscience compels me to acknowledge not only my intellectual influences and sources of inspiration, but my spiritual-musical ones as well. In the most heartfelt and humble way I say *asante sana* to each of the musical prophets mentioned above.

My editor, Michael Sisskin, and the Lexington Books editorial board deserve very special thanks (*nashukuru sana*) for seeing the potential in this book project and prodding me along during the many months it took me to revise the manuscript and prepare it for production. Michael's keen eye and constructive criticisms of the manuscript have certainly helped me to compose what I have come to think of as my most accessible book to date. I would like to formally thank Michael and my publisher Julie Kirsch for the promptness and professionalism with which they have handled my book projects, and for their patience with my extremely erratic (if not a bit eccentric) research and writing regimen, which in this instance took me to dozens of university and public libraries, archives, and research centers in Africa, Europe, and the United States. I am not by any means the easiest person to correspond with when I am working, but throughout the entire research and writing process they have calmly fielded my inquiries and coolly encouraged me to complete my book.

This book is offered as an emblem of my deep and abiding intellectual admiration for Lucius Outlaw, William King, and Lewis Gordon. During my graduate school days Professor Outlaw exposed me to Africana philosophy and methodically guided me through a wide range of philosophy of race, philosophy of culture, social and political philosophy, Marxism, critical theory, and hermeneutics. It was our weekly meetings and his extremely constructive criticisms of several drafts of my doctoral dissertation that led me to the archaeology of the Africana tradition of critical theory. It was also Professor Outlaw who, more than any of my other graduate school professors, encouraged me to develop my own distinct and decidedly dialectical relationship with W. E. B. Du Bois's insurgent intellectual and radical political legacies. In so many ways he served as a sort of methodological "midwife," helping me to conceptually conceive Africana critical theory and constantly encouraging me to go above and beyond monodisciplinary musings on Du Bois in particular, and Africana studies in general.

Working with Professor William King enabled me to deepen and further develop my relationship with Du Bois's interdisciplinary social scientific legacy. King's encyclopedic knowledge of African American contributions to social science, historical sociology, political sociology, sociology of race, and sociology of knowledge helped to add a deeper, more profoundly social scientific dimension to my articulation of Africana critical theory. He repeatedly reminded me that W. E. B. Du Bois's conception of "black studies" was grounded in both the social sciences and the humanities, and that the growing tendency among contemporary Africana studies scholars to narrowly focus on either the social sciences or the humanities is actually antithetical to the initial mission and message of, first, "black studies," then "African American studies," and now "Africana studies" (i.e., comparative continental and diasporan African studies). King's criticisms ultimately led me to more explicitly emphasize and articulate the need for increased intellectual openness, interdisciplinarity, and intersectionality within the twenty-first-century world of Africana studies in particular, and the academy in general. It is on this basis that I have built many of my more recent ideas surrounding Africana studies as a trenchant transdisciplinary human science.

Lastly, Professor Lewis Gordon has consistently encouraged me to not simply build on but earnestly attempt to go beyond Du Bois's (and Fanon's) interdisciplinary legacy. He was an early advocate of my articulation of Africana critical theory, and over the years unequivocally urged me to continue my archaeology of the Africana tradition of critical theory. His emphasis on the existential-phenomenological aspects of Africana philosophy provided me with both a paradigm and point of departure with which to document and discursively develop the Africana tradition of critical theory. Moreover, Gordon's philosophy of the human sciences has indelibly informed my conception of Africana critical theory in general, and epistemic apartheid in particular. As will be witnessed, in this book's introduction I openly acknowledge epistemic apartheid as an intellectual offshoot of Gordon's conception of "disciplinary decadence."

Where Outlaw's articulation of Africana philosophy enabled me to discursively develop Africana critical theory, Gordon's conception of disciplinary decadence allowed me to extend and expand my discursive domain beyond the intellectual arena of Africana studies and create a critical dialogue with the social sciences in general, and sociology in particular. Furthermore, King grounded me in both the history of sociology and historical sociology, adding a decidedly deeper, more historical and social scientific dimension to my articulation of Africana critical theory. Taken together, then, Outlaw,

King, and Gordon's collective contributions to Africana critical theory have helped me deconstruct and reconstruct both Du Bois's sociology and my own insurgent intersectional sociology and critical social theory. Therefore, I find it only fitting to solemnly dedicate this book to them and to the collegiality and camaraderie they have generously offered me over the years. This book, I solemnly say, is as much theirs' as it is mine.

If, then, my gentle readers, any inspiration or insights are gathered from my journey through the jungles of critical social theory and the haunted history of sociology, I pray you will attribute them to each of the aforementioned. However, if (and when) you find foibles and intellectual idiosyncrasies, I humbly hope you will associate them with neither any of the forenamed nor, most especially, W. E. B. Du Bois. I, and I alone, am responsible for what herein is written. As is my custom, then, I begin by softly saying, almost silently singing my earnest and eternal prayer: *Nkosi Sikelel' iAfrika*.

Reiland Rabaka
W. E. B. Du Bois Memorial Center for Pan-African Culture, Accra, Ghana
W. E. B. Du Bois Library, University of Massachusetts at Amherst
W. E. B. Du Bois Collection, Beinecke Rare Book and Manuscript Library, Yale University
W. E. B. Du Bois Collection, Fisk University Library
W. E. B. Du Bois Collection, Robert W. Woodruff Library, Atlanta University Center

Introduction

On the Beginning(s) of Epistemic Apartheid

Du Bois, Intellectual Segregation, Conceptual Incarceration, and the Disciplinary Decadence of Sociology

> The Present condition of sociological study is peculiar and in many respects critical. Amid a multitude of interesting facts and conditions we are groping after a science—after reliable methods of observation and measurement, and after some enlightening way of systematizing and arranging the mass of accumulated material. Moreover, the very immensity of the task gives us pause. What after all are we trying to do but make a science of human action? And yet such a task seems so preposterous that there is scarce a sociologist the world over that would acknowledge such a plan. Rather, turning from so startling a task, they have assured the world that their object is to study a certain metaphysical entity called "society"—and when they have been asked earnestly and rather insistently just what society is, they have replied in language at once curious, mystical and at times contradictory. Has not the time come however when we should face our problem? In reality we seek to know how much of natural law there is in human conduct. Sociology is the science that seeks to measure the limits of chance in human action, or if you will excuse the paradox, it is the science of free will.
>
> W. E. B. Du Bois, "The Atlanta Conferences," 85

INTRODUCTION: ON DU BOIS, HORROR IN, AND THE HAUNTING OF THE HISTORY OF SOCIOLOGY

A storm has been brewing, boldly building since the first hallowed history of sociology was written. As the first history of anything may be forgiven for omissions and elisions, yet and still it is extremely important to create critical inventories and thoroughly interrogate *what was included* versus *what was excluded* in the first history or, rather, the first series of histories of the phenomenon in question. What is more, if the phenomenon in question eventually comes to pretentiously pride itself on its liberalism, scientism and objectivism, but in reality actually historically and currently continues to violate all but the most racist and sexist versions of liberalism, scientism and objectivism, then credence is given to those who would or those who, in fact, have constructively critiqued the falseness of the phenomenon in question. Truth be told, such is the sad story of the disciplinary development of sociology or, rather, the haunted history of sociology.

To say that sociology has a long and shameful history of excluding women and nonwhites' (which, of course, includes nonwhite women's) contributions from its developmental or intellectual history is, quite simply, to say nothing that has not already been repeatedly said time and time again (Blackwell and Janowitz, 1974; Hare, 2002; Ladner, 1998; Lengermann and Niebrugge-Brantley, 1998; Washington and Cunnigen, 2002). However, what *Against Epistemic Apartheid: W. E. B. Du Bois and the Disciplinary Decadence of Sociology* offers that is wholly innovative and distinctive is that it brings new and intensive archival research into critical dialogue with the watershed work of classical and contemporary, male and female, black and white, national and international sociologists and social theorists' Du Bois studies. Moreover, what is even more distinctive is that it does all of this under the interpretive auspices of *Africana critical theory* with the express intent of creating critical inventories and thoroughly interrogating *what has been included* and *what has been excluded* when and where we come to W. E. B. Du Bois's contributions to the discipline of sociology.[1] It could be easily argued, echoing the sociological Du Bois studies of the past, that he has yet to receive the due recognition he deserves for his innovative and awe-inspiring contributions to sociology in general, and American sociology in particular.

For instance, I am inclined to utterly agree with Dan Green and Edwin Driver (1976) in "W. E. B. Du Bois: A Case in the Sociology of Sociological Negation" when they sternly stated: "The sociology of W. E. B. Du Bois stands out as a prophetic and progressive conception of sociology. Ironically, his viewpoint is, with few exceptions, now mainstream as contrasted with the era in which he was writing when he stood on the periphery of the discipline" (319). Furthermore, they quickly continued: "Important and valuable as his contributions may be, historically or currently, Du Bois has not been accorded by early or later white sociologists one iota of the respect and recognition that he deserves. His continuous neglect by the sociological fraternity (hereafter meaning white sociologists only) constitutes an interesting and perhaps instructive datum for the 'sociology of sociology'" (320). Again, I could not agree with Green and Driver more when they characterized Du Bois's ragged relationship with the "sociological fraternity"—moreover, "meaning white sociologists only" they candidly contended—as one fraught with a series of "sociological negation[s]." It is absolutely amazing that almost thirty-five years after Green and Driver bellowed about Du Bois's despicable "sociological negation," he still "has not been accorded . . . one iota of the respect and recognition that he deserves." In fact, it seems almost safe to say that the lone constant concerning Du Bois's sociological legacy has been its incessant and insidious omission from, or, at best, its dogged distortion in the history of sociology. Green and Driver critically and cogently presented a "case" (i.e., as in their subtitle, "A Case in the Sociology of Sociological Negation") that seems to have fallen, decade after decade, on deaf ears:

> Du Bois rightly deserves a place among the giants of sociology during the era 1896–1914 when he made most of his substantial, direct contributions to the sociological enterprise. He established at Atlanta University one of the first departments of sociology in the United States, created the first Laboratory of Sociology, instituted a program of systematic research, founded two journals (*Crisis* and *Phylon: A Review of Race and Culture*), attempted to organize a sociological society in 1897, or eight years before the American Sociological Society developed out of the American Economic Association, and he established a record of valuable publications which has rarely ever been equaled by sociologists. His study of *The Philadelphia Negro* was probably the first sociological research replicated when Howard Odum did a similar study in Philadelphia about two decades later. Atlanta University over the years became the site where such renowned sociologists as E. Franklin Frazier (the first . . . black president of ASA), Ira De [Augustine] Reid, Mozell Hill, and others could find employment in the early years of their sociological careers. (319; see also Key, 1978)

Against Epistemic Apartheid will hopefully indicate that I have not only *heard*, but intend to humbly *heed* Green and Driver's intellectual history-making observations with respect to Du Bois's sociologically negated seminal sociological discourse. The irony, of course, at the heart of his sociological negation is that Du Bois, as Earl Wright (2002a, 2002b, 2002c, 2005, 2008) has astutely asserted, arguably established the "first American school of sociology." Phil Zuckerman (2004) corroborates this claim with his contention that "years before the famous studies of the Chicago School, Du Bois's sociological output was characterized by a hands-on, empirical research methodology to a much greater and more respectable degree than that of his more famous contemporaries" (6). What is more, Zuckerman observed, Du Bois's "courses in sociology at Atlanta University were among the earliest offered in the United States" (6). It is, perhaps, a little more than ironic then that Du Bois's contributions historically have been and currently continue to be excluded from, or distorted when and where they are included in the history of sociology. Zuckerman's weighted words, once again, find their way into the fray when he critically comments on the processes of canonization, relating that they "invariably reflect political relations, racial fissures, class differences, national hierarchies, gender biases, and a host of other related imbalances of power, authority, and access to the means of scholarly production, distribution, and recognition" (2).

With regard to the innumerable issues beyond those of racism, sexism, and classism at the heart of the process(es) of canonization, and speaking directly of the "host of other related imbalances of power, authority, and access to the means of scholarly production, distribution, and recognition" involved in the process(es) of canonization, renowned Du Bois scholar Elliott Rudwick (1974) reported:

> Sociological theory on race prevalent before World War I generally stressed the biological superiority of the white race and the "primitiveness" of the "inferior" black's "racial temperament," which predisposed him toward "shiftlessness and sensuality," rendering him basically unassimilable. . . . The Chicago School of urban sociology that began about the time of World War I did not consider Du Bois's work significant, even though its leader, Robert Park, was deeply interested in the study of race relations. . . . But in the United States of the early twentieth century, white sociologists were not likely to recognize the contribution made by a study of the black community [i.e., *The Philadelphia Negro*]. . . . Thus, ironically, Du Bois, who by training and research orientation toward both empiricism and reform was part of the mainstream of American sociology as it evolved at the turn of the century, found himself relegated to the periphery of his profession. (48–49; see also Marshall, 1994)

In "The 'Philadelphia Negro' Then and Now," the critically acclaimed sociologist and Africana Studies scholar Tufuku Zuberi corroborates Rudwick's above assertions by simultaneously critiquing his (i.e., Zuberi's) alma mater (i.e., the University of Chicago) and his current intellectual headquarters (i.e., the University of Pennsylvania) when he discusses the myriad ways in which the Chicago School, the Department of Sociology at the University of Pennsylvania, and white "academic sociologists" in general ignored Du Bois's inauguration of, and contributions to, empirical sociology in the United States. Zuberi (1998) revealingly wrote:

> Unfortunately, Du Bois's model of investigation was not appreciated by scholars in the field of sociology, particularly those at the University of Chicago who, as the "Chicago School," came to dominate urban sociology. *The Philadelphia Negro* received glowing reviews in the popular press and from liberal historians, but it was ignored by academic sociologists. The prestigious *America Journal of Sociology* did not even bother to review the book. Furthermore, Du Bois was never offered a professional appointment in a major "mainstream" university department, including the sociology department at the University

of Pennsylvania, which had grudgingly extended him the title of "assistant in sociology" for the duration of his study of the Seventh Ward [i.e., *The Philadelphia Negro*].

Decades before the Chicago School of Sociology rose to prominence, Du Bois had shown the uniqueness of the African experience in the United States generally and in the urban setting in particular. He described the illogical nature and historic impact of racism, and argued in an eloquent voice that it was a mistake to consider the problems of the African American population as parallel to those of European immigrants. However, these insights were in large part ignored by European American sociologists. (183)

Openly and honestly, then, it needs to be admitted that neither the sociological canon nor the histories of sociology are neutral, purely "objective" affairs of academicians who observe social phenomena and/or disciplinary development in some sort of social-political-historical-cultural-racial-sexual vacuum. One would think that I need not write this, and certainly not in a volume aimed at sociologists, but the roguish reality, the horrid history of sociology's intellectual exclusions and erasures, especially with respect to W. E. B. Du Bois's legacy, on principle, leaves me no other recourse. Even more intellectually irritating is the fact that as late as the dawn of the twenty-first century, undergraduate and graduate students, almost as a rule, are granted degrees in sociology in the United States of America and not only do the majority of them not read a single word Du Bois wrote but, even more maliciously, they never even hear his name "mentioned in any" of their "sociology classes" (Zuckerman, 2004, 3, 12). *Against Epistemic Apartheid*, then, is in part a critique of, and in part a complementary corrective for the longstanding and nefarious negation of Du Bois's sociological legacy.

There has long been a growing discussion concerning the gross intellectual injustice of Du Bois's sociological negation, especially with respect to the disciplinary development and professionalization of sociology in the United States. However, there is only so long Du Bois scholars, sociologically oriented or otherwise, can continue to hem and haw about the ways in which he has been ignored, excluded, and erased by the "white sociological fraternity" (Green and Driver, 1976, 319). Believe me, I also bemoan and sing a sorrow song, a bitter blues about Du Bois's fate at the hands of the "white sociological fraternity," but there is another part of me, a part that humbly acknowledges him as an intellectual ancestor, which knows that he would want contemporary Du Bois scholars, especially critical sociologists, to move beyond their meditations on his sociological negation and make concrete contributions, not simply to sociology but to the radical democratic transformation of our respective societies and the wider world. This book then, in addition, serves as a kind of caveat: one which simultaneously warns against *epistemic apartheid* (to be defined and discussed in detail below) and also excessive deconstructive criticism without reconstructive correctives or, at the least, without the offering of reconstructive alternatives.

In essence, what we have here is a dialectical deconstruction and reconstruction of sociology; in other words, a *critical sociology of sociology*, if you will. However, and not wanting to appear too intellectually audacious, in the critical spirit of W. E. B. Du Bois my conscience compels me to honestly and openly admit that *Against Epistemic Apartheid* is also intended as a critique of what has come to be called "Du Bois studies." Where one is wont to rail against Du Bois's sociological negation in the history of sociology, it should also be borne in mind that he was, in fact, a *transdisciplinary critical social theorist*, one whose work is not easily situated in the nice and neat conceptions and categories of classical or contemporary sociology, or any other discipline, to strike while the iron is hot. In order to seriously grasp and grapple with my contention that Du Bois was, in fact, a *transdisciplinary critical social theorist*, it will be necessary for us to briefly revisit his innovative intellectual biography, where the real roots of his transdisciplinary critical social theory can be said to lie.

MONETARY POVERTY, ALBEIT INTELLECTUALLY WEALTHY: ON DU BOIS'S INTELLECTUAL BIOGRAPHY AND LATE NINETEENTH-CENTURY TRANSDISCIPLINARY UNDERGRADUATE AND GRADUATE TRAINING

William Edward Burghardt Du Bois (pronounced "Due-Boyss") was born five years after the Emancipation Proclamation on 23 February 1868, in Great Barrington, Massachusetts, a tiny mill town in the Berkshire Mountains. The few African Americans in the area worked as domestics in homes or servants at summer resorts, while the Irish, German, and Czech Catholics worked in the town's factories. Du Bois was raised solely by his mother, as his delinquent father went absent before his toddling son turned two years old. His mother was a domestic and washerwoman, and supported her precocious son through other odd jobs and outright charity from the well-to-do white town residents. Du Bois's father's absence greatly affected him, although perhaps not as much as his mother's paralytic stroke, which his biographer David Levering Lewis (1993) reports "impaired her left leg or arm, or both" (29). Du Bois's early life, Lewis laments, was "a milieu circumscribed by immiseration, dementia, and deformity" (29). As with so many black children born in the shameful shadow of American slavery, he grew up very poor and, consequently, developed a consciousness of his lower-class status before he was aware of his race and American racism, even though he was the only black child in his all-white school. It was not long, however, before race and racism unforgivingly entered his life, and from his first unforgettable and life-altering experience of anti-black racism he defiantly decided to "prove to the world that Negroes were just like other people" (Du Bois, 1972b, 5; see also Lewis, 1993, 32–34; Horne, 2009, 1–16; Marable, 1986, 5–8).

Where Du Bois was excited and excelled in the classroom, he and his mother struggled financially to make ends meet. School was the one place he did not feel the burden and bondage of poverty, and his grades reflected his sense of freedom. In fact, his high school principal, Frank Alvin Hosmer, thought enough of Du Bois's intellectual aptitude to ask one of the wealthy women of Great Barrington to buy the boy's much-needed textbooks. When Du Bois was torn between quitting school and getting a steady job to support himself and his ailing mother, who "frequently . . . suffered from [bouts of] severe depression," according to Manning Marable (1986), Du Bois's mother insisted that he get his education, and the townsfolk found odd jobs for the gifted lad that did not conflict with his schoolwork (3). Upon graduating from high school Du Bois had his heart set on going to Harvard, but his high school did not meet Harvard's academic standards and he, quite frankly, did not have the money to go. The townsfolk, however, decided that he should go to college, and Fisk University, an all-black Congregational institution in Nashville, Tennessee, was deemed more appropriate for a promising young "Negro" of Du Bois's caliber and comportment.

At Fisk Du Bois discovered the rich diversity of African American culture and he enthusiastically studied Greek, Latin, German, classical literature, philosophy, ethics, chemistry, and physics, earning a bachelor's degree in 1888. Still determined to go to Harvard, Du Bois audaciously applied and was accepted as a scholarship student, but Harvard would not accept him as a graduate student because Fisk's curriculum did not meet their entrance requirements. He, therefore, undauntedly entered Harvard as a junior majoring in philosophy. Where Harvard was academically welcoming to Du Bois, socially it was as racially segregated as the rest of the United States at the time. In his autobiographical writings he reiterated how he was barred from white students' cliques and clubs at Harvard, revealingly writing, "I was in Harvard, but not of it" (Du Bois, 1968a, 136; see also Du Bois, 1960b). Ironically, where he was rejected by Harvard's students he was warmly embraced by many of its professors, several of whom are acknowledged intellectual luminaries, such as William James, Josiah Royce, George Santayana, and Frank Taussig (Lewis, 1993, 85–103; Horne, 2009, 1–16; Marable, 1986, 13–20; Rampersad, 1990, 19–47). Three months before he earned his second bachelor's degree—*cum laude*, in philosophy, in 1890—Du Bois petitioned the Harvard Academic Council for scholarship assistance to pursue a PhD in social science. Even at this early age he was already clear on how he wanted to use his PhD in "the field of *social science* under *political science*," he unapologetically announced, "with a view to the ultimate application of its principles to the social and economic advancement of the Negro people" (Du Bois, 1997a, 7, all emphasis in original; see also Du Bois, 1968a, 148–50).

For his graduate studies Du Bois switched from philosophy to history on the advice of his mentor William James, who candidly cautioned the youth, saying (according to Du Bois) "there is not much chance for anyone earning a living as a philosopher," let alone a Negro at the end of the nineteenth century. The die was cast, and Du Bois (1968a) completed his master's degree in 1892 under the tutelage of Albert Bushnell Hart, "studying in history and political science and what would have been sociology if Harvard had yet recognized such a field" (149). After earning his master's degree he "had already made up [his] mind that what was needed was further training in Europe. The German universities were at the top of their reputation," he contended, and "[a]ny American scholar who wanted preferment went to Germany for study" (150). And to Germany the intellectually indefatigable Du Bois went, studying at the Friedrich-Wilhelm III Universität in Berlin, now known as the University of Berlin, with highly acclaimed social historians and political economists Gustav von Schmoller, Heinrich von Treitschke, and Adolf Wagner, among others. One of Friedrich-Wilhelm III Universität's most illustrious graduates, a young fellow by the name of Max Weber, even received a temporary lectureship at his alma mater during Du Bois's second year at the university, before he went on to accept an appointment as a professor of economics at Freiburg University in 1894. Although Du Bois did not officially take any classes with Weber, as is often incorrectly reported, he was extremely impressed with the young German's universalist-leaning lectures (162). Later the two developed a remarkable mutual respect for each other's work, which resulted in Du Bois's invitation to Weber to participate in the 1904 Atlanta University conference on crime, and Weber's invitation to Du Bois to publish an article on race in the United States (*Die Negerfrage in den Vereinigten Staaten*) in the *Archiv für Sozialwissenschaft und Sozialpolitik* (Du Bois, 1906a, 2006; see also Chandler, 2006, 2007). Weber also had *The Souls of Black Folk* translated into German.

Although he completed all of the course requirements and his doctoral dissertation, Du Bois was denied a PhD from Friedrich-Wilhelm III Universität because he ran out of scholarship money, which would have enabled him to stay in Berlin for the additional academic year needed before a doctoral student could defend their dissertation. In other words, his deeply desired dream of earning a PhD in "the field of *social science*" from one of the preeminent European universities was, unfortunately, dashed only on account of his lack of scholarship funds and a residency requirement. Dejected but not hopelessly disheartened, Du Bois resolutely returned to Harvard and took his PhD in history and political science in 1895 with a dissertation entitled *The Suppression of the African Slave Trade to the United*

States of America, 1638–1870 (1954), which synthesized his graduate studies in history, sociology, and political economy to such an unprecedented and sophisticated extent that it was published as the first volume of the Harvard Historical Monograph Series in 1896. However, even though Du Bois was armed to the teeth with degrees from the most prestigious national and international institutions of his epoch, he encountered great difficulty in landing a job. In his autobiography he wryly wrote, "I just got down on my knees and begged for work, anything and anywhere. I began a systematic mail campaign." However, "I wrote to no white institution," he exclaimed, perhaps recollecting William James's advice, because "I knew there were no openings there" (184).

Eventually Du Bois was granted a position as a professor of classics, teaching Latin, Greek, German, and English, at Wilberforce University, an African Methodist Episcopal institution in Ohio. He unsuccessfully attempted to add sociology to the curriculum in 1894, and left the school in frustration for the University of Pennsylvania in 1896, where he was hired as an "assistant instructor" to research and write a study on the African Americans of Philadelphia (see Lewis, 1993, 150–78). At the University of Pennsylvania, however, he was still not free from frustration, writing in his autobiography, "I ignored my pitiful stipend" and "it goes without saying that I did no instructing, save once to pilot a pack of idiots through the Negro slums" (Du Bois, 1968a, 197; see also Lewis, 1993, 179–80). As will be witnessed in the subsequent chapter, his Philadelphia study, *The Philadelphia Negro*, although long-overlooked in the history of sociology, was upon its publication in 1899 an utterly unprecedented and undeniably innovative work in urban sociology, industrial sociology, historical sociology, political sociology, sociology of race, and sociology of culture. The eminent African American sociologist Elijah Anderson (1996) has recently asserted in his introduction to a reprint edition of *The Philadelphia Negro*, "W. E. B. Du Bois is a founding father of American sociology, but, unfortunately, neither this masterpiece nor much of Du Bois's other work has been given proper recognition; in fact, it is possible to advance through a graduate program in sociology in this country without ever hearing about Du Bois" (xiv).

Anderson's weighted words here help to highlight why the book you now hold in your hands, perhaps, has an added importance. To put it plainly, what *Against Epistemic Apartheid* offers that is wholly innovative and distinctive is that it weaves fresh and intensive archival research and the watershed work of classical and contemporary, male and female, black and white, national and international sociologists and social theorists' Du Bois studies together with the express interpretive intent of creating critical inventories and thoroughly interrogating *what has been included* and *what has been excluded* when and where we come to W. E. B. Du Bois's contributions to the discipline of sociology. At the conceptual core of this study, then, is a set of crucial questions, questions which I believe continue to haunt the history of sociology: why is it imperative for contemporary or, rather, twenty-first-century sociologists to know *who* Du Bois was and *what* he contributed to sociology—and, even more methodologically speaking, why is it important to not only know *what* but *how*, in his own innovative intellectual history-making manner, Du Bois contributed what he contributed to sociology? It ought to be stated outright here at the outset: the real answers to these questions do not lay so much in who Du Bois was, but more in his—however long-overlooked—sociological legacy, which is to say the answers lie in the lasting contributions of his discursive formations and discursive praxes to posterity's critical comprehension of the ways in which classical social inequalities and injustices are very often inextricable from and indelibly connected to contemporary social inequalities and injustices—and, faithfully following Du Bois's innovative intersectional sociology, especially with regard to the ways in which race, gender, and class frequently overlap and transmute to form the interlocking systems of oppression of racism *and* sexism *and* capitalism.

As stated above, *Against Epistemic Apartheid* is only partially and preliminarily concerned with Du Bois's exclusion from the history of sociology. Again I say, there is only so long Du Boisian sociologists can condemn Du Bois's absence from "mainstream" sociological discourse. As a *critical sociology of sociology*, *Against Epistemic Apartheid* ultimately is much more interested in demonstrating Du Bois's undeniable contributions to the history, discourse, and development of American sociology in particular, and the wider world of sociology in general. This dialectical, Africana critical theoretical approach to Du Bois's sociological discourse will enable objective interpreters of his work to see that, when compared and contrasted with the monumental work of Karl Marx, Max Weber, and Emile Durkheim, what was and what remains really and truly distinctive about Du Bois's sociology is precisely his unpretentious preoccupation with uniquely and unequivocally *American* social, political, and cultural issues, such as, for example, race and anti-black racism in the context of slavery, lynching, Jim Crow laws, black codes, segregation, and other forms of racial oppression in the United States; racial capitalism and the racial colonization of social classes in the United States; the racial colonization of gender and sexuality in the United States; the racial colonization of religion in the United States; the racial colonization of education in the United States; and the racial criminalization of blacks, among other poverty-stricken people, in the United States.

In the series of studies to follow, I essentially devote a chapter to each of the above issues, except, however, the discussion of racial capitalism and the racial colonization of social classes is carried out through an intense engagement of Du Bois's contributions to rural and urban sociology, respectively. Ultimately, then, *Against Epistemic Apartheid* does much more (a whole lot more!) than rail against Du Bois's exclusion from the hallowed history of sociology. It indefatigably and sincerely seeks to answer the crucial questions above concerning *who* Du Bois was, *what* he contributed to sociology, and *how* he contributed what he contributed to sociology remains relevant. In answering, or even in earnestly attempting to answer these questions it seems almost safe to say that the long-lingering and overarching question as to *why* twentieth-first-century sociologists should be exposed to Du Bois's sociological discourse will at last be laid to rest. However, before engaging Du Bois's major contributions to sociology it will be extremely important to briefly provide my readers with conceptual contours of the philosophical frameworks and *leitmotifs* (or, rather, the recurring critical theoretical themes) of the book: sociology's *disciplinary decadence* and *intellectual historical amnesia* as a consequence of its longstanding practice of *epistemic apartheid*. But, just what, pray tell, is *disciplinary decadence, intellectual historical amnesia*, and, most importantly with regard to the discussion at hand, *epistemic apartheid*? In answering this question my readers may come to see that *Against Epistemic Apartheid* is not simply aimed at *disciplinary decadence, intellectual historical amnesia*, and *epistemic apartheid* in sociology exclusively, but also—and this should be unapologetically emphasized—each of the aforementioned in the academy of the twenty-first century more generally.

DISCIPLINARY DECADENCE, INTELLECTUAL HISTORICAL AMNESIA, AND THE ANGUISH OF EPISTEMIC APARTHEID: TOWARD A TRANSDISCIPLINARY TRAJECTORY AND AN UNCOMPROMISING CRITICAL THEORY OF THE HUMAN SCIENCES

What has long bothered me about Du Bois studies, and one of the main reasons I have humbly returned to this important area of critical inquiry, is because of the longstanding tendency to downplay and diminish Du Bois's contributions to, not simply sociology but, as quiet as it is kept, to Africana studies, or the dimwitted disposition that seems to always and everywhere sever Du Bois from Africana studies or, worst of all, the inclination to render Africana studies utterly invisible or altogether nonexistent. Here I am saying as simply as I possibly can that Du Bois has been left in an intellectual vacuum because the transdisciplinary intellectual legacy he bequeathed does not fit into the monodisciplinary motifs of much of contemporary academic discourse. What if when one performs an intellectual archaeology of the development of "disciplines" and the "academy," one comes to the uncomfortable conclusion that the contemporary intense emphasis on "multidisciplinarity" or "interdisciplinarity" is not so new at all, but was quite common in the intellectual milieux of bygone epochs? Think for a moment. Think about the ways in which a wide range of academic disciplines have long had critical relationships with, to raise the most obvious example, Karl Marx's intellectual and political legacy.

Most modern—and even some so-called postmodern—academics are willing to concede Marx's seminal contributions to the discourse and development of disciplines as varied as, say, sociology, philosophy, history, political science, and economics. Why then is my assertion of Du Bois's transdisciplinary contributions so difficult to conceive, let alone concede? Is this symptomatic of a kind of treason against Du Bois's true trandisciplinarity in favor of a faux allegiance to his supposed monodisciplinary, sociologically negated legacy? Basically, the flat-footed line of logic is as follows: "*Either* Du Bois is a sociologist *or* he is a historian, but he cannot be *both* a sociologist *and* a historian. He cannot contribute to both sociology and history." What is more, it would seem to me that a one-dimensional, monodisciplinary approach to a multidimensional, transdisciplinary critical social theorist such as Du Bois smacks of the very diabolical double-dealing and double standard that ultimately led him to leave academic sociology—only after, as will be witnessed throughout this book, two decades (from 1895 to 1915) of intellectual history-making at Wilberforce University, the University of Pennsylvania, and Atlanta University—for Pan-Africanism, civil rights activism, and antiwar activism, among other social causes. Du Bois (1968b) detailed the reasons for his departure from academic sociology in *Dusk of Dawn*, sternly stating:

> Two considerations thereafter broke in upon my work and eventually disrupted it: first, one could not be a calm, cool, and detached scientist while Negroes were lynched, murdered and starved; and, secondly, there was no such definite demand for scientific work of the sort that I was doing, as I had confidently assumed would be easily forthcoming. I regarded it as axiomatic that the world wanted to learn the truth and if the truth was sought with even approximate accuracy and painstaking devotion, the world would gladly support the effort. This was, of course, but a young man's idealism, not by any means false, but also never universally true. (67–68)

Could it be the case, then, that Du Bois should more properly be dialectically and simultaneously considered an integral part of the inauguration of sociology *and* an innovative contributor to disciplines as diverse as, say, Africana studies, anthropology, history, philosophy, political science, economics, religion, and education? What if concrete examples of Du Bois's seminal contributions to each of the aforementioned fields or disciplines have long been documented and critically debated, but—and here's the real rub—utterly unknown to the large majority of sociologists because they have historically negated or dismissed Du Bois and his discourse, sociological or otherwise? Admittedly, we tread here on treacherous critical theoretical terrain, because to concede Du Bois's transdisciplinary contributions would also mean that we are willing to acknowledge that he was not simply a classical sociologist and that his thought and texts should be rightfully considered alongside the work of Karl Marx, Max Weber, Emile Durkheim, Vilfredo Pareto, Georg Simmel, George Herbert Mead, Auguste Comte, Herbert Spencer, Ferdinand Tönnies, and Thorstein Veblen, among others, but, even more, that Du Bois's thought and texts, similar to several of the aforementioned, go above and beyond or, rather, *transgress, transcend,* and *transverse* academic disciplines or specific fields of scholarly inquiry—hence, my above characterization of Du Bois as a *transdisciplinary critical social theorist.* The series of critical questions and answers emphasized above points us to the prickly practice of what the critically acclaimed Caribbean American philosopher Lewis Gordon (2006b) has correctly called "disciplinary decadence." In his own words:

> *Disciplinary decadence* is the ontologizing or reification of a discipline. In such an attitude, we treat our discipline as though it was never born and has always existed and will never change or, in some cases, die. More than immortal, it is eternal. Yet as something that came into being, it lives, in such an attitude, as a monstrosity, as an instance of a human creation that can never die. Such a perspective brings with it a special fallacy. Its assertion as absolute eventually leads to no room for other disciplinary perspectives, the result of which is the rejection of them for not being one's own. Thus, if one's discipline has foreclosed the question of its scope, all that is left for it is a form of "applied" work. Such work militates against thinking. (4–5, emphasis in original; see also Gordon, 2006a, 2006c)

What is in question here are the borders and boundaries of disciplinary knowledge and the ways in which many, if not most, academicians have repeatedly and unrepentantly rejected *discipline-transcending* or, rather, *transdisciplinary knowledge*—that is, knowledge which *transgresses, transcends,* and *transverses* disciplines or specific fields of scholarly inquiry. This is, also, I should add, symptomatic of what we could call *epistemic closure,* where one is only open to, or seriously engages knowledge emanating from their respective discipline or field and, in the most closed-minded and claustrophobic manner imaginable, xenophobically considers knowledge from "outside" of their discipline or field pure folly, "foreign" foolishness, as it were. Continuing his discourse on disciplinary decadence, Gordon (2006b) importantly concludes:

> Disciplinary decadence, as we have seen, is the process of critical decay within a field or discipline. In such instances, the proponent ontologizes his or her discipline far beyond its scope. Thus, a decadent scientist criticizes the humanities

for not being scientific; a decadent literary scholar criticizes scientists and social scientists for not being literary or textual; a decadent social scientist sins in two directions—by criticizing either the humanities for not being social scientific or social science for not being scientific in accord with, say, physics or biology. And, of course, the decadent historian criticizes all for not being historical; the decadent philosopher criticizes all for not being philosophical. The public dimension of evidence is here subordinated by the discipline or field's functioning, literally, as the world. Thus, although another discipline or field may offer evidence to the contrary, it could, literally, be ignored simply on the basis of not being the point of view of one's discipline or field. (33)

Here we have returned to the question of canonization. Processes of canonization, as renowned sociologist George Ritzer (2006) observed, are not neutral, and histories of sociology are not now and never have been free from the social inequalities and injustices—for example, the racism, sexism, and/or classism—of the respective intellectual milieux and societies in which sociologists live and work. When Gordon observes the *epistemic closure* of decadent disciplines, we are given occasion to think long and hard about the ways in which nonwhite and non-male contributors to sociology have been incessantly ignored, excluded, and/or erased from the history of sociology because of the gatekeeping and disciplinary decadence of the "white sociological fraternity." The question which exasperatingly emerges, then, is this: Is the "white sociological fraternity" still willing to deny the seminal sociological contributions of nonwhites, and in this instance, specifically the contributions of W. E. B. Du Bois? Also, a corollary critical question begs to be asked: Is the "white sociological fraternity" still willing to deny the seminal sociological contributions of women, such as, say, Harriet Martineau, Jane Addams, Anna Julia Cooper, Charlotte Perkins Gilman, Marianne Weber, Ida B. Wells, Elsie Clews Parsons, Beatrice Potter Webb, and, finally, "The Chicago Women's School" (e.g., Florence Kelley, Edith Abbot, Grace Abbot, Sophonisba Breckinridge, Frances Kellor, Julia Lathrop, Anne Marion MacLean, and Marion Talbot)?[2] Sad to say, it seems so, and that is precisely why *Against Epistemic Apartheid* holds a heightened intellectual historical (and intellectual *herstorical*!) importance. However, this book is also concerned with the ways in which the minority of Du Bois scholars who have been willing to concede his seminal contributions to sociology have repeatedly ignored or erased his undisputed inauguration of Africana studies and, by default, Africana studies altogether.

When I register my complaint concerning the fact that many, if not most, of the work in Du Bois studies has consistently either, at best, overlooked Du Bois's contributions to Africana studies or, at worst, rendered his contributions to, *and* Africana studies in and of itself invisible or entirely nonexistent, I am not putting into practice that awful ideology or foul "perspective" that "brings with it a special fallacy" that Gordon observed above. Quite the contrary, I am pointing to something altogether different, something a little more illusive or subtle that has seemed to slip through the cracks and crevices of the scholarship on Du Bois. This, therefore, is not a simple case of "disciplinary decadence" where I incorrigibly argue that "my discipline is better than yours, you ignoramus!" and where I sanctimoniously believe that my discipline is the end all and be all or, rather, the definitive "last word" (hallelujah!) in terms of human studies.

What I wish to do here is circumvent the very tired tendency to read or, rather, misread Du Bois in reductive disciplinary terms where his thought is validated and legitimated only insofar as it can be roguishly reframed and/or forced to fit into the arbitrary and artificial academic confines of this or that decadent discipline. The lingering *leitmotif* of *Against Epistemic Apartheid*, therefore, is that Du Bois's larger transdisciplinary legacy situates his thought and texts somewhere between and *beyond* sociology and a host of other disciplines—Africana studies, anthropology, history, philosophy, political science, economics, religion, and education quickly come to mind. Indeed, Du Bois has been hailed as a historian, sociologist, Marxist, Pan-Africanist, and political activist, but never as an early transdisciplinary critical social theorist with concrete political commitments to, not simply black liberation and racial justice, but to women's liberation and gender justice, the crudely criminalized poor masses and poverty-stricken working classes, and racially colonized nonwhites worldwide. He has long been praised and criticized by legions of scholars who have interpreted and rigorously reinterpreted his work, often overlooking its deep critical social theoretical dimensions. Here for the first time Du Bois's transdisciplinary critical social theory is not simply put on display but also placed into critical dialogue with a wide range of disciplinary perspectives: from sociology and history to Africana studies and women's studies; from economics and education to philosophy and religion; and, finally, from political science and cultural anthropology to communications and criminology.

However, unlike my previous Du Bois studies (i.e., *W. E. B. Du Bois and the Problems of the Twenty-First Century* and *Du Bois's Dialectics*), *Against Epistemic Apartheid* was researched and written specifically with the contemporary sociological audience in mind—in essence, inverting my earlier intellectual exercises where I sought to demonstrate Du Bois's contributions to Africana studies, radical politics, and critical social theory. Instead of examining what Du Bois contributes to marginalized and/or emerging interdisciplinary areas of critical inquiry, here I decidedly take a no-holds-barred approach to his long-overlooked offerings to arguably one of the oldest and most august "mainstream" or "traditional" disciplines in the academy of the twenty-first century: sociology. In order to really come to terms with, let alone critically comprehend Du Bois's sociological negation and then, more importantly, the crucial contributions of Du Bois's sociological discourse, it will be necessary for us to discuss the unmitigated unpleasantness of the many ways in which various forms of social segregation, oppression, and exploitation (e.g., racism, sexism, and capitalism) *exterior to the American academy*, however illusively or inadvertently, have in fact informed and influenced *the interior of the American academy* and, especially, as I emphasize throughout *Against Epistemic Apartheid*, the discursive formations and discursive practices of American sociology—from its inception and inchoate institutionalization at the end of the nineteenth century all the way through to its present sociological pretensions and practices. This, of course, is what I have repeatedly made reference to above as *epistemic apartheid*.

Conceptually speaking, what I am currently calling *epistemic apartheid* is an intellectual offshoot of what Lewis Gordon has dubbed "disciplinary decadence." With *epistemic apartheid*, however, I am earnestly attempting to take Gordon's concept of disciplinary decadence one step (or, perhaps, a couple of steps) further by emphasizing that when one carefully and critically reads his brilliant book *Disciplinary Decadence: Living Thought in Trying Times* (2006b) closely and carefully, it is possible to "slightly stretch"—to borrow an apt phrase from Frantz Fanon (1968, 40) in *The Wretched of the Earth*—Gordon's theory to intellectually encompass or conceptually capture, not only "the process of critical decay within a field or discipline" but, even more, *the processes of institutional racism or, rather, academic racial colonization and conceptual quarantining of knowledge, anti-imperial thought, and/or radical political praxis produced and presented by nonwhite—and, I am tempted to sardonically say, "especially black"—intellectual-activists*. It would seem to me that this is a major source for much of the "disciplinary decadence" that has long intellectually asphyxiated the academy, although my conscience compels me to also acknowledge that *epistemic apartheid* is not simply about institutional racism and racial colonization. It includes and seeks to raise critical consciousness about the ways in which knowledge is, in addition, *conceptually quarantined* along *racially gendered*, religious, sexual orientation, and economic class lines, which ultimately and truculently translates into the dim disciplinary borders and boundaries that Gordon contends cause "disciplinary decadence." In other words, my *critical theory of epistemic apartheid* seeks to respectfully build on and go beyond my much intellectually adored and deeply admired colleague Lewis Gordon's concept of "disciplinary decadence" by doing away with some of its abstractness and denseness, and by more concretely and social scientifically applying it to a specific "field or discipline" (i.e., sociology) and a specific intellectual or critical theorist (i.e., W. E. B. Du Bois).[3]

Truth be told, there is a sense in which Gordon's conception of "disciplinary decadence," almost in a postmodernesque manner, meta-philosophically free-floats from discipline to discipline, or, rather, hauntingly hovers above disciplines without ever really touching down to actually *apply* or put into *practice* its innovative, intellectual history-making assertions. It would seem that at this point in his articulation of the concept of disciplinary decadence Gordon privileges analysis of (mono)disciplinary theories and knowledge production *within the academy* over the ways in which (mono)disciplinary discursive formations and discursive practices have been (and, to a certain extent, continue to be) simultaneously influenced and impacted by social institutions and social practices *without the academy* and, what is more, increasingly influence and impact social institutions and social practices *without the academy*. Hence, here we have the vicious, academically insular hermeneutic circle *Against Epistemic Apartheid* seeks to audaciously accent and discursively disrupt. However, it must be openly admitted, by limiting the initial focus of disciplinary decadence to the hallowed walls and lofty lecture halls of the academy, Gordon undeniably has a greater philosophical justification for his critique of (mono)disciplinary knowledge production and immanent clarification of the intelligibility of interdisciplinary discourse in terms of the rules and regulations of (mono)disciplinary border- and boundary-building. Even so, a more critical theoretically thoroughgoing analysis of the epistemic undercurrents emerging from the border- and boundary-building of "traditional" disciplines and their influence and impact on social institutions and social practices (again, absolutely *outside of the academy*) needs to be explicitly undertaken and historically and culturally situated within its full social and political context(s). Which is also to say that even though *epistemic apartheid* greatly appreciates disciplinary decadence's ability to illuminate the intellectual insularity and clannishness of various academic disciplines' discursive communities, yet and still more concrete (i.e., critical theoretical) connections need to be made with respect to the "real life" power relations and the overarching effects that the *intellectual segregating of epistemes* or *conceptual quarantining of knowledge(s)* has on and has in the social and political world(s) well beyond the walls of the academy. Therefore, working from the peripheral point of view of W. E. B. Du Bois's sociological discourse offers us an opportunity to simultaneously identify and critically analyze instances of *epistemic apartheid* in the history and disciplinary development of sociology, as well as an important opportunity to concretely connect sociology's *epistemic apartheid* with the wider world of American apartheid, which at the very least includes the "real life" power relations and overarching effects of racial injustice (racism), gender injustice (sexism), and economic injustice (capitalism).

Against Epistemic Apartheid unequivocally is not in any way a critique of Lewis Gordon or his conception of disciplinary decadence as much as it is more a timely textual display of my profound respect for an intellectually inspiring colleague whose work I take seriously enough to build on and create a critical dialogue with. Clearly Professor Gordon and I have several shared and/or overlapping areas of intellectual interest (e.g., Africana studies, Du Bois studies, Fanon studies, Africana philosophy, philosophy of the human sciences, etc.), so I would sincerely hope and pray that readers take me seriously when I say that *epistemic apartheid* earnestly seeks to extend and expand "disciplinary decadence" not simply to the social sciences, which admittedly Gordon himself does in *Disciplinary Decadence*, but to keenly include the dialectical impact and influence of social, political, and cultural history *outside of the academy* on the intellectual history, disciplinary development, discursive formations, and discursive practices *inside of the academy*. It would seem to me that with all of its emphasis on the intricate innerworkings of specific disciplines and their particular discursive formations and discursive practices, Gordon's concept of disciplinary decadence could be easily (albeit erroneously, I honestly believe) misinterpreted as purely meta-theoretical or, rather, merely meta-philosophical, without in any way (in the fashion of Michel Foucault) critically connecting intellectual history, disciplinary development, discursive formations, and discursive practices to the wider social, political, and cultural world(s) outside of, but unfathomably and undeniably influential on, the academic world.

Gordon's work is extremely *epistemically elastic*, which is one of the reasons my work has consistently kept up a critical dialogue and dialectical rapport with it. However, here I take his critique of disciplinary decadence and philosophy of the human sciences in a different discursive direction by intensely applying it to the social sciences, specifically sociology, all the while conceptually conceiving and incisively expatiating *epistemic apartheid*. In fact, it could be said that where Gordon's concept of disciplinary decadence is a philosophy of the human sciences, *epistemic apartheid* is offered as a *critical theory of the human sciences*, which in this specific instance focuses on the intellectual history, disciplinary development, discursive formations, and discursive practices of sociology. To say that *epistemic apartheid* is a *critical theory of the human sciences* as opposed to a philosophy of the human sciences should shamelessly signal to my readers that *epistemic apartheid* is not simply another name for disciplinary decadence insofar as disciplinary decadence, although not exclusively, is indeed a philosophy of the human sciences with mind-boggling meta-philosophical (among many other) implications, and *epistemic apartheid* is a *critical theory of the human sciences* that unequivocally and unceasingly seeks to unite the intellectual insurgency and radical research of the human sciences *interior to the academy* with radical political praxis and revolutionary social movements *exterior to the academy*. It is in this sense, then, that *epistemic apartheid*, as an unabashed *critical theory of the human sciences*, can be considered a conceptual counterpart or, even more, an integral aspect of the ongoing evolution of my body of work to date—that is, of course, *Africana critical theory* (Rabaka, 2007b, 2008a, 2009a, 2010a, forthcoming).

From a methodological point of view, critical theory seeks to simultaneously 1) comprehend the established society; 2) criticize its contradictions and conflicts; and 3) create ethical and egalitarian (most often radical/revolutionary democratic socialist) alternatives.[4] The ultimate emphasis on the creation and offering of ethical and egalitarian alternatives brings to the fore another core concept of critical theory: its *theory of human liberation and radical/revolutionary democratic social(ist) transformation*. The paradigms and points of departure for critical theorists vary depending on the theorists' race, gender, class, sexual orientation, religious affiliation, and nation, among other intellectual interests and political persuasions. For instance, many European critical theorists turn to Hegel, Marx, Weber, Freud, and/or the Frankfurt School (e.g., Adorno, Benjamin, Fromm, Habermas, Horkheimer, and Marcuse), among others, because they understand these thinkers' thoughts and texts to speak in special ways to European modern and/or "postmodern" lifeworlds and lived experiences (see Held, 1980; Jay, 1996; Kellner, 1989; Wiggerhaus, 1995).

My conception of critical theory, *Africana critical theory*, utilizes the thought and texts of Africana intellectual-activist ancestors as critical theoretical paradigms and radical political points of departure because so much of their thought is not simply *problem-posing* but *solution-providing* where the specific life struggles of persons of African origin and/or descent (or, if I must, "black people") are concerned—humble human life struggles, it should be said with no hyperbole and high-sounding words, which European critical theorists (who are usually Eurocentric and often unwittingly white supremacist) have, for the most part, woefully neglected in their classical and contemporary critical theoretical discourse—a discourse that ironically has consistently congratulated itself on the universality of its interests, all the while (again, for the most part) sidestepping the centrality of racism and colonialism within its own discursive communities and out in the wider social, political, and cultural world(s). Moreover, my conception of critical theory is critically preoccupied with classical Africana intellectual-activists and the thought-traditions they inaugurated, not only because of the long-unlearned lessons they have to teach contemporary critical theorists about the dialectics of being simultaneously radically humanist and morally committed agents of a specific continent, nation, or cultural groups' liberation and democratic social(ist) transformation, but also because the ideas and ideals of continental and diasporan African intellectual-activists of the past indisputably prefigure and provide a foundation for contemporary Africana studies, and Africana philosophy in particular. In fact, in many ways, Africana critical theory, besides being grounded in and growing out of the transdisciplinary discourse(s) of Africana studies, can be said to be a critical theoretical offshoot of Africana philosophy, which according to the acclaimed African American philosopher, Lucius Outlaw (1997a), is

> a "gathering" notion under which to situate the articulations (writings, speeches, etc.), and traditions of the same, of Africans and peoples of African descent collectively, as well as the sub-discipline or field-forming, tradition-defining, tradition-organizing reconstructive efforts which are (to be) regarded as philosophy. However, "Africana philosophy" is to include, as well, the work of those persons who are neither African nor of African descent but who recognize the legitimacy and importance of the issues and endeavors that constitute the disciplinary activities of African or [African Caribbean or] African American philosophy and contribute to the efforts—persons whose work justifies their being called "Africanists." Use of the qualifier "Africana" is consistent with the practice of naming intellectual traditions and practices in terms of the national, geographic, cultural, racial, and/or ethnic descriptor or identity of the persons who initiated and were/are the primary practitioners—and/or are the subjects and objects—of the practices and traditions in question (e.g., "American," "British," "French," "German," or "continental" philosophy). (64)

Africana critical theory is distinguished from Africana philosophy by the fact that critical theory cannot be situated within the world of conventional academic disciplines and disciplinary divisions of labor. It transverses and transgresses boundaries between traditional disciplines and accents the interconnections and intersections of, for example, philosophy, history, politics, economics, psychology, sociology, anthropology, and the humanities, among other disciplines and/or areas of critical inquiry. Critical theory is contrasted with mainstream, monodisciplinary social theory through its mixed and multidisciplinary methodology and its efforts to develop a comprehensive dialectical theory of domination and liberation specific to the special needs of contemporary society. Africana philosophy has a very different agenda, one that seems to me more meta-philosophical than philosophical at this point, because it entails theorizing-on-tradition and tradition-reconstruction more than tradition extension and expansion through the production of normative theory and critical pedagogical praxis aimed at earnest *application* (i.e., immediate radical/revolutionary self- and social-transformation).

The primary purpose of critical theory is to relate radical thought to revolutionary practice, which is to say that its focus—philosophical, social, and political—is always and ever the search for ethical alternatives and viable moral solutions to the most pressing problems of our present age. Critical theory is not about, or rather *should not* be about allegiance to intellectual ancestors and/or ancient schools of thought, but about using *all* (without regard to race, gender, class, sexual orientation, and/or religious affiliation) accumulated radical thought and revolutionary practices in the interest of human liberation and democratic social(ist) transformation. With this in mind, Cornel West's (1982) classic contentions concerning "Afro-American critical thought" offer an outline for the type of theorizing that Africana critical theory endeavors:

> The object of inquiry for Afro-American critical thought is the past and present, the doings and the sufferings of African people in the United States. Rather than a new scientific discipline or field of study, it is a genre of writing, a textuality, a mode of discourse that interprets, describes, and evaluates Afro-American life in order comprehensively to understand and effectively to transform it. It is not concerned with "foundations" or transcendental "grounds" but with how to build its language in such a way that the configuration of sentences and the constellation of paragraphs themselves create a textuality and distinctive discourse which are a material force for Afro-American freedom. (15)

Though Africana critical theory encompasses and is concerned with much more than the lifeworlds and life struggles of "African people in the United States," West's comments here are helpful, as they give us a glimpse at the kinds of transdisciplinary connections critical theorists make or, rather, *should* make in terms of their ideas having a radical political impact and significant influence on society. Africana critical theory is not thought for thought's sake (as it often seems is the case with so much contemporary philosophy—Africana philosophy notwithstanding), but *critical thought for life and liberation's sake*. It is not only a style of writing which focuses on radicalism and revolution but, even more, it (re)presents a new way of *thinking* about and *doing* revolution that is based and constantly being built on the best of the radicalisms and revolutions of the past, and the black radical and black revolutionary past in particular.

From West's frame of reference, "Afro-American philosophy expresses the particular American variation of European modernity that Afro-Americans helped shape in this country and must contend with in the future. While it might be possible to articulate a competing Afro-American philosophy based principally on African norms and notions, it is likely that the result would be theoretically thin" (24). Quite contrary to West's comments, Africana critical theory intrepidly represents and registers as that "possible articulat[ion] of a competing [Africana] philosophy based principally on African norms and notions," and although he thinks that the results will be "theoretically thin," Africana critical theory—faithfully following Fanon (1965, 1967, 1968, 1969) and Cabral (1972, 1973, 1979)—understands this risk to be part of the price the wretched of the earth must be willing to pay for their (intellectual, political, psychological, and physical) freedom.[5] Intellectually audacious, especially considering the widespread Eurocentrism and white supremacism of contemporary conceptual generation, Africana critical theory does not acquiesce or give priority and special privilege to European history, culture, and thought. It turns to the long-overlooked thought and texts of women and men of African descent who have developed and contributed radical thought and revolutionary practices that could possibly aid us in our endeavors to continuously create an *antiracist, antisexist, anticapitalist, anticolonialist, and sexual orientation-sensitive critical theory of contemporary society.*

Above and beyond all of the aforementioned, Africana critical theory is about offering alternatives to *what is* (domination and discrimination), by projecting possibilities of *what ought to be* and/or *what could be* (human liberation and radical/revolutionary democratic social transformation). To reiterate, Africana critical theory is not afraid, to put it as plainly as possible, to critically engage and dialogue deeply with European and/or other cultural groups' thought-traditions. In fact, it often finds critical cross-cultural dialogue and astute appropriation (i.e., *Africanization*) necessary considering the historical conundrums and current shared conditions and shared crises of the modern or postmodern, transnational, and almost completely multicultural world. Africana critical theory, quite simply, does not privilege or give priority to European and/or other cultural groups' thought-traditions since its philosophical foci and primary purpose revolves around the search for solutions to the most pressing social and political problems in continental and diasporan African lifeworlds and lived experiences in the present age.

All of this brings us to the intricacies of applying Africana critical theory—in this incarnation under the guise of a *critical theory of epistemic apartheid*—to the intellectual history, disciplinary development, discursive formations, and discursive practices of sociology in general, and American sociology in particular. If, indeed, as I have been arguing above and intend to continue contending in the chapters to follow, W. E. B. Du Bois is central to the discourse and development of sociology, especially American sociology, why then has his work suffered "sociological negation"? How is it possible that a pioneering sociologist of Du Bois's stature has been all but ignored, excluded, and erased from the history and curriculum of sociology, even as late as the first decade of the twenty-first century? If Du Bois's sociological discourse can be shown to have been marginalized or, at the least, *academically ghettoized* on account of not only his race, but also because of the subjects he opted to sociologically (and often empirically) investigate, would not this paradox decidedly and almost definitively demonstrate that sociology or, at minimum, American sociology should on principle reevaluate and revise its intellectual history, disciplinary development, discursive formations, and discursive practices? These crucial questions are at the conceptual core of this intellectual exercise in identifying, critically analyzing, and offering ethical and egalitarian alternatives to sociology's longstanding practice(s) of what I have conceptually conceived of as, and, quite calmly, have come to call *epistemic apartheid*.

EXPATIATING EPISTEMIC APARTHEID: ON THE ONGOING EVOLUTION OF THE AFRICANA TRADITION OF CRITICAL THEORY

Since its inception more than one hundred years ago, and in light of constantly changing social, political, and cultural conditions, American sociology has studied race, gender, and class from myriad methodological and discursive directions: for example, the inchoate discursive formations and discursive practices of the late nineteenth and early twentieth century; the inauguration of symbolic interactionism in the 1930s; the forays into functionalism in the 1940s and 1950s; the radicalization of sociology as a result of the social unrest in the 1960s and 1970s; and the increasing advent of, and emphasis on, sociological specialization in race, gender, and class studies in the 1980s and 1990s. However, closely mirroring the race, gender, and class segregation of American society, throughout its history American sociology has been sometimes subtly, and sometimes not so subtly shaped and shaded by a furtive form of *epistemic apartheid*.

Indeed, American sociology's *conceptual quarantining* has, again however subtly, consistently reflected the racial segregation, gender injustice, and class struggles of American society, most frequently treating studies of race, gender, and class separately—that is, *intellectually segregating* racial studies from gender studies, and both racial and gender studies from class studies. The myriad social and symbolic borders and boundaries that defined and deformed the United States of the late nineteenth and early twentieth century are many of the very same borders and boundaries that have historically fueled American sociology's *epistemic apartheid*.[6] For instance, early U.S. social policymakers sought to create social hierarchies in which to differentially and definitively mark, categorize, and grade people and places—especially continents, colonies, nations, and neighborhoods—utilizing a crude, nefariously negative criteria of race, gender, and class. Echoing European imperial powers' *racial colonial* social categories and conventions, the United States offered up its own vicious version of the concept of "divide and conquer" by creating its own brutal brand of apartheid (i.e., "American apartheid") and socially segregated its population along race, gender, and class lines. As will be witnessed in our discussion of *The Philadelphia Negro* to follow, industrial capitalism in the United States spurred the increasing concentration of "ethnic" and working-class populations in inner cities and urban areas. African Americans, in particular, were considered the lowest of the low: not only were they the epitome of poverty in a society predicated on carpetbagger capitalist wealth, they were unceasingly and, therefore, unforgivably black in a society that glorified, deified, and, quite literally, worshipped whiteness. Perhaps there is no better example of African Americans' peculiar predicament in late nineteenth- and early twentieth-century

America than the 1896 Supreme Court decision *Plessy v. Ferguson*, which in no uncertain terms legalized and, therefore, institutionalized the "separate but equal" doctrine of social inequality and injustice—what we in Africana studies, à la Lewis Gordon (1995a), are wont to call *anti-black racism* (see Thomas, 1997).

In essence, *Plessy v. Ferguson* roguishly represents not simply one of the greatest symbols of American apartheid, but also a bitter and brutal reminder that the United States government, in fact, sanctioned, was patently part and parcel of the racial formation and racial segregation processes at the end of the nineteenth century, which, as will be witnessed in our discussion of *The Souls of Black Folk* to follow, led W. E. B. Du Bois to famously prophesy, "The problem of the twentieth century is the problem of the color-line,—the relation of the darker to the lighter races of men in Asia and Africa, in America and the islands of the sea." As stated above, *epistemic apartheid* is not simply centered on the study of race and the critique of racism but, equally important, it was created to conceptually capture the ways in which patriarchy, and gender injustice in general, has historically and continues currently to (re)define and deform the study of women's lifeworlds and lived experiences. Very few academics in the twenty-first century will deny the myriad ways in which women's (let alone openly or radically feminist!) discursive formations and discursive practices have been marginalized in the seemingly (and more often obviously!) male supremacist discourses and histories of various disciplines, and the academy more generally. In addition, *epistemic apartheid* is also aimed at critiquing the crude, insensitive, and frequently sensational ways in which elite and unabashedly bourgeois academics objectify and disreputably report on the lifeworlds and life struggles of working-class and poverty-stricken people. Instead of *intellectually segregated* or separate areas of inquiry, *epistemic apartheid* seeks to incessantly and insurgently *intellectually desegregate* and critically connect race, gender, and class studies and, in this specific instance, demonstrate that in spite of the unprecedented changes at the turn of the twentieth century—or, perhaps, maybe even because of those vicissitudes—the race, gender, and class borders and boundaries of late nineteenth- and early twentieth-century American culture and society simultaneously *and* surreptitiously formed and deformed the frame and foci of American sociology from its inception, which in turn led to despicable discursive practices of marginalization and exclusion or, rather, the *intellectual historical amnesia* that has been carried over to, and continues to haunt, sociology in the twenty-first century.

Sociology's longstanding *intellectual historical amnesia*, therefore, is almost undeniably consequent to its *epistemic apartheid*. Although often articulated through dual interpretive-theoretical thrusts (qualitative methods) and empirical-positivistic paradigms (quantitative methods), in their efforts to study the meaning and aftermath of the Enlightenment and European modernity in the United States (i.e., "New Europe") most early European American sociologists often unrepentantly participated in, exacerbated, and perpetuated—literally, refined and repugnantly reproduced—the racial, gendered, and class social segregation outside of the academy and simply transferred and transformed it to suit their "scholastic" or "scientific" whims and wishes inside of the academy, ultimately creating an academic world that very much mirrored the undeniably undemocratic (i.e., with respect to nonwhites, non-males, and the poor) social, political, and cultural world(s) of late nineteenth- and early twentieth-century America. Continuing with this line of logic leads us to an open admission and brief discussion of the fact that *epistemic apartheid* is conceptually connected to, and was conceptually conceived in the aftermath of Michel Foucault's articulation of an archaeology of various discursive formations and discursive practices. For instance, *epistemic apartheid* critically follows Foucault's philosophical histories and/or historicist philosophies: from his critique of psychiatry in *The History of Madness in the Classical Age* to his critique of the evolution of the medical industry in *The Birth of the Clinic: An Archaeology of Medical Perception*; from his critique of the evolution of the human sciences in *The Order of Things: An Archaeology of the Human Sciences* to his critique of the historical-situatedness of truth, meaning, and reason (i.e., the *episteme* of an epoch), and the very methodologies through which they are arrived at or comprehended in his extremely innovative *The Archaeology of Knowledge* (see Foucault, 1971, 1973, 1974, 1994, 2009).[7]

According to Foucault (1994), archaeology is distinguished from "the confused, under-structured, and ill-structured domain of the history of ideas" (195). He, therefore, rejects the history of ideas as an idealist and liberal humanist, purely academic or ivory tower mode of writing that traces an uninterrupted evolution of thought in terms of the conscious construction of a tradition or the conscious production of subjects and objects. Against the bourgeois liberalism of the history of ideas approach, Foucaultian archaeology endeavors to identify the states and stages for the creation and critique of ongoing and open-ended or, rather, more nuanced knowledge, as well as the hidden rules and regulations (re)structuring and ultimately determining the form and focus of discursive rationality that are deeply embedded within and often obfuscatingly operate below the perceived borders and boundaries of disciplinary development, methodological maneuvers, or interpretive intention. At the outset of *The Order of Things*, Foucault (1971) contended: "It is these rules of formation, which were never formulated in their own right, but are to be found only in widely differing theories, concepts, and objects of study, that I have tried to reveal, by isolating, as their specific locus, a level that I have called . . . archaeological" (xi).

Moreover, *epistemic apartheid* also draws from Foucault's more mature materialist genealogies, such as *Discipline and Punish: The Birth of the Prison*; *The History of Sexuality, Vol. 1: The Will to Knowledge*; *The History of Sexuality, Vol. 2: The Use of Pleasure*; and *The History of Sexuality, Vol. 3: The Care of the Self*, where he deepened and developed his articulation of archaeology and evolved it into a unique conception of genealogy, which signaled an intensification of his critical theorization of power relations, social institutions, and social practices (see Foucault, 1979, 1990a, 1990b, 1990c). However, *epistemic apartheid* does not understand Foucault's later focus on genealogy to be a break with his earlier archaeological studies as much as it is taken to represent a shift of discursive direction and, even more, an extension and expansion of his discursive domain. Similar to his archaeologies, Foucault characterized his later genealogical studies as a new method of investigation, a new means of interpretation, and a new mode of historical writing. Truth be told, then, both of these Foucaultian methodologies endeavor to radically reinterpret the social world from a micrological standpoint that allows one to identify discursive discontinuity and discursive dispersion instead of what has been commonly understood to be continuity and uninterrupted identity evolution and, as a consequence, Foucault's methodologies enable us to grapple with and eventually firmly grasp historical happenings, cultural crises, political power plays, and social situations in their complete and concrete complexity. Furthermore, both Foucaultian methodologies also attempt to invalidate and offer more nuanced narratives to commonly held conceptions of master narratives and great chains of historical continuity and their teleological destinations, as well as to hyperhistoricize what has been long thought to be indelibly etched into the heart of human history. In other words, and more meta-methodologically speaking, in discursively deploying archaeology and/or genealogy Foucault sought to disrupt and eventually destroy hard and fast bourgeois humanist historical identities, power relations, and imperial institutions by critically complicating, by profoundly problematizing and pluralizing the entire arena of discursive formations and discursive practices—hence, freeing historical writing from its hidden bourgeois humanist social and political hierarchies, by disavowing and displacing the bourgeois humanist (and, therefore, "socially acceptable") subject, and critically theorizing modern reason and increasing rationalization through reinterpreting and rewriting the history of the human sciences.

By focusing on a specific critical theorist (i.e., W. E. B. Du Bois) and a specific discipline within the human sciences (i.e., sociology), in this instance *epistemic apartheid* reinterprets and rewrites the history of American sociology from the peripheral point of view of nonwhite, non-male, and working-class "organic intellectual" social theorist-activists and (traditionally trained) academic sociologists. Closely following Foucault's archaeological and genealogical endeavors, then, I am not so much interested in contributing the definitive statement on Du Bois's sociological discourse, as much as I am simply seeking to offer an *intellectual tool, discursive device* or, rather, *critical theoretical construct*, which may allow others much more knowledgeable than I with respect to Du Bois and sociology to build bridges between disciplines and connect disparate discursive communities—if not eventually do away with the discursive practices of *conceptually quarantining* and/or *disciplining* knowledge altogether. Hence, in all intellectual honesty, I openly admit that no single method of investigation or mode of analysis in and of itself can definitively grapple with and grasp the cornucopia of concepts and plurality of paradigms that correlate with the wide range of power relations, social institutions, and social practices which currently constitute contemporary society. Accordingly, while I have been indelibly influenced by, for example, philosophy of the human sciences, Africana philosophy, Pan-Africanism, Marxism, Frankfurt School critical theory, phenomenology, existentialism, feminism, womanism, Fanonian philosophy, Foucaultian philosophy, hermeneutics, and semiotics, faithfully following the work of William King (1990, 1995, 2009) I resolutely and unrepentantly reject a monodisciplinary or single phenomenon-focused super-theory approach and instead analyze classical and contemporary society from a transdisciplinary critical theoretical frame of reference which brings disparate discursive formations and discursive practices into critical dialogue in an effort to provide an *alternative optic* on, and *alternative options* to past, present, and future humanity, history, culture, and society.

That being said, here I have not hesitated to bring the dialectic to bear on and, literally, deconstruct and reconstruct Africana critical theory in an earnest effort to demonstrate that in my conception critical theories and critical methodologies must unceasingly be subordinated to the timely and tactical necessities of the particular project, subject, or object in question. Authentic critical theory is always and ever concerned with the complexities, specificities, and/or historical-situatedness of real, flesh and blood human lifeworlds and life struggles; therefore, it is not a visceral, free-floating war machine revved up and ever ready to attack any old target the racists, and/or sexists, and/or bourgeoisie happen to leave vulnerable. The intellectual life-altering lessons I have learned from critically and systematically studying Foucault's archaeological and genealogical method(s) have radically reinvigorated my articulation of Africana critical theory and enabled me to inaugurate and expatiate a new, discursively deeper dimension of the Africana tradition of critical theory (i.e., *epistemic apartheid*), which brings a decidedly more transdisciplinary critical theoretical approach to disciplinary development, discursive formations, and discursive practices in the academy of the twenty-first century. Just as I asserted above with respect to Foucault's methodological shift from archaeology to genealogy, *epistemic apartheid* should not be taken as and is not in any way intended to be a replacement for, or an abandonment of, my articulation of Africana critical theory as much as it is meant to signal and symbolize an intensification of its evolution and an even more radical methodological extension and expansion of the Africana tradition of critical theory's discursive practices and discursive domains.

Bearing the above in mind, it should also be stated outright that I do not in any way intend Africana critical theory or *epistemic apartheid* as definitive conceptual solutions to the problems plaguing sociology, or any other discipline for that matter, and, just for the sake of clarity, it should be equally emphasized that I am most certainly not interested in founding a new discipline—truth be told, following Du Bois, Fanon, and Foucault, I have come to think of my work as insurgently *antidisciplinary* but, however ironically, *ever epistemically open* to knowledge emerging from single subject-focused disciplines if—and this is an extremely important *if*—the specific disciplinary knowledge in question is deemed useful for the project at hand. As stated in almost all of my previous work, one of the reasons I was initially and remain intellectually attracted to, and intellectually enthusiastic about, Africana studies is because of its *epistemic openness* and complete disregard for conventional conceptions of disciplinary development. At this point, then, it will be helpful to briefly operationalize my (new or, rather, more current) conception of Africana studies for the specific discursive purposes of *Against Epistemic Apartheid*: from an Africana critical theoretical frame of reference, Africana studies is the body of knowledge based on and built around critically and systematically studying a specific human group, continental and diasporan Africans, and their particular and peculiar lifeworlds and life struggles which is most modeled on or, at the very least, seems to perfectly parallel Du Bois and Fanon's extensive and diverse insurgent intellectual activity and revolutionary praxis because at its conceptual core it is a *transdisciplinary human science*. Here, I should like to take this line of logic one step further and more concretely synthesize Du Bois and Fanon's respective philosophies of the human sciences with Africana studies, which in this instance roughly translates into *a form of human studies incorrigibly obsessed with eradicating the blight on the souls of black folk, the wretchedness of the wretched of the earth, and indefatigably geared toward the ultimate goal of deepening and developing the Africana tradition of critical theory*. That being said, then, Africana studies is unequivocally the area of investigation, as opposed to the "academic discipline," that has most inspired Africana critical theory's unique research methods and modes of analysis—"unique" especially when compared to other forms of critical theory that emerge from traditional, single subject-focused disciplines—because Africana studies is a *transdisciplinary human science*—that is, *an area of critical inquiry that transgresses, transverses, and ultimately transcends the arbitrary and artificial academic and disciplinary borders and boundaries, the conflicted color-lines and yawning racial chasms, and the jingoism and gender injustice of traditional single phenomenon-focused, monodisciplinary disciplines, owing to the fact that at its best it poses problems and incessantly seeks solutions on behalf of the souls of black folk and the other wretched of the earth employing the theoretic innovations of both the social sciences and the humanities, as well as the political breakthroughs of grassroots radical and revolutionary social movements.*[8]

I have long critically comprehended the myriad dangers that, literally, *disciplining* knowledge has done and continues to do to knowledge production and knowledge dissemination in particular, and to human culture and civilization in general. Africana critical theory, here under the guise of a *critical theory of epistemic apartheid*, is aimed at and unapologetically attacks the epistemological presuppositions and methodological procedures at the historical heart of narrow-minded (mono)disciplinary development, discursive formations, and discursive practices, and deftly demonstrates the ways in which they continue to influence and inform contemporary (mono)disciplinary development, discursive formations, and discursive practices. Therefore, I honestly believe that Du Bois's transdisciplinary and deeply *sociological* discourse offers us an ideal alternative history of sociology in general, and American sociology in particular, because the bulk of his work seems to have escaped a great many (albeit not all) of the (racist, sexist, and classist) assumptions of mainstream (classical) sociology on account of it being simultaneously *academically marginalized* and a *sociology of the socially marginalized*.

To continue the long-standing discursive practice of (dis)placing Du Bois's discourse utterly outside of the history and disciplinary development of sociology in general, and American sociology in particular, is to patently participate in and discursively perpetuate *epistemic apartheid*, which, as was witnessed above, has most frequently hinged upon a coarse combination of Eurocentric, patriarchal, and bourgeois conceptions of "science," "social science," and "sociology." This briskly brings us to the watershed work of the noted feminist philosopher of science Sandra Harding, and the influence her version of "standpoint theory" and articulation of "strong objectivity" has exerted on *epistemic apartheid*'s conception of the human sciences in general and the social sciences in particular.[9] Overall it would seem that at the conceptual core of Harding's (1994) critique of "traditional" histories, philosophies, and sociologies of science is her controversial claim that "there could be many universally valid but culturally-distinctive sciences" (357; see also Fay, 1996). She contentiously contends that "[t]aking a standpoint 'outside' European culture enables the identification of aspects of the conceptual frameworks, paradigms, and epistemes of European sciences and technologies not so easily detected from 'inside' European culture" (Harding, 1997, 52). In suspending Eurocentrism and panoramically viewing the history of European sciences and technologies from peripheral points of view "outside" of, and most often ardently oppressed by European culture, an alternative vision and alternative version of European science and technology is offered up, and we are able to critically comprehend, in Harding's (1994) well-founded words, that "[m]odern sciences have been enriched by contributions not only from the so-called 'complex' cultures of China, India, and others in east-Asian and Islamic societies, but also from the so-called 'simpler' ones of Africa, pre-Columbian Americas, and others that interacted with the expansion of European cultures. . . . Some knowledge traditions that were appropriated and fully integrated into modern sciences are not acknowledged at all" (347).

Obviously here Harding is critically turning our attention to the fact that, as quiet as it has been kept, "[p]rior to European expansion African, Asian, and indigenous American cultures had long traded scientific and technological ideas among themselves as they exchanged other products, but this possibility was reduced or eliminated for them and transferred to Europe during the 'voyages of discovery'" (356).[10] Indeed, a critical question begs, "In what ways have the existing projects in physics, chemistry, engineering, biology, geology, and the history, sociology, anthropology, and philosophies of the sciences been excessively contained [and, even more, *conceptually incarcerated*] by Eurocentric assumptions and goals?" (363) This is an extremely important question, and one that is at the conceptual core of *Against Epistemic Apartheid*, although with an exclusive focus on the ways in which Du Bois's sociological discourse, by "[t]aking a standpoint 'outside' European [American sociological] culture enables the identification of aspects of the conceptual frameworks, paradigms, and epistemes of European [American social] sciences and technologies not so easily detected from 'inside' European [American sociological] culture." By expanding Harding's critique of "traditional" conceptions of the "hard sciences" and intensely applying it to the so-called soft sciences, and sociology in particular, *Against Epistemic Apartheid* critically accents and intensely engages *the distinctive dialectic of systematic knowledge and systematic ignorance* that has come to characterize modern (Eurocentric) sciences (i.e., both "hard" and "soft" sciences). Moreover, sociology has long sought to model itself after the "hard sciences," whether with regard to its methods of investigation and modes of analysis or, rather, through its pretensions to, and pontifications of, strictly adhering to experimental, empirical, quantifiable data and/or "the scientific method," as well as its obvious obsession with accuracy and, seemingly above all else, objectivity. This means, then, that many of the very same patterns of systematic knowledge and systematic ignorance that Harding, among others, maintains plagues the "hard sciences" may be surreptitiously embedded in the intellectual origins, methods of investigation, and modes of analysis of the "soft sciences," and especially sociology. Having strongly stressed all of this, however, I simply could not agree with Harding more when she earnestly asserts that the "point here is not that non-Western cultures and their scientific traditions are all good and Western ones are all bad, but that all of us can learn and benefit from the achievements of non-European civilizations' traditions also" (362).

Against Epistemic Apartheid is essentially an extension and expansion of Harding's contention that "all of us can learn and benefit from the achievements of non-European civilizations' traditions also," and here the main point is to move beyond the meta-philosophical and meta-methodological contentions of Gordon's critique of disciplinary decadence, Foucault's early archaeological studies, and Harding's standpoint theory, and—à la Fanon's *A Dying Colonialism* and Foucault's later genealogical studies, especially *Discipline and Punish*—critically retheorize and more concretely complicate the intellectual history, disciplinary development, discursive formations, and discursive practices of a specific European and European American scientific tradition (i.e., sociology), by deftly demonstrating what a specific non-European social scientist's (i.e., W. E. B. Du Bois's) discourse has to offer that "all of us can learn and benefit from." It can almost be undeniably asserted that Du Bois has been and remains something akin to European and European American sociology's quintessential Other, and his sociological "Otherness" has long hinged on *the diabolical dialectic of white superiority and black inferiority*. However, as will be observed in the chapters to follow, Du Bois increasingly came to reject the black/white dichotomy—what Fanon (1968, 1969), in *The Wretched of the Earth* and *Toward the African Revolution*, referred to as the "Manichaeanism" of the racially colonized world—and he refused to invest his intellectual energy into the doomed *dialectic of white superiority and black inferiority* (see, especially, the discussion of Du Bois's concept of "double-consciousness" in chapter 2).[11] With regard to "science," Du Bois (1898b) sternly stated: "Students must be careful to insist that science as such—be it physics, chemistry, psychology, or sociology—has but one simple aim: the discovery of truth. Its results lie open for the use of all men [and women]—merchants, physicians, [women and] men of letters, and philanthropists, but the aim of science itself is simple truth" (16). According to Harding (1994), it would seem that Du Bois's conception of science runs counter to commonly held European conceptions of science in light of the fact that, for the most part, European sciences have long had Eurocentrism, if not outright white supremacism and other elements of imperialism, at their conceptual core:

> Nobody has discovered an eleventh commandment handed down from the heavens specifying what may and may not be counted as a science. Obviously the project of drawing a line between science and non-science is undertaken because it emphasizes a contrast thought to be important. Belief in the reality of this demarcation, as in the reality of the science versus pseudoscience duality,

is necessary to preserve the mystique of the uniqueness and purity of the West's knowledge-seeking. Thus the sciences, as well as the philosophies that are focused on describing and explaining that kind of rationality so highly valued in the modern West, have been partners with anthropology in maintaining a whole series of Eurocentric contrasts, whether or not individual scientists, philosophers, or anthropologists so intended. The self-image of the West depends on contrasts not only between the rational and the irrational, but also between civilization and the savage or primitive, the advanced or progressive and the backwards, dynamic and static societies, developed and undeveloped, the historical and the natural, and other contrasts through which the European Self has contrasted its Other, and thereby justified its exploitative treatment of various peoples. My point here is that even though there clearly are obvious and large differences between modern sciences and the traditions of seeking systematic knowledge of the natural world to be found in other cultures, it is useful to think of them all as sciences to gain a more objective understanding of the causes of Western successes, the achievements of other sciences, and possible directions for future local and global sciences. (350)

Against Epistemic Apartheid is not about denying the "successes" or overall validity of many aspects of European sciences any more than it is about accenting each and every intellectual insult European American sociologists have inflicted upon non-European American—and especially African American—sociologists and/or contributors to American sociology. This is also to say that *Against Epistemic Apartheid* is not another intellectual exercise in "negative dialectics," but a book about the ways in which Du Bois's sociological negation at the hands of the "white sociological fraternity" has thwarted sociology in general, and American sociology in particular, from developing to its fullest potential and making more substantial or concrete contributions to the democratic, more multicultural, and genuinely transgendered transformation of contemporary society. Taking Harding's words to heart, *Against Epistemic Apartheid* aims to disrupt the ongoing Othering of nonwhite sociologists and/or contributors to sociology by explicitly illustrating why it is important to think of non-European/non-white "traditions of seeking systematic knowledge of the natural [and social] world[s] . . . as sciences to gain a more objective understanding of the causes of Western successes [and failures], the achievements [and pitfalls] of other sciences, and possible directions for future local and global sciences." Du Bois's sociological discourse certainly offers us an irrefutable example of one of the "achievements of other sciences, and possible directions for future local and global sciences." Furthermore, as a new discursive device especially created to conceptually capture, not only "the process of critical decay within a field or discipline" (à la Gordon's disciplinary decadence) but, even more, *the processes of institutional racism or, rather, academic racial colonization and conceptual quarantining of knowledge, anti-imperial thought,* and/or radical political praxis produced and presented by nonwhite—and, I am tempted to sardonically say again, "especially black"—intellectual-activists, *epistemic apartheid* also makes an important contribution to the discourse on the "achievements of other sciences, and possible directions for future local and global sciences."

As an offshoot of Africana critical theory created to conceptually capture, not only the ways in which the social borders and political boundaries built around race, gender, and class within American society have been egregiously grafted onto American sociology, but also *the intellectual segregation of knowledge* throughout the academy in general (i.e., above and beyond issues revolving around race, gender, and class), *epistemic apartheid* has several distinguishing features that should be briefly discussed. First, within the world of *epistemic apartheid*, everything has a particular place or quarantined space, *one* place or *single* space, as places and spaces are coarsely catalogued and have meaning only in relation to each other or to an "Other," which is also to say that every place or space must be mercilessly and mechanically ranked and registered. Hence, *epistemic apartheid*—whether overt or covert, visible or invisible—is integral to, and inextricable from, the social construction of the social segregation(s) surrounding and the social hierarchies (re)defining and deforming race, gender, and class in American culture and society.

Second, within the world of *epistemic apartheid* cultural conventions and social practices compulsorily categorize and designate individuals to segregated places and quarantined spaces. Nonwhites, women, and working-class people often appear to voluntarily embrace their prescribed places, spaces, and identities, but it must always be borne in mind that they involuntarily inherited their ranked and registered social statuses and social identities, and must perpetually wrestle with the, whether positive or negative, actual or alleged attributes associated with the places, spaces and identities they have been involuntarily assigned. We witness here exactly where Foucault's conceptions of, not only "counter-identities" but, equally important throughout *Against Epistemic Apartheid*, "counter-sciences" comes into play (see Foucault, 1971, 1974, 1977a, 1977b, 1984, 1988).

Third, *epistemic apartheid* revolves around an often illusive form of essentialism (albeit not only racial essentialism), which in the most unscientific and objectionable manners imaginable absurdly assumes that nonwhites, non-males, and the poor who have been compulsorily categorized and who share involuntarily assigned ranked and registered social statuses and social identities actually (i.e., in reality) have a "collective mind" and share many (keep in mind, coercively conceived) common characteristics. In fact, for the elite and privileged few with access to, or, in most instances, who *own* proper places and spaces (recall Cheryl Harris's 1993 critical discussion of "whiteness as property") within the world of *epistemic apartheid*, embracing this all-encompassing brand of essentialism breeds and rewardingly reinforces the foresaid social hierarchies and, most importantly here, a perceived homogeneity. As will be seen in the discussion of *The Philadelphia Negro* to follow, whites—whether willfully or unwittingly—often embrace what Jean-Paul Sartre called "bad faith" when they fool themselves into believing and/or thinking of, in Du Bois's words, "Negroes as composing one practically homogenous mass"; in addition, men who attempt to gloss over the glaring differences within women's lifeworlds and life struggles can be said to be in "bad faith"; and the rich, too, who rob the poor of their human right to be different, to be humble and hardworking on their own terms—indeed, they also bathe in the murky waters of "bad faith."

Lastly, sustaining intellectually and/or socially segregated places, spaces and identities necessitates an enormous amount of border and boundary maintenance, policing and patrolling, which at this point in American intellectual and social history seems almost as "American" as apple pie, baseball, and a McDonald's "Big Mac." In order to exacerbate and perpetuate *epistemic apartheid*, the spoils of the intellectual and cultural wars historically and currently being waged must be touted and distributed to those faithful (*badly faithful*, if you will) to its tenets, which means that crude (albeit often clandestine) racist, sexist, and classist criteria have been and continue to be employed to distinguish between those who are authentic apartheidists (intellectual, social, or otherwise apartheidists), and those who are interlopers—thus, the latter designation (i.e., interlopers) usually approximates and encompasses the position(s) of the white liberals (academics or otherwise) who roguishly ride the line between white supremacist conservatism and authentic white antiracist radicalism. Therefore, and as will be critically discussed at length throughout this book, in American sociology in general, and in its subdisciplines in particular, Du Bois's sociological negation has most frequently revolved around *a dialectic of discursive formations and discursive practices of inclusion and exclusion* (mostly exclusion), which reveal that *epistemic apartheid* has been indispensable to and, even more, at the heart of the myriad ways in which sociology has historically and continues currently to *conceptually quarantine* and *conceptually colonize* not only the sociological study of race, gender, and class, but also its (i.e., sociology's) intellectual history, curriculum, discursive formations, and discursive practices.

One the one hand, it could be said that at its inception American sociology, of all the disciplines in the American academy, was almost perfectly poised to grasp and grapple with the various versions of *social and epistemic apartheid* running rampant, because its *raison d'être* revolved around identifying and critically analyzing the rules and regulations of social institutions and social practices that were invisible or long ignored in conventional social etiquette and social exchanges. Clearly, race, gender, and class relations in America have been defined and deformed by a fusion of different forms of, whether implicit or explicit, *apartheid*—that is, domination and discrimination, as well as colonization and segregation—which, when carefully and critically contemplated, helps to highlight a systematic synthesis or super-structural combination of the rules and regulations (often invisibly) embedded in American social institutions and social practices. Turn-of-the-twentieth-century American culture and society offered seemingly limitless new angles for critical sociological analysis, from class struggle and urbanization as a consequence of industrial capitalism to explorations of the regulations of race in the aftermath of African American enslavement and emancipation, and to the problems surrounding unwed working-class women—early twentieth-century sociologists had an ideal opportunity to chart and challenge both the intellectual and social segregation of American race, gender, and class relations. In 1904, a year after he published *The Souls of Black Folk*, Du Bois (1904a) sternly stated: "[T]here lies before the sociologist of the United States a peculiar opportunity. We have here going on before our eyes the evolution of a vast group of men from simpler primitive conditions to higher more complex civilization" (85–86). Then, speaking directly of the sociological significance of the African American experience, he contended: "I think it may safely be asserted that never in the history of the modern world has there been presented to men of a great nation so rare an opportunity to observe and measure and study the evolution of a great branch of the human race as is given to Americans in the study of the American Negro" (86). Obviously Du Bois's references to "men" and "primitive" people is indicative of some of the ways in which he himself participated in and perpetuated *epistemic apartheid*, which will be critically revisited in the chapters to follow.

On the other hand, and directly connecting with Du Bois's observations above, it must be earnestly admitted that American sociology was in fact founded and formed within a world where race, gender, and class discrimination and segregation were the rule and, thus, these deformed and colonized social relations in turn informed the intellectual history and institutionalization of sociology. American sociology simultaneously internalized and intellectually incorporated the assumptions of the overarching American apartheid(s)—e.g., racism, sexism, and capitalism—into its intellectual history, disciplinary development, discursive formations, and discursive practices, as well as its research methods and conception(s) of knowledge production. For instance, the symbolic and disciplinary organization of American sociology in and of itself seems to smack of *epistemic apartheid*.

First, take the tendency among American sociologists to *conceptually quarantine* ideas hard and fast in *one*, and only *one*, preestablished category, which means, then, that ideas only register when and where they fall within or can be forced to fit within the predetermined concepts and categories of a rote ranking symbolic order predicated on socially segregated race, gender, and class relations. What is more, some sociological work amasses greater rewards and recognition, whereas other sociological work, for whatever reason deemed unworthy of such reward and recognition in light of the socially segregated race, gender, and class relations, is academically ghettoized or sociologically stigmatized. Within the world of *epistemic apartheid*, then, whole subdisciplines or entire specializations can academically rise or fall depending on their perceived contribution to continued intellectual colonization and their place within the rote ranking symbolic hierarchies of disciplinary knowledge production.

Second, forcing ideas to fit into predetermined, intellectually colonized categories or conceptually incarcerating spaces most often devalues and distorts the theory or concept in question, because processes of classification, as with processes of canonization, in and of themselves entail a certain species of *epistemic reductionism* where ideas are stridently stripped down to what is understood to be their essential attributes. However, keep in mind that this "strident stripping down" is usually performed by a sociologist who, whether consciously or unconsciously, adheres to the axioms of *epistemic apartheid* and, therefore, the rote ranking of people, places, and things (e.g., theories). Obviously intricate (and, especially, insurgent!) ideas may not be able to be easily or quickly reduced to *conceptual cliff's notes*—which is also one of the cardinal rules of *epistemic apartheid*, especially with regard to the study of race, gender, and class—and they are, therefore, *discursively dismissed, intellectually segregated,* and/or *conceptually quarantined* from sociology's "official" intellectual history, discursive formations, and discursive practices.

Finally, if, in fact, many early American sociologists, whether consciously or unconsciously, embraced *epistemic apartheid*, then, earnest efforts to introduce necessary or entirely new areas of sociological inquiry, research methods, and modes of interpretation emerging from the sociological margins and other academically ghettoized enclaves (e.g., Africana studies and women's studies, etc.) may have (and I honestly believe *have*) been ignored, excluded, or rendered invisible since the inception of American sociology. As a consequence, the intellectual history and disciplinary development of sociology has been and continues to be haunted by a disguised, but nonetheless diabolical, *dialectic of homogenous discursive formations and hegemonic discursive practices*. Hence, the question begs: How has sociology's participation in the maintenance, policing, and patrolling of both the social and symbolic borders and boundaries of American society influenced and informed, defined and deformed the discourse and development of American sociology? How has the incessant search for homogenous sociological work to fit into its predetermined conceptually colonized paradigms predicated on *epistemic apartheid* retarded the discourse and development (let alone the radical social transformation implications and radical political potential!) of American sociology? And, even more, how has sociology's disguised, but nonetheless diabolical, *dialectic of homogenous discursive formations and hegemonic discursive practices* influenced the ongoing ignoring, exclusion, and intellectual invisibility of W. E. B. Du Bois's sociological discourse?

Considering the above discussion of disciplinary decadence, archaeology, genealogy, and standpoint theory, it will be important for my readers to bear in mind that each of the subsequent chapters has been endeavored with the critical understanding that Du Bois's transdisciplinarity, especially where his contributions to sociology are concerned, demands that we commit monodisciplinary treason and suspend our academic allegiances to this or that discipline in favor of a fuller and more nuanced comprehension of his intellectually innovative thought and texts, which, if truth be told, continue to *transgress, transcend,* and *transverse* the arbitrary and artificial academic and disciplinary borders and boundaries, the conflicted color-lines and yawning racial chasms, and the jingoism and gender injustice of traditional single phenomenon-focused, monodisciplinary disciplines. Du Bois's conception of sociology is, indeed, different from much of what currently passes as sociology, and part of what is genuinely distinctive about his contributions to sociology is his unrepentant disregard for disciplinary borders and boundaries. Methodologically, however, his innovative sociological roots come rushing to the fore. The bulk of his body of work speaks in a special way to his unique sociological heritage.

Therefore, the subsequent series of studies undeniably demonstrate that Du Bois employed a wide range of sociological research methods: from quantitative methods to qualitative methods; from archival methods to ethnographic methods; from content analysis to longitudinal study; and from participant observation to experimental methods. What is more, Robert Wortham's "W. E. B. Du Bois's Urban Sociology" (2008) even goes so far as to accent Du Bois's "early 'trademark' approach to sociological research design, *methodological triangulation,*" emphasizing Du Bois's innovative methodological sophistication (2–3; see also Wortham, 2009b). Clearly, then, it is not the intention of *Against Epistemic Apartheid* to attempt to finalize Du Bois's "imminent canonization" (Zuckerman, 2004, 7) within sociology, but something altogether different: first, to demonstrate that his thought and texts simultaneously and seminally contributed to the discourse and development of sociology, and spawned several subdisciplines within sociology in which it has been either ignored, excluded, or erased; second, to emphasize not simply Du Bois's transdisciplinarity, but also the transdisciplinarity of "early" or "classical" sociology in general; and, finally, to call into question the *intellectual historical amnesia, epistemic apartheid* and inherently exclusive nature of the process(es) of canonization, sociological or otherwise. Du Bois's distinctive transdisciplinary contributions to the discourse and development of sociology are, perhaps, best explored by critically engaging the ways in which Du Bois scholars have utilized his work as paradigms and points of departure within several of the subdisciplines of sociology. Many of the sociological subdisciplines that prominently engage Du Bois's thought and texts help to highlight the distinctiveness of his contributions to sociology and, ironically, his characteristic transdisciplinarity, which simultaneously places him both *within* and *without* sociology.

To say that Du Bois's thought and texts stand both *within* and *without* sociology is, quite simply, to say that "traditional" disciplinary and subdisciplinary definitions of sociology, or any other discipline for that matter, are not now and never have been "pure" and/or neutral. Neither Marx, nor Weber, nor Durkheim held "pure" and/or neutral conceptions of sociology, which means, then, that there is room or, rather, there is enough intellectual space for the conceptions and contributions of innumerable sociologically negated nonwhite, non-male, and organic intellectual sociologists and social theorists. It is, therefore, with keeping this critical understanding in mind that *Against Epistemic Apartheid* is divided into six chapters, each of which highlights a different subdiscipline—or, in most instances, set of subdisciplinary themes—predicated on, or pertinent to, Du Bois's distinct transdisciplinary contributions to sociology. The remainder of this introduction, therefore, will offer the reader brief synopses of the book's six ensuing chapters.

ON DU BOIS'S DISTINCT CONTRIBUTIONS TO SEVEN SUBDISCIPLINES WITHIN SOCIOLOGY: CHAPTER SUMMARIES AND CHALLENGES TO THE HISTORY OF SOCIOLOGY

When compared with the work of his pioneering sociological peers, especially the work of Marx, Weber, and Durkheim, the distinctiveness of Du Bois's contributions lie not in the fact that he was African American, or that he trekked from Fisk to Harvard to the University of Berlin and, then, back to Harvard to ultimately become the first African American to earn a PhD from that auspicious institution in 1895. Quite the contrary, what remains remarkable about his contributions has nothing to do with his race, gender, or class, but more to do with the often-overlooked fact that unlike Marx, Weber, or Durkheim, Du Bois's primary sociological preoccupation was to develop a social science specific to the special needs of the United States of America. As several of the subsequent chapters in *Against Epistemic Apartheid* illustrate, Du Bois arguably endeavored the first major studies, empirical or otherwise, in the history of American sociology. Also, he established the "first American school of sociology," with the Atlanta University school of sociology (1895–1925), predating the University of Chicago's school of sociology (1915-1930) by two decades (Du Bois, 1940, 1969b, 1969c). The following chapters gathered here, then, have three main objectives: first, to provide readers with a sense of Du Bois's unique personal, political, and intellectual pedigree; second, to demonstrate how he utilized what he learned at Fisk, Harvard, and the University of Berlin in ways and for purposes often not fully fathomed by his professors and peers (none of whom were "sociologists" in the sense in which the term is used today and, in point of fact, none of whom have been canonized, or are being considered for canonization within the discipline of sociology à la Du Bois); and, third, to emphasize that no matter what Du Bois appropriated from his professors and peers at Fisk, Harvard, and the University of Berlin, it is extremely intellectually disingenuous and indicative of an intense *intellectual historical amnesia* and *epistemic apartheid* to incessantly seek to interpret his contributions to sociology as somehow, always and ever, derivative of or consequent to his having studied with European (e.g., Gustav von Schmoller, Heinrich von Treitschke, and Adolf Wagner) and European American (e.g., William James, Josiah Royce, George Santayana, and Albert Bushnell Hart) professors (Lewis, 1993, 179-210; see also Edwards, 2001). None of the aforementioned—no, not a single one of them—dared to do what Du Bois did: which is to say—and here I purposely repeat myself—he inaugurated a tradition or "school" of empirical social scientific research primarily preoccupied with the most pressing problems confronting the citizens of the United States of America. What is even more impressive is the wide range and wide reach of Du Bois's contributions to sociology, which, as will be witnessed in this volume, include undeniable offerings to urban sociology, rural sociology, sociology of race, sociology of class, sociology of culture, sociology of religion, sociology of education, sociology of crime, and—undoubtedly unlike any of his fabled professors or the long-sanctioned "sociological trinity" of Marx, Weber, and Durkheim—seminal and significant male-feminist/male-womanist contributions to sociology of gender and intersectional sociology (Bologh, 1990; Di Stephano, 1991; Erickson, 1993; Hearn, 1987, 1991; Lehmann, 1994; Sargent, 1981).

If we were to momentarily entertain the lame but longstanding assertion that Du Bois's contributions to sociology are consequent to his studies with his European and European American professors, then a couple of critical questions continue to linger: Why is it that his professors, who lived lives unsullied by American apartheid, anti-black racism, lynching, racial colonialism, and other forms of racial oppression, didn't inaugurate sociology in the United States? Why is it that, with all of the unhampered access to intellectual resources and research opportunities, one of them didn't place the sociology of race on the inchoate sociological agenda? Could it be that Du Bois's contributions to sociology are much more than mere derivatives of his professors' thought and texts and, more plausibly, intellectual artifacts which reveal that he developed a dialectical relationship and critical rapport, not simply with his professors' work, but with the thought and texts of the early establishers of what has come to be called "sociology"? The ensuing studies in *Against Epistemic Apartheid* provide answers to these questions, often while simultaneously raising other alternative critical questions. Admittedly, the dialectical thought that Du Bois's discourse and many of the better texts in Du Bois's studies inspires is part of the reason why his legacy has been repeatedly resuscitated, not simply with respect to sociology but, even more, with regard to a wide range of intellectual enterprises and political pursuits.

Chapter 1, "Du Bois and the Early Development of Urban and Rural Sociology: *The Philadelphia Negro* and the Sociology of the Souls of Black Farming Folk," reinterprets Du Bois's contributions to urban and rural sociology from an Africana critical theoretical frame of reference that is sensitive to the ways in which his emphasis on the horrors of the African holocaust and African American enslavement, as well as the aftereffects of African American enslavement and the ongoing effects of American apartheid simultaneously helped to *epistemically emancipate* and *conceptually incarcerate* his work within the world of late nineteenth-century white sociology. It first offers a reinterpretation of Du Bois's contributions to rural sociology that contends that his empirical study "The Negroes of Farmville" not simply predated *The Philadelphia Negro* but, even more, prefigured and provided a methodological model and interpretive exemplar that was extremely influential on his subsequent sociological discourse. Second, chapter 1 critically engages *The Philadelphia Negro* along the lines of its methodological innovations and elitist misinterpretations—innovations and misinterpretations that have intellectually illuminated *and* discursively darkened its sociological salience.

The second chapter, "Du Bois and the Sociology of Race: The Sociology of the Souls of Black and White (Among Other) Folk," endeavors an entirely new angle on Du Bois's contributions to the sociology of race by working through several of his seminal writings on race and racism with a keen eye on the ways in which he, literally, laid the foundation for what is currently being called, not simply the "sociology of race," but also "critical race theory" and "critical white studies." As to be expected, Du Bois's immortal *The Souls of Black Folk* is critically examined, especially the discursive devices he created—such as the "Veil," "second-sight," "double-consciousness," and the "color-line"—to simultaneously capture the dilemmas and dualities or, rather, the conundrums and complexities of what it means to be black in a white world *and* to deepen and develop early twentieth-century sociology of race. Then, juxtaposing the interrogation of *The Souls of Black Folk* with the archaeological analysis of works such as "The Conservation of Races," "The Study of the Negro Problems," "The Souls of White Folk," and *The Gift of Black Folk*, the chapter gives way to an extended discussion of Du Bois's long-overlooked "gift theory," and the ways in which it informed his critical theory of race and racism.

Chapter 3, "Du Bois and the Sociology of Gender: 'The Damnation of Women,' 'The Freedom of Womanhood,' and the Insurgent Intersectional Sociology of the Souls of Black (Among Other) Female Folk," is divided into three sections, each of which corresponds with one of Du Bois's major contributions to black feminist sociology, *the sociology of racially gendered classes*, and/or intersectional sociology. The first section performs an intellectual archaeology of Du Bois's early life and thought and identifies the black women's club movement, and Josephine Ruffin's radicalism in particular, as a central site and source of his paradigm(s) for social organization; political education; black feminism; public intellectualism; and radical journalism. The second section acutely explores Du Bois's (re)presentation and (re)positioning of black women and black mothers. It accents his efforts to counter both white and male supremacists' contentions concerning black women, and illustrates the importance of emphasizing the category of *racially gendered women* within the discursive world of the sociology of gender. The third section focuses on Du Bois's classic male-feminist manifesto, "The Damnation of Women." It brings together the insights from the previous sections and seeks to provide a radical reinterpretation of his male-feminism with an eye on the ways in which it prefigured and continues to provide a foundation for intersectional sociology and comparative and conjunctive transdisciplinary race, gender, and class analysis in the twenty-first century. The third chapter concludes with an intellectual autobiographical interlude where the author encourages men, and specifically more male sociologists, to solemnly deconstruct and reconstruct modern masculinity by taking sociology of gender, black feminist sociology, feminist theory, and women's studies more seriously in their sociological research (and their personal lives).

The fourth chapter, "Du Bois and the Sociology of Religion: The Sociology of the Souls of Religious Black (Among Other) Folk," explores Du Bois's sociological discourse on spirituality and religion. It argues that his religious thought—being distinguished by its emphasis on Africana religiosity and spirituality; the relationship between and the political economy of religion and racism; and the ways oppressing and oppressed people use and/or abuse religion either as a form of social pacification or social protest—simultaneously deconstructs and reconstructs the conventional analytical categories of sociology of religion and liberation theology. Du Bois's work in this area will be shown to make a profound contribution to both classical and contemporary sociology of religion insofar as it provides a paradigm that enables twenty-first-century sociologists to critique the ideological elements of religion while simultaneously accenting its more emancipatory aspects. Du Bois's sociology of religion, like his critical social theory in general, is shown to be self-reflexive, constantly exhibiting the ability to revise and refine itself and, as a result, is shown to be remarkably relevant for contemporary sociology of religion, religious studies, and religious criticism.

Chapter 5, "Du Bois and the Sociology of Education: Critiquing the (Mis)Education of Black (Among Other) Folk," first discusses Du Bois's development of a critical theory of history (as opposed to, or contrasted with, a conventional "philosophy of history") and its impact on his sociology of education. Next, it examines Du Bois's sociology of culture and the distinct style of cultural criticism he developed for its centrality to his sociology of education, critical pedagogy, and critical educational theory more generally. Third, it endeavors to objectively analyze some of the major deficiencies and limitations of Du Bois's sociology of education by contrasting his 1903 theory of the "Talented Tenth" with his 1948 revision of the Talented Tenth thesis into a more Marxist and/or democratic socialist theory of "the Guiding Hundredth." Finally, the fifth chapter concludes by commenting on the contributions Du Bois's sociology of education makes to contemporary critical educational theory and critical pedagogical praxis.

The sixth chapter, "Du Bois and the Sociology of Crime: Critiquing the Criminalization of Black (Among Other) Folk," engages Du Bois's sprawling, but extremely important, contributions to the sociology of crime, and American criminology in general. The bulk of his best work in this area is contained in "The Negro and Crime," *The Philadelphia Negro*, "The Problem of Negro Crime," "Crime and Our Colored Population," and, of course, his intellectual history-making edited volume *Some Notes on Negro Crime*. After undertaking an intellectual archaeology of his sociology of crime, the chapter then develops a critical discussion of what Du Bois's discourse contributes to contemporary sociology of crime.

Finally, the book quickly concludes with a brief discussion of the ways in which ending *epistemic apartheid* and seriously engaging Du Bois's sociological discourse, among others who have been *intellectually segregated* and *conceptually quarantined*, could transform sociology and epistemically open it to transdisciplinary discourses. Hence, *Against Epistemic Apartheid* ends as it began: resolutely and unrepentantly rejecting a monodisciplinary or single phenomenon-focused super-theory approach and instead emphasizing the analysis of classical and contemporary society from a transdisciplinary critical theoretical frame of reference that brings disparate discursive formations and discursive practices into critical dialogue in an effort to earnestly provide *alternative optics* on (and *alternative options* to) past, present, and future humanity, history, culture, and society. Let us, then, turn to the first chapter, where we will witness the genesis of Du Bois's distinct sociological discourse and controversial conceptual generations, which he (in the most unprecedented manner imaginable) utilized to document and empirically study African Americans' particular and peculiar urban and rural experiences at the turn of the twentieth century.

NOTES

1. The Africana Critical Theory (ACT) intellectual archaeology project, which includes my previous works, *W. E. B. Du Bois and the Problems of the Twenty-First Century*, *Du Bois's Dialectics*, *Africana Critical Theory*, and *Forms of Fanonism*, is discussed in detail below.

2. For further discussion of women's contributions to sociology or, rather, feminist intellectual *herstories* of sociology, as well as the noteworthy works that have informed my analysis here, please see: Aldridge (2008), P. H. Collins (1998, 2000a), Delamont (2003), Goetting and Fenstermaker (1995), Lengermann and Niebrugge-Brantley (1998), Myers, Anderson, and Risman (1998), Rege (2003), Stanley (1990), Sydie (1987), and R. A. Wallace (1989).

3. It should be pointed out that I undertook a similar intellectual archaeological endeavor with respect to Frantz Fanon's contributions to Africana studies, radical politics, and critical social theory in *Forms of Fanonism: Frantz Fanon's Critical Theory and the Dialectics of Decolonization* (2010a). However, there I only hinted at the profound critical theoretical and critical praxiological implications of *epistemic apartheid*, whereas here I turn from Fanon to Du Bois, from an implicit emphasis on *epistemic apartheid* to an intense explicit exploration and critique of *epistemic apartheid*, and, finally, from emerging interdisciplinary fields of critical inquiry to an age-old and august fully established discipline. In unhurried hindsight, then, I have now come to conceive of my work in *Forms of Fanonism*—as well as *Africana Critical Theory* (2009a), which immediately preceded the Fanon book—as, of course, integral to the evolution of Africana critical theory but, even more importantly here, imperative for the emergence and unambiguous articulation of *epistemic apartheid*. Below I discuss the critical relationship and dialectical rapport between Africana critical theory and *epistemic apartheid*.

4. Along with Africana studies and more general critical social scientific research methods (see the in-text citations), Africana critical theory has also been deeply influenced by the monumental meta-methodological studies of Bonilla-Silva and Zuberi (2008), Bulmer and Solomos (2004), Sefa Dei and Johal (2005), Fong (2008), Gunaratnam (2003), Ramji (2009), Sandoval (2000), L. T. Smith (1999), and Twine and Warren (2000), which collectively seek to decolonize research methods and emphasize their importance for developing *critical theories of white supremacist patriarchal colonial capitalist societies*. The influence of these works on Africana critical theory's mixed- or multi-methodological orientation cannot be overstated. For further discussion, see my previous work *Africana Critical Theory* (2009a).

5. Africana critical theory is not alone in its critique of West's lack of faith in the conceptual generation capacities of black folk in particular, and the other wretched of the earth in general. Several scholars, many working within Africana studies, have advanced constructive criticisms of his work. See, for example, Cowan (2003), Gilyard (2008), C. S. Johnson (2003), D. Wood (2000), and Yancy (2001).

6. Clearly, my conception of *epistemic apartheid* has been indelibly informed by a wide range of "American apartheid studies" encompassing much more than race relations, racism and white supremacy, but also, and most distinctively, the intersecting and overlapping impact and influence of American apartheid on religion, education, employment, entertainment, medicine, realty, and so forth in the United States. Therefore, well beyond the esteemed sociologists Douglas Massey and Nancy Denton's watershed work, *American Apartheid: Segregation and the Making of the Underclass* (1993), I have also relied on the following research to conceptually conceive the present *critical theory of epistemic apartheid*: Bullard, Grisby, and Lee (1994), Collins and Yeskel (2005), Grady-Willis (2006), J. P. Jackson (2001, 2002, 2005), Jackson and Weidman (2004), Khatri and Hughes (2002), Kozol (2005), Kushner (1980), Street (2005), Twine and Warren (2000), H. A. Washington (2006), Whitehead (1994), and Young and Braziel (2006).

7. As is well-known, *episteme* is a Greek word for knowledge, but because it was taken up by Kant, Foucault went out of his way to distinguish his conception of *episteme* from the Kantian conception. In *Foucault Live* he made it clear that he was employing the term to simply denote "all those relationships which existed between the various sectors of science during a given epoch" (Foucault, 1996, 76). Therefore, anything labeled with the adjective "epistemic," which is derived from "epistemological," has some relation to knowledge, or to a general theory of knowledge (hence, "epistemological").

8. The literature on Africana studies, which in its most comprehensive sense includes African, African American, Afro-American, Afro-Asian, Afro-European, Afro-Latino (a.k.a. Latino Negro), Afro-Native American, Caribbean, Pan-African, black British, and, of course, black studies, is diverse and extensive. However, for quick comprehensive overviews, see Asante and Karenga (2006), Gordon and Gordon (2006a, 2006b), Rabaka (2009a, 2010a), Rojas (2007), and Rooks (2006).

9. Although my analysis here primarily centers around Sandra Harding's (1976, 1986, 1987, 1991, 1998, 2004, 2006, 2008) feminist philosophy of science, it has also gathered additional insights from the work of several other prominent feminist philosophers of science, feminist sociologists of science, and/or "standpoint theorists"—for example, P. H. Collins (1998, 2000a, 2005, 2006), Haraway (1989, 1997, 2004), Harding and Figueroa (2003), Harding and Narayan (2000), Harding and O'Barr (1987), Hartsock (1998), Hawkesworth (1990, 2006a, 2006b), Kincaid, Dupre, and Wylie (2007), Narayan (1997), Pinsky and Wylie (1989), D. E. Smith (1990, 1993, 1999), and Wylie (2002).

10. For further discussion of the outright imperial violence and exploitation involved in Europe's "explorations" of, or "voyages of discovery" to non-European continents and cultures, and for the most noteworthy works which have informed my analysis here, please see Blaut (1987, 1993, 2000), Boone and Mignolo (1994), Mignolo (2000, 2003, 2005), and Greer, Mignolo, and Quilligan (2007).

11. With regard to "Manichaeanism," it is important to point out that this term was popularized by Abdul JanMohamed in "The Economy of Manichean Allegory: The Function of Racial Difference in Colonialist Literature" (1985) and *Manichean Aesthetics: The Politics of Literature in Colonial Africa* (1988), where he accented Frantz Fanon's identification and critique of the Manichaean nature of the unyielding conflict between the colonizer and the colonized. Within the worlds of

Africana, cultural, and postcolonial studies, Manichaeanism is usually taken as a term for the implacable and ever-antagonistic binary anatomy of imperial ideology. JanMohamed utilizes the doggedly dualistic meaning of the term to conceptually capture the process(es) through which imperial discourse "divides and conquers," or, rather, polarizes society, culture, and each and every lived experience and lived endurance of both the colonizer and the colonized into Manichaean categories of good and evil (as in the "Manichaean heresy"—see Mirecki and BeDuhn, 2001; Runciman, 1982; Tardieu, 2008). In a world coarsely conceived through Manichaean categories, the colonized who are constantly quarantined to the borders and outer-boundaries of "civilization" are perceived as uncivilized, uncontrollable, unassimilable, and ultimately evil, while the colonizer's culture is perceived as the epitome of "civilization," sanctity, and good. For further discussion, and the first critical theoretical (re)interpretation of Fanon and his conception and critique of Manichaeanism, see Rabaka (2010a).

1

Du Bois and the Early Development of Urban and Rural Sociology

The Philadelphia Negro and the Sociology of the Souls of Black Farming Folk

> Nothing more exasperates the better class of Negroes than this tendency to ignore utterly their existence... In many respects it is right and proper to judge a people by its best classes rather than by its worst classes or middle ranks. The highest class of any group represents its possibilities rather than its exceptions, as is so often assumed in regard to the Negro.
>
> W. E. B. Du Bois, *The Philadelphia Negro*, 310, 316–17

INTRODUCTION: (INTER)CONNECTING DU BOIS'S URBAN AND RURAL SOCIOLOGICAL DISCOURSES

Although *The Philadelphia Negro* has long been regarded as W. E. B. Du Bois's quintessential contribution to sociology, especially empirical sociology, contemporary reassessments of the text often overlook its trenchant transdisciplinarity and the real reasons it has resiliently risen to "classical"—I dare not say "canonical"—status in disciplines as varied as Africana studies, anthropology, sociology, history, political science, and economics, among others. Undoubtedly, Du Bois was one of the earliest innovators of, and critical contributors to empirical social science research at the dawn of the discipline of sociology in the United States, especially during its formative phase spanning the years 1895–1915 (Lemert, 2000b; Wortham, 2009b; Zuckerman, 2004). However, where most sociologists, in essence, start and stop with *The Philadelphia Negro*, which was published in 1899, Du Bois made several seminal sociological contributions that predate and prefigure his watershed Philadelphia work. The most noteworthy among his pre-*Philadelphia Negro* publications include "The Conservation of Races"

(1897), "A Program for a Sociological Society" (1897), "The Strivings of the Negro People" (1897), "The Study of the Negro Problems" (1898), "The Negroes of Farmville, Virginia: A Social Study" (1898), "Careers Open to College-Bred Negroes" (1898), and *Some Efforts of American Negroes for Their Own Social Betterment* (1898).

Years before, and for more than a decade after *The Philadelphia Negro* was published, Du Bois resoundingly rejected the anti-black racist grand theorizing commonplace in the sociological circles of his day and he, hinting at his own hard-nosed historical sociology, arraigned several of the leading sociological lights of his epoch—sociological theorists such as Herbert Spencer, Charles Ellwood, and Lester Ward—for confusing their own racial hierarchal and racial colonial (mis)understandings of society with empirical observation of human behavior, especially African and African American cultures and practices.[1] Unrepentantly challenging the ungrounded anti-black racist grand theorizing of renowned Cornell University professor Walter Francis Wilcox, author of *Negroes in the United States* (1904), Du Bois's riposte to Wilcox's work, which seemed to be completely divorced from the actual lifeworlds and life struggles of African Americans, is directly related to his disdain for Spencerian anti-black racism disguised as "high science" sociological theorizing. Du Bois (1997a) responded to Wilcox with words that continue to cut to the core more than a century after they were written:

> The fundamental difficulty in your opinion is that you are trying to spin a solution of the Negro problem out of the inside of your office. It can never be done. You have simply no adequate conception of the Negro problem in the South and of Negro character and capacity. When you have sat, as I have, ten years in intimate soul contact with all kinds and conditions of black men [and women] you will be less agnostic [concerning black folk]. I have prejudices but they are backed by knowledge if not supported. . . . If you insist on writing about and pronouncing judgment on this problem why not study it? Not from a car-window and associated press dispatches . . . but get down here and really study it firsthand. Is it a sufficient answer to a problem to say the data are not sufficient when they lie all about us? There is enough easily obtainable data to take you off the fence if you will study it firsthand and not [through] prejudiced eyes—my eyes, or those of others. (75)

Du Bois's words here help to highlight many of the major issues involved in interpreting or, rather, reinterpreting his sociological legacy. Important epistemic issues, issues ranging from his "ten years in intimate soul contact with all kinds and conditions of black men [and women]" to his intense emphasis on the need for "firsthand" or empirical studies of African American lifeworlds and life struggles free from "prejudiced eyes" or anti-black racist perspectives, lie at the heart of Du Bois's sociological discourse, and especially his contributions to urban and rural sociology. Du Bois challenges those sociologists, among others, who continue to theorize African American lived experiences and lived endurances through their "car-window[s] and associated press dispatches," as well as through "prejudiced eyes." His innovative sociological empiricism, however, was not always guided by "[un]prejudiced eyes," and he himself seems to allude to as much when he wrote, "I have prejudices but they are backed by knowledge if not supported." The "knowledge" that Du Bois based his "prejudices" on, as will be critically discussed below, was frequently and ironically drawn from white middle-class culture and Victorian values, which should remind contemporary readers that innovative empiricism and the most copious data collection is a sorry substitute for *conceptual criteria, methods of interpretation,* and *modes of analysis* grounded in and growing out of classical and contemporary, continental and diasporan African history, culture, and struggle.

This chapter reinterprets Du Bois's contributions to urban and rural sociology from an Africana critical theoretical frame of reference that is sensitive to the ways in which his emphasis on the horrors of the African holocaust and African American enslavement, as well as the aftereffects of African American enslavement and the ongoing effects of American apartheid simultaneously helped to *epistemically emancipate* and *conceptually incarcerate* his work within the world of late nineteenth-century white sociology. Du Bois's early sociological discourse lucidly demonstrates the difficulties he faced in his efforts to employ empirical social scientific research in the interest of social reform, and it also points to the difficulties he encountered as he attempted to simultaneously reach black and white audiences, both within and beyond the American academy. First, I offer a reinterpretation of Du Bois's contributions to rural sociology that contends that his "The Negroes of Farmville" not only predated *The Philadelphia Negro* but, even more, prefigured and provided a methodological model and interpretive exemplar that was extremely influential on his subsequent sociological discourse. Second, and building on the previous section, I critically engage *The Philadelphia Negro* along the lines of its methodological innovations and elitist misinterpretations—innovations and misinterpretations that have intellectually illuminated *and* discursively darkened its sociological salience. Accenting *The Philadelphia Negro*'s contributions to urban sociology, historical sociology, industrial sociology, sociology of work, sociology of the family, sociology of race, sociology of gender, and sociology of culture, I intentionally suspend any extended discussion of the ways in which *The Philadelphia Negro* contributes to sociology of religion, sociology of education, and sociology of crime, preferring instead to treat them respectively in the subsequent chapters of this book devoted exclusively to each of the aforementioned. Finally, I conclude this chapter with a critical discussion of the methodological innovations and interpretive limitations of Du Bois's contributions to urban and rural sociology, purposely giving *The Philadelphia Negro* the lion's share of my attention since it is the more detailed and more widely read of his early social scientific research. We begin, then, with Du Bois's unrecognized contributions to rural sociology.

DU BOIS'S SOCIOLOGICAL ROSETTA STONE: "THE NEGROES OF FARMVILLE, VIRGINIA" AND RUMINATIONS ON AFRICAN AMERICAN RURAL SOCIOLOGY

While working on *The Philadelphia Negro* Du Bois managed to research, write, and publish his first major contribution to rural sociology, "The Negroes of Farmville, Virginia: A Social Study." Although long overlooked, "The Negroes of Farmville" is something of a Rosetta Stone in terms of deciphering, not simply Du Bois's contributions to rural sociology, but also his innovative offerings to urban sociology. Contacted early in 1897 by the U.S. Department of Labor, Du Bois was extended an invitation to conduct a series of studies "relating to the economic progress of the colored people" in the South. "The Negroes of Farmville" was the first of five stellar studies for the Department of Labor. After "The Negroes of Farmville" was published in 1898 there was "The Negro in the Black Belt: Some Social Sketches" in 1899, which presented investigations of "[s]ix small groups, containing a total of 920 Negroes," all in Georgia except for one in Alabama (Du Bois, 1980a, 47). Then, in 1901 he published "The Negro Landholder of Georgia," which was followed by "The Negro Farmer" in 1906. "The Sharecropping System in Lowndes County, Alabama," the fifth and final study of the "economic conditions of the American Negro" conducted under the auspices of the Department of Labor, was, according to Herbert Aptheker (1980a), "lost" and/or "destroyed," Du Bois believed, "due to the radical nature of its findings and its condemnation of the then dominant system under which the vast majority of black people—and many white people—lived in the South" (1). With regard to rural sociology, Du Bois also published "The Relation of the Negroes to the Whites of the South" (1901), "The Spawn of Slavery: The Convict Lease-System in the South" (1901), "The Negroes of Dougherty County, Georgia" (1901), "The Development of a People" (1904), "The Negro South and North" (1905), and "Sociology and Industry in Southern Education" (1907).

As representative examples of Du Bois's contributions to rural sociology I would like to focus on and limit my comments to the first two studies, "The Negroes of Farmville" and "The Negro in the Black Belt," as these studies where published prior to, and directly influenced *The Philadelphia Negro* and Du Bois's subsequent Atlanta University studies (see Du Bois, 1969b). Undoubtedly, the Farmville study exerted the greatest influence on *The Philadelphia Negro* but, yet and still, the Black Belt investigation's impact should not be downplayed and was, at the time, equally indicative of Du Bois's signature sociology, rural or otherwise. The bulk of the discussion below, therefore, will revolve around the ways in which "The Negroes of Farmville" represents one of Du Bois's often-overlooked contributions to rural sociology and, also, how his rural sociology informed—indeed, discursively dovetailed with—his more renowned urban sociology. Less attention will be given to "The Negro in the Black Belt" intentionally, then, as my main objective here is to introduce my readers to the most representative example of Du Bois's contributions to rural sociology and the ways in which it intersects and overlaps with his urban sociology.

The first major remarkable feature of "The Negroes of Farmville" is how much it methodologically resembles *The Philadelphia Negro*. Undertaken during the era when Spencerian sociology dominated sociological discourse, the Farmville study was refreshingly free from the ungrounded grand theorizing that seemed to always and everywhere privilege conjectural commentary over the kind of empirical sociological inquiry that Du Bois had been trained in and was willfully determined to develop in the United States, especially with regard to the "Negro Problem." However, I should quickly quip, even in light of his adherence to empirical sociology, Du Bois (1980a), too, was often inclined to making sweeping, condescending, and perfectly paternalistic statements privileging the "better class" of "country Negroes" over the "lowest classes" of "country Negroes"—an unsavory practice he was equally prone to in *The Philadelphia Negro*, as will be witnessed below (47).

The tobacco-trading center of six counties, Farmville, Virginia, in 1897 was, Du Bois (1898a) waxed, "thoroughly Virginian in character—easygoing, gossipy, and conservative, with respect for family traditions and landed property" (4-5). Methodologically borrowing from his urban sociological and historical studies soon to be published as *The Philadelphia Negro*, Du Bois responded to the Department of Labor's invitation to investigate the industrial and economic conditions of the "colored" people in the South with a research plan that offers contemporary rural sociologists a window into his innovative and ever evolving methodological world. Writing to the first U.S. Commissioner of Labor, Carroll Davidson Wright—an eminent economist in his own right, known for his comprehensive *Evolution of the United States* (1897) and prodigious *Outline of Practical Sociology* (1902)—Du Bois's (1997a) proposed research plan, dated 5 May 1897, stated in part:

> In accordance with your suggestion I have been for the last month giving considerable thought as to methods of studying certain aspects of the industrial development of the Negro. It seems to me that the difficulties of studying so

vast and varied a subject are so large that the first work to be done should be rather of an experimental or preliminary nature calculated to locate and define the difficulties and to indicate lines upon which a larger investigation could be carried to success. At the same time the results of a series of preliminary studies could be published and would by allaying false notions and prejudices prepare the public mind for the larger work. Both the preliminary and the main work must of course be strictly limited in scope; great care must be taken to avoid giving offence to white or black, to raise no suspicions and at the same time to get definite accurate information. (41)

Scholars and students of rural sociology should observe, first and foremost, that Du Bois gave "considerable thought as to [the] methods of studying certain aspects of the industrial development of the Negro" in the South and nonmetropolitan areas. His rural sociology did not suffer from an unsophisticated superimposition of his urban sociological research methods. Indeed, his "considerable thought" concerning "Negro" conditions in rural regions seems to have indelibly inspired his methodological innovations, not only in the Farmville study, but also in *The Philadelphia Negro*. It should also be observed that considering "the difficulties of studying so vast and varied a subject" as African Americans' industrial and economic conditions in rural regions, similar to his Philadelphia study, Du Bois proposed that the "preliminary" rural studies be "strictly limited in scope," emphasizing that "great care must be taken to avoid giving offence to white or black, to raise no suspicions and at the same time to get definite accurate information." It was not the "strictly limited ... scope" of "The Negroes of Farmville," or any of his other contributions to rural sociology, that ultimately proved problematic, but the almost impossibility of "avoid[ing] giving offence to white or black" and "rais[ing] no suspicions." How could his research "raise no suspicions" when neither blacks nor whites knew, as he himself put it, "the real condition of the Negro"? What we have here, then, is a curious case of rural sociology with metropolitan measures and mannerisms. In some senses, Du Bois recenters city life and a metropolitan mindset, especially urban race relations and white middle-class morals and manners, as he analyzes the American apartheid conditions of black folk far removed from metropolises. However, despite his often Eurocentric, elitist, and assimilationist interpretations of African American life and culture in his major contributions to rural sociology, Du Bois's work continues to offer rural sociologists much on a methodological level and as an early sociological portrait of black life at the turn of the twentieth century.

It is only by reading between the lines of Du Bois's early work, especially "The Negroes of Farmville," that one can begin to appreciate the intense emphasis I am placing on its importance for understanding his sociological oeuvre. Du Bois's definitive biographer, David Levering Lewis (1993), went so far as to say that "The Negroes of Farmville" "was a small masterpiece of great range and depth, influencing the conclusions of the Seventh Ward monograph [i.e., *The Philadelphia Negro*] and serving as the standard for the Atlanta University Studies which he was then planning to take charge" (195). Above I characterized "The Negroes of Farmville" as a sort of Rosetta Stone that can—and, I argue, *should*—be used to decode Du Bois's sociological contributions. I make this assertion based on the fact that "The Negroes of Farmville," however subtly, influenced all of Du Bois's subsequent major contributions to the discourse and development of sociology in the United States. The fact that the Farmville study has received so little—actually, virtually *no*—critical commentary says a lot about, not simply Du Bois's "sociological negation," but African Americans' "sociological negation" and/or pathological presence when and where they were discussed in early sociological inquiry in the United States.[2]

A year before *The Philadelphia Negro* was published, Du Bois (1898a) found a "small, well-defined group . . . of Negroes" that he believed would provide him with an almost ideal environment to examine, "with as near an approach to scientific accuracy as possible, the real condition of the Negro" (7). While working on *The Philadelphia Negro*, the intellectually indefatigable Du Bois went to Farmville and copiously collected the data that would ultimately be published as what can now be properly considered the prelude to his larger body of sociological research. He assertively intoned, "The investigator spent the months of July and August [of 1897] in the town; he lived with the colored people, joined in their social life, and visited their homes" (12). As was quickly becoming his custom, with regard to both his urban and rural sociological research, Du Bois "plunged into the backwater community with gusto," Lewis (1993) notes, "determined to explore the place from the bottom up" (195).

In exploring Farmville "from the bottom up" Du Bois (1898a) employed an amazingly wide range of research methods, such as participant observation, survey research, archival research, ethnographic research, and statistical analysis, tellingly writing in a footnote: "Letters of introduction and some personal acquaintances among the people rendered intercourse easy. The information gathered in the schedules was supplemented by conversations with townspeople and school teachers, by general observation, and by the records in the County Clerk's Office" (7). He literally studied Farmville "from the bottom up," although he seems to have incessantly favored the "highest" or "better" class of "country colored people" (37–38). As will soon be explained in greater detail below, from Du Bois's early sociological optic the "highest" or "better" class of "country colored people" was usually those black folk who were not only middle-class but, beyond their bourgeois status, further along in their assimilation of white middle-class culture and values. His work hints at the myriad ways in which Farmville's black folk at the turn of the twentieth century were situated at the "geographic center of an historic slave State," and how most of their parents experienced firsthand the "rise and fall of the plantation slave system . . . and the moral and economic revolution of emancipation in a county where the slave property was worth at least $2,500,000" (4). However, his early work here does not engage the pitfalls of pandering to the Eurocentrism and elitism of white middle-class culture and Victorian values; that kind of critique, which Du Bois did eventually develop, would be registered later, a lot later by many accounts (Gooding-Williams, 2009; Horne, 1986, 2009; Marable, 1986; A. L. Reed, 1997; C. J. Robinson, 2000).

Even so, Du Bois's Farmville study proves prescient when one considers the fact that the first Great Migration of African Americans (from 1910 to 1940) was more than a decade in the future (Grossman, 1991; Harrison, 1991; Lemann, 1991; Marks, 1989). Couched among the carefully conceived and constructed tables and charts outlining every aspect of Farmville life from business and employment to schooling and literacy, from mortality and family structure to conjugal conditions and sex habits are undoubtedly some of the first sociological observations of African American "rural exodus"—that is, African American migration from rural regions to urban areas in search of better opportunities and employment. Du Bois (1898a) deftly wrote:

> Naturally such a town in the midst of a large farming district has a great attraction for young countrymen, on account of its larger life and the prospect of better wages in its manufacturing and trading establishments. A steady influx of immigrants thus adds annually to the population of the town. At the same time Farmville boys and girls are attracted by the large city life of Richmond, Norfolk, Baltimore, and New York. In this manner Farmville acts as a sort of clearinghouse, taking the raw country lad from the farm to train in industrial life, and sending North and East more or less well-equipped recruits for metropolitan life. This gives the town an atmosphere of change and unrest rather unusual in so small a place, and at the same time often acts as a check to schemes of permanent prosperity. (5)

Perhaps the most telling part of the above passage with regard to Du Bois's rural sociology is this: "Farmville acts as a sort of clearinghouse, taking the raw country lad from the farm to train in industrial life, and sending North and East more or less well-equipped recruits for metropolitan life." "Farmville," Du Bois observed, "is the trading center of six counties," and as such it held a "great attraction for young countrymen" because of its promise of a "larger life and the prospect of better wages in its manufacturing and trading establishments." Better wages, but also "train[ing] in industrial life" lured many a "raw country lad from the farm." With their new industrial training, many of Farmville's young black folk moved on to larger cities and urban life, creating what I am wont to call a *revolving-door community and culture* in Farmville. Building on Du Bois's above assertion that Farmville "acts as a sort of clearinghouse," it seems almost safe to say that Farmville represented a stepping stone town which many African Americans used to get entry into more metropolitan environments. This is extremely sociologically significant when we consider that by most accounts Du Bois is openly acknowledged as one of the major establishers of urban sociology in the United States. What if when one carefully and closely reads "The Negroes of Farmville," she is left with the distinct impression that Du Bois should more properly be considered simultaneously a key innovator in both urban *and* rural sociology? What if the ignoble ignoring or erasure of Du Bois's contributions to rural sociology now, after acknowledging the sociological significance of "The Negroes of Farmville," reeks of the very same stench that has so long been the calling card of the "sociological negation" that Green and Driver (1976) audaciously observed more than thirty-five years ago?

Beyond it being one of the earliest assessments of African American "rural exodus," "The Negroes of Farmville" also offers contemporary rural sociologists a "social sketch" of rural African American family life and structure, as well as rural African American conjugal conditions and sex habits. It would be difficult to explain with any certainty why Du Bois placed his discussion of conjugal conditions and sex habits before his discussion of family life and structure in Farmville or, even more puzzling, why he separated the two sections with discussions of education and illiteracy, as well as work and wages. Perhaps this is merely another example of the eccentric and idiosyncratic nature of his early sociological innovations or, perhaps, it is intentional and illustrative, indicative of the disjointed and dire conditions of African American rural life and culture at the turn of the twentieth century. No matter what Du Bois may have meant by bookending the Farmville study with discussions of, first, conjugal conditions and sex habits and then family life and structure, it is readily apparent that he wanted to expose his readers to the heterogeneity and complexity of rural African American life and culture. His emphasis on *black heterogeneity* is especially noteworthy when we turn, as we will below, to his discussion of labor and what he termed the "[t]hree pretty distinctly differentiated social classes" in Farmville (Du Bois, 1898a, 36).

With regard to African American rural conjugal conditions at the turn of the twentieth century, Du Bois made one of his more remarkable discoveries when his research revealed that "[i]n slavery days marriage or cohabitation was entered upon very early, and the first generation of freedmen did the same. The second generation, however, is postponing marriage largely for economic reasons, and is migrating to better its condition" (11). Here we come back to Du Bois's emphasis on African American "rural exodus," but we also move forward to his assessment of African American rural married life. Although he asserted, in the most Eurocentric and assimilationist manner one can imagine, that in terms of African American conjugal culture "we find . . . a race young in civilization," it could be alternatively argued that the very fact that African Americans were "postponing marriage largely for economic reasons" undoubtedly demonstrates the seriousness with which and the sanctity in which marriage was held by black folk not far removed from enslavement. This, indeed, is sociologically significant because it demonstrates that African Americans were arguably developing their own unique conjugal culture post-Emancipation, just has they had done during their desperate period of enslavement. Much more than a "mass of ignorant freedman," and in spite of Du Bois's "double-conscious" moralizing from a white middle-class cultural perspective, "The Negroes of Farmville" reveals the inner-workings of an African American rural world where African cultural retention and African cultural regeneration was often subtly and simultaneously taking place, or doggedly developing in such an unusual and unconventional manner—again, from a white middle-class cultural perspective—that one of, as Henry Louis Gates Jr. put it, "the most deeply read, most widely traveled, and most broadly and impeccably educated human beings in the world" seemed nearly completely confused as to how to assess the data that he himself copiously collected (Du Bois, 1898a, 4; Gates, 1996, 119). Comparing the "race young in civilization" with the conjugal conditions of the people of England, France, Germany, Hungary, and Italy, Du Bois concluded, as he did in *The Philadelphia Negro*, that because the women significantly outnumbered the men in Farmville, then serious marital and sexual problems were certain to abound. This conclusion in and of itself is not sociologically problematic, and it seems to be grounded in and in sync with Du Bois's data. However, when one engages this conclusion from an Africana critical theoretical perspective, then Du Bois's "double-conscious" dogmatizing rushes to the fore and rears its extremely ugly and aristocratic head. Projecting patently Victorian values onto African American conjugal conditions in Farmville, Du Bois (1898a) went on to declare:

> This leads to two evils—illicit sexual intercourse and restricted influence of family life. When among any people a low inherited standard of sexual morals is coincident with an economic situation tending to prevent early marriage and to promote abnormal migrations to the irresponsibility and temptations of city life, then the inevitable result is prostitution and illegitimacy. Thus, it is quite possible to see these evils increase among a people during a period when great general advance is being made. They are the evils inseparable from a transition period, and they will remain until the industrial situation becomes satisfactory, migration becomes normal, and moral standards become settled. (11)

After reading this, the question—again, from an Africana critical theoretical perspective—on the tip of most tongues is or, rather, *should be*, "To whose moral standards is Du Bois referring?" We could go further to ask: "Why should African Americans adhere to moral standards that most middle-class white folk seem to unrepentantly disregard?" We could go even further to ask: "Why are whites not examining African American and other non-white cultures in order to discover what moral lessons they could possibly learn about this great 'transition period' closing the nineteenth and welcoming the twentieth century?" Part of the answer, I suspect, lies in Du Bois's conception of postemancipation African Americans as being "a race young in civilization." Paradoxically, with all of his reading and traveling, and his broad and impeccable education, as Gates exclaimed above, Du Bois's conception of culture, at least in "The Negroes of Farmville" and *The Philadelphia Negro*, was fundamentally flawed because it privileged white middle-class culture and Victorian values, seemingly almost always and everywhere projecting them onto African Americans a mere two generations removed from enslavement and in the process of earnestly attempting to eke out an existence in the midst of one of the most unforgiving periods of American apartheid. Nevertheless, it is not enough to quickly label Du Bois "elitist" or "Eurocentric," and then lethargically leave the matter lying there. His contributions to sociology (or any other discipline for that matter), especially as they appear in "The Negroes of Farmville" and *The Philadelphia Negro*, demand that we bring what I have termed elsewhere "the Du Boisian dialectic" to bear on them, simultaneously critiquing and appreciating, teasing out and testing the positive and negative, or progressive and retrogressive aspects of his thought and texts from an Africana critical theoretical perspective, which is to say, in the earnest interests of continental and diasporan African liberation and democratic social transformation (see Rabaka, 2008a).

Undoubtedly Du Bois's discussion of "illegitimate births" and "low inherited standard[s] of sexual morals" is problematic, if not outright aristocratic, but, by the same token, it is to his credit that he provided an even more detailed discussion of miscegenation, ultimately relating it back to African Americans' enslavement and the hypocrisy of America's racial hierarchy. Although he does not directly engage the question of how African Americans' enslavement altered their traditional African conjugal culture, nor does he make any reference whatsoever to indigenous African marital practices, he does hint at how *white men in particular were willing to sexually cross the color-line in a way that they were not willing to socially cross the color-line*. What remains amazing, even as we engage this study after the first decade of the twenty-first century, is Du Bois's blatant disregard for his stated intention to "avoid giving offence to white or black" and "to raise no suspicions." Clearly Du Bois said what he felt he needed to in order for the

Department of Labor to approve and provide the funding for his Farmville study. However, when one calmly and carefully combs through this work, there are, to be sure, moments of intense textual tension that reveal his elitism and Eurocentrism, but there are also often muted moments where Du Bois audaciously broached disreputable subjects that would have easily offended most of his white readers. Even as he leveled one Eurocentric or elitist label after another on to the African Americans of Farmville, his words, however subtly, seemed to betray the "double-conscious" war soon to consume his dark and distressed, excruciating anxiety-filled soul in *The Souls of Black Folk* in particular, and in several of his subsequent works in general. With weighted words that surely distinguish his rural sociology from that of his contemporaries, Du Bois (1898a) took historical and sociological aim at the often-unreported ironies of miscegenation:

> While facts bearing on miscegenation between whites and blacks are difficult to obtain and interpret, yet they are of interest. Of the 44 illegitimate children mentioned, 10 were, in all probability, children of white men; 4 of these belonged to one mother, who was openly known to be the concubine of a white man who had a white family; 2 of the children belonged to another mother, and there were four mothers each having 1 illegitimate child, making six mothers in all having such children. There is no doubt that this illicit intercourse has greatly decreased in recent years. Curiously enough, there are in the vicinity of the town two cases of intermarriage of colored men and white women, which are undisturbed, despite the law. (12)[3]

The most obvious critique of the foregoing revolves around Du Bois's discussion of "illegitimate children." To twenty-first-century eyes and ears, this passage smacks of elitism, and rightly so. However, if one were to not only acknowledge Du Bois's aristocratic pontifications but also his seminal sociological contributions by reading between the lines and not stopping at the first sign of elitism, then—and, I am tempted to say in quick succession, only then—can one come to appreciate the fact that by simply being a "Negro" at the end of the nineteenth century and broaching the taboo topic of miscegenation in a social scientific and statistical manner, Du Bois was actually breaking new ground. Without in any way apologizing for Du Bois's elitism and Eurocentrism—something sensitive readers who are familiar with my body of work, especially my Du Bois studies, know that I will never concede—my conscience compels me to calmly and coolly say that even in the midst of his most elitist moments Du Bois seems to be double-consciously double-dealing his white readers. I will not go so far to say that he used the lame language and Victorian values of the white middle class to camouflage his critiques of the hypocrisy of their racial hierarchy, but I can, with a clear conscience, contend that when the passage above is read without the knee-jerk reaction to his aristocratic acrobatics Du Bois's revelations about miscegenation can and should be considered devastating from and to a white supremacist, anti-black racist, and/or pro-American apartheid perspective.

What if, in his own subtle way, the "two evils" of "illicit sexual intercourse and restricted influence of family life" that Du Bois discussed above were not simply the sole property and liability of "irresponsible" blacks, but also whites—and, even more damning, white males, the supposed supreme racial rulers of nineteenth-century America? Fast and firm, Du Bois's data reveals as much, especially when we are reminded that he wrote, "[o]f the 44 illegitimate children mentioned, 10 were, in all probability, children of white men," and then he observed, "4 of these belonged to one mother, who was openly known to be the concubine of a white man who had a white family; 2 of the children belonged to another mother, and there were four mothers each having 1 illegitimate child, making six mothers in all having such children." Once we digest the first and most immediate critique, which is, of course, aimed at Du Bois's elitist language (i.e., "illegitimate children"), is it possible that this sentence can be interpreted as anything other than a critique of white *and* male supremacy? This statement clearly illustrates the "irresponsibility" and cowardice of the white men who, I reiterate, were willing to sexually cross the color-line but not socially willing to cross it. Du Bois went one step further to deliver the social scientific deathblow to the chivalrous image of the white male by accenting two interracial marriages between black men and white women, stating, "Curiously enough, there are in the vicinity of the town two cases of intermarriage of colored men and white women, which are undisturbed, despite the law." In essence, Du Bois was demonstrating—in a way that decidedly prefigures Frantz Fanon's *Black Skin, White Masks*—that where white men were willing to unrepentantly practice concubinage with black women, black men were willing to practice a proper "Christian" rite and enter into "holy matrimony" with white women.

Transitioning from African American rural conjugal conditions to education, Du Bois painted a stark social portrait of the impact of "child labor" on African American rural education. "The town of Farmville has no schools for colored children," Du Bois wrote with disdain, but "sends them to the district school just outside the corporation limits. . . . It is not at present, if the general testimony of the townspeople is to be taken, a very successful school" (18). Then, hitting at the heart of the matter, he observed, "[i]t is practically ungraded," and "the teachers are not particularly well-equipped." Here, his comments suggest that, not only were African American children in rural regions not receiving education comparable to their European American counterparts, but that—and equally depressing—African American teachers, as a consequence of the poor quality of their own educational experiences, were not as "well-equipped" or well-prepared to meet the needs of students who, literally, had no formal educational familial traditions to model their educational ambitions on.

Shifting from the impact of the political economy of race and racism on African American rural education, to the impact of the political economy of gender and sexism on African American rural education, Du Bois shared, "Between the ages of 5 and 15 years the boys and girls attend school in about the same proportion; after that the boys largely drop out and go to work. As compared with the boys, a larger proportion of the girls receive some training above that of common grades" (13). The culprit of the alarmingly high dropout rate, Du Bois revealed, was not simply the impact of the political economy of race and racism, but also the crude zero-sum calculus of the intersections and interconnections of racism *and* capitalism within the world of American apartheid. "The effect of child labor in housework and in the tobacco factories," he wrote, "is easily traced . . . to the length of school attendance. . . . One noticeable change in the later generation is that the excess of illiteracy which was formerly among the women is now among the men" (13). Then, as if falling back into his aristocratic frame of reference, Du Bois wrote, "The better classes of women do not like to work in the factories, and the surroundings are said to be unsuitable for girls. Many children are kept from school all or part of the time to enable them to help in this factory work" (19). Purposely sidestepping for the moment Du Bois's comments concerning "[t]he better classes of women," which is obviously yet another sign of his elitist optic, the point I would like to drive home here has to do with the impact of child labor on African American rural education, or lack thereof. African American children in rural regions were born into a world where they were socially disadvantaged and discriminated against because of the color of their skins, and Du Bois's research accents their restricted access to education and the poor quality of the education they did receive. The calamitous conclusions of the Farmville study concerning education would be incessantly corroborated throughout the twentieth century and well into the twenty-first century by Africana historians, philosophers, sociologists, psychologists, and anthropologists of education both far and wide.

Education, in many senses, is virtually inextricable from class, and class is also often determined by occupation. However, what if no matter how well-educated an African American might be, certain occupations remained restricted to them based on the racial rules of nineteenth-century American apartheid? Such was the case, sad to say, when Du Bois collected the data for the Farmville study, and one of the most remarkable features of his work in this instance was its assertion and conception of inchoate African American class formations. "The opportunities for employment in Farmville," he asserted, "explain much as to the present condition of its Negro citizens, as, for example, the migration from country to town and from town to city, the postponement of marriage, the ownership of property, and the general relations between whites and blacks" (15). In essence, Du Bois went from highlighting the connections between African American rural education and employment to the ways in which African American "work and wages" was creating "[t]hree pretty distinctly differentiated social classes": the "highest" or "better" class; the "laboring" or "working" class; and, the "lowest," "criminal" or "semi-criminal" class (15–23).[4]

In terms of the "highest" or "better" class, Du Bois included entrepreneurs, preachers, teachers, caterers, grocers, barbers, farmers, and artisans. The "laboring" or "working" class was mostly made up of those employed in domestic service, cooperage, tobacco manufacturing, fruit-canning, feed-grinding, railroading, woodworking, and brickmaking. The "lowest," "criminal," or "semi-criminal" class was primarily composed of those who occupy the status of the "lumpenproletariat," to use Marxist terminology—that is, those legally unemployed but illegally employed, such as loafers, panhandlers, thieves, pimps, and prostitutes. Concerning the "better" class, Du Bois wrote, they "own their own homes, and do not usually go out to domestic service; the majority of them can read and write, and many of the young ones have been away to school" (36). With weighted words, which surely prefigure E. Franklin Frazier's *The Black Bourgeoisie* (1962), Du Bois (1898a) moralizes one moment, and then points to the "better" class's prickly practices the next moment:

> Among this class of people the investigator failed to notice a single instance of any action not indicating a thoroughly good moral tone. There was no drinking, no lewdness, no questionable conversation, nor was there any well-founded accusation. The circle was, to be sure, rather small, and there was a scarcity of young men. It was particularly noticeable that three families in the town, who, by reason of their incomes and education would have naturally moved in the best circle, were rightly excluded. In two of these there were illegitimate children, and in the third a wayward wife. Of the Farmville families about 40—possibly fewer—belonged to this highest class. (37)

Take note that Du Bois remarked that Farmville's "highest" class was "rather small" and clannish, similar to the bourgeoisie in Marx's conception of class. They purportedly possessed a "thoroughly good moral tone," but inexplicably Du Bois fell into the fantastic world of the black bourgeoisie's Victorian values when he overlooked the irony of beginning this passage characterizing this class as being in possession of a "thoroughly good moral tone," and then ending the passage with a discussion of how three families "who, by reason of their incomes and education would have naturally moved in the best circle, were rightly excluded" because they did not live up to the black bourgeoisie's strict adherence to the white bourgeoisie's Victorian values. Education and income, then, did not, and do not now, automatically assure one sound moral standing or entry into the wicked world of the bourgeoisie—black, white, or otherwise. What this paradox almost perfectly illustrates is the deep "double-consciousness" of the black bourgeoisie and its inability to earnestly engage other classes of African Americans on their own unique socioeconomic and cultural terms—terms, truth be told, partly retained or inherited from the syncretization of indigenous African customs and cultures, but also terms equally informed by African lifeworlds and life struggles in the cruel context of the racial colonialism and racial capitalism of the aftermath of African enslavement and the initiation of American apartheid.

In his discussion of "The Economics of the Family," Du Bois goes to great pains to describe the "three conceptions of the word 'family'" that could be applied to Farmville families: the "possible" family, the "real" family, and the "economic" family. Blinded by both his Eurocentrism and elitism, Du Bois failed to see that the data that he himself collected allowed for a broader conception of family than the Victorian value-informed one privileged by the black bourgeoisie. For instance, Du Bois (1898a) defined the "three conceptions of the word 'family'" as follows: "1. The possible family, i.e., the parents and all children ever born to them living. 2. The real family, i.e., the parents and all children living at present. 3. The economic family, i.e., all persons, related and unrelated, living in one home under conditions of family life" (23–24). Du Bois thought long and hard enough about his conception of family to sociologically redefine it to speak to the special needs of Farmville families. However, his redefinition of family was not critical of the ways in which Victorian values could possibly lead to the ostracization of certain African American families because, to put it plainly, African Americans were not then and are not now white families with long-term skin tans or permanently pigmented complexions. By being either unaware of, or ignoring, African and African American conceptions of the "extended family," Du Bois may have made a sociological move forward, in terms of redefining "family" for African American families, but he certainly made a cultural move backward by not widening his working comprehension of African American culture beyond the pretentious world of the black bourgeoisie.[5] In other words, in a strictly sociological sense, Du Bois contributed to the sociology of the African American family with his tripartite conception but, in a cultural sense, he did not historically and culturally ground his redefinition and conception of the African American family in the distinct diversity of African and African American lifeworlds and life struggles beyond the vantage point of both the white and black bourgeoisies. Conceptually incarcerated within the world of bourgeois thought and culture, Du Bois's sociology of the African American family privileged the "highest" or "better" class's conception of family without critically calling into question whether *their* familial paradigm, which was almost in every instance nothing more than a mere mimicking of the white middle-class familial model, was in the best interest of African American, not simply social survival, but cultural-social-political-psychological-educational development.[6]

According to Du Bois, Farmville's "laboring" or "working" class was at a crossroads, caught somewhere between the occupations associated with African American enslavement and the occupations resulting from the Second Industrial Revolution then ushering in the twentieth century (Bernal, 1970; Hudson, 1983; Rutledge, 1989). Domestic service, in particular, was frowned upon and only grudgingly entered into by this class, but, I reiterate, the cold calculus of the racial colonialism and racial capitalism of American apartheid made it virtually impossible for many members of this class to escape the economic necessity of entering into such work, no matter how demeaning they may have found it. Again, the occupations open to African Americans in rural regions at the turn of the twentieth century were extremely limited, and almost perfectly point to the racial rules of American apartheid. Explaining the working class's disdain for domestic service, Du Bois (1898a) revealingly wrote:

> There is considerable dissatisfaction over the state of domestic service. The Negroes are coming to regard the work as a relic of slavery and as degrading, and only enter it from sheer necessity, and then as a temporary makeshift. Parents hate to expose their sons to the early lessons of servility, which are thus learned, and their daughters to the ever-possible fate of concubinage. Employers, on the other hand, find an increasing number of careless and impudent young people who neglect their work, and in some cases show vicious tendencies, and demoralize the children of the family. They pay low wages, partly because the Southern custom compels families, who ought to do their own work, to hire help, and they cannot afford to pay much; partly, too, because they do not believe the service rendered is worth more. The servants, receiving less than they think they ought, are often careful to render as little for it as possible. They grow to despise the menial work they do, partly because their employers themselves despise it and teach their daughters to do the same. (21)

What Du Bois does here is demonstrate the sociocultural and political-economic aftereffects of African American enslavement, the ongoing effects of American apartheid, and the rising racial consciousness of what was then termed the "New Negro."[7] His rural sociology here reveals that unlike most African Americans in urban environments, African Americans in rural regions lived in the shadow of enslavement long after the Emancipation Proclamation was issued and the Civil War was won. They intentionally sought to distance themselves and shield their families from the horrific hangovers of the African holocaust and African American enslavement. Anything associated with enslavement, whether occupational or social, was entered into only out of "sheer necessity," and then only "as a temporary makeshift." This is extremely telling and distinguishing with regard to Du Bois's rural sociology insofar as it reveals that the "race young in civilization," as he put it, consciously resisted—on their own terms, and in their own way—their continued racial colonization and dehumanization, which was perpetuated by the supposed superior white race and white "civilization." Farmville's domestic servants performed work that was despised by black and white alike. However, Du Bois asserted, these workers were not inherently "careless and impudent young people who neglect[ed] their work" as much as they, on their own antiracist terms, resented the sociohistorical fact that for most white Southerners the "term 'Negro' and 'servant'" were rendered "synonymous" as a result of African American enslavement, racial colonization, and American apartheid (21).

Beneath Farmville's working class, according to Du Bois, was the "lowest" class; a class of folk who were either unemployed or unemployable. Speaking of the unemployed first, Du Bois points to the problems of Farmville's "industrial situation" as the culprit causing the intense economic distress of many an "industrious man." For the most part, the unemployed were not blamed for their dire situation, and Du Bois found fault with the process of industrialization as it was then taking place in rural regions: "A considerable number of idlers and loafers shows that the industrial situation in Farmville is not altogether satisfactory and that the moral tone of the Negroes has room for great improvement. One of the principle causes of idleness is the irregular employment" (22). Again, it should be emphasized that Du Bois was not arguing that this class of Farmville folk was inherently "idle," but that their "idleness" was inextricable from the political economy of the industrialization process in rural regions. However, going back to his menacing white middle-class moralizing, Du Bois reiterated his belief that "the moral tone of the Negroes has room for great improvement" even as he was asserting that the "industrial situation" of African Americans also "has room for great improvement." Such was the "double-conscious" sociological discourse that came to be characteristic of Du Bois's work during this early period.

On behalf of the humble and hardworking, although unemployed, of Farmville, Du Bois plainly pleaded: "A really industrious man who desires work is apt to be thrown out of employment from one-third to one-half of the year by the shutting up of the tobacco factories, the brickyard, or the cannery." Then, commenting on the far-reaching effects of being perpetually and, in a sense, schizophrenically partially employed and partially unemployed, Du Bois emotionally argued, "If the man be of ordinary caliber he easily lapses into the habit of working part of the year and loafing the rest. This habit is especially pernicious for half-grown boys, and leads to much evil." Notice that Farmville's working class was willing to—for lack of a better word—*work*, and that the fault was not found with the earnestly unemployed, but with the ways in which the "irregular employment" of the "industrial situation" was taking its toll on African American uplift and, in some senses, returning African Americans to the period of, and practices endured during, their enslavement.[8]

Conscious of the myriad ways in which whites, then as now, either ignore or downplay the horrors of the African holocaust and African American enslavement, as well as the aftereffects of African American enslavement and the ongoing effects of American apartheid, Du Bois climatically concluded: "Undoubtedly the present situation prolongs some of the evils of the slave system, and is the cause of much of that apparent laziness and irresponsibility for which so many Negroes are justly criticized. . . . The great demand is for steady employment which is not menial, [and] at fair wages" (22). Farmville's unemployed were not asking for handouts or any form of welfare. What they deeply desired was work and, what is more, work that was not demeaning and, seemingly in some way, a constant reminder or return to their dehumanizing lived experiences and lived endurances during African American enslavement. Du Bois's *sociological sensitivity* with regard to African American history, culture, and struggle here must be highlighted. When compared with the work of his rural sociological contemporaries at the end of the nineteenth century, Du Bois undeniably made a lasting contribution, especially when his sociological sensitivity to African American history, culture, and struggle is taken into account. However, as has been repeatedly observed above and as will continue to be the case throughout this book, Du Bois could be just as *sociologically insensitive* as he was sociologically sensitive with respect to African American history, culture, and struggle. Observe his comments on "that apparent laziness and irresponsibility for which so many Negroes are justly criticized." Certainly there are "idle" African Americans, as there are such folk in each and every human group, but one must always be careful and, even more, culturally sensitive when and where we come to African American lifeworlds and life struggles because of the long-denied acknowledgement of, I purposely repeat, the horrors of the African holocaust and African American enslavement, as well as the aftereffects of African American enslavement and the ongoing effects of American apartheid.

Du Bois's sociological insensitivity with regard to African American history, culture and struggle is undoubtedly on display when we turn to his discussion of the "slum elements" of Farmville, the "usual substratum of loafers and semi-criminals who will not work" (23). Admittedly, there is an important distinction that Du Bois made in his study between the "willing workers, or those capable of training," and those "able-bodied men who gamble, and fish, and drink" (23). However, when engaged from an Africana critical theoretical frame of reference, crucial historical-cultural-social-political questions remain, such as: How did the "irregular employment" opportunities impact Farmville's "slum elements?" What of the sociocultural and political economic impact of the black codes, the Jim Crow "separate but equal" laws, the peonage system, the crop-lien system, and/or the convict-lease system? How many of the folk who constituted Farmville's "slum elements" would have or could have been "willing workers, or those capable of training" if only they had had adequate education and honest employment opportunities? Du Bois's study did not adequately answer these questions, but instead depressingly predicted the growth of this class and painted a portrait of it as a sort of "breeding ground," if you will, for the "lowest" and "worst criminal classes." He wrote, the "slum elements of Farmville are as yet small in number, but they are destined to grow with the town. They receive recruits from the lazy, shiftless, and dissolute of the country around; they send them on to Washington, Philadelphia, and Baltimore as fit candidates for the worst criminal classes of those cities" (23).

"The Negroes of Farmville" remains sociologically significant more than a century after its publication because it not only hinted at African Americans' distinct growth and development a mere thirty years after the Emancipation Proclamation, but also what was to quickly become Du Bois's signature sociological discourse. "A study of a community like Farmville," Du Bois concluded, "brings to light facts favorable and unfavorable, and conditions good, bad, and indifferent. Just how the whole should be interpreted is perhaps doubtful" (38). As we are now well into the twenty-first century, it seems almost safe to say that although there is no consensus on "[j]ust how the whole" of African American history, culture and struggle "should be interpreted," the development and discourse of black-African American-Africana studies has consistently identified ways in which African American history, culture, and struggle should *not* be interpreted. Eurocentric, elitist, and assimilationist, to name only a few, interpretations of African American history, culture, and struggle have been repeatedly rejected, if not downright denounced. *Conceptual decolonization* has been and remains on the rise, and the Africana critical theoretical perspective is part and parcel of this intellectual evolution. Du Bois's rural sociology is a significant aspect of this evolution as well and, as we have witnessed above, almost perfectly places both the pitfalls and enormous potential of, not simply his sociological thought, but also classical African American intellectual history and culture into bold relief.

Perhaps above and beyond all the other aspects of his documentation and analysis in the Farmville study, Du Bois believed his discovery of, and emphasis on class formation among African Americans a mere thirty years after the Emancipation Proclamation was sociologically significant. African American social classes may not, then as now, resemble Marxian, Weberian, or Durkheimian social classes, but for Du Bois and the majority of the mass of African American sociologists who were to conduct their work in his wake, that was all beside the point. The point, if I may put it plainly, was to sociologically engage every pertinent aspect of African American lifeworlds and life struggles in the interest of human liberation and democratic social transformation. Du Bois declared: "One thing, however, is clear, and that is the growing differentiation of classes among Negroes, even in small communities. This most natural and encouraging result of 30 years' development has not yet been sufficiently impressed upon general students of the subject, and leads to endless contradiction and confusion" (38). Indeed, "endless contradiction and confusion" have plagued African American sociology and/or the sociology of African Americans. However, and in all intellectual honesty, it must be conceded that Du Bois's work has often added to, and sat at the heart of the "endless contradiction and confusion" surrounding African American sociology and/or the sociology of African Americans. Perhaps his conclusion to the Farmville study best puts the, literally, "endless contradiction and confusion" into perspective:

> [A] visitor might tell us that the Negroes of Farmville are idle, unreliable, careless with their earnings, and lewd; another visitor, a month later, might say that Farmville Negroes are industrious, owners of property, and slowly but steadily advancing in education and morals. The apparently contradictory statements made continually of Negro groups all over the land are both true to a degree, and become mischievous and misleading only when they are stated without reservation as true of a whole community, when they are in reality true of only certain classes in the community. The question then becomes, not whether the Negro is lazy and criminal, or industrious and ambitious, but rather what, in a given community, is the proportion of lazy to industrious Negroes, of paupers to property-holders, and what is the tendency of development in these classes. Bearing this in mind, it seems fair to conclude, after an impartial study of Farmville conditions, that the industrious and property-accumulating class of the Negro citizens best represents, on the whole, the general tendencies of the group. At the same time, the mass of sloth and immorality is still large and threatening. (38)

Observe that Du Bois ended by exclaiming that "it seems fair to conclude, after an impartial study of Farmville conditions, that the industrious and property-accumulating class of the Negro citizens best represents, on the whole, the general tendencies of the group," while almost every preceding word of the study points to the paucity of the "highest class" of Farmville's black folk. How can so few "best represent" so many, especially considering the sociocultural and political economic diversity of Farmville's black masses? What about the assimilationist tendencies of Farmville's "highest class" of black folk? How can their incessant whitewashing of, and dogged distancing of themselves from, black culture, as produced and practiced by Farmville's masses, "best represent" the future of "Negro groups all over the land"? Again, it seems as though Du Bois's "double-conscious" sociological discourse decidedly took a step forward by acknowledging the hardships and harsh labor conditions of Farmville's masses, but there is another sense in which his rural sociology unmistakably took a step backward by failing to acutely acknowledge the fact that the black bourgeoisie had developed the disgusting habit of mimicking the white middle class's morals and culture. This pathological paradox is, perhaps, nowhere more evident than it is in Du Bois's innovative and, by some accounts, infamous study of African American Philadelphians: *The Philadelphia Negro*.

DU BOIS'S URBAN SOCIOLOGY: *THE PHILADELPHIA NEGRO*

Building on and decidedly going beyond the methodological outline and orientation of "The Negroes of Farmville," Du Bois's *The Philadelphia Negro* confirms the rural study's Rosetta Stone status in his sociological discourse. Discursively mirroring his discussion of the distinct history and heritage, racialization and criminalization, family life and conjugal conditions, education and illiteracy, and work and wages of the "country Negro," *The Philadelphia Negro* added in-depth investigations of the disease and death rate, alcoholism and pauperism, electoral politics, and religious practices of the "city Negro" as well. Much more methodical and meticulous than the rural study, over the century since its publication *The Philadelphia Negro* has garnered a unique place for itself in the annals of American social science. Lionized historian David Levering Lewis (1993) declared, "Some have made the debatable claim that *The Philadelphia Negro* is the first study of its kind in America, but its pride of place as the first scientific urban study of African Americans is as secure as the charge is misconceived that Du Bois's book is largely derivative" (190). Appearing to offer Lewis a rejoinder, the eminent African American sociologist Elijah Anderson (1996) exclaimed, "Du Bois's work takes on seminal status not only for the study of the urban poor but also for the study of race in urban America. Indeed, it is in this sense that *The Philadelphia Negro* was truly the first work of its kind" (xix). Then, concluding his contention with words that seem to dovetail with Lewis's views, Anderson asserted, "It was the first [study] to seriously address and profoundly illuminate what was then known as "the Negro problem."[9]

Researched, written, and published under the auspices of the University of Pennsylvania and its affiliated welfare organization, the College Settlement Association (CSA), *The Philadelphia Negro* bears the marks of Du Bois's distinct "double-conscious" sociological discourse at the turn the twentieth century. Partly on account of the white middle-class feminist paternalist reformism of CSA which, Lewis (1993) asserted, "was a feminist force to reckon with for civic leaders," and partly owing to his own Eurocentrism, elitism, and assimilationism, Du Bois wrote "what amounted to two books in one—one that would not be immediately denounced or ridiculed by the arbiters of mainstream knowledge, influence, and order for its transparent heterodoxy; and a second one that would, over time, deeply penetrate the social sciences and gradually improve race relations policy through its not-immediately apparent interpretive radicalism" (188–89).[10] It was Du Bois's "interpretive radicalism" that, although quite often condescendingly conservative throughout the text, registers as the greatest challenge to those who claim, as they have repeatedly and with glowing glee for more than a century, that his study is derivative of the English capitalist Charles Booth's *Life and Labor of the People in London* (1889–1902) and U.S. Settlement House movement pioneer Jane Addams's *Hull House Maps and Papers* (1895).

Undeniably Booth and Addams's studies, as well as city surveys of poverty-stricken communities in New York, Boston, Washington, and Chicago, served as methodological models for *The Philadelphia Negro*. In fact, it has been argued that Booth's work provided both Addams and Du Bois with intellectual inspiration. However, no matter what Du Bois may have methodologically drawn from Booth, Addams, or others conducting serious social scientific research at the turn of the twentieth century, one thing is for certain and that is that no one else was applying social scientific research methods to, and conducting empirical sociology in the interests of African Americans. What is more, Du Bois's distinction is doubled when we take into account that where Booth and Addams's studies focused on city life and urban environments, Du Bois undertook studies of both African American city life and urban environments *and* African American country life and rural environments. Lewis (1993) proudly proclaimed that the "thoroughness with which Du Bois refined and applied what he borrowed, however, was characteristically remarkable" (190).

More recently the esteemed French sociologist, Pierre Saint Arnaud (2009), has asserted that Addams's work, in particular, "offered Du Bois a template, but he proceeded much more systematically, innovating with his deliberate melding of methodical fact-finding and theorization" (138). Where Lewis wrote "[s]ome have made the debatable claim that *The Philadelphia Negro* is the first study of its kind in America," similar to Anderson above, Saint-Arnaud audaciously offered the riposte that Du Bois's work was "the first work of social science to focus on race in the 'urban' American setting." Furthermore, Saint-Arnaud said "it was the first community study in the United States to be performed by a scholar" (139). The minor textual tension between Lewis and Saint-Arnaud's studies is telling insofar as their respective interpretations speak volumes about their methodological orientations and disciplinary perspectives, as well as Du Bois's innovative "two books in one"—as Lewis aptly put it—approach in *The Philadelphia Negro*.

Whether Lewis and Saint-Arnaud disagree as to the exact nature of Du Bois's historical (à la Lewis) and/or sociological (à la Saint-Arnaud) distinction is ultimately beside the point, as both seem to unanimously agree that in the century since its publication *The Philadelphia Negro* has "deeply penetrate[d] the social sciences and gradually improve[d] race relations policy" by historicizing the horrors of the African holocaust and African American enslavement, as well as the aftereffects of African American enslavement and the ongoing effects of American apartheid.[11]

In other words, armed to the teeth with innovative empirical research methods gathered from his graduate studies in history, political science, and economics at Harvard and the University of Berlin, Du Bois lent the historical, sociological, and political economic study of race, racialization, and racism an academic legitimacy and analytical validity that was not simply rare, but virtually unprecedented nationally and internationally at the turn of the twentieth century. This is a point that must be emphasized because it goes well beyond the coarse claim that Du Bois's Philadelphia study is somehow "derivative" of Booth's, Addams's, or others' studies, and it gets to the meat of the matter by acknowledging, first and foremost, that Du Bois, indeed, did conceptually and methodologically "borrow" from the aforementioned. However, instead of getting stuck on or, worse, stopping at a discussion of what Du Bois "borrowed" from others, an Africana critical theoretical approach to his contributions to sociology accents *how* and *the myriads innovative ways in which* he "refined and applied what he borrowed," as Lewis asserted above, which "was characteristically remarkable." Again, what makes Du Bois's early sociological studies "characteristically remarkable" is the incontrovertible fact that where others applied empirical social scientific research methods to the English working class in London (Booth), or the European immigrant working class in Chicago (Addams), or the white working class in Boston—à la amateur sociologist Robert Woods in *The City Wilderness* (1898)—Du Bois's distinction is to be found in his, literally, deconstructing and reconstructing social scientific research methods and inaugurating empirical sociology in the interest of African American liberation and antiracist social transformation. As was observed earlier, this last point is one on which Lewis, Anderson, and Saint-Arnaud, among others, agree. Lewis's (1993) sharp-witted words are worthy of quotation:

> *The Philadelphia Negro* was remarkable as an example of the new empiricism that was fundamentally transforming the social sciences at the beginning of the twentieth century. Although Du Bois's novel sociological insights would soon become conventional wisdom, as one of the last books of the nineteenth century and the first of the twentieth century, the Philadelphia study would be a breakthrough achievement, an important and virtually solitary departure from the hereditarian theorizing of the times. The armchair cerebrations of sociology's great nineteenth-century system-builders—Auguste Comte, Karl

Marx, and Herbert Spencer—would continue to inform, challenge, and inspire, but the watchword of the discipline was becoming *investigation*, followed by induction—facts before theory. More than any other leading American sociologist during the decade after 1898, Du Bois undertook for a time the working out of an authentic objectivity in social science, "to put science into sociology through a study of the conditions and problems of [his] own group." (201–2, emphasis in original; see also Du Bois, 1968b, 50–51)

Lewis's work is especially important here in terms of highlighting, not only the ways in which Du Bois's empirical research was distinguished from the "armchair cerebrations of sociology's great nineteenth-century system-builders—Auguste Comte, Karl Marx, and Herbert Spencer," but also the historicization of Du Bois's sociology within the developing world of American sociology. No mention need be made of the fact that all three of the aforementioned were European sociologists whose primary preoccupations involved sociological theory in the interest of the social transformation of their respective locales. Indubitably, Du Bois was one of the first sociologists to earnestly endeavor a sociology to speak to the special needs of the United States, which—it could almost go without saying—at the turn of the twentieth century had its own particular and peculiar set of social problems. Part of what really and truly distinguished the United States' turn-of-the-twentieth-century social problems from those of Europe was, of course, its notorious "Negro problem." What Du Bois's work sought to do was historicize or, rather, rehistoricize the "Negro problem," in essence, countering the European American academic conventions of his milieu, which seemed to always and everywhere view African Americans from an ahistorical—albeit Eurocentric—perspective that incessantly either ignored or abated the horrors of the African holocaust and African American enslavement, as well as the aftereffects of African American enslavement and the ongoing effects of American apartheid.

Intellectually indefatigable and doggedly determined, as a response to the customary ahistorical and Eurocentric academic approach to African American history, culture, and struggle, Du Bois had no other recourse but to develop—he, literally, intellectually *invented*—*a distinct history, culture, and political economy-informed sociology*, which simultaneously revolutionized sociology in general, and made much-needed conceptual room for what would come to be called "African American sociology" (Blackwell and Janowitz, 1974; Conyers and Barnett, 1999; Staples, 1975; Wright and Calhoun, 2006; Young and Deskins, 2001). Saint-Arnaud (2009) hit the nail on its head when he earnestly rhetorically asked, "What choice did he [Du Bois] have but to invent a counter-sociology, perhaps even an anti-sociology, in an intellectual context in which the Anglo-American founding fathers indulged in broad theoretical speculation on race relations, championing a theoretical model—Social Darwinism—that 'instinctively placed blacks at the primitive end of the evolutionary scale'?" Once more, mention must be made of Lewis and Saint-Arnaud's agreement on Du Bois's challenge to the "armchair cerebrations" and Social Darwinism of sociology's "great nineteenth-century system-builders." Speaking directly to Du Bois's paradoxical predicament as he simultaneously sought entry into and to unerringly overhaul sociology, Saint-Arnaud said, "When listening to the sages explain racial inequality as the inevitable result of grand natural laws, or invoke Spencer, their favorite prophet, Du Bois simply had no theoretical corpus on which to base a contrary position. He had to build a new science from the ground up, a science devoted to the advancement, as opposed to the near-term extinction, of black Americans" (140).[12]

African Americans's turn-of-the-twentieth-century situation was indeed dire, and Du Bois's sociohistorical testimony in *The Philadelphia Negro* corroborates Saint-Arnaud's claims. However, "even with the terribly adverse circumstances under which Negroes live," Du Bois (1899) unapologetically exclaimed in the face of Social Darwinism and Spencerian social thought, "There is not the slightest likelihood of their dying out." He reassured his readers that "a nation that has endured the slave trade, slavery, reconstruction, and present prejudice three hundred years, and under it increased in numbers and efficiency, is not in any immediate danger of extinction" (388). *The Philadelphia Negro* was, therefore, more than a mere sociological catalogue of a diseased and dying race and its peculiar "problems." Much more, it was intended as a salvo signaling African Americans' tragic past and the possibility of their triumphant future. Additionally, it might also be said, *The Philadelphia Negro* was one of Du Bois's earliest and most sustained efforts to synthesize social science and social reform in the interests of African Americans.

Saint-Arnaud's emphasis on Du Bois having "no theoretical corpus on which to base a contrary position" and his "build[ing] a new science from the ground up, a science devoted to the advancement, as opposed to the near-term extinction, of black Americans" deserves to be discursively accented, as does Du Bois's development of a "counter-sociology," or "perhaps even an anti-sociology." Du Bois's "counter-sociology" or, perhaps more properly, *counter-anti-black racist sociology* is often at once contradictory and controversial: contradictory, in the sense that it frequently used white middle-class morals and culture as the criteria in which to identify and offer solutions to "Negro problems"; controversial, in terms of its almost complete rejection of the "armchair cerebrations" and Social Darwinism of sociology's "great nineteenth-century system-builders." However, it should be said in all intellectual honesty, Du Bois's urban sociology could be quite conservative, as we have witnessed was the case with his rural sociology. Suffice to say, it seems as though the "double-conscious" and schizophrenic nature of Du Bois's sociology could be interpreted as a conceptual consequence of his having "no theoretical corpus on which to base a contrary position" and his efforts to "build a new science from the ground up." In this vein, Elijah Anderson (1996) goes so far as to say:

> At the same time, it is provocative to consider what part Du Bois's own identity played in the contradictory perspectives he presents—that of the elite Victorian young gentleman committed to the ideas of meritocracy and universalism, and that of a son of a people struggling to live in freedom after two hundred years of a bondage justified on racial grounds. Du Bois's struggle to reconcile these two orientations is one of the fascinating aspects of *The Philadelphia Negro*. One gets the sense that it was very difficult for him to accept the idea that blacks were second-class citizens because at the time he wrote the book he still considered himself to be a full citizen of the United States, even a member of the elite. This tension may account for the ultimately ambivalent assessment of the Philadelphia Negro's situation with which Du Bois leaves the reader. (xxiii)

In essence, the contradictory and controversial aspects of Du Bois's early sociology cannot be completely said to be a consequence of his having "no theoretical corpus on which to base a contrary position" and his efforts to "build a new science from the ground up." Beyond the problems inherent in his Eurocentrism and embrace of white middle-class morals and Victorian values were his homespun black elitist orientation and his incessant advocacy of the African American aristocracy as the "best representatives" of his people, which will be discussed in detail in the succeeding section. It is ultimately Du Bois's "struggle to reconcile these two orientations"—both bourgeois, although one black and one white—that simultaneously defines and deforms *The Philadelphia Negro* and, as Anderson asserted, offers one of the most "fascinating aspects of *The Philadelphia Negro*" in particular, and Du Bois's early sociological discourse in general.

It is important for us to openly acknowledge that Du Bois did not simply "refine and apply" the innovative methodological orientations of the early sociological world to African America, as his work also shows traces of his, however subtle, digestion and indelicate application of a homespun intraracial Social Darwinistic elitism where the "better class" of blacks, "the talented few," were purportedly destined to rise above and eventually rule over the "low civilization" of the "great mass of Negroes." For instance, Du Bois (1899) ironically wrote, "There are many Negroes who are as bright, talented and reliable as any class of [white] workmen, and who in untrammeled competition would soon rise high in the economic scale, and thus by the law of the survival of the fittest we should soon have left at the bottom those inefficient and lazy drones who did not deserve a better fate" (98, 141, 147, 193). Inexcusable elitism and assimilationism fill the pages of *The Philadelphia Negro* but, yet and still, it has been repeatedly hailed—by black and white alike, bourgeois and proletarian—as a hallowed text in the history and discursive development of American sociology.

Unquestionably contradictory and controversial, Du Bois's sociology was ultimately *social policy–preoccupied* and *social praxis–promoting*. Seemingly more concerned with "getting the facts straight" than with avoiding hurting black or white folks' feelings, *The Philadelphia Negro* spared nothing and no one in its unquenchable quest to provide new, empirically based knowledge in the interests of social, political, and institutional transformation. Long before European American sociology sought to couple social theory with social praxis, Du Bois literally laid the foundations for liberation sociology in the United States. On the prescient and praxis-oriented nature of Du Bois's sociology in general, and *The Philadelphia Negro* in particular, Saint-Arnaud's (2009) words, once again, prove noteworthy:

> The work [i.e., *The Philadelphia Negro*] was exceptional, in sum—nothing less than a landmark of social science—in that it anticipated by many years the moment when mainstream Anglo-American sociology would emerge from its amorphous state to become a less pompously declamatory science, one more rooted in social praxis and historical experience. Du Bois's sociology was, in most respects, far ahead of its "scientific time"—measured, it must always be remembered, on the clock of the Anglo-American intelligentsia. But in one respect—his mixing of the agendas of sociological science and social reform—Du Bois was very much of his time, cast in the same mold as [Lester Frank] Ward, [Charles Horton] Cooley, [Franklin Henry] Giddings, or [Edward Alsworth] Ross. He presented himself as both a disinterested analyst of society and an enlightened contributor to the easing of racial friction. This combination of science and reform inevitably led him into ambiguities, exaggerations, and biases. (139–40)

It should be, again, reiterated that neither Ward, Cooley, Giddings, nor Ross, nor any other European American sociologist for that matter, sought to systematically "refine and apply" social scientific research methods and conduct empirical sociology in the interests of African Americans. Therefore, although Saint-Arnaud is clearly correct when he argues that *The Philadelphia Negro* "anticipated by many years the moment when mainstream Anglo-American sociology would emerge from its amorphous state to become a less pompously declamatory science, one more rooted in social praxis and historical experience," his analysis seems to go awkwardly astray when he quickly casts Du Bois in the "same mold" as Ward, Cooley, Giddings, and Ross, as well as when he Eurocentrically maintains that Du Bois's sociology should be "measured, it must always be remembered, on the clock of the Anglo-American intelligentsia." With all due respect to the sociological legacies of each of the aforementioned, part of what really and truly distinguishes Du Bois's sociological legacy from those of his European and European American sociological forebears and contemporaries is his indelible and still easily detected dogged determination, and the persistent passion with which he deconstructed and reconstructed the then inchoate empirical social scientific research methods in the interests of African Americans and innovatively inaugurated what Saint-Arnaud's research refers to as "an authentically black sociology" (125). This, of course, leaves Saint-Arnaud's assertion that Du Bois's sociology must be "measured, it must always be remembered, on the clock of the Anglo-American intelligentsia" in the lurch, at best, or an inexplicable and lame lapse into Eurocentrism, at worst. Needless to say, it is truly intellectually amazing and more than a little ironic that, in this instance, Saint-Arnaud seems to almost completely ignore and render invisible Africana intellectual and cultural history in general, and the aberrant evolution of the African American intelligentsia in particular, which has been copiously documented and critically discussed by Earl Thorpe (1961), Harold Cruse (1967), William Banks (1996), Joy James (1997), Manning Marable (2000), Anthony Bogues (2003), Jerry Watts (2004), and Kristin Waters and Carol Conway (2007), among others.

If, indeed, we are willing to concede Saint-Arnaud's assertion that Du Bois was "the creator of an authentically black sociology," then we need to think long and laboriously about precisely what makes "black sociology"—to put it plainly—*black*. I can say outright that it is not necessarily the methodological orientation that makes "black sociology" *black*, because many "black" sociologists have been trained in and employ exactly the same or, at the least, very similar methodological tools when compared with their nonblack sociological peers; it is, most certainly, not a biologically determined or racial essentialist affair, as several nonblack or sociologists *not* of African descent have made immeasurable contributions, which have been openly acknowledged and accepted, to the discourse and ongoing development of "black sociology"; and, to be sure, it is not a sociology that is simply the opposite of white sociology, or white sociology in blackface, if you will, as the collective research of Joyce Ladner (1998), Bruce Hare (2002), and Jonathan Holloway and Ben Keppel (2007) reveals. Hence, here we have come right back to what Lewis referred to above as the "interpretive radicalism" of Du Bois's sociology in particular, and African American sociology in general.

In other words, when all the smoke clears and all the dust settles, it is the distinct *conceptual criteria, methods of interpretation,* and *modes of analysis* that distinguish African American sociology from other versions of sociology. Furthermore, although it may not need to be said but, perhaps, it should be said for the sake of sanity, integrity, and clarity, African American sociologists and/or sociologists of African American lifeworlds and life struggles should not be "measured . . . on the [racial-colonial-bourgeois cuckoo] clock of the Anglo-American intelligentsia" but, with sincere and solemn respect for the subjects of their work (i.e., African Americans), African American sociologists' thought and texts should more properly be "measured . . . on the clock of the [African American] intelligentsia." When this is done, first and foremost, then African American sociological thought can, and perhaps *should*, be compared and contrasted with European American, among other, sociological trends and traditions—which is also to say that an Africana critical theoretical approach to African American sociology does not in any way preclude deep, discursive dialogue between African American and European American sociology but, instead, openly and earnestly encourages it, as well as critical comparisons with the sociological trends and traditions of the wider nonwhite world.

In essence, what Du Bois's early sociological work presents us with are the theoretical trials and tribulations, the conceptual growing pains of his earnest efforts to conceive, first, an African American and, later, a Pan-African critical perspective specific to the special sociopolitical needs, the lifeworlds and life struggles of continental and diasporan Africans or, if I must, "blacks" living in an anti-black racist and white supremacist world. Recall, I wrote above that it seems as though the "double-conscious" and schizophrenic nature of Du Bois's sociology could be interpreted as a conceptual consequence of his having "no theoretical corpus on which to base a contrary position" and equally indicative of his stab at "build[ing] a new science from the ground up." Furthermore, Saint-Arnaud asserted that Du Bois had no other recourse but to create a "counter-sociology," where I argued that Du Bois inaugurated what might be more properly called a *counter-anti-black racist sociology*. It is important, then, here and now to reemphasize the unique conceptual difficulties Du Bois surely faced in his endeavors to establish an empirical sociology in the interest of African American liberation and democratic social transformation.

I utterly agree with Saint-Arnaud when he concluded the passage above by stating that Du Bois's idiosyncratic "combination of science and reform inevitably led him into ambiguities, exaggerations, and biases." However, it should be underscored that it was not merely Du Bois's "combination of science and reform" that "led him into ambiguities, exaggerations, and biases," because Saint-Arnaud himself said that on this account Du Bois was very much in the "same mold" as other early American sociologists. More critically, and emerging from an Africana critical theoretical perspective, what makes Du Bois's "ambiguities, exaggerations, and biases" even more ironic and perfectly paradoxical is that even though he was diligently endeavoring to establish an empirical sociology in the interests of African Americans, his work, quite literally, *his words* betray the fact that he was intellectually infected with Eurocentrism, elitism, assimilationism, certain elements of Social Darwinism, and a very subtle form of sexism which privileged the patriarchal conception of the African American family. Here, then, we have returned to Africana critical theory's intense emphasis on *conceptual criteria, methods of interpretation,* and *modes of analysis* that are grounded in, and speak to the special needs of continental and diasporan African lifeworlds and life struggles. In what follows, let us look at *The Philadelphia Negro* through the lens of Africana critical theory, accenting its prefiguring and pivotal place in Du Bois's sociological discourse. By dividing our discussion along the lines of the book's primary themes, which coincide with its major chapters, we will be able to better grasp and grapple with its innovative and influential findings and more easily explore its "interpretive radicalism," as well as its *interpretive elitism* and *conceptual conservatism.*

ON THE "TALENTED FEW" AND THE "SUBMERGED TENTH": DU BOIS'S HISTORICAL SOCIOLOGY OF RACIALLY OPPRESSED AND ECONOMICALLY EXPLOITED SOCIAL CLASSES

Undoubtedly, one of the major breakthroughs of *The Philadelphia Negro* was its detailed discussion of class formation among African Americans a mere three decades since the signing of the Emancipation Proclamation. Even more meticulously than in "The Negroes of Farmville," Du Bois (1899) ventured into the uncharted regions of African American social classes and unprecedentedly determined that class formation and class conflict on the part of African Americans was a consequence of, of course, economics, employment, education, property ownership, morals, and manners, but also, and even more tellingly, racialization and assimilation—what he termed "color prejudice," the "color-line," "discrimination against Negroes," "the tangible form of Negro prejudice," "a silent policy against Negroes," "veiled discrimination," and "social ostracism" (322–67). Seeming to simultaneously draw from and commit a *conceptual coup d'état* in the midst of Weber and Marx's conceptions of class, Du Bois's concept of class, even in this early instance, is distinguished on account of its critical attention to the ways in which the political economy of race and anti-black racism in a white supremacist capitalist society such as the United States dictated and determined that social classes amongst African Americans could more properly be viewed as *racial classes.*

Even if all of the other sociological innovations of *The Philadelphia Negro* were to be overlooked, as they frequently have been, Du Bois's dogged insistence on the ways in which African American social classes have been and remain degradingly racialized and, therefore, are always and everywhere more than mere socioeconomic classes—à la the conventional sociological conception of class—should be calmly and cautiously considered for both its classical and contemporary sociological significance. Du Bois's sociology of racial classes reaches from the nineteenth century, across the twentieth century, and resonates with both the sociology of race and the sociology of class in the twenty-first century with its intense emphasis on African Americans' particular and peculiar class formations and class cultures. His sociology of racial classes registers as an early reminder that Weberian and Marxian conceptions of class, no matter how "universal" many sociologists believe them to be, were primarily tailored to meet the needs and greeds of Europeans, and not those of a non-European group such as African Americans who were, truth be told, enslaved and colonized or, rather, *racially colonized* by Europeans from a wide range of class backgrounds: from bourgeoisie and petit-bourgeoisie to proletariat and lumpenproletariat.

Part of what made African American social classes *racial classes* was not simply their racialization at the hands of whites but, even more, the continued racial colonization of their lifeworlds and lived experiences under American apartheid. Du Bois (1899) unrepentantly retorted at the outset of *The Philadelphia Negro*:

> Here is a large group of people—perhaps forty-five thousand, a city within a city—who do not form an integral part of the larger social group. This in itself is not altogether unusual; there are other unassimilated groups: Jews, Italians, even [other white] Americans; and yet in the case of the Negroes the segregation is more conspicuous, more patent to the eye, and so intertwined with a long historic evolution, with peculiarly pressing social problems of poverty, ignorance, crime and labor, that the Negro problem far surpasses in scientific interest and social gravity, most of the other race or class questions. (5)

Acknowledging the inextricable nature of racial segregation from African Americans' other "peculiarly pressing social problems," Du Bois ultimately declared that "the Negro problem far surpasses in scientific interest and social gravity, most of the other race or class questions."

For those who have wrongly claimed that Du Bois's class consciousness was a consequence of his later Marxist studies, here is proof-positive to the contrary. However, I would be one of the first to openly admit—as he did in his final autobiography, *The Autobiography of W. E. B. Du Bois*—that when Du Bois's early sociology of class is placed under scrutiny it is found woefully wanting, especially with regard to every class of African Americans other than the "better class of Negroes" or, rather, the "Negro aristocracy," as he put it. For Du Bois, the "Negro problem," the *Negroization* or *process(es) of Negroizing* African Americans went well above and well beyond "other race or class questions," because intentionally immigrating to America, without in any way diminishing the hardships and harsh conditions immigrants experienced, is extremely different from having endured the African holocaust, the Middle Passage, and African American enslavement, as well as the aftereffects of African American enslavement and the ongoing effects of American apartheid. African American social classes, therefore, did not then and do not now solely revolve around income, employment, and education, but also pivot on an axis involving the political economy of black lives lived in anti-black racist and white supremacist environments.

Du Bois made a major methodological contribution by emphasizing the importance of contextualizing the "Negro problem" within the various environments in which African American lifeworlds and life struggles were persistently pathologized or problematized. "The student of these questions," Du Bois (1899) asserted in referring to his contention that "the Negro problem far surpasses in scientific interest and social gravity, most of the other race or class questions," "must first ask, What is the real condition of this group of human beings? [O]f whom is it composed, what subgroups and classes exist, what sort of individuals are being considered?" He went further to hit at the heart of his emphasis on contextualizing African Americans within the various environments in which they eke out their existences, sternly stating, "The student must clearly recognize that a complete study must not confine itself to the group, but must specially notice the environment; the physical environment of city, sections and houses, the far mightier social environment—the surrounding world of custom, wish, whim, and thought which envelops this group and powerfully influences its social development" (5). In any effort, then, with pretensions to present a "complete study" of African Americans it is necessary to "specially notice [their] environment," as it is crucial to understanding their "social development." Above Du Bois wrote of the "long historic evolution" of the "Negro problem" and American apartheid. His remarks here point to the deeply historical dimension of his sociology, which has been collectively commented on by Manning Marable (1986), David Levering Lewis (1993), Robert Gregg (1998), and Gerald Horne (2009).

Indeed, other ethnic and cultural groups had gone through their own unique trials and tribulations in their efforts to socioeconomically adjust and "assimilate" to the new context of American industrial capitalist culture—*The Philadelphia Negro* offers brief discussions of the socioeconomic histories of various "ethnic European" groups, such as the Jews and Italians mentioned above. However, according to Du Bois, what made their respective situations perpetually and distinctly different from the situation of African Americans was the incessant and insidious interplay of the political economy of race and anti-black racism in a white supremacist society. It is this comparative historical dimension in *The Philadelphia Negro* that further distinguishes Du Bois's sociological discourse from the "armchair cerebrations of sociology's nineteenth-century system-builders" and gave its innovative interpretations their critical theoretical thrust. For Du Bois, sociology was so much more than merely "history abstracted" and isolated to tease out and examine its social problematics, as if the social can somehow be fancifully suspended from, not only the historical, but also the political and the economic (Lewis, 1993, 203). In his 1898 classic "The Study of the Negro Problems," with which he undeniably laid the foundation on which contemporary Africana studies has been built, Du Bois (1898b) observed that the "study of the Negro as a social group may be, for convenience, divided into four not exactly logical but seemingly most practicable divisions, viz: 1. Historical study. 2. Statistical investigation. 3. Anthropological measurement. 4. Sociological interpretation" (18). Note that "Historical study" is first and foremost, and then "Statistical investigation" and "Anthropological measurement" are to be undertaken before "Sociological interpretation." This should be stressed, or else Du Bois's cutting-edge conception of racial classes, not to mention his homespun *historical sociology*, is bound to be overlooked.

Throughout *The Philadelphia Negro*, Du Bois relentlessly reminded his readers that race and racism shaped and shaded or, rather, distorted and deformed African American social development. Sometimes assuming the passive voice of an objective and disinterested social scientist rattling off facts and figures, and at other times unequivocally and aggressively arguing in the interests of African Americans, Du Bois's (1899) *Africana history, culture, and political economy-informed sociology* repeatedly returned to comparative history to give its sociological interpretations in-depth acuity and unprecedented authority. For example, he thundered:

> We grant full citizenship in the World-Commonwealth to the "Anglo-Saxon" (whatever that may mean), the Teuton and the Latin; then with just a shade of reluctance we extend it to the Celt and Slav. We half deny it to the yellow races of Asia, admit the brown Indians to an ante-room only on the strength of an undeniable past; but with the Negroes of Africa we come to a full stop, and in its heart the civilized world with one accord denies that these come within the pale of nineteenth-century Humanity. This feeling, widespread and deep-seated, is, in America, the vastest of the Negro problems; we have, to be sure, a threatening problem of ignorance but the ancestors of most Americans were far more ignorant than the freedmen's sons; these ex-slaves are poor but not as poor as the Irish peasants used to be; crime is rampant but not more so, if as much, as in Italy; but the difference is that the ancestors of the English and the Irish and the Italians were felt to be worth educating, helping and guiding because they were men and brothers, while in America a census which gives a slight indication of the utter disappearance of the American Negro from the earth is greeted with ill-concealed delight. (386–87)

It is within this context of overt anti-black racism and American apartheid that African American social classes formed and fluttered here and there. Their classes could not and would not be "classes" in a Weberian or Marxian sense so long as the political economy of race and anti-black racism in a white supremacist capitalist society was—whether intentionally or unintentionally, consciously or unconsciously—embraced by whites (including "ethnic European" immigrants) from a wide range of class backgrounds: again, from bourgeoisie and petit-bourgeoisie to proletariat and lumpenproletariat. As the work of Davis and Haller (1973), Hershberg (1981), Scranton (1986), and Warner (1984) demonstrates, there has long been an historical and sociological discourse surrounding the "late" urban "arrival time" of African Americans—that is, when compared with "ethnic European" immigrants—as the fundamental factor explaining their maladjustment within industrial cities and urban environments, consequently reducing or, in several cases, rendering invisible the salience of the political economy of race and anti-black racism in a white supremacist society. *The Philadelphia Negro* unflinchingly challenges such mealy-minded and misguided hypotheses by turning to the history of American apartheid and pointing out that long before the Industrial Revolution, and long after the Emancipation Proclamation and Reconstruction, African Americans were not allowed any form of individuation within the world of white supremacy, which, as the twentieth-century works of Richard Wright, Ralph Ellison, James Baldwin, Aime Cesaire, and Frantz Fanon eloquently illustrate, ultimately existentially translates into black invisibility and black anonymity. "No differences of social condition" or social class, Du Bois (1899) declared, "allowed any Negro to escape from the group, although such escape was continually the rule among Irish, Germans and other whites" (11).

In other words, elite African Americans' degraded racial status trumped their purportedly privileged class status—that is, their, theoretically, socially privileged position based on their education, employment, and income—and it is from this frame of reference that Du Bois delivered what was undeniably the first extended foray into African American class formation and class conflict.[13] "Before it was identified and described in *The Philadelphia Negro*, the class structure of Afro-America was mostly unknown, utterly mysterious, and even widely assumed as nonexistent," David Levering Lewis (1993) quipped (209). He caustically continued, "Most white people supposed that the periodic appearance of exceptional or 'representative' black people was due to providence, 'mixed blood,' or some mysterious current passing through a dark, undifferentiated mass. Otherwise, there were only good Negroes and bad ones." Almost assuredly to the awe of his white readers, Du Bois identified four omnipresent classes or "grades," as he put it, of African Americans easily eyed in Philadelphia, New York, Farmville, or Atlanta.

Almost as if preparing his readers for his intellectual history-making report, Du Bois (1899) softly intoned, "There is always a strong tendency on the part of the [white] community to consider the Negroes as composing one practically homogenous mass. This view has of course a certain justification" after all, he solemnly said, because "the people of Negro descent in this land have had a common history, suffer today common disabilities, and contribute to one general set of social problems" (309). Then, like a lion calmly luring his prey into his lair, he sardonically said, "Yet if the foregoing statistics have emphasized any one fact it is that wide variations in antecedents, wealth, intelligence and general efficiency have already been differentiated within this group." Which, in other words, is to say that long before the births of Marx and Weber, African American social classes had "already been differentiated" and did not—and certainly not always and in every instance—quickly coincide with European or European American social classes or class struggles. Here we have returned to what I referred to above as Du Bois's *conceptual coup d'état* in the midst of Weber and Marx's conceptions of class.

The first social class among African Americans was variously termed "the better class of Negroes," the "Negro aristocracy," and, most tellingly, the "talented few." They were, Du Bois delightfully disclosed, "[f]amilies of undoubted respectability earning sufficient income to live well; not engaged in menial service of any kind; the wife engaged in no occupation save that of house-wife, except in a few cases where she had special employment at home. The children not compelled to be bread-winners, but found in school; the family living in a well-kept home" (310–11). Of course, note should be made of Du Bois's, however demure, embrace of the patriarchal family model. Essentially, the husband and father was to be the breadwinner, and only, as Du Bois himself put it, "unworthy" or "unfortunate" women were left to protect and provide for themselves and, if applicable, their poor, fatherless children. Although I hate to say it, however my conscience compels me to, one gets the distinct impression from reading *The Philadelphia Negro* that Du Bois beguilingly believed that "a woman's place is in the home." In holding that backward belief, though, he never offered viable options for the supposedly "unworthy" or "unfortunate" women who did not have homes and courageously struck out on their own to build a home or, as bell hooks (1990) has said, to create a "home-place." Where Du Bois attributed a great deal of agency to African American men, his work was woefully weak when it came to identifying and, even more, embracing African American women's agency, their *womanist lifeworlds* and *lifeworks*, if you will. We will return to Du Bois's ignorance of African American women's agency below, but I implore my readers to constantly bear this issue in mind in the meantime.[14]

The second class of African Americans were "the respectable workingclass." They lived "in comfortable circumstances, with a good home, and having steady remunerative work. The younger children in school" (311). The third class was candidly called the "poor." They were, Du Bois glibbed, "persons not earning enough to keep them at all times above want; honest, although not always energetic or thrifty, and with no touch of gross immorality or crime. Including the very poor, and the poor." The last and, as Du Bois disdainfully put it, "the lowest class" was one comprised of "criminals, prostitutes and loafers," the so-called "submerged tenth." Therefore, in Du Bois's early articulation of African American social classes there was a black bourgeoisie, a "Talented Few" or "Talented Tenth" at the top, a "Submerged Tenth" at the bottom and, sandwiched in-between, the black working class, on the one hand, and the black poor and "very poor," on the other hand.

It could be easily averred that Du Bois's early articulation of African American social classes most readily resembles Marx's infamous conception of social classes—that is, bourgeoisie, petit-bourgeoisie, proletariat, and lumpenproletariat. However, to make too much of this—that is, the external or schematic similarities of the trappings of their conceptions of class—would be to make a grave mistake and commit an unpardonable conceptual crime against W. E. B. Du Bois. For example, Saint-Arnaud (2009) said, "Du Bois's approach to stratification reflected the influence of late nineteenth-century American social reformers, as well as Weber and, in the background, Marx," but then he went on to do nothing more than attempt to demonstrate how Du Bois's conception of class fits, often too nicely and too neatly, into preexisting or "conventional" sociological categories of class (135). Du Bois's innovative emphasis on the political economy of race and anti-black racism in dictating and determining African American class formation and African American class struggle is inexplicably given short shrift, and Saint-Arnaud's readers are treated to a rather bland analysis of *The Philadelphia Negro* that seems to blatantly neglect the nuances of Du Bois's breakthroughs in an effort to reveal the "sources of Du Bois's innovations," which are curiously always and everywhere attributed to, and/or are derivatives of European or European American sociological pioneers (140–44).

In downplaying Du Bois's emphasis on the political economy of race and anti-black racism in dictating and determining African American class formation and African American class struggle, Saint-Arnaud, however unintentionally, excludes or, at the very least, renders invisible the aberrant evolution, history, and culture of the African American intelligentsia. Only Du Bois's intellectual history-making debate with Booker T. Washington, the most accommodating of African American leaders, is discussed, and then only in passing. Frederick Douglass, Anna Julia Cooper, Alexander Crummell, and Ida B. Wells's influence on Du Bois is placed in the background, as if they were quarantined and forced to sit in the "Colored Section," while the influence of Max Weber, Karl Marx, Gustav von Schmoller, William James, Charles Booth, and Jane Addams, to name only a few, is placed in the foreground, as if they were courteously escorted to the sociological section reserved for "Whites Only." *Epistemic apartheid* abounds, yet and still, in contemporary sociological discourse, and especially when and where we turn to nonwhite (and non-male) sociologists' contributions to the classical discourse and development or, rather, the haunted history of sociology.

This comment may seem a bit blunt, perhaps even blistering but, I say honestly and with every amount of intellectual integrity I can muster, such are the wicked ways of *sociological negation, disciplinary decadence, intellectual historical amnesia,* and *epistemic apartheid* that Africana critical theory is conscientiously committed to countering. European and European American sociologists are long overdue in discursively developing, not simply a knowledge of, but also respectful critical relationships with Africana intellectual history and culture, just as many African and African American sociologists have developed detailed and dialectical working relationships with European and European American sociological histories and heritages. Africana critical theorists, therefore, are not asking European and European American sociologists to do something that they, Africana critical theorists, have not already done, but only earnestly making a plea to white sociologists to end *intellectual disingenuousness* and *epistemic apartheid* by placing non-European/nonwhite—and, in this instance, Africana—intellectual histories and cultures on their own terms and, then, on equal terms with the intellectual ancestors and innovators of their (that is, white sociologists') hallowed intellectual history and culture. What is more, Africana critical theorists again earnestly emphasize that non-European/nonwhite intellectual artifacts should be approached and interpreted, first and foremost, employing the *conceptual criteria, methods of interpretation,* and *modes of analysis* of their respective intellectual and cultural milieux before they are compared and contrasted with European and European American intellectual histories and cultures.

Immediately following Du Bois's (1899) discussion of African American social classes in *The Philadelphia Negro* is a chapter on "Color Prejudice" (322–67). The fact that Du Bois placed a chapter on anti-black racism directly after his unprecedented discussion of African American social classes speaks in no uncertain terms about the ways in which he was attempting to share with his readers, not only the evolution and inner workings of African American social classes, but also the distinct ways in which the political economy of race and anti-black racism dictated and determined African American class formation and African American class struggle in ways unfathomed by Weber, Marx, "late nineteenth-century American social reformers," and most certainly, if I may, European and European American social classes: from bourgeoisie and petit-bourgeoisie to proletariat and lumpenproletariat. Again, I solemnly say, this is precisely why Africana critical theory's intense emphasis on Africana history, culture, and political-economy-informed *conceptual criteria, methods of interpretation,* and *modes of analysis* remain relevant with respect to the (re)interpretation of Du Bois's sociological discourse. Too often, Africana critical theorists—whether W. E. B. Du Bois and Frantz Fanon, or Anna Julia Cooper and Angela Davis—are analyzed from a, however well-intentioned and well-meaning, Eurocentric perspective that, by its very nefarious nature, cannot possibly intellectually expatiate Africana critical theorists, because a Eurocentric interpretive frame of reference always and in every instance, no matter how seemingly subtle, lamely liberal or weak-willed, superimposes and privileges European history and culture, European conceptions of science and civilization *over* and *onto* non-European history and culture, as well as non-European conceptions of science and civilization.

All the while acknowledging the political economy of race and anti-black racism within a white supremacist society, Du Bois acutely identified the ways in which anti-black racism was inextricable from the political economy of African American occupations in late nineteenth-century Philadelphia. There was great difficulty, Du Bois reported, in "getting work," "keeping work," and "entering new lines of work," and this created a dire situation where African Americans not only socioeconomically suffered and resented whites but also, eventually, resented and reviled each other and their (from their paradoxical perspective) "damn-blasted!" blackness (323–24; see also Licht, 1992). "It is one of the paradoxes of this question," Du Bois (1899) divulged, "to see a people so discriminated against sometimes add to their misfortunes by discriminating against themselves" (347). Unequivocally, then, Du Bois documented African Americans' own unique *racialized class struggles*, which were equally unequivocally exacerbated and perpetuated, not only by variations in education, employment and income, but, perhaps even more intensely, by the political economy of race and anti-black racism within a white supremacist society. For instance, and to expose Du Bois's problematic privileging of the "better class of Negroes," let us turn to his discussion of the "aristocracy of the Negro." In his own unmistakably elitist words.

> Nothing more exasperates the better class of Negroes than this tendency to ignore utterly their existence.... In many respects it is right and proper to judge a people by its best classes rather than by its worst classes or middle ranks. The highest class of any group represents its possibilities rather than its exceptions, as is so often assumed in regard to the Negro. The colored people are seldom judged by their best classes, and often the very existence of classes among them is ignored. This is partly due in the North to the anomalous position of those who compose this class: they are not leaders or the ideal-makers of their own group in thought, work, or morals. They teach the masses to a very small extent, mingle with them but little, do not largely hire their labor. Instead then of social classes held together by strong ties of mutual interest we have in the case of the Negroes, classes who have much to keep them apart, and only community of blood and color prejudice to bind them together. (310, 316–17)

We have established that Du Bois's early sociological work, especially *The Philadelphia Negro*, was shot through and through with Eurocentrism, elitism, and assimilationism; therefore, I need not rehearse here how incredibly elitist he was to assert, in essence, that the frequently backward-thinking black bourgeoisie—who, as he himself acknowledged, did not in any way fulfill the central mission of the bourgeoisie, which is to invent, be "leaders," and be "ideal-makers"—best represented African Americans. In addition, I will forego a full discussion of Du Bois's contention that the African American aristocracy, who ironically does not "mingle with" and, even more damning, does not "hire" members of the black working class and the black masses, should "teach the masses." Issues such as these will be engaged in greater detail below; however, here I would like to highlight the last sentence of the passage above: "Instead then of social classes held together by strong ties of mutual interest we have in the case of the Negroes, classes who have much to keep them apart, and only community of blood and color prejudice to bind them together." Here Du Bois slightly overstated his case when he claimed, almost as if attempting to directly counter Marx's conception of class, that "instead . . . of social classes held together by strong ties of mutual interest," in the case of African Americans *"only* community of blood and color prejudice . . . bind them together."

It was not "only" black biology and anti-black racism that led to and held African American social classes together, but also intra-racial conflicts and contradictions, many stemming from African Americans' historical and cultural evolution from enslaved "house Negroes" and "field Negroes" to emancipated black integrationists and black nationalists. Ironically, Du Bois's (1899) deep sense of history in *The Philadelphia Negro* penetratingly documented much of this historical and cultural evolution but, once again, his inchoate mode of analysis and interpretive framework displayed serious limitations, which ultimately altered his analysis, tipping it toward *conceptual conservatism* even in the midst of his *interpretive radicalism* and sociological innovations (10–46, 318–21). Consciously seeking to go above and beyond Du Bois's conception of class, from an Africana critical theoretical frame of reference *racial classes* can be said to be classes in the conventional sense, as they are conscious of their own class interests and harbor hostility toward other classes and their interests. However, *racial classes* are also classes in an unconventional sense, insofar as *racialization* and *racial colonization* uncouthly collapse the respective nonwhite social classes into "one practically homogenous mass," as Du Bois said above, which makes *racial classes* socially, politically, and economically impotent and impedes the pursuit of their various class interests in a white supremacist society.

It is, indeed, the "community of blood and color prejudice" that "binds" racial classes "together," and certainly their respective socioeconomic statuses seem to be secondary, if not altogether trumped by the political economy of race and racism within a white supremacist capitalist society.

On the one hand, racial classes *are* and *are not* classes in the conventional sociological sense, because although they evolved in the context of capitalism, just as many European and European American social classes, the political economy of race and racism within white supremacist capitalist societies, literally, racially dehumanized and deformed their class formations and class struggles. On the other hand, Du Bois's *interpretive elitism* blinded him from seeing the ways in which it was not "*only* community of blood and color prejudice" that bound African American social classes "together," but also intra-racial class conflicts and contradictions ranging from the "impulse of the best, the wisest and the richest . . . to segregate themselves from the masses" to the clannishness of "the mass of the servant class, the porters and waiters, and the best of the laborers" (315-17).

It could possibly go without saying that members of the various African American social classes resented being confused with, or collapsed into a social class other than their own or, worse, "one practically homogenous mass" by whites. However, what Du Bois, with his *interpretive elitism* in tow, overlooked was the fact that above and beyond their "community of blood" and common experience of "color prejudice," intra-racially and intra-culturally African American social classes had incessantly seething and simmering relationships with one another that, admittedly, were exacerbated and perpetuated by African American enslavement and its aftereffects, but also, truth be told, possibly built on preexisting "traditional" (i.e., precolonial and precapitalist) African conceptions of social classes. In fact, Du Bois himself hinted at as much when he revealingly wrote: "If the Negroes were by themselves either a strong aristocratic system or a dictatorship would for the present prevail. With, however, democracy thus prematurely thrust upon them, the first impulse of the best, the wisest and richest is to segregate themselves from the mass." He concluded, "This action, however, causes more of dislike and jealousy on the part of the masses than usual, because those masses look to whites for ideals and largely for leadership" (317). The black working class and the black masses, then, do not look to the African American aristocracy, who sickly and insultingly "segregate themselves from the mass," but rather the black masses remonstratively and repugnantly, however unconsciously and covertly, frequently turn to whites for "ideals" and "leadership," perhaps in the twisted logic of, as the saying goes, "If you can't beat 'em, join 'em." This is indicative of not "*only* community of blood and color prejudice" binding the black working class and the black masses together, but also a deep-seated sense of denial and betrayal at the hands of, yes, of course, whites, but the black bourgeoisie as well. Special note must be made of the intensity of *the diabolical dialectic of white superiority and black inferiority* that led, not simply W. E. B. Du Bois and the African American aristocracy to embrace and assimilate certain aspects of white middle-class culture and Victorian values, but also, as quiet as it is kept and as the above revoltingly reveals, the black working class and the black masses were also induced to imbibe the vulgar values and corrosive culture of the white middle class.

Returning the black working class and the black masses' resentment, their "dislike and jealousy," the black bourgeoisie takes a page out of the white world's book and coarsely collapses the black working class and the "worthy poor" into the "Submerged Tenth," the black lumpenproletariat of criminals, pimps, and prostitutes (311–21). Displaying his palpable elitist disdain, Du Bois wrote, "It is just as natural for the well-educated and well-to-do Negroes to feel themselves far above the criminals and prostitutes of Seventh and Lombard Streets, and even above the servant girls and porters of the middle-class workers. So far they are justified; but they make their mistake in failing to recognize that however laudable an ambition to rise may be, the first duty of an upper-class is to serve the lowest class" (317). Here Du Bois seems to "double-consciously" go simultaneously backward and forward—*backward*, of course, with his claim that "the well-educated and well-to-do Negroes" have a right to look down on, not only the "criminals and prostitutes," but also "the servant girls and porters of the middle-class workers"; *forward*, perhaps, in the sense that here we witness him wrestling with his conception of the responsibility or "duty" of the African American aristocracy, which he unequivocally concluded, was "to serve the lowest class." Of course, Du Bois would go on wrestling with the question of the responsibility or "duty" of the African American aristocracy for the remainder of his life—first, putting forward his theory of the "Talented Tenth," and then deconstructing and reconstructing it into his often-overlooked doctrine of the "Guiding Hundredth" (Rabaka, 2008a).

Although primarily known as a sociologist of race, and even more an innovator within the world of urban sociology, Du Bois's sociology of racial classes has been and remains lamentably ignored and excluded. Partly on account of his own *interpretive elitism*, and partly on account of his sociological negation, Du Bois's sociology of racial classes' relegation to the periphery of the sociology of class has undeniably distorted, if not deformed, the discourse and development of this subdisciplinary area within sociology. A similar assertion could be made about his sociology of the African American family and, consequently, it is the main subject of the next section.

DU BOIS'S SOCIOLOGY OF THE URBAN AFRICAN AMERICAN FAMILY: BLACK BOURGEOIS PATRIARCHY, WHITE MIDDLE-CLASS MORALITY, AND THE BURDEN OF BLACK WOMEN'S SEXUALITY

Critically building on our understanding of Du Bois's sociology of racial classes, now we temporarily turn to his equally innovative and awe-inspiring, as well as controversial and contradictory, sociology of the African American family. Similar to his sociology of racial classes, Du Bois's *conceptual conservatism* and *interpretive elitism* loudly leaps from the pages of *The Philadelphia Negro* in ways that enable us to not simply take stock of his elitism and assimilationism, but also his subtle sexism. For instance, Du Bois often linked poverty with immorality, frequently equating the alarming presence of unmarried African American women, especially unmarried mothers and husbandless wives, with promiscuity and degeneracy. As was witnessed with his Farmville study, in *The Philadelphia Negro* unemployment was unerringly associated with "shrewd laziness, shameless lewdness," and "cunning crime" (311-12). The unemployed were essentially "good natured, but unreliable and shiftless persons who cannot keep work or spend their earnings thoughtfully" (314). From Du Bois's elitist frame of reference, and coming in a close second to the political economy of race and anti-black racism within a white supremacist society, many, if not most, of African Americans' social problems stemmed from "the large proportion of single men" and the "larger number of widowed and separated" women, which indicated the "widespread and early breaking up of family life" (66-67).

The "early breaking up of family life" was the consequence of several sociocultural or, rather, socioracial factors ranging from the history of the "lax moral habits of the slave regime" to "economic difficulties." As the "conditions of life for men are much harder than for women," Du Bois reported, "desertion and separation" are almost understandable for "a people comparatively low in the scale of civilization" (66-68). However, this was nothing other than a veiled, shockingly Eurocentric reference to the absence of the African American family based on the bourgeois patriarchal paradigm. Du Bois's subtle sexism seeped into his analysis of the African American family and, ultimately, made his *interpretive elitism* all the more intense, especially with regard to African American women's conjugal conditions. He audaciously asserted that "a large number of these widows are simply unmarried mothers and thus represent the unchastity of a large number of women." In other words, Du Bois straightforwardly and haughtily labeled unmarried African American mothers slightly better than "sluts"—actually he, indeed, did sociologically designate them as "sluts"—but, with equally unmitigated imperiousness, he quickly went on to add insult to injury by claiming that unmarried African American mothers and their often "unkept" and "undisciplined" children were likely to lapse into welfarism and crime: "The result of this large number of homes without husbands is to increase the burden of charity and benevolence, and also on account of their poor home-life to increase crime" (68). With words that seem to sadly prefigure the twentieth-century discourse on African American "welfare queens," Du Bois did not simply condemn poor black mothers to lives of promiscuity and unchaste charity, which was already condescendingly bourgeois and otherwise bad enough, but he also foretold the future of their children as one irrevocably bound up with the aforementioned "shrewd laziness, shameless lewdness," and "cunning crime."

Although Du Bois ardently insisted on compassion in comprehending social scientific research as an instrument in the interest of social reform (especially African American uplift), his elitist, assimilationist, and, sometimes, sexist approach was not always empathetic with poor blacks in general, and unwed African American women and mothers' lifeworlds and life struggles in particular. Consequently, he frequently explained the life struggles and low status of every social class of African Americans other than the "well-educated and well-to-do Negroes" in terms of their alleged improper sexual behavior, which eventually always ended with an elitist exegesis on what I have termed *the burden of black women's sexuality*—that is, the supposed heightened or hyperactive *sociosexual deviance* of those condemned women, much like my own most beloved grandmothers and mother, who were "unmarried mothers" and, therefore, allegedly roguishly "represent[ed] the unchastity of a large number of women." It was not only a bourgeois patriarchal family paradigm that Du Bois used as his point of departure here, but also what he dubbed "the monogamic ideal" (72). African American men's complicity in African American women and African American mothers' "unchastity" is given short shrift, if Du Bois can be said to have confessed it at all. Ironically, it is almost as if late nineteenth-century African American women had miraculously (albeit not immaculately) developed a way to artificially inseminate themselves, and late nineteenth-century African American men's promiscuity and "desertion" is rendered invisible, at best, or erased from the narrative of Du Bois's historical sociology altogether, at worst. In other words, where African American women and African American mothers's "unchastity" appears in *The Philadelphia Negro*, African American men's "desertion" and, let it be solemnly said, their dastardly promiscuous and polygamous double-dealing disappears.

Because, as Du Bois audaciously said above, the "conditions of life for men are much harder than for women," black men's exclusion from industrial occupations and unions was taken as an unambiguous assault on the African American patriarchal family ideal. Unceasing stereotypical caricatures, emanating from white working-class minstrelsy to white middle-class highbrow journalism, proclaimed the patriarchal absence in African American families as proof-positive of black men's emasculation, black women's licentiousness, and the arrant inferiority of black culture. Formed and deformed by white middle-class conceptions of the patriarchal family, black men and women twistedly sought to embrace and bring their conjugal conditions and traditions in line with white patriarchal sex roles and gender norms, and it was these warped "norms" which ultimately became the *sine qua non* of African American uplift, cultural development, and social survival. Du Bois's early sociological discourse—especially as found in "The Negroes of Farmville" and *The Philadelphia Negro*—is, however uncomfortably, conceptually situated at the center of a discursive universe that was informed by white bourgeois patriarchal sex roles and gender norms, and also black nationalist intellectual-activists' agonizing acknowledgement of the horrid history of African American enslavement, anti-black racist sexual violence against black women, and the degradation of the African American family. Ironically, however, many, if not most New Negro "race men"—Du Bois not withstanding—attempted to counter minstrelesque mischaracterizations of the patriarchal absence in the African American family with their own homespun and hard-edged black bourgeois patriarchy and hypermasculinity, which always seemed to register more as a knee-jerk reaction to minstrelesque mischaracterizations than an authentic and autonomous articulation of African American manhood and the African American family (M. B. Ross, 2004; Summers, 2004).

Caught within the double-bind of white *and* black bourgeois conceptions of the African American family, many New Negro "race men" desperately desired to prove whites' minstrelesque mischaracterizations wrong by demonstrating that they were, indeed, the masters of their houses and the heads of their families, which from their banal bourgeois-informed perspectives translated into irrefutable evidence of African American civilization, humanity, dignity, and piety (Hine and Jenkins, 1999, 2001). However, the New Negro "race men," patently pursuing an African American patriarchal family paradigm, did not realize that their obsessive preoccupations with achieving the patriarchal family, bourgeois morality, and Jeffersonian individuality in their incessant efforts to counter minstrelesque mischaracterizations was unwittingly leading them to embrace a *white middle-class patriarchal family model in blackface*, which, again unwittingly, distracted them from and distorted their critical comprehension of the political economy of race and anti-black racism within a *white supremacist patriarchal capitalist society*. In other words, their reactionary black patriarchy was inadvertently playing right into the hostile hands of the white supremacist capitalist patriarchs who put forward the minstrelesque mischaracterizations in the first place and who knew, furthermore, that as long as African Americans, among other nonwhites, viewed racism, sexism, and capitalism in isolation and disconnection—instead of as incessantly interconnecting, interlocking, and overlapping systems of exploitation, oppression, and violence—then no true antiracist, antisexist, and anticapitalist social transformation would be quickly forthcoming.

Du Bois doggedly attempted to situate his sociology of the African American family within the wider context of the urban environment. For example, his references to the instability and weaknesses of the black family were parlously placed somewhere between the political economy of anti-black racism and black moral turpitude: "The causes of desertion are partly laxity in morals and partly the difficulty of supporting a family" (Du Bois, 1899, 67). Du Bois, to be sure, did not downplay the incessantly interlocking nature of racial oppression and economic exploitation on African American families, illuminating the "economic stress" and the "grave physical, economic and moral disorder" they cause (68, 70). It sickened him that "the sorts of work open to Negroes [is] not only restricted by their own lack of training but also by discrimination against them on account of their race; that their economic rise is not only hindered by their present poverty, but also by widespread inclination to shut against them many doors open to the talented and efficient of other races." What is more, Du Bois unapologetically declared, "Everyone knows that in a city like Philadelphia a Negro does not have the same chance to exercise ability or secure work according to his talents as a white man" (98).

It was ultimately a combination of racial, sexual, moral, and economic factors, Du Bois concluded, that destabilized and degraded the African American family. Returning to his historical sociological lens, and also returning to his subtle sexism *against* black women and *for* black patriarchy, Du Bois sternly stated:

> [I]t must be remembered that the Negro home and the stable marriage state is for the mass of the colored people of the country and for a large per cent of those of Philadelphia, a new institution. The strictly guarded savage home-life of Africa, which with all its shortcomings protected womanhood, was broken up completely by the slave ship, and the promiscuous herding of the West Indian plantation put in its stead. From this evolved the Virginia plantation where the double row of little slave cabins were but parts of a communistic paternalism centering in the Big House which was the real center of the family life. Even in Pennsylvania where the plantation system never was developed the slave family was dependent in morals as well as work upon the master. With emancipation the Negro family was first made independent and with the migration to cities we see for the first time the thoroughly independent Negro family. On the whole it is a more successful institution than we had right to expect, even though the Negro has had a couple of centuries of contact with some phases of the monogamic ideal. The greatest weakness of the Negro family is still lack of respect for the marriage bond, inconsiderate entrance into it, and bad household economy and family government. Sexual looseness then arises as a secondary consequence, bringing adultery and prostitution in its train. And these results come largely from the postponement of marriage among the young. Such are the fruits of a sudden social revolution. (71–72)

Foregoing a full discussion of Du Bois's obviously Eurocentric and patriarchal statement concerning the "strictly guarded savage home-life of Africa, which with all its shortcomings protected womanhood," I would like to conclude my analysis of Du Bois's sociology of the African American family by focusing on his assertion that "[s]exual looseness then arises as a secondary consequence" to African Americans' "lack of respect for the marriage bond, inconsiderate entrance into it, and bad household economy and family government." Irritatingly Du Bois seems to deemphasize the enormous role European imperialism (via *white supremacist patriarchal capitalist colonialism*) played in dehumanizing and degrading African Americans and the African American family. Admittedly, and to his credit, he did invoke the "slave ship[s]," the "promiscuous herding of the West Indian plantation[s]," the "Virginia plantation[s]," the "little slave cabins," the "Big House," and the "plantation system" in general. However, to his discredit, Du Bois ultimately placed the crises of African American conjugal conditions almost squarely on African Americans, and especial black women. Again, the fault is not to be found with Du Bois's historical and sociological research methods, which were indubitably impeccable and innovative for his intellectual milieu. It was Du Bois's constantly recurring *conceptual conservatism* and *interpretive elitism*, reeking of both sexism and assimilationism, that repeatedly rendered his sociology of the African American family a *sociology of black deviance*: a *sociology of black women's promiscuity*, a *sociology of black men's emasculation*, and, even more despicably, a *sociology of black children's criminalization*. Here, we have come back, once again, to Africana critical theory's emphasis on the importance of *conceptual criteria*, *methods of interpretation*, and *modes of analysis* grounded in and growing out of continental and diasporan African history, culture, and struggle.

Du Bois developed a merciless critique of "[un]protected womanhood" that spared neither "unmarried mothers," husbandless wives, widows, nor "well-to-do" married women who worked outside of their homes. Black bourgeois patriarchal familial and social etiquette dictated that "a woman's place is in the home," but this ideal, like most ideals the black bourgeoisie borrowed from the white middle class, was not easily attainable for African American men and women considering their dual racial oppression *and* economic exploitation. It would be almost impossible to deny Du Bois's disdain for the moral failings of black men, repeatedly referring to them as "criminals," "gamblers," "idlers," "rogues," "rascals," "shrewd abettors," and "shiftless and lazy ne'er-do-wells," but, yet and still, black women who struggled to meet the white middle-class standards for womanhood and motherhood, which the black bourgeoisie superimposed on African American womanhood and motherhood, were summarily dismissed and scapegoated as the major contributors to, and essentially the continuing causes for, the instability of the African American family. The sick social stratification and moral hierarchy of the black bourgeoisie rushes to the fore when we turn to Du Bois's rote ranking of African American women: humble and hard-working married women who worked outside of their homes had only a slightly higher moral and social standing than unmarried women. Indeed, they were respectable, but not as vividly virtuous as those wives who were "engaged in no occupation save that of house-wife." It was these families "of undoubted respectability," and "earning sufficient income to live well," which Du Bois believed best represented African Americans (310–11). However, these families were few and far between (i.e., the "Talented Few"), and yet Du Bois, blinded by his *interpretive elitism*, continued to encourage African Americans, the large majority of whom were extremely economically exploited and poverty-stricken, to placidly pursue this *white middle-class patriarchal family model in blackface*. Why did Du Bois incessantly advocate that African Americans assimilate white middle-class culture and values? How could he not have seen how blatantly sexist many of his sociological assessments of black women's lifeworlds and life struggles were? What role did internalized anti-black racism play in forming and deforming Du Bois's research methods, sociological observations, and sociological theorizations? This chapter concludes by briefly offering answers to each of these questions.

DU BOIS'S METHODOLOGICAL INNOVATIONS AND INTERPRETIVE LIMITATIONS IN *THE PHILADELPHIA NEGRO*

As discussed above, many have made mention of Du Bois's methodological innovations in *The Philadelphia Negro*. However, few have moved beyond merely mentioning Du Bois's methodological innovations to critically detailing the ways in which his classical research methods laid the foundation for contemporary research methods. More attention has been given to what Du Bois borrowed or, in many instances, how his methods were allegedly uncritically derived from European and European American early sociologists, but rarely has Du Bois's borrowings from African American intellectual and cultural history been discussed, and even rarer do discussions of Du Bois as a mixed or multimethodological innovator register. Along with the inadequate attention that Du Bois's methodological innovations have received has been the tendency on the part of the few who have accented and engaged his remarkable research methods to almost completely overlook his *conceptual conservatism* and *interpretive elitism*. It is highly plausible, especially from an Africana critical theoretical perspective, that Du Bois may have been simultaneously *methodologically progressive* and *interpretively regressive*. In other words, and in many illustrative instances throughout *The Philadelphia Negro*, his thinking shows lucid signs of *sociological breakthrough* and, again from an Africana critical theoretical framework, it also symbolizes an *Africological setback* consequent to his seemingly unrepentant reliance on Eurocentric, elitist, and assimilationist frames of reference; hence, what I have referred to throughout this chapter as Du Bois's *conceptual conservatism* and *interpretive elitism*. This, to be sure, created a curious paradox in the ways in which Du Bois's sociological legacy has been interpreted and continues to be reinterpreted.

In terms of Du Bois's methodological innovations, the influence of Charles Booth and Jane Addams seems to be easily detected in *The Philadelphia Negro*, but the myriad influential texts emanating from African American intellectual and cultural history have been conspicuously and consistently left in the lurch. Sociological research methods that sensitively engaged African American lifeworlds and life struggles in the late nineteenth century were virtually nonexistent, and white sociology's "natural laws" and negative assessments of black culture were almost always based on Eurocentric evolutionary grand theorizing rather than empirical evidence. There was no other recourse for Du Bois if, indeed, he wanted to critically study African Americans. He would have to, literally, invent research methods tailored to the particular and often peculiar lifeworlds and life struggles of African Americans, which he knew from his graduate studies at the University of Berlin and Harvard, as well as his earlier research, went well beyond rote racial oppression and included economic exploitation, miseducation, continued racial colonization, and the innumerable absurdities and agonies of American apartheid. As if directly refuting those who have repeatedly argued that his research methods were derivative of late nineteenth-century white sociological research methods, in his posthumously published autobiography, Du Bois (1968a) declared:

> I started [*The Philadelphia Negro*] with no "research methods" and I asked little advice as to procedure. The problem lay before me. Study it. I studied it personally and not by proxy. I sent out no canvassers. I went myself. Personally I visited and talked with 5,000 persons. What I could, I set down in orderly sequence on schedules which I made out and submitted to the University [of Pennsylvania] for criticism. Other information I stored in my memory or wrote out as memoranda. I went through the Philadelphia libraries for data, gained access in many instances to private libraries of colored folk and got individual information. I mapped the district, classifying it by condition; I compiled two centuries of history of the Negro in Philadelphia and in the Seventh Ward. (198)

Even when placed alongside *Life and Labor of the People of London* and *Hull House Maps and Papers*, methodologically *The Philadelphia Negro* remains distinguished. What is more, if we were to situate *The Philadelphia Negro* within the context of early sociological inquiry in the United States, then we come back to Phil Zuckerman's (2004) contention that "[y]ears before the famous studies of the Chicago School, Du Bois's sociological output was characterized by a hands-on, empirical research methodology to a much greater and more respectable degree than that of his more famous contemporaries" (6). Alluding to those who have compared *The Philadelphia Negro* with Florence Kelley's watershed Hull House work, the eminent English sociologist Martin Bulmer (1991) writes, "More important, his [i.e., Du Bois's] conception of science was a more rigorous one than that of Florence Kelley, and it precluded too close identification with philanthropy and social intervention" (174).[15] Synthesizing disparate parts of early white sociological discourse with strands of embryonic Pan-Africanist, black nationalist, black Christian, black bourgeois, and black ethnological uplift thought, Du Bois's sociological perspective and experiences were unlike those of his "more famous contemporaries," partly because many of them worked within intellectual and social reform communities which fostered constant sociological dialogue, and partly because Du Bois neither had the luxury nor largess of long-term research funding or a research team. The fact that with *The Philadelphia Negro* Du Bois can be said to have, literally, singlehandedly inaugurated empirical sociology in the United States has not been completely lost. For example, all the way from England, Bulmer (1991) bawled:

> For fifteen months, Du Bois immersed himself in the detailed empirical study of the Seventh Ward, the largest concentration of black people in a city which at that time had a black population of 45,000, the largest anywhere in the North. His experience of carrying out the study was different from that of Charles Booth or Florence Kelley, for he worked on his own with little support from others. Although nominally attached to the University [of Pennsylvania] with the position of "Assistant Instructor," he had a one-year appointment which was not renewed, no office there, his name did not appear in the university catalogue, he taught no students, and he had only peripheral contact with members of the sociology department. His time was spent entirely in the black district, his principal social contacts, perforce, were with black rather than white Philadelphians. Color distanced him too from the white philanthropists who had initiated the study, and [this] meant that his contact with them was not on a regular basis. . . . The contrast between the Seventh Ward study and Hull House was marked. Florence Kelley was a resident of Hull House and full participant, W. E. B. Du Bois resided above a cafeteria belonging to the Philadelphia Settlement and was not a participant in the work of the Settlement. (174)

Those seeking to render methodological comparisons or interpretations of *The Philadelphia Negro*, then, should do so cautiously, because, as Bulmer observed, Du Bois labored "morning, noon, and night" under comparably different conditions than those of his "more famous contemporaries." The "comparably different conditions" that I am calling my readers' attention to here have been either unintentionally overlooked or intentional erased by those sociologists who, for whatever reason, refuse to sincerely and sensitively consider the horrors of the African holocaust and African American enslavement, as well as the aftereffects of African American enslavement and the ongoing effects of American apartheid on the discourse and development of sociology in the United States. Basic logic tells us that it is extremely possible that the Native American holocaust may have altered or had some sort of significant impact on the ways in which sociologists approach the lifeworlds and life struggles of Native Americans; basic logic also tells us that it is extremely possible that the Jewish holocaust may have altered or had some sort of significant impact on the ways in which sociologists approach the lifeworlds and life struggles of Jews; and, finally, basic logic tells us that it is extremely possible that the Armenian holocaust may have altered or had some sort of significant impact on the ways in which sociologists approach the life worlds and life struggles of Armenians—why then is Africana critical theory's emphasis on the horrors of the African holocaust and African American enslavement, as well as the aftereffects of African American enslavement and the ongoing effects of American apartheid, not considered with the same spirit of sociological seriousness that "basic logic" reveals that we should hold with regard to the aforementioned?

Part of Du Bois's methodological innovation revolved around his intense emphasis on a comprehensive history of African Americans' heterogeneity and the gathering of empirical evidence prior to sociological theorizing concerning their lifeworlds and life struggles. In his 1898 classic "The Study of the Negro Problems," Du Bois (1898b) exclaimed, "One cannot study the Negro in freedom and come to general conclusions about his destiny without knowing his history in slavery" (12). When viewed from the sociological world of the early twenty-first century, *The Philadelphia Negro*, with its dull facts and figures, seems like a fairly typical empirical sociological investigation of African Americans in Philadelphia at the turn of the twentieth century. However, when situated within the sociological world it evolved out of and, in several senses, eventually epistemically exploded, *The Philadelphia Negro*'s trenchant transdisciplinarity not only took the "master's tools" and initiated the work of dismantling the "master's house"—to poorly paraphrase Audre Lorde (1984)—but it also deftly demonstrated the *disciplinary decadence* and *epistemic apartheid* of sociology, especially American sociology, at its inception.

In "The World Was Thinking Wrong About Race," the acclaimed African American intellectual historian Mia Bay (1998) unapologetically announced:

> Du Bois's study of the Philadelphia Negro has emerged as a classic across the disciplines precisely because it was written before the modern disciplines of sociology, anthropology, history, and economics were fully formed. Although justly celebrated for its contributions to all these fields, *The Philadelphia Negro*'s relationship to the more amorphous social science of its own day has been

overshadowed by the retrospective appreciations it has received from scholars intent on establishing it as a pioneering work within their various nascent disciplines. (41)

Bay's last point should be emphasized, as it helps to directly highlight sociology's, among other traditional disciplines, *disciplinary decadence* and *epistemic apartheid,* and it also highlights the immense importance of Africana critical theory's emphasis on reinterpreting Du Bois's employing transdisciplinary *conceptual criteria, methods of interpretation,* and *modes of analysis* that have been grounded in, and continue to grow out of, classical and contemporary, continental and diasporan African lifeworlds and life struggles. After all, to speak candidly, since continental and diasporan Africans were, in most instances, at the heart of Du Bois's various discourses, is it then too much to contend that continental and diasporan African histories, cultures, and struggles *should have been* placed not only at the conceptual core of Du Bois's methods of interpretation and modes of analysis but, even more, that continental and diasporan African histories, cultures, and struggles *should be* placed at the conceptual core of Du Bois scholars and students' methods of interpretation and modes of analysis if, indeed, their Du Bois studies are to be free from the *interpretive Eurocentrism, interpretive elitism,* and *interpretive assimilationism* that Du Bois unwittingly bequeathed to seemingly every generation of Africana intellectuals since *The Philadelphia Negro*'s publication?

The Philadelphia Negro boldly blurred the boundaries between sociology, anthropology, history, and political economy in their intellectual infancy, and it put forward a pioneering empiricism that continues to inspire awe. "Its intellectual achievement has been assessed, above all," Bay argues, "in terms of its innovative use of social science practices that became commonplace long after it was published, such as participant observation, census-taking, the interview, and the historical and economic analysis of government data. Yet such appreciations tend to measure mostly the symbolic significance—as a 'black first'—of a book so neglected in its own day that most of its innovations were not so much picked up as rediscovered by later social scientists" (41–42). More than merely "a 'black first,'" *The Philadelphia Negro* challenges those who have either completely ignored it within the world of white sociology or attempted to ghettoize it within the world of "black sociology." With implications for sociology, anthropology, history, and political economy in general, and urban sociology, historical sociology, industrial sociology, sociology of work, sociology of economics, sociology of race, sociology of culture, sociology of deviance, sociology of religion, sociology of education, and sociology of crime specifically, *The Philadelphia Negro*'s sociological empiricism seems to hold it together in the same way that its aforementioned *interpretive Eurocentrism, interpretive elitism,* and *interpretive assimilationism* incessantly threatens to tear it apart.

Du Bois's methodological innovations and sociological empiricism were, in many instances, muted by his *conceptual conservatism* and *interpretive elitism*. It would be virtually impossible to deny Du Bois's uneasy intellectual adherence to white middle-class culture and Victorian values, as well as his internalization of anti-black racist myths and subtle sexist stereotypes. As mentioned above, Du Bois sometimes employed the crude characterizations of African Americans—especially African American women, wives, and mothers—rampantly running throughout the white sociological discourse of his era. With the very dispassionate and disinterested social scientific detachment he would later mercilessly criticize, Du Bois (1899) Eurocentrically referred to African Americans as a "half-developed race" and "a people comparatively low in the scale of civilization" (351, 66). He essentially accepted white middle-class culture, and in particular the white middle class's Victorian values and gender norms of family life, as universal "civilized" and "high culture" criteria by which to, literally, "judge" black behavior, regardless of social class. Therefore, ironically, even as he pointed out that "[t]here is always a strong tendency on the part of the [white] community to consider the Negroes as composing one practically homogenous mass," Du Bois himself seemed susceptible to white bourgeois and anti-black racist thinking concerning African American social classes.

Du Bois was explicitly Eurocentric, elitist, and assimilationist throughout *The Philadelphia Negro* and, in effect, advocated that African Americans should openly embrace and assimilate European and European American "civilization" and culture as quickly as possible if they were to survive the endless onslaught of American apartheid and European global imperialism. Here, then, we have returned to Du Bois's lame "If you can't beat 'em, join 'em" logic, which both pervades and perplexes *The Philadelphia Negro*. At this early point in his intellectual and political development he did not dare demand a radical democratic transformation of the *white supremacist patriarchal capitalist colonial system* that Europeans and European Americans had insidiously erected—a system that either ignored or erased the horrors of the African holocaust and African American enslavement, as well as the aftereffects of African American enslavement and the ongoing effects of American apartheid. Explicit evidence of Du Bois's *interpretive Eurocentrism, interpretive elitism,* and *interpretive assimilationism* recurringly surfaces when and where we come to his condescending comments concerning African American social classes, especially the differences in their conjugal conditions and family life. Du Bois's various interpretive limitations caused him to neglect the nuances of African American culture, at best, or completely disregard the distinctiveness of African American culture, at worst—and the real rub is that his various interpretive limitations led him to these myopic misinterpretations of African American culture even as he methodically and meticulously chronicled it in innovative and unprecedented ways. Here, then, we have come full circle and returned to the crux of my contention that in *The Philadelphia Negro* Du Bois was simultaneously *methodologically progressive* and *interpretively regressive*.

We turn now to an exploration of Du Bois's sociology of race, where once again his research reveals itself to be both *methodologically progressive* and *interpretively regressive*. Although much more consistent than his urban and rural sociology, Du Bois's sociology of race nonetheless is not free from controversy and contradictions. Race and racism, as he said so long ago, have historically and continue currently to present contemporary society in general, and contemporary sociology in particular, with one of its greatest "problems." Let us, then, consciously cross the color-line and enter the racially colonized world within the Veil.

NOTES

1. In "'The World Was Thinking Wrong About Race': *The Philadelphia Negro* and Nineteenth Century Science," African American intellectual historian Mia Bay (1998) paints a portrait of the intellectual milieu, especially the social scientific scene, which Du Bois, with his intense emphasis on empirical research, was working against:

> In its analysis of race relations, especially, 1890s sociology was based on theoretical speculations rather than on empirical research. Bent on creating 'grand theories' of society that could be employed to analyze and solve the social problems of Gilded Age America, the founding fathers of American sociology invariably explained racial inequities with reference to natural laws. These natural laws offered little support to Du Bois's search for the scientific principles that would foster black progress. (44)

This last point is one that should be ardently accented, as it speaks directly to the discourse surrounding Du Bois's "borrowings" from the sociological figures of his day. I reiterate, no matter what Du Bois may have "borrowed" from his professors at the University of Berlin or Harvard, and also no matter what he may have "borrowed" from Marx, Weber, or Durkheim, or the myriad other late nineteenth-century usual sociological suspects, it is important to bear in mind that his *sociological subjects*, his *sociological agenda*, and his *sociological goals* were distinctly different from all of the aforementioned insofar as Du Bois's sociology was devoted to social reform and, eventually, radical social transformation primarily in the interest of black folk living in white supremacist societies. Bay went on to bellow:

> Although Northern sociologists held out more hope than Southern sociologists that natural law did not forever bar the development and assimilation of the Negro, even the most liberal Northern sociologists held low opinions of the capabilities of nonwhites and "were unable to envision an egalitarian society in the foreseeable future." In the

South and North, alike, sociological inferences about black capacities owed a great deal to [the] ideas of Herbert Spencer and other American evolutionists, who popularized a Social Darwinism that "placed blacks at the primitive end of the evolutionary scale." Gloomily interpreted, as they frequently were in the 1890s, the Darwinian laws governing race development heralded nothing short of the extinction of American blacks, a prediction not uncommon in 1890s social science. (44)

As will be witnessed in the sections to follow, it will be extremely important to critically and constantly consider the context(s) within which Du Bois was developing his sociological methods and interpretations; hence, a critical and comprehensive engagement of *both* African American *and* European American intellectual and cultural history is a prerequisite in order to adequately assess Du Bois's sociological discourse and the legacy it left in its wake. Few scholars have faced a more daunting intellectual environment with as much sociological sophistication and intellectual eloquence as Du Bois did at the end of the nineteenth century. His efforts to reach and have his work seriously read by both black and white audiences, as well as his collegiate experiences in both black and white institutions of higher education, frequently led Du Bois to contradictory positions and controversial claims. The subsequent sections of this chapter, therefore, chart Du Bois's contradictions and controversies with an eye toward the ways in which they continue to contribute to the deconstruction and reconstruction of urban and rural sociology in particular, and Africana critical theory of contemporary society in general.

2. Besides Lewis (1993), "The Negroes of Farmville" is briefly mentioned, although not thoroughly engaged, by Bulmer (1991), Outlaw (2000), and R. W. Williams (2006), and it appears to have completely escaped the scholarly scrutiny of several of Du Bois's more noted biographers, such as Broderick (1959), Horne (2009), Marable (1986), Rampersad (1990), and Rudwick (1960a, 1968, 1982a).

3. My interpretation of miscegenation has been informed by Lemire (2002), Pascoe (2009), J. D. Smith (1993d, 1993e), and Williamson (1995).

4. It is interesting to compare and contrast Du Bois's foregoing contention of "[t]hree pretty distinctly differentiated social classes" with his discussion of "three pretty clearly differentiated classes" in "The Negro in the Black Belt" and his identification of "four grades," or classes, of black Philadelphians in *The Philadelphia Negro*, where he deepened and developed his conception of the "[t]hree pretty distinctly differentiated social classes" and added the "submerged tenth" class of criminals, pimps, and prostitutes (Du Bois, 1980a, 59, 62–63). The "submerged tenth" clearly correlates with the lumpenproletariat in Marx's concept of class. Du Bois's concept of class is engaged in greater detail in the subsequent sections of this chapter.

5. Sociological inquiry focusing on the African American family has greatly developed since Du Bois's early African American family studies, which culminated with his 1908 edited volume *The American Negro Family*. My interpretation of the African American family, here and throughout the remainder of this chapter, has been influenced by Billingsley (1988, 1992), Dunaway (2003), D. L. Franklin (1997), Gutman (1976), Hattery and Smith (2007), McAdoo (2006), Staples (1999), and Taylor, Jackson, and Chatters (1997). In terms of my conception of the African American "extended family," I have relied on several of the above, but also, more specifically, Sims (1978) and Shimkin, Shimkin, and Frate (1978).

6. Du Bois's issues of Eurocentric and elitist interpretation seem to be deeply embedded within his working conception of the African American family, and these issues extend to, not only *The Philadelphia Negro*, but also his "The Negro in the Black Belt" and his edited volume *The Negro American Family* (Du Bois, 1908, 1980a). Discussion of the faulty and elitist elements of his analysis of the African American family in *The Philadelphia Negro* will be provided in the subsequent sections of this chapter. However, since "The Negro in the Black Belt" so closely resembles "The Negroes of Farmville," in both content and form, there is no need to give an extended analysis of it here; suffice it to say that Du Bois (1980a) discusses "the development of the Negro from country to city life, from semi-barbarism to a fair degree of culture" (47). He continued, "Here we get a glimpse of the real Negro problem; of poverty and degradation of the country Negro, which means the mass of Negroes in the United States" (48). Note that Du Bois, in essence, claimed that "the mass of Negroes in the United States" were basically living lives of "semi-barbarism" in the late nineteenth century. In fact, if I were pressed to make a distinction between "The Negro in the Black Belt" and "The Negroes of Farmville," perhaps I would assert that in the Black Belt study Du Bois's condescending (mis)characterizations of the African American family seem to be even more abrasive and unbridled than in the Farmville study. For instance, he unflinchingly wrote in "The Negro in the Black Belt": "The character of home life varies with the different families. The family of 21 [persons] is a poverty-stricken, reckless, dirty set. The children are stupid and repulsive, and fight for their food at the table. They are poorly dressed, sickly, and cross. The table dishes stand from one meal to another unwashed, and the house is in perpetual disorder. Now and then the father and mother engage in a hand-to-hand fight. In some respects this family is exceptionally bad, but several others are nearly as barbarous" (49). It is unconscionable to condone unsanitary living conditions or "hand-to-hand fight[ing]" within any family. However, perhaps there has never been a more mean-spirited description of African American children penned by an African American than Du Bois's characterization of the children of this family of twenty-one as "cross," "stupid and repulsive." He went further to share with his readers that the family was "exceptionally bad, but several others are nearly as barbarous." What distinguishes *The Philadelphia Negro* from both "The Negroes of Farmville" and "The Negro in the Black Belt" is the Philadelphia study's deeper historical dimension. Part historical, part sociological, *The Philadelphia Negro* discursively historicizes the African American urban experience with an emphasis on the impact that anti-black racism and industrial capitalism were having on black Philadelphian culture, community, and society. Again, though, many issues arise surrounding Du Bois's Eurocentric, elitist, and often assimilationist methods of interpretation and angles of analysis in *The Philadelphia Negro*, which will be discussed in detail in the succeeding sections of this chapter.

7. The New Negro movement is generally understood to have its origins in the emergence of the black women's club movement in 1893, as well as Frederick Douglass's death, W. E. B. Du Bois's graduation from Harvard with a PhD, and Booker T. Washington's "Atlanta Exposition Address," all occurring in 1895. In 1896 the black women's club movement reached a climax with the merging of the National Federation of Afro-American Women, the Women's Era Club of Boston, and the National League of Colored Women, which established the National Association of Colored

Women (NACW), the first nationally networked African American organization outside of the African American church (see chapter 3). The rising racial consciousness of the "New Negroes" was sparked by the infamous Hayes-Tilden compromise of 1877, which subsequently led to the 1896 Supreme Court "separate but equal" verdict in the *Plessy v. Ferguson* case. Between 1895 and 1925, African Americans experienced an intense period of social transformation, which had an enormous impact on their social and political consciousness, and it is this evolution of African Americans' cultural, social and political consciousness during the period ending the nineteenth century and beginning the twentieth century that is commonly called the New Negro movement. African American historian Rayford Logan (1954) famously referred to the decade closing the nineteenth century as the "nadir" of African American history, and his work, along with the work of several other scholars, has brought to light more than three thousand documented lynchings during this unfortunate era (see Brundage, 1993, 1997; Gonzales-Day, 2006; Ifill, 2007; Nevels, 2007; Pfeifer, 2004; Waldrep, 2006; Zangrando, 1980). The New Negro movement culminated with the wide and varied political cultures and aesthetic innovations of the Harlem Renaissance, and it is interesting to note that Du Bois's work was at the center of both the New Negro movement and the Harlem Renaissance. In essence, the "New Negro" was distinguished from the "Old Negro" by their resistance to African American reenslavement and American apartheid. They rejected the *minstrelesque mischaracterizations* of African Americans and the whitewashed revisionist interpretations of the African holocaust and African American enslavement, which made white enslavers appear as though they were patently pious, benevolent Christians who "civilized" and "Christianized" the "heathen" and "barbarous" Africans they ruled over on their palatial antebellum plantations. New Negro studies, then, is an extremely important area of inquiry within Africana studies, even though it is frequently folded into Harlem Renaissance studies. Undoubtedly New Negro studies and Harlem Renaissance studies discursively dovetail but, yet and still, it is important to distinguish between the two because, to put it plainly, the aesthetic innovations of the Harlem Renaissance are virtually incomprehensible without first engaging the historical, cultural, social, and political coming-to-critical consciousness that the New Negro movement fostered. For my (re)interpretation of the New Negro movement, I have drawn from A. E. Carroll (2005), A. P. Davis (1975), Foley (2003), Gates and Jarrett (2007), Hutchinson (1995, 2007), Lewis (1989), Locke (1968), and Wintz (1996).

8. Assessments of African American employment and occupations tend to be free-floating affairs. Therefore, in keeping with Africana critical theory's emphasis on a panoramic portrait of classical and contemporary, continental and diasporan African histories, cultures, and struggles, I have tapped both old and new scholarship. Several noteworthy works in African American labor studies, therefore, have informed my interpretation of black labor struggles at the end of the nineteenth century and the beginning of the twentieth century—for instance, Arnesen (2002), Cantor (1969), Flynn (1983), Foner (1982), Nieman (1994a, 1994b), and Novak (1978).

9. It may be difficult for many of my readers to comprehend the complexities and contradictions of what was commonly called the "Negro Problem" between the waning years of the Civil War through to the increased militancy of the civil

rights movement, a period roughly running from 1855 to 1965. However, it is extremely important to highlight this often overlooked discourse within African American intellectual history and culture because it helped to shape and define Du Bois's discursive formations and practices, from his Fisk years through to his death in Kwame Nkrumah's Pan-African socialist Ghana. Major "New Negro" intellectuals and activists weighed in on the "Negro Problem," each seeming to offer their own unique solutions. For instance, besides Du Bois's classic 1898 "The Study of the Negro Problems," among his many other contributions to this discourse, Sutton Griggs (1969), Booker T. Washington (1900), and Marcus Garvey (1966) each averred solutions to the "Negro Problem." For further discussion of this discourse, which I am wont to call "Negro Problem studies," see Myrdal (1944), J. D. Smith (1993a, 1993b, 1993c, 1993d, 1993e, 1993f), and A. A. Young (1993).

10. Two of the largest and most influential settlement houses were Chicago's Hull House, which was established by Jane Addams and Ellen Gates Starr in 1889, and New York City's Henry Street Settlement, which was founded by Lillian Wald in 1893. The settlement movement coincided with the white middle-class social reform agendas and activities of the Progressive Era (1890–1920). During this same period, as mentioned above, black middle-class social reform efforts were situated under the rubric of what is now known as the "New Negro" movement. For further discussion of the settlement movement, especially the feminists and suffragettes alluded to earlier, see Beauman (1996), Carson (1990), Crocker (1992), Lasch-Quinn (1993), and Trolander (1987). It is interesting to observe the ways in which Du Bois's thought dovetails with both the settlement movement and the general tenor of Progressivism. African American political scientist Adolph Reed's *W. E. B. Du Bois and American Political Thought* (1997) has provided the most informed engagement of Du Bois's relationship with the settlement movement and Progressivism to date (see esp. 91–125).

11. Although it is arguable whether or not *The Philadelphia Negro* has, indeed, "gradually improve[d] race relations policy," one can be certain that actual or, rather, "real-life" race relations seem to have remained obstinately immune, not only to Du Bois and others' sociology of race, but also to the historic election of the first African American president of the United States of America, Barack Obama (see Roediger, 2008). In his introduction to the 1996 edition of *The Philadelphia Negro*, Elijah Anderson (1996) asserted the following:

> Nearly a hundred years have passed since W. E. B. Du Bois wrote *The Philadelphia Negro*. Have his insights contributed to the amelioration of the conditions he studied? Is the African American today, in Philadelphia or anywhere in the United States, free of the forces Du Bois chronicled? Despite undeniable progress, the answer must be no. By considering the status of blacks then and now, the entrenched nature of the forces of both white racism and black victimization can be seen in even sharper relief than was visible to Du Bois. Du Bois's keen observations should make it clear to all that much additional effort will be needed before our society approaches real equality of opportunity or the rational benevolence envisioned by this eloquent, humane, and seminal thinker. (xxxv)

I could not agree more with Anderson when he emphasizes that today "the entrenched nature of the forces of both white racism and black victimization can be seen in even sharper relief than was visible to Du Bois" in his era and that "much additional effort will be needed before our society approaches real equality of opportunity." I cannot help but to bring up the fact that after more than a decade and a half of developing "deeply penetrat[ing] . . . social science" aimed at "gradually improv[ing] race relations policy," Du Bois decided that "much additional effort" was still "needed." Before the close of the first decade of the twentieth century, he left social science and instead solemnly committed himself to social activism in the interest of radical social transformation: first, cofounding the NAACP; then, publicly supporting the suffragettes and other feminist causes; next, resuscitating his Pan-Africanism and intensifying his interests in Africa and Africans; and, finally, deepening and developing his critique of the political economy of race and anti-black racism by undertaking an intellectual history-making critical exploration of Marxism—ultimately synthesizing it with his antiracism, antisexism, and anticolonialism (see Rabaka, 2007b).

12. To get a sense of what Du Bois was up against in terms of Social Darwinism and Spencerian social thought under the guise of conventional sociological wisdom at the turn of the twentieth century, please see Bannister (1979), Dickens (2000), Hawkins (1997), Hofstadter (1944), Rumney (1966), and Ruse and Richards (2009).

13. Prior to Du Bois's foray into African American class formation there was Joseph Willson's 1841 study, *Sketches of the Higher Classes of Colored Society in Philadelphia*, which was recently retitled and republished in 2000 as *The Elite of Our People: Joseph Willson's Sketches of the Black Upper-Class in Antebellum Philadelphia*. However, Du Bois, it would seem, still holds the distinction of offering us the first extended analysis of African American class formation insofar as his work, however elitist, attempted to paint portraits of not only the African American upper class, but also the black middle, working, and "submerged tenth" classes, as well as to strike at African American class conflict.

14. It is also important here to observe that in Du Bois's early articulation of African American social classes he seems to blur the boundaries between the African American upper class and the African American middle class; they are essentially one and the same at this point in his thinking. I have come to think that this collapse of African American upper and middle classes is more a consequence of African Americans' historical and cultural evolution out of enslavement and into the social setting of American apartheid. However, part of the lapse in the lines between the upper and middle classes of black folk of the late nineteenth century might also have to do with their clannishness and incessant efforts to exclude working-class and lower class blacks from their social world. In other words, I am arguing that African American social classes were still forming when Du Bois collected the data for *The Philadelphia Negro* and, as his research and analysis clearly indicate and advocate, the only blacks worthy of "representing" the "race" were those who had assimilated, at the least, white middle-class culture and Victorian values—hence, the culture, values, and behaviors of the African American aristocracy and the African American middle class combined were famously referred to by the eminent African American sociologist E. Franklin Frazier (1962) as the "black bourgeoisie." For further discussion of the black bourgeoisie, see Banner-Haley (1993, 1994), Bowser (2007), Feagin (1994), Frazier (1951, 1957, 1968), Lacy (2007), Landry (1987), Pattillo (2000), and Teele (2002). An alternative interpretation of Du Bois's early

articulation of African American social classes might also emphasize that the group that Du Bois refers to as "the respectable working-class" in *The Philadelphia Negro* coincides with the contemporary black middle class. This is a plausible interpretation insofar as in his early articulation of African American social classes, Du Bois does not use the term "upper-class" as much as he uses terms such as "the better class of Negroes," the "Negro aristocracy," and, more tellingly, the "talented few."

15. It is important to observe that the influential social reformer Florence Kelley eventually became one of Du Bois's colleagues and a cofounder of the NAACP, which was established on 12 February 1909 by a diverse group of dissidents, which included Du Bois, Kelley, Ida B. Wells, Archibald Grimké, Henry Moscowitz, Mary White Ovington, Oswald Garrison Villard, and William English Walling.

2

Du Bois and the Sociology of Race

The Sociology of the Souls of Black and White (Among Other) Folk

> The problem of the twentieth century is the problem of the color-line—the relation of the darker to the lighter races of men in Asia and Africa, in America and the islands of the sea.
>
> W. E. B. Du Bois, *The Souls of Black Folk*, 29

INTRODUCTION: DU BOIS'S SOCIOLOGICAL DISCOURSE ON RACE AND RACISM

Du Bois's corpus contains an astounding body of literature on, and nuanced knowledge of, race and racism. His sociology of race figures prominently, and has been consistently featured in critical racial discourse: from late nineteenth-century controversies surrounding the "Negro problem" through to twenty-first-century rearticulations of many of his innovative ideas under the rubric of "critical race theory." Moreover, race theorists have chronicled his concepts of race from a multiplicity of disciplinary and theoretical perspectives, often arguing against and, at other times, agreeing with his critical writings on race and racism, which have been documented to have undeniably dominated racial discourse during the twentieth century.

The history of Du Bois's sociology of race and antiracist theorizing is not an easy tale to tell but, nonetheless, it is a tale that must be told. Why? One may ask. Why do we need yet another (re)interpretation of Du Bois's concept(s) of race and critique(s) of racism? Why should we revisit the discourse of race and racism anyway? Isn't race, and therefore racism, a thing of the past or, at the least, a superstitious social construction that "science" tells us has never existed, or certainly no longer exists—especially considering the election of Barack Obama as the first African American president of the United States of America? Didn't Anthony Appiah's analytic philosophical assault debunk Du Bois's concept of race once and for all, exposing its pseudo-scientific and narrow nationalistic underpinnings? And, after all the smoke has cleared and the dust settled, isn't Du Bois just another over-engaged "race man" posthumously positioned (primarily by the present author) as a critical race theorist?[1]

Throughout this chapter I will address these questions (and probably problematize and raise many others) by arguing that Du Bois's writings on race remain relevant and contribute to contemporary racial discourse, especially sociology of race, for four fundamental reasons. First, his sociology of race has been often interpreted as an "ideology of race"—that is, as an inert, inflexible, fixed and fast, singular notion of what race is, and which groups constitute constituent races. This is not only a gross misinterpretation of Du Bois's ever evolving sociology of race, but an example of the type of intellectual disingenuousness and, let it be said, *epistemic apartheid* that has long plagued Africana intellectuals of every political persuasion and social station.

Critically engaging Du Bois's sociology of race offers objective interpreters and critics of race and racism an opportunity to analyze a theoretically rich and thoroughgoing series of ruminations on race and racism by an undisputed pioneer (critical!) race theorist who almost infinitely harbored a hardnosed skepticism toward the supposed scientific and/or biological bases of race. This skepticism, coupled with his own homegrown pragmatism, often led Du Bois to contradictory conclusions regarding race. However, he repetitiously reminded his readers that he was not searching for a sound, "scientific" concept of race as much as he was on a quest to either locate or create a vehicle for Pan-African cultural development and black social survival.

The meaning of race has always meandered, as the very idea of race has consistently traveled far and wide since its inception. As we witnessed with the discussion of "The Negroes of Farmville" and *The Philadelphia Negro* in the previous chapter, Du Bois has the distinction of being one of the first persons of African descent to empirically research and write on race and anti-black racism. His Africanity or blackness is important insofar as Africans or blacks have historically and continue currently to be considered one of the most thoroughly and oppressively racially colonized groups—although undertheorized from their own cultural perspectives and radical political positions—in the history of race and racism. From an increasingly insurgent empirical and critical theoretical perspective, he studied the history of race with an intense interest in its origins and originators, and the purpose(s) of its origination. This alone should distinguish Du Bois's writings on race as more than mere intellectual artifacts but, truth be told, there is much more, so much more.

Du Bois's concepts of race harbor an inherent and radical humanism that is often complex and seemingly contradictory, but which nonetheless is part and parcel of his overarching transdisciplinary trajectory. In particular, he developed what I have crudely called a "gift theory" which, in short, elaborated that each race has specific and special "gifts" to contribute to national and international culture and civilization. As will be witnessed below, in works such as *The Souls of Black Folk*, "The People of Peoples and Their Gifts to Men," *Darkwater*, and, most especially, in later works like *The Gift of Black Folk*, "The Black Man Brings His Gifts," *Black Reconstruction, Black Folk, Then and Now, Dusk of Dawn*, and *The World and Africa*, Du Bois put forward concepts of race that were not biologically based, but predicated on social, political, historical, and cultural "common" characteristics and "common" experiences shared by continental and diasporan Africans. In Du Bois's "gift theory," these characteristics represent Pan-African peoples' "gifts" or race- and culture-specific contributions to the wider world and the ongoing development of civilization.

Second, and falling fast on the heels of the first point, it is important for us to revisit Du Bois's concepts of race because what we now know of his sociology of race is almost utterly predicated on, and relegated to his early writings. For instance, most contemporary critics of Du Bois's sociology of race begin and often end with his 1897 address to the American Negro Academy, "The Conservation of Races." Some critics go as far as his early career classics, "The Study of the Negro Problems," *The Philadelphia Negro*, and, of course, *The Souls of Black Folk*. Further than these texts, however, contemporary race critics do not dare venture, which to my mind seems absurd considering the fact that Du Bois continued to publish for another sixty years. Scant attention has been given to Du Bois's writings on race and racism after *The Souls of Black Folk*, and when on rare occasions they are engaged more is made of his infamously alleged and highly controversial collapsing of race into class in his 1935 classic, *Black Reconstruction of Democracy in America*. Maybe those who argue that Du Bois (1982d) collapsed race into class, and that he uncritically accepted communism have never read his 1936 essay "Social Planning for the Negro, Past and Present," where he roared against the supposed racelessness and political panacea thesis of white socialists and communists: "There is no automatic power in socialism to override and suppress race prejudice. . . . One of the worst things that Negroes could do today would be to join the American Communist Party or any of its many branches" (38). Du Bois, then, was a much more astute interpreter of Marxian philosophy and class theory than many contemporary race theorists, especially sociologists of race and critical race theorists, may be aware of. Without a thorough understanding of why, and the ways in which he critically engaged—as opposed to uncritically embraced—Marxism many critics of his concepts of race are doomed to do Du Bois a disservice by misinterpreting his motivations for emphasizing certain aspects of race and racism at specific sociohistoric and politico-economic intervals. It may not be too much of an overstatement to say that Du Bois empirically developed a discourse on race in order to critique racism and provide a philosophical foundation for antiracist radical politics and social movements. This is the second reason his work has import for contemporary race and racism discourse, especially sociology of race: because it may offer models for us to further our critiques of race and to combat the seemingly omnipresent and omnipotent racism of the twenty-first century.

The third reason Du Bois's writings on race are important for contemporary race and racism discourse is because of the recent emergence of critical white studies and the emphasis on whiteness, white racelessness or white racial neutrality and universality, and white supremacy. In several pioneering publications in historical sociology, sociology of race, sociology of culture, and political economy he deftly and defiantly hit at the heart of whiteness, chronicling its rise alongside the concept of race, noting that to be white is to be raceless, to be powerful or, at the least, to have privileged access to power or people in positions of power. In the logic of the white world, race is something that soils the social status of subhumans—that is, nonwhites; it politically pollutes their thinking, thus rendering them powerless, irrational, and in need of clear conceptions concerning themselves and the world. Since whites are the only group purportedly not plagued by race, they then have been burdened by God (who, within the racist logic of the white supremacist world, is also, of course, white) with the task of leading the lost, raced "natives," "barbarians," "savages," and subhumans to the higher level or lily-white "heaven" of humanity. Du Bois resented whites' racial mythmaking, and directed a significant portion of his writings on race and racism to critiquing whiteness and white supremacy. His writings, such as "Race Friction Between Black and White," "The Souls of White Folk," "Of The Culture of White Folk," "White Co-Workers," "The Superior Race," "The White Worker," "The White Proletariat in Alabama, Georgia, and Florida," "The White World," and "The White Folk Have a Right to Be Ashamed," represent and register as early innovative efforts aimed at critiquing and combating whiteness and white supremacy. Du Bois's work in this area, then, can be said to prefigure and provide a paradigm and point of departure for the contemporary discourse and debates of critical white studies.

Finally, Du Bois's writings on race are relevant with regard to contemporary race and racism criticism as they contribute significantly to the discursive arena of critical race theory. No longer considered the exclusive domain of legal studies scholars and radical civil rights lawyers and law professors, critical race theory has blossomed and currently encompasses and includes a wide range of theory and theorists from diverse academic disciplines. In a nutshell, the core concerns of critical race theory include race and racism's centrality to European imperial expansion and modernity; racism's intersections and interconnections with sexism, capitalism, and colonialism; white supremacy; white normativity and white neutrality; state-sanctioned (or, legal) racial domination and discrimination; and revolutionary antiracist race and cultural consciousness amongst nonwhites (Crenshaw, Gotanda, Peller, and Thomas, 1995; Delgado, 1995; Delgado and Stefancic, 2001; Essed and Goldberg, 2001; Goldberg and Solomos, 2002). Du Bois's sociology of race in many senses foreshadows contemporary critical race theory and, therefore, contributes several paradigms and points of departure to its discursive community as well. However, as with so many other aspects of his thought, Du Bois's writings on race and racism have been relegated to the realm, at best, of ethnic and racial studies, which downplays and diminishes their trenchant transdisciplinarity and significance for sociology of race and sociology of culture in particular, and contemporary radical politics and critical social theory in general. Therefore, his writings on race have been virtually overlooked and/or rendered intellectually invisible by critical race theorists.

As Susan Gillman and Alys Eve Weinbaum recently argued in their groundbreaking anthology *Next to the Color-Line: Gender, Sexuality, and W. E. B. Du Bois* (2007), and, as I will discuss in greater detail in the next chapter, Du Bois was critically conscious of many of the ways in which *race is gendered* and *gender is raced*. Emerging in the fifteenth century, and coinciding with European imperial expansion around the globe, racial domination threw fuel on the wildfire of preexisting gender discrimination. An astute student of gender relations, Du Bois eventually accented the intersections and interconnections of racism and sexism, specifically white supremacy and patriarchy. This means, then, that at the least some of his antiracist social theorizing may serve as a model for contemporary critical race theory in the sense that it seeks a similar goal: To make visible the long invisible connections between racial, gender and class domination and discrimination, not only in law but in medicine, politics, education, and religion, among other aspects and areas of contemporary society. What is intellectually amazing and seminally significant is that Du Bois developed *a sexism-sensitive conception of race and racism* almost a hundred years prior to the current critical race theory movement, which is to say that much of Du Bois's work in sociology of race and sociology of culture, for all theoretical and practical purposes, could (and, I honestly believe, should) be considered *classical critical race theory*.

Du Bois was also an early exponent of the race/class thesis that contended that although class struggle had been a part of human history for several centuries, the modern concept of race and the insidious sociopolitical practice of racism—of course, coupled with capitalism and colonialism—exacerbated class conflicts among both the racial colonizers and the racially colonized. Although often unacknowledged, similar to C. L. R. James (1994, 1996, 1999) and Oliver C. Cox (1948, 1976, 1987), Du Bois was a pioneer in terms of analyzing the political economy of race and racism, which is to say that he often argued against studying race independent of class. Race and class, as we have seen with race and gender in Du Bois's *sexism-sensitive* and/or *gender-centered conception of race*, are inextricable and incessantly intersecting and reconfiguring, constantly forming and reforming, creating a racial or racist dimension in modern class theory and class struggle, and a classist or economically exploitive dimension in racial politics and racial struggle.

Race and racism were European modernity's weapons of choice in its efforts to establish global (racial colonial) capitalism. A (sub)person, from the modern white world's frame of reference, was capitalized on or, rather, economically exploited based on biology or ethnicity. That is to say, the degree(s) to which one was dominated and/or discriminated against was predicated on European-invented racial classifications and ethnocultural categorizations. Du Bois's writings on the political economy of race and racism, therefore, provide an alternative paradigm for contemporary critical race theory to build on and bolster its calls for racial, economic, and gender justice.

In what follows, I will further elaborate on each of the four fundamental reasons Du Bois's concepts of race and critiques of racism remain relevant for contemporary sociology of race. Devoting a section to each issue, the remainder of this chapter is divided into four sections and begins with a close reading of Du Bois's early conception of race as articulated in his classic essay "The Conservation of Races." In the subsequent section I continue the close reading of "The Conservation of Races," but acutely alter my interpretation by placing the essay into discursive dialogue with several of Du Bois's other seminal works in sociology of race, specifically *Dusk of Dawn*, in an effort to judiciously juxtapose his concept of race with his core critique of racism. This section ultimately seeks to deftly demonstrate several of the ways in which Du Bois's discourse on race and racism prefigured and has direct (albeit often overlooked) relevance for contemporary critical race theory. The next section engages Du Bois's immortal *The Souls of Black Folk* with an eye on the ways in which he created discursive devices, such as the "Veil," "second-sight," "double-consciousness," and the "color-line," to simultaneously capture the dilemmas and dualities or, rather, the conundrums and complexities of what it means to be black in a white world *and* to deepen and develop early twentieth-century sociology of race. If, indeed, Du Bois arguably inaugurated the sociology of race in the United States, this section queries, how might the sociology of race and actual, real-life race relations be different today if his sociological discourse had not fallen prey to "sociological negation" and "the logic of segregation"—in other words, *epistemic apartheid*? Then, I conclude the chapter by examining both the textual tension and conceptual camaraderie between *The Souls of Black Folk*, "The Souls of White Folk," and *The Gift of Black Folk*, audaciously asserting that Du Bois not simply established the sociology of race in general, but more specifically *both* the sociology of black folk *and* the sociology of white folk as well. This section ultimately focuses on the evolution of Du Bois's "gift theory" in the aforementioned works and his unprecedented critical social theory of whites' *racial theft* and *cultural banditry* of *black folk and black gifts as property*. In short, I end the chapter accenting Du Bois's innovative contributions to classical and contemporary critical white studies.

ON THE DIABOLICAL DIALECTIC OF WHITE SUPERIORITY AND BLACK INFERIORITY: DU BOIS'S CONCEPTION(S) OF RACE IN "THE CONSERVATION OF RACES"

There have been so many interpretations, reinterpretations, and misinterpretations of Du Bois's "The Conservation of Races" over the last century that I am tempted to forego a discussion of it here (see, e.g., Appiah, 1992; Goodin, 2002; Gooding-Williams, 1996, 2009; Lott, 2001; Outlaw, 1995, 1996a; P. C. Taylor, 2000; Zamir, 1995, 2008). However, as Tommy Lott in *The Invention of Race* (1999) tells us, it remains one of the best points of departure for the undaunted contemporary critical race theorist who dares venture into the vortex of Du Bois's discourse on race and racism and the barrage of commentary and criticism it has elicited. In "The Conservation of Races," Du Bois set out to simultaneously deconstruct and reconstruct "race." In 1897, when he delivered this address, race was something for which science had no "final word" and no "definite conclusion[s]" (Du Bois, 1897a, 6). Race science was actually *racist science*—that is, a bunch of purportedly biologically determined, "scientific" categories created by white supremacist "scientists" with an eye aimed at maintaining and magnifying white world supremacy and *the diabolical dialectic of white superiority and black inferiority* (Jackson and Weidman, 2004; Moses, 1978; Poliakov, 1974; Stepan, 1982; Ward and Lott, 2002). Du Bois's (1897a) deconstruction of race, then, was geared toward debunking late nineteenth-century pseudo-scientific notions of race based on "physical characteristics" and *the diabolical dialectic of white superiority and black inferiority* (6).

Although this very well may have been Du Bois's intention, and I honestly think that it was, when he rendered his reconstruction of race he was caught in a quagmire and series of contradictions because he relied on the very "physical characteristics" he claimed had no biological basis for race. Many critics have questioned why Du Bois did not leave the language of race altogether, where others have asked if it would not have been better for him to emphasize social or political alternatives outside of the racial arena. To these queries Du Bois's (1897a) text seems quick to quip: Because "there can be no doubt, first, as to the widespread, nay, universal, prevalence of the race idea, the race spirit, the race ideal, and as to its efficiency as the vastest and most ingenious invention for human progress" (7). The "vastest and most ingenious invention for human progress"? But didn't race lead to racism? Hasn't "the race idea" harmed more than it has ever helped people of African origin and descent, and humanity as a whole, for that matter? What, with high-sounding tones, is he talking about? Has Du Bois gone off the deep end? I answer emphatically: No! No, Du Bois didn't lose himself to lunacy. No, he is not a narrow-minded nationalist (at least not in this instance). And, no, just for the hell of it, to the white supremacists and liberal white racists who would fix their faces to say this sounds even remotely like "reverse racism" (whatever that is).

In order to understand why Du Bois deconstructed and reconstructed race, as opposed to creating or advocating another alternative for black radical politics, black cultural development, and black social survival, we will have to quickly examine his concepts of race and critiques of racism. This section will be devoted to his concepts of race, and the subsequent section will treat his critiques of racism—although I should observe that it will be very difficult, if not impossible, to discuss race without discussing racism to a certain extent. Also, I must admit, it would be backbreaking to discuss classical conceptions of race without comparing them, however unconsciously, to contemporary conceptions of race. Therefore, this section, much like each of the chapters in this book, uses Du Bois's thought and texts as a critical paradigm and point of departure to revisit and revise both classical and contemporary sociological discourse.

"The Conservation of Races" is an almost ideal essay to engage Du Bois's sociology of race because he maintained and routinely revised many of the views he espoused here throughout his career. In this sense, "The Conservation of Races" not only serves contemporary critical race theorists as an entry to Du Bois's sociology of race, but it apparently served a similar function for Du Bois himself as well. For instance, in *Dusk of Dawn*, in the chapter "The Concept of Race," he reflected:

> I was born in the century when the walls of race were clear and straight; when the world consisted of mutually exclusive races; and even though the edges might be blurred, there was no question of exact definition and understanding of meaning of the word. One of the first pamphlets that I wrote in 1897 was on "The Conservation of Races" wherein I set down as the first article of a proposed racial creed: "We believe that the Negro people as a race have a

contribution to make to civilization and humanity which no other race can make." (Du Bois, 1968b, 116)

Over forty years after he penned "The Conservation of Races," Du Bois was still clinging to some of the "essential" (as opposed to "essentialist") ideas he set down in it; ideas that continue to impact and influence sociological and critical race theoretical discourse and debates in the twenty-first century. Du Bois (1897a) boldly began the essay asking "What is the real meaning of Race; what has, in the past, been the law of race development, and what lessons has the past history of race development to teach the rising Negro people?" (5). He then proceeded to deconstruct then prevalent late nineteenth-century notions of race based on biology (i.e., "physical characteristics" and "physical differences," such as "cranial measurements . . . color, hair, [and] bone") (6). "All these physical characteristics," Du Bois declared, "are patent enough, and if they agreed with each other it would be very easy to classify mankind. Unfortunately for scientists, however, these criteria of race are most exasperatingly intermingled" (6). On the one hand, the "final word of science, so far, is that we have at least two, perhaps three great families of human beings—whites and Negroes, possibly the yellow races" (6). On the other hand, he perplexingly pondered: "We find upon the world's stage today eight distinctly differentiated races, in the sense in which History tells us the word must be used. They are the Slavs of eastern Europe, the Teutons of middle Europe, the English of Great Britain and America, the Romance nations of Southern and Western Europe, the Negroes of Africa and America, the Semitic people of Western Asia and Northern Africa, the Hindoos of Central Asia and the Mongolians of Eastern Asia" (8).

Within each of the "eight distinctly differentiated races," Du Bois reported, there were "minor race groups," which seemed to confound him as much as I am almost certain they will contemporary sociologists of race and critical race theorists (7). The science of race, he curtly concluded at the outset of his essay, was then as now predicated on confusing and "contradictory criteria" that may never be clear-cut because of the sociohistoric reality of racial "intermingling" (6). Early in "The Conservation of Races," then, Du Bois made it clear that he was not interested in rendering a biologically determined or pseudo-scientific definition of race, and that it had been and remained "racial intermingling" that dumbfounded the dimwitted pretensions to pristine races of late nineteenth-century racial discourse.

According to the twenty-nine-year-old Du Bois, stepping outside of the realm of race science and taking an enormous intellectual risk; a race is "a vast family of human beings, generally of common blood and language, always of common history, traditions and impulses, who are both voluntarily and involuntarily striving together for the accomplishment of certain more or less vividly conceived ideals of life" (7). As I intimated earlier, part of Du Bois's reconstructed concept of race rests on biological factors—that is, a claim of "common blood." However, we would do well to note that he wrote that persons who belong to a specific race are "*generally* of common blood," but "*always* of common history, traditions and impulses." Du Bois patently put more emphasis on peoples' "common history, traditions and impulses" than he did on their "common blood and language" in his definition of race because his definition was neither for scientific nor biological designs, but for social and political purposes.

In Du Bois's sociology of race "common history, traditions and impulses" mattered much more than "common blood and language" because, as he made clear in his 1906 volume *The Health and Physique of the Negro American*, he was well aware of racial "intermingling" and the sociohistoric fact that there are now and historically have been few, if any, "pure" and "unmixed" races (Du Bois, 1906b, 13–18). This is an extremely important and—at the time and, perhaps, even today—*radical* point to make because, as he put it in his often overlooked 1935 essay, "Miscegenation," "Most American students have the curious habit of studying Negroes indiscriminately without reference to their blood mixture and calling the result a study of the Negro race" (Du Bois, 1985a, 98). Du Bois (1968b) sought to sidestep biology-based concepts of race because he knew that "all members of the Negro race were not black," or purely or wholly of African origin or descent (100). By which he, however contradictorily and controversially, meant that all blacks are not, to put it plainly, "black." Or, put another way, all people classified and categorized as "black" do not have "the rich, dark brown [skin] of the Zulu[s]" (Du Bois, 1897a, 6). What is more, the texture of their hair and the size and shape of their heads, noses, lips, and so on vary widely and are not always similar or shared common or shared characteristic physical features. Here Du Bois was hinting at the sheer diversity of *Africanity* (i.e., African humanity and African identity), which he had previously engaged in his 1915 cultural anthropological classic, *The Negro*. After this devastating discursive deconstruction of race, contemporary sociologists of race and critical race theorists are probably left exasperatingly wondering exactly what Du Bois did a century ago when he earnestly asked, "What, then, is a race?"

This question was meant to be rhetorical more than it was meant to be anything else, although much else has been made of it. As he illustrated, Du Bois was critically conscious of the ways in which white race scientists conceived of race. Referring to many of the major turn-of-the-twentieth-century white race theorists, such as Charles Darwin, Johann Friedrich Blumenbach, Thomas Henry Huxley, and Friedrich Ratzel, Du Bois exposed inconsistencies in their biology-based theories of race and offered what has been repeatedly referred to by several, at times, sophisticated philosophers of race, as a "sociohistorical" reconception of race. In response to his rhetorical question, "What, then, is a race?" Du Bois (1897a) infamously answered, "It is a vast family of human beings, generally of common blood and language, always of common history, traditions and impulses, who are both voluntarily and involuntarily striving together for the accomplishment of certain more or less vividly conceived ideals of life" (7). Above I examined his use of "generally" and "always" in this passage, so I will not spend much time on it here. What I am more interested in at this point is the latter part of Du Bois's (re)definition of race and its simultaneously problematic and promising critical theoretical, social, and political possibilities.

According to Du Bois, members of a specific race *always* share history, culture ("traditions"), and sociopolitical views and values ("impulses" and "striving[s]") that, though "subtle, delicate and elusive," are "clearly defined to the eye of the Historian and Sociologist" (7). Biologists and racist scientists, Du Bois was hinting at here, have missed perhaps the most significant element of race: its historical, cultural, social, and political points of intersection and interconnection. Races are only *generally* of "common blood," but they are *always* of "common history, traditions and impulses." The "common blood" or biological bit of Du Bois's (re)definition of race is just that—a small or minor piece of the puzzle, of the riddle of race, of his overall antiracist racial reconstruction project that is easily eclipsed by major historical, cultural, and sociopolitical factors. A claim of "common blood" is *not* always and in every instance a necessary factor for ascertaining racial membership and/or ethnocultural inclusion. When and where Du Bois uses "always" above to measure and magnify the "subtle, delicate and elusive" differences of history, culture, and struggle, "which have silently but definitely separated men into groups," he is simultaneously sidestepping and critiquing white supremacist conceptions of race and demonstrating that his (re)definition of race is *primarily* predicated on historical, cultural, and sociopolitical factors as opposed to purely physiological phenomena. In other words, persons are members of the same race if, and only if, they share or have in common history, culture, and sociopolitical struggle(s) or, rather, shared lifeworlds and life struggles. But it is not the case, in Du Bois's conception of race, that persons are members of the same race if, and only if, they share "common blood and language."

The latter part of Du Bois's (re)definition of race stated above, the part which asserts that races are "always of common history, traditions and impulses, who are both voluntarily and involuntarily striving together for the accomplishment of certain more or less vividly conceived ideals of life," reveals his major motivation for clinging to the language of late nineteenth-century racial discourse and the accoutrements of race. At this juncture Du Bois was directing his readers to the "deeper differences" that distinguish one race from another—the "spiritual" and "psychical" differences (8). Recall, Du Bois stated that "the race idea [is] . . . the vastest and most ingenious invention for human progress." This is so because to "the eye of the Historian and Sociologist," the "history of the world is the history, not of individuals, but of groups, not of nations but of races, and he who ignores or seeks to override the race idea in human history ignores and overrides the central thought of all history" (7). Aside from the fact that Du Bois may have overstated his case by claiming that "the race idea" is "the central thought of *all* history"—because race actually was not "invented" and put to racist purposes in the manner in which we are currently familiar with it until European modernity, which also spawned capitalism to accompany the age-old practices of sexism and colonialism—his statement, nevertheless, highlights the antiracist and radical political dimension(s) of his (re)definition of race.

Flying in the face of biology-based concepts of race, Du Bois declared, "So far as purely physical characteristics are concerned, the differences between men do not explain all the differences of their history," and "physical differences of color, hair and bone go but a short way toward explaining the different roles which groups of men have played in Human Progress" (6–7). When and where Du Bois wrote of the "different roles which groups of men have played in Human Progress," he clearly revealed that he conceived of *race* as *a sociopolitical vehicle, as a medium through which to accent African agency and humble humanity*. Although many sociologists and historians of race have remarked on Du Bois's "sociohistorical" reconception of race, I do not think that this characterization does his antiracist concept of race justice, since it also contained a definite and distinct political and, as we will soon see, ethical dimension. The political dimension of Du Bois's (re)definition of race has been commented on above. However, it is also extremely evident when we come to the passage in "The Conservation of Races" where he invoked historical-political figures, who he claimed represented not themselves individually, but symbolized the collective "strivings" of sociocultural and political-economic groups and civilizations. For instance, Du Bois declared, "We see the Pharaohs, Caesars, Toussaints and Napoleans of history and forget the vast races of which they were but epitomized expressions" (7).

Here, then, Du Bois was pointing out that even in the historical scheme of racial things it was not only "whites" (the "Caesars" and "Napoleans") but "blacks" (the "Pharaohs" and "Toussaints") as well who used race (or, at the least something with the precolonial semblances of race) as a tool for political progress and social survival. However, we should quickly be clear here: using race as *a group-organizing and movement-mobilizing concept* against racial oppression, as opposed to using race to psychopathically practice and promote racial oppression, racial exploitation, and racist exclusions, are two interrelated but distinctively different things. Take, for example, the "Toussaints" that Du Bois invoked above. Toussaint L'Ouveture, in Du Bois's critical race theorizing here, utilized Haitians' common experience of racial oppression, racial exploitation, and racist exclusion at the hands of several European colonial powers to forge the first modern black revolution against white supremacy and various forms of racism, such as colonial racism, cultural racism, class or economic racism, deracinative racism, and exterminative racism. In contrast to the "Caesars" and "Napoleans" of history who utilized race as a gateway and bridge to racial and other forms of ethnocultural exploitation, oppression, and violence, here Du Bois was hipping his antiracist readers to the fact that historically there were precedents for, literally, *using* race to combat racism. Now, I am almost certain that the question that is on the tip of a lot of my readers' tongues is this: But, can we really combat racism by utilizing race in a morally mature manner? And, even if we can, are we willing to place our humanity in jeopardy by traveling down the tragic roads and through the tricky back and side streets of the racial state?

As Goldberg (1993, 1997, 2001, 2008), Omi and Winant (1994), and Winant (1994, 2001, 2004) have astutely observed, the reality of the racial matter is that we are already in the racial state. We were born into a racial colonial-capitalist world; born on the racial colonial-capitalist battlefield where Frantz Fanon (1965, 1968) waged a valiant war in the anti-imperialist interests of *the wretched of the earth* against *a dying colonialism*. Consequently, whether we consciously or unconsciously contribute to its perpetuation or its destruction, we, in so many subtle and not so subtle ways, currently and will continue for the foreseeable future to contribute either to its recreation and reconstruction, or to its downfall and ultimate destruction. It is a frightening thought, but one that must be critically thought out and ethically acted on. Hence, as a hotly contested concept, race harbors a certain malleability and instrumentality which no group, or elite, or aristocracy within a group, has a monopoly on. Race is not a set of singular, tried and true transhistorical and transcultural meanings and expressions but, even more, it is a continuously transforming and transmutating entity, ever breaking with its former definitions and redefinitions, insidiously extending and expanding its range and reach in light of rapidly changing political patterns, social situations, cultural contexts, and economic episodes. Therefore, theoretically race, as a sociopolitical concept and not a pseudo-scientific conjecture, could technically and pragmatically be utilized by the racially colonized to combat racism—that is, an oppressive economic, social, political, and cultural condition and system. This will be the recurring theme and primary point of departure of the subsequent section.

ON THE IRONIES OF RALLYING AROUND RACE IN THE INTEREST OF REVOLUTIONARY ANTIRACISM: DU BOIS'S RACE CONSERVATION, CRITIQUES OF RACISM, AND CONTRIBUTIONS TO CRITICAL RACE THEORY

It must be unequivocally asserted outright: Du Bois did not have any deep and abiding love of race as a concept. In fact, Tommy Lott (2001) observes that in "The Conservation of Races," Du Bois "seems to have meant to undermine the whole business of constructing racial categories" (69). What attracted Du Bois to, and excited him about, the concept of race was the radical political possibilities it offered for Pan-African, especially African American, social survival and cultural development. He argued in "The Conservation of Races" that just as other races had utilized race as an "instrument of progress," so too would continental and diasporan Africans have to (or, at the least, should have the liberty to) use race to forge what was surely a new idea in 1897, "the van of Pan-Negroism" (Du Bois, 1897a, 7, 10). However, Du Bois was well aware that because Pan-African peoples' primary exposure to race was the wicked ways in which Europeans used or, rather, abused it—that is, as an instrument of oppression and excruciating exploitation—blacks developed a tendency to "deprecate and minimize race distinctions" (5). The young Du Bois, perhaps paradoxically, believed that race could be put to antiracist purposes, and especially in anti-African/anti-black, racially segregated, multiracial, and multicultural societies. In "The Conservation of Races" he counseled the American Negro Academy to reconsider the possible uses and historic abuses of race, stating, "We are apt to think in our American impatience, that while it may have been true in the past that closed race groups made history, that here in conglomerate America *nous avons changer tout cela*—we have changed all that, and have no need of this ancient instrument of progress. This assumption of which the Negro people are especially fond, cannot be established by a careful consideration of history" (7).

For Du Bois, "the Historian and Sociologist" (and, we might add, the "Political Economist"), a radically reconstructed concept of race could be used by continental and diasporan Africans as an "instrument of progress" and a weapon against racial oppression, racial exploitation, and racist exclusions. Race, like so many European inventions and European-derived devices, can be adopted and adapted for Africana and other non-European interests. Think for a moment. Think about the ways in which Pan-African peoples have historically employed non-African technological advances, such as, say, cars and computers, or telephones and televisions. Think about Africana appropriations of various non-African religious traditions, and not simply European religious traditions but Asian and Native American religious traditions. What is more, think about what you are reading and, more importantly, who it has been researched and written by. Which is to say, think about how I—perhaps not "purely," but surely a person of African descent—am using a European language, English, in the interest of the wretched of the earth's struggle for human rights and racial justice.

People of African descent have a long history of *Africanizing* non-African concepts, tools, and technologies. Continental and diasporan Africans often use these, among other thought-complexes and intellectual instruments, in ways inconsistent with their inventors' intentions, but also in ways that speak volumes about Africana lifeworlds and life struggles. Therefore, *a concept, tool, or type of technology need not be created by a specific human group in order for that group to effectively and/or progressively utilize it.* Culture quickly comes into play here. And it is culture that determines how a concept, tool, or type of technology is viewed, valued and put to use. Race concepts, though by no means open-ended or value-free, can be deconstructed and reconstructed by the racially colonized in the interest of human liberation and democratic social transformation. For instance, in *Racist Culture*, my colleague David Theo Goldberg (1993) makes an interesting point concerning race in this regard:

> A person need not be a racist, then, merely by use of some version of the concept "race." So it cannot be mere use of race which is objectionable. . . . This prevailing historical legacy of thinking racially does not necessitate that any conceptual use of or appeal to race to characterize social circumstance is inherently unjustifiable. What renders an appeal to racial categorization racist is not that it need be arbitrary. Rather, its racism turns on whether the categorization is constitutive and promotive in the case at hand of racialized exclusions. In other words, what distinguishes a racist from a nonracist appeal to the category of race is the *use* into which the categorization enters, the exclusions it sustains, prompts, promotes, and extends. Foucault argues instructively that no technology, technique, or architecture necessarily restricts freedom or is naturally liberative. In the final analysis, the only and necessarily contingent guarantee of freedom is the practice of freedom itself, is freely living out the conditions of expressive space. Analogously, I want to suggest that though race has tended historically to define conditions of oppression, it could, under a culturalist interpretation—and under some conditions must—be the site of a counterassault, a ground or field for launching liberatory projects or from which to expand freedom(s) and open up emancipatory spaces. (125, 211, emphasis in original)

Race concepts, then, can be progressively utilized by the racially colonized to combat their racial oppression and racial objectification. The racially colonized approach and employ race differently—and, one is even tempted to say, *diametrically*—than their racial oppressors because their sociopolitical agendas are different and diametric: the latter has an agenda of domination, while the former has an agenda of liberation. Concepts of race, as with racial identities, have historically and continue currently to be constructed in contexts of racial domination and discrimination. This means, then, that the ruling racial group's view of, and ideological stance toward, race (when and where it is acknowledged) has been and remains one where it is understood to be direly divisive and utterly oppressive. All of this makes pure and perfect sense in the logic of the racial rulers because their entire history of and power relations to race have been, to put it plainly, a history of and power relations predicated on racial oppression, racial exploitation, and racist exclusion. The ruling race cannot conceive of the racially ruled using race in good conscience because they, the ruling race, have never used race with any ethical or emancipatory intent.

For the self-righteous racial rulers it is not a question that race can be used in any other way than they have used it. From their point of view, race-consciousness logically leads to racism, to racial domination and racist exclusions. However, for the racially dominated, race is malleable and motive, and neither the racially privileged at present nor even the historic inventors of race have exclusive control over the idea and concept.[2] Du Bois was an early advocate of "race action," "race responsibility," and "race enterprise" in the interest of the racially oppressed, but he advocated all of this with an eye toward and an emphasis on social ethics. For instance, in "The Conservation of Races" he sternly stated, "[I]t is our duty to conserve our physical powers, our intellectual endowments, our spiritual ideals; as a race we must strive by race organization, by race solidarity, by race unity to the realization of that broader humanity which freely recognizes differences in men, but sternly deprecates inequality in the opportunities of development" (Du Bois, 1897a, 12). In Du Bois's sociology of race, race was about antiracist democratic social transformation, as opposed to racist or, rather, white supremacist social domination. Race was (or could be) liberative, as opposed to oppressive. For Du Bois, the world simply did not have to be the way the white supremacists and racist social (and other) scientists said it was or had to be.

In embracing race as an emancipatory sociopolitical tool, Du Bois was criticized by whites and, as he painfully admitted, shunned by many bourgeois blacks. With regard to whites' reactions to his rebellious embrace of race, he recollected in *Dusk of Dawn*: "'Chauvinism!' they said, when I urged Pan-African solidarity for the accomplishment of universal democracy. 'Race prejudice,' they intimated, was just as reprehensible when shown by black toward white as when shown by white toward black" (Du Bois, 1968b, 311).[3] Moreover, much to his mortification, many persons of African descent resented his embrace of race as well. From his point of view, they seemed not to have understood what he had characterized over forty years earlier, in "The Conservation of Races," as "the central thought of all human history"—"the race idea." Writing revealingly of blacks' reactions to his embrace of race in *Dusk of Dawn*, Du Bois remarked, "There were plenty of my colored friends who resented my ultra 'race' loyalty and ridiculed it" (628). Undeterred, Du Bois continued his ruminations on race, amazingly prefiguring Fanon's emphasis on revolutionary decolonization and revolutionary humanism, by placing a greater emphasis on the ethical responsibilities of both the racially colonized *and* the racial colonizers (see Rabaka, 2010a). Race, then, is a chameleonic and controversial concept whose uses and abuses neither the ruling race nor the racially ruled have come to interracial or intraracial consensus or definite conclusions concerning. It is also, and perhaps more importantly with respect to Du Bois's sociology of race, an idea and concept which must be approached morally, with every effort being made to maintain the dignity and inherent value of each and every human group and human being. It is here, then, that we witness what I have come to call Du Bois's "radical humanism."

I am not arguing here that Du Bois understood race to be neutral or nonpolitical, but that he, like Goldberg above, understood race's almost inherent instrumentality to the racially dominated. Looking at race from the eyes of the racially oppressed, Du Bois argued that although "the master's tools will not dismantle the master's house," as Audre Lorde (1984) would have it, if put to proper antiracist purposes the racially enslaved certainly could make it very hard for the racial masters to live in and enjoy their racial colonial-capitalist plantations. Further, it is the master's discomfort in his once cozy racial colonial-capitalist abode that antiracist radicals bank on when and where they employ race in the interest of antiracist struggle.

However, all involved in the struggle against racial oppression are not open to using race to combat racism. For some, it is quite simply erroneous and absurd, and symbolizes antiracists' lowering themselves and their ideals to the level of racists. It is as simple, they say, as the age-old contradiction of "an eye for an eye" or "fight fire with fire." What will be the outcome? What lessons will humanity have learned? Will the world be a better place? Some even go so far as to ask: Will we (i.e., the well-meaning and morally conscious of the world) still be human after behaving so inhumanely? For others, embracing race for antiracist purposes is a temporal and extremely time-sensitive tactic, one that must be employed morally and sparingly because using race to combat racial oppression more often than not does not remove racism as much as it temporarily relieves racial tension by rewriting and reinscribing, countering and contradicting dominant racial concepts and codes. In other words, I am saying that race-based antiracism may be at best a momentary strategy that is applicable at specific sociohistoric and politico-economic intervals, but that it should not now nor ever become the most privileged and primary liberatory tool or emancipatory tactic the racially oppressed utilize in their quest for racial justice. Race-based antiracism will ultimately reify—that is, move from the level of an idea or abstraction to the level of the concrete and material, to inevitable inertia—because the historical horizon and cultural context in which it is undertaken will not last indefinitely. Race-based antiracism, if endeavored on a mass movement scale, will rapidly alter racial attitudes, thus requiring new (perhaps nonracial) replacement views and values. And this is one of the major issues that many antiracist advocates of raced-based politics often overlook.

As Goldberg (2001) points out in *The Racial State*, "Race can be mobilized to antiracist purposes at best only as a short-term and contingent strategy." Why? Because "racial invocation likely reinscribes elements of the very presumptions promoting racist exclusions it is committed to ending" (113–14). This is something that Du Bois's sociology of race and critical race theory anticipated, and that is why he was careful to emphasize that the struggle against racial oppression must never degenerate into any morally reprehensible ideas or acts on the part of the racially oppressed. Racial justice seekers must morally and cautiously use race as an organizing instrument or, rather, antiracist rallying point. In *Dusk of Dawn*, Du Bois (1968b) offered this advice: "So long as we [are] fighting a color-line, we must strive by color organization. We have no choice. If in time, the fight for Negro equality degenerates into organized murder for the suppression of whites, then our last case is no better than our first; but this need not be, if we are level-headed and clear-sighted, and work for the emancipation of all men from caste through the organization and determination of the present victims of caste" (311). Du Bois's concepts of race and racial struggle, then, were almost utterly the antithesis of white supremacist social scientists' conceptions of race. In conceiving of race from an Africana perspective—that is, from the perspective of one thoroughly racially dominated in the (post)modern moment—Du Bois sought to redefine and reconceptualize race. As a result, he offered *a race-based antiracist alternative* that destabilized and deconstructed the established imperial order's concepts of race.

As discussed above, historically racial classifications and ethno-cultural categorizations were invented and assigned primarily by scientists and bureaucrats belonging to the dominant racial group. These white agents of the established imperial order usually understood themselves to be racially superior to nonwhite inferiors. Consequently, and as was witnessed in the discussion of *The Philadelphia Negro* in the previous chapter, the racially dominated have imposed on them, and often intensely internalize, white supremacist racial schemas and social hierarchies. These racial schemas and social hierarchies quickly rub the racially dominated wrong, and at such time one of two things usually takes place: The racially dominated either accept and sometimes subtly embrace white supremacist views and values, or they reject and resist them. In the latter case, the excruciating experience of racism and the forging of a distinct racial identity provide the fertile soil in which the seeds of antiracist critical social theory and antiracist radical political praxis are planted.

As the racially oppressed begin to use race for their own antiracist purposes they must beware of what Cornel West (1993b) has called "the pitfalls of racial reasoning." Race-based antiracism, as stated above, is only a short-term tactic that must be employed morally and sparingly. Eventually and increasingly greater emphasis should be placed on social ethics and not purely on rebellious race-based antiracist identity politics and struggles. A new politics, perhaps, based more on shared cultural crises, economic injustices, educational issues, and threatening social situations should be consciously developed and ultimately replace race-based antiracist rallying and organization. Prolonged political mobilization centered on race will eventually weaken the struggle for racial justice because race offers a preexisting and historically problematic identity that was prefabricated and prefashioned by racists, and specifically white supremacists. There simply is no substitute for the racially oppressed forming their own social organizations, political movements, and cultural or ethnic identities independent of racism. At this point, identity will be formed in the face of shared sociohistoric and politico-economic issues and common lived experiences, as opposed to solely being based on reactions to racial oppression, which could potentially lead the racially oppressed right back down the road to racial essentialism and racial exclusionism. The new politics, then, will be based on new ethical identities and issues as opposed to purely racial or primarily race-based identities and issues.[4]

This brings us full circle, back to the fact that Du Bois developed a discourse on race only insofar as he sought to critique racism and provide a philosophical foundation and rallying point for insurgent antiracist struggle. In the aftermath of "The Conservation of Races" and *The Philadelphia Negro*, among his other early work, he intensified and extended his discourse on race and racism by doing something that virtually no other sociologists at the inception of sociology could do or did: He relied on his innovative empirical studies on, and lived experiences of, race and racism to paint sophisticated historical-sociological portraits of race and racism's impact on society. Du Bois left the dull, detached, and learned language of *The Philadelphia Negro* and audaciously synthesized sociology, philosophy, history, and political economy with the intricacies of the African American experience and (à la his idol Frederick Douglass) his own awe-inspiring autobiography. By most accounts between 1897 and 1903 he became one of the most extensively published authors in the United States, publishing not only in the prominent black publications but, unprecedentedly, in many of the prominent white publications as well. An abbreviated list of the publications Du Bois's articles and essays appeared in during this pivotal period includes *The Atlantic Monthly, The Chicago Tribune, The Independent, The Nation, The New York Times Magazine Supplement, The Southern Workman, Harper's Weekly, The World's Work, The Outlook, The Missionary Review of the World, The Spelman Messenger, The New World, The Literary Digest, The Advance, Annals of the American Academy of Political and Social Sciences, American Historical Review, Political Science Quarterly, Charities, Booklover's Magazine,* and *The Dial.* This groundswell of intellectual activity can be taken as a consequence of three things: first, Du Bois's disappointment with the way that he and his beloved book, *The Philadelphia Negro,* was treated at the hands of the white gatekeepers of the American academy; second, his efforts to emulate his (although self-educated) well-read, well-published, and well-traveled idol, Frederick Douglass; and, third, his growing disaffection with what he saw as Booker T. Washington's unscrupulous efforts to assume the leadership role left in the wake of Douglass's sudden death in 1895.

Washington was not called the "Wizard" for nothing, from Du Bois's increasingly critical point of view. The "Wizard," as it were, was making the already bad social situation of blacks at the turn of the twentieth century worse by incessantly advocating accommodationism and assimilationism. Hence, there is a sense in which Du Bois's prolificacy between 1897 and 1903 can be seen as his ongoing effort to counter Washington's accommodationism and assimilationism, and all of this even though, as was discussed in the previous chapter, Du Bois exhibited his own homespun assimilationism (not to mention Eurocentrism and elitism) throughout *The Philadelphia Negro.*

The Du Bois–Washington debate, then, represents something of a turning point for Du Bois, not simply politically (as I [Rabaka, 2008a] have argued elsewhere), but also, and most pertinent to the present discussion, sociologically. Indeed, his wrangling with Washington helped to quicken his political radicalization and *debourgeoisification*—and, truth be told, the large majority of his views during the period in question (i.e., 1897 to 1903) were definitely considered politically radical to both whites and blacks (and especially by Washington and the "Tuskegee Machine") at the turn of the twentieth century—but the dispute with Washington also forced him to radically rethink his relationship with his research, writing style, and intended audience. As innovative as *The Philadelphia Negro* may have been, and I should say it was, Du Bois quickly came to the realization that a "calm, cool, and detached" social scientific book of that sort would not win his cause—for example, voting rights, civil rights, and social justice—as many supporters as an accessibly written volume of essays vividly reflecting on the state of the "race problem" at the dawn of the promising new century. In other words, he desperately desired to reach a wider audience and naggingly knew that *The Philadelphia Negro* and his other academic writings up to that point would not do the trick. Faced with this dilemma, Du Bois at first reluctantly, and then resolutely transformed himself into the "discipline's first preeminent public sociologist," according to the acclaimed African American sociologist and civil rights scholar Aldon Morris. Morris (2007) importantly mused,

> Before the turn of the twentieth century Du Bois was well on his way to becoming a public intellectual and using sociology to emancipate the oppressed. In so doing, Du Bois broke radically from the Chicago School, whose practitioners followed Robert Park's advice that "their role instead was to be that of the calm, detached scientist who investigates race relations with the same objectivity and detachment with which the zoologist dissects the potato bug." But Du Bois lived in a completely different world from that of most Chicago School sociologists; he was often the victim of racism, and he abhorred the pain it inflicted on both himself and his race. Speaking of a particularly gut-wrenching lynching, after which he saw the victim's knuckles on display in the window of a local grocer, Du Bois wrote: "One could not be a calm, cool, and detached scientist while Negroes were lynched, murdered and starved." This stance led him to pioneer American public sociology and to become the discipline's first preeminent public sociologist long before it was lucrative and celebratory to be a public intellectual. (526; see also Du Bois, 1968a, 222, 1968b, 67–68)

Morris maintains that Du Bois was simultaneously a pioneer public sociologist and innovative public intellectual more than a century before the contemporary upsurge and advocacy of public intellectualism and public sociology. In addition, Morris makes a critical distinction between Du Bois's classical public sociology and insurgent public intellectualism and the academic acrobatics and word-wizardry of contemporary public intellectualism by strongly stressing that Du Bois's public intellectualism and public sociology was always and ever aimed at "emancipat[ing] the oppressed," and not filling his personal coffers like a good little capitalist and bourgeois intellectual. Du Bois's intense period of public sociological gestation and conceptual generation culminated with the publication of undoubtedly his most widely read work, *The Souls of Black Folk*. In the subsequent section I will examine *The Souls of Black Folk* exclusively with reference to its contributions to the sociology of race, bearing in mind, of course, that Du Bois's primary objective in the book was not to contribute to the development of sociology, or the discourse of any other academic discipline, as much as it was to "emancipate the oppressed," as Morris correctly contended above.

THE SOULS OF BLACK FOLK AND THE SOCIOLOGY OF RACE: DU BOIS'S VISION OF THE VEIL, SAGA OF SECOND-SIGHT, GIFT THEORY OF CULTURAL GIVING, CONCEPT OF DOUBLE-CONSCIOUSNESS, AND DOUBLE-CROSSING OF THE COLOR-LINE

For more than a century *The Souls of Black Folk* has been praised and criticized, interpreted and misinterpreted by so many scholars from so many different disciplines that it gives one pause before penning yet another piece on it. For instance, *The Souls of Black Folk* has been the subject of entire books of critical commentary, and innumerable essays, countless journal articles, and stacks of book chapters (see, e.g., W. L. Andrews, 1985; Bloom, 2001; R. Carroll, 2003; Crouch and Benjamin, 2002; Fontenot, 2001; Fontenot and Keller, 2007; Hubbard, 2003; Wolfenstein, 2007). Scholars working in diverse disciplines, such as history, philosophy, political science, psychology, anthropology, economics, education, literature, and religion, among others, have hailed it as a hallowed and timeless tome. However, much like the sociological reception of *The Philadelphia Negro, The Souls of Black Folk*'s sociological significance has been and remains conspicuously contemptible, partly owing to Du Bois's "sociological negation" at the hands of the white sociological fraternity, and partly on account of academia's ongoing lame "logic of segregation," both of which crudely combined constitute promptly and precisely what I am currently calling *epistemic apartheid*. Renowned sociologist of race Howard Winant (2007) pulls no punches and unapologetically maintains that Du Bois was "long relegated to sociology's margins because of his radicalism as well as his race" (555). Even after the publication of both *The Philadelphia Negro* and *The Souls of Black Folk*, Winant went further to observe, as late as "1905 and for a long time thereafter, the sociology of race took shape almost exclusively as a conversation among whites, even though this required the marginalization of W. E. B. Du Bois, who was not only the founder of the field in its modern, empirical, and theoretically sophisticated form but also arguably the founder of modern American sociology *tout court*" (538).

From Winant's critical frame of reference, Du Bois was marginalized in sociological discourse because of his "radicalism as well as his race," which not only gives credence to my above assertion that Du Bois's early work, however conservative it might seem to the eyes of twenty-first-century sociologists, was quite "radical" during its day, but also his work was always already considered too "political" and too "polemical" by white sociologists because he was ironically and oxymoronically a "black sociologist" or, rather, as Du Bois (1968a) put it in his *Autobiography*, he was merely a "Negro . . . studying Negroes, and after all, what had Negroes to do with America or [social] science?" (228). Because Du Bois was a "Negro . . .

studying Negroes," his social scientific objectivity was immediately and incessantly called into question in ways that white sociologists who conduct sociological studies on white society and white culture rarely, if ever, have been (Cross, 2000; B. R. Hare, 2002; Ladner, 1998; McKee, 1993; Pettigrew, 1980; Wacker, 1983). This disreputable double standard on the part of the white sociological world in particular, and the wider white social world in general instilled in the "souls of black folk," intellectuals or otherwise, what Du Bois dubbed "double-consciousness"—that is, *the psychological condition and social state where blacks incessantly and uncritically engage and judge their lifeworlds and life struggles exclusively utilizing the white world's anti-black racist culture and conceptions of civilization*. Hence, the concept of "double-consciousness" discursively captures the ways in which blacks, however subtly, unceasingly accept and internalize *the diabolical dialectic of white superiority and black inferiority* (Mocombe, 2008; Rawls, 2000; Tomisawa, 2003; Travis, 1996).

The Souls of Black Folk, as is often said of Duke Ellington's music or Romare Bearden's artistry, is "beyond category." In 1904, writing in response to the already growing body of commentary on and criticism of his beloved "little book," Du Bois rather self-effacingly explained: "*The Souls of Black Folk* is a series of fourteen essays written under various circumstances and for different purposes during a period of seven years. It has, therefore, considerable, perhaps too great, diversity. There are bits of history and biography, some description of scenes and persons, something of controversy and criticism, some statistics and a bit of storytelling. All this leads to rather abrupt transitions of style, tone and viewpoint and, too, without doubt, to a distinct sense of incompleteness and sketchiness" (Du Bois, 1997d, 255). Some of the early reviewers commented on the sprawling nature of the book, hence Du Bois's concession that it has "considerable, perhaps too great, diversity." In fact, many of the turn-of-the-twentieth-century historians found *The Souls of Black Folk* too "literary" to be counted as truly "historical"; many of the sociologists decried its lyricism and historicalness, thus making it sociologically insignificant or, at the least, sociologically inauthentic; and, for sundry philosophers it was, of course, too historical and sociological, thus not properly philosophical—*disciplinary decadence*, indeed, has intellectual historical precedent.

However, other early reviewers, both black and white, read unblemished words of genius in *The Souls of Black Folk*—words that, when closely read and carefully contemplated, were conceptually held together by the common thread of several innovative discursive devices Du Bois developed to accessibly articulate, first, the beauty and the poetry, as well as "the strange meaning of being black here in the dawning of the Twentieth Century"; second, the vision and viciousness of the "Veil"; third, the dilemmas of "double-consciousness"; fourth, the saga of "second-sight"; and, fifth and finally, the cruelty of life lived along the "color-line." Alluding to each of the aforementioned, Du Bois wrote in further response to his early critics: "There is a unity in the book, not simply the general unity of the larger topic, but a unity of purpose in the distinctly subjective note that runs in each essay. Through all the book runs a personal and intimate tone of self-revelation. In each essay I sought to speak from within—to depict a world as we see it who dwell therein. In thus giving up the usual impersonal and judicial attitude of the traditional author I have lost in authority but gained in vividness" (255). In so many words, Du Bois was letting his critics know that *The Souls of Black Folk* was neither written exclusively for a black audience nor exclusively for a white audience but, as his concept of "double-consciousness" seems to suggest, it was carefully composed with a combination of both blacks and whites, and ultimately a harmonious synthesis of both black and white history, culture, and society in mind. In *The Souls of Black Folk*, then, by breaking free from the "usual impersonal and judicial attitude of the traditional author" and social scientist, and by coupling African American culture-laden lyricism or poetry with passion and acute intellect with unbridled emotion, Du Bois (1903c) amazingly managed to achieve his goal of raising awareness of the "soul-life" or, rather, the lifeworlds and life struggles of the "souls of black folk" and reaching a wider audience (79, 191, 201).

It was not an easy task, Du Bois sternly stated in response to his early critics, walking between the "two worlds within and without the Veil," tactfully taking notes and tirelessly talking with both black and white folk who would much rather not be bothered with the bumptious business of studying race. But even with its "penumbra of vagueness and half-veiled allusion," he honestly believed that *The Souls of Black Folk* would reward its readers with exceptional insights into the "two worlds within and without the Veil," lives damaged by the duplicity of "double-consciousness," and the lunacy of life lived along the "color-line" (Du Bois, 1997d, 255). Concluding his rejoinder to his initial critics, Du Bois reminded them that it was, indeed, "difficult, strangely difficult, to translate the finer feelings of men into words. . . . Nevertheless, as the feeling is deep the greater the impelling force to seek to express it. And here the feeling was deep," which brings us back to Morris's assertion above that Du Bois's sociology was primarily preoccupied with "emancipat[ing] the oppressed" and not simply discursively developing sociology, or any other academic discipline for that matter (255). "In its larger aspects the style" and substance of *The Souls of Black Folk*, "is tropical—African," Du Bois impenitently declared. "This needs no apology," he caustically continued. Then, as if directly channeling the *soul-lives* of David Walker, Robert Alexander Young, Frederick Douglass, Martin Delany, Henry Highland Garnet, and Alexander Crummell, among other unnamed "black bards" and unsung black radical soldiers, Du Bois wrote, perhaps, the most candid self-reflection on his "little book" committed to the printed page: "The blood of my fathers spoke through me and cast off the English restraint of my training and surroundings. The resulting accomplishment is a matter of taste. Sometimes I think very well of it, and sometimes I do not" (255).

The Souls of Black Folk's trenchant transdisciplinarity is easily detected, even in revered African American biographer Arnold Rampersad's (1990, 70) tripartite discursive division of the text: chapters 1–3 ("Of Our Spiritual Strivings," "Of the Dawn of Freedom," and "Of Mr. Booker T. Washington and Others") hinge on the historical "strivings" of the "souls of black folk"; chapters 4–9 ("Of the Meaning of Progress," "Of the Wings of Atalanta," "Of the Training of Black Men," "Of the Black Belt," and "Of the Quest of the Golden Fleece") symbolize the sociological "strivings" of the "souls of black folk"; and chapters 10–14 ("Of the Sons of Master and Man," "Of the Faith of the Fathers," "Of the Passing of the First-Born," "Of Alexander Crummell," and "The Sorrow Songs") represent the spiritual and religious "strivings" of the "souls of black folk." However, and in all intellectual honesty, as useful as Rampersad's three-part (re)conceptualization of *The Souls of Black Folk* may have been for his specific interpretive intentions, it should be said that his scheme seems to mask as much as it reveals, especially when viewed from Africana critical theory's transdisciplinary frame of reference. Rampersad's tripartite conceptual (re)configuration of *The Souls of Black Folk* does not go far enough, and downplays and diminishes what I referred to above as Du Bois's "trenchant transdisciplinarity" insofar as his scheme seems to skim over the fact that almost each and every chapter of the book boldly blurs the arbitrary and artificial (and, let it also be unapologetically said, *Eurocentric*) academic disciplinary borders and boundaries that routinely revamp and wreak the havoc of *epistemic apartheid*. For instance, and as I (Rabaka, 2008a) have argued elsewhere, "Of Mr. Booker T. Washington and Others" is not only historical, but also significantly sociological and patently political (and, even more, it was considered to be *radically political* from Booker T. Washington's accommodationist point of view); "Of the Training of Black Men" is not simply sociological, but it also has profound implications for African American education and, therefore, accents the educational "strivings" of the "souls of black folk"; and, lastly, similar to the essay on Booker T. Washington, "Of Alexander Crummell" is not only important for African American religious studies, but equally indicative of the historical, cultural, social, and political "strivings" of the "souls of black folk."

Du Bois's discourse, here and throughout his *oeuvre*, was much more *transdisciplinary* than many Du Bois scholars have been willing to concede: partly owing to their monodisciplinary maneuvers to roguishly reclaim and reframe Du Bois for their own respective (or, rather, *disrespective*) single subject-focused fields or disciplines, and partly on account of the fact that, truth be told, W. E. B. Du Bois and Du Bois studies have yet to be seriously situated within the intellectual-historical and political-cultural context(s) of *Africana academia*—which is to say, *that often academically ghettoized and, therefore, intellectually invisible, nonwhite world within the ivory towers that has historically and currently continues to remorselessly and treasonously transgress, transverse, and transcend the longstanding "logic of segregation" and epistemic apartheid that has asphyxiated the earnest intellectual exchange and deep discursive dialogue of virtually each and every academic discipline in the interest of critically, empirically, and systematically studying the lifeworlds and life struggles of classical and contemporary, continental and diasporan Africans' lived experiences and lived endurances in light of the horrors of the African holocaust, African colonization, and African diasporan enslavement, as well as their strident struggles against the aftereffects of African colonization, African diasporan enslavement, and the ongoing effects of the advent of worldwide white supremacist patriarchal capitalist colonialism.*

Rampersad's initial tripartite conceptual (re)configuration of *The Souls of Black Folk*, which has been widely accepted in Du Bois studies, neglects more nuanced and transdisciplinary interpretations of Du Bois's thought and texts that might actually be more properly termed, as Rampersad's (1996, 290) later Du Bois studies revealed, "antidisciplinary" (see also Rabaka, 2006b). This means, then, that although Rampersad's early Du Bois studies may have neglected more nuanced and transdisciplinary interpretations of Du Bois's thought and texts, I am not in any way suggesting that his work smacks of *epistemic closure*. In fact, quite the contrary, I am saying that Rampersad's later Du Bois studies reveal him to be an *epistemically open* scholar who is not afraid to put his evolving relationship with the work of a much-misinterpreted intellectual icon into print for all the world to witness and deeply meditate on. My comments on Rampersad's early tripartite conceptual (re)configuration of *The Souls of Black Folk* are also intended to dispel the longstanding tendency among Du Bois studies scholars to overlook the fact that—as even Rampersad's own later Du Bois studies reveal—his three-part paradigm for critically engaging *The Souls of Black Folk* was specific to his interpretive intentions in *The Art and Imagination of W. E. B. Du Bois* and should not be taken as the definitive or most exclusive way to interpret Du Bois's watershed work.

Now, after establishing the fact that *The Souls of Black Folk* is truly a transdisciplinary work, with many insurgent "antidisciplinary" aspects (à la Rampersad's research), I would like to remind my readers that I am concerned here only with those elements of the book deemed to directly contribute to the sociology of race and antiracist social movements. Admittedly, then, what follows is not intended as an exhaustive examination of *The Souls of Black Folk* in any way whatsoever, but more as an *instrumental interpretation* or, rather, as a brief (albeit critical) overview of what the work offers to contemporary sociology of race *and* ongoing antiracist struggles. It is extremely important to bear in mind the latter intention of my "instrumental interpretation" here (i.e., to explore what *The Souls of Black Folk* offers to ongoing, twenty-first-century antiracist struggles), because if one focuses only on the former at the expense of the latter, then, intellectual disingenuousness and mealy-minded misinterpretations of my intended "instrumental interpretation" will, I am almost certain, abound.

Du Bois's contributions to the sociology of race in *The Souls of Black Folk* revolve around the dilemmas and dualities or, rather, the conundrums and complexities of what it means to be black in a white world—what was commonly called at the turn of the twentieth century, the "Negro Problem." In *The Souls of Black Folk* he created several seminal concepts of race and critiques of racism to complement his earlier efforts to establish the social scientific study of race in the interest of "emancipat[ing] the oppressed" or, rather—in Du Bois's own words, which seem to amazingly prefigure the language of Fanon's *Les damnés de la terre* by nearly six decades—"the earthly damned" (Du Bois, 1903c, 227). Many of the concepts of racial lived experience that Du Bois articulated in *The Souls of Black Folk* are intellectually interconnected and endlessly intersect, and they ultimately offer several of his most enduring contributions to the subtleties of the sociology of race. Undoubtedly his concepts of "double-consciousness" and the "color-line" are sociologically significant; however, I would also assert that his theory of blacks' "Veiled" visibility and invisibility, as well as his emphasis on blacks' unique "second-sight" in the white world are equally relevant with regard to the sociology of race.

Literary theorists have frequently commented on the "Veil" and "second-sight" in *The Souls of Black Folk*, but few sociologists have offered nuanced interpretations of the ways in which Du Bois's vision of the Veil, along with its corollary concept of the color-line, was "prophetic" in the sense that it continues to capture the conundrums of the trajectory and transmutation of American apartheid: from late nineteenth-century black codes and Jim Crow laws, to the twentieth-century rabid racial segregation which led to the civil rights movement and the twenty-first-century liberal racism of the post–civil rights period—as well as the *epistemic apartheid* of postmodernism and postcolonialism. Where the color-line calls to mind the racially segregated, Jim Crowed separate and unequal (as opposed to "separate but equal") white and black worlds of the late nineteenth and early twentieth centuries, Du Bois's discourse on the Veil points to the ways in which racial colonization does not render the racially oppressed completely devoid of human agency and cultural creativity. In fact, in some ways Du Bois's work here suggests that the Veiled quality of the color-line at best *blurs*, and at worst *blinds* whites to blacks' human agency and capacity for cultural creation. Thus, the Veil's sociological significance is dual or, rather, doubled, and although both whites' and blacks' lifeworlds and lived experiences revolve around the very same color-line, it is their divergent relationships to the Veil, and the ways in which the Veil racially (re)structures their psychological, social, and cultural worlds that determines their self-conceptions and, quite literally, the quality of their *soul-lives*.

Du Bois's discourse on the Veil not only accents African Americans' agency, but also their ability to create an antiracist culture of resistance and human redemption in the midst of the mayhem of the white supremacist capitalist colonial world. The Veil has been and can continue to be used by the racially oppressed to *conceal*, but it can also be used by the racially oppressed to *reveal*, if—and this is an extremely important "if"—an earnest opportunity presents itself, as Du Bois (1903c) deemed it did in *The Souls of Black Folk*, stating in "The Forethought": "Herein lie buried many things if read with patience may show the strange meaning of being black here at the dawning of the Twentieth Century. . . . I have sketched in swift outline the two worlds within and without the Veil" (vii). Du Bois's theory of the Veil, then, is essentially a trope that sociologically symbolizes *white (hyper)visibility* and *black (hyper)invisibility*, white humanity and black subhumanity in a white supremacist capitalist colonial world.

The "strange meaning of being black," Du Bois declared, "is not without interest to you, Gentle Reader," which refers to both black and white "Gentle Reader[s]," because "the problem of the Twentieth Century," he prophesied with words that continue to resonate and ring true, "is the problem of the color-line" (vii). *The Souls of Black Folk*, therefore, was written with "Gentle Reader[s]" from both the world "within" and the world "without the Veil" in mind—that is, for those blacks who unceasingly searched for the "strange meaning of being black" in a white world and for those whites who had consciously or unconsciously drawn the color-line after the collapse of Reconstruction and the rising tidal wave of anti-black racial violence that rolled across the United States as the twentieth century dawned.[5] If there were any doubts as to Du Bois's sincerity on the part of whites, he blithely wrote, "I pray you, then, receive my little book in all charity, studying my words with me, forgiving mistake and foible for sake of the faith and passion that is in me, and seeking the grain of truth hidden there" (vii). He equally assuaged the potential suspicions of his black readers by bluntly asserting, "And, finally, need I add that I who speak here am bone of the bone and flesh of the flesh of them that live within the Veil?" (viii)

Du Bois's discourses on the Veil and the color-line are sociologically significant because they represent some of the first efforts by a sociologist to articulate a *critical social theory of racial oppression, racial exploitation, and racial violence*—that is, a critical social theory of the ways in which racial oppression, racial exploitation, and racial violence, first, racially divide and socially separate (the color-line); second, distort cultural communications and human relations between those they racially divide along the color-line (the Veil); and, third, as a result of each of the aforementioned, cause blacks to suffer from a severe inferiority complex that insidiously induces them to constantly view themselves from whites' supposed "superior" points of view (double-consciousness). The Veil's processes and practices of concealment racially (re)organize, literally, everything that crosses the color-line, every interaction between "the two worlds within and without the Veil," thus *blurring* or, more frequently, *blinding* those who are white and who negligently and nonchalantly wish not to view nonwhites (i.e., nonwhites' humanity, history, and culture). Here, Du Bois's work prefigures the discourse on black anonymity and black invisibility in white societies developed by Ralph Ellison (1980), Toni Morrison (1990), and Lewis Gordon (1995a, 1997a, 1997b, 2000b), among others. Although whites may render blacks anonymous and invisible in the white world, blacks are never invisible to each other; as Du Bois pointed out in *The Philadelphia Negro* blacks are not a "homogenous mass," and especially not within the world of the Veil. However, one of the consequences of whites' sociopolitical dominance and their ability to amplify their *ideology of black invisibility* is that blacks begin to internalize *the diabolical dialectic of white superiority and black inferiority*, which in turn leads to what Du Bois cryptically called "double-consciousness."

In their efforts to combat the internalization of *the diabolical dialectic of white superiority and black inferiority* Du Bois seems to suggest that blacks need to become critically aware of their "double-consciousness" and how their utilization of white values and white culture as a criteria to judge black lifeworlds and black life struggles is extremely impertinent with respect to blacks' humanity, history, and culture. I could not agree more with Rampersad (1990, 74) when he correctly contends that the "term 'soul'" throughout *The Souls of Black Folk* "was used synonymously with consciousness," which is to say that Du Bois advocated that African Americans dialectically deconstruct and radically reconstruct their "double-consciousness" into a *critical black consciousness* or, rather, a *critical Africana consciousness*—that is, *a critical and, let it be said, compassionate consciousness grounded in and growing out of continental and diasporan African history, culture, and struggle, and always and ever harboring a humble radical humanism that righteously refuses to denigrate or demonize whites or other nonwhites but instead is unceasingly open to aiding and abetting all human beings who sincerely seek to reclaim and rehabilitate their long-denied and/or long-deformed humanity as a consequence of* white supremacist patriarchal capitalist colonialism. A *critical Africana consciousness* would enable African Americans to combat double-consciousness: first, by becoming aware of their own distinct history, culture, and struggle on their own terms—that is, without the interference of whites and their, whether conscious or unconscious, *anti-black racist and white supremacist (mis)conceptions of blacks and blackness*; second, by (re)learning to love, critique, and appreciate authentic continental and diasporan African history, culture, and struggle; and third, and only after each of the foresaid, by sharing the wisdom of their lifeworlds and the lessons of their life struggles with the wider world of human culture and civilization.

As for whites living within racially divided worlds or, rather, *color-lined* societies, Du Bois audaciously argued that they are affected just as much as blacks. The striking difference, however, was that whites seemed willing to accept a blithe blindness to black social suffering, black political disenfranchisement, and black economic exploitation and the myriad ways in which each of the aforementioned is inextricable from white privilege, white social wealth, and white political power as a consequence of whites' cruel creation of the color-line and, then, their racial colonization of blacks and other nonwhites along that despicable dividing line. As will be witnessed in the concluding section below, Du Bois was one of the first sociologists to seriously consider the recurring effect that whites', whether active or passive, complicity in the construction and maintenance of the color-line had on the "souls of white folk" (see below). From Du Bois's perspective, race and racism have never been simply black or nonwhite peoples' problem, but a human problem that should concern all humanity. Anywhere societies are racially divided, even though they may not be "legally" or "officially" racially divided anymore, the quality of both white and nonwhite life suffers, and all humanity is repetitiously, even if sometimes surreptitiously, haunted by the gnawing knowledge that it has not fulfilled the liberated future that so many of the exalted ancients fought and died for.

In *The Souls of Black Folk* Du Bois deployed the vivid and oft-times lyrical language of the Veil, as well as its conceptual complement the "color-line" to make his sociology of race accessible to as wide an audience as possible. And, although I may be roundly ridiculed for writing this, I owe it to W. E. B. Du Bois to state outright that there, indeed, are some sentiments, some "finer feelings," especially certain lived experiences and lived endurances prevalent in the nonwhite world, which simply cannot be captured in the academese and twisted tongue of—to use, once again, Du Bois's still-resounding words—"calm, cool, and detached" white social science. Recall, above Du Bois asserted that in writing *The Souls of Black Folk* he found that it was "difficult, strangely difficult, to translate the finer feelings of men into words." Early twentieth-century America did not view the Veiled race (i.e., his beloved "black folk") as "men," by which Du Bois meant *human beings*, so his task was doubly difficult when compared and contrasted with the work of his white sociological peers at the turn of the twentieth century. Du Bois biographer David Levering Lewis (1993) hit the nail on its head when he revealingly wrote, "Three years into yet another century of seeming unassailable European supremacy, *Souls* countered with the voices of the dark submerged and unheard" (278). The marvelous meaning of *The Souls of Black Folk* was (or, at the least, should have been) crystal clear, according to Lewis: Until Du Bois's "Gentle Reader[s]" "appreciated the message of the songs sung in bondage by black people," which was one of the only ways enslaved Africans could express themselves, then, "Du Bois was saying, the words written in freedom by white people would remain hollow and counterfeit" (278). Lewis went on to point to the personal pain, severe suffering and, I should say, *soul-searching* Du Bois endured to compose a work of such simultaneous gruesomeness and grandeur—or, rather, what I am accustomed to calling, faithfully following Thelonious Monk, the *ugly beauty* of *The Souls of Black Folk*. Observing Du Bois's extraordinary "courage in abundance," especially considering the lynching-laden historical moment in which he composed *The Souls of Black Folk*, a usually cool-penned Lewis, palpably bristling with intellectual enthusiasm and excitement, exclaims:

> He also possessed in equal measure—passion mediated by the written word. The shaping empire of intellect reigned over both. From the first page of *The Souls of Black Folk*, Du Bois's mind, courage, and passion interact to create a splendid diapason. It is as though the small hurts and large insults of his own life . . . have fused with those of the Sam Hoses and Ida B. Welles and ten millions more to merge Du Bois, for a noetic moment in history, uniquely with the souls of all black people. (279)

Certain sociologists may have overlooked the sociological significance of *The Souls of Black Folk* on account of its remarkable lyricism. However, their visceral reaction to the volume unequivocally reinforces precisely why Du Bois's discourse on the Veil has resonated with so many, both within and without academia. The theory of the Veil is interconnected with the concept of the color-line, but they should not be, as they frequently have been, collapsed into one and the same thing or, more simply, they should not be made synonymous. Du Bois uses the metaphor of the Veil to expatiate racially colonized and racially divided life along the color-line, and to explain the ways in which an invisible social construction such as the "color-line" actually becomes highly visible when viewed from the long-veiled perspective of blacks in a white supremacist world. Because blacks are veiled in invisibility in a white supremacist world, Du Bois brought whites' tendency to approach blacks more as problems than as human persons to his readers' attention at the outset of *The Souls of Black Folk*, thereby innovatively inverting whites' pathological approach to black humanity, history, and culture. In other words, Du Bois problematized whites' problematic conceptions or, rather, misconceptions of blacks by audaciously asserting blacks' humanity and autonomous agency. Cautiously lifting the Veil so that whites might have a window into the black world, he wryly wrote:

> Between me and the other world there is ever an unasked question: unasked by some through feelings of delicacy; by others through the difficulty of rightly framing it. All, nevertheless, flutter round it. They approach me in a half-hesitant sort of way, eye me curiously or compassionately, and then, instead of saying directly, How does it feel to be a problem? they say, I know an excellent colored man in my town; or, I fought at Mechanicsville; or, Do not these Southern outrages make your blood boil? At these I smile, or am interested, or reduce the boiling to a simmer, as the occasion may require. To the real question, How does it feel to be a problem? I answer seldom a word. (Du Bois, 1903c, 1–2)

Although Du Bois deceptively claims that he seldom answers a word in response to the often unasked and insulting question "How does it feel to be a problem?" *The Souls of Black Folk* should be seen as part of his ever evolving and often intricate answer or, rather, his synoptic *solution* to what could be called the "White Problem" or, rather, the "Problem of white folk"—that is, whites' problematic, (hyper)racial colonial approach to black lifeworlds and black life struggles. Both the Veil and the color-line are invisibly (to most whites) and visibly (to most blacks) present in each and every one of their interactions; in all of the cracks and crevices of the crucial questions that could have and should have been earnestly asked of one another; in the many millions of racial myths and cultural stereotypes that the media produces for mass consumption and, as far as one can see, for mass confusion. Du Bois's vision of the Veil, then, is also a *critical theory of willful white blindness to black humanity, history, and culture*. With the phrase "willful white blindness to black humanity, history, and culture" I wish to emphasize *whites' ability, theoretically and technically speaking, to see blacks and their humanity, history, and culture if*—and, again I say, this is an extremely important "*if*"—*they choose to do so but*, and here's the real rub, *whites' tendency to intentionally turn a blind eye to black humanity, history, and culture*—or, further, *whites' custom to selectively see certain "exceptional" blacks (usually black entertainers and black athletes), but whites' apparent inability to authentically see the ongoing suffering and social misery of the black masses, who continue to live within the world of the Veil and whose lives are cruelly quarantined to the color-line.*

Faithfully following Du Bois's discourse, I honestly believe that if whites wanted to, or even needed to really and truly *see* and appreciate blacks' (not just "exceptional" blacks') humanity they could (through protracted processes of learning to love and appreciate blacks on blacks' own terms) transgress and transcend their *white blindness to blacks and blackness*—that is, whites' blindness to real (as opposed to their unreal or fictitious fantasies of) blacks and blackness or, rather, authentic Africans and Africanity. However, in order to do this, whites would have to open themselves, not just to blacks', but to all nonwhites' humanity, history, culture and, most importantly, their respective ongoing struggles for racial and social justice. Du Bois, an avowed radical humanist, was willing to aid those whites who were willing to undertake the protracted processes of learning to love and appreciate blacks on blacks' own terms by introducing them to the world within the Veil, the blighted black world. He stated to his "Gentle Reader[s]," "Leaving, then, the world of the white man, I have stepped within the Veil, raising it that you may view faintly its deeper recesses—the meaning of its religion, the passion of its human sorrow, and the struggle of its greater souls" (viii).

Du Bois, as his work undoubtedly demonstrates, was willing to raise the Veil and cross the color-line but, the question begs, how many whites at the turn of the twentieth century were willing to cross with him? It could go without saying that there was for the most part a stubborn refusal to cross the color-line on the part of most whites and, perceptively anticipating that this would be the case, Du Bois developed his concept of double-consciousness to capture the excruciating anguish that *the diabolical dialectic of white superiority and black inferiority* inflicted on blacks; his theory of second-sight explained the unique insight or "subjugated knowledge" (à la Foucault's phrase) blacks gained as a result of their experience and endurance of *the diabolical dialectic of white superiority and black inferiority*.[6] Du Bois's discourse on the Veil dovetails with his concept of double-consciousness insofar as it also seeks to explain that blacks' efforts to gain self-consciousness in a white supremacist world will be, by default, always and everywhere damaged and distorted because the most prevalent and pervasive ideas and images of blacks and blackness (or, rather, Africans and Africanity) in white supremacist societies are those predicated on, and prefabricated by *the diabolical dialectic of white superiority and black inferiority*. In other words, where the Veil metaphorically represents the ways in which the color-line is constantly cloaked in a dark cloud of misconceptions, miscommunications, and misgivings between "the two worlds within and without the Veil," double-consciousness conceptually captures the often-overlooked fact that blacks not only internalize *the diabolical dialectic of white superiority and black inferiority* in the white supremacist world, but also the fact that part and parcel of the white supremacist world's "ideological hegemony" (in the Gramscian sense) is the constant blanketing of the white-dominated black world with *anti-black racist and white supremacist (mis)conceptions of blacks and blackness* (i.e., Africans and Africanity).[7] The concept of double-consciousness, therefore, boldly broaches the taboo topic (among both blacks and whites) of blacks' intense internalization of white supremacist anti-black racist creations and disseminations of blackness or, as Du Bois said above, "the strange meaning of being black here in the dawning of the Twentieth Century."

Du Bois's vision of the Veil astutely affords his "Gentle Reader[s]" the opportunity to transgress *willful white blindness to blackness*, and to actually see blacks and their history, culture, and struggle with new eyes, perhaps, from the vantage points of Pan-Africanism and radical humanism. However, and going back to what I (Rabaka, 2008a) have elsewhere termed "Du Bois's dialectics," his vision of the Veil is also about revealing the truth long-buried in the blood-soaked soil of a racially colonized and racially divided nation and world. In *The Souls of Black Folk* the trope of the Veil is certainly about mourning and memorializing those who agonizingly endured the "holocaust of war, the terrors of the Ku-Klux Klan, the lies of carpet-baggers, the disorganization of industry, and the contradictory advice of friends and foes," only to be "left . . . bewildered serf[s] with no new watchword beyond the old cry for freedom" (Du Bois, 1903c, 7). But the Veil also represents all of those veiled figures, especially women in African, African American, and Caribbean cultures and societies, who for so long have passed unnoticed, attentively observing without being respectfully observed or acknowledged, always seemingly concealing more than they are revealing (Cooper, 1998, 114; Rabaka, 2007b, 156–60; also see the next chapter).

Even though Du Bois was willing to work with whites in their earnest efforts to transgress their blindness to black humanity, history, and culture, he was not willing to do so at the expense of downplaying or diminishing the physical and psychological damage that life within the Veil and life along the color-line, as well as *the diabolical dialectic of white superiority and black inferiority* and *anti-black racist and white supremacist (mis)conceptions of blacks and blackness* had on the "souls of black folk." The conceptual culmination of Du Bois's insurgent efforts to make both blacks and whites aware of the physical and psychological damage that life within the Veil and life along the color-line had on the "souls of black folk" was, of course, his intellectual history-making discourse on double-consciousness and its corollary concept of second-sight. He revealingly wrote, in perhaps the most widely commented upon passage in *The Souls of Black Folk*:

> After the Egyptian and Indian, the Greek and Roman, the Teuton and Mongolian, the Negro is a sort of seventh son, born with a veil, and gifted with second-sight in this American world—a world which yields him no true self-consciousness, but only lets him see himself through the revelation of the other world. It is a peculiar sensation, this double-consciousness, this sense of always looking at one's self through the eyes of others, of measuring one's soul by the tape of a world that looks on in amused contempt and pity. One ever feels his two-ness—an American, a Negro; two souls, two thoughts, two unreconciled strivings; two warring ideals in one dark body, whose dogged strength alone keeps it from being torn asunder.

The history of the American Negro is the history of this strife—this longing to attain self-conscious manhood, to merge his double self into a better and truer self. In this merging he wishes neither of the older selves to be lost. He would not Africanize America, for America has too much to teach the world and Africa. He would not bleach his Negro soul in a flood of white Americanism, for he knows that Negro blood has a message for the world. He simply wishes to make it possible for a man to be both a Negro and an American, without being cursed and spit upon by his fellows, without having the doors of Opportunity closed roughly in his face. (Du Bois, 1903c, 3–4)

Here, with these hallowed words, Du Bois indelibly etched his name into the annals of American literary and cultural history. Although the Veil and the color-line are central tropes in *The Souls of Black Folk*, Du Bois's concept of double-consciousness and its corollary concept of second-sight are simultaneously essential to understanding *The Souls of Black Folk* and, albeit often overlooked by the white sociological fraternity, vital to sociologically comprehending the conundrums and contradictions of racial colonization and racial segregation in a nation, nay, in a world which pretentiously prides itself on its cultural liberalism and commitment to unfettered democracy. Observe that Du Bois's doubling discourse connected the Veil with second-sight ("the Negro is a sort of seventh son, born with a veil, and gifted with second-sight in this American world"), and America (i.e., the United States), representing the white supremacist capitalist colonial world in deep-seated denial, was to those "born with a veil," "a world which yield[ed] [them] no true self-consciousness, but only lets [them] see [themselves] through the revelation of the other world."

Then, as if faithfully harking back to his stated intention at the book's opening—that is, to candidly explore the "strange meaning of being black here in the dawning of the Twentieth Century"—Du Bois articulated his own homespun *ontology of black life worlds and black life struggles* in a white supremacist capitalist colonial world. "It is a peculiar sensation, this double-consciousness, this sense of always looking at one's self through the eyes of others." Indeed, Du Bois's concept of double-consciousness also seems to have profound implications for a *social psychology of black life worlds and black life struggles* in a white supremacist capitalist colonial world. For example, and bearing Frantz Fanon's (1965, 1967, 1968, 1969) watershed work in mind, it might be useful to quickly list some of the psychological concepts and conditions that double-consciousness appears to be conceptually connected to—if not during its day, then certainly currently: schizophrenia, paranoia, dysmorphophobia, inferiority complex, and anxiety disorder, among others.[8]

Black life worlds, Du Bois correctly assumed, would be "strange" and "peculiar" to whites because of *the ideology of black invisibility, the diabolical dialectic of white superiority and black inferiority*, and *anti-black racist and white supremacist (mis)conceptions of blacks and blackness*. The concept of double-consciousness asserts that the very color-line that racially divides the white world from the black world simultaneously creates a tortured "two-ness" in blacks' souls. In fact, the "racial faultlines" of the color-line ultimately drive blacks to constantly question whether they are Africans or Americans (and even whether they are human) to such a doggedly excruciating degree that their souls become doubled and divided like the loveless racially colonized world that they are forced to live in or, rather, endure (Almaguer, 1994). Du Bois's concept of double-consciousness, then, is also a discursive *doppelgänger*, textually representing the consequences of blacks' racial colonization and the ways in which the color-line not only racially divides society but, even more, black souls and black selves.[9]

Du Bois distressingly wrote of "two souls, two thoughts, two unreconciled strivings; two warring ideals in one dark body, whose dogged strength alone keeps it from being torn asunder." But a question begs: Where do blacks' get the "dogged strength" that keeps their souls and bodies "from being torn asunder"? After painting such a bleak picture of the "souls of black folk," and their trials and tribulations in the white supremacist world, this seems like a fair question and, indeed, it is a query which Du Bois ingeniously answered with his *saga of blacks' second-sight*.[10] Second-sight symbolizes blacks' ability, even in the face of adversity (i.e., holocaust, enslavement, colonization, segregation, and neo-apartheid), to see both Africa (the black world) and America's (the white world's) strengths and weaknesses, and the ways in which these two worlds could and should learn from and, even more, aid each other. Du Bois described African Americans in the passage above as being "gifted with second-sight," and it is their experiences in and visions of "the two worlds within and without the Veil" that ultimately distinguish their special contributions to American and world culture and civilization. In essence, where the majority of whites suffer from *white blindness to blackness*, blacks have been blessed (or "gifted," as it were) with second-sight as an ironic consequence of their having endured racial colonization and other forms of racial oppression at the hands of whites. But blacks, it should solemnly be said, should never take their giftedness for granted, as it is neither automatic nor axiomatic: because double-consciousness, truth be told, constantly makes second-sight dangerously double-edged and always and ever enervating on account of both the intensity and depth of blacks' internalization of *anti-black racist and white supremacist (mis)conceptions of blacks and blackness* and the paradoxes of the trajectory and transmutations of American and global apartheid. It is with this in mind that I argue that double-consciousness at its conceptual core is about *double or divided selves in the process of spiritually, psychologically, and socially evolving out of tortured "two-ness" into "self-conscious manhood"*—which is to say, *self-conscious humanhood*. However, it must be emphasized, the only way to achieve *self-conscious humanhood* is through ongoing insurrectionary antiracist and radical pro-humanist struggle or, as Du Bois put it, "strife" and "striving."

Second-sight provides blacks with a window into the "two worlds within and without the Veil," and it also enables them to begin *the dialectical process(es) of revolutionary decolonization and human liberation* by critically calling into question double-consciousness. Once this process is initiated it, literally, gives African Americans *second-sight*—that is, *first, the ability to view the world from within and without the Veil; second, to see the special contributions that both the "souls of black folk" and the "souls of white folk" have made to America and the wider world; and, ultimately and most importantly, to sift through and synthesize the best of the "souls of black folk" with the best of the "souls of white folk" in the interest of creating*, as Du Bois said, "a better and truer self," a "better and truer" nation, and a "better and truer" world. This was Du Bois's sensational solution to the problem of double-consciousness. The "Negro," armed with second-sight, would have to "merge his double self into a better and truer self." However, in this "merging he wishes neither of the older selves to be lost. He would not Africanize America, for America has too much to teach the world and Africa. He would not bleach his Negro soul in a flood of white Americanism, for he knows that Negro blood has a message for the world." In the end, then, second-sight would/will enable African Americans, not simply to *see* but also to *synthesize* black and white "gifts" and "messages" and, in the fullness of time, to *articulate*, literally, to speak anew America's special truths to the wider world.

However, in order to fulfill the consecrated mission that Du Bois charged black folk with, they, first and foremost, needed to familiarize themselves with their history, culture, and struggle without the insidious intrusions of Eurocentric interpretations of their lived experiences and lived endurances. It is in this sense that *The Souls of Black Folk* is steeped with impressively abridged swaths of African American history, which represent according to Lewis (1993), "the kind of feat that was to become [Du Bois's] signature" (280). As it relates to African Americans' discovering their "gifts" to the United States, Du Bois's forays in social, political, and cultural history were meant to expose his "Gentle Reader[s]" to the "truth hidden there" at the heart of America and American history since the nation's inception. In the last chapter of *The Souls of Black Folk*, "The Sorrow Songs," Du Bois (1903c) unapologetically argued that African Americans had given America three preeminent "gifts," and that America would not be America "without her Negro people":

> Your country? How came it yours? Before the Pilgrims landed we were here. Here we have brought our three gifts and mingled them with yours: a gift of story and song—soft, stirring melody in an ill-harmonized and unmelodious

land; the gift of sweat and brawn to beat back the wilderness, conquer the soil, and lay the foundations of this vast economic empire two hundred years earlier than your weak hands could have done it; the third, a gift of the Spirit. Around us the history of the land has centered for thrice a hundred years; out of the nation's heart we have called all that was best to throttle and subdue all that was worst; fire and blood, prayer and sacrifice, have billowed over this people, and they have found peace only in the altars of the God of Right. Nor has our gift of the Spirit been merely passive. Actively we have woven ourselves with the very warp and woof of this nation—we fought their battles, shared their sorrow, mingled our blood with theirs, and generation after generation have pleaded with a headstrong, careless people to despise not Justice, Mercy, and Truth, lest the nation be smitten with a curse. Our song, our toil, our cheer, and warning have been given to this nation in blood-brotherhood. Are not these gifts worth the giving? Is not this work and striving? Would America have been America without her Negro people? (262–63)

Here I would like to highlight how Du Bois's *gift theory* hinges on his theory of second-sight, so much so that second-sight, it could be argued, is a subtle subtextual theme that informs each and every sentence of *The Souls of Black Folk*. Take note above of Du Bois's discourse on *the dialectic of black gifts and white indebtedness*, which in a white supremacist world means that whites neither acknowledge blacks' gifts nor their white indebtedness to the black givers of the gifts. Second-sight is not simply about blacks' ability to identify and appreciate their gifts to America and the wider world, but also about blacks sharing the wisdom of their lifeworlds and the lessons of their lived experiences with others, especially other nonwhites struggling against the various forms of European imperialism and authentic antiracist white allies insurgently involved in the struggle for racial and social justice. This, of course, means that someway and somehow blacks will have to counter double-consciousness and *the diabolical dialectic of white superiority and black inferiority*, because without breaking free from double-consciousness blacks will not be able to fully embrace or appreciate their second-sight or self-consciously see that their peculiar and particular lived experiences and lived endurances of the horrors of the African holocaust and African American enslavement, as well as their strident struggles against the aftereffects of African American enslavement and the ongoing effects of American apartheid could make an incalculable contribution to human culture and civilization. In other words, the cure (second-sight and self-consciousness) is partially contained in the poison (the Veil and double-consciousness). Indeed, African Americans' lived experiences and lived endurances of the horrors of the African holocaust and African American enslavement, as well as their more recent struggles against the aftereffects of African American enslavement and the ongoing effects of American apartheid represent a deconstruction and reconstruction of what it means, not simply to be black in a white supremacist world, but it also critically calls into question whites' historic and hegemonic racial classifications and ethno-cultural categorizations which disgustingly denote which *human beings* count as "human," "subhuman," and/or "non-human" within the white supremacist world.

With whites undeniably wielding enormous (if not unparalleled) power within the black world, and with their complicated complicity in, and irrational relationships with the concept of double-consciousness, the racial colonization of the color-line, *the ideology of black invisibility, the diabolical dialectic of white superiority and black inferiority*, and *anti-black racist and white supremacist (mis)conceptions of blacks and blackness*, Du Bois tersely turned his attention to developing a sociology of the "souls of white folk." In fact, soon after the publication of *The Souls of Black Folk* Du Bois came to the realization that in order to really and truly grasp and seriously grapple with the "souls of black folk" he would also have to critically engage the "souls of white folk"—the dark den that crudely created the doomed concept of race and spawned racism, or, rather more politely, race's originators and their reasons for its origination. He intensely deepened and developed his discourse on race and critique of racism by unswervingly critiquing the specific race and type of racism that continued to plague the racially colonized and racially divided (especially blacks) along the color-line: whites and white supremacy. Perhaps the first sociologist of race to systematically explore the imperial international, national, regional, and local dimensions of white supremacy, Du Bois's work in this area can be said to contribute to what many contemporary sociologists of race, political scientists of race, anthropologists of race, philosophers of race, historians of race, and, of course, critical race theorists are currently calling critical white studies.

"THE SOULS OF WHITE FOLK" AND *THE GIFT OF BLACK FOLK*: DU BOIS'S SOCIOLOGY OF WHITENESS, CRITIQUE OF WHITE SUPREMACY, AND CONTRIBUTIONS TO CRITICAL WHITE STUDIES

Traditionally, "white supremacy" has been treated in race and racism discourse as *white domination of and white discrimination against nonwhites*, and especially blacks. It is a term that often carries a primarily legal and political connotation, which has been claimed time and time again to be best exemplified by the historic events and contemporary effects of, first, the African holocaust, African colonization, and African American enslavement; second, the "failure" of Reconstruction, the racist ritual of late nineteenth- and early twentieth-century lynching, and the rise of black codes and Jim Crow segregation in the United States; and third, post–civil rights liberal racism in America and continued white neo-colonial and racial rule throughout Africa, and especially apartheid in South Africa. Considering the fact that state-sanctioned racial segregation and black political disenfranchisement have seemed to come to an end, "white supremacy" is now seen as classical nomenclature which no longer refers to contemporary racial and social conditions. However, instead of being a relic of the past that refers to an odd or embarrassing moment in the United States and South Africa's (among many other anti-black racist nations and empires') march toward transethnic and multicultural democracy, it remains one of the most appropriate ways to characterize current racial colonial national and international conditions. Which, in other words, is to say that white supremacy has been and remains central to modernity (and "postmodernity"), because "modernity" (especially in the sense in which this term is being used in European and American academic and aesthetic discourse) reeks of racial domination and discrimination. It is an epoch (or aggregate of eras) which symbolize not simply the invention of race, but the perfection of a particular species of *global* racism: white supremacy. Hence, European modernity is not merely the moment of the invention of race, but even more, as Theodore Allen (1994, 1997) argues in *The Invention of the White Race*, it served as an incubator for the invention of the white race and a peculiar Pan-European imperialism predicated on the racial ruling, economic exploitation, cultural degradation, and, at times, physical decimation of the lifeworlds of nonwhites.

In "The Souls of White Folk," which was initially published in the *Independent* in 1910, then substantially revised and republished in *Darkwater* in 1920, Du Bois (1920) stated, "Everything considered, the title to the universe claimed by White Folk is faulty" (31). Long before the recent discourse on critical race theory and critical white studies, Du Bois called into question white superiority and white privilege, and the possibility of white racelessness and/or white racial neutrality and white universality. He was one of the first critical race theorists to chart the changes in race relations from *de jure* to *de facto* forms of white supremacy, referring to it, as early as 1910, as "the new religion of whiteness" (31).

White supremacy had not and would not end unless and until the values and views endemic to it and associated with it were or are rejected and replaced by radical antiracist, critical multicultural, and uncompromising ethical views and values. The rejection of white supremacy and the replacement of white supremacist views and values involves not only blacks and other nonwhites but, truth be told, whites as well. As the examples of the Emancipation Proclamation, Reconstruction, and the civil rights movement indicate, changes in the law and its interpretation and application do not always translate into racial justice and radical democratic social transformation. White supremacist social views and values linger long after amendments have been made and laws changed. Therefore, law-focused critical white studies and critical race theory, as I (Rabaka, 2006c, 2006d) have argued elsewhere, provide at best only a partial solution to the seemingly unceasing and more surreptitious problem of white supremacy in the twenty-first century.

The conception and critique of white supremacy that I develop here does not seek to sidestep socio-legal race discourse as much as it intends to supplement it with Du Bois and others' work in radical politics and critical social theory. One of the main reasons this supplemental approach to critical white studies and critical race theory is important is because typically legal studies of race confine theorists to particular national social and political arenas, which is problematic considering the fact that white supremacy is a global racist system (Bonilla-Silva, 2001, 2003; Bonilla-Silva and Doane, 2003; C. W. Mills, 1997, 1998). In fact, Du Bois (1920) declared, "Whiteness is the ownership of the earth forever and ever, Amen!" (30). Here he is sardonically hinting at the cardinal difference between white supremacy and most other forms of racism: its worldwide or global historical, cultural, social, political, legal, and economic influence and impact. White supremacy serves as the glue that connects and combines racism to colonialism, and racism to capitalism and, logically then, each of the aforementioned to one another. It has also been illustrated that white supremacy exacerbates sexism by *sexing racism* and *racing sexism*, to put it unpretentiously. Thus, white supremacy as a global racism intersects and interconnects with sexism, and particularly patriarchy as a global system that oppresses and denies women's human dignity and right to be humanly different from men, the ruling gender. At this interval I am intentionally suspending my usual emphasis on, and criticisms of racism, colonialism, and capitalism's interconnections and intersections with sexism, as that would, first, require more room than I have here and, second, it might appear a bit redundant since I have opted to offer a fuller and more detailed discussion of the interconnections and intersections of racism, sexism, and capitalism in the subsequent chapter.

With regard to Du Bois's critique of white supremacy, it is not simply a global and social phenomenon, but a personal and political one as well. That is to say that for Du Bois white supremacy is simultaneously systemic and systematic, and also a matter of racist cultural mores and manners, which teeter-totter between idealist, materialist, and constructionist accounts of race. For example, an idealist account of race says simply (or not so simply) that white racism against nonwhites, and especially blacks, is not so much a matter of race as it is of culture. Racial idealists argue that European culture and its precolonial history of color-symbolism and religious views—such as Europeans' conceptions of themselves as "civilized" whites and nonwhites as "wild," "savage," "heathen," or "ethnic" Others; the positive and negative associations regarding the colors white and black;

and the ways in which their racist cultural interpretations of Christianity support not only the white/black color valuations and devaluations but the "civilize and Christianize" missions of European racial colonialism and imperialism—set the stage for what would later become racism and white supremacy.

Materialist accounts of race, which are primarily inspired by Marxist theory, maintain that racism does not have to do with culture as much as it does with political economy. Europeans needed a cheap labor force to extra-exploit and work their newly and imperially acquired continents, countries, colonial settlements, and plantations. For the racial materialists it was not about "religion" or "civilization" or "science," but an obscene economics and politics predicated on super-exploitation, which was always and everywhere reduced to its lowest and most racist level. Finally, racial constructionists contend that *race* is an outgrowth of human beings' inherent ethnocentrism, but that *racism* is a result of Europe's push for global dominance and white world supremacy. In this view, no matter who invented race, its reasons for origination, and whether it is scientifically sound, it is an historical artifact that most modern (and "postmodern") human beings use, either consciously or unconsciously, to make interpersonal, sociocultural, and politico-economic decisions. "Whites" and "non-whites" do not exist prior to the imperial expansion that helped to birth, raise and rear European modernity. But this is all beside the point to the constructionists. What is relevant is *the invention of whiteness* and its classical and contemporary uses and abuses, and the ways it has evolved over several centuries, transitioning from *de jure* to *de facto* form, and transforming the racial rules and ethnic ethics of who counts as "white" and "non-white" or, more properly, "human" and "non-human."

Du Bois's writings on race do not fit nicely or neatly into any of the aforementioned accounts of race. As even a cursory review of his concepts of race and critiques of racism reveals, at different intervals throughout his long life and career he harbored what would currently be considered aspects of each of the three accounts of race discussed above. For Du Bois, as I intimated earlier, white supremacy was not simply a global and social phenomenon, but a personal and political one as well. Hence, his assertion, in "The Souls of White Folk": "The discovery of personal whiteness among the world's peoples is a very modern thing" (29). Take special note of the connection Du Bois makes between "personal whiteness" and "modernity," to use the latter term loosely. His dialectical approach to white supremacy accents its interconnections and intersections with other systems of exploitation, oppression, and violence because in his critical socio-theoretical framework racism is one of several "very modern" interconnecting and intersecting hegemonic variables. But it is white supremacy's *globality*, the fact that it is a racist global system or "racial polity," as the acclaimed Caribbean philosopher of race Charles Mills (1999) maintains, that marks it for much-needed critical theoretical consideration.

In his critique of the global aspects of white supremacy, Du Bois critically engaged its origins and evolution, locating its genesis, uniqueness, and ubiquitousness in European imperial global expansion, domination, and colonization. What distinguished white supremacy from local, national and regional racisms, such as those that have historically existed and currently continue to exist between certain nonwhite groups, is its international imperial nature and modern world-historic influence and effects. At the heart of the history of white supremacy, as quiet as it is kept, is a prolonged practice and promotion of an extremely acute form of *cultural racism* and *cultural theft*. For Du Bois (1920), whites were "super-men" and "world-mastering demi-gods" with "feet of clay" (35). By which he meant, whites, with all their claims of superiority and "super-humanity," were or appeared to be super-strong because they built their empire(s) on the "gifts," which is to say, on the inventions and innovations, on the sciences and civilizations, and on the cultures and contributions of the hyper-raced and transethnic others—the folk now known as "non-whites"—whom whites, generation after jostling generation, whether actively or passively, have racially colonized and quarantined to the world within the Veil and life along the color-line (36). But as the "super-men" with "feet of clay" comment reveals, and as Du Bois's saga of second-sight above suggests, the colored and colonized were well aware of whites' weakness(es), of their Achilles' heel(s): Their imperial push for global domination—that is, their century-spanning project(s) of setting up systems of exploitation, oppression, and violence—unwittingly and ironically created intra-imperial cultural tensions, racist sibling rivalries among whites themselves, and also created the context and laid the foundation for the very anti-imperial colored/colonized hammer that Du Bois boldly believed would smash the imperial white "super men's" "feet of clay." In "The Souls of White Folk," Du Bois audaciously asserted:

> The greatness of Europe has lain in the width of the stage on which she has played her part, the strength of the foundations on which she has builded, and a natural, human ability no whit greater (if as great) than that of other days and races. In other words, the deeper reasons for the triumph of European civilization lie quite outside and beyond Europe—back in the universal struggles of all mankind.
>
> Why, then, is Europe great? Because of the foundations which the mighty past have furnished her to build upon: the iron trade of ancient, black Africa, the religion and empire-building of yellow Asia, the art and sciences of the "dago" Mediterranean shore, east, south, and west, as well as north. And, where she had builded securely upon this great past and learned from it she has gone forward to greater and more splendid human triumph; but where

she has ignored this past and forgotten and sneered at it, she has shown the cloven hoof of poor, crucified humanity—she has played, like other empires gone, the world fool!

If, then, European triumphs in culture have been greater, so, too, may her failures have been greater. (40)

Here Du Bois notes major "gifts" or contributions to culture and civilization that various nonwhites have made throughout human history, many of them in their precolonial (or, rather, pre-*European* colonial) periods.[11] He does not diminish or attempt to downplay the "greatness of Europe," but observed that "the triumph of European civilization lie quite outside and beyond Europe." From Du Bois's (1897a) critical racial frame of reference, each ethno-cultural group or, rather, each "race" has a "great message . . . for humanity" (11). He was extremely confident in the greatness of black folk's past and present "gifts" *and* spirit of giving, even in the face of and often, it seemed, in spite of their lived experiences and lived endurances of holocaust, enslavement, colonization, segregation, and so forth.

One of the main reasons Du Bois believed blacks' were uniquely "gifted," and their "gifts" were especially valuable with regard to world culture and civilization was because their antiracist (and anticolonial) struggle strategies and tactics had historically and have consistently been markedly different from those of any other human group with respect to the development of modern democracy (i.e., "European" and "American" democracy). This is so, in Du Bois's *gift theory of cultural giving*, on account of the fact that within white supremacist social hierarchy Africans are the antithesis of Europeans or, rather, blacks are the subhuman, at best, or nonhuman, at worst, opposite of white humans. Four years after publishing "The Souls of White Folk" in *Darkwater*, Du Bois fully developed his *gift theory of cultural giving* in his often-overlooked 1924 classic, *The Gift of Black Folk: The Negroes in the Making of America*. Admittedly, not as well-written and certainly lacking the lyricism of *The Souls of Black Folk*, *The Gift of Black Folk* was aimed at a separate (albeit intensely interconnected) set of historical and sociological circumstances. Where *The Souls of Black Folk* sought to inspiringly introduce blacks to their history, culture, and struggle and to counter Booker T. Washington's accommodationism and assimilationism, as well as to introduce well-meaning whites and counter willful white blindness to black folk's humanity, history, and culture, *The Gift of Black Folk* was geared toward revealing African Americans' major contributions to American culture and civilization in light of several historical factors that shaped and shaded the first quarter of the twentieth century—for example, the New Negro movement's evolution into the Harlem Renaissance; the Niagara movement's transformation into the National Association for the Advancement of Colored People (NAACP); the growing black consciousness and deepening commitment to civil rights, racial justice, and social justice; the heightened rise of anti-black racist terrorist groups (e.g., the Klu Klux Klan, the Knights of the White Camelia, White Citizens' Parties) and anti-black racist violence (e.g., the racist ritual of lynching, race riots, anti-black racist pogroms); the eugenicist movement in the United States; the backward-thinking white Baptists, Methodists, and Episcopalians, among other white religious denominations, who callously combined a subtle white supremacy (but white supremacy nonetheless) with Christianity; and the anti-black racist propaganda spewing from Henry Ford's extremely popular *Dearborn Independent* in particular, and the white press in general.

The Gift of Black Folk should surely be seen as a conceptual complement to "The Conservation of Races," *The Souls of Black Folk*, and "The Souls of White Folk" insofar as it harks back to, first, Du Bois's early insistence in "The Conservation of Races" that "the Negro people, as a race, have a contribution to make to civilization and humanity, which no other race can make." Second, *The Gift of Black Folk* seems to literally pick up where *The Souls of Black Folk* left off when, after revealing black folk's three great "gifts" (the "gift of story and song," the "gift of sweat and brawn," and the "gift of the Spirit"), Du Bois asked, "Would America have been America without her Negro people?" Third, and as was observed in the passage from "The Souls of White Folk" above, Du Bois intensely accented Africa's contributions to world culture and civilization in the face of worldwide white denial of their indebtedness, not simply to blacks, but to other nonwhites as well. In essence, "The Conservation of Races" and *The Souls of Black Folk* can be seen as the groping beginnings of Du Bois's *gift theory of cultural giving* with a faithful focus on black lifeworlds and black life struggles in the aftermath of the Civil War, the Emancipation Proclamation, Reconstruction, and the rise of black codes and Jim Crow laws; where "The Souls of White Folk" symbolizes Du Bois's efforts to critically offset the supposed universality of whiteness and the surreptitiousness of white supremacy in an early twentieth-century white world which stubbornly refused to acknowledge its long-standing psychopathic and schizophrenic obsession with race, racelessness, and racial theft, *The Gift of Black Folk* represents Du Bois's radical reassessment, and most sophisticated and sustained articulation, of African Americans' distinct contributions to American history, culture, and society.

As was observed above, in *The Souls of Black Folk* Du Bois emphasized three major "gifts" African Americans have historically given to America. In *The Gift of Black Folk* he updated his gift theory and systematically chronicled ten major, as well as several minor, "gifts" that enabled him to more concretely answer the question which climactically closed *The Souls of Black Folk*: "Would America have been America without her Negro people?" As if seeking to directly answer this crucial question, perhaps because it had been on his mind a great deal during the two decades that separate *The*

Souls of Black Folk and *The Gift of Black Folk*, Du Bois (1924) declared with weighted words:

> This essay is an attempt to set forth more clearly than has hitherto been done the effect which the Negro has had upon American life. Its thesis is that despite slavery, war and caste, and despite our present Negro problem, the American Negro is and has been a distinct asset to this country and has brought a contribution without which America could not have been; and that perhaps the essence of our so-called Negro problem is the failure to recognize this fact and to continue to act as though the Negro was what we once imagined and wanted to imagine him—a representative of a subhuman species fitted only for subordination. (ii–iii)

Bearing in mind the question, "Would America have been America without her Negro people?" it is important to connect this query to the sentence above, which reads as follows: the "American Negro is and has been a distinct asset to this country and has brought a contribution without which America could not have been." Herein lies Du Bois's discursive challenge to the ideals and the "souls of white folk"—that is, their need to openly acknowledge their *white indebtedness* in order to see blacks as human beings, as fellow citizens, as more than mere field-hands, hewers of wood and drawers of water. After the publication and critical acclaim of *The Souls of Black Folk* it appeared as though the majority of whites, even liberal and well-meaning whites, were willing to, at most, acknowledge what Du Bois referred to as the "gift of sweat and brawn," but they seemed to be stubbornly and shamefully blind to blacks' other "gifts."

The Gift of Black Folk asserts that the African contribution to the upbuilding of America was much more than their labor, whether in bondage or in so-called freedom. Du Bois unequivocally intoned: "It must not be assumed, however, that the labor of the Negro has been simply the muscle-straining unintelligent work of the lowest grade. On the contrary, he has appeared as both personal servant, skilled laborer, and inventor . . . the Negroes of the colonial times were not all ignorant savages." In fact, as illustrated by "the advertisements concerning them," he thundered, "[c]ontinually runaway slaves are described as speaking very good English; sometimes as speaking not only English but Dutch and French. Some could read and write" (64). Here, then, is a direct challenge to the myth of the "happy slaves" and "good darkies" that dot page after page of antebellum American literature and revisionist history. Even if whites, especially liberal or well-meaning whites, had taken the time to read Frederick Douglass—who, along with Harriet Tubman, Sojourner Truth, and Charles Lenox Remond, Du Bois asserted, represented "living refutations of the whole doctrine of slavery" or, more specifically, white supremacy—they would have come to the uncomfortable realization that the great bulk of what they thought they knew so well about "Negroes" and the "Negro's" "true nature" was nothing more than figments of their own faulty imaginations, fallacious racializations, flawed colonizations, and on and on *ad infinitum* (147–48, 174).

Beyond their labor, according to Du Bois's updated gift theory in *The Gift of Black Folk*, blacks had also contributed to pioneering exploration, military service, more inclusive democratic government, the first system of public education, social welfare, women's liberation, music, literature, and the moral and spiritual reconstruction of religion in American culture and society. Essentially devoting a chapter to each of the aforesaid, by the book's end Du Bois's readers are left with the distinct impression that African Americans are the quintessential Americans because of their contribution to, but ongoing exclusion from, "American" democracy, and their dogged efforts to, literally, deconstruct and reconstruct democracy in the interest of the inclusion of blacks and other nonwhites. Their exclusion from the theory and practice of democracy in America enabled it to be defined (and, in a sense, distorted and deformed) at the expense of African Americans' lived experiences and lived endurances, thus casting a long, dark, and doomed shadow over American democracy until such time that all human souls who humbly share *their* cultural gifts with America can benefit from *their* concrete contributions to the *shared human project* and *shared human product* of a profoundly, intensely inclusive, multicultural, and transethnic democratic United States of America, *their* new nation.

A hard-hitting Du Bois went so far as to assert that America may have never come to be if it were not for the singular role enslaved Africans (*not* "Negroes," *not* "blacks," and *not* "colored people") were forced to play in forging the new nation. Furthermore, Du Bois fumed, the so-called democracy created by the black "slave-holding" (and Native American mass murdering) white "Founding Fathers" was never designed to be a democracy "for the masses of men" and women, but instead an inept, imitation Athenian democracy, a *herrenrasse demokratie* (i.e., a master race democracy) in which African American enslavement (not to mention the Native American holocaust), as well as capitalist and sexist exploitation, oppression, and violence, became as supposedly "normal" and "natural" as Mary Shelley's "Frankenstein" monster or Friedrich Nietzsche's "blond beast."

Boldly building on his research in "The Conservation of Races," *The Souls of Black Folk*, and "The Souls of White Folk," in *The Gift of Black Folk* Du Bois appeared to be more determined than ever before to drive home the point that African Americans' contributions to America extended well beyond their invaluable labor and, truth be told, actually cut to the core of the very meaning and mission of "democracy" in America and the wider world. He blasted, "One cannot think then of democracy in America or in the modern world without reference to the American Negro." Extremely critical of the tired tendency on the part of whites to make whiteness synonymous with Americanness and, even more, white supremacist nationalist-patriotism synonymous with upholding American democracy, Du Bois challenged the longstanding white lie that whites were the sole architects of American democracy, arguing instead that the "democracy established in America in the eighteenth century was not, and was not designed to be, a democracy of the masses of men [and women] and it was thus singularly easy for people to fail to see the incongruity of democracy and slavery." Unequivocally critiquing whites' intertwining or, rather, their ignominious efforts at a sick synthesis of democracy and white supremacy ("slavery"), Du Bois (1924) intrepidly accented African Americans' agency and centrality in both the theoretical and practical development of democracy in America: "It was the Negro himself who forced the consideration of this incongruity [of democracy and slavery], who made emancipation inevitable and made the modern world at least consider if not wholly accept the idea of a democracy including men [and women] of all races and colors" (139).

Du Bois's conception of democracy was "radical" in the sense that it emphasized that at its heart democracy involves *inclusive ethical and egalitarian interactions* (as opposed to *exclusive exploitative exchanges*) with others, such as sharing social space, the creation and constant re-creation of culture, and community caretaking, and not simply the routines of voting rights, political procedures, and rallying soldiers to defend doomed exclusive and elitist ideals. African Americans' opening up, as it were, of the "idea of democracy" to include "men [and women] of all races and colors" patently places them smack dab in the middle, not only of the creation, but also the forward march of American and world democracy. In fact, it could easily be averred that the conceptual thread that runs throughout *The Gift of Black Folk* revolves around the centrality of African Americans in American history, culture, and society. From Du Bois's (1924) frame of reference it was obvious that

> dramatically the Negro is the central thread of American history. The whole story turns on him whether we think of the dark and flying slave ship in the sixteenth century, the expanding plantations of the seventeenth, the swelling commerce of the eighteenth, or the fight for freedom in the nineteenth. It was the black man that raised a vision of democracy in America such as neither [white] Americans nor Europeans conceived in the eighteenth century and such as they have not even accepted in the twentieth century; and yet a conception which every clear-sighted man knows is true and inevitable. (135–36)

If, indeed, we are willing to accept Du Bois's contention that African Americans are at the heart of American history, culture, and society, then, a lingering question irritatingly remains: Why have black folk's gifts to America been left in the lurch for so long? In addition, we may also want to ask: If African Americans' contributions to American history, culture, and society have not been, and are not now being attributed to them, then who, pray tell, is reaping the recognition and reward for the gifts they gave to America? Here we have come back to what I referred to above variously as "racial theft" or "cultural theft." In truth, it must be admitted that in *The Gift of Black Folk* Du Bois laced most of his words with his own homespun naïve liberalism in an effort to appeal to a wider white audience. Seeming to reach back to the intellectual intentions of *The Philadelphia Negro*, he almost innocently believed that if African Americans' gifts to America were laid before whites in a less strident and more straightforward manner (as compared and contrasted with his increasingly radical writings in *The Crisis* during this period), then they would rethink race, if not repudiate anti-black racism and their racist relationships with blacks (and other nonwhites). How else can one explain his answer to the rhetorical question, "Who made America?" with which he begins the prescript of the book? In his answer to this question he clearly demonstrates that he is neither the Du Bois of *The Philadelphia Negro* nor *The Souls of Black Folk*, but an altogether different Du Bois somewhere between the Pan-African radicalism of *Darkwater* (which, it will be recollected, houses "The Souls of White Folk") and the intellectual history-making "black Marxism" and radical democratic socialism of *Black Reconstruction* (which houses unprecedented critiques of white supremacist capitalist colonialism in chapters such as "The White Worker," "The Transubstantiation of the White Poor," and "The White Proletariat in Alabama, Georgia, and Florida").

Observe here how Du Bois deceptively developed what I referred to in the preceding section as a *critical theory of willful white blindness to black humanity, history, and culture* in the Prescript, where in answer to the foresaid rhetorical question (i.e., "Who made America?") he responded, "Now that [America's] foundations are laid, deep but bare, there are those who would forget the humble builders, toiling wan mornings and blazing noons, and picture America as the last reasoned blossom of mighty ancestors; of those great and glorious world builders and rulers who know and see and do all things forever and ever, Amen! How singular and blind!" (33). Whites' blindness to blacks' gifts to America, Du Bois contended, not only had implications for race relations but also the very meaning and ongoing development of democracy in America and the wider world. Nobly acknowledging the efforts of white abolitionists, he reminded his readers that authentic white antiracists were in the minority among whites, and that no matter which whites may have been willing to see and commemorate blacks' contributions in the past, somewhere along the way whites *lost sight* of blacks' indispensable contributions to the formation and "foundations" of the United States in the present. "How singular and blind!" indeed. *The Gift of Black Folk*, then, was about bringing sight (or, rather, sharing blacks' "second-sight") with the blind white world.

However, the book is also about remembering or, rather, *the gift of remembering*. Recall above Du Bois's assertion that "there are those who would forget the humble builders, toiling wan mornings and blazing noons" to, literally, lay the "foundations" of America, especially "democracy" in America. Obviously here he is referring to the long-forgotten black folk of America's past but, perhaps even more, he is also highlighting both *white forgetfulness* and, as a result of their forgetfulness, *white indebtedness*. Hence, he went on to state, "For the glory of the world is the possibilities of the common place and America is America even because it shows, as never before, the power of the common, ordinary lovely man"—by which he means the humble, hard-working, beautiful "human being." And then, returning to his critical discourse on American democracy, Du Bois announced, "This is real democracy and not vain and eternal striving to regard the world as the abiding place of exceptional genius with great black wastes of hereditary idiots" (33). In order to achieve what Du Bois termed "real democracy," it would be necessary for whites to actively participate in "black" or, now, "African American" studies—that is, whites would need to systematically and critically (and, I would assert, *transdisciplinarily*) study African American lifeworlds and life struggles: from their precolonial lives and abduction in Africa through to their horrific experiences during the Middle Passage; from their hardships and hard labor conditions during enslavement through to their ongoing quest(s) for racial and social justice.

There simply is no substitute for whites' remembering blacks' contributions because, as the past and present state of affairs cogently demonstrates, without blacks' reminding whites of blacks' gifts to America, white supremacy, the Veil, and the color-line would continue to cause *white forgetfulness*—not to mention blacks' double-consciousness. In other words, Du Bois told whites that the great "land of the free" and the "home of the brave" (mis)conception of America that they take so much pride in and unquestionably take *all* the credit for creating would not exist without the incalculable contributions of not simply blacks but, as he emphasized in "The Souls of White Folk," other nonwhites who have also been rendered anonymous, at best, or invisible, at worst, in the "official" white-washed, narcissistic narrative of how America came to be. To this he responded with words which continue to resonate: "We who know may not forget but must forever spread the splendid sordid truth that out of the most lowly and persecuted of men, Man made America. And that what Man has here begun with all its want and imperfection, with all its magnificent promise and grotesque failure will some day blossom in the souls of the Lowly" (33). Flashes of critical optimism creep across the pages of *The Gift of Black Folk* to such a great extent that one cannot help but to come to the conclusion that through all of his biting criticisms of *white blindness*, *white forgetfulness*, and *white indebtedness*, Du Bois honestly believed that if whites would open their eyes to blacks' (and other nonwhites') gifts to America and the wider world they would in that very moment, almost as if miraculously or baptismally, take a much-needed step toward regaining their sight and memory; reclaiming their humanity and redeeming themselves (human redemption); and, last but not least, they would take a step toward "real democracy" by acknowledging the allegedly long-lost "souls of the Lowly."

In *The Gift of Black Folk* Du Bois's historical and sociological analysis controversially and seemingly contradictorily seesaws between optimism and pessimism regarding *white blindness, white forgetfulness,* and *white indebtedness*. In some passages Du Bois could be interpreted as problematically assuming that racism actually operates primarily or even wholly on the level of conscious racist beliefs and conscious racist commitments, and that all that is needed (à la his naiveté in *The Philadelphia Negro*) is for the folly of racist beliefs and racist commitments to be brought to their adherents' attention. Thus, nonracist (although not antiracist) thought and behavior will be the result. However, when viewed from the Africana critical theoretical framework, even in 1924 Du Bois's efforts to offset whites' longstanding ill-treatment of blacks was much more complex and complicated than the foregoing lamely liberal interpretation. *The Gift of Black Folk* complicates those liberal interpretations that would exclusively focus on Du Bois's optimism or, rather, his *critical optimism* without sufficiently juxtaposing it with his *critical pessimism* with regard to whites remembering blacks' gifts, because throughout the book he repeatedly reminded his readers that, for the most part, *white forgetfulness,* as with *white blindness,* was and remains *willful*—which is to say, *white forgetfulness* and *white blindness* have been and remain intentional and iniquitous, and not, as is so often clamorously claimed by liberal and so-called well-meaning whites, accidental and innocent.

A clear textual marker of my above contention concerning the dialectical complexity of Du Bois's *critical theory of willful white forgetfulness* can be found in his constant criticisms of whites' historic and current (mis)treatment of *blacks as property* or, rather, *racial real estate,* which innovatively inverts, and patently paved the way for, Cheryl Harris's (1993) discourse on "whiteness as property." If black folk were "legally" and literally property or pieces of real estate owned by white folk, then the countless contributions blacks made to the formation and "foundations" of America were historically and are currently viewed as white contributions from the perspective of the white world. Because blacks were bought, sold, and owned by whites, whites looked at blacks as their *racial real estate,* their "investments" and they, therefore, were able to capitalize on and attribute any contribution that their black "property" may have made or, indeed, did make to America to their villainously vain selves. This means, then, that black contributions to America, through *white supremacist sorcery* or *anti-black racist alchemy*, surreptitiously and duplicitously became white contributions to America—hence, my assertion above of *willful white blindness* to, and *willful white forgetfulness* of blacks' gifts to America, as well as blacks' humanity, history, and culture.

It should also be pointed out that *The Gift of Black Folk* also shows Du Bois in the throes of developing a more nuanced critical theory of white supremacist capitalist colonialism. Far from "going soft," as it were, with respect to his critique of whites' appropriations, whether conscious or unconscious, of blacks' gifts to America, he also accented the intersecting and interconnecting aspects and effects of racism, capitalism, and colonialism on black lifeworlds and black life struggles, which is a caveat as needed now at the dawn of the twenty-first century as it was at the close of the first quarter of the twentieth century when he published the book. Du Bois's use of the discursive device of black "gifts" simultaneously enabled him to rhetorically and conceptually deepen and develop his critique of *blacks and black gifts as property* in particular, and white supremacist and anti-black racist capitalist economic exploitation in general. The "gift of labor," he somberly said, is "one of the greatest that the Negro has made to American nationality. It was in part involuntary, but whether given willingly or not, it was given and America profited by the gift. This labor was always of the highest economic and even spiritual importance" (Du Bois, 1924, 76). *The Gift of Black Folk*, then, was meant to serve as a textual reminder to both white *and* black America, as well as the wider world, reminding them that black folk's gifts were gifts that were given, in spite of racial theft, cultural banditry, or officially sanctioned and legalized anti-black racist exploitation, oppression, and violence that shaped and shaded the historical, cultural, and social contexts under which the gifts were given. The main point is that the gifts were given, and Du Bois's emphasis here, like most of his theses throughout his corpus, is dual: on the one hand, he is simultaneously accenting African Americans' agency and centrality in American history, culture, and society; and, on the other hand, he is underscoring the *white blindness, white forgetfulness*, and *white indebtedness* that white America and the white world have long been content to loathsomely live with and innocently claim to know nothing about.

In *Black Reconstruction*, Du Bois continued his critique of *blacks and black gifts as property* by synthesizing his sociology of race with Marxism's critique of capitalism, class, and property, ultimately centering on black racial identity and white anti-black racist class solidarity.[12] "Property involves theft by the Rich from the Poor," he announced. However, even amongst the poorest of the white poor, enslaved African Americans' lived experiences and lived endurances were distinctly different because they were, literally, regarded *as* property. Poor whites were yet and still considered human beings in the white world, but blacks were considered *racial real estate*:

"Indeed, the system [of African American enslavement] was so reactionary, so utterly inconsistent with modern progress," Du Bois loudly (1995a) lamented, that "we simply cannot grasp it today." What is more, "No matter how degraded the [white] factory hand, he is not real estate. The tragedy of the black slave's position was precisely this" (10).[13] In no uncertain terms, white supremacist capitalism revolved around *racial theft* and *cultural banditry*—utilizing the color-line, "slave codes," black codes, Jim Crow laws, the crop-lien system, the convict lease system, racial segregation, and the racist ritual of lynching, among other forms of racial exploitation, racial oppression, and racial violence. White supremacist capitalism incessantly severed blacks' culturally developed gifts from their black givers, and using *anti-black racist alchemy* reduced (à la *reductio ad absurdum*) both the black gifts and the black givers to "legally" appropriated *white property* or, rather, whites' own *white gifts* to not only America, but also to the wider world. Through *anti-black racist alchemy* or, rather, *white supremacist sorcery*, African Americans *and* their contributions to America were seized or appropriated by whites and then rearticulated and accepted as either extremely important and innovative extensions of whites themselves or authentic expressions of their own white culture or, even more, as property in which they had invested and, therefore, were "legally" and absolutely within their rights to claim credit for.

In *Black Reconstruction*, Du Bois reminded his readers that "[s]laves were not considered men. They had no right of petition." Furthermore, "[t]hey could own nothing; they could make no contracts; they could hold no property, nor traffic in property; they could not hire out; they could not legally marry nor constitute families; they could not control their children; they could not appeal from their master; [and] they could be punished at will" (10). All of this means, then, that when viewed from the perspective of *blacks and black gifts as white people's property*, when whites sequestered black gifts as their own, and then rearticulated those gifts as their own lily white enhancements and expressions of themselves it was *by no means*, from their putrid perspective, *racial theft* or *cultural banditry*. This was logically and "legally" so because of blacks' simultaneous subhuman *and* nonhuman status within the social hierarchy of the white supremacist world: logically, if blacks were considered less than human (i.e., subhuman) there was no recognized human agent to make the contribution, or *to do the giving*; and legally, therefore, since blacks' human rights were not recognized by white supremacist law, they were considered not simply subhuman but, even more frequently, nonhuman, which means that they could not possibly make contributions, or *could not possibly give gifts* to the upbuilding of America and human culture and civilization worldwide. Continuing with the twisted logic of the *blacks and black gifts as white people's property* perspective, we may conclude that there was not racial theft or cultural banditry from black people on the part of white people insofar as whites, literally, viewed blacks as their property; therefore, blacks' contributions to America are whites' contributions to America because enslaved Africans were nothing more than extensions of their white masters—as clearly stated in *Dred Scott v. Emerson* in 1852, and again in *Dred Scott v. Sandford* in 1857.

However, when the Veil is lifted and African Americans, whether enslaved or emancipated, are viewed *as people* and *not as property* (during enslavement) or *not as problems* (during the post-Emancipation period), then, we have grounds to assert that African Americans' human rights and civil rights were violated and that they were, indeed, robbed in the most roguish manner imaginable by white enslavers and their contemporary descendants who not only attribute blacks' gifts to whites, but also, and however unwittingly, add insult to injury by attributing blacks' gifts to whites while they deny the humble humanity of African Americans during both their enslavement and post-Emancipation periods. When viewed from the Africana critical theoretical framework, whites did not then and do not now simply *appropriate* blacks' gifts to American history, culture, and society, but they actually, and more specifically, *expropriate* blacks' gifts because *appropriate* means *to take something for ones' own use, typically without the owner's permission*, but *expropriate* means *to take something from its rightful owner with the backing of the law and, therefore, with the sanction of the government or the state*. This means, then, that we must be careful with the terms in which we talk about whites' *racial theft* and *cultural banditry* of blacks' gifts to America, because it is extremely important to bring the U.S. government's complicity in this most malicious matter to twenty-first-century Americans'—*all* contemporary Americans (i.e., African, Asian, European, Latin, and Native, among other Americans)—attention. From the optic of the Africana critical theoretical framework, the language of "appropriation" is too neutral and may mislead many to believe that African Americans are seeking redress or reparations from individual whites, whereas the utilization of the language of "expropriation" more clearly conveys African Americans' indictment of the U.S. government for sanctioning such atrocious and blatantly undemocratic laws which enabled whites to violate blacks' human rights and civil rights with impunity (see my "Critical Reparations Theory," in Rabaka, 2008a).

Someday, someway, and somehow white America and the wider world must come to or be brought to the realization that black folk are not racial real estate or pieces of white people's property, neither during their enslavement nor post-Emancipation period, but rather African Americans, past and present, are humble human beings who have long expressed their autonomous human agency and capacity for human creativity, both of which have undeniably contributed to the United States' history, culture, society, and conception of democracy. It is only by problematicizing and, ultimately, doggedly denying *blacks and black gifts as white people's property* that we can come to genuinely critique and/or appreciate blacks' contributions to America as the invaluable "gifts" that they really and truly are. If whites are allowed to continue to sever the gifts from the givers, then, logically, from a white perspective suffering from black historical amnesia, black gifts and their black givers will continue to be reduced to pieces of racial real estate. The white racist capitalist commodification of blacks and their contributions to America ultimately translate into the white racist capitalist consumption of both black folk and their black gifts for white cultural exchange, white capitalist profit, and, it must be admitted, white sensual and sexual pleasure.

Du Bois's critical discourse on whiteness points to the fact that whites' anti-black racist capitalism revolves around the mistreatment of *black folk and black gifts as property* not only in their efforts to offer up black products for anti-black racist capitalist consumption and profit, but also to provide much-needed protection for their simultaneously psychopathic *and* sociopathic white psyches, whether liberal and well-meaning white psyches or full-fledged white supremacist psyches. Bringing the Du Boisian dialectic to bear here, it could be further explained as follows: If, on the one hand, black folk are *racial real estate*, they are logically and legally disqualified from making contributions to human culture and civilization and, thus, they are *prime property* expressly available for exchange on the white supremacist and anti-black racist capitalist marketplace or, more bluntly, on the auction block. If this, indeed, is the case, then whites' anti-black racist and, however sometimes subtle or surreptitious, white supremacist violation of blacks' human rights and civil rights need not cause their consciences to either fear or fret. If, on the other hand, black folk are *people* or *human persons*, then mistreating them as though they were *prime property* or *racial real estate* and, even more, committing *racial theft* and *cultural banditry* against them would more than likely cause guilt—perhaps, what is commonly called *white guilt*—and worry whites' consciences. Whites' anti-black racist ruse is that in order to *see* themselves, which is to say their history, culture, society and conception of democracy, as "good," then they must become and remain *blind* to blacks as human persons, and blacks and any black gift that racial theft and cultural banditry cannot be committed against becomes and remains "bad," "barbaric," "savage," and/or "uncivilized." Consequently, *white blindness* and *white forgetfulness* have long enabled whites, whether consciously or unconsciously, to repulsively reduce blacks to property and incessantly steal and take credit for virtually anything and everything blacks contribute to national and global culture.

Ending racist domination and discrimination against blacks involves an unprecedented transformation of the white psyche, and not simply—as so many white Marxists never cease saying—the eradication of capitalist society in and of itself. Du Bois's sociological discourse intensely emphasizes the fact that racism is inextricable from capitalism, they are incessantly intersecting and overlapping systems of exploitation, oppression, and violence, and his work further demonstrates that there is no such thing as toppling capitalism without also terminating racism: a war must be simultaneously waged on multiple fronts, against capitalism *and* racism (*and*, as will be discussed in the next chapter, against sexism as well). The contemporary discourse on "color blindness," from a Du Boisian perspective, is sociologically symptomatic of the ongoing racial theft and cultural banditry of blacks' gifts under the guise of an allegedly "new" antiracism that does not in any significant way connect past or present racism to capitalism. It is, in so many words, a new defensive device that opens up an alternative avenue for whites to evasively wiggle their way out of "soul-searching" and critically examining their "souls" and their psychopathic and sociopathic psyches, which would more than likely irrefutably reveal to them that they are not only raced (i.e., white) but anti-black racist (i.e., white supremacist), and that they, rich and poor, or, rather, both bourgeois and proletariat whites, have profited from and have been privileged as a result of the racial theft and cultural banditry, as well as the simultaneously racist *and* capitalist commodification and consumption of black folk and black gifts.

Du Bois's gifts theory is part and parcel of his sociological discourse and, although often overlooked, it evolved a great deal: from his early work discussed above, through to his most sustained discussion of the theory in *The Gift of Black Folk*. For instance, in "The Conservation of Races," it will be recalled that Du Bois (1897a) declared, "We believe that the Negro people, as a race, have a contribution to make to civilization and humanity, which no other race can make" (15). He held this belief primarily for two reasons. First, it was based on Africa's past, "one of the richest and most intriguing which the world has known." Most race and/or racist scientists at the turn of the twentieth century either had no knowledge of Africa's past, or they were aware of it and developed their racist theories to counter claims of the greatness of African antiquity. As Du Bois (1995b) put it in "The Superior Race," which was published in 1923, "Lions have no historians" (474), by which he wished to imply that even though the lion is universally revered as the "king of the jungle," it is nonetheless an animal and, therefore, has no history and thus no need of historians. It is only human beings who can make history and create culture, and in a white supremacist world blacks are not human but, as observed above, subhuman at best, or nonhuman at worst. Therefore, the history and culture that Africans did in fact produce in ancient epochs, or in the "precolonial" period, as it were, is viewed as either influenced by or derivative of European culture, or a "primitive" attempt to imitate and emulate European culture, usually Greco-Roman culture. Du Bois's critique of, and counter to, these claims can be found in his watershed works in the areas of African historical sociology, African historiography, and African cultural anthropology—for example, works such as *The Negro*, *Africa, Its Geography, People and Products*; *Africa—Its Place in Modern History*; *Black Folk Then and Now: An Essay on the History and Sociology of the Negro Race*; *Color and Democracy: Colonies and Peace*; *The World and Africa*; and *Africa: An Essay Toward a History of the Continent of Africa and Its Inhabitants*.

The second reason Du Bois believed that Pan-African people had a significant contribution to make to human culture and civilization was because their endurance and experiences of holocaust, enslavement, colonization, segregation, and so on, had "gifted" them with "second-sight," as he put it above in *The Souls of Black Folk*. In this instance, "second-sight" enabled black folk to see things that others could not on account of the specificities of African and African American historicity. That is to say, Du Bois believed that blacks' contemporary "gift" to human culture and civilization had to do with their particular and peculiar position in and struggle(s) against one of the major systems of exploitation, oppression, and violence plaguing the large majority of humanity in the (post)modern moment: white supremacy. Du Bois's belief that black folk have a "great message . . . for humanity" led him to a lifelong critique of white supremacy that is best exemplified by works such as "Race Friction Between Black and White," "Of The Culture of White Folk," "White Co-Workers," "The Souls of White Folk," "The Superior Race," "The White Worker," "The White Proletariat in Alabama, Georgia, and Florida," "The White World," and "The White Folk Have a Right to Be Ashamed." Of these works, "The Souls of White Folk," published in *Darkwater: Voices Within the Veil* in 1920, which recasts and combines Du Bois's 1910 essay by that name and his freshly penned piece, "Of the Culture of White Folk" (published in 1917), offers his most sustained and sophisticated statement against white supremacy, as it not only critiques white supremacy, but also represents and registers as one of the first attempts to expose white supremacy's influences on and interconnections with other systems of exploitation, oppression, and violence, such as colonialism and capitalism.

As his sociology of race and critique of white supremacy evolved, so too did Du Bois's gift theory. It began innocently enough as a claim that black folk, "as a race, have a contribution to make to civilization and humanity, which no other race can make." Then, it grew gradually into a charge to contemporary Pan-African people to emulate and audaciously endeavor to surpass their august ancestors' contributions to human culture and civilization. In "The Conservation of Races," Du Bois (1897a) declared:

> Manifestly some of the great races of today—particularly the Negro race—have not as yet given to civilization the full spiritual message which they are capable of giving. I will not say that the Negro race has as yet given no message to

the world, for it is still a mooted question among scientists as to just how far Egyptian civilization was Negro in its origin; if it was not wholly Negro, it was certainly very closely allied. Be that as it may, however, the fact still remains that the full, complete Negro message of the whole Negro race has not as yet been given to the world. (9-10)

From Du Bois's view, blacks had been unable to give "civilization the full spiritual message which they are capable of giving" primarily because of white supremacy and its enormous and unfathomable effects on black lifeworlds and black lived experiences. His early uncertainty regarding the African origins of ancient Egyptian civilization was laid to rest as a result of the research of Franz Boas, Leo Frobenius, and Harry Johnston, among others. If Egypt, undoubtedly one of the greatest classical civilizations, was African or, at the least, initiated by Africans—as Du Bois documented in *The Negro, Black Folk, Then and Now,* and *The World and Africa*—then, it would be a great disservice to modern Pan-African people to argue that they have "given no message to the world." As he studied and learned more of Africa's ancient and precolonial past, Du Bois's gift theory shifted its emphasis from Pan-African people giving "the full, complete Negro message . . . to the world" to accenting and highlighting classical African contributions to human culture and civilization with an eye toward, first, confronting and combating the white supremacist theses of, of course, white superiority and black inferiority and, also, blacks' purported lack of history and culture; second, providing contemporary Pan-African people with classical African cultural paradigms and traditional motifs; and, finally, offering a caveat to continental and diasporan Africans that their task is not so much to give the definitive Africana message to the world (something, on second thought, that may never really be possible), but to contribute to and continue the Pan-African struggle for freedom and justice in their own age and leave a legacy for succeeding generations.

Generic racism, if there is such a thing, essentially entails racial domination and discrimination. White supremacy does not simply racially oppress, as Du Bois asserted above. Being the fraternal twin (or, at the least, a sibling of some sort) of capitalism, it racially oppresses in the interest of nonpareil racial colonial economic exploitation. It symbolizes the intensification of economic exploitation by adding a racist dimension to capitalist greed and colonial gain. Hinging on a diabolical dialectic that sees whites as superior and nonwhites as inferior, white supremacy consumes the nonwhite world and claims nonwhites' contributions to human culture and civilization as European or white contributions to culture and civilization. This is so because, as discussed earlier, from the white supremacist point of view, nonwhites have never and do not now possess culture or civilization and, therefore, could not possibly contribute to the upbuilding of something they have never and do not now possess. Further, white supremacy enables and utterly encourages whites to theoretically and culturally loot the knowledge banks and cultural treasure troves of the nonwhite world, similar to the way they did when they established *racial colonialism* and *colonial capitalism*, because it is a global system that recognizes and rewards based on the embrace of white hegemonic views and values, white conquest, and racial colonization.

Moving beyond a strictly materialist (politico-economic and/or class-centered) account of race and racism, and hitting at the heart of white supremacy, Du Bois (1920), in "The Souls of White Folk," queried the "colored world" and those whites who would open themselves to moral and materialist questions: "How many of us today fully realize the current theory of colonial expansion, of the relation of Europe which is white, to the world which is black and brown and yellow? Bluntly put, that theory is this: It is the duty of white Europe to divide up the darker world and administer it for Europe's good" (41). Part of Du Bois's critique of white supremacy reveals his reliance on racial materialist arguments, where the other portion of his critique revolves around his own homegrown cultural nationalism, which later in his life evolved into a combination of *Pan-Africanism, cultural internationalism, democratic socialism,* and *radical humanism* that sought to accent and highlight commonalities and kinships among nonwhites based on their lived experiences and lived endurances of, and struggles against European imperial expansion and all-out white (cultural, social, political, legal, educational, religious, aesthetic, and economic) domination and discrimination. Du Bois's critical comments in "The Souls of White Folk" deserve quotation at length here, as his argument is elaborated throughout several carefully constructed paragraphs that poignantly capture the crux of his critique of white supremacy:

> The European world is using black and brown men for all the uses which men know. Slowly but surely white culture is evolving the theory that "darkies" are born beasts of burden for white folk. It were silly to think otherwise, cries the cultured world, with stronger and shriller accord. The supporting arguments grow and twist themselves in the mouths of merchant, scientist, soldier, traveler, writer, and missionary: Darker peoples are dark in mind as well as in body; of dark, uncertain, and imperfect descent; of frailer, cheaper stuff; they are cowards in the face of mausers and maxims; they have no feelings, aspirations, and loves; they are fools, illogical idiots—"half-devil and half-child." (41–42)

Emphasis must be placed on Du Bois's slight discursive shifts here. He undeniably touches on racial colonialism's intersections and interconnections with capitalism by pointing to "all the uses" whites have put nonwhites to: field work, house work, military work, sex work, and so on. He, then, highlights the ways in which the white world had/has a tendency to view nonwhites as either "devils" or "children," bringing issues of nonwhites' perceived nonhumanity ("devils") or their "minority" status ("children") to the fore, simultaneously exposing both whites' inhumanity, at worst, or paternalism, at best, toward their racial colonial subjects, or newly discovered "property." Continuing his discourse on white folk's dehumanization of nonwhites, Du Bois sternly stated:

> Such as they [i.e., nonwhites] are civilization must, naturally, raise them, but soberly and in limited ways. They are not simply dark white men. They are not "men" in the sense that Europeans are men. To the very limited extent of their shallow capacities lift them to be useful to whites, to raise cotton, gather rubber, fetch ivory, dig diamonds—and let them be paid what men think they are worth—white men who know them to be well-nigh worthless.
>
> Such degrading of men by men is as old as mankind and the invention of no one race or people. Ever have men striven to conceive of their victims as different from the victors, endlessly different, in soul and blood, strength and cunning, race and lineage. It has been left, however, to Europe and to modern days to discover the eternal world-wide mark of meanness—color!
>
> Such is the silent revolution that has gripped modern European culture in the later nineteenth and twentieth centuries. Its zenith came in Boxer times: White supremacy was all but world-wide, Africa was dead, India conquered, Japan isolated, and China prostrate, while white America whetted her sword for mongrel Mexico and mulatto South America, lynching her own Negroes the while. (42)

The "civilized" (read: whites) are simultaneously a race in a sociocultural and politico-economic sense, though they do not think of themselves in racial terms, and they throw temper tantrums when they are thought of in racial terms or as being racialized or raced. They can steal and kill the "uncivilized" (read: nonwhites) without regard to rank or reason, and they can at any moment change the rules of the racial hierarchy and racial history because they alone are decidedly and definitively the authors of human culture and civilization, and most certainly the architects of science and technology. As Du Bois demonstrated above, white supremacy is not simply about racial domination and discrimination, which is to say, white supremacy cannot quickly be reduced to racism, and especially as it is understood in contemporary racial discourse. Much more, white supremacy robs the raced or nonwhites of their right to be human, of their right to self-definition and self-determination. It reduces human beings to the status of things, which is one of the reasons, as Frantz Fanon observed in *The Wretched of the Earth*, when they are discussed by the white world, nonwhites are frequently referred to in "zoological terms," in the terms in which animals are discussed and dissected. Fanon (1968) fumed:

In fact, the terms the [white racial colonial] settler uses when he mentions the native [i.e., the raced or the nonwhite] are zoological terms. He speaks of the yellow man's reptilian motions, of the stink of the native quarter, of breeding swarms, of foulness, of spawn, of gesticulations. When the settler seeks to describe the native fully in exact terms he constantly refers to the bestiary. (42; see also Rabaka 2010a)

Du Bois's critique of white supremacy also hits head-on the issue of white personhood and black (or nonwhite) subpersonhood. Recall above he asserted, "They [the colored and colonized] are not simply dark white men. They are not 'men' in the sense that Europeans are men." Whiteness and maleness are prerequisites for personhood in the world that modernity made. A person, in this world, is one who is rational, self-directing, and morally and legally equal with a white male. Since white males created the laws of this world, none but white males are equal and given moral, legal and extralegal consideration. Therefore, as the *Dred Scott* 1857 decision mentioned above demonstrates, "a black man has no rights which a white man is legally bound to respect" (see *Dred Scott*, 1857, 403–7). White rights are intimately intertwined with the denial of black rights. Or, to put it another way, white personhood is inextricable from black subpersonhood.

In *The Racial Contract*, Charles Mills (1997) contends: "Whiteness is defined in part in respect to an oppositional darkness, so that white self-conceptions of identity, personhood, and self-respect are then intimately tied up with repudiation of the black Other. No matter how poor one was, one was still able to affirm the whiteness that distinguished one from the subpersons on the other side of the color-line" (58–59). And who or what are these "human things," to borrow a phrase from Du Bois's (1995b) discourse, on the "other side of the color-line" (20)? Mills (1997) maintains, "Subpersons are humanoid entities who because of racial phenotype/genealogy/culture, are not fully human and therefore have a different and inferior schedule of rights and liberties applying to them. In other words, it is possible to get away with doing things to subpersons that one could not do to persons, because they do not have the same rights as persons" (56).

Even in its mildest and most unconscious forms, white supremacy is one of the most extreme and vicious human rights violations in history because it plants false seeds of white superiority and black inferiority in the fertile ground of the future. It takes human beings and turns them into the subhuman or nonhuman "things," making them nonwhite means to a white imperial end. Du Bois's sociology of the "souls of white folk," gift theory, and critique of white supremacy registers, then, as not only a radical criticism of an increasingly illusive and nebulous racism, but an affirmation of black humanity and an epoch-spanning assertion of Pan-African and other oppressed people's inherent right to human rights, civil rights, and social justice.

Du Bois's sociology of race, perhaps above all else, is distinguished by its commitment to nonwhites' humanity and whites' human redemption. It was not simply the Veil, the color-line, or double-consciousness that impeded a truly democratic society, but equally *white blindness, white forgetfulness*, and whites' treatment of *blacks and black gifts as property*. Where he began his adventures in the sociology of race toying with partially essentialist, reformist, and gradualist strains, historical happenings on the world scene and the acute and increasing economic exploitation of blacks in white supremacist societies led him to couple his sociology of race and critical race theory with a more concerted Marxist critique of capitalism's connections with racism. As a consequence, Du Bois developed many of the first major critical concepts in the sociology of race. However, racism and capitalism were not the only issues Du Bois believed were deterring an authentically multicultural and transethnic democratic society. There was also the problem of gender domination and discrimination, something he consistently sociologically engaged, but an issue that most Du Bois scholars have buried beneath a barrage of criticism regarding his black radicalness, critical coquetry with Marxism, and sociological deviations when compared and contrasted with the work of his white male peers. The next chapter, then, will be devoted to the often overlooked antisexist and male-feminist dimensions of Du Bois's sociological discourse.

NOTES

1. With regard to Anthony Appiah's assault on Du Bois's historical sociology of race, his "The Uncompleted Argument: Du Bois and the Illusion of Race," originally published in *Critical Inquiry* in 1985, was revised, retitled, and reprinted as "Illusions of Race" in his *In My Father's House: Africa in the Philosophy of Culture* (Appiah, 1992, 28–46). In "Race, Culture, Identity: Misunderstood Connections" (1996), Appiah amends some his argument(s) against Du Bois's so-called sociohistorical conception of race, and claims that Du Bois was up to much more than he, Appiah, had initially realized. For hard-hitting critiques of Appiah's criticisms of Du Bois's concepts of race and critiques of racism, see Patrick Goodin's "Du Bois and Appiah: The Politics of Race and Racial Identity" (2002), Paul Taylor's "Appiah's Uncompleted Argument: W. E. B. Du Bois and the Reality of Race" (2000), and Lucius Outlaw's legendary and heatedly debated "defense" of Du Bois, "'Conserve' Races?: In Defense of W. E. B. Du Bois" (1996a). Further, for a vociferous yet not vicious critique of Du Bois, Appiah and Outlaw's discourse and debates on Du Bois, race, culture, and identity, see Robert Gooding-Williams's "Outlaw, Appiah, and Du Bois's 'The Conservation of Races'"(1996). Concerning the claim that Du Bois may very well be "just another over-engaged 'race man' posthumously positioned as a radical theorist," see Rabaka (2007b, 2008a) where I discuss the disingenuousness and difficulties of reading a multidimensional theorist such as Du Bois from a one-dimensional frame of reference.

2. I am well aware of the fact that part of my interpretation here sounds a little "postmodern," especially with my claims concerning race's malleability and fluidity. However, the reality of the racial matter is that there is a stream of the black radical thought-tradition that is, to put it plainly, *anti-European modernity*. If Euro-modernity is predicated on the exploitation, death and destruction of Africana peoples and cultures, then it seems logical that an Africana "antimodern," as opposed to "postmodern" tradition would arise. Indeed it did, and one of the primary tasks of Africana critical theory has been and remains to document and develop this discourse (see Rabaka, 2007b, 2008a, 2009a, 2010a). What "modernity" means in the African world is very different from that of the European world, and we could aver the Asian, Latin American, and Native American worlds as well. The Ghanaian philosopher Kwame Gyekye has eloquently argued, in *An Essay on African Philosophical Thought* (1995) and *Tradition and Modernity: Philosophical Reflections of the African Experience* (1997), that where Europeans may have been trying to free themselves from many of their more oppressive traditions during their "Enlightenment" (all the while racially colonizing and enslaving non-European "Others"!), Africans have spent most of European modernity asserting their humanity and attempting to modernize what they could from their past. It is not as though Africana peoples were or are inherently against modernity or modernization, but unequivocally against the Europeanization (and/or imperialization) of their modernity. For further discussion of Africana antimodernism, and Du Bois's antimodernism specifically, see Wilson Jeremiah Moses's *Afrotopia* (1998), and especially the chapter "W. E. B. Du Bois and Anti-Modernism."

3. White criticism of black race-consciousness is a theme that runs throughout Du Bois's discourse. Whatever he felt about it at any given historical interval, it made no matter to him when examined in light of an Africana history-, culture-, and struggle-informed sociopolitical perspective. Du Bois, a doyen in Africana historical discourse, consistently counseled blacks, as well as whites, to study continental and diasporan African history, culture, and struggle. With no knowledge of Africana history, even well-meaning (white and/or black) interpreters were doomed to misinterpret Africana lifeworlds and life struggles. Regarding the white criticism of the black race-consciousness theme that runs throughout Du Bois's discourse, see not only *Dusk of Dawn*, as quoted in the text, but also his *John Brown, Color and Democracy: Colonies and Peace, The Autobiography of W. E. B. Du Bois*, and *Against Racism*, among other pieces published in periodicals (Du Bois, 1945, 1962, 1968a, 1985a).

4. My interpretation of Du Bois's social ethics, as well as my general argument throughout the preceding paragraphs, has been deeply influenced by Ramona Edelin's doctoral dissertation, "The Philosophical Foundations and Implications of William Edward Burghardt Du Bois's Social Ethic" (1981), which carefully and critically elaborates Du Bois's lifelong preoccupation with and predilection for social ethics.

5. On Du Bois and the NAACP's crusade against anti-black racist violence, especially lynching, see Bernstein (2005) and Zangrando (1980). For discussions of anti-black racist violence—again, with special attention paid to the racist ritual of lynching—which reached across the Reconstruction years into the heart of the twentieth century, see first and foremost Du Bois's *Black Reconstruction* (1995a), as well as Apel (2004), Brundage (1993, 1997), Markovitz (2004), Nevels, (2007), Shapiro (1988), Waldrep (2006), and Williamson (1984, 1986).

6. With regard to "subjugated knowledge," Foucault (2003) offered this explanation during one of his legendary College de France lectures in 1975:

> When I say "subjugated knowledges" I mean two things. On the one hand, I am referring to historical contents that have been buried or masked in functional coherences or formal systemizations. [In other words, I am referring to] blocks of historical knowledges that were present in the functional and systematic ensembles, but which were masked, and the critique was able to reveal their existence by using, obviously enough, the tools of scholarship. Second, when I say "subjugated knowledges" I am also referring to a whole series of knowledges that have been disqualified as . . . insufficiently elaborated knowledges: naive knowleges, hierarchically inferior knowledges, knowledges that are below the required level of erudition or scientificity. (7)

The conceptual correlation that I am making between Du Bois's theory of "second-sight" and Foucault's conception of "subjugated knowledges" is important insofar as it enables us to see, not simply an instance where a nonwhite intellectual's thought prefigures that of a white intellectual but, much more importantly, here we have an instance in which we can clearly see that *epistemic apartheid* is not solely predicated on race, but that it extends well beyond race and cuts to the very core of issues revolving around conceptual incarceration and distorted discursive formations; it could probably go without saying that racism, sexism, capitalism, colonialism, heterosexism, religious intolerance, and so forth have significantly impacted academic and the wider social world's conception of what constitutes "knowledge" and what counts as "naïve" or "inferior" "knowledge." When Foucault points to "knowledges that have been disqualified," knowledges that were "masked," and knowledges that have been rendered "hierarchically inferior," it would seem to me that his explanation of "subjugated knowledges" lends itself to the (re)definition of Du Bois's saga of blacks' "second-sight." For further discussion, see below.

7. By "ideological hegemony," Gramsci essentially sought to emphasize that the ruling race-class and established order's ideas, attitudes, values, beliefs, morality, and so on permeate every aspect of civil society—including a wide range of social institutions and social activities: from churches and schools to family functions and the medical industry—therefore, seemingly neutral institutions and aspects of civil society actually hinge on and help to foster unconscious conformity and commitment to views and values that uphold the status quo and that are, ultimately, antithetical to social transformation in the interest of the economically exploited and racially oppressed. Hegemony, in the Gramscian sense, then, could be loosely defined as a worldview or organizing principle that is propagated by the ruling race-class's agencies of indoctrination and socialization, both "sacred" and secular, which touch every area of daily and social life, like the intemperate tentacles of a hungry octopus. The internalization of the dominant culture's belief system and values, usually unconscious, on the part of the racially oppressed and economically exploited causes the ruling race-class's ideologies to appear to be logical or "common sense"; thus, as the ruling race-class seeks to maintain its privilege, power, and wealth, they of necessity attempt to popularize and perpetuate their worldview, culture, values, morality, and so on, and repetitiously render them omnipotent and omnipresent, making them appear to be a part of the "divine" and "natural" order of things, part of both a "sacred" heritage and "sacred" history. To successfully take hold, however, the ruling

race-class's "ideological hegemony"—literally, their indoctrination and socialization campaign, or their unscrupulous ideological warfare—must operate and penetrate on two different levels: on the first level, as a seemingly "innocent," "normal," and "neutral" worldview and conception of life and society for the common folk; and on the second level, as an allegedly objective "social scientific" and "scholarly" program and set of principles which is unceasingly propagated and reproduced by a cadre of elite intellectuals and their minions, who, of course, benefit from the preservation of the established order. By casting Gramsci's conception of "ideological hegemony" into the discussion of Du Bois's conceptions of double-consciousness and the Veil I seek to illustrate the fact that blacks' double-conscious internalization of white-propagated *anti-black racist and white supremacist (mis)conceptions of blacks and blackness* is politically and sociologically symptomatic of white supremacy's intersection and interconnection with the political economy of race and anti-black racism in anti-black racist capitalist culture and society. Almost as if in direct dialogue with Du Bois (especially the later, more "black Marxist" Du Bois), in his *Prison Notebooks* Gramsci wrote of the "great variety of morbid symptoms" that "appear" when ideologically dominated cultures and societies began to lose their hold on the masses' minds. There is a sense in which Du Bois's concept of double-consciousness can be read as a sociological diagnosis of the masses' (in this instance, the black masses') continued unconscious internalization of the dominant group's anti-black racist ideology. Gramsci (1971) explained the next stage, the stage in which the masses begin to call the existing culture and society into question, although they do not yet consciously embrace a counter-ideology—sort of a social limbo state, somewhere between the old and the new society: "If the ruling class has lost its consensus, i.e., is no longer 'leading' but only 'dominating,' exercising force alone, this means precisely that the great masses have become detached from their traditional ideologies, and no longer believe what they used to believe previously, etc. The crisis consists precisely in the fact that the old is dying and the new cannot be born; in this interregnum a great variety of morbid symptoms appear" (275–76). It might be possible to point to double-consciousness as an extremely early "morbid symptom," one still very steeped in the old society and "their traditional ideologies"—that is, the society dominated by *the diabolical dialectic of white superiority and black inferiority.* Although only hinted at throughout *The Souls of Black Folk*, Du Bois's sociological discourse did eventually come to explicitly critique the intersection and interconnection of racism and capitalism as dual and inextricable systems of exploitation, oppression, and violence in black lifeworlds and black life struggles. For further discussion of Du Bois's increasingly radical politics after the publication of *The Souls of Black Folk*, see Horne (1986, 2009), Marable (1986), and Rabaka (2007b, 2008a, 2010b). And, for further discussion of Gramsci's conception of ideological hegemony, see Gramsci (1971, 206–76, 2000, 189–221) specifically, and Gramsci (1977, 1978, 1985, 1992, 1995, 1996) more generally.

8. My interpretation of the cultural and social psychological implications of Du Bois's concept of double-consciousness in particular, and *The Souls of Black Folk* in general, has been influenced by A. Davis (1983), S. O. Gaines (1996), Gaines and Reed (1994), Jennings (1998), and Wolfenstein (2007).

9. In *The Wretched of the Earth*, Fanon argues that it is primarily because of colonialism's violent denial of the racially colonized's humanity and history that the

"wretched of the earth" *must* rescue and reclaim their humanity and history from the dark, dank dungeon that the racial colonizer has confined it to, and completely topple the racial colonial world. The racially colonized, therefore, must be mentally and physically prepared to *violate* the "dividing line[s]"—social, political, cultural, metaphysical, physical, epistemological, and ethical—imposed by the racial colonizer if they are to "return to the upwards paths of their own culture," as Cabral contended, and in like fashion, as Fanon importantly asserted, *rehumanize* the racial colonizers and return them to their long-lost humanity as well (Cabral, 1979, 143; Fanon, 1968, 38; see also Bernasconi, 1996; Rabaka, 2010a). Du Bois's concept of double-consciousness continues to resonate with sociologists of race, philosophers of race, and psychologists of race because, similar to Fanon's work, whether discussing black lifeworlds in capitalist or colonialist societies, it aids in accenting the racial or racist dimensions of the political economies of these societies, which divide and doubly problematize blacks' lived experiences in the said societies.

10. I emphasize the epic aspects of Du Bois's theory of second-sight here by referring to it as the *"saga* of second-sight" in an effort to accent the fact that, first, if indeed a saga is a "story of heroic achievement" and, second, as David Levering Lewis (1993) observed, if Du Bois's writings, especially his memoirs, utilized the "language of the saga," then, it is important for us to make a connection between his autobiography and his African and African American historiography (19). In other words, Du Bois's "saga of second-sight" demonstrates not only that his soul is bound up with those of the "souls of black folk," but also that he boldly believed that just as he was able to arrive at the critical black consciousness (as opposed to double-consciousness) of second-sight, so too could and would his beloved black folk break free from the gruesome grasp of double-consciousness. In order to wrench themselves free from the clutches of double-consciousness, like Du Bois, black folk would have to systematically and critically study continental and diasporan African history, culture and struggle on their own terms—that is, consciously countering the "ideological hegemony" of anti-black racist capitalism, which is also to say that there are serious implications for what we are currently calling "Africana studies" scattered throughout Du Bois's oeuvre but especially apparent in his critique of double-consciousness and saga of second-sight. Further commenting on Du Bois's distinct synthesis of his personal history with the nuances of national African American and international Pan-African history, Lewis announced, "In those lyrical memoirs, whether *Darkwater, A Pageant of Seven Decades, Dusk of Dawn,* or the *Autobiography* [*of W. E. B. Du Bois*], we are drawn to participate in a chronicle of epic sweep, at once familial, racial, national, global, and prophetic" (19). All of this, then, should be borne in mind in the discussion below concerning second-sight as a possible solution to the problem of double-consciousness.

11. Here, I am hinting at the fact that nonwhites have a long history of colonizing one another, albeit never in the world-imperial and white supremacist fashion of European imperialism and global domination. This, of course, is a fact that the recondite historical researcher, Du Bois, did not allow to fall through the cracks in his more mature historical writing. For, perhaps, the best examples from his oeuvre, see *The Negro, Black Folk Then and Now,* and *The World and Africa* (Du Bois, 1939, 1965, 1970b).

12. Joel Olson (2005) offers a clarifying point with regard to my assertion that Du Bois's work here cannot be counted as either purely "black nationalist" or purely "white Marxist" but ultimately "centered on black racial identity and white anti-black racist class solidarity," in stating that even when Du Bois did dabble with black nationalism it served more "internationalist and humanist objectives" (125). In terms of what I am referring to here as "white anti-black racist class solidarity," Olson corroborates my claim by announcing that the "white world is a product of a peculiar cross-class alliance between capitalists and a section of the working-class, which receives certain privileges in exchange for its complicity with the system of capitalism. The black or dark world, meanwhile, consists of those excluded from and subordinated by this alliance. Membership in either world, Du Bois emphasizes, is less the result of biology or ancestry than of a social-political system that collects humans into 'races' or 'worlds' for the purpose of class rule" (119). Indeed, Du Bois's sociology of race did take a Marxist turn and increasingly considered class and class struggle more and more, but it is important to always acknowledge the ways in which Du Bois extended and expanded Marxism to meet the special needs of nonwhites, and especially blacks, who were/are being simultaneously exploited and oppressed by both capitalism *and* racism. For further discussion, see Olson (2004), C. J. Robinson (2000), and Roediger (1994, 2002, 2007).

13. My comments here should not in any way be (mis)interpreted as criticisms of "poor whites," but as part of my ongoing critique of capitalism and racism as interlocking systems of exploitation, oppression, and violence that distorts and deforms whites' humanity just as much as they do nonwhites' humanity. Africana critical theory's unrepentant radical humanism incessantly insists on its adherents remaining open to working with anyone (without regard to race, gender, class, sexual orientation, religious affiliation, or country of origin) who is sincerely and consistently struggling to achieve racial, gender, economic, and social justice. With regard to the noteworthy works on poor whites and the ways in which racism and capitalism impact whites' lifeworlds and lived experiences, see Flynt (1979), Forret (2006), K. Moss (2003), Wray (2006), and Wray and Newitz (1997).

3

Du Bois and the Sociology of Gender

"The Damnation of Women," "The Freedom of Womanhood," and the Insurgent Intersectional Sociology of the Souls of Black (Among Other) Female Folk

> The meaning of the twentieth century is the freeing of the individual soul; the soul longest in slavery and still in the most disgusting and indefensible slavery is the soul of womanhood.
>
> W. E. B. Du Bois, "Women Suffrage," 298

> The uplift of women is, next to the problem of the color-line and the peace movement, our greatest modern cause.
>
> W. E. B. Du Bois, *Darkwater: Voices From Within the Veil*, 181

INTRODUCTION: DU BOIS'S SOCIOLOGY OF RACIALLY GENDERED CLASSES AND THE PARADOXES OF RADICAL ANTIRACIST POLITICS

Although many have interpreted him as an archetypal "race man," according to African American feminist political philosopher Joy James (1997) in *Transcending the Talented Tenth*, Du Bois actually practiced "a politics remarkably progressive for his time and ours" (36). James went on to note that "Du Bois confronted race, class, and gender oppression while maintaining conceptual and political linkages between the struggles to end racism, sexism, and war" (36–37). His sociological framework, therefore, was dynamic and constantly integrated diverse components of African American liberation theory, Pan-Africanism and anticolonial theory, feminist and women's liberation theory, peace and international political theory, and Marxist and non-Marxist anticapitalist and class theory, among others.

In "The Souls of Black Women Folk in the Writings of W. E. B. Du Bois," the late African American feminist literary theorist Nellie McKay (1990) contended, "At a time when black male writers concentrated their efforts on the social, economic, and educational advancement of black men as the 'leaders' of the race, Du Bois is something of an anomaly in his recognition that black women were equal partners in the struggle to claim the human dignity all black people were seeking" (236). Moreover, in *Daughters of Sorrow: Attitudes Toward Black Women, 1880–1920*, African American women's studies professor Beverly Guy-Sheftall (1990) maintains that Du Bois was not only one of "the most passionate defenders of black women," but also one of the "most outspoken [male-]feminists" in African American history and, more generally, in American history (13). In fact, in Guy-Sheftall's greatly respected opinion, Du Bois "devote[d] his life's work to the emancipation of blacks *and* women" (161, emphasis in original).[1]

Further, in *W. E. B. Du Bois: Black Radical Democrat*, esteemed African American historian Manning Marable (1986) echoes Guy-Sheftall's observations, declaring that "[l]ike [Frederick] Douglass, Du Bois was probably the most advanced male leader of his era on the question of gender inequality" and woman suffrage, although he was deeply "troubled by the racism within the white women's movement" (85). Particularly perplexing for Du Bois was the white women's movement's inattention to, and perpetuation of, racism, especially anti-black racism. For instance, Du Bois was deeply bothered by the racial politics of the National American Woman Suffrage Association (NAWSA), whose president, Carrie Chapman Catt, asserted that democratic rights had been granted to African American men "with possibly ill-advised haste," producing "[p]erilous conditions" in U.S. society as it introduced "into the body politic vast numbers of irresponsible citizens." Belle Kearney, the Mississippi suffragist leader, practiced an even more overtly anti-black racist politics by advocating that white women's enfranchisement would guarantee, among other things, an "immediate and [more] durable white supremacy" (cited in Marable, 1986, 85). Du Bois (1995b), in his characteristic male-feminist fashion, shot back: "Every argument for Negro suffrage is an argument for woman's suffrage; every argument for woman's suffrage is an argument for Negro suffrage; both are great movements in democracy" (298).

Because Du Bois has been most frequently viewed from monodisciplinary perspectives, his previously noted transdisciplinary contributions have been consistently downplayed and diminished. In many sociologists' minds (if Du Bois ever even crosses their minds), he is, *au mieux*, perhaps a "pioneering" sociologist of race, but further than that no concession can be or has been made. Even in Du Bois studies, prior to his death and most certainly posthumously, Du Bois's work, even when it has been acknowledged to have a wide-ranging reach and intellectual influence well beyond sociology of race, has been still relegated or, to use the critical language of *epistemic apartheid, conceptually quarantined* to race- and ethnicity-focused subfields within "traditional" disciplines. However, and as I have argued in *W. E. B. Du Bois and the Problems of the Twenty-First Century*, many of the social and political problems of the twentieth century have been carried over into the twenty-first century, especially the problems of racism, sexism, capitalism, and colonialism. Amazingly, particularly when compared with the work of others of his era, Du Bois's discourse eventually evolved into an inchoate intersectional framework that, according to Susan Gillman and Alys Eve Weinbaum in *Next to the Color-Line: Gender, Sexuality, and W. E. B. Du Bois* (2007), "juxtaposed" race *with* gender *with* class to such an innovative extent that they audaciously announced "there could hardly be a more opportune time than the present to reengage his writings from the widest possible conceptual and historical vantage point" (1–2).

In Du Bois studies there has been a long history of disrupting and disconnecting (as opposed to, à la Du Bois himself, *intersecting, interconnecting,* and *juxtaposing*) the various social variables or social problems he critiqued and sought solutions to, which in many ways erases or, at the least, renders invisible the implicit or veiled *racially gendered critical logic and language* at play in, and that is part and parcel of, his renowned discourse on race and racism. In other words, Gillman and Weinbaum weigh in again, "As readers of Du Bois, we have finally arrived at a historical juncture when the daunting expansiveness of Du Bois's grammar—not to mention his life and work, spanning two centuries and straddling the globe—requires reinvigoration and renewal by scholarly and political concerns that have, over the past three decades, become inextricable from 'the problem of the color-line' that Du Bois formulated and against which he fought on multiple fronts" (2). Indeed, Du Bois did fight "on multiple fronts," and one of the pitfalls of attempting to force his work to fit into Eurocentric, patriarchal, and/or bourgeois conceptions of who counts as a sociologist, or what counts as sociology, is that much of Du Bois's sociological (and, not to mention, his transdisciplinary) distinctiveness is lost in monodisciplinary translation. This chapter takes its cue from Gillman and Weinbaum, among several of the other contributors to their anthology, by not simply reframing Du Bois's comparative and conjunctive analysis within the context of women and gender studies, but also in light of the fact that their anthology seems to completely overlook Du Bois's contributions to sociology of gender in general, and black feminist sociology in particular. Not one single sociologist or political scientist, or social scientist of any sort, contributed to *Next to the Color-Line*, which does not so much intellectually indict Gillman and Weinbaum as much as it, once again, highlights how social scientists, and sociologists in particular, have put into play *epistemic apartheid* when and where we come to the work of W. E. B. Du Bois. How else can one explain the fact that sociology has not in its long and august history produced a solitary book-length review of, or anthology of critical commentary on, his contributions to sociology? What is it about Du Bois's embryonic intersectional framework that Gillman, Weinbaum, and their colleagues in the humanities can see that sociologists well into the twenty-first century continue to be blind to?

In terms of identifying and analyzing Du Bois's contributions to the sociology of gender in general, and black feminist sociology in particular, what I am most interested in here is how Du Bois maintained, as James put it above, "conceptual and political linkages" between various antiracist, antisexist, anticolonialist, and anticapitalist thought-traditions and sociopolitical movements. Unlike most of his white male sociological peers, Du Bois did not downplay or attempt to erase gender domination and discrimination. On the contrary, over time his work placed the critique of sexism and racism right alongside or, rather, *in juxtaposition to* the critique of capitalism, class analysis, and class conflict theory. In tune with the thinking of many Marxist feminists and socialist feminists, Du Bois grew to be critical of both capitalism and patriarchy. He came to understand that women, in a general sense, have great potential as agents of democratic social transformation because of their simultaneous experience of capitalist exploitation and sexist oppression. However, similar in many respects to most contemporary black feminist sociologists, Du Bois ultimately understood black women in particular to have even greater potential as agents of radical democratic social change on account of their simultaneous experience of racism, sexism, and economic exploitation, whether under capitalism or colonialism. Du Bois's socio-theoretical framework, therefore, has immense import for the discussion at hand so far as it provides contemporary sociologists of race *and* gender *and* class with a paradigm and point of departure for developing a *transdisciplinary* and *transgendered intersectional sociology* that is simultaneously critical of racism, sexism, capitalism, and colonialism.

Although there is much in Du Bois's male-feminist writings that warrants our attention, this chapter will limit its focus to those aspects of his social thought that register as seminal and significant contributions to the discourse and development of black feminist sociology, the *sociology of racially gendered classes*, and *insurgent intersectional sociology* that is conscious of and critiques racism, sexism, and capitalism as overlapping and interlocking systems of exploitation, oppression, and violence. Therefore, for the purpose of coherence the chapter will be divided into three sections, each of which corresponds with one of Du Bois's major contributions to black feminist sociology, the sociology of racially gendered classes, and/or intersectional sociology. The first section, "The Roots of Du Bois's Male-Feminist Radicalism: Josephine St. Pierre Ruffin and the Black Women's Club Movement," performs an intellectual archaeology of Du Bois's early life and thought and identifies the black women's club movement, and Josephine Ruffin's radicalism in particular, as a central site and source of his paradigm(s) for social organization, political education, black feminism, public intellectualism, and radical journalism. The second section, "'The Uplift of Women Is, Next to the Problem of the Color-Line . . . Our Greatest Modern Cause': Du Bois's Sociology of Black Womanhood and Black Motherhood," acutely explores Du Bois's (re)presentation and (re)positioning of black women and black mothers. It accents his efforts to counter both white and male supremacists' contentions concerning black women, and illustrates the importance of emphasizing the category of *racially gendered women* within the discursive world of the sociology of gender. The third section, "Du Bois, 'The Damnation of Women,' and the Advent of Insurgent Intersectional Sociology," focuses on Du Bois's classic male-feminist manifesto "The Damnation of Women." It brings together the insights from the previous sections and seeks to provide a radical reinterpretation of his male-feminism with an eye on the ways in which it prefigured and continues to provide a foundation for intersectional sociology and comparative and conjunctive transdisciplinary race, gender, and class analysis in the twenty-first century. The chapter quickly closes with "Du Bois, 'The Soul of Womanhood,' and the Sociology of Gender," which is in essence an intellectual autobiographical interlude where the author encourages men, and specifically more male sociologists, to solemnly deconstruct and reconstruct modern masculinity by taking sociology of gender, black feminist sociology, feminist theory, and women's studies more seriously in their sociological research. We begin, then, with what could be called the "roots" of Du Bois's male-feminist radicalism, the black women's club movement.

THE ROOTS OF DU BOIS'S MALE-FEMINIST RADICALISM: JOSEPHINE ST. PIERRE RUFFIN AND THE BLACK WOMEN'S CLUB MOVEMENT

There is a subtle pro-feminist subtext that shades and colors Du Bois's sociological discourse. It runs through his thought like an age-old river cutting through the earth on its way to the ocean. Although his social thought gives way at times to both the mythical and the mystical, especially where black women are concerned, it can be said with no hyperbole and high-sounding words that the philosophical foundation of Du Bois's male-feminism was the black women's club movement. In fact, I would go so far as to say that Du Bois's sociology at many intervals is incomprehensible without serious consideration being given to the impact and influence of several of the central intellectual-activists of the black women's club movement on his thought throughout his long life. Secondly, and continuing this line of thinking, I would also suggest that the black women's club movement provided Du Bois with concrete and culturally grounded paradigms and points of departure for social organization, social and political activism, interorganizational cooperation, radical journalism, public intellectualism, critical education for black liberation, black womanhood, black motherhood, and the black family.

Du Bois's male-feminist politics neither begins nor ends with his 1920 publication of "The Damnation of Women" in *Darkwater*. On the contrary, black feminist sociologist Cheryl Gilkes (1996) has asserted that as far back as his 1883 to 1885 articles for the *New York Globe*, Du Bois displayed a rare "sensitivity to the contributions of black women to community life" (118; see also Lewis, 1993, 38–39). He advocated women's equality and engaged "women's issues" in the *Fisk Herald* in 1885, responding to an article on women's liberation by observing that the "column on woman's work is interesting, and a first rate woman's rights argument." Further, after becoming the editor-in-chief of the *Fisk Herald* in 1887, Du Bois published a semi-autobiographical novella, *Tom Brown at Fisk*, which featured a female schoolteacher protagonist who exclaimed in the opening paragraph of the piece, "It's hard to be a woman, but a black one—!," which clearly indicates his early interest in black women's lifeworlds and life struggles (Lewis, 1993, 62, 73–75).

By 1892 the young Du Bois was publishing his "Harvard Daily Themes" in the *Courant*, "a weekly newspaper of women's rights, civil rights, and informed opinion," which was edited by the noted African American "militant suffragette," Josephine St. Pierre Ruffin (105). Ruffin would go on to found the Women's Era Club in 1893, and edit its newspaper, the *Women's Era*. She also co-organized a national convention of black women's clubs that would lead to the formation of the National Federation of Afro-American Women (NFAAW) and, ultimately, the National Association of Colored Women (NACW).

David Levering Lewis argues, "Nowhere does Du Bois suggest that Mrs. Ruffin's feminist politics influenced his own precocious views about the rights of women. Mary Silvina's son had already arrived at them independently by then, yet the distinguished personalities and articulate opinions he met in Charles Street [i.e., in Ruffin's house] may well have quickened and sharpened the positive views he had come to hold" (105). Gilkes makes a strong counterclaim concerning the editorial relationship between Ruffin and the young Du Bois. According to Gilkes (1996), their editorial relationship "was highly significant," because it was Ruffin who introduced the young Du Bois to the world of the black women's club movement and to Ida B. Wells, another cofounder of the Women's Era Club, and "a prime mover in the Black Women's Club Movement" (118). In dialoguing with Ruffin and Wells, among other "clubbers," Du Bois observed firsthand African American social organization, political activism, and, most importantly with regard to the present discussion, black feminism and black women's liberation thought and practice. Consequently, he developed an unusual sensitivity to African American women's sufferings and their contributions to American history, culture, and society in general, and African American history, culture, and community specifically.

In fact, the influence of Ruffin in particular on Du Bois's thought should not be downplayed because, as Gilkes (1996) crucially contends, "It was Ruffin who provided the classic definition of a woman's movement from an African American perspective: she defined the black women's movement as a movement for the benefit of women and men, and she invited men to join women's work and struggles" (118). In her address to the First National Conference of Colored Women, convened under her leadership and held in Boston in 1895, Ruffin hit at the heart of the black women's club movement. Her remarks set the parameters and in several senses served as moral and sociopolitical principles to guide black women's club activities and social uplift efforts: from the National Association of Colored Women through to the National Council of Negro Women. At the First National Conference of Colored Women, Ruffin (1895) stated, in part:

> Our woman's movement is a woman's movement in that it is led and directed by women for the good of women and men, for the benefit of *all* humanity, which is more than any one branch or section of it. We want, [and] we ask the active interest of our men, and, too, we are not drawing the color-line; we are women, American women, as intensely interested in all that pertains to us as such as all other American women; we are not alienating or withdrawing, we are only coming to the front, willing to join any others in the same work and cordially inviting and welcoming any others to join us. (14, emphasis in original)

Ruffin's black feminist/womanist principles allowed the young Du Bois to perceive the importance of not simply getting more men involved in the black women's club movement, but also of black men developing more critical, self-reflexive stances toward patriarchy and their internalization of white male bourgeois thought and practices. Of all the things Du Bois learned from and admired about the black women of the club movement and some of their progressive white counterparts, it was, according to Gilkes (1996), "their ability to work together across class and color-lines in spite of their disagreements" (130). Clearly Ruffin intimates as much with her above contention—"we are not drawing the color-line"—and her additional assertion—"we are women, American women, as intensely interested in all that pertains to us as such as all other American women." After the anti-black feminist foibles of *The Philadelphia Negro* and the sundry masculinisms of *The Souls of Black Folk*, a more socially and politically mature Du

Bois would later emerge and employ many of the womanist principles and practices, as well as many of the members of the black women's club movement, to establish the Niagara movement and, ultimately, cofound the first national civil rights organization and movement in the United States: the National Association for the Advancement of Colored People (NAACP).

It is far from a coincidence that two of the foundational figures of the black women's club movement contributed to the founding and initial formation of the NAACP: Mary Church Terrell and Ida B. Wells (Lewis, 1993, 391). Further, politically active until the end of her life and always keeping a keen and critical eye on her surrogate son (i.e., Du Bois), Ruffin helped to found the Boston branch of the NAACP. In fact, so enduring was Ruffin's influence on Du Bois (1968a) that half a century after their initial encounter he recollected in *The Autobiography of W. E. B. Du Bois*, "Mrs. Ruffin of Charles Street, Boston . . . was a widow of the first colored judge appointed in Massachusetts, an aristocratic lady. . . . She began a national organization of colored women and published the *Courant*, a type of small colored weekly paper which was spreading over the nation. In this I published many of my Harvard daily themes" (137).

Du Bois's commitment to women's rights, although full of controversy and contradictions, was as consistent later in his intellectual life as it was inconsistent at the inception of his storied career. What many Du Bois scholars and critics have often overlooked is the simple, although central fact that for Du Bois women—and African American women in particular—were integral to the development of democracy because "Du Bois's vision" was one that "pointed to" and attempted to produce "a society that could confront, respect, and embrace the gifts of all" (Gilkes, 1996, 133). Observe how similar Du Bois's radical democratic theory sounds against the backdrop of Ruffin's black radical feminist dictum: "Our woman's movement is a woman's movement in that it is led and directed by women for the good of women and men, for the benefit of *all* humanity, which is more than any one branch or section of it." Du Bois's radical democratic theory has a deep, although sometimes subtle pro-feminist dimension to it, a dimension that helps to highlight both its roots in the incipient radical politics and social activism of the black women's club movement, and also its relevance for contemporary black feminist sociology that is simultaneously antisexist and antiracist, as well as critical of the ways in which racism and sexism intersect and interconnect with capitalism.

In brief, Du Bois's discourse, on deep and diverse levels, prefigures and provides a paradigm for the development of both black feminist and intersectional sociology because it simultaneously sought black liberation *and* gender equality *and* the "economic emancipation" and "democratization of modern society" (Du Bois, 1985a, 181, 1995b, 615). Du Bois's male-feminism, inextricable from his critiques of racism, colonialism, capitalism, and Marxism, took into serious consideration the "subjugated" and/or "suppressed" knowledge of a particular social, historical, and cultural group or racially gendered class (i.e., black women), and attempted to apply it towards the goal of human liberation and democratic social transformation (P. H. Collins, 1990, 221–38). Nowhere is this more evident in Du Bois's emerging antisexist social thought, and specifically with regard to the sociology of gender, than in his sociology of black womanhood and black motherhood.

"THE UPLIFT OF WOMEN IS, NEXT TO THE PROBLEM OF THE COLOR-LINE . . . OUR GREATEST MODERN CAUSE!": DU BOIS'S SOCIOLOGY OF BLACK WOMANHOOD AND BLACK MOTHERHOOD

Du Bois is known to have developed a critical social theory that was simultaneously critical of racism, colonialism, capitalism, and traditional Marxism. Here it will be important to bring this thought into dialogue with his maturing male-feminism and critique of sexism in our efforts to identify and analyze his contributions to the sociology of black womanhood and black motherhood. Similar to Frederick Douglass (1992), Du Bois demanded that women's human and civil rights be respected and protected. Beyond Douglass, however, Du Bois also thoroughly theorized and "strategized woman suffrage and female equality," argues Gary Lemons (2001, 2009) and Nellie McKay (1985, 1990), "from a standpoint grounded in the lived-experiences" and literature of black women (Lemons, 2001, 74). Bringing his critique of capitalism and careful study of modern political economy to bear on "this man-ruled world" and its absurd "sex conditions," Du Bois advocated that women have "equal pay for equal work," stating, "We cannot abolish the new economic freedom of women. We cannot imprison women again in a home or require them all on pain of death to be nurses and housekeepers" (Du Bois, 1995b, 289, 297, 309).

As discussed in the previous chapter, many Du Bois scholars have pointed out that Du Bois prophesied that "the problem of the twentieth century" would be "the problem of the color-line" (see, e.g., Anderson and Zuberi, 2000; Bell, Grosholz, and Stewart, 1996; Fontenot, 2001). However, what many of these otherwise thorough scholars have failed to grapple with is the fact that Du Bois made this statement in 1900 (in "To the Nations of the World"), and that he augmented and revised this thesis several times within the remaining sixty-three years of his life (Du Bois, 1995b, 639–41). In fact, by the time he published *Darkwater* in 1920, Du Bois (1920) stressed not only the "sex conditions," "sex equality," and "sex freedom" of women, but he also asserted that "women are passing through, not only a moral, but an economic revolution" (180, 181, 184). Further, forty-three years before his death, Du Bois—seemingly unbeknownst to the great majority of past and present Du Bois scholars—stated, "The uplift of women is, next to the problem of the color-line and the peace movement, our greatest modern cause" (181).[2]

It will be important for us to begin by, first, examining Du Bois's conception of how black women and black womanhood are shaped by society and, even more, how in turn society is influenced and impacted by black women and black womanhood. Then, our discussion will turn to Du Bois's sociology of black mothers and black motherhood, exploring their impact on society, and society's impact on them. Throughout the analysis here it will be extremely important to observe the ways in which the white and male supremacy of U.S. society doubly distorts and deforms black womanhood and black motherhood, and how, as quiet as it has been kept, Du Bois's discourse on black women and black mothers, which often unwittingly shows traces of both male-feminism and male-chauvinism, was aimed at disrupting these distortions and deformations.

Certainly some of Du Bois's women-focused work, and specifically his thoughts on motherhood, borders on a mythic idealization of the maternal. For instance, he invokes "Neith, the primal mother of all," as a universal symbol of maternalism. She is "the primal black All-Mother of men . . . whose feet rest on hell, and whose almighty hands uphold the heavens; all religions, from beauty to beast, lies on her eager breasts; her body bears the stars, while her shoulders are necklaced by the dragon" (165–66). Neith's spirit, classically embodied in African queens, those "dusky Cleopatras, dark Candaces, and the darker, fiercer Zinghas," has made its way down to "our own day and our own land—in gentle Phillis [Wheatley]; Harriet [Tubman], the crude Moses; the sibyl Sojourner Truth; and the martyr, Louise De Mortie" (166).

Out of Africa came many contributions to human culture and civilization, but none, according to Du Bois, greater than Africa's "peculiar emphasis" on "the mother-idea." Where he related to his readers that the "father and his worship is Asia" and "Europe is the precocious, self-centered, forward-striving child . . . the land of the mother is and was Africa" (166). Although Du Bois is certainly to be commended for his efforts to accent and highlight African and African American women's lived experiences and lived endurances in "this man-ruled world"—as he sternly stated in "Woman Suffrage"—there may also be a sense in which he overstated his case and, consequently, unintentionally aided in the reification and perpetuation of what Michele Wallace (1990a) terms "the myth of the superwoman," and/or what Patricia Hill Collins (2000a, 174–75) more recently referred to as "mother glorification" and the myth of "the superstrong Black mother."

It was Du Bois (1920) himself who stated, "They [black women] existed not for themselves, but for men" (163). He painted a portrait of black women as strong, self-sacrificing, and long-suffering, but did not detail how these, among other, quintessentially black female character traits can be and historically have been abused, and not only by white men and white women, but by black men as well. On this point Du Bois's analysis does not take into consideration the concrete issues involved in many black mothers' lived experiences and lived endurances; issues which demand that we acknowledge black mothers' strengths, but also their all too human weaknesses and limitations. That is to say, for example, that we should keep cognizant of the fact that black mothers simply cannot do it all, and the fact that though some may very well be "superstrong," no human being, male or female, can be "superstrong" at every interval in human experience. Life, quite simply, remains too much of a mystery for it to be otherwise.

Du Bois wrote affectionately of "a vast group of women of Negro blood who for strength of character, cleanness of soul, and unselfish devotion of purpose, is today easily the peer of any group of women in the civilized world" (185). Here he was attributing to black mothers many characteristics associated with archetypal or universal motherhood. In doing this he was attempting to construct what he believed to be a positive image for African American women in general, and black mothers in particular. However, Du Bois failed to see that he was constructing what Patricia Hill Collins (2000a), in "Mammies, Matriarchs, and Other Controlling Images," calls a "controlling image" of African American women, one which praises black mothers' resilience ("super-strength") in a white and male supremacist society that has historically labeled them as not only "bad" mothers, but emasculating matriarchs, "bitches," and whores (69–96). In his subtle gender-blindness, Du Bois did not see that in order for African American women to remain on the pedestal he placed them on, black mothers would have to continue to be super strong, self sacrificing, and long-suffering, especially with regard to the men in their lives, whether father, brother, son, husband, lover, or traditional black church pastor.

What is more, by viewing black women primarily as mothers or essentially in their maternal mode, Du Bois also limited black women to a biological function or "sex role" and, in a sense, he quarantined them to the domestic domain or private sphere. This is not only problematic, but seems contradictory considering his assertion that "the future woman must have life-work and economic independence. She must have knowledge. She must have the right of motherhood at her own discretion" (Du Bois, 1920, 164).[3] How will women, and African American women in particular, ever achieve "economic independence" and/or pursue their "life-work" if, first, they are to be "good mothers" on the terms in which Du Bois outlined above (self-sacrificing and long-suffering, among several others) and, second, men (and African American men notwithstanding) are not taken to task for their faults with regard to fathering and fatherhood?

By placing such a strong emphasis on black women's experience as mothers, Du Bois, inadvertently I think but nonetheless, downplays the multidimensionality, the very variegations of African American women's lifeworlds and lived experiences. It is not that Du Bois did not advocate that women be more than mothers and have the right to be more than mothers, but that he did not develop this aspect of his male-feminism to the depth and detail that he did his concept of motherhood. In addition, it could also be averred that Du Bois's overemphasis on motherhood, his "mother glorification," as it were, also led him to level several lopsided (mis)interpretations of black women's lifeworlds and life struggles. Lame (mis)interpretations speak volumes about how "sex roles" discourse often provides a subtle subtext for many "gender progressive" men's articulations of, and approaches to feminist and/or women's liberation theory. For example, when Du Bois wrote of Toussaint Le'Ouverture, Frederick Douglass, and Alexander Crummell in *Darkwater*—the text which houses his most sustained treatment of "the woman question" and motherhood, "The Damnation of Women"—there was no talk of fatherhood or fathering. Which is to say that Du Bois did not see noted black men one-dimensionally or simply as fathers, but in multidimensional terms, as revolutionists, political radicals, great writers, eloquent orators, and the like. The "sex roles" subtext can be seen to be at work in this instance, and it certainly seems to have informed Du Bois's, albeit problematic, *pro*-feminist politics.

There is, however, also another way that we could analyze this. Let us begin with a rhetorical question: Could it be that Du Bois understood African American women to be so "socially damned" (his words) that he felt that the only way to get both his black and white readers of 1920 to sympathize with his subject, black women, was to situate their lifeworlds and lived experiences in an area of the human experience which many regard as universally respected and virtually irreproachable—motherhood? Think about it for a moment. At the turn of the twentieth century and well into its first quarter—which is to say, from the height of the New Negro movement through to the Harlem Renaissance—who chronicled the lived experiences and lived endurances of black women besides, well, black women? Certainly not prominent black male intellectuals and leaders. Ask yourself: Where is Booker T. Washington's work on women's rights? What was Marcus Garvey's position on the liberation of women? Additionally, we are left wondering what Alain Locke or James Weldon Johnson, or any number of esteemed black male intellectuals and leaders at the turn of the twentieth century through to the 1920s, thought of the struggle for women's rights.

Now, as I see it, there are several ways we could approach this, but keeping the overall objective of the identification and critique of *epistemic apartheid* in mind, I am not so interested in pointing out what this or that thinker did not theorize, as much as I am with providing a paradigm for an insurgent intersectional sociology that soberly and seriously critiques racism and sexism, just as intensely as it does capitalism and class struggle. With that being said, I feel compelled to state outright, Du Bois was doing a little literary double-dealing here, and in some ways it works, but in other respects it quite honestly does not and, consequently, it reveals some of the lacunae and serious limitations of his male-feminism and sociology of black womanhood and black motherhood. I want to suggest that Du Bois perhaps could have sidestepped some of the seeming contradictions of his construction of a "primal black All-Mother of men" myth had he emphasized and passionately advocated the very real need for men (and, again, African American men notwithstanding) to take fatherhood as sincerely and seriously as most women seem to take motherhood. This would have epistemically opened his argument up for critical discussions of female/male complementarity, sociopolitical co-creation, community caretaking, and collective cultural working—which in my mind remains important whether one is heterosexual or homosexual, because anti-black racism continues to bind black men to black women, and vice versa, as it is a form of domination and discrimination that affects persons of African origin and descent across the wide spectrum of the various ways of being *African* in the world.

A second way of engaging some of the stereotypes in Du Bois's womanist work here is to critically and epistemically open ourselves to the idea that it is highly plausible that he purposely constructed a "super black woman," a "primal black All-Mother of men," in an attempt to counter claims of white women's superiority and black women's inferiority (recall the discussion of *the diabolical dialectic of white superiority and black inferiority* in the previous chapter). Du Bois wanted to offset the anti-black racist images of black womanhood and black motherhood; therefore, he advanced almost the exact antithesis of those images. In *To Wake the Nations: Race in the Making of American Literature,* lionized literary theorist Eric Sundquist (1993) observes that although Du Bois's views on women and sexuality were "sometimes prudish," they "were hardly unbending. . . . Rather, they were frequently strategic and in any event must be judged in the context of his reaction to white racist attacks on African American sexuality and family morality" (586). Du Bois, Sundquist continues, understood himself to be "countering the contemporary archetype of the Negro as licentious or race-mixing 'beast,'" by highlighting African American women's humble humanity and reconstructing an image of black women, black mothers, and the black family, therefore theoretically rescuing and reclaiming for them the "moral integrity that had been undermined by the social effects of slavery and by racist theory" (584).

In his efforts to counter the racist myths about black womanhood and black motherhood, Du Bois, in his classic 1912 essay "The Black Mother," challenged "the master class['s]" conception of "the black mammy" in no uncertain terms (Du Bois, 1995b, 294). For those of "the master class," such as Thomas Nelson Page, who "after—with wet eyelids—recounting the virtues of his mammy, declares petulantly that she did not care for her own children," Du Bois reminded them that "the black mammy" is a perpetual "perversion of motherhood" (294). Why, my readers may ask? Because "the black mammy" always and ever "existed under a false social system," one that "deprived her of [both] husband and child," not to mention her right to *self-determination* and *self-definition*—two cornerstone characteristics of the conceptual universes of both black feminism and womanism (294; see also Guy-Sheftall, 1995; L. Phillips, 2006).

The "master class"—following in the fashion of white supremacist patriarchy—only appreciated black women and black motherhood when they could exploit and control or, rather, racially colonize black women's lifeworlds and lived experiences. But they had little or no respect for the black mother "in her own home, attending to her own babies." In fact, Du Bois (1995b) exclaimed, "As the colored mother . . . retreated to her own home, the master class . . . cried out against her. 'She is thriftless and stupid'" (294).

It is in the context of these racist assaults, both physically and psychologically, on black women that Du Bois developed his continental and diasporan African culture-based antisexist counterclaims. These claims were both grounded in and grew out of his knowledge of African American women's lived experiences and their sociopolitical theory and praxis. As much is evinced when we turn to his tutelage under and, eventually, more mature work with the black women's club movement, which it will be recalled was discussed above. Against those theorists and critics who customarily read Du Bois primarily and one-dimensionally as a "race man," I think that it is extremely important at this point to observe along with Gary Lemons (2001) that "not only was his [Du Bois's] conception of anti-racist resistance feminist-inspired, his worldview was profoundly influenced by black women" (73).

In fact, few scholars, black feminists and womanists notwithstanding, have pointed out that in many instances in his writings, pro-feminist or otherwise, Du Bois placed black women's sociopolitical theory and praxis on a par with and, at certain intervals, *over* that of black men. A prime example is the following passage from "The Damnation of Women," where he solemnly said:

> As I look about me today in this veiled world of mine, despite the noise and more spectacular advance of my brothers, I instinctively feel and know that

it is the five million women of my race who really count. Black women (and women whose grandmothers were black) are today furnishing our teachers; they are the main pillars of those social settlements which we call churches; and they have with small doubt raised three-fourths of our church property. If we have today, as seems likely, over a billion dollars of accumulated goods, who shall say how much of it has been wrung from the hearts of servant girls and washerwomen and women toilers in the fields? As makers of two million homes these women are today seeking marvelous ways to show forth our strength and beauty and our conception of truth. (Du Bois, 1920, 179)

Here, Du Bois was making a veiled reference to the black women's club movement, which was the very same movement that fueled and provided a foundation for his burgeoning male-feminist politics and a paradigm for his, literally, lifelong social and political activism. The black women's club movement, moreover, introduced and exposed Du Bois not simply to the black feminist social theory and praxis of luminaries such as Frances Harper, Anna Julia Cooper, Josephine Ruffin, Ida B. Wells, and Mary Church Terrell—all founding figures in the black women's club movement—but it also introduced him to "the first truly national black organization that functioned with strength and unity": the National Association of Colored Women (Hine and Thompson, 1998, 180).

It was one of the great tragedies of Du Bois's early life that his mother, Mary Silvina Burghardt Du Bois, died on 23 March 1885, approximately one month after her son's sixteenth birthday. In *W. E. B. Du Bois: Biography of a Race, 1868–1919*, David Levering Lewis (1993) paints a picture of the relationship between the "crippled" single mother and precocious son as being "laconic" and financially troubled, but extremely caring and close: "They were a regular feature of town life, occasioning well-intentioned remarks about their mutual devotion. Willie was always 'a little surprised because people said how nice I was to my mother.' 'I just grew up that way. We were companions,' he said, pure and simple" (30). Some time before her death, Mary Silvina suffered a paralytic stroke that "impaired her left leg or arm, or both," but even with her disabilities she "invested what was left of herself in Willie" (29–30). She continued to work, and with the help of her brother and some of Great Barrington's prominent citizens, she cared for her son until he graduated from high school, in 1884.

As Arnold Rampersad (1990) pointed out, in *The Art and Imagination of W. E. B. Du Bois*, "There can be little doubt that Du Bois's remarkable regard for women, especially black women, had its roots in his deep regard for his mother" (4). With the death of his mother, Du Bois began to deepen his burgeoning male-feminist consciousness, perhaps as a mute tribute to his dearly departed mother, by becoming more involved in black women's social uplift efforts, and specifically the black women's club movement. As we have seen, the women of the black women's club movement became, in many senses, surrogate mothers for the now motherless and fatherless Du Bois. As a result, early in his long life he became keenly aware of the sacrifices and compromises that many black women made for black men, black children, and the overall black liberation struggle. Du Bois felt compelled to not only acknowledge the sacrifices and compromises that black women made for black freedom, but he was also motivated to expand his own and others' understanding of these sacrifices and compromises. One of the ways Du Bois did this was by documenting and developing black women's social theory and political activism. Perhaps his greatest work in this vein is his immortal "The Damnation of Women."

DU BOIS, "THE DAMNATION OF WOMEN," AND THE ADVENT OF INSURGENT INTERSECTIONAL SOCIOLOGY: TOWARD A CRITICAL SOCIOLOGY OF OVERLAPPING AND INTERLOCKING SYSTEMS OF EXPLOITATION, OPPRESSION, AND VIOLENCE

In his enduring essay "The Damnation of Women," Du Bois (1920) stated that there are three "great causes" in the modern world to which every human being should devote special concern and careful consideration: "the problem of the color-line," "the uplift of women," and "the peace movement" (181). Women in general, and black women in particular, Du Bois sardonically remarked, "existed not for themselves, but for men." He went on to say, "They were not beings, they were relations and these relations were enfilmed [sic] with mystery and secrecy" (163). Where the majority of his black male contemporaries argued "a woman's place is in the home," sociologically Du Bois did not associate femininity with fragility or domesticity. He was an increasingly consistent defender of black womanhood, criticizing both white supremacist and black masculinist myths and stereotypes aimed at black women. As discussed above, in his 1912 essay "The Black Mother," Du Bois defended black women, and black motherhood in particular, against the race supremacist assaults and assumptions of both white men and white women. Three years later, a galled Du Bois called black men's open and uncritical acceptance of male supremacy into question. His brothers in black were thinking and doing the unpardonable: disenfranchising their sisters in black in much the same manner that whites did to blacks, and the rich did to the poor. Even if it meant becoming the laughingstock of the land, Du Bois (1995b) would—in the venerable spirit of Frederick Douglass and Charles Lenox Remond long before him—be disloyal to the putrid patriarchal privileges and practices of "this man-ruled world" (297).

In his classic 1915 *Crisis* essay, "Woman Suffrage," which was a defense of women's right to vote and pursue political offices, Du Bois (1995b) took Howard University dean and professor Kelly Miller to task for comments he made against women's suffrage and feminist political practice (297–98). Du Bois, an ardent advocate of women's rights and women's suffrage, stated that Dean Miller and men of his ilk who contended that "the bearing and rearing of the young is a function which makes it practically impossible for women to take any large part in general, industrial and public affairs; that women are weaker than men; that women are adequately protected under man's suffrage; that no adequate results have appeared from woman suffrage and that office-holding by women is 'risky,'" are not only aping the assertions of white masculinists and white supremacists, but also putting forward "ancient" arguments. From Du Bois's black male-feminist sociological perspective, "The actual work of the world today depends more largely upon women than upon men" (297).

Just as Du Bois argued in *The Philadelphia Negro* that "[t]he world was thinking wrong about race," in "Woman Suffrage" he intended to show Kelly Miller and his black male-chauvinist colleagues that "this man-ruled world" was thinking wrong about gender (the "problem of gender"), and the "woman question" in particular (Du Bois, 1968a, 197). He chided with his unique male-womanist wisdom: "The statement that woman is weaker than man is sheer rot: It is the same sort of thing that we hear about 'darker races' and 'lower classes.' Difference, either physical or spiritual, does not argue weakness or inferiority" (Du Bois, 1995b, 297). Here, by comparing masculinist sentiment ("woman is weaker than man") with white supremacist ideology (aimed at the "darker races") and bourgeois thought (on the "lower classes"), Du Bois innovatively accentuates the intersections and interconnections between sexism, racism, and classism, thus laying the groundwork for the race, gender, and class paradigm currently utilized within contemporary intersectional sociology decades before the major intersectional sociologists of the late twentieth and early twenty-first century were born. From Du Bois's inchoate intersectional sociological optic, black men who argue women's inferiority wish to dominate and discriminate against women based on their differences from men. This, however, is no different than the white racist theorist who theorizes black inferiority and subhumanity, and no different than the bourgeois thinker who theorizes the vices and vulgarities of urban underclass(es), and especially nonwhite inner-city youth—now primarily the "hip hop generation," which just so happens to be, it must be unapologetically admitted, the present author's jostling generation.

The connection that Du Bois made between sexism, racism, and classism also indicates that he was, to a certain extent, not only conscious but also critical of the supposed gender neutrality and universality of men's patriarchal thought and practice. What is more, Du Bois's male-feminist thought in this instance demonstrates that he was aware that the black men who argued women's inferiority wished to dominate and discriminate against women based on women's differences *not* simply from "men"—in some supposed "general," "neutral," or "universal" sense—but from the vantage point and sociopolitical position of *white* and *wealthy* men. "Men," as with "women," only exist in archetypal form, as pure classless and raceless entities, in the heads of established order academicians and in the one-dimensional, whitewashed books that they research and write.

Du Bois's male-feminist critical social thought points to a set of subtle prereflective parenthetical signifiers (adjectives), which are subtextual markers included along with the purportedly neutral and universal terms (i.e., "man," "woman," "boy," and "girl"). So, in all actuality when Kelly Miller and other patently pro-patriarchal men argue against women's equality based on their perceived differences (read: deficiencies and deviations) from the supposed male norm, they are arguing against women's equality based on the *white* male as the archetype. Moreover, Miller and men of his ilk do not simply take the *white* male as the mean by which to measure women's humanity (or lack thereof), but they also, whether unwittingly or otherwise, use the *bourgeois* or *wealthy* white male as the model male or, even more, as the universal embodiment of authentic humanity.

The foregoing analysis reveals, at the least, two things: first, that most men's worldview in white and male supremacist capitalist societies is simultaneously race-, gender-, and class-specific and hegemonic; and, second, the aforementioned helps to highlight the fact that although many black men may be deeply devoted to the struggle against white supremacy and for black liberation, without serious, sustained, and simultaneous intersectional struggle against racism *and* sexism *and* capitalism, black liberation will be nothing more than, as Fanon (1968) put it in *The Wretched of the Earth*, "a fancy-dress parade and the blare of the trumpets" (147). Domination and discrimination would still be with us, part and parcel of our daily lived experiences and lived endurances, and nothing will have changed except for the color (and class or caste in some respects) of the oppressors. In Fanon's words, "There's nothing save a minimum of readaptation, a few reforms at the top, a flag waving: and down there at the bottom an undivided mass [of women, especially nonwhite women], still living in the middle ages, endlessly marking time" (147; see also "Feminist Fanonism" in Rabaka, 2010a, 217–70).

In "The Damnation of Women," as he invoked the names of the Haitian revolutionists Toussaint L'Ouverture and Jean Jacques Dessalines, Du Bois also called on Harriet Tubman, Sojourner Truth, and Mary Ann Shadd;

quoted anonymously his contemporary Anna Julia Cooper; and made veiled reference to Ida B. Wells (Du Bois, 1920, 175-78). Further, in an audacious turn of phrase, Du Bois placed the resistance activities of black women on a par with those of black men, going so far as to recall Sojourner Truth's classic query to Frederick Douglass—"Frederick, is God dead?"—when the black male-feminist abolitionist, in a moment of desperation, declared that African Americans would have to fight for their freedom by force of arms. Douglass is reported to have stated, "It must come to blood; they [enslaved Africans] must fight for themselves, and redeem themselves, or it would never be done." Truth was apparently troubled, according to Harriet Beecher Stowe and a host of white writers, by Douglass's radical tenor and questioned his faith in God, who—as Stowe's recounting of the story goes—she fervently believed would guide African Americans to an imminent victory over their enslavers and white supremacy (Douglass, 1994, 719; Painter, 1996, 160-63).

In recounting black history, Du Bois cast black women in revolutionary roles, not only in "The Damnation of Women," but also in "The Freedom of Womanhood" from *The Gift of Black Folk*. The struggle against African American enslavement and white supremacy was not simply waged by black men, but by black men *and* black women for all people of African descent and humanity as a whole. Du Bois (1995b) reminded his readers that although black women, those "long-suffering victims" and "burdened sisters," were "sweetly feminine," "unswervingly loyal," "desperately earnest" and "instinctively pure in body and soul," they were still an "army" leading "not only a moral, but an economic revolution" (298, 308). We witness here, once again, his recurring theme of highlighting the interconnections of racism, sexism, and capitalism by engaging the lifeworlds and life struggles of black women, consequently contributing to both black feminist sociology and intersectional sociology. Moreover, in his efforts to further emphasize the strength, resilience, and distinct social world of black women, Du Bois (1920) declared:

> No other women on earth could have emerged from the hell of force and temptation which once engulfed and still surrounds black women in America with half the modesty and womanliness that they retain. I have always felt like bowing myself before them in all abasement, searching to bring some tribute to these long-suffering victims, these burdened sisters of mine, whom the world, the wise, white world, loves to affront and ridicule and wantonly to insult. I have known the women of many lands and nations—I have known and seen and lived beside them, but none have I known more sweetly feminine, more unswervingly loyal, more desperately earnest, and more instinctively pure in body and in soul than the daughters of my black mothers. This, then—a little thing—to their memory and inspiration. (186)

Keeping in mind our above discussion of Du Bois's efforts to counter racist *and* sexist claims concerning black womanhood, note here how he highlighted "the wise, white world['s]" *anti-black racist misogyny*. The "wise, white world" includes both white men *and* white women. So, to speak of "the wise, white world['s]" *anti-black racist misogyny* is to speak of both white men and white women's hatred and domination of, or, at the least, their unceasing discrimination against black women. In this instance, Du Bois's pro-feminist politics points to the ways in which *race is gendered* and *gender is raced*, which, in other words, is to say that his black woman-centered social thought keeps a keen eye on the ways in which the combination of both white *and* male supremacy targets those persons who are black *and* female in a manner and to a degree much different than it does those persons who are white and female or black and male. Additionally, emphasis should be placed on the fact that Du Bois's work here does not in any way attempt to deny the sexism that white women have been forced to endure, or diminish the anti-black racism that black men have been plagued with. Du Bois is not so much concerned here with denying others' oppression as with turning his readers' attention to and accenting black women's *multiple oppressions* as a result of the intersections of racism *and* sexism *and* classism. Here we have come back to his emphasis on the heterogeneity of black lifeworlds and black lived experiences.

Where we saw that his focus in *The Philadelphia Negro* was on empirically and critically differentiating African American social classes, especially as they revolved around income, employment, and education, in "The Damnation of Women" Du Bois seemed to be determined to draw distinctions between the lifeworlds and life struggles of black women and white women, as well as black women and black men. This is sociologically significant insofar as in making distinctions between black women's lived experiences and lived endurances and those of either white women or black men, Du Bois not only demonstrated the ways in which *race is gendered* and *gender is raced* but, even more intellectually incendiary, he strongly stressed the ways in which black women constitute a *racially gendered class* whose lifeworlds and life struggles are markedly different from the other women of their gender, and the men of their race. If we were to interject into this analysis the fact that both white women and black men can and often do exploit, oppress, and violate black women as a result of their respective privileged relationships with one or more of the major interlocking systems of oppression (i.e., racism, sexism, capitalism, and/or colonialism), then we may be able to more clearly see why Du Bois's early intersectional sociology was simultaneously *inaugural*, *innovative*, and *insurgent*. To be black in a white supremacist society, as Du Bois argued in *The Souls of Black Folk*, is indeed to be seen and approached more as a problem than a person. Further, to be black in such a social world is to be perpetually plagued by that ever unasked question that is seemingly on the tip of every tongue at every turn: "How does it feel to be a problem?"

To be a woman in a male supremacist society, as Carole Pateman (1988) put it in *The Sexual Contract*, is to be seen and treated as a semi-citizen, if women are seen and treated as sometime-citizens at all. It is an experience that affords few luxuries and little or no illusions about ones' socially supposed place and "sex role," about men's power to discipline and punish women with impunity. However, to be a black woman in a white *and* male supremacist society, as Audre Lorde (1984) asserted in *Sister Outsider*, is to be seen and ever approached, not as one who is humanly different, but as one who is subhuman, one who is humanly deviant and deficient. Black women in white and male supremacist societies experience different, perhaps deeper forms of racist and sexist domination and discrimination because they register as the antithesis, as the combined embodiment of the negation of both whiteness and maleness.[4] To acknowledge *anti-black racist misogyny*, then, is to simply say as Lorde (1984) did, "Some problems we share as women, some we do not" (119). It is to talk of that long taboo topic in both feminist and womanist theory and praxis revolving around the difference(s) that race, racism, and antiracist struggle historically have made and continue currently to make in the lifeworlds and life struggles of nonwhite women, and African American women in particular.

Du Bois's contributions to black feminist and intersectional sociology are further distinguished by their emphasis on the political economy of racism and sexism in white and male supremacist capitalist societies. Early in his career, Du Bois noted the connections between capitalism, racism, and sexism. This is extremely unique when one considers the rigid racist and sexist sociological framework that most turn-of-the-twentieth-century social theorists (male and female) were operating out of (see introduction and chapter 1). Although in many respects quite crude by contemporary standards, Du Bois's sociological discourse can be said to have prefigured and provided a foundation for the study of race, gender, and class, as well as the critique of racism, sexism, and capitalism long touted by late twentieth- and early twenty-first-century intersectional sociologists. According to black feminist sociologist Cheryl Gilkes (1996), Du Bois developed a "critical sociology," which "emphasized that gender, race, and class intersected in the lives of black women to foster an important critical perspective or standpoint" (117, 112).

"Standpoint epistemology" is a term coined by feminist philosopher of science Sandra Harding (1991) in the mid-1980s to conceptually capture the fact that there are many different ways of knowing or coming to cognition.[5] Outside of academic philosophy, epistemology is often collapsed into methodology, even within the world of the sociology of knowledge, but where *methodology* generally refers to a specific set of rules or techniques utilized to guide the "scientific" study of, and the collection of data about, particular phenomena, in contrast, *epistemology* usually refers to what is already known about, and the different ways in which "scientific" researchers arrive at and critically analyze further knowledge—or, even more, what constitutes knowledge about or deeper knowledge—of particular phenomena.[6] "Standpoint epistemology," in essence, insurgently emerged as a philosophy of science in an effort to address not only the different ways in which researchers come to "know" something but, even more, it emphasizes the importance of the angle or perspective or "standpoint" from which certain phenomena is approached or engaged and in many instances changes or alters one's knowledge and experience of that phenomena. As has been repeatedly documented in the history of American sociology, African Americans and women (and especially *African American women*) who have advanced sociologies of their own lifeworlds and life struggles have been criticized for not being "disinterested," "detached," and "objective" enough in their studies. Constantly reprimanded for being "too close" to the subjects of their sociological inquiries, black and feminist (again, especially *black feminist*) sociologists were reminded of the insider/outsider research model, and because they lived and worked within blacks' or women's or black women's lifeworlds their intimacy with their subjects was ever ungraciously understood to automatically translate into researcher bias; the fact that blacks or women or, again, *black women* could be "objective" when utilizing the "scientific method" to gather and analyze data on blacks or women or black women, of course, went without saying. It was, indeed, a moot point, and suspicion of blacks' or women's or black women's "substandard" data collection and analysis, therefore, was raised as the reason for the sociological fraternity's *epistemic closure* or, rather, *epistemic unreceptiveness* to the "subjugated knowledge" that blacks, women, and, especially, black women produced.

Harding's work, however, points to the countless studies by white men studying white men, which have been very rarely called into question, let alone seriously "scientifically" problematized with regard to researcher bias. Admittedly, renowned sociologist of science Robert Merton addressed this issue in "Insiders and Outsiders: A Chapter in the Sociology of Knowledge" (1972), but, let us be clear here, he was obviously making a case for "outsiders"—meaning, white males studying, especially, nonwhites and non-males—from their supposed sociologically superior "objective" and more "scientific" standpoint. In other words, Merton was contending that those who are not members of a group can study and develop techniques to study (i.e., methodology) that group, as well as come to know (i.e., epistemology) the social problems or issues of that group with seemingly greater "scientific" objectivity and accuracy than members or, rather, the "insiders" of the group. Harding's standpoint theory, as well as the work of others, does not completely condemn Merton's sociology of knowledge as much as it challenges his emphasis on "outsiders'" supposed "greater" "objectivity" and his, whether implicit or explicit, critique of the "insider" within the sociological world. For example, she emphasizes that human beings' lifeworlds and lived experiences both configure and constrain what they can come to know and, I would assert, their lifeworlds and lived experiences also impact and influence their cognition—that is, the process or processes through which they come to know what they know. In other words, the knowers are inextricable from their knowledge and, even more, they are inextricable from the knowledge they produce and share with others. Furthermore, something very similar could be said about the process(es) through which they come to acquire their knowledge (cognition).

As the previous chapters on Du Bois's rural and urban sociology and sociology of race revealed, he was quite cognizant of the fact that he was frequently both an "insider" and an "outsider" in his investigations of the "Negro problem." For instance, *The Souls of Black Folk* clearly indicates that his lived experiences and lived endurances of anti-black racism qualified him as an "insider." Recall that in *The Souls of Black Folk* he went so far as to write, "And, finally, need I add that I who speak here am bone of the bone and flesh of the flesh of them that live within the Veil." However, in *The Philadelphia Negro* his *interpretive elitism* and *bourgeois Eurocentrism* unquestionably qualified him as an "outsider" with respect to many aspects of the black masses and black working class's lifeworlds and life struggles. However, what is truly striking about Du Bois's evolving transdisciplinary discourse is that it demonstrates that he was able to transcend a great deal of his early *interpretive elitism* and *bourgeois Eurocentrism* to such an elevated extent that he was eventually able to not only inaugurate *intersectional sociology centered around the study of race, gender, and class and the critique of racism, sexism, and capitalism*, but also he was ultimately able make both *innovative epistemological and methodology contributions* to the discursive communities of history, sociology, political science, economics, and what we now know as "African American studies," among others. For example, buried in the January 1942 edition of *American Historical Review* is a long-overlooked book review by Du Bois (1942) in which he upbraids Robert Austin Warner, one of the most prominent political scientists of his epoch, for "almost flippantly" writing a "rambling social study [*New Haven Negroes: A Social History*] of over three hundred pages of which less than half are really germane to the subject" (377).

Du Bois began his barrage by stating outright, "I do not think that Mr. Warner's book is an adequate study of any of these problems [i.e., 'Negro problems'], and least of all does it give a picture of the inner psychological development of this group of Negroes" (376). Obviously referring to what he dubbed "double-consciousness" in *The Souls of Black Folk*, Du Bois asserted that it is important to always consider the "inner psychological development" of black folk when undertaking critical studies of any aspect of black lifeworlds and black life struggles. His critique of Warner, and by extension his critique of white social scientists who claim to be cloaked in "scientific objectivity," was two-fold: both epistemological and methodological. On the one hand, Du Bois was critical of Warner's methodology, unequivocally contending: "I find in Mr. Warner's study no sense of unity or growth, no careful digestion or arrangement of his material, no conception of the inner reactions of this changing and developing group of human beings, and no comprehension of the drama involved. Some social students seem to think that because the scientist may not be emotional he has, therefore, no call to study emotion. This, of course, is a ridiculous *non sequitur*" (377). By calling into question Warner's "digestion and arrangement of his material," Du Bois was clearly taking a swipe at what he felt was Warner's technical and analytical inattention to the "inner reactions of this changing and developing group of human beings." There are in fact rules which must guide scientific research conducted on human beings (i.e., their humanity, history and culture must be acknowledged at the outset of the study, especially with regard to investigations of exploited and oppressed groups) and, in so many words, Du Bois was saying that Warner and his white social scientist colleagues frequently failed to observe these basic "scientific" regulations when they investigated black lifeworlds and black lived experiences. This meant that the bulk of their so-called scientific studies on the "Negro Problem" were discursively deformed as a result of methodological deficiencies stemming from a—whether conscious or unconscious—disregard for black humanity, black history, and black culture and the ways in which anti-black racism encouraged blacks' internalization of *the diabolical dialectic of white superiority and black inferiority* and deformed their "inner psychological development" and "inner reactions," once again, both of which are clearly conceptually connected to what Du Bois famously dubbed "double-consciousness" in *The Souls of Black Folk*.

On the other hand, Du Bois's critique of Warner and white social scientists' supposed "objectivity" was unswervingly aimed at the epistemological issues inherent in their methodologically deficient and discursively deformed studies of black lifeworlds and black lived experiences. Almost as if directly critiquing Merton's "Insiders and Outsiders" article close to a quarter of a century before it was published, Du Bois leveled his assault against the exclusive and uncritical utilization of the "outsider" approach to acquire alleged "unemotional" and "objective" epistemological insights. Concluding his review of Warner's work, he sternly stated:

> Mr. Warner impresses me as writing of the Negro group from the outside looking in, which is almost inevitable. I do not say that the only person who can

write of England must be an Englishman, or that only Japanese should write of Japan; but I would insist that if a person is writing of a group to which he is socially and culturally alien, he must have some extraordinary gifts of insight. This Mr. Warner conspicuously lacks. He is not unsympathetic with Negroes nor in the slightest way inimical, but, on the other hand, he betrays no iota of real comprehension of what it meant to be a Negro in New Haven during the eighteenth, nineteenth, and twentieth centuries. The New Haven Negroes deserve a better study than Mr. Warner has given them. (377)

So that there is no misunderstanding here, emphasis should be placed on the fact that Du Bois did not in any way argue that "if a person is writing of a group to which he [or she] is socially and culturally alien," he or she simply should not research or write on that group. Quite the contrary, Du Bois's contention cuts to the core of the epistemological issues at hand because it stresses the need for researchers to not only thoroughly familiarize themselves with the lifeworlds and life struggles (i.e., the humanity, history, and culture) of the group they seek to study, but it also emphasizes that researchers need to always and ever remain *epistemically open* to the "subjugated knowledge" emerging from the "insiders'" own interpretations of their lived experiences and lived endurances. In essence, Du Bois concluded by saying that both the "insider" and the "outsider" approaches to social phenomena have their conceptual and cognitive strengths and weaknesses. Hence, he said that the "outsider" approach to "alien" or foreign cultures and societies is viable, but only if the researcher has "extraordinary gifts of insight." In order to obtain "extraordinary gifts of insight" the researcher must sincerely and intensely immerse himself in the history and culture of the group he seeks to study.

As was witnessed in our discussion of "The Negroes of Farmville" and *The Philadelphia Negro*, Du Bois's early sociological discourse demonstrates that he was conscious of his status as an "insider," as one who dwelled within the world of the Veil. He used his "insider's" insight to conduct many of the first empirical social scientific studies of African American lifeworlds, life chances, and life struggles. However, as our discussion of *The Philadelphia Negro* also revealed, he recognized the value of social scientific objectivity and, consequently, innovatively developed several research methods that enabled him to epistemologically take advantage of his "insider" status while simultaneously methodologically making the most of social scientific objectivity. My readers must bear in mind that Du Bois's initial empirical social scientific research (between 1895 and 1915) was squarely situated within the world of "objective," "dispassionate," and "detached" late nineteenth- and early twentieth-century social science, as he himself admitted in both *Dusk of Dawn* and *The Autobiography of W. E. B. Du Bois*, sternly stating, "One could not be a calm, cool, and detached scientist while Negroes were lynched, murdered and starved" (Du Bois, 1968a, 222, 1968b, 67–68). In other words, African Americans' lived experiences and lived endurances, especially of white supremacist and anti-black racist exploitation, oppression, and violence, at the turn of the twentieth century demanded much more than an "outsider's" social scientific "objectivity" but also an "insider's" insurgent intersectional sociology that was capable of *connecting* and *combining* the study of race and the critique of racism with the study of gender and class and the critique of sexism and capitalism. As the Atlanta University studies conducted and published under his auspices reveal, Du Bois employed both an "insider's" and "outsider's" methodology to inaugurate both intersectional sociology and his own inchoate and extremely early version of what we now know as "standpoint epistemology." It is in this way that Du Bois's dialectical social science contributes to both sociological meta-methodology and transdisciplinary standpoint epistemology. And, although his work indicates that his own "extraordinary gifts of insight" with respect to black women's lifeworlds and life struggles were frequently crude and riddled with contradictions and controversy, it is extremely important to acknowledge that Du Bois's dialectical sociology indeed does contribute to contemporary standpoint epistemology, sociology of knowledge, black feminist sociology, and intersectional sociology.

Feminist sociologist Betsy Lucal (1996) asserts that "[h]ad Du Bois ignored women in his work, he would not have been exceptional. The fact that women figure prominently in so much of his work sets him apart from his contemporaries, and, indeed, from not a small number of sociologists today" (199). Du Bois believed that women, and black women in particular, were (within white and male supremacist societies) a "subordinate group," who by dint of hard labor and harsh living conditions had developed a distinct and ever-intersecting race, gender, and class consciousness. With "[a]ll the virtues of her sex . . . utterly ignored," "the primal black All-Mother of men," "the African mother" endured, in Du Bois's (1920) account, "[t]he crushing weight of slavery" only to be resubjugated in a world that claimed to "worship both virgins and mothers," but "in the end despises motherhood and despoils virgins" (164–66, 169, 171). African American women, in the period after *de jure* American slavery, were flung into a world where they were dominated and discriminated against simultaneously on account of their race and their gender. Their subordination, then, was inherent—though implicit on many accounts—in the evolving social ontology of white and male supremacist U.S. society.[7] The chronic experience and effects of the interlocking and intersecting nature of racism, sexism, classism, and, as of late, heterosexism have led many black feminists to posit that black women experience a reality that is distinctly different from the lived experiences and lived endurances of those persons who are not black *and* female. Theories of "double," "triple," and "multiple" jeopardy abound but curiously, rarely if ever has Du Bois's male-feminism and innovative intersectional sociology figured prominently in this discourse.

From his early empirical studies through to his posthumously published autobiography, Du Bois spent the great bulk of his life and intellectual energy wrestling with various social "problems," different forms of domination and discrimination, and although he often missed the mark in his personal life (I am almost tempted to say, in his personal "affairs") with women, specifically with respect to his wife and daughter, there remains much that can be and, I honestly believe, should be salvaged from his long-overlooked innovative intersectional sociology and contributions to black feminist sociology.[8] To leave Du Bois to the traditional "great race man" or "pioneering" sociologist of race line of thinking is, to my logic, to throw the baby out with the bath water (or, at the least, to clandestinely and repeatedly bathe the baby in dirty water while claiming that the water is clean). The more radical and critical thing to do is to search for and salvage what we can from Du Bois's sociological discourse that can aid us in our current endeavors to develop black feminist sociology, the sociology of racially gendered classes, and intersectional sociology. This chapter, then, is an earnest effort to build on and go beyond Du Bois's often unformed (and at some points seemingly uninformed) male-feminism, as it is aimed at bringing his antisexist social thought into discursive dialogue with the work of several of the key black feminist and intersectional sociologists (e.g., Gloria Anzaldúa, Patricia Hill Collins, Delores Aldridge, Rose Brewer, Deborah King, Bonnie Thornton Dill, and Maxine Baca Zinn) who have popularized the interlocking and intersecting race-gender-class-sexuality paradigm within the world of contemporary sociology.

As with any epistemological standpoint or sociological method there are things that are positive and others that are negative in Du Bois's discourse, which, of course, brings us back to the question of dialectics. A dialectical approach to Du Bois enables us to simultaneously acknowledge and critique the sexism he practiced at specific intervals in his private life, while appreciatively focusing on his production and promotion of male-feminist and other antisexist positions and policies in his public and political life. This dialectical approach also opens objective interpreters of Du Bois's discourse to the fact that he—as is common with many men struggling against their sexist socialization and internalization of sexism—may very well have had instances of sexist thought and behavior in both his public and private lives.

Were we to highlight Du Bois's sexism without accenting his antisexism (or vice versa) we would be practicing and producing the very type of one-dimensional interpretation and uncritical thought that standpoint epistemology and intersectional sociology purport to be combating and offering ethical, epistemological, and radical political alternatives. Because he has long been cast in the "great race man" cloak, it is difficult for many Du Bois scholars and critics to look at his life and work from multidimensional and transdisciplinary angles. What I wish to accent here, above all else, are those aspects of Du Bois's lifework that contribute to the development of black feminist sociology, the sociology of racially gendered classes, and intersectional sociology, which means that I am primarily concerned with those aspects of his discourse that critique domination and provide the promise of liberation. The Du Bois that I am interested in did not shy away from the forms of domination that women, and particularly black women, experienced as a result of white and male supremacy. Surely his essays such as "The Work of Negro Women in Society," "The Black Mother," "Hail Columbia!," "Woman Suffrage," "The Damnation of Women," and "Sex and Racism," to name only a few, are sincere testimonies and somber testaments that affirm his claim in the last paragraph of "The Damnation of Women": "I honor the women of my race" (Du Bois, 1920, 185).[9]

Observing the fact that "women of African descent have struggled with the multiple realities of gender, racial, and economic or caste oppression," Joy James, similar to Cheryl Gilkes, contends that black women have "created . . . space for a more viable democracy" (James and Sharpley-Whiting, 2000, 1; see also Gilkes, 1996, 114, 116–17). Democracy, as we witnessed in the previous chapter, was one of the most prevalent and pervasive themes in Du Bois's discourse, and he argued that it has not and will never exist so long as any human group, no matter how small or so-called minority, is excluded from the civic decision-making processes of its respective national and international communities. Du Bois included women when he spoke of "peasants," "laborers," and "socially damned" persons who must always be considered if the United States, or any nation for that matter, is to achieve anything remotely close to "real" democracy. For instance, in *Darkwater* in the chapter entitled "Of the Ruling of Men," Du Bois (1920) asserted:

> Today we are gradually coming to realize that government by temporary coalition of small and diverse groups may easily become the most efficient method of expressing the will of man and of setting the human soul free. . . . [N]o nation, race, or sex, has a monopoly of ability or ideas . . . no human group is so small as to deserve to be ignored as a part, and as an integral and respected part, of the mass of men . . . above all, no group of twelve million black folk, even though they are at the physical mercy of a hundred million white majority, can be deprived of a voice in government and of the right to self-development without a blow at the very foundations of all democracy and all human uplift. . . . [N]o modern nation can shut the gates of opportunity in the face of its women, its peasants, its laborers, or its socially damned. How astounded the future world-citizen will be to know that as late as 1918 great and civilized

nations were making desperate endeavor to confine the development of ability and individuality to one sex,—that is, to one-half of the nation; and he [or she] will probably learn that a similar effort to confine humanity to one race lasted a hundred years longer. (153–54)

We see here an emphasis not only on racial oppression, but also on "sex" or gender domination, as well as a critique of many whites and males' belief that they somehow have a "monopoly of ability or ideas." Du Bois directed his intellectual attention to the plight of black women, and they were, so far as he was concerned, "an integral and respected part" of his beloved "black folk." In fact, the black woman, "the primal black All-Mother of men," could not and would not be held in check, neither by white nor male supremacy because, Du Bois sociologically surmised, she was leading both a "moral" and an "economic" revolution (179). Although often rendered invisible within the white male-dominated sociological world of late nineteenth- and early twentieth-century America, Gilkes (1996) contends that "for Du Bois, black women represent a unique force for progressive change in the United States" because of the degree(s) to which they experience and endure various forms of racial oppression, gender domination and discrimination, and economic exploitation (113).

Where most of the male social theorists of his age placed a greater emphasis on class theory, class formation, class consciousness, and the impact of political economy on culture and society, Du Bois innovatively engaged the intersections of class, race, *and* gender utilizing black lived experiences and black liberation thought and practices as a paradigm for his sociological theories and conception of an ever-expanding, all-inclusive democracy. Which is also to say that Du Bois's ever evolving conception of an all-inclusive democracy (as opposed to a *herrenrasse demokratie*, or master race democracy) was dialectically informed by his innovative intersectional sociology. Gilkes goes further to note that "Du Bois's vision pointed to a society that could confront, respect, and embrace the gifts of all" (133). His was a sociological imagination that did not limit itself to the issues of the white male working class(es), as was the custom in his day, but audaciously sought to develop "a broad theory of history that concerned itself with the development of democracy and of American culture" (114). Going against the sociological grain of his times, Du Bois staunchly opposed the "subordination of the problems of gender and race in the development of sociological theory," Gilkes importantly observes (117). Hence, here again, we see that Du Bois's sociological discourse is distinguished from that of classical European and European American sociologists, who by most accounts relegated race and gender, as well as racism and sexism, not merely to the sociological margin, but to intellectual oblivion. When race and gender did or does register in classical and contemporary Eurocentric and patriarchal sociological discourse they are seen as social negatives that somehow, almost miraculously, fell from the sky, as though Europeans were not the architects of the concept of race and racism (as we now experience and endure them), and as though men were not the masterminds behind gender domination and discrimination against women and other men who embrace and endorse what bell hooks (1991) calls "alternative masculinities."

It was precisely "the problems of gender and race" that Karl Marx, Emile Durkheim, and Max Weber—the "three names [that] rank above all others," according to esteemed British sociologist Anthony Giddens (1971, vii)—downplayed in their "development of sociological theory." Du Bois's sociological discourse is distinguished by the fact that it sought solutions to the problems of racism and sexism, while keeping a keen and critical eye on the ways in which capitalism deforms and ultimately destroys the prospects for an authentically multicultural, transethnic, and transgendered democracy. On the preoccupation with, and prevalence of "the problem of class" in early modern social theory, Gilkes (1996) caustically comments, "Although issues of class, race, and gender ought to be addressed, most early social theory only focused on class and not on gender or race. In spite of its prominence in American society, the problem of race relations was not accorded the same theoretical importance as were issues centered on class, change, and social structure" (113).

Considering Du Bois's intense emphasis on both race and gender, it is not hard to see how his early intersectional sociology was seen to be suspect by sociology's early fraternity—that is, when or if his work was deemed to be "sociology" at all. This, however, leads us to call into question sociology's early, almost obsessive interest in "class, change, and social structure," while willfully overlooking the ways in which each of the aforementioned interconnected and intersected with race and gender or, more specifically, racism and sexism. Questions concerning what kind of "change" and, further, for which "class" early sociologists were seeking such "change," abound. Considering the many levels and shifting dynamics of the "social structure," we are also left wondering which aspects of the "social structure" the early sociologists were seeking to "change," and in which class's interest. Why is it that sociology's white "founding fathers" were unable to see what Du Bois's early intersectional sociology indicates that he so clearly saw and, even more, experienced and endured? It seems to be the case that what Du Bois identified as "social problems" were distinctly different from what white sociologists at the turn of the twentieth century deemed to be "social problems." From his early intersectional sociological perspective, "social problems" did not only emerge from the consequences of capitalism and class struggle, although he indeed did come to critically understand the importance of capitalism's "multiple" inextricable interconnections with racism and sexism. The "social problems" revolving around race and racism *and* gender and sexism were equally important, from Du Bois's early intersectional sociological angle, and they desperately demanded "solutions" right along with the "social problems" emerging from capitalism and class struggle. Recall, if you will, in "The Damnation of Women," Du Bois succinctly said, "The uplift of women is, *next to* the problem of the color-line and the peace movement, our greatest modern cause" (emphasis added).

Above when he employs the phrase "next to," Du Bois highlights how several "social problems" are not casually related simply because they are "social problems" in some free-floating general sense but, even more, they are intensely inextricable and unequivocally interrelated because they incessantly intersect and interconnect, influencing and informing (or, rather, *reforming*) each other, thus making their impact and effects as "social problems" that much more pervasive and profound, that much more diabolical and socially detrimental. The sentence that immediately follows the above quote from "The Damnation of Women" reads, "When, now, two of these movements—women and color—combine in one, the combination has deep meaning." In light of his express emphasis on "two of these movements—women and color," it would seem, then, that I would not be stretching it too much to say that the previously quoted sentence could be interpreted as Du Bois saying that the "uplift of women" and the "problem of the color-line" present sociologists with two of "our greatest modern cause[s]" and, what is more, when these two "great modern cause[s]" are "combined in one"—as they are in the lifeworlds and life struggles of nonwhite women, and I am thinking here especially of black women—then the "combination has deep meaning" and, perhaps, even deeper discursive and intersectional sociological significance.

If we are willing to concede that Gilkes—who, by the way, is an endowed MacArthur professor of sociology at Colby College—has assessed the history of sociology correctly when she contends that most early sociologists were preoccupied with and primarily focused on "class, change, and social structure," then the implications for standpoint epistemology and the intersectional emphasis of Du Bois's sociological discourse need no further explanation. Clearly, as the chapter on his rural and urban sociology demonstrated, Du Bois was no stranger to the sociology of social class and, I must remind my readers, even within the world of the sociology of class his work is distinguished by its emphasis on *the inseparable interconnections of industrial, monopoly, corporate, and/or advanced industrial capitalism with the rote racialization and impact of anti-black racism on African American class formations and class struggles.* Here, then, is precisely and exactly why I have characterized Du Bois's sociology as early and innovative intersectional sociology that, from what I can gather, helped to establish *the simultaneous study of race, gender, and class,* and *the simultaneous critique of racism, sexism, and capitalism* within the world of sociology before the close of the first quarter of the twentieth century.

Emphasis on, and astute articulations of, intersectional sociology reemerged in the last quarter of the twentieth century, primarily under the guise of black feminist, Latina/Chicana, and other nonwhite women's sociology. However, the late twentieth-century reemergence of intersectional sociology all but left Du Bois's embryonic intersectional sociological discourse in the lurch and, as a result, we witness here once again the ways in which *epistemic apartheid* extends beyond the white sociological fraternity and reaches across several sociological subdisciplines to touch the sociology of gender in general, and black feminist sociology in particular. Angela Hattery and Earl Smith (2005) correctly contend that "Du Bois influenced the discipline of sociology to the extent that . . . his work in the area of race, class and gender conceptually and cognitively," although long-overlooked, demands that contemporary intersectional sociologists "not only recognize . . . him, pulling him from the dustbin of American sociology for pioneering these theoretical arguments (and empirical studies) but, more so, showing the *contemporaneous* nature of his work" (3, emphasis in original). The "contemporaneous nature" of Du Bois's work, and specifically his *comparative and conjunctive analysis* that combined the social scientific study of race, gender, and class with the systematic critique of racism, sexism, and capitalism, continues to distinguish his sociological discourse not simply from the large majority of the sociologists of his turbulent times but from the large majority of the sociologists of the late twentieth century and early twenty-first century.

As discussed in the previous chapter, when and where Du Bois is discussed in sociology his work is usually *conceptually quarantined* to the "Negro Question" or, rather, the "Race Problem." The interpretation, reception, and rearticulation of his polymathic and polyvocal historical sociology, political sociology, rural sociology, urban sociology, sociology of culture, sociology of class, sociology of gender, sociology of religion, sociology of education, and sociology of crime are, thus, one-dimensionally and in the most intellectually disingenuous manners reduced to and rendered "sociology of race" or "black sociology," which ultimately translates into the *academic ghettoization*, at best, or the *intellectual niggerification*, at worst, of Du Bois and his sociological discourse. Of course, the academic ghettoization of Du Bois's sociological discourse makes it that much easier and "acceptable" for highbrow sociology professors and students of each and every human hue (including mentally misguided and conceptually incarcerated black sociology professors and students) to ignore, exclude, or completely erase Du Bois from their sociological discourses.

This means, then, that because Du Bois has long been either absent from most of the sociological curriculum, especially in the United States, and also because when and where his work is engaged it is approached primarily and almost exclusively with regard to its contribution to the sociology of race, his innovative intersectional sociology has been rendered intellectually invisible and he has never received the recognition he is due for inaugurating one of the most intellectually extraordinary and conceptually compelling critical paradigms in both the national and international history of sociology. I write all of this quite solemnly, without one hint of hagiography or hyperbole, which anyone who has ever read any of my Du Bois studies will surely tell you is absolutely not a part of the critical relationship and dialectical rapport that I have developed with Du Bois and his discourse over the years, but, even more, this is written with an intense emphasis on intellectual honesty, intellectual integrity and, of course, my earnest efforts to continue the struggle *against epistemic apartheid*.

With all of the brouhaha surrounding, and the brandishing of esoteric analyses regarding the centennial of *The Souls of Black Folk* in 2003 it is easy to lose sight of the fact that Du Bois was so much more than an extremely eloquent "essayist" or "founding father" of the modern civil rights movement. Truth be told, several sociological circles joined in the centenary commemorations, convening panels at professional symposia and commissioning distinguished lectures on Du Bois (a couple of which, it should be very humbly said, featured the present author). However, I could not agree with Hattery and Smith more when they critically contend that contemporary Du Boisian sociologists must move beyond repeatedly railing about how horribly Du Bois's discourse has been ignored or neglected within the world of sociology—a world which, I remind my readers, he undeniably helped to establish in the United States—and begin to astutely and eruditely identify *why, how*, and *what*, in the most amazing intellectual history-making manner, he contributed to sociology. Staying stuck on Du Bois's sociological negation will never be enough and, in point of fact, it does not in any way provide answers to the aforementioned questions. Hattery and Smith (2005) insistently interject:

> Yet, what is not addressed is not so much the absence of Du Bois from mainstream sociology but rather, why is it that we need to know who he was and what he did? Conversely, it is not enough to repeat over and over the aforementioned but begin to situate that Du Bois made considerable contributions to the main canon of sociology similar in ways to the work of Max Weber, Karl Marx, and Emile Durkheim. For Du Bois the real answer lays not so much in who he was but the lasting contributions of his work for understanding long-term, systematic, structured inequities that unfold along race, class, and gender lines. (6)

Sociologically black women's lifeworlds and life struggles provided Du Bois with an almost ideal set of social variables through which to critically comprehend the "long-term, systematic, structured inequities that unfold along race, class, and gender lines." Because of the sociohistorical fact of their suffering, what black feminist sociologist Deborah King (1995) calls the "multiple jeopardy" of being black, female, poor, and perpetually hypersexualized—which, in other words, is to say that black women to varying degrees simultaneously experience and endure racism, sexism, and the ravaging effects of economic exploitation, whether under capitalism or colonialism, among other existential issues—Du Bois understood women of African descent to be the almost ideal agents of radical democratic social (and later *radical democratic socialist*) change. In black women and their lived experiences and lived endurances, Du Bois found radical subjects for social change and the spreading of radical democratic thought and practice. Although rarely referred to, Gilkes (1996) importantly asserts, "Du Bois's perspectives on African American women anticipated and influenced concepts and ideas we currently use to examine the intersection of gender, race, and class with reference to African American women" (132). Helping to corroborate my above contentions concerning Du Bois's inauguration of intersectional sociology, she continues, "his work is the earliest self-consciously sociological interpretation of the role of African American women as agents of social change" and, therefore, offers contemporary sociologists of gender in general, and black feminist sociologists in particular, a multiperspective and transdiscplinary model on which to build an unrepentant and openly insurgent antiracist, antisexist, and anticapitalist intersectional sociology (134).

In fact, when Du Bois's work on women is taken together and juxtaposed with his research on race and class, African American women irrefutably emerge as integral parts of all three of the "great revolutions" he prophesied (e.g., in *Darkwater, The Gift of Black Folk, Dark Princess, Black Reconstruction, Black Folk, Then and Now, Color and Democracy,* and *The World and Africa*) which must take place if America (and the wider world) was to truly achieve democracy. Observe below how each of the social "revolutions" that he contended black women would be central to emerged out if his overarching intersectional sociology: the first was the revolution against racism or the color-line; second was the revolution against sexism, and specifically patriarchy; and third and finally was the revolution against economic exploitation, which, from Du Bois's perspective, included both capitalism and racial colonialism. Here we see most clearly how Du Bois went about confronting and contesting the major existential issues of his epoch (and ours): racism, sexism, and capitalism.

Of the "great revolutions," first there was the revolt of the masses of nonwhite folk against racism, racial colonialism, and the color-line. This, of course, translated itself in Du Bois's discourse into his anticolonialist and antiracist writings in *The Moon, The Horizon, The Crisis, Phylon,* and *The*

National Guardian, among other publications, and into public intellectualism and political activism. Black women were cast in a "messianic" or "prophetic" role in the revolution against racial domination and discrimination because Du Bois believed that their sufferings "provided them with a legitimate voice of challenge" (Gilkes, 1996, 120). Who knew then, and who would know now, perhaps more so than most other classes of citizens, the deficiencies of U.S. democracy than those persons simultaneously experiencing white and male supremacy, as well as economic super-exploitation? Prefiguring Patricia Collins's conception of "subjugated knowledge" (which she borrows from Foucault), Du Bois attempted to accent and highlight the "hidden" and/or "suppressed" knowledge produced by black women as they confronted, combated, and often contradicted both white and male supremacy, as well as the conundrums of capitalism (see Collins, 1998, 95–123; 2000a, 51–90).

The second "great revolution" that black women were to participate in, according to Du Bois, especially in "The Damnation of Women" and "The Freedom of Womanhood," was the revolution of the "freeing" of womanhood. In his 1915 classic "Woman Suffrage," he unequivocally asserted, "The actual work of the world today depends more largely upon women than upon men." Consequently, he continued with weighted words, "this man-ruled world faces an astonishing dilemma. . . . The meaning of the twentieth century is the freeing of the individual soul; the soul longest in slavery and still in the most disgusting and indefensible slavery is the soul of womanhood" (Du Bois, 1995b, 297–98). He contended that it was the "new revolutionary ideals" of women, and especially African American women, "which must in time have vast influence on the thought and action of this land [the United States]" (311). Here he is clearly drawing from the social theories of several pioneering black feminist theorists of his era, almost all associated with the black women's club movement in one way or another—for example, Anna Julia Cooper, Ida B. Wells, Josephine St. Pierre Ruffin, Frances Ellen Watkins Harper, and Maria Stewart, among others. Ever the serious student of African American sociopolitical thought and culture, Du Bois was keenly conscious of African American women's liberation thought traditions: from the feminist abolitionism of Maria Stewart, Sojourner Truth, and Frances Harper to the black women's club and civil rights activism of Anna Julia Cooper, Ida. B. Wells, and Mary Church Terrell. In fact, taken by themselves, "The Damnation of Women" and "The Freedom of Womanhood" make it virtually impossible to deny Du Bois's—again, however contradictory and controversial—relationship with late nineteenth- and early twentieth-century black feminist theory and praxis. As was discussed above, the black women's club movement's central organization, the National Association of Colored Women (NACW), literally provided Du Bois with a paradigm and point of departure in which to not only develop his own distinct brand of male-feminism and inaugurate intersectional sociology but it also ultimately enabled him to link his increasingly insurgent intersectional sociology to radical political praxis: first, with his leadership in the Niagara movement, and then, second, with his leadership in the National Association for the Advancement of Colored People (NAACP). All of this helps to highlight, once again, that "Du Bois believed in the importance of an activist social science for the growth and development of democracy," as Gilkes (1996, 115) correctly contends, which also connects with Aldon Morris's assertion in the previous chapter that Du Bois was most interested in "using sociology to emancipate the oppressed." As we have witnessed throughout this chapter, Du Bois certainly considered women as an integral part of "the oppressed" and also as special contributors to not only women's decolonization and women's liberation but, even more, to human liberation and democratic social transformation.

The last of the "three great revolutions" Du Bois maintained that black women were to play a pivotal role in was the revolution against economic exploitation, particularly contemporary capitalism. Du Bois (1995b) asserted that "[t]he emancipation of man is the emancipation of labor and the emancipation of labor is the freeing of that basic majority of workers who are yellow, brown, and black" (606). Moreover, in "slavery," in "concubinage," as cooks, nurses, and washerwomen, Du Bois (1970a) recognized the significance of black women as workers, stating in "The Freedom of Womanhood," that the issue of "economic independence is . . . the central fact in the struggle of women for equality. In the earlier days the slave woman was found to be economically as efficient as the man" (142). Then, historically moving from the past to the present, he reiterated the significance of black women as workers and the ways in which their work disrupted the psychopathic sanctions of the white supremacist patriarchal capitalist social world: "In our modern industrial organization the work of women is being found as valuable as that of men. . . . The Negro woman as laborer, as seamstress, as servant and cook, has come into competition with the white male laborer and with the white woman worker." Furthermore, he stated, directly hitting the heart of the matter, the "fact that she could and did replace the white man as laborer, artisan and servant, showed the possibility of the white women doing the same thing, and led to it." In fact, he thundered in conclusion, "The usual sentimental arguments against women at work were not brought forward in the case of Negro womanhood." With these often-overlooked words, Du Bois revealed that black women workers were *racially gendered* in such a way that their race trumped their gender in *the white supremacist patriarchal capitalist public sphere*, while their centuries-spanning endurance of *anti-black racist rape* and other forms of *white supremacist sexual violence* as "concubines" and the like illustrated the ways in which their gender trumped their race in *the white supremacist patriarchal capitalist private sphere*. In addition, Du

Bois's historical sociological discourse here also inverts the conventional white feminist revisionist histories where white women are always and ever seen as the gender conscious "wonder women" and "women warriors" leading the gender unconscious and sexism-submissive black (and other nonwhite) women to critical gender or feminist consciousness. Quite the contrary, Du Bois historically documented that it was African American women who were arguably the first women to be a part of the U.S. workforce en masse and that it was black women who paved the way for other women to be seen and taken seriously as workers. Additionally, this last point helps to highlight how black women's lived experiences and lived endurances challenged not only white supremacist patriarchal notions of "a woman's place," but also, more specifically, many black men, white women, and other nonwhite women's misconceptions about "a woman's place" (142).

Du Bois's contributions to black feminist sociology point to the historical fact that black women were attempting to grasp and grapple with distinctly different social and political issues than their white counterparts, although he openly acknowledged that both groups of women were discriminated against on account of their gender. Race, racism, and antiracist struggle made and continues to make distinct differences in the lifeworlds, life struggles, and liberation theory and praxis of African American women, and this is especially true when coupled with their simultaneous struggles for gender justice and an end to economic exploitation. To put it another way, gender *and* racial domination and discrimination, and the theory and praxis developed to combat these oppressions, have historically and continue currently to serve as central determining factors in African American women's lifeworlds and lived experiences, and it is this stubborn sociohistorical fact, combined with the contradictions of capitalism and/or colonialism, that have routinely put many black feminists at loggerheads with the inexcusable racial lethargy and lacunae of ruling race/class or, rather, white feminists and their brand of feminism.

In many ways black women's lifeworlds and life struggles are unique when one critically considers that they have been not only relegated to the margins within feminist theory, women's studies, and the wider women's liberation movement, but also, truth be told, they have been frequently ignored or rendered invisible in African American studies, the civil rights movement, the black power movement, and, as of late, the hip hop generation. In "Grounding with My Sisters: Patriarchy and the Exploitation of Black Women," Manning Marable (1983) discusses the double dilemma of black women both *within* and *without* their race, and *within* and *without* their gender:

> Black social history, as it has been written to date, has been profoundly patriarchal. The sexist critical framework of American white history has been accepted

by black male scholars; the reconstruction of our past, the reclamation of our history from the ruins, has been an enterprise wherein women have been too long segregated. Obligatory references are generally made to those "outstanding sisters" who gave some special contribution to the liberation of the "black man." Even these token footnotes probably do more harm than good, because they reinforce the false belief that the most oppressed victim of white racial tyranny has been *the black man*. . . . From the dawn of the slave trade until today, U.S. capitalism was both racist and sexist. The super-exploitation of black women became a permanent feature in American social and economic life, because sisters were assaulted simultaneously as workers, as blacks, and as women. (70, emphasis in original)

As we have witnessed throughout this chapter, Du Bois's insurgent intersectional sociological framework was one of the first to critically engage black women's simultaneous social statuses "as workers, as blacks, and as women." He increasingly focused on black women's role(s) in the "economic revolution," stating, our "black women toil and toil hard," and they "are a group of workers, fighting for their daily bread like men; independent and approaching economic freedom" (Du Bois, 1920, 180). It was not enough for black liberationists to struggle against anti-black racism and white supremacy; it was not enough for women liberationists to struggle against patriarchy or male supremacy; and it was not enough for Marxists and other left-leaning radicals to struggle against capitalist exploitation. What was needed was a critical comparative and conjunctive historical, political, sociological, and economic (i.e., a transdisciplinary) framework that took into consideration each of the aforementioned forms of domination and discrimination. For Du Bois, as a critical social theorist and radical political activist, a *real revolutionist* has the onerous task of critiquing society as a whole, not simply the parts of it that most inhibit and encumber the theorist's particular race, gender, and/or class. In "The Damnation of Women" and "The Freedom of Womanhood," among other articles and essays, Du Bois turned his readers' attention to the plight of black women, thus putting into principled practice his admonition that a truly *critical* social theorist critique society as a whole, not simply selected parts of it which most hinder and harm the theorist and their closest kin and kith.

CONCLUSION: DU BOIS, "THE SOUL OF WOMANHOOD," AND THE SOCIOLOGY OF GENDER—OR, A CONCLUDING ALMOST AUTOBIOGRAPHICAL COMMENT FROM A BLACK RADICAL POLITICAL MALE-FEMINIST SOCIOLOGIST

I began this chapter with an epigraph from Du Bois: "The meaning of the twentieth century is the freeing of the individual soul; the soul longest in slavery and still in the most disgusting and indefensible slavery is *the soul of womanhood*" (emphasis added). As I researched, wrote, and revised this chapter I was disheartened and, if I can be candid here, slipped in and out of states of deep depression when I came to the incontrovertible conclusion that this statement was equally as prophetic and profound as Du Bois's oft-quoted prophecy from *The Souls of Black Folk*: "The problem of the twentieth century is the problem of the color-line—the relation of the darker to the lighter races of men in Asia and Africa, in America and the islands of the sea." Both of these statements by Du Bois continue to ring true and remain as relevant at the opening of the twenty-first century as they were at the close of the twentieth century; hence, my previous emphasis on Du Bois and "the problems of the twenty-first century" (Rabaka, 2007b).

As we conclude, a couple of the recurring critical questions which we must solemnly ask ourselves present themselves: If, as the above commentary revealed, Du Bois indeed does make several contributions to the sociology of gender, how can these contributions be incorporated into, or boldly brought into critical dialogue with the major discursive communities of contemporary sociology of gender in particular, and contemporary sociology in general? If we are willing to concede Du Bois's contributions—one last time, however contradictory and controversial—to what is currently being called "black feminist sociology," then what would be the best way (or ways), in the most patently nonpaternalistic and earnestly antisexist manner, to assert that Du Bois's sociological discourse possibly offers contemporary black feminist sociologists an alternative paradigm and point of departure to deepen and develop their extremely important area of sociological inquiry? And, lastly, if any aspects of my contention concerning Du Bois's inauguration of intersectional sociology were found to be compelling (and I humbly pray that they were), then, does not Du Bois deserve long-overdue recognition for establishing arguably one of the most intellectually extraordinary critical paradigms and series of methodological procedures in the history of not simply American sociology, but in the history of the wider world of sociology? How could contemporary intersectional sociology be strengthened by developing a critical dialogue with Du Bois's sociological discourse which, as was witnessed above, engaged many of the very same or, at the least, very similar social problems to which twenty-first-century intersectional sociologists are sincerely searching for solutions?

Du Bois seems to have possessed the ability to synthesize disparate discourses into his own somewhat sophisticated intersectional sociology. For instance, it is interesting to point out that although he initially drew from elite black women's work that cast bourgeois black women in leadership roles, work such as that of Anna Julia Cooper and many of the other members of the black women's club movement, he continued to deepen and develop his concepts of race, gender, and class, as well as his critiques of the political economy of racism and sexism in white supremacist patriarchal capitalist cultures and societies. Ultimately, Du Bois developed an insurgent intersectional sociological framework that transcended and transgressed, if you will, the gender (male) and class (bourgeois) elitism of his younger years (e.g., "The Negroes of Farmville," *The Philadelphia Negro*, and "The Talented Tenth"). Critically comparing Cooper and Du Bois's social theory, Joy James (1997) helps to drive this point home:

> Cooper's gender politics revolved around poor black women's struggles and elite black women's agency. But Du Bois's evolving class politics allowed him to, theoretically, attribute greater agency to *poor* black women workers and laborers. Du Bois's later writings surpass Cooper's 1892 work in democratizing agency. Cooper repudiates masculine elites, or privileged black male intellectuals. However, her repudiations do not extend to feminine elites, or privileged black female intellectuals. Cooper countered the dominance of male elites with that of female elites and remained somewhat oblivious of the limitations of her caste and class-based ideology. Cooper's 1892 book [*A Voice from the South*] failed to argue that the intellectual and leadership abilities of black women laborers equaled those of black women college graduates, whereas Du Bois's later revisions of the Talented Tenth included non-elite black women and men. In this respect, we see that Du Bois's maturing politics were less hampered by the cultural conservatism of bourgeois notions of respectability for (black) women. (45, emphasis in original)

It is not my intention here to (re)interpret and (re)inscribe Du Bois as some sort of super antisexist social theorist. I am well aware of the ways in which an antisexist male perspective in a male supremacist society is not as suspect as an antisexist female perspective—although I would concede that an antisexist male perspective *is* suspect to a certain degree and that gender-progressive males are marginalized and ostracized in such a social world, despite the fact that they have never been marginalized and ostracized to the extent to which (openly antisexist) women have historically been in the said social world. However, and in all intellectual honesty, an antisexist male (with the most minute amount of academic credentials and/or institutional affiliation) can quickly become, in the minds of the ruling race/gender/class and their media machines in a male supremacist social world, an authoritative antisexist voice of reason. This, of course, is similar in many senses to the ways in which white "race traitors" and white antiracists are exalted as the definitive voices of antiracist reason and radical antiracist political practice in white supremacist society. Du Bois's discourse destabilizes and resists efforts to position him purely (and disingenuously I believe) as "race man" *or* "male-feminist," "Pan-Africanist" *or* "Marxist," or "black nationalist" *or* "integrationist" because—as I have elaborated above—he continuously deepened and developed the basic concepts and categories of his insurgent intersectional sociological framework and synthesized disparate radical political discourses into his own original critical theory of contemporary society: what I have referred to elsewhere as *Africana critical theory* or, rather, *the Africana tradition of critical theory* (Rabaka, 2007b, 2008a, 2009a, 2010a).

To read "The Conservation of Races," *The Souls of Black Folk*, *Darkwater*, and *Dusk of Dawn* is to read not merely studies in race, but also studies in class and caste. To read *Black Reconstruction*, *Color and Democracy* and *The World and Africa* is not simply to read studies in race, caste and class, but also studies in Pan-Africanism and anticolonialism. And, finally, when "The Damnation of Women," "The Freedom of Womanhood," "The Work of Negro Women in Society," "The Black Mother," "Suffering Suffragettes," "Hail Columbia!," "The Burden of Black Women," and "Sex and Racism" are read, what one is reading are not just studies in race and class theory, but also critical analyses of gender domination and discrimination, and especially as these interlocking systems of exploitation, oppression, and violence affect the lifeworlds and life struggles, the lived experiences and lived endurances of black women. It is the multidimensionality and transdisciplinarity of Du Bois's insurgent intersectional sociological discourse that make it difficult for opportunistic interpreters to (mis)appropriate and (re)articulate his thought and texts in a monodimensional and monodisciplinary manner. Moreover, it is the same multidimensionality and transdisciplinarity in Du Bois's discourse that provide paradigmatic examples of some of the ways male-feminists in general, and male-feminist sociologists in particular, can simultaneously avoid being appropriated as "the" authoritative and most rational voices of gender justice, and employ intersectional sociology to cogently connect critiques of sexism with those of racism and classism.

If male antisexist social theorists and activists openly and honestly dialogue with, and document and disseminate the community and campus work of, female antisexist social theorists and activists, then it will be very hard for male supremacist media machines to project the gender-progressive male voice as the definitive voice of gender justice. Critically engaging women's liberation theory and practice by actively and earnestly participating in the said theory and practice, male antisexist social theorists and activists can and should expand the range and use(s) of women's liberation theory and other antisexist social theory to include the work of both women *and* men who sought and are seeking gender justice, especially women's decolonization and women's liberation. Male antisexist social theorists and activists must simultaneously and dialectically deconstruct and reconstruct male antisexist, gender justice, and women's liberation theory and praxis traditions, and share the knowledge they discover and create with gender-justice-seeking women and men. In fact, one of the special tasks of antisexist men is to encourage our brother-friends to critically examine the ways in which they embrace patriarchy and perpetuate and exacerbate sexism and female domination and discrimination. Male antisexist social theorists and activists are long overdue in astutely and accessibly articulating to sexist men the violent psychological and physical consequences of male supremacist thought and behavior, and how, as quiet as it is kept, this thought and behavior not only robs women of their human and civil rights, but also often causes serious life-threatening conflicts and contradictions among men.

What I am calling for here is for antisexist men to unflinchingly encourage sexist men to self-consciously confront and correct their sexist socialization and sexist thought and behavior. Antisexist men must embrace the revolutionary responsibility of providing new paradigms for modern masculinity. We must show the world, and especially women, our sister-friends, that patriarchal, phallocentric, militaristic, and misogynistic masculinity are not definitive practices or modes of masculinity but, truth be told, deformations and destructions of masculinity. Masculinity, henceforth and forevermore, must be predicated on moral practice and the magic of male/female complementarity. What it means to be a "man" must begin to be bound up with males' embrace of the ethical obligation to end female domination and discrimination and their promotion of women's decolonization, women's liberation, and radical/revolutionary antisexist social reorganization.

African American male antisexist social theorists and activists must be bold enough and brave enough to take our cue from our male-feminist forefathers, men ("father figures") such as Charles Lenox Remond, Frederick Douglass, and W. E. B. Du Bois, among others, who—as I have endeavored to illustrate above—possessed problematic but nonetheless progressive stances on gender justice and, specifically, African American women's decolonization and liberation. However, and even more than turning to the antisexist thought and practice traditions of our male-feminist forefathers, antisexist men of African descent must learn the many lessons our freedom-fighting foremothers' legacies of liberation thought and practice have to teach. This impulse to learn radical lifesaving and life-enhancing lessons from our foremothers must on principle also extend to the thought, texts and practices of openly antisexist African American women in our present age. A common characteristic of both black feminist and intersectional sociological discourse is the principle that theory and praxis must simultaneously speak to the special needs of women and the poor, especially poor nonwhite women, and the emancipatory aspirations of humanity as a whole. This means, then, that most modern black feminist and insurgent intersectional sociologists do not adhere to the constraints of Eurocentric, bourgeois, or otherwise elitist constructions of gender and/or socialized "sex roles." The only "role" that twenty-first-century black feminist and insurgent intersectional sociologists have is that of *epistemically open* (i.e., transdisciplinary), politically committed intellectual-activists: *antiracist, antisexist, and anticapitalist intellectual insurrectionists.*

Du Bois's sociology of gender, as we have witnessed throughout this chapter, was critical of the patriarchal pretensions and practices of both white and black men, as well as both white and male supremacy. Ultimately he applied his intersectional sociology to other pressing social problems, in a sense, taking his work in new discursive directions. Deeply connected to his critique of the racial colonization of gender, class, and labor is Du Bois's intellectual history-making critique of the racial colonization of religion. Although not as widely discussed within the world of the sociology of religion as warranted, Du Bois put forward some of the most severe, albeit constructive, criticisms of American religion, especially African American religion, in the history of sociology. Here, as with his sociological discourse in general, he passionately danced with the dialectic, bringing it to bear on American and African American religious history and culture. Even though he was not "religious" in the traditional sense, many of Du Bois's biographers have commented on his profound spirituality, which leads us to ask: What were his thoughts on the religion of "black folk"? What were his critical views on the black church and black preachers? What were his thoughts on the religion of "white folk"? What were his critical views on the white church and white preachers? What does Du Bois's sociology of religion have to offer to the sociology of religion in the twenty-first century? It is to these questions that we now turn.

NOTES

1. Some may find Guy-Sheftall's (re)construction of Du Bois as a male-"feminist" troubling. However, as Hazel Carby (1998) contends, it should be held in mind that Du Bois means "many things to many people" (14). He is one of the many male and female "rediscovered ancestors" whose thought and texts are currently being engaged by contemporary theorists "in response to the needs of various agendas," academic and otherwise (14). Where Guy-Sheftall (1990) and McKay (1990) read Du Bois as a male-"feminist," Joy James (1996, 1997) proffered a "pro-feminist" Du Bois. More recently, Gary Lemons (2001) argued that Du Bois's pro-women's rights and women's suffrage work can actually be read as both "black feminist" *and* "womanist." It is not the intention of this chapter to argue whether Du Bois was a "womanist" or a "feminist"—two terms, it should be pointed out, that were not *en vogue* in Africana intellectual arenas until after his death. The primary purpose here is to discover what implications Du Bois's pro-women's rights and women's suffrage work has for the development of an antiracist, antisexist, anticapitalist, and anticolonial critical theory of contemporary society. Therefore, this study will draw from the women's liberation theory of a wide range of women *and* men of African descent

who self-describe and self-define themselves as "womanists," "Africana womanists," "black feminists," and "African feminists," among other nomenclature.

2. Nellie McKay, Gary Lemons, and Hazel Carby each bemoan the fact that there is a strong tendency in Du Bois studies to read him primarily as a "race man" and downplay his "feminist" and/or "womanist" discourse. In her essay, "The Souls of Black Women Folk in the Writings of W. E. B. Du Bois," McKay (1990) claims that Du Bois was one of very few black men who wrote "feminist autobiography": "More than any other black man in our history, his three autobiographies [*Darkwater, Dusk of Dawn*, and *The Autobiography of W. E. B. Du Bois*] demonstrate that black women have been central to the development of his intellectual thought" (229, 231). McKay, who is a literary theorist and critic, argues that one of the reasons that so many Du Bois scholars read him as a "race man" is because they often overlook his "more creative, less sociological works, where most of his thoughts on women and his own fundamental spirituality are expressed" (230). "Few people, even those who have spent years reading and studying Du Bois," quips McKay, "know that he wrote five novels and published a volume of poetry" (231). In "'When and Where [We] Enter': In Search of a Feminist Forefather—Reclaiming the Womanist Legacy of W. E. B. Du Bois," Lemons (2001) laments that Du Bois's "womanist activism remains to be fully claimed by contemporary Black men, as he continues to be viewed primarily as a 'race man'" (72). What perplexes Lemons is the fact that the critics who elide and erase Du Bois's women's liberation work do not simply do Du Bois a disservice, but also rob contemporary men, and men of African descent in particular, of an Africana male *antisexist* role model. According to Lemons, "not only" was Du Bois's "conception of antiracist resistance feminist-inspired, his worldview was profoundly influenced by Black women" (73). Finally, in the first chapter of her book, *Race Men*, "The Souls of Black Men," Hazel Carby (1998) offers contemporary academics and political activists a deconstruction of Du Bois as "race man" that acknowledges that he "advocated equality for women and consistently supported feminist causes" (12). Carby, who asserts that it is not her intention to claim that Du Bois was "a sexist male individual," is not, however, as concerned with Du Bois's "male-feminist" thought—though she gives it a highly critical treatment—as with many black male intellectuals' erasure and omission of his feminist thought from their discourse on Du Bois and their obsessive concerns with "the reproduction of Race Men" (12, 25). She states, "If, as intellectuals and as activists, we are committed, like Du Bois, to struggles for liberation and democratic egalitarianism, then surely it is not contradictory also to struggle to be critically aware of the ways in which *ideologies of gender* have undermined our egalitarian visions in the past and continue to do so in the present" (12, my emphasis). Carby's caveat, like the cautions of McKay and Lemons, essentially asks that we be cognizant of not only the "ideologies of gender" in the present, but also the "ideologies of gender" of the past, and how this specific species of ideology may have and/or, more than likely, indeed did influence the ways our intellectual ancestors theorized about this or that issue. In other words, we must make ourselves and others critically conscious of sexist sentiment in both classical and contemporary Africana liberation thought and practices. My work here, then, registers as an effort to simultaneously deepen and develop the antisexist aspects of Africana critical theory, and an attempt to move beyond one-dimensional interpretations of Du Bois which downplay the multidi-

mensionality of his thought and texts. It is important here to note that because of the richness and wide range and reach of Du Bois's thought, within Du Bois studies there are various research areas and agendas—for example, history, philosophy, social theory, politics, economics, aesthetics, religion, education, and so forth. Depending on one's intellectual orientation and academic training and discipline, his thought and texts may serve a multiplicity of purposes and may be approached from a wide array of discursive directions. Needless to say, my interpretations of Du Bois have been deeply influenced by my training in and trek through Africana studies, and specifically Africana philosophy, critical social theory, and radical politics.

3. Here Du Bois is hinting at his long-held position, which Guy-Sheftall (1995) terms a "progressive stance," that maintains that black women should have the right to choose motherhood as opposed to having it forced upon them by white and/or male supremacist social standards (12). His most developed statement on this issue is "Black Folk and Birth Control" (1932), in which he states that African Americans, with the aid of "the American Birth Control League and other agencies," have a "difficult and insistent problem" before them as to discerning the best method by which to spread "among Negroes an intelligent and clearly recognized concept of proper birth control, so that the young people can marry, have companionship and natural health, and yet not have children until they are able to take care of them" (Du Bois, 1982c, 320–21). Du Bois, like many African Americans during his long lifespan, "want[ed] the black race to survive" (321). However, he was quick to offer a caveat: "[We] must learn that among human races and groups, as among vegetables, quality and not mere quantity really counts" (321). His argument was that during enslavement "every incentive was furnished to raise the largest number of children possible"—this, of course, was in the best interest of the white ruling race/class, as they would then have more workers and, thus, more wealth (320). But, in the post-Emancipation period, Du Bois observed, African Americans had to reclaim and reconstruct family and extended family traditions that were conducive to their new social situations and circumstances. Part of Du Bois's argument was predicated on economic considerations—keep in mind that he was writing during the height of the so-called Great Depression. But other aspects of Du Bois's argument rest on a radical cultural philosophy that privileged African American social development and cultural survival. According to Du Bois, African Americans must not be fooled by "the fallacy of numbers"; they must think practically and take into consideration the historical and cultural context in which their children will be born (321). African American children will perish or prosper based on their parents' preparation and maturation: cultural, social, political, educational, economic, and so forth.

4. In "Sex, Race, and the Matrices of Desire in an Anti-Black World," the Jamaican American philosopher Lewis Gordon (1997b) argues that the normative desire in an anti-black world is to avoid "*being* the black and feminized," because "in such a world a rational person wants to be white and masculine" (77, emphasis in original). Why, one may ask? In a word, an "anti-black world is also a misogynist world," but, we must bear in mind, "a misogynist world is not necessarily an anti-black one," on account of the mobile, reversible, and unstable nature of intra-racial power relations among white males and females (76). What this means is that an anti-black world is almost inherently and most likely an anti-woman world. White and masculine are positive and privileged sociopolitical variables in such a world. When

this line of thinking is taken to its extreme, white and masculine are collapsed into each other and callously combined; hence, as if magically, they are made to appear to be inextricable; and, for all practical purposes, then, white *equals* masculine and masculine *equals* white. Therefore, those farthest from *being* white and masculine in a white and male supremacist society (i.e., those humble human beings who happen to be both *black* and *female*) almost inevitably and invariably experience and endure deeper and comparably different forms of domination and discrimination when compared with both their black male and white female counterparts.

5. It would be virtually impossible for me to overstate Harding's influence on my interpretation of the epistemological and methodological implications of intersectional social science, not simply for sociology but also for the human sciences in general. Therefore, beyond her groundbreaking book *Whose Science? Whose Knowledge?: Thinking from Women's Lives* (1991), I have turned to Harding (1976, 1986, 1987, 1993, 1998, 2006, 2008), as well as Harding and O'Barr (1987), Harding and Hintikka (1983), and Harding and Narayan (2000). Furthermore, in terms of the works that I turned to for my interpretation of the interconnections between standpoint epistemology, feminist epistemology, and feminist sociology of knowledge, please see Alcoff and Potter (1993), Alexander and Mohanty (1997), Duran (1991), Mohanty (2003), Narayan (1997), Rege (2003), and D. E. Smith (1990, 1993, 1999).

6. With regard to my interpretation of methodology, and specifically the ways in which feminist methodology disrupts and deconstructs the discursive formations and practices of male supremacist methodologies, I have relied on Harding (1987), Harding and Hintikka (1983), Hesse-Biber (2007), Hesse-Biber, Gilmartin, and Lydenberg (1999), Lather (2007), Naples (2003), and Nielsen (1990). In terms of my conception of the sociology of knowledge, I turned to the following noteworthy works: Bailey (1994), Fuhrman (1980), Mannheim (1972), E. D. McCarthy (1996), and Stehr and Meja (2005).

7. For further discussion, consult Angela Davis's (1995) essay "Reflections on the Black Woman's Role in the Community of Slaves," which remains one of the best introductions to African American women's existential universe during enslavement. In "Sexism and the Black Female Slave Experience," and in *Ain't I A Woman* generally, bell hooks (1981) provides a provocative and penetrating analysis of sexual stereotypes and racial myth-making that were/are continually created in white and male supremacist efforts to sociopolitically control and "steer" black women away from the sites and sources of power, and also the people in/with power away from black women's lived experiences and lifeworlds (15–49). Patricia Hill Collins (2000a) also comments on sexual stereotypes and racial myth-making, and particularly with regard to "the politics of the maternal" in "Mammies, Matriarchs, and Other Controlling Images" (69–96). She, too, is critical of white and male supremacist efforts to sociopolitically control and "steer" African American women and has put forward a blistering critique in "The More Things Change, the More They Stay the Same: African American Women and the New Politics of Containment" (P. H. Collins, 1998, 11–43). In a similar spirit, Hammond (1997) and Towns (1974) offer a couple of the best critical genealogies of the mythologization of black women's sexuality. And finally, Joy James (1999), in "Depoliticizing Representations: Sexual-Racial Stereotypes," critiques some of the ways African American

women's radicalism (during and after enslavement) has been downplayed because of the hypersexualization, "mammification," and "bitchification" of black women in modern mass media and print (123–50).

8. As a matter of intellectual integrity, my conscience compels me to bring a couple of episodes in Du Bois's private life or, rather, his "private affairs" to my readers' attention. Widely considered Du Bois's "definitive" biographer, two-time Pulitzer Prize–winning historian David Levering Lewis (1993) controversially gets into the thick of things with regard to Du Bois's public male-feminism and private male chauvinism (including his "womanizing," haphazard husbandhood, and faltering fatherhood) in *W. E. B. Du Bois: Biography of a Race, 1868–1919* (see especially 449–65). "The episodic dalliances, the star-crossed love affair with Fauset, the comfortable arrangements with Georgia Johnson and Mildred Jones began to be replicated with a seeming insatiety that yielded nothing to advancing years, and may, perhaps, have been a spectacular version of the generalized male late-life crisis," announced Lewis (2000), righteously returning to this sordid subject in the massive second volume of his Du Bois biography, *W. E. B. Du Bois: The Fight for Equality and the American Century, 1919–1963* (267). If his hinting at Du Bois's adulterous behavior in the first volume shocked and awed his readers, in the second volume Lewis was surely hoping to create a *cause célèbre* by painstakingly documenting and detailing Du Bois's extramarital affairs with novelist and poet Jessie Fauset (49–50, 188–90); schoolteacher Mildred Bryant Jones (128, 267); poet Georgia Douglas Johnson (183–85); dramatist Anne Cooke (186); his secretary Marvel Jackson Cooke (186–87); *Opportunity* secretary Ethel Ray (189, 268); sculptor Elizabeth Prophet (268–69); the infamous "other Mrs. Du Bois," white high schoolteacher Rachel Davis Du Bois (189, 270–72); New York City white socialite Nora Waring (272); widow Louie Shivery (382–84); Atlanta University graduate student and, later, Du Bois's research assistant, Ellen Irene Diggs (305, 383–84); and, perhaps most famously, the woman to whom he dedicated *Black Reconstruction*, medical doctor Virginia Alexander (267–74).

9. Each of the aforementioned essays can be found in Du Bois (1995b), with the exception of "The Work of Negro Women in Society," which was originally published in the *Spelman Messenger* in February 1902 and is included in Du Bois (1982b, 139–44)

4

Du Bois and the Sociology of Religion

The Sociology of the Souls of Religious Black (Among Other) Folk*

> Here, then, is the problem of the color-line and it is not only the most pressing social question of the modern world; it is an ethical question that confronts every religion and every conscience.
>
> W. E. B. Du Bois, "Will the Church Remove the Color-Line?," 174

INTRODUCTION: DU BOIS'S SOCIOLOGY OF THE DIVINE AND THE DEMONIC

While W. E. B. Du Bois's pioneering work as a historian, sociologist, political scientist, and race theorist has been heavily lauded and heatedly debated over the ensuing decades since his death in 1963, few social theorists, and especially *critical* social theorists, have sought to connect his wide-ranging antiracism with his unrepentant criticisms of religion. As Edward Blum's *W. E. B. Du Bois: American Prophet* (2007), Brian Johnson's *W. E. B. Du Bois: Toward Agnosticism, 1868–1934* (2008), Jonathon Kahn's *The Divine Discontent: The Religious Imagination of W. E. B. Du Bois* (2009), and Edward Blum and Jason Young's *The Souls of W. E. B. Du Bois* (2009) have each recently revealed, Du Bois had a lifelong, critical, and often contradictory relationship with religion, and particularly religion as it has historically been used, or rather abused, for Eurocentric-ideological-imperial purposes. His sociological discourse, however subtly, highlights a distinct Africana history-, culture-, philosophy-, and struggle-informed perspective on religion that simultaneously accents the advances it has inspired, and highlights the hurt and harm it has caused throughout human history. Du Bois's approach to religion was rarely one that could be quickly or easily quarantined to traditional religious studies because of his *transdisciplinarity* and consistent emphasis on race, gender, class, and caste (i.e., "intersectional") issues within the realm of religion. The emphasis on secular issues within the sacred world of religion led Du Bois to develop a distinct style of critical religious thought that paid more attention to the earthly deeds than the ethereal words of a religious tradition, institution, or adherent. This shift of focus, along with his disaffection for any specific religious denomination, gave Du Bois enormous insight into the ways in which religion has been and continues to be (ab)used in the interest of Eurocentric-ideological-imperial domination and discrimination.

Often Du Bois's writings on religion reveal as much about the political economy of race and racism as they do about the "religious economy" or tenets of the religious tradition in question (R. A. Wortham, 2009a). He was apparently more preoccupied with, to use his words, "the problem of race and religion" than the problem of religion in any isolated or narrow-minded sense (Du Bois, 2000a, 199). In fact, as many of his major studies in this area demonstrate, religion and racism have long been inextricable in the modern moment, and some of his work in this vein supports a similar claim with regard to religion and sexism.[1] That being said, Du Bois's sociology of religion consistently emphasized African American religion (i.e., the "Negro Church") as a medium through which to critique white domination and promote black liberation. For instance, in *The Philadelphia Negro* he identified six fundamental functions of the African American Church: raising the annual budget; maintaining organizational membership; social interaction and planned activities (amusements); setting moral standards; promoting general education; and stimulating social betterment (Du Bois, 1899, 202–7). If, indeed, functional analyses of religion frequently emphasize the ways in which religious organizations magnify meaning, encourage unity, and supply social support, along with offering a sense of belonging and identity, then it can be easily argued that Du Bois's sociology of religion prefigured several of the foci of functionalist analyses of religion. Ultimately, however, Du Bois's sociology of religion ironically centers more on earthly liberation than heavenly salvation.

For more than half a century religion has been conceived of as a site of and source for liberation, with many theologians and religious studies scholars calling for a *theology of liberation* or *liberation theology* (see Berryman, 1987; Boff and Boff, 1987; Cone, 1970; Gutierrez, 1988; Segundo, 1976; C. Smith, 1991). In brief, *liberation theology* is *theology deeply rooted in lived experience, lived endurance and, perhaps most importantly, anti-imperial social and political praxis*, and imperialism—any form of imperialism, whether racism, sexism, capitalism, or colonialism—is adamantly opposed. It is primarily concerned with relating religion (usually some form of Christianity) to poor, poverty-stricken, and oppressed peoples' social and political problems, those persons that liberation theologians call "the least of Christ's brothers and sisters" (Rowland, 1999, 3). Liberation theology is highly critical of the scholasticism of traditional Christian theology and seeks to make the words and deeds of Jesus Christ more accessible to the poor masses and working classes of the world, especially those of the so-called Third World and/or "underdeveloped" countries. It enables and encourages the poor and marginalized masses to relate their suffering and social misery to Christ's suffering, crucifixion, and resurrection. According to liberation theologians, Christ always communed with the most needy and vulnerable (i.e., "the masses"); consequently, Christ's "presence is hidden in the poor," and it is the poor who have a special lesson to teach church leaders and the politically powerful, not simply vice versa (12).

Like liberation theology, Africana religious thought is primarily preoccupied with liberating the lives of the poor and dispossessed. However, unlike liberation theology, Africana religious thought has since its inception dialogued deeply with indigenous (dare I say "precolonial") African religious traditions and spirituality, and contained a critical antiracist and anticolonialist component that has consistently problematized, if not downright dialecticized, religion as a realm of potential good or bad. Religion has never and does not now guarantee Good or that "God's will" will be done. And it is this conundrum, coupled with the contradictions of combining racism and religion for imperial purposes, that lies at the heart of Africana critical religious thought.

As early texts attest—texts such as Robert Alexander Young's *The Ethiopian Manifesto*, David Walker's *An Appeal in Four Articles*, Maria Stewart's *Meditations From the Pen of Mrs. Maria Stewart*, Frederick Douglass's *Narrative of the Life of Frederick Douglass*, Edward Blyden's *Christianity, Islam, and the Negro Race*, and numerous others—Africana theorists have constantly criticized the (ab)use of religion for the purposes of domination and discrimination (Blyden, 1994; Douglass, 1994; M. W. Stewart, 1987; D. Walker, 1993; R. A. Young, 1996). This is to say that Africana theorists have long developed a habit of viewing religion dialectically—that is, simultaneously as *both* a site of spiritual liberation *and* a source of social domination. Although often overlooked, Du Bois greatly contributed to this tradition and, what is more, his empirical studies of African American religion may be regarded as some of the first efforts to develop a sociology of American religion and, most especially, a sociology of African American religion. The greatly respected sociologist of religion Phil Zuckerman (2002) maintained that "it is without question that the sociological study of African American religion (and by extension, significant aspects of white religion) begins with the work of Du

Bois" (247). Importantly building on Zuckerman's work, Robert Wortham (2005a) went so far as to say:

> Sociologists of religion routinely discuss the classic contributions of Durkheim, Weber, and Simmel while virtually ignoring Du Bois. This is unfortunate because Du Bois's early work on religion moves well beyond ethnographic description and philosophical-theoretical formulation. In fact, the section on religion in *The Philadelphia Negro* and the Atlanta University Conference study on *The Negro Church* are based on data obtained from ethnographic studies of congregations, field interviews, surveys, and *Census of Religious Bodies* data. Furthermore, *The Negro Church* appears to be the first empirically based book-length sociological study of a religious group. Given Du Bois's ultilization of multiple empirical approaches in these classic studies of religion in the United States, he should be included as one of the field's founding figures. . . . Although Du Bois wrote about a variety of sociological topics, his early work on religion is seminal. His empirical approach to the study of religious phenomena was unprecedented. The classic studies on religion by Durkheim, Weber, and Simmel do not integrate qualitative and quantitative approaches to data analysis as extensively as does Du Bois. Today researchers speak of meta-analysis and methodological triangulation as if these concepts were something new. In many respects, *The Negro Church* is a pioneering example of each of these approaches. (434, 448)

In an effort to build on and go beyond both Zuckerman and Wortham's work, here it is important to not simply restate the obvious (i.e., Du Bois's sociological negation as a consequence of *disciplinary decadence, intellectual historical amnesia,* and, of course, ultimately *epistemic apartheid*) but, keeping with the critical theoretical theme of this book, it is more important to identify and analyze *what* and *how* Du Bois contributed to the inauguration and ongoing development of the sociology of religion in the United States. This chapter, therefore, offers a transdisciplinary exploration of Du Bois's sociology of religion. It argues that his sociological discourse on religion—being distinguished by its emphasis on Africana religiosity and spirituality; the relationship between, and the political economy of, religion and racism; and the ways oppressing and oppressed people use and/or abuse religion either as a form of social pacification or social protest—simultaneously deconstructs and reconstructs the conventional analytical categories of philosophy of religion, sociology of religion, and liberation theology. Du Bois's work in this area makes a profound contribution to contemporary sociology of religion, and critical religious studies more generally, insofar as it provides a paradigm that enables twenty-first-century sociologists to critique the ideological elements of religion while simultaneously accenting its more emancipatory aspects. His sociology of religion, like his sociology in general, is ultimately shown to be self-reflexive, constantly exhibiting the ability to revise and refine itself and, as a result, continues to be remarkably relevant for contemporary sociology of religion.

DU BOIS'S PHILOSOPHY OF RELIGION

In "W. E. B. Du Bois and Religion," esteemed Du Bois studies scholar Herbert Aptheker (1982) argued, "[W]hile Du Bois was an agnostic in his last years, he never was an atheist. Though the record shows a diminution as time passed in the confidence with which he held some religious concepts . . . he never quite rejected a belief in some creative and persistent force" (5). Moreover, African American historian Manning Marable (1998) maintains, "Du Bois was simultaneously an agnostic and an Anglican, a staunch critic of religious dogma and a passionate convert to the black version of Christianity. His belief in his people was expressed in his own black faith for the world" (60). As a child, Du Bois enjoyed church and, according to Aptheker (1982), "outside of his school his major contact with the people of his town was through church" (6). Du Bois (1968a) and his mother Mary Silvina "were the only colored communicants" of the Congregational church of his childhood, and he writes that his mother had "many acquaintances there" and that "the minister, [Reverend Evarts] Scudder, was especially friendly" (88). In fact, in *The Autobiography of W. E. B. Du Bois*, he goes so far as to say, "I felt absolutely no discrimination, and I do not think there was any, or any thought" (89). It was in the context of this thoroughly New England, although "especially friendly," congregation that Du Bois received most of his early religious instruction. However, as he pointed out a little later, "While I was in high school, the colored folk of the town, mostly newcomers . . . organized a small branch of the A. M. E. [African Methodist Episcopal] Zion church," which "we used to attend" from time to time (90; see also B. L. Johnson, 2008; D. Levinson, 2006).

He fondly remembered the annual church festivals, its Sunday school, instruction in Hebrew and Greek, and the Sunday sermons. Arnold Rampersad (1990) has remarked that the foundation of Du Bois's "moral fervor was the iron of Puritan Ethics, initially instilled in him in the First Congregational Church of Great Barrington" (5). The Congregationalism of Du Bois's boyhood was "deeply orthodox" and "[i]n its doctrine, if not its style, it reflected [a] severe Calvinism," with all its "seriousness and combativeness" (5). It is important to observe with Rampersad that "[e]ven though Du Bois later scorned organized religion, these early Great Barrington years probably had a lasting impact on him and on the nebula of philosophic speculation surrounding his views of mankind" (5). However, it should also be held in mind that even from an early age Du Bois exhibited a critical disposition toward religion and was an extremely independent ecumenical thinker.[2] Much later in his life Du Bois (1968a) maintained, "I have seen miracles in my life. As a boy we did not have the possibility of miracles emphasized in our schools. In the weekly Sunday School, we studied the bible with its tales of the impossible but I remember distinctly that I questioned the validity of some of them, like that story of Jonah" (413).

Throughout his long life Du Bois drew from his strict religious rearing, peppering his writings with religious themes, religious metaphors, and references to God (see Blum, 2007; Forney, 2002; Kahn, 2009). Although he was extremely critical of Christianity, he did not hesitate to use it to combat an unjust issue, provocatively explain a point, or ethically ground an argument. He had a peculiar predilection for religion, as the religiosity and profound spirituality of even his earliest writings reveal, and it was a constant source of both personal and professional inspiration and frustration (Blum and Young, 2009).[3] Many of his religious writings harbor an autobiographical element, and are marked by a deep personal commitment to aligning the gentle words of Jesus with the deeds of those who claim to follow in His faithful footsteps. Moreover, Du Bois's religious writings are not immune to moral outrage and often display the critical questioning that ultimately became the cornerstone of his corpus. In "A Litany of Atlanta," for example, written in the aftermath of the 1906 Atlanta pogrom, he thundered:

> We are not better than our fellows. Lord; we are but weak and human men. When our devils do deviltry, curse Thou the doer and the deed—curse them as we curse them, do to them all and more than ever they have done to innocence and weakness, to womanhood and home.
> *Have mercy upon us, miserable sinners!*
> And yet, whose is the deeper guilt? Who made these devils? Who nursed them in crime and fed them on injustice? Who ravished and debauched their mothers and their grandmothers? Who bought and sold their crime and waxed fat and rich on public iniquity?
> *Thou knowest, good God!* (Du Bois, 2000a, 65, emphasis in original)[4]

Du Bois (1997c) consistently affirmed his belief in "a vague Force which, in some incomprehensible way, dominates all life and change" (223). However, he was quick to correct anyone who might attempt to ascribe his beliefs—his liberation theology, if you will—to a specific organized religion or religious denomination. Perhaps the epitome of a heretic in the eyes of "good," God-fearing, church-going folk, he began his "Credo," originally published in 1904, with the somber words "I believe in God," and then unapologetically went on to announce, "I believe in the Devil and his angels, who wantonly work to narrow the opportunity of struggling human beings, especially if they be black; who spit in the faces of the fallen, strike them that cannot strike again, believe the worst and work to prove it, hating the image which their Master stamped on a brother's soul" (Du Bois, 1920, 3).[5]

What bothered Du Bois (1968a) most was religious hypocrisy or, in his words, "religious lies" (412). He quite simply had no tolerance for the abuse of religion, or for those who used religion as a tool to oppress or pacify. As Aptheker (1980b), a personal friend of Du Bois and his literary executor, observed, "Du Bois's honesty was fierce" and "no one dared impugn his integrity" (x). Therefore, when he found fault with a religious tradition (mostly Christianity, since it was the dominant religion of the United States during his lifetime), Du Bois was merely demanding an honesty and level of integrity from it, its leaders, and its adherents which he himself lived by. He consistently contended that religion was being used systematically to deceive, particularly the poor and children, thus socializing them to accept the lies and larceny of those in (Eurocentric-ideological-imperial) authority. His remarks are worth recollecting here at length:

> [T]he Soviet Union does not allow any church of any kind to interfere with education, and religion is not taught in the public schools. It seems to me that this is the greatest gift of the Russian Revolution to the modern world. Most educated modern men no longer believe in religious dogma. If questioned they will usually resort to double-talk before admitting the fact. But who today actually believes that this world is ruled and directed by a benevolent person of great power who, on humble appeal, will change the course of events at our request? Who believes in miracles? Many folk follow religious ceremonies and services; and allow their children to learn fairy tales and so-called religious truth, which in time the children come to recognize as conventional lies told by their parents and teachers for the children's good. One can hardly exaggerate the moral disaster of this custom. We have to thank the Soviet Union for the courage to stop it. (Du Bois, 1968a, 42)

Furthermore, critically continuing in the same vein, Du Bois stated:

> It is our great debt to the Soviet Union that it alone of nations dared stop that lying to children which so long disgraced our schools. We filled little minds with fairy tales of religious dogma which we ourselves never believed. We filled their thoughts with pictures of barbarous revenge called God which contradicted all their inner sense of decency. We repeated folk tales of children without fathers, of death which was life, of sacrifice which was shrewd investment and ridiculous pictures of an endless future. The Soviets have stopped this. They allow a child to grow up without religious lies and with mature mind make his own decision about the world without scaring him into Hell or rewarding him with a silly Heaven. (412)

Du Bois's dialectical relationship with religion changed dramatically throughout his life, and where in his youth he was more or less quite content with the teachings of Jesus Christ, in adulthood he came to not only question basic "Christian" tenets, but also many of the more mischievous people who claimed to be "Christians." His was a complex and seemingly contradictory relationship with religion, one that went from earnestly affirming his faith in God, Jesus, and the redemption of "miserable sinners" to leveling some of the staunchest criticisms of Christianity, and religion in general, in modern memory—one need not mention his previously cited passionate praise of the Soviet Union's antireligion public policies. What is more, his many autobiographical writings are chock-full of discussions of his religious development and, therefore, attest to the importance of religion in his critical universe and corroborate the accuracy of the foregoing claims.

In his five major autobiographical works, *The Souls of Black Folk* (1903), *Darkwater* (1920), *Dusk of Dawn* (1940), *In Battle for Peace* (1952), and *The Autobiography of W. E. B. Du Bois* (1968), Du Bois detailed his consecutive withdrawal and final cleavage from religion. Arriving for study at Fisk University in the autumn of 1885, he reported that he almost immediately joined the campus Congregational church, eagerly "volunteering to teach Sunday school" (Lewis, 1993, 65). After settling into college life he penned a letter to his former congregation back in Great Barrington, in which he was proud to announce, "I am glad to tell you that I have united with the Church here and hope that the prayers of my Sunday School may help guide me on the path of Christian duty" (Du Bois, 1968a, 110). However, his fellowship with the Congregationalists at Fisk was fleeting, as he soon "became critical of religion and resentful of its practice" (Du Bois, 1968b, 33). What prompted the sudden change in Du Bois's religious outlook? What could have possibly happened at Fisk, an African American *religious* university, to make Du Bois resent the very practice of religion? According to award-winning Du Bois biographer, David Levering Lewis (1993), the "course of events defies clear reconstruction" and, to make matters worse, Du Bois himself "never got the story quite straight," recollecting it differently in each of his autobiographical works (65). What does seem certain, though, is that Du Bois's disdain for organized religion grew out of, believe it or not, a controversy surrounding dancing. In his last autobiography he candidly recalled that

> "Pop" Miller did not allow my church membership to progress as placidly as I planned. He was an official of the church and a fundamentalist in religion. He soon had me and others accused before the church for dancing. I was astonished. I had danced all my life quite as naturally as I sang and ran. In Great Barrington there was little chance to dance on the part of anyone but in the small group of colored folk there was always some dancing along with playing games at homes. When I came South and was among my own young folk who not only danced but danced beautifully and with effortless joy, I joined and

Du Bois and the Sociology of Religion 231

learned eagerly. I never attended public dance halls, but at the homes of colored friends in the city, we nearly always danced and a more innocent pastime I could not imagine. But Miller was outraged. What kind of dancing he was acquainted with I do not know, but at any rate in his mind dancing figured as a particularly heinous form of sin. I resented this and said so in very plain terms. The teachers intervened and tried to reconcile matters in a way which for years afterward made me resentful and led to my eventual refusal to join a religious organization. They admitted that my dancing might well be quite innocent, but said that my example might lead others astray. They quoted Paul "If meat maketh my brothers to offend, I will eat no meat while the world standeth." I tried to accept this for years, and for years I wrestled with this problem. Then I resented this kind of sophistry. I began again to dance and I have never since had much respect for Paul. (Du Bois, 1968a, 110–11)

Falsely accused of heresy, the young, popular black New Englander ("my popularity rather went to my head") was surrounded by Southern sophists, and where Fisk gave him his first exposure to "the South: the South of slavery, rebellion and black folk" and to "the scientific attitude," it also offered him an acute awareness of the dormant dogma and ideological aspects of religion (Du Bois, 1968a, 105–9, 1968b, 50). Du Bois had long held religion in high esteem, and now, in his first year at Fisk, the motherless and fatherless lad's newfound Southern home away from home, he was compelled to question his religious foundation. His religious questioning continued at Harvard and, as he noted in *Dusk of Dawn*, it did not wane when he went to Germany to study at the University of Berlin, where he "turned still further from religious dogma" (Du Bois, 1968b, 50). In his final autobiography Du Bois (1968a) painted a picture of himself as a constant critic of religion and narrates a rather nuanced ecumenical adventure:

My religious development has been slow and uncertain. I grew up in a liberal Congregational Sunday School and listened once a week to a sermon on doing good as a reasonable duty. Theology played a minor part and our teachers had to face some searching questions. At 17 I was in a missionary college where religious orthodoxy was stressed; but I was more developed to meet it with argument, which I did. My "morals" were sound, even a bit puritanic, but when a hidebound old deacon inveighed against dancing I rebelled. By the time of graduation I was still a "believer" in orthodox religion, but had strong questions which were encouraged at Harvard. In Germany I became a freethinker and when I came to teach at an orthodox Methodist Negro school I was soon regarded with suspicion, especially when I refused to lead the students in public prayer. When I became head of a department at Atlanta, the engagement was held up because again I balked at leading in prayer, but the liberal president let me substitute the Episcopal prayer book on most occasions. Later I improvised prayers [i.e., *Prayers for Dark People*] on my own. . . . From my 30th year on I have increasingly regarded the church as an institution which defended such evils as slavery, color caste, exploitation of labor and war.

I think the greatest gift of the Soviet Union to modern civilization was the dethronement of the clergy and the refusal to let religion be taught in the public schools. (285; see also Du Bois, 1980c)

For Du Bois, part of the problem of religion was the fact that it was being used as a tool for social pacification and to suppress forces for radical democratic socialist transformation. Throughout its long history, religion has been contracted to uphold "such evils as slavery, color caste, exploitation of labor and war" and, we should on principle add, the violent oppression of women and virulent hatred of homosexuals. He was not against religion, but against the way many of its adherents interpreted or, rather, misinterpreted it for ideological-imperial purposes. In all of his religious questioning, including his increasingly radical criticisms of religion at the end of his life, Du Bois seems to have maintained an unfeigned and heartfelt belief in God.

It may be difficult for many of the more religious to digest, but the fact of the matter is: *God did not create religion*. God created human beings, who in turn created religion, but, I should unrepentantly reiterate, *God did not create religion*. Therefore, Du Bois felt no ethical obligation to follow the worldly whims and wishes of so-called religious leaders or institutions, especially when these leaders and institutions did not live by their own sacred texts and tenets. In one of the most significant summaries of Du Bois's (anti- and/or critical) religious development during his collegiate years, Du Bois biographer Arnold Rampersad (1990) has tellingly written:

> The omniscient God of Du Bois's Congregational youth was slowly but surely displaced by the Unknowable of Herbert Spencer. Paradoxically, the search for truth was also the gospel of those who acknowledged this unknowable. For them, man scrutinized the universe unclouded by religious dogma: secular learning was religion enough. To those faithful to the old God, the new learning led almost inevitably to amorality and eventually to fatalism. As in his religion, so in his formal education, Du Bois would make a significant but unsteady transition between the old and new orders. (19–20)

Plowing his own radical spiritual path through the realm of religion, Du Bois brought his increasingly dialectical thought to bear on religious leaders, institutions, and practices.[6] He was particularly perplexed by the imperial-ideological aspects of modern religion, yet seemed to hold out a silent hope that it could be contracted not simply for heavenly salvation but for earthly liberation and radical democratic socialist transformation as well.[7] No matter what his personal views concerning religion, the dogged social scientist W. E. B. Du Bois (1899) never lost sight of the fact that the African American church, as he marveled in *The Philadelphia Negro*, "is by long odds the vastest and most remarkable product of American Negro civilization"

(21). In fact, for Du Bois, the African American church was distinguished not so much for the sacred communion it provided blacks, but for the educational initiatives, social services, and political power it bequeathed to successive struggling generations of black folk. Thus, as observed by Phil Zuckerman (2009) in "The Irreligiosity of W. E. B. Du Bois," however ironically, the "irreligious" Du Bois undertook several unprecedented empirical social scientific studies of religion. These studies focused more on the secular impact and temporal role religion played in history, culture, politics, and society, and over time they have come to be characterized as some of the crowning achievements of Du Bois's sociology of religion.

DU BOIS'S SOCIOLOGY OF RELIGION

Religion is a recurring theme throughout Du Bois's wide and varied writings, and he has recently been recognized as "the first American sociologist of religion" for his pioneering 1903 volume, *The Negro Church* (see Zuckerman, Barnes, and Cady, 2003; see also Blum, 2005a; C. Evans, 2007; Savage, 2000; R. A. Wortham, 2005a, 2009; Zuckerman, 2002). Although I am generally critical of work that seeks to situate Du Bois's discourse within a specific (mono)disciplinary matrix, because his writings reveal him to be a trenchant *transdisciplinary* critical social theorist, I do think it important to engage interpretations of his thought and texts that subtly chronicle how he simultaneously contributed to the social sciences and humanities, broadly speaking. Looking at Du Bois from the lens of the sociology of religion should epistemically open those scholars skeptical of my thesis that Du Bois was an important transdisciplinary critical social theorist to the fact that he produced knowledge that not only combined the insights of sociology and religion but, as was discussed in the previous chapters, he generated a new kind of knowledge that discursively disrupted the boundaries and cut across these disciplines, creating a new transdisciplinary discursive domain or, at times, an antidisciplinary field of critical inquiry.

The bulk of what Du Bois had to say concerning religion is buried in miscellaneous speeches, magazine articles, newspaper columns, novels, and book chapters. *The Negro Church* (1903a) was his only book-length work on religion and, although he wrote much of it, it still stands in the final analysis as an edited volume. However, there are many additional major sources of Du Bois's sociology of religion, including 1) his autobiographical writings discussed above; 2) chapters from his well-known works, such as *The Philadelphia Negro* and *The Souls of Black Folk*, which specifically address religion; 3) his less popular and little-known texts, such as *The Negro in the South*, *John Brown*, and *The Gift of Black Folk*; 4) his creative writings, including five novels, numerous short stories, poems, and plays, which have been collected in *The Creative Writings of W. E. B. Du Bois*; and 5) his posthumously published volume of prayers, *Prayers for Dark People*, and three volumes of correspondence, *The Correspondence of W. E. B. Du Bois, 1877–1963*.

As with Du Bois's philosophy of religion, a major preoccupation of his sociology of religion revolved around the problem(s) of race and racism. Africans were not "black," or assigned the racial designation of "blackness," in a color-blind and politically neutral social world (V. Anderson, 1995; J. K. Carter, 2008, Prentiss, 2003; J. R. Washington, 1984). Far from it—and speaking with words bequeathed by the black existentialists—persons of African descent were "black" and only *became*, or were forced to *be*, "black" in response and in resistance to white supremacist anti-black racist imperialism (Gordon, 1997a, 1997b, 2000b, 2008). Du Bois's sociology of religion, therefore, harbors a deeply historical dimension, one that charts the changes and challenges of Africana religious thought and practices in traditional Africa, during the African holocaust and African American enslavement, and in so-called freedom (i.e., after the physical enslavement and material colonization of Africans and Africa—if we dare speak of anything after the horrors of holocaust, or as if it is possible to dream of a world in the wake of white supremacist global imperialism).

Du Bois's sociological treatment of Africana religion fundamentally centers on *syncretism*—that is, on how enslaved Africans, as the Princeton professor of religion Albert Raboteau (1978) observed in *Slave Religion*, fused their traditional religious thought and practices with the Christian theology of their white enslavers. It is in the explanation of this protracted sociocultural and historical process that Du Bois distinguished himself not simply as a sociologist of religion, but also a historian of religion and political theologian. Without a doubt, argued Du Bois, there were white and black Christians, but they were bound together not by religion as much as by theology. In other words, I am hinting here at what womanist theologian Jacquelyn Grant (1989) eloquently argued in *White Women's Christ and Black Women's Jesus*—that is, that blacks and whites may be employing similar religious language and drawing from the same sacred text (the Bible), but their lived experiences and lived endurances, their histories, cultural contexts, and social situations inspire them to draw comparably different conclusions as to the nature and power of God. What Du Bois's work demonstrates is that racial colonization and enslavement changed black folk's theology, but it did not in every instance, and certainly it did not completely, destroy their religious thought and practices. This is an insight Du Bois culled from his lived experiences, sociological observations, and data collection at Fisk, in Philadelphia's black community (under the auspices of the University of Pennsylvania), and at Atlanta University, among other sites, where black Christians practiced or, literally, *lived* a wide variety of Africanized versions of Christianity and where, in their daily lives, conscious and unconscious African retentions reigned.[8]

As an historian of religion with strong sociological leanings, Du Bois chronicled, 1) the radical thought and rebellious lives of early African American religious leaders; 2) intra-African American class divisions and how secular distinctions such as these played themselves out in the realm of religion; 3) the dual sacred and secular nature of African American religion and the black church; 4) the conflicts within several white Christian denominations over the issue of whether enslaved Africans could or should be baptized; and 5) why the white Baptists and Methodists were more successful in sowing the seeds of Christianity in the hearts and minds of the enslaved. Along with these issues, among others, Du Bois strongly stressed that African American religion, particularly as embodied in and flowing out of the black church, was not only "the first distinctively Negro American social institution" but, and most importantly, "the sole surviving social institution of the African fatherland." Religion, he wrote in *The Negro Church*, was the lone social sphere in which enslaved Africans had any agency, and even in this realm they were severely regulated. Du Bois (1903a), writing with a sense of unmitigated awe and critical discovery, declared:

> At first sight it would seem that slavery completely destroyed every vestige of spontaneous social movement among Negroes; the home had deteriorated; political authority and economic initiative was in the hands of the masters, property, as a social institution, did not exist on the plantation, and, indeed, it is usually assumed by historians and sociologists that every vestige of internal development disappeared, leaving the slaves no means of expression for their common life, thought, and striving. This is not strictly true; the vast power of the priest in the African state has already been noted; his realm alone—the province of religion and medicine—remained largely unaffected by the plantation system in many important particulars. The Negro priest, therefore, early became an important figure on the plantation and found his function as the interpreter of the supernatural, the comforter of the sorrowing, and as the one who expressed, rudely, but picturesquely, the longing and disappointment and resentment of a stolen people. From such beginnings arose and spread with marvelous rapidity the Negro Church, the first distinctively Negro American social institution. It was not at first by any means a Christian Church, but a mere adaptation of those heathen rites which we roughly designate by the term Obe Worship, or "Voodoism." Association and missionary effort soon gave these rites a veneer of Christianity, and gradually, after two centuries, the Church became Christian, with a simple Calvinistic creed, but with many of the old customs still clinging to the services. It is this historic fact that the Negro Church of today bases itself upon the sole surviving social institution of the African fatherland, that accounts for its extraordinary growth and vitality.... This institution, therefore, naturally assumed many functions which the other harshly suppressed social organs had to surrender; the Church became the

center of amusements, of what little spontaneous economic activity remained, of education, and of all social intercourse. (5)

African American religion was forged in the fires of abolitionist struggle, and the quest for freedom was not quenched by the bellowing, but weak-willed words of the Emancipation Proclamation. Therefore, Du Bois studied the impact of African American religion, basically the black church, on African American social development and cultural survival postenslavement. African American religious thought and practices, Du Bois had a hunch, changed during the decades after enslavement because, although they had *de jure* freedom, blacks were still in a white supremacist, hyper-racially ruled social world and did not have *de facto* freedom. Hence, American apartheid lingered on, leaving its stench and stain on everyone and everything it came into contact with, even religion, and, as will be witnessed in the chapter to follow, also education (Whitehead, 1994; see also Kushner, 1980; Massey and Denton, 1993; H. A. Washington, 2006).

In *The Philadelphia Negro* (1899), Du Bois analyzed a wide range of African American religious practices that illustrated the dramatic (sacred *and* secular) changes in black church life in the three and a half decades since the issuing of the Emancipation Proclamation. Beginning with the history of the black church, Du Bois then turned his attention to its organizational structures and social functions, and was undoubtedly the first to systematically study and document its political positions, educational initiatives, amusement/entertainment activities, missionary efforts, charitable organizations, insurance societies, and homes for the aged and the infirmed. He examined congregational economic life, what Robert Wortham (2009a) has recently referred to as "religious economy": from debts and membership contributions to the value of church properties and pastors' salaries. Further, Du Bois critically observed how black class divisions within the churches and various denominations played themselves out, causing continuous stratification and discontinuous congregational affiliation. He painstakingly detailed an intricate interrelation of church and/or religion-related social and political programs, and the lingering leitmotif of African retentions, which I have come to think is one of the hallmarks of his work, is ubiquitous. With words that read more like a sorrow-filled sinner testifying in a black church at Sunday morning service, Du Bois (1899) wrote:

> We often forget that the rise of a church organization among Negroes was a curious phenomenon. The church really represented all that was left of African tribal life, and was the sole expression of the organized efforts of the slaves. It was natural that any movement among freedmen should center about their religious life, the sole remaining element of their former tribal system. . . . The Negro is, to be sure, a religious creature—most primitive folk are—but his rapid and even extraordinary founding of churches is not due to this fact

alone, but is rather a measure of his development, an indication of the increasing intricacy of his social life and the consequent multiplication of the organ which is the function of his group life—the church.... The Negro church is the peculiar and characteristic product of the transplanted African, and deserves especial study. As a social group the Negro church may be said to have antedated the Negro family on American soil; as such it has preserved, on the one hand, many functions of tribal organization, and on the other hand, many of the family functions. Its tribal functions are shown in its religious activity, its social authority and general guiding and coordinating work; its family functions are shown by the fact that the church is a center of social life and intercourse; acts as newspaper and intelligence bureau, is the center of amusements—indeed, is the world in which the Negro moves and acts. So far-reaching are these functions of the church that its organization is almost political. (197, 201)

His inexcusable politically incorrect language aside ("The Negro is, to be sure, a religious creature—most primitive folk are")—which demonstrates that one of the major architects of Africana studies was not immune to internalized anti-black racism and *the diabolical dialectic of white superiority and black inferiority!*—Du Bois accentuated both the social and political functions of the black church. In his estimate, it is "the most remarkable product of American Negro civilization" because "[i]t is a democratic church; a church where the governing power is largely in the hands of the mass of membership" (Du Bois, 1985a, 84). The democratic nature of the black church is a recurring theme in Du Bois's writings on religion, especially when he compared it with the white church, because, in spite of what he was wont to term its "primitivisms" and "nativisms," yet and still, he stated, "The Negro church is at least democratic. It welcomes everybody. It draws no color-line" (Du Bois, 2000a, 141). He asserted that the black church is further distinguished because it serves as *a multipurpose site for moral instruction, political education, social development, and racial/cultural awareness.*

As intimated in the previous chapter, African American women's special role in creating and sustaining the black church was not lost on Du Bois, and they received unprecedented praise from his pen. Radical religious convictions were not simply the cornerstone of individual black women's struggles against various forms of oppression, but they were also at the heart of their collective efforts to organize African Americans in the interest of social uplift. In *Darkwater*, Du Bois put forward the oft-noted names of Harriet Tubman and Sojourner Truth, fervently recalling not merely their profound religiosity, but also how their religious beliefs inspired and, perhaps, even invoked their legendary "feminist-abolitionism" (Du Bois, 1920, 175-77; see also Guy-Sheftall, 1990; Yee, 1992). The organizations that ultimately came to be collectively called the "black women's club movement" all emerged from the religious cultural context of the black church and, it should be reiterated, the National Association of Colored Women

(NACW)—i.e., the national association of black women's clubs—was "the first truly black national organization that functioned with strength and unity" (Hine and Thompson, 1998, 180). So powerful and pervasive was the influence of the black women's club movement on Du Bois, when he turned to social organization and radical political activism, he used the black women's club movement as a model, going so far as to name the social organization he helped to found (along with two of the major leaders of the black women's club movement, Ida B. Wells and Mary Church Terrell), the National Association for the Advancement of Colored People (NAACP). In *The Gift of Black Folk*, he candidly conceded:

> We have noted then the Negro woman in America as a worker tending to emancipate all women workers; as a mother nursing the white race and uniting the black and white races; as a conspirator urging forward emancipation in various sorts of ways; and we have finally only to remember that today the women of America who are doing humble but on the whole the most effective work in the social uplift of the lowly, not so much by money as by personal contact, are the colored women. Little is said or known about it but in thousands of churches and social clubs, in missionary societies and fraternal organizations, in unions like the National Association of Colored Women, these workers are founding and sustaining orphanages and old folk homes; distributing personal charity and relief; visiting prisoners; helping hospitals; teaching children; and ministering to all sorts of needs. Their work, as it comes now and then in special cases to the attention of individuals of the white world, forms a splendid bond of encouragement and sympathy, and helps more than most realize in minimizing racial difficulties and encouraging human sympathy. (Du Bois, 1970a, 149)

Without a doubt, Du Bois (1920) declared in *Darkwater*, "It was . . . strong women that laid the foundations of the great Negro church of today, with its five million members and ninety millions of dollars in property" (174). He acknowledged the role of "early church mothers," such as Mary Still, in the establishment of the African Methodist Episcopal Church (174). Moreover, he suggested that "such [was the] spiritual ancestry" that spurred Harriet Tubman's legendary efforts to liberate the enslaved, sympathize with John Brown's revolutionary abolitionism, and enlist in the Union Army (174).

In an audacious turn of phrase, Du Bois further accentuated black women's special "spiritual ancestry" by placing the religious and resistance activities of black women on a par with those of black men. As discussed in detail in the previous chapter, he went so far as to recall Sojourner Truth's classic query to Frederick Douglass—"Frederick, *is God dead?*"—when the male-feminist abolitionist, in a moment of desperation, declared that African Americans would have to fight for their freedom by force of arms. Du Bois also acknowledged the work of Kate Ferguson, a nineteen-year-old African American widow, who "took the children of the streets of New York, white and black, into her empty arms, taught them, found them homes," and, most pertinent to the present discussion, she "established the first modern Sunday School in Manhattan" (177-78).

In his writings on religion Du Bois also spoke highly of African American clergy, and often exhibited a great deal of sympathy for their peculiar simultaneous positions as "spiritual guides" and social leaders of their people. For instance, in his chapter on Alexander Crummell and in "Of the Faith of the Fathers," both in *The Souls of Black Folk*, he heartily advanced, "The Preacher is the most unique personality developed by the Negro on American soil. A leader, a politician, an orator, a 'boss,' an idealist—all these he is, and ever, too, the center of a group of men" (Du Bois, 1903c, 190; see also Du Bois, 1899, 205-7, 1982b, 328-29, 2000a, 21-22). Black ministers were often misunderstood, he argued, and very few were qualified to criticize them, as there were no serious studies (antedating Du Bois's) of their dual religious and social roles. In perhaps his earliest essay on religion, "The Problem of Amusement" (originally published in 1897), Du Bois (1978) contended:

> The minister who directs this peculiar and anomalous institution must not be criticized with full knowledge of his difficult role. He is in reality the mayor, the chief magistrate of a community, ruling to be sure, but ruling according to the dictates of a not over-intelligent town council, according to time honored custom and law; and above all, hampered by the necessities of his budget; he may be a spiritual guide, he must be a social organizer, a leader of actual men; he may desire to enrich and reform the spiritual life of his flock, but above all he must have church members; he may desire to revolutionize church methods, to elevate the ideals of the people, to tell the hard, honest truth to a people who need a little more truth and a little less flattery—but how can he do this when the people of this social organism demand that he shall take from the purely spiritual activities of his flock, time to minister to their amusements, diversion, and physical comfort; when he sees the picnic masquerading as a camp-meeting, the revival becoming the social event of the season, the day of worship turned into a day of general reception and dining out, the rival church organizations plunging into debt to furnish their houses of worship with an elegance that far outruns the financial ability of a poverty-stricken people; when the church door becomes the trysting place for all the lovers and Lotharios of the community; when a ceaseless round of entertainments, socials, and necktie parties chase the week through—what minister can be more than most ministers are coming to be, the business managers of a picnic ground? (229)

Finally, with regard to Du Bois's reverence for African American religion, it must be said that he held black church music in especial high esteem. He frequently wrote beamingly and bemusingly of African American religious music, calling it "the most original and beautiful expression of human life and longing yet born on American soil" (Du Bois, 1903c, 191). What is more, few scholars of African American religious music, or black music in general, can resist commenting on that hauntingly famous passage from *The Souls of Black Folk* where Du Bois wrote:

> Little of beauty has America given the world save the rude grandeur God himself stamped on her bosom; the human spirit in this new world has expressed itself in vigor and ingenuity rather than in beauty. And so by fateful chance the Negro folk-song—the rhythmic cry of the slave—stands today not simply as the sole American music, but as the most beautiful expression of human experience born this side the seas. It has been neglected, it has been, and is, half despised, and above all it has been persistently mistaken and misunderstood; but notwithstanding, it still remains as the singular spiritual heritage of the nation and the greatest gift of the Negro people. (251)

From the Du Boisian perspective, the black church was the cornerstone of African American culture, and in his studies he traced its connections to the spiritual and broader cultural traditions of Africa, while simultaneously demonstrating the process (i.e., syncretism) by which various disparate groups of enslaved Africans miraculously became a multicultural and transethnic diasporan community, a many-sided single people—in other words, *African Americans*. In *Slave Culture*, Sterling Stuckey (1987) pointed out that even before enslaved Africans reached the shores of North America, they began to create a new culture, one where traditional "tribalisms" were nothing more than "a lingering memory in the minds of American slaves" (3). People from as far north as Senegal were piled onto people from Namibia and Angola in the south, people from Kenya in the east were sandwiched between Ghanaians and Nigerians from the west, and in their long and horror-filled voyage to the Americas they initiated the protracted and arduous process of creating a new culture. This new culture was primarily one of resistance, but it must be borne in mind that the bulk of this defiance was grounded in and grew out of the enslaved Africans' harkening back to the religions and social justice traditions of their ancestors, which, for all of the reasons observed above, are historically embodied in the black church.

DU BOIS'S SOCIOLOGY OF THE RACIAL COLONIZATION OF RELIGION

For Du Bois the African American church was based as much on African religious thought and practices as it was on European and European American Christian theology, and its contributions to African American culture, both sacred and secular, were not only worthy of religious and social study, but, he believed, provided a paradigm and should be recounted for present and future generations of African Americans and others struggling against oppression and exploitation. He, therefore, often acknowledged and emphasized what he understood to be the overarching achievements of African American religion, and the black church in particular. In weighted words from one of his classic passages from the pages of the *Crisis*, he sternly stated:

> Before such an organization [i.e., the black church] one must bow with respect. It has accomplished much. It has instilled and conserved morals, it has helped family life, it has taught and developed ability and given the colored man his best business training. It has planted in every city and town of the Union, with few exemptions, meeting places for colored folk which vary from shelters to luxurious and beautiful edifices. (Du Bois, 1972c, 332)

However, here the Du Boisian dialectic rears its head. One of the many things that distinguish Du Bois's sociology of religion is that it exposes both the positives *and* negatives of religion. In other words, his sociology of religion is deeply dialectical, as with the best of his work. As we have seen above, Du Bois undoubtedly saw a certain value and had a deep and sincere respect for religion. But, by the same token, he was also one of its harshest critics, especially when religion was (ab)used to uphold racism, sexism, classism, or militarism. Aptheker's (1980b) work offers great insight on this issue:

> Neither in his youth nor in later life did Du Bois attend any church with any regularity, but he was well aware of the enormous influence of the church upon the history and lives of black people and upon his own life. . . . The fact is that Du Bois disliked denominational religion and detested that "Christianity" which became an excuse for the status quo—whether slavery or racism or war: the religion, as he once put it, of J. P. Morgan rather than of Jesus Christ. A reason for this sharp feeling was Du Bois's admiration for what he took to be the revolutionary, or at least radical and challenging, character of the actual teachings of Jesus. . . . [H]e viewed the black church as, at its best, the "basic rock" of his people, their shield and sword, their solace and goad; an indispensable source of their persistence and historical confidence despite all oppression. (vii–viii)

The fact of the matter is Du Bois problematicized more than he praised religion. To be sure, he acknowledged its positive historical, cultural, and social significance, but his comments were often more critical and condemning than they were congratulatory and commending. Few sociologists of religion have recognized the potential *and* actual (or historical) pitfalls of religion as long and as loudly as Du Bois did and, even more, few have exhibited the kind of care he did in discussing tough and taboo topics in a critical language laced with love and fiery words filled with a radical humanism that would make both Mohandas Gandhi and Martin Luther King blush. Du Bois, fiercely dancing with the dialectic, criticized black and white religious leaders and institutions alike. He argued that religious hypocrisy, as with other vices and vulgarities emerging from the bowels of human existence, is not the exclusive domain of a single racial group, gender, or social class, but remains open to any and all who would enter into its evil.

His cautious contempt for the black church and its bourgeois practices was notorious, as was his critical disdain for its leadership. From the Du Boisian dialectical perspective, the black church seemed to be involved in and promoting everything but its "chief duty," that of "character building" (Du Bois, 1973, 114). Part of the problem, to be sure, was with its leadership. The "average Negro preacher," Du Bois (1899) put it plainly, "is a shrewd manager, a respectable man, a good talker, a pleasant companion, but neither learned nor spiritual, nor a reformer" (206). In "The Minister," an address delivered at the 1906 Hampton Annual Conference, Du Bois (1906c) boldly criticized African American ministers, saying, as only he could, the too-often "Unsaid Thing" on the tip of most black folk's tongues:

> On the whole the Negroes of the United States are not satisfied with their ministers.... [O]n the whole there is deep and wide-spread dissatisfaction with the average Negro minister.... There have been among Negro ministers in the past so many men of immoral life and men so lacking in dignity and high purpose that continually the educated classes of the race, the young aspiring graduates of our schools, the fathers of rising families have been dissatisfied with this class of men and have withdrawn themselves from them. (91)

However, here it is important to highlight the fact that Du Bois did not lay the blame completely on the black clergy; black congregations were also at fault. They were, to be sure, a difficult and contradictory group to lead and, as Du Bois observed, increasingly the traditional leaders of the church were being led, if not by the entire congregation, then by the rich and politically powerful of the church (i.e., the black bourgeoisie). This is an intricate issue, one that points to the pitfalls of African American religion in general, the relationship between black clergy and black congregations more specifically, and, most importantly from a Du Boisian dialectical perspective, the moral mission of black folk. In words that brilliantly capture this conundrum, Du Bois (1899) wrote:

> In direct moral teaching and in setting moral standards for the people.... the church is timid, and naturally so, for its constitution is democracy tempered by custom. Negro preachers are often condemned for poor leadership and empty sermons, and it is said that men with so much power and influence could

make striking moral reforms. This is but partially true. The congregation does not follow the moral precepts of the preacher, but rather the preacher follows the standard of his flock, and only exceptional men dare seek to change this. And here it must be remembered that the Negro preacher is primarily an executive officer, rather than a spiritual guide. (205-6)

On the one hand, Du Bois praised the social function of the black church, acknowledging it as the cornerstone of African American culture and commending it for its contributions to African American social development and cultural survival. On the other hand, he criticized the black church for failing to develop the special moral mission of African Americans. He was highly disappointed with the pomp and circumstance of black church life, and said so in clear and critical terms. The "reform of the pulpit" was only part of the work that Du Bois (1982b) saw at hand (329). If the black church was to truly embrace both its sacred and secular obligations and live out its creed, then it must not only demand that its clergy be persons (men *and* women) of "integrity, learning, and deep spiritual earnestness" (Du Bois, 1899, 206). It must also call upon its congregations to be persons of "integrity, learning, and deep spiritual earnestness."[9] In the 1938 classic commencement address, "The Revelation of Saint Orgne the Damned," which he was invited to deliver in commemoration of the fiftieth anniversary of his graduation from Fisk, Du Bois (1973) put forward perhaps his most trenchant criticisms of the black church:

> [B]ehold . . . the Black Churches of America. . . . Their five millions of members in 40,000 groups, holding $2,000,000,000 in their hands, are the most strongly organized body among us; the first source of our group culture, the beginning of our education—what is this church doing today towards its primary task of teaching men right and wrong, and the duty of doing right? The flat answer is nothing if not less than nothing. Like other churches and other religions of other peoples and ages, our church has veered off on every conceivable side path, which interferes with and nullifies its chief duty of character building. It has built up a body of dogma and fairy tales, fantastic fables of sin and salvation, impossible creeds and impossible demands for ignorant unquestioning belief and obedience. Ask any thorough churchman today and he will tell you, not that the object of the church is to get men to do right and make the majority of mankind happy, but rather that the whole duty of man is to "believe in the Lord Jesus Christ and be saved;" or to believe in the "one Holy Catholic church," infallible and omniscient. (113-14)

In response to the issues he raised Du Bois boldly restated the fundamental role of the black church, and it is interesting to note that his position was remarkably consistent with that of his initial sociology of African American religion in "The Problem of Amusement" and *The Philadelphia Negro*, pieces which he penned four decades prior to "The Revelation of Saint Orgne the

Damned." He audaciously asserted, "The function of the Negro Church, instead of being that of building edifices, paying old debts, holding revivals and staging entertainments, has got to be brought back, or shall we say forward, to the simple duty of teaching ethics. For this purpose the Hebrew scriptures and the New Testament canon will not suffice" (114).

Why would a strictly scriptural or "religious" response to African American problems not be a viable solution? Because clergy and laity alike for hundreds of years had been interpreting and misinterpreting, using and abusing both Christian theology and religion in general, not for the spreading of a spirit of selflessness and loving-kindness, but very frequently to teach selfishness, competitiveness, and the diabolical "good" of guile. Moreover, even more than the black church, the white church was not only guilty of the foregoing but, according to Du Bois, served in many respects as a model for much of the religious mayhem of the black church. For example, in his 1907 essay "Religion in the South," he railed against white religion and whites' tendency to disingenuously blame blacks (among other racially colonized nonwhites) for their own social degradation and political disenfranchisement:

> Not only is there . . . falseness when the [white] South excuses its ethical paradox by pointing to the low condition of the Negro masses, but there is also a strange blindness in failing to see that every pound of evidence to prove the present degradation of black men but adds to the crushing weight of indictment against their past treatment of this race. A race is not made in a single generation. If they accuse Negro women of lewdness and Negro men of monstrous crime, what are they doing but advertising to the world the shameless lewdness of those Southern men who brought millions of mulattoes into the world, and whose deeds throughout the South and particularly in Virginia, the mother of slavery, have left but few prominent families whose blood does not today course in black veins? Suppose today Negroes do steal; who was it that for centuries made stealing a virtue by stealing their labor? Have not laziness and listlessness always been the followers of slavery? If these ten millions are ignorant by whose past law and mandate and present practice is this true? (Du Bois, 1982a, 92–93)

To be sure, black religion historically had and currently continues to have its problems and, as was witnessed above, Du Bois did not mince any words bringing his concerns to the attention of the black church. However, he importantly emphasized, the black church and the white church had different kinds of problems, perhaps not at every instance, but enough to level comparably different critiques. His major criticism of the white church revolved around its claim of *agapē* (i.e., selfless love) or, rather, what has come to be called "Christian love." How is it possible that white clergy and white laity could avow the cardinal creed of Christian love (*agapē*), and then schizophrenically, psychopathically, and systematically sanction and perpetually participate in the violation, oppression, and exploitation of their enslaved and/or racially segregated black Christian brethren and sistren?

Christianity, it could be said, has been the subterfuge through which whites have religiously disarmed blacks, among racially colonized others. In fact, Christianity was utilized to spread the spirit of Europe and its imperial push for global dominance much more than it has ever actually imparted Christian ethics. No matter what the "true" tenets of Christianity may be or are soberly understood to be, many of its historical manifestations and cultural expressions have violently and repetitiously registered in the all too familiar hegemonic language(s) of racism, sexism, colonialism, and, of course, capitalism—for instance, the early imperial expansion of "Christendom" (*Christendomiensis* in Latin) or the Christian Empire, and, of course, the long catalogue of Christian Crusades (Hindley, 2003; MacEvitt, 2008; Mastnak, 2002; Riley-Smith, 2008). The corroboration of this claim is written all over racialized and colonized people's faces (*and* their bodies as well). Thus, the theodicean question returns: How could a religion that has unleashed such evil in the world be good or, at the least, be used for good in the present? The time for timid talk was long gone, if ever there was a time to talk to enslavers and oppressors in such a way. Du Bois offered his studied answer to this question more times than many white Christians would care to recall. On what he called, the "utter failure of white religion," Du Bois (1970d) austerely stated, "A nation's religion is its life and as such white Christianity is a miserable failure" (309). In connection to this, he asserted elsewhere:

> It is painfully true that White Christianity has in the twentieth century been curiously discredited. . . . Here in the twentieth century of the Prince of Peace the leading nations representing His religion have been murdering, maiming and hurting each other on a scale unprecedented in the history of Mankind . . . into the White Church of Christ race prejudice has crept to such an extent it is openly recognized and in the United States at least it is considered the natural and normal thing that white and colored people should belong mostly to different organizations and almost entirely to different congregations. . . . These facts do not impugn Christianity but they do make terrible comment upon the failure of its white followers. (Du Bois, 1985a, 84)

Du Bois was careful not to condemn Christianity outright but, more particularly, his contempt was critically aimed at *white* Christianity, which could more properly be called *white supremacist patriarchal capitalist colonial* Christianity. It was what seemed to be the inherently white supremacist nature of white religion that bothered him. He perplexingly mused, white Christianity "theoretically opens the door to all men and yet closes it forcibly and insultingly in the face of black men" (Du Bois, 1982a, 92). He noted a recurring theme of religious hypocrisy in the way whites (mis)interpreted and practiced Christianity. In his 1929 essay "The Church and the Color-Line," he thundered:

> [W]hen the church meets the Negro problem, it writes itself down as a deliberate and systematic liar. It does not say "Come unto me all ye that labor"; it does not "love its neighbor as itself"; it does not welcome "Jew and Gentile, barbarian, Scythian, bond and free;" and yet it openly and blatantly professes all this. . . . [T]he church has opposed every great modern social reform; it opposed the spread of democracy, universal education, trade unionism, the abolition of poverty, the emancipation of women, the spread of science, the freedom of art and literature, and the emancipation of the Negro slave. When the reform was gained, the church righted itself, led usually by some schismatic and heretical part of itself, came over on the Lord's side and usually did not hesitate both to claim a preponderant share of the glory of victory and again to emphasize its supernatural claims. (Du Bois, 1970d, 217)

Du Bois's critique of the hypocrisy of white Christianity did not end here; there was more. Indeed, there was much more that he took issue with. Many of his criticisms centered on how the white church sanctioned the African holocaust, racial colonization, African American enslavement, and post-Emancipation racial segregation—a historical fact that many black Christians had (and continue to have) a hard time coming to terms with. For example, in his 1931 essay "Will the Church Remove the Color-Line?" there stands a little-known passage that says more about white Christian hypocrisy in one paragraph than many are likely to be exposed to attending the most "progressive" black churches of the present age faithfully for a number of years. Du Bois (2000a) revealingly wrote:

> [P]erhaps many of us would rather forget it [i.e., African holocaust and African American enslavement]; yet we cannot forget that under the aegis and protection of the religion of the Prince of Peace—of a religion which was meant for the lowly and unfortunate—there arose in America one of the most stupendous institutions of human slavery that the world has seen. The Christian Church sponsored and defended this institution, despite occasional protest and effort at amelioration here and there. The Catholic church approved of and defended slavery; the Episcopal church defended and protected slavery; the Puritans and Congregationalists recognized and upheld slavery; the Methodists and Baptists stood staunchly behind it; the Quakers gave their consent to it. Indeed, there was not a single branch of the Christian Church that did not in the end become part of an impregnable bulwark defending the trade in human beings and the holding of them as chattel. (174–75)

Here Du Bois is unequivocally discursively disrupting and unapologetically challenging what John Whitehead (1994) has identified as the long-standing "religious apartheid" centered around "the Curse of Ham" myth and other "Bible-based" white supremacist anti-black racist misinterpretations and morally repugnant justifications of the African holocaust, racial colonization, African American enslavement, and post-Emancipation racial segregation. Indeed, as the work of Hans Baer (1984), Mark Chapman (1996), Cain Felder (2002), David Goldenberg (2003), Stephen Haynes (2002), Robert Hood (1990), David Howard-Pitney (2005), John David Smith (1993c), and Joseph Washington (1984) illustrate, there is a growing body of contemporary research that seems to point to, and acutely accent the prescient nature of Du Bois's critical sociology of the racial colonization of religion. Du Bois had harsh, but morally justified, words to say with regard to the white church's position on racial segregation or, rather, American apartheid. Not only did the white church want to conveniently and cowardly omit its role in the holocaust and enslavement of African people, but it wanted to do so while slyly supporting twentieth-century racial segregation and, therefore, blacks' ongoing dehumanization and social degradation. In his 1913 essay "The Church and the Negro," Du Bois (2000a) declared: "The church aided and abetted the Negro slave trade; the church was the bulwark of American slavery; and the church is the strongest seat of racial and color prejudice. If one hundred of the best and purest colored folk of the United States should seek to apply for membership in any white church in this land tomorrow, 999 out of every 1,000 ministers would lie to keep them out. They would not only do this, but would openly and brazenly defend their action as worthy of followers of Jesus Christ" (99).

In his 1929 article "The Color-Line and the Church," Du Bois continued this line of criticism, demonstrating in it and the various writings cited above his undeniable contributions to the sociology of religion: principally, that religion is inextricable from the history, culture, and political economy of society, and always intersects with and informs the general thought and practices of society. He put it plainly: "The American Church of Christ is Jim Crowed from top to bottom. No other institution in America is built so thoroughly or more absolutely on the color-line. Everybody knows this" (169).

A major assertion of the sociology of religion is that religion is not simply about the sacred or transcendent, the intangible or otherworldly (i.e., God, angels, heaven, the soul, faith, belief, miracles, and prayer), but that religion is also concerned with everyday reality and social phenomena. Moreover, the sociology of religion grapples with (or *should* wrestle with) the ways in which religion hints at the fact that it is a human product, perhaps divinely inspired, but a human product nonetheless, and one that plays itself out, not in heaven, but here on earth within the web of the wider social world. From this view, religion may be conceived of as being meticulously marked by particular sociohistorical events, social thought, social practices, social organizations, and social institutions, and it is precisely the way in which Du Bois critically engaged religion and religious institutions, focusing on their *sociality*, that distinguish his writings on religion and places the bulk of his work in this area under the rubric of the sociology of religion.

In Du Bois's dialectical treatment of religion he was able to touch on and turn his readers' attention to its potential for good *or* bad. Religion has never been neutral, but always and ever an alternative site where knowledge and power are contested and acquired. Du Bois composed some of the most beautiful passages one could possibly read concerning African American religion and the black church. However, he also leveled some of the harshest criticisms of African American religion and the black church ever recorded. What is it about Du Bois's dialectic that makes him seem so schizophrenic, praising the black church on one page and then caustically condemning it on the next? And what of his work on white Christianity and the white church? He certainly does not seem schizophrenic or two-tongued in that regard. He is straightforward and to the point: he thinks white Christians and white Christianity reek of religious hypocrisy, to put it plainly.

Because religion, as with any area of culture, is a shared human project and a social construction, it almost inherently points to human potentials and moral pitfalls. Du Bois's writings on religion seek to simultaneously salvage its good and, literally, excommunicate its bad. Many scholars of religion and social scientists have misunderstood his work in this area, among several other areas, because, as he put it, "so far as the American world of science and letters was concerned, we [i.e., African American social scientists] never 'belonged'; we remained unrecognized in learned societies and academic groups" (Du Bois, 1968a, 228). His work, as I am certain many must wryly contend concerning the work of contemporary Africana studies scholars, is merely the work of "Negroes studying Negroes, and after all, what [have] Negroes to do with America or science [or human culture and civilization, some might even sardonically add]?" (228)

In short, from his research on African American religion during enslavement, to his portraits of radical black religious leaders; from his pioneering studies of black congregational life, to his critiques of both black and white Christianity; from his discussions of the role of African American women in the black church, to his passionate praise of African American religious music, there can be little doubt that Du Bois significantly contributed to the sociology of religion (and by extension, religious studies and sociology, in the broader sense). He was not simply the first black sociologist of religion, or the first sociologist of black religion, but the first sociologist to analyze the role of religion in American society, which, I should reiterate, is purportedly the central point of the sociology of religion in the United States.

CRITICAL THEORY OF LIBERATION THEOLOGY: DU BOIS, SOCIOLOGY, AND LIBERATION THEOLOGY

Du Bois's philosophy of religion and sociology of religion lend themselves to the development of a *critical theory of liberation theology* insofar as, first, critical social theory seeks to employ every available resource to critique all forms of domination and provide a basis for the radical democratic socialist transformation of contemporary society. Second, a critical theory of liberation theology is premised on a theology of liberation, which, of course, begins with thought on God (*theologia* in Latin), but it is also rooted in the social and political realities of poor and marginalized people, those struggling against the contemporary beasts of burden: capitalism, colonialism, racism, and sexism, among other imperial issues. A critical theory of liberation theology, then, draws from the discourses of both critical theory and liberation theology in the interest of critiquing the ideological and oppressive aspects of religion and their role in and relationship to contemporary society. Moreover, a critical theory of liberation theology contains the characteristic dialectical and self-reflexive quality of the best of critical social theory and, therefore, seeks to deconstruct and reconstruct both critical theory and liberation theology through theoretical synthesis and deep discursive dialogue on social domination and human liberation.

An Africana critical theory of liberation theology places liberation theology in dialogue with classical and contemporary critical social theory, and particularly the Africana tradition of critical theory. It challenges traditional liberation theologians to epistemically open themselves to the contributions of black radical politics and black revolutionary social movements. From the view of Africana critical theory, this dialogue will be philosophically fruitful insofar as black radical political theory and black revolutionary social movements have been frequently omitted from the social theories and political thought that most mainstream liberation theologians employ in their efforts to bridge the growing gap between "church and state" or, rather, religion and society. Further, many of the social problems that liberation theologians currently seek to address have been, or are being, brilliantly engaged in the discursive formations and discursive practices of Africana philosophy, Africana religious studies, and Africana social and political thought (J. K. Carter, 2008; R. M. Franklin, 1990; Lott and Pittman, 2003; Palmié, 2008; Trost, 2007; Wiredu, 2004).

Traditionally, liberation theology has prided itself on the fact that it is not quarantined to luxurious church sanctuaries and university lecture halls, but rather emerges in the midst of sufferers' quests for salvation, concrete social conflicts, and anti-imperialist struggles (C. Boff, 1987; McGovern, 1989; Milbank, 1990). Oxford theologian Christopher Rowland (1999) contends, "The key thing is that one first of all *does* liberation theology rather than learns about it. Or, put another way, one can only learn about it by embarking on it" (4, emphasis in original). Embarking on liberation theology means, first of all, coming to terms with the fact that it is a very varied intellectual and political tradition that seeks to situate theology and religion in contemporary social contexts and cultural conditions. It means acknowledging the wide range of theoretical and political practices that have come to be identified as "liberation theology," practices which, it should be emphasized, have consistently dialogued with the discourses of the academy (though not necessarily the discursive formations and discursive practices of Africana intellectuals in the academy, or the social and political theories and praxes of black organic intellectual-activists working outside the orbit of the academy). Hence, among the more popular versions of liberation theology there are Marxist, feminist, postmodernist, and postcolonialist schools of thought, as well as racial and cultural studies–based liberation theologies, which accent issues of ethnicity, history, and cultural geography often along with the class and gender analysis of Marxist and feminist liberation theologies (Berryman, 1987; Boff and Boff, 1987; Hennelly, 1995; Rowland, 1999; Segundo, 1976).

By focusing on the progressive and regressive aspects of religion, Du Bois's sociology of religion demonstrates its *dialecticality* and, like the liberation theologians, he places *human liberation* at the heart of his discourse on theology and religion. Where liberation theologians conventionally stress poor and vulnerable peoples' struggles against secular oppression, Du Bois (1972c) criticized, not simply imperial society, but the church for acquiescing to the whims and wishes of rich and ruling-class congregants and betraying the "working man" (330). In *The Philadelphia Negro*, he also criticized the church for taking too great a portion of poor families' income, money he maintained that could be better spent on bare necessities and much-needed family possessions, such as homes. Du Bois (1899) declared: "Much of the money that should have gone into homes has gone into costly church edifices, dues to societies, dress and entertainment. If the Negroes had bought little homes as persistently as they have worked to develop a church and secret society system, and had invested more of their earnings in savings-banks and less in clothes they would be in far better condition to demand industrial opportunity than they are today" (185).

A critical theory of liberation theology does not simply use sacred texts to point to secular wrongs, as it seems is the case with so much of modern theology, progressive or otherwise. It does not see religion or the church as politically neutral, nor does it understand the Bible or any other sacred text (e.g., the Odu Ifa, the Tanakh, the Qur'an, the Vedas, the Vinaya Pitaka, or the first four Nikayas of the Sutta Pitaka) to be sources free from the trappings of a particular race, gender, or class's all too human heavenly and/or earthly desires. It is, to put it plainly, a critical theory of liberation theology primarily preoccupied with the deconstruction and reconstruction of theology and religion in the interest of human liberation and radical democratic socialist transformation.

Du Bois's philosophy of religion and sociology of religion are relevant with regard to the development of a critical theory of liberation theology insofar as his writings on religion exhibit a *theodicean openness* to the role that not only Christianity, but also indigenous African religions and Islam have played in continental and diasporan African history and culture—in essence, therefore, antedating Ali Mazrui's (1986) "triple heritage" thesis by well over half a century. In *The Souls of W. E. B. Du Bois* (2009), religious historians Edward Blum and Jason Young maintain that "Du Bois demonstrated a multicultural approach to religion, often invoking sacred concepts and histories from all over the world. In the history of Islam, for instance, he saw Muslim societies throughout the Middle East and North Africa as complex societies comprised of varied races, religions, and cultures that might serve to guide the twentieth-century United States into more equitable social and racial interactions" (xx). In other words, "Du Bois's range of religious thought was not in the least limited to Christianity. He was well-versed in a variety of religious traditions, histories, and mythologies. In his writing, Du Bois imagined and articulated a cultural and social pluralism of interaction and creation" (xx). Indeed, Du Bois's articulation of a "cultural and social pluralism of interaction and creation" not only accents the ubiquitous radical democratic dimension of his sociological discourse, but it also decidedly distinguishes his sociology of religion from those of Durkheim, Weber, and Simmel, among others. What is more, Du Bois's sociology of religion, as I have repeatedly said of his sociology in general, may be further distinguished from those of his more famous contemporaries insofar as his was simultaneously a sociology of world religions and, even more unequivocally, a sociology of religion preoccupied with religion in the United States or, rather, "American religion" in general, and African American religion in particular. Blum and Young help to drive the point home:

> Just as Du Bois explored the economic, social, and psychological roots of American racism and discrimination in a century marred by lynching, segregation, and race riots, so also he delved into the role of religion in the modern world in fascinating ways. He anticipated, for instance, the rise of the contemporary tensions that seem to be tearing the world apart: the global circulation of corporate capital and commerce, religious fundamentalism, and evangelical theologies. Indeed, Du Bois identified the crucial paradox and presumed contradiction between America's religious legacy—built on morality, justice, and equality—with the country's devotion to progress, modernity, and economic gain. Throughout his life and writings, Du Bois paid special attention to the tensions that erupted in a nation lying prone before two gods, and he labored to the very end hoping that the deity of justice and brotherhood would prevail over the god of violence and hate. (xviii; see also R. C. Henry, 2009; Sevitch, 2002, 2009; J. R. Young, 2009)

It is important here, then, to observe the ways in which Du Bois's classical sociology of religion simultaneously transgresses and transcends the *theocentric* (God the Father–centered), *Christocentric* (Jesus Christ–centered), and *pneumocentric* (Holy Spirit–centered) trinity of both traditional Christianity and most contemporary sociology of religion. For example, in *The Negro Church* Du Bois (1903a) discussed "primitive Negro religion," by which he meant the religion of "the African tribes," and made dazzling claims concerning retentions of ancient African religious beliefs and practices (1). He stated with clear confidence, "There can be no reasonable doubt, however, but that the scattered remains of religious systems in Africa today among the Negro tribes are survivals of the religious ideas upon which the Egyptian religion was based" (1–2).

In *Black Folk, Then and Now*, Du Bois (1939) continued to chronicle the character of traditional African religions, stating again, "The basis of Egyptian religion was 'of a purely Nigritian character,' and, in its developed form, Sudanese tribal gods were invoked and venerated by the priest" (108). He went on to discuss the religions of the Bori, Yoruba, Hausa, and Ewe, among other African cultural groups, asserting:

> The religion of Africa is the universal animism or fetishism of primitive peoples, rising to polytheism and approaching monotheism chiefly, but not wholly, as a result of Christianity and Islamic missions. Of fetishism there is much misapprehension. It is not mere senseless degradation. It is a philosophy of life. Among primitive Negroes there can be . . . no such divorce of religion from practical life as is common in civilized lands. Religion is life, and fetish an expression of the practical recognition of the dominant natural forces which surround the Negro. (106)

With regard to Islam, Du Bois claimed, it "came by conquest, trade, and proselytism. As a conqueror it reached Egypt in the seventh century and had by the end of the fourteenth century firm footing in the Egyptian Sudan" (108). In addition, he acknowledged Islam (which he referred to throughout his early works as "Mohammedism") as a religion which "[t]oday . . . dominates Africa north of ten degrees north latitude and is strong between five and ten degrees north latitude. In the east it reaches below the Victoria Nyanza" (108). In *The World and Africa*, Du Bois (1965) wrote at length about Islam's imperial legacy in Africa, what he called "the process of Arabization in North Africa" and the "Arabization of the Nile valley" (185). He even went so far as to discuss the extremely taboo topic concerning the Prophet Muhammad personally enslaving Africans, but then, he quickly claimed, "He [the Prophet Muhammad] liberated all his slaves, and they were all well-known figures in the early history of Islam" (183). Although he despised the imperial legacy of Islam in Africa, Du Bois often posed it as a counter to the crass Christianity of Africa's European racial colonizers. In *The Negro Church*, he wrote, "Mohammedism entered Africa in the seventh and eighth centuries and has since that time conquered nearly all North

Africa, the Sudan, and made inroads into the populations of the west coast ... and especially is it preserving the natives against the desolations of Christian rum" (Du Bois, 1903a, 2).

Du Bois's *theodicean openness* to non-Christian theologies and religions, particularly indigenous African theologies and religions, is also evident in his own personal beliefs and worship practices, which, as mentioned above, cannot be quickly characterized as "Christian" in any conventional sense. Noted African American theologian Gayraud Wilmore (1983) perhaps put it best when he stated that Du Bois "was a religious man in the broadest sense, but one who did not regard himself as a churchman" (136). Wilmore continued:

> His religion obtrudes through his secular writings under a nimbus of African spirituality and transcendental mystique. He was once Knight Commander of the Liberian Order of African Redemption, which had strong religious overtones. On his 25th birthday he vowed to become the Moses of black people and improvised a ritual of regeneration, using wine, candles, oil, and oranges. In the throes of the rite he prayed, sang, and made "a sacrifice to the *Zeitgeist* of Work, God and Mercy." (258-59; see also Du Bois, 1985a, 26-29)

Du Bois, therefore, aids in the development of a critical theory of liberation theology insofar as his writings on religion compare and contrast the wide range of theologies and religions throughout the African world. His philosophy of religion and sociology of religion constantly dovetailed with his increasingly critical dialectic, and this enabled him to highlight both the positive and negative impact of theology and/or religion on black folk, their histories, cultures, and struggles. Indeed, Christianity garnered the bulk of his religious criticism because it was, and remains, the dominant religion of the United States and the religion to which most people of African descent adhere in the Western hemisphere. His critique of Christianity, then, must be viewed as nothing less than a continuation of his critique of Western European and white American imperialist thought and culture and, equally important, accommodationist and assimilationist tendencies in African American religious thought and practices.

Liberation theology, in the "traditional" sense, is often content to leave its central theological components as they are; which is to say, "conventional" liberation theology's Christological core is rarely critically called into question, and in this sense it seems utterly unaware of non-Christian liberation theologies and religious realities (Dabashi, 2008; Engineer, 1990; Hennelly, 1990; McGovern, 1989; Naseef, 2007). The critical theory of liberation theology that I am developing here, then, seeks to challenge conventional liberation theology to dialogue with the wide range of theologies and religions in the world, especially the African world. It, therefore, neither begins nor ends with Jesus Christ and Christianity, but is theodiceanly open to the prophets and prophetesses, priests and priestesses, and theologies of other spiritual traditions and religions. In this sense, critical theory of liberation theology, as I envision it, is not quarantined to Jesus Christ and Christianity but, I should add, it is also not anti-Christian. It is, in a word, more of a meta-theoretical and radical methodological move toward our current (I could say *continental* and *diasporan African*, but it is certainly applicable to racially colonized and oppressed others') religious reality—a reality that historically has been and currently continues to be marked and molded by unprecedented diasporan diversity (L. E. Barrett, 1974; Olupona and Gemignani, 2007; Pinn, 2009; Schmidt, 2008; Trost, 2007).

Critical theory of liberation theology hinges on hermeneutics and *emancipatory epistemology*—that is, *a theory of knowledge deeply concerned with critical interpretation and concrete struggles for human liberation*. A major goal of *emancipatory epistemology* is to contest flatfooted, reductionistic, and absolutist conceptions of meaning, what we call in Africana philosophy—borrowing the buzzwords of the black existentialists and postmodernists—"essentializing" and "totalizing" meanings. In essence, and more meta-methodologically speaking, this means warding off narrow-minded and totalizing thought that resists or rejects difference and diversity, whether religious, cultural, racial, sexual, or what have you. *Emancipatory epistemology* sidesteps the psychopathic policing and other pitfalls of *epistemic apartheid* (whether within or without the realm of religion), and stubbornly struggles to combat *epistemic closure* with *epistemic openness* and the ongoing development of progressive discursive formations and discursive practices predicated on human liberation and democratic socialist transformation.

Theology, religion, and the church have long been immune, in the minds of many, to even the most sincere constructive criticism, but Du Bois dialectically points us in a different direction. His critique of Christianity, again the dominant religion of the society in which he lived and worked, contributes to the development of a critical theory of liberation theology in that it prefigures and provides a paradigm for the deconstruction and reconstruction of liberation theology, the role of religion in society, and the ways in which Africana religious thought broadens the epistemic base of both critical social theory and liberation theology. Long before the liberation theologians began their discourse on those who are "poor and Christian," "the weakest and the insignificant"; before liberation theologians began to use the Bible to buttress their claim that it is important to "understand the grace and salvation of Jesus in the context of the present and from the situation of the poor"; before the liberation theologians pointed out that poverty-stricken people's "faith affects in many different ways their experience of poverty and oppression, and this experience of poverty and oppression makes its mark on their experience of the gospel," W. E. B. Du Bois developed a critical discourse on theology and religion that accentuated the often overlooked situation of persons who are poor, black, and Christian (Gutierrez, 1999, 19, 25-26). He chastised the Christian church for not living by its creed, for allowing racism and segregation (i.e., the "color-line") to creep into its congregations, and for bastardizing the life and legacy of Jesus Christ. How could they call themselves "Christians," Du Bois furiously wondered, if they do not adhere to the cardinal principles of Christianity: Christ's word and the Golden Rule? In his 1913 *Crisis* essay, "The Church and the Negro," he wrote:

> The relation of the church to the Negro is, or should be, a very simple proposition. Leaving aside the supernatural significance of the church, we have here groups of people working for human uplift and professing the highest and most unselfish morality as exemplified by the life and teaching of Jesus of Nazareth and the Golden Rule. By this standard all church members should treat Negroes as they themselves would wish to be treated if they were colored. They should do this and teach this, and, if need be, die for this creed. (Du Bois, 2000a, 99)

Like liberation theologians, Du Bois conceived of Christ as someone who would side with the poor and the most marginalized in society. In his writings on religion Du Bois illustrated time and time again how the teachings of Jesus could be used to combat the increasing invisibility of poverty and the ongoing oppression of the poor. In this sense, his work connects with contemporary liberation theology, especially the thought of leading Latin American liberation theologian Gustavo Gutierrez (1999), where he writes:

> These times . . . bear the imprint of a new presence of the poor, the marginalized and the oppressed. Those who were for so long "absent" in our society and in the Church have made themselves—and are continuing to make themselves—present. It is not a matter of physical absence: we are talking of those who have had scant or no significance, and who therefore have not felt (and in many cases still do not feel) in a position to make plain their suffering, their aspirations, and their hopes. (20; see also Gutierrez, 1996)

Not simply in society, but within the hallowed walls of the Christian church, African Americans have been (and in some senses remain) invisible and "have not felt (and in many cases still do not feel) in a position to make plain their suffering, their aspirations, and their hopes." The situation sometimes seems worse when we turn to the discourse of liberation theology where, once again, race and racism have reared their ugly heads. Which is to say that liberation theology is often locked along a racial divide or, rather, the "color-line" with each theologian shepherding his or her own racially colonized and poverty-stricken flock, often forgetting that religion at its best does not condone racial (or gender or class or sexual orientation) distinctions and/or oppression but critically combats any and all forms of imperialist thought and practices.

In contrast with most mainstream liberation theologians who have a longstanding tendency of focusing almost exclusively on Latin America and the Caribbean, Du Bois's liberation theology centers on the poor and, perhaps, the most vulnerable members of U.S. society, African Americans. With words that will surely shock many contemporary liberation theologians and liberal white Christians alike, in "The Church and the Negro," Du Bois (2000a) provocatively declared that "Jesus Christ was a laborer and black men are laborers; He was poor and we are poor; He was despised of his fellow men and we are despised; He was persecuted and crucified, and we are mobbed and lynched. If Jesus Christ came to America He would associate with Negroes . . . and working people; He would eat and pray with them, and He would seldom see the interior of the Cathedral of Saint John the Divine" (99–100).

Prefiguring the discourse of black theology by nearly half a century, Du Bois's words capture one of its core concerns—that is, the contradictions of coupling racism and religion, particularly Christianity (Cone and Wilmore, 1993; Hopkins, 1999a; 1999b; Kunnie, 1994; Pinn, 2003). Black theology, as defined by one of its founding figures, James Cone (1969), begins with "the Black condition" (18): "It is a theology which confronts white society as racist Antichrist, communicating to the oppressor that nothing will be spared in the fight for freedom" (135). A central issue in the discourse of black theology is the racial colonization of God and, therefore, God's racial identity and racial depictions of God are of prime importance to black liberation theologians. Cone (1970) contends, "The Blackness of God and everything implied by it in a racist society is at the heart of Black Theology's doctrine of God," in that "there is no place for a colorless God in a society where people suffer precisely because of their color" (120).

In order to understand black liberation theology's concept of blackness, one must first explore the history of race and anti-black racism, and the social significance of skin color in Western culture and social consciousness (Jordan, 1968; Pieterse, 1992; Goldberg, 1993). Another founding figure in black theology, Deotis Roberts (2003), pointed out long ago that in a white supremacist society, such as the United States, whiteness is the opposite of blackness, even in the realm of religion. Where whiteness represents all that is good, beautiful, and divine, blackness signifies all that is bad, ugly, and evil. What is more, in white supremacist society blackness symbolizes subhumanity and intellectual inferiority, the exact opposite of what whiteness means (i.e., the highest mark of humanity and super-superiority, not simply intellectually but in every imaginable area).

Black liberation theology begins with the black condition because it is a condition not of continental and diasporan African people's creation or social construction, but a condition of continued coercion, violence, and oppression. Blackness, then, for the black liberation theologians, is not necessarily a biological concept, but an existential-phenomenological paradigm and point of departure. It is, in a word, a concept that captures the historical and cultural legacy of black people's resistance to white supremacy and anti-black racism, among other imperialisms unleashed by Europe's push for global dominance. Therefore, when the black liberation theologians argue for Jesus' blackness, they are not putting forward a biological or crude racial claim as much as they are contending, as Cone (1970) did in his classic *A Black Theology of Liberation*, that the ministry and moral life and legacy of Jesus are more meaningful if it is acknowledged that, according to the New Testament of the Bible, the image of Jesus which has precedence over all others is that of Christ as "the Oppressed One," and that his entire life and legacy rest squarely on his identification with the poor, downtrodden and dispossessed (202–10).

The God of black liberation theology, then, is "the God of and for the oppressed of the land who makes himself known through their liberation" (116; see also Cone, 1975). Cone's (1969) conception of black liberation theology, as a consequence, means nothing less than "doing God's work in history by righting the wrongs done against his people" (47). Hence, based on this interpretation, blacks—undoubtedly a group of the most oppressed people in the world—are one of God's covenant communities. This is a theme that runs throughout Du Bois's writings on religion, and its similarity with Conian theology is striking. Herbert Aptheker (1980b) observed, "If Du Bois is not the first who writes of a Black God, he is certainly among the earliest to express this view and he repeatedly draws a parallel between lynching as practiced by Americans and crucifixion as practiced by the Romans" (viii; see also Blum, 2007, 2009).

For Du Bois, as for Cone and contemporary black liberation theologians, religion should foster not simply a love of God (*theophilia*), but a love for oneself, all humanity, all creatures, and all creation (*agapē*). Too often Christianity has been used to crush and enslave the human spirit encased in black (and especially black women's) bodies and, even though black liberation theologians have yet to acknowledge it, Du Bois was one of the first to systematically criticize both white and black Christianity's supposed colorblindness and religious racial neutrality. He called on the black church to remember its rebellious roots and insurgent abolitionist activities, which is one of the reasons he continuously chronicled the contributions of black religious leaders to black radical thought and revolutionary struggles. Coincidently, Cone (1969) makes a similar claim, pleading with black clergy and laity to recall that "the Black church was born in protest," has a "heritage of radical involvement in the world," and, therefore, possesses a past that "is a symbol of what is actively needed in the present" (112–13).

CONCLUSION: DU BOIS, BLACK LIBERATION THEOLOGY, AND CRITICAL THEORY OF CONTEMPORARY SOCIETY

It would be very difficult to say with any precision "what is actively needed in the present"; however, I believe that Du Bois, Gutierrez, Cone, and many of the liberation theologians point us in some promising directions. The "this-world" or earthly focus of liberation theologians' brand of Christianity is certainly a move in a more propitious direction, but their blindness to other forms of faith, religions, spiritual traditions, and non-Christian prophets and prophetesses, or priests and priestesses speaks volumes about the ways in which Christianity is continually being (ab)used for global imperial and cultural hegemonic purposes. Where I am perplexed by the intellectual insularity of some of the liberation theologians' discursive formations and discursive practices, I am also deeply moved by their awe-inspiring efforts to encourage contemporary Christians and Christianity to not simply speak truth *to* global imperial power, but to speak truth *about* global imperial power. Speaking truth to power in more ways than one places the powerful at the discursive center. It presumes that the powerful possess a moral consciousness and an ethical authority which history has hinted again and again they simply do not. Du Bois and the liberation theologians, then, are not as interested in speaking truth to the powerful as much as they are concerned with speaking truth about the powerful to the powerless. This practice promotes the empowerment of the powerless in a way that speaking truth to the powerful often only flatters them and warns them of what they need to alter in their efforts to maintain the apartheid(s)—epistemic or otherwise—of the established imperial order.

Du Bois's philosophy of religion and sociology of religion, although primarily preoccupied with the critique of Christianity and its impact on U.S. society, could be extremely useful in deconstructing and reconstructing liberation theology, broadening its base to more acutely encompass critical race theory, radical politics, social analysis, political economy, cultural criticism, anticolonialism, and feminism. His writings on religion could also aid in epistemically opening liberation theology to the spiritual knowledge(s) of non-Christian, albeit still God-loving laities. What is more, Du Bois's emphasis on social ethics in his writings on religion certainly stands as a testament and offers a prodigious moral model of what religion should really be about: *not* about saving souls and using guile to get into heaven; *not* about religious chauvinism or racial exclusionism in the realm of religion; *not* about building big churches or worship centers; and, most certainly, *not* about promoting patriarchal and bourgeois (and/or heterosexist) views and values. Quite the contrary, as we have witnessed, and as he himself testified with his own words above, Du Bois believed that religion at its best should really be about enhancing the quality of life on earth, about promoting and practicing loving-kindness and compassion, about being selfless as opposed to selfish, and about respecting and valuing the wide range of human diversity and human difference that God has omnisciently placed on earth.

In 1910, while a professor of history, sociology, and economics at Atlanta University, the allegedly agnostic Du Bois composed a prayer that beautifully captures his overarching belief, not in any specific religion or spiritual tradition, but in the God of and for the oppressed and struggling people of the world. Here, then, I solemnly conclude this chapter with his heartfelt prayer:

> Give us grace, O God, to dare to do the deed which we well know cries to be done. Let us not hesitate because of ease, or the words of men's mouths, or our own lives. Mighty causes are calling us—the freeing of women, the training of children, the putting down of hate and murder and poverty—all these and more. But they call with voices that mean work and sacrifice and death. Mercifully grant us, O God, the spirit of Esther, that we say: I will go unto the King and if I perish, I perish—Amen. (Du Bois, 1980c, 21)

Du Bois's critical religious thought was part of his diverse and ongoing efforts to bring dialectical sociological thought to bear on not only the ideologies of imperialism, but also the institutions of imperialism. Inextricable from his critiques of racism, sexism, and American capitalism, and along with the various institutions and social practices that each of the aforementioned spawned, stands Du Bois's staunch critique of the racial colonization (and otherwise imperialization) of U.S. education. Similar to his sociology of religion, Du Bois's sociology of education can be said to offer contemporary sociologists an important and critical engagement of the ways in which the racial colonization of American education has historically informed and deformed U.S. culture and society. Du Bois's sociological discourse, as observed in the previous chapter, is insurgently intersectional and seems to incessantly interconnect the assorted apartheids of American racism, sexism, and capitalism with major American social institutions and conventions, such as religion, education, and criminal justice in the United States. Although it has not received as much scholarly attention as his urban sociology or sociology of race, Du Bois's sociology of education makes a distinct contribution to contemporary sociology of education insofar as it was undoubtedly one of the first to identify and critique the causes and consequences of *epistemic apartheid* and the ways in which the racial colonization of education not only negatively impacts nonwhites in general, and African Americans in particular, but also the democratic development of American society as a whole. Has America matured to the point where it can be openly admitted that much of what historically passed as "education" was decidedly Eurocentric, patriarchal, bourgeois, heterosexist, and unrepentantly intolerant of non-Christian religions and, therefore, had serious social consequences with regard to the inception and ongoing development of American democracy? How did U.S. government-sanctioned laws prohibiting African Americans from receiving any form of education during their enslavement deform American democracy and American society? Have the Eurocentric, patriarchal, bourgeois, heterosexist, and religiously intolerant elements of past American education been exorcised from present American education? What does Du Bois's work in this area offer in answer to these crucial queries? An intense exploration of these critical questions and an earnest offering of answers will, accordingly, constitute the primary preoccupation of the next chapter.

NOTES

*This chapter is lovingly dedicated to my mother, Reverend Marilyn Giles, who has been an ordained Baptist minister for more than a quarter of a century, and who continues to struggle with the constant intentional erasure or, at the very least, the intense invisibility of African American women, especially womanist theologians and ministers, in the Southern Baptist black church. Her indelible influence on my philosophy of religion, sociology of religion, and conceptions of both black liberation and womanist theology cannot be overstated. Iwori Meji 3:2; Owonrin Meji 6:1; Iwori Odi 75:1; Oturupon Bara 176:1; Oturupon Ogunda 206:1; Exodus 20:12; Deuteronomy 5:16; Matthew 15:4; Matthew 19:19; Mark 7:10; Mark 10:19; Luke 18:20; Ephesians 6:2.

1. With regard to Du Bois's work that connects not simply racism, but also sexism to religion, see, for example, "The Burden of Black Women," "The Gospel According to Mary Brown," "The Damnation of Women," and "The Freedom of Womanhood" in Du Bois (1969a, 1970a, 1982b, 1982c).

2. Brain Johnson's *W. E. B. Du Bois: Toward Agnosticism, 1868–1934* (2008) helps to corroborate my claims here. For a discussion of black ecumenism, see Sawyer (1994).

3. With regard to religion being both an "inspiration and frustration" for Du Bois, I observe below his acute and pioneering awareness of the black church as the center of African American life and culture, and I also note how perplexed he was, as early as his teenage years at Fisk, with dogmatic religion, religious hypocrisy, religion that prohibits or restricts progressive social and political theory and praxis, and religion being (ab)used to dehumanize or dispossess. The pertinent passages from his texts are presented and commented on below.

4. For further discussion of what has come to be called the "Atlanta Race Riot," see Bauerlin (2001), Burns (2006), Godshalk (2005), and Mixon (2005).

5. Du Bois's "Credo" has a pivotal place in his oeuvre for several reasons. First, it was one of the only published pieces in his long literary career in which he openly espoused a belief in God. Second, it was one of the first to blazon out at the dawn of the twentieth century expressing a growing spirit of black nationalism and

critical opposition to Booker T. Washington's accommodationism. Du Bois (1920) declared that he believed in God and in "all men, black and brown and white," who, from his perceptive point of view, "are brothers, varying through time and opportunity, in form and gift and feature, but different in no essential particular, and alike in soul and the possibility of infinite development" (3). And then, his radical humanism took a back seat to what he saw at the time as the necessity of black nationalism (and, I would include, Pan-Africanism) in the face of European imperialism, and specifically white supremacy and anti-black racism. He unapologetically announced:

> Especially do I believe in the Negro Race: in the beauty of its genius, the sweetness of its soul, and its strength in that meekness which shall yet inherit this turbulent earth. I believe in Pride of race and lineage and self: in pride of self so deep as to scorn injustice to other selves; in pride of lineage so great as to despise no man's father; in pride of race so chivalrous as neither to offer bastardy to the weak nor beg wedlock of the strong, knowing that men may be brothers in Christ, even though they may not be brothers-in-law. (3)

A final reason Du Bois's "Credo" is distinguished amongst his other writings is because of its unprecedented popularity. Du Bois biographer David Levering Lewis noted that the piece was literally celebrated by blacks of all political persuasions and white conservatives and white liberals alike. So popular was Du Bois's "Credo" that, Lewis (1993) claims, it was "reprinted widely in the African American press and made available on cardboard rectangles slightly larger than playing-card size by a Memphis printing establishment" (313). An extremely important piece with regard to Du Bois's writings on religion, Lewis offers a succinct synopsis of the historical context in which it was produced, its personal and political purposes, and its impact on blacks as wells as whites during those turbulent times. His words are worth quoting at length:

> Like so much else that he wrote, the "Credo" was meant to serve a dual purpose: manifesto to a few thousand influential whites outlining the social and civil rights ideals Du Bois and his few supporters embodied; and catechism for great numbers of ordinary men and women of his race whose beleaguered pride was faltering. . . . Du Bois sprinkled it with pieties about peace and beauty and goodness—patience, even—and appeared to profess a belief in God and spoke of green pastures beside still waters, for he especially needed to persuade a white public schooled in the black world by *Up From Slavery* [Booker T. Washington's 1901 accommodationist autobiography] that he was not a rash and godless intellectual, but a committed exponent of Judeo-Christian harmony and justice. "Credo" was a majestic incantation whose surface and subliminal meanings were easily misread. White readers of a sanctimonious or myopic bent were profoundly gratified by the expression of religious sentiments, as were the overwhelming majority of his own people. Perceptive readers, on the other hand, heard, in a staccato modeled on Zola's *J'accuse*, distinct sounds of white supremacy crumbling. A good many black people heard the thunder of avenging racial parity. They would hang the "Credo" on their living room walls after Du Bois included it in *Darkwater* sixteen years later, just as their grandchildren would mount "I Have a Dream" on theirs. (312)

6. A note on the dialectical nature of Du Bois's thought is necessary in order to quell longstanding confusion. Francis Broderick (1955, 1958c, 1959), August Meier

(1959, 1963), and Elliot Rudwick (1956, 1958a, 1959a, 1968), among others, have each made mention of the contradictory character of Du Bois thought. However, in their criticisms they fail to adequately acknowledge and assess the social forces and social phenomena, public policies and political programs—which Du Bois apparently was consistently conscious of—that continental and diasporan Africans were struggling against. Africana history has shown that blacks exist in a totalitarian reality that is simultaneously and thoroughly white supremacist, sexist, capitalist, and colonialist, a reality extremely arduous to explain to whites primarily because one of the fundamental features of being white in a white supremacist world is an exaggerated and over-inflated sense of self and (whether consciously or unconsciously) participating in the public practice of racistly rendering blacks nonexistent or, as Ralph Ellison (1980) might put it, invisible. It is this invisibility that most members of the ruling race (and we could add *gender* and *class*) literally do not detect which makes many of Du Bois's positions seem contradictory and intellectually incoherent. The duality that Du Bois's critics describe is actually quite common in Africana social and political thought, and it neither began nor ended with Du Bois, but is symptomatic of blacks' efforts to live (not simply survive) and work in a world ravaged by racism and other forms of imperialism, in societies where white supremacy and capitalist patriarchy are institutionally sanctioned and socially accepted. The dialectical nature of Du Bois's thought, to be sure, is one of his greatest contributions to the Africana tradition of critical theory, and his search for solutions to the most pressing social problems, along with his ability to consistently put forward radical political programs and ethical alternatives, remains unparalleled. For further discussion of "Du Bois's dialectics," please see Rabaka (2008a).

7. Du Bois believed that religion, and Christianity in particular, could be employed as an instrument in both the quest to achieve black liberation and radical democratic socialist transformation. In *W. E. B. Du Bois: American Prophet*, the noted religious historian Edward Blum (2007) importantly observed:

> At first glance, Du Bois's assertion that religious leaders and ideas helped rationalize and legitimate capitalistic exploitation seems to show that he was using a fairly simple Marxian approach. But looking at a variety of Du Bois's other texts suggests that he broke with the Marxian base-superstructure analysis by claiming that an ideological value, "true Christianity," could make social change; if a renewal of true Christianity struck society and masses of people subscribed to the radical teachings of Christ, a new economic base could result, one of economic justice and brotherhood. By focusing on racism and religion as powerful social forces, Du Bois offered a sophisticated revision of Marxian theory. In Du Bois's scholarly writing, a religious renewal could have the power to change economic structures, a position that would have been anathema to any strict Marxist. (111; see also Blum, 2005b)

8. For further discussion of African retentions in African American religious thought and practices, please see Bascom (1980), L. E. Barrett (1974), Bastide (1971, 1978), J. E. Holloway (1991), J. M. Murphy (1994), Sernett, (1999), G. E. Simpson (1978), Trost (2007), and C. S. Wilder (2001).

9. In *Afrotopia*, Moses (1998), who argues that Du Bois was "[p]reeminently a dialectician" that "frequently championed opposing positions, sometimes within the scope of a single paragraph," gives us a bird's-eye view of Du Bois's dialectical

approach to African American religion. He states that because Du Bois's thought was primarily dialectical,

> [i]t is therefore not surprising that from time to time Du Bois wrote optimistically of the church's past and present role in organizing the political and economic consciousness of black communities. In his assessment of African American religion, Du Bois represented contradictory tendencies toward modernism and traditionalism. Toward the end of his chapter entitled "The Faith of the Fathers" in *The Souls of Black Folk*, he spoke as the prophet of a new "awakening . . . when the pent-up vigor of ten million souls shall sweep irresistibly toward the Goal." At other locations in that same essay, he wrote almost nostalgically of the waning of a mythical Afro-Christian virtue, which was supposedly giving way to the tawdry values of modern capitalism. He was ambivalent with respect to the role that religion played in African American acculturation, suggesting at times that it symbolized the retention of African traditions, at others viewing it as evidence of African American acceptance of American values. He posed the question of whether religion had functioned historically as a force for social reform or as a form of escapism. (136–37)

5

Du Bois and the Sociology of Education

Critiquing the (Mis)Education of Black (Among Other) Folk

> There are going to be schools which do not discriminate against colored people and the number is going to increase slowly in the present, but rapidly in the future until long before the year 2000, there will be no school segregation on the basis of race. The deficiency in knowledge of Negro history and culture, however, will remain and this danger must be met or else American Negroes will disappear. Their history and culture will be lost. Their connection with the rising African world will be impossible. What then can we do or should we try to do?
>
> W. E. B. Du Bois, "Whither Now and Why?," 151–52

INTRODUCTION: DU BOIS'S SOCIOLOGY OF EDUCATION

Educational and intellectual historian Derrick Alridge (2008) opens his watershed work *The Educational Thought of W. E. B. Du Bois* stating, "No other African American or other American scholar has ever offered as comprehensive a set of educational ideas for black people as did Du Bois" (1). However, Alridge quickly quips, "Despite his contributions . . . Du Bois has been for the most part neglected as an educational thinker in twentieth-century American history, and his educational ideas have been largely ignored by the fields of educational and intellectual history" (1). Something similar could be said concerning the ongoing omission of Du Bois's critical educational theory with regard to the sociology of education. When Du Bois is acknowledged within the sociology of education, it is most frequently in reference to his intellectual history-making debate with Booker T. Washington concerning an optimal educational strategy for African Americans, or completely collapsed into what can be gathered from his most popular publications, *The Souls of Black Folk* and "The Talented Tenth," both published in 1903.

In 1903, Du Bois was thirty-five years old, and would go on to live another extremely eventful sixty years. Needless to say, his ideas grew and changed greatly over the course of his long and productive life. To start and stop investigations of Du Bois's educational thought with *The Souls of Black Folk* and "The Talented Tenth" is to put into play a kind of logical reductionism that seems to be almost exclusively reserved for either nonwhite or non-male intellectuals. In order to seriously grasp and grapple with Du Bois's educational thought, one must be willing to go into discursive depth and to rigorously research not only Du Bois's educational ideas, but also the epoch in which he put forward his educational theories and praxes. In other words, to start and stop investigations of Du Bois's educational thought with *The Souls of Black Folk* and "The Talented Tenth" would mean overlooking important contributions to the sociology of education published both prior to and long after *The Souls of Black Folk* and "The Talented Tenth." For instance, prior to his aforementioned 1903 classics, Du Bois published "Careers Open to College-Bred Negroes," *The Philadelphia Negro*, *The College-Bred Negro*, *Memorial to the Legislature of Georgia on Negro Common Schools*, "The Freedmen's Bureau," *The Common School*, "The Burden of Negro Schooling," and "The Higher Education of the Negro," among many others. Special mention must be made of the often-overlooked fact that *The College-Bred Negro* was the first social scientific study of African Americans in higher education.

Du Bois's major contributions to educational thought after the publication of *The Souls of Black Folk* and "The Talented Tenth" include "What Intellectual Training Is Doing for the Negro," "Atlanta University," "The Hampton Idea," *College-Bred Negro Communities*, *The College-Bred Negro American*, *The Common School and the Negro American*, "Negro Education," "Education in Africa," "Education and Work," *The Field and Function of a Negro College*, "Does the Negro Need Separate Schools?," "A Program for Land-Grant Colleges," and "The Freedom to Learn," among many others. It is, of course, important to observe the fact that five of the fourteen chapters of *The Souls of Black Folk* were exclusively devoted to education, which made the book the most audacious and eloquent statement concerning African American education at the turn of the twentieth century. However, it is equally important to observe that of the sixteen Atlanta University studies Du Bois edited, four were exclusively focused on education: *The College-Bred Negro*, *The Common School*, *The College-Bred Negro American*, and *The Common School and the Negro American*. Although the Atlanta University studies on African American education are not in any way unblemished, they are indisputably the first comprehensive studies of African American education. Often lacking adequate data and revealing serious interpretive limitations (i.e., elitist, Eurocentric, and masculinist interpretive limitations), the Atlanta University studies on African American education still represent an unprecedented achievement. This fact is even more obvious when Du Bois's lack of research funds, the recentness of social scientific research methodologies at the turn of the twentieth century, and his undeniably overambitious intellectual aspirations are taken into critical consideration.

It is, perhaps, common knowledge at this point that at the conceptual core of Du Bois's social scientific discourse lies his searing search for solutions to social, political, and cultural "problems." In fact, it could be easily averred that Du Bois spent the sweep of his publishing life, an almost unfathomable eighty years (from 1883 to 1963), searching for solutions to problems, and not just "Negro" or black problems, but problems that plagued humanity as a whole. These "problems" varied in nature and nuance, but each emerged from the incontrovertible fact(s) of modern (and/or postmodern) imperialism—and specifically as experienced and endured in various forms of racism, sexism, capitalism, and colonialism. According to Du Bois, one of the most pressing problems confronting humanity, and nonwhites (in capitalist, communist, and colonialist countries) in particular, is, as he himself put it, "the problem of education."

Education, for Du Bois, is "by derivation and in fact a drawing out of human powers." It involves, or, at the least, education according to Du Bois *should* involve, essentially three things. First, education requires a critical knowledge of the past—that is, critical study of history, continental and diasporan African as well as "world" history. Du Bois argued that *history*, as conventionally conceived in white supremacist capitalist and colonialist contexts, was often an ideological ruse in the hands of the ruling race/gender/class/religion. Over time he, therefore, developed a critical theory of history, a historical sociology or *counterhistory*, if you will, that chronicled the insidious agenda of European imperialism and Africana and other progressive peoples' radical politics and unceasing social movements *against apartheid*, epistemic or otherwise.

Second, education entails questions of culture, "cultural study"—as Du Bois (1973, 9, 28) put it long before Stuart Hall (1996) and his cultural studies colleagues—and critical cultural inquiry. History and culture go hand-in-hand, and to rob and reframe a people's history and culture from an oppressive point of view, or in the interest of imperialism, is to distort and deny that which is most human in each of us: our right to live decent and dignified lives, to walk unmolested in the world, and to develop (freely and to our fullest potential) our own unique contributions to the various traditions and heritages that constitute human culture and civilization.

Lastly, Du Bois's sociology of education demands a critical understanding of present and future vital needs—the needs of not simply this or that specific cultural group, class, race, or gender, but humanity and our fragile ecology as a whole. This means, then, that Du Bois's sociology of education (as with Du Bois's sociological discourse in general) is inherently and radically humanist, multicultural, and transethnic, and often uses history and culture as a basis to apprehend, interpret, and create critical consciousness concerning life- and world-threatening conflicts and contradictions. Considering Du Bois's definition of education—a process by which persons are taught to draw out and draw upon human powers and human potentialities in the interest of radical (if not revolutionary) self- and social-transformation—this chapter takes as one of its central tasks an exploration of Du Bois's evolving sociology of education and considers its import for contemporary sociology of education, critical educational theory, and what I have elsewhere termed *Africana critical pedagogy*.[1]

In what follows I will, first, discuss Du Bois's historical sociology and its impact on his sociology of education. Next, I examine Du Bois's sociology of culture and the distinct style of cultural criticism he developed for its centrality to his sociology of education, and critical educational theory more generally. Third, I endeavor to objectively analyze some of the major deficiencies and limitations of Du Bois's sociology of education by quickly contrasting his 1903 theory of the Talented Tenth with his 1948 revision of the Talented Tenth thesis into a more Marxist and/or democratic socialist theory of "the Guiding Hundredth." Finally, I conclude the chapter commenting on the contributions Du Bois's sociology of education makes to contemporary critical educational theory and praxis. Let us begin, then, by hitting at the heart of Du Bois's sociology of education, his historical sociology.

DU BOIS, HISTORICAL SOCIOLOGY, EDUCATIONAL HISTORY, AND THE SOCIOLOGY OF EDUCATION

For Du Bois, Africana education—i.e., the education of persons of African origin and descent and others about "the part which Africa has played in world history" (Du Bois, 1965)—"should be founded on a knowledge of the history of their people in Africa and in the United States [and other parts of the African diaspora], and their present condition[s]" (Du Bois, 1973, 93). Du Bois's sociology of education is distinguished in that it was one of (if not "the") first to maintain that "the whole cultural history of Africans in the world" should be taken into consideration when one is seeking to grasp and grapple with the "present condition[s]" of continental and diasporan Africans. To begin, according to Du Bois, one needs to know about "the history of their people in Africa," "the slave trade and slavery," "abolition," and "the struggle for emancipation" (150). Only after a careful and critical study of classical, colonial, and contemporary continental and diasporan African history did Du Bois deem an educator minimally prepared to proceed with the pedagogical process where continental and diasporan Africans are concerned.

Knowledge of "the whole cultural history of Africans in the world" is a necessity in Du Bois's sociology of education on account of the complexities and conundrums of the colonial, neocolonial, and, some would go so far to add, "postcolonial" Africana condition (see Eze, 1997b; Olaniyan, 1992, 2000; Quayson, 2000a, 2000b; Rabaka, 2007b). Africana education "starts from a different point" because continental and diasporan Africans' historicity—that is, their concrete historical endurances and cultural experiences—have been and continue to be ones which require, and often demand, as Du Bois (1973) put it, "a different starting point" (95). Du Bois's demand for a different point of departure for Africana education rests on the realities of continental and diasporan Africans' situatedness in the modern world. In other words, he understood continental and diasporan Africans to be "facing a serious and difficult situation," one that was at once "baffling and contradictory," and "made all the more difficult for us because we are by blood and descent and popular opinion an integral part of that vast majority of mankind which is the Victim and not the Beneficiary of present conditions; which is today working at starvation wages and on a level of brute toil and without voice in its own government or education in its ignorance, for the benefit, the enormous profit, and the dazzling luxury of the white world" (48, 75).

As the Eritrean philosopher Tsenay Serequeberhan (1994) has pointed out, "Philosophy, African or otherwise, is a critical and systematic interpretative exploration of our lived historico-cultural actuality," and it is a "critical and explorative engagement of one's own cultural specificity and lived historicalness" (3, 23). This means, then, that Du Bois's (1973) philosophy of education is on point when and where it emphasizes "cultural specificity" and Africans' particular and peculiar historicity (11). Du Bois's sociology of culture and its connections to his educational thought will be the subject of the succeeding section. Therefore, I will sidestep direct discussions of culture here and focus primarily on how history is regarded by Du Bois, among other Africana educators, as the prime point of departure for interpretation and analysis where continental and diasporan African lifeworlds and life struggles are concerned.

Africana education, according to Du Bois, "cannot begin with history and lead to Negro history. It cannot start with sociology and end with Negro sociology" (95). It "must be grounded in the condition and work of . . . black men [and women]" (95), which is to say that Africana education, educators, and students "must start where we are and not where we wish to be" (94). Drawing parallels between African American education and European education, Du Bois argued that much in the same manner that education and educational institutions function in England, France, Spain, and Russia, they have a similar task and must play a comparable role in African American life and culture. As he understood it, education and educational centers in the aforementioned countries used the history of the country and the culture of its people as aids in the socialization and acculturation of its citizens. Like education and educational centers elsewhere, Du Bois admonished Africana educators and educational institutions to utilize continental and diasporan African history and culture as their foundation and grounding point of departure. Employing the educational atmosphere in Spain as an initial example, Du Bois (1996a) sternly stated:

> A university in Spain is not simply a university. It is a Spanish university. It is a university located in Spain. It uses the Spanish language. It starts with Spanish history and makes conditions in Spain the starting point of its teaching. Its education is for Spaniards, not for them as they may be or ought to be, but as they are with their present problems and disadvantages and opportunities. (416)

Building on the above, and bearing both historical and cultural context in mind, Du Bois then turned toward the French intellectual environment and contended with critical candor:

> In other words, the Spanish university is founded and ground in Spain, just as surely as a French university is French. There are some people who have difficulty in apprehending this very clear truth. They assume, for instance, that the French university is in a singular sense universal, and is based on a comprehension and inclusion of all mankind and of their problems. But it is not, and the assumption that it is arises simply because so much of French culture has been built into universal civilization. A French university is founded in France; it uses the French language and assumes a knowledge of French history. The present problems of the French people are its major problems and it becomes universal only so far as other peoples of the world comprehend and are at one with France in its mighty and beautiful history. (416)

When and where the education and educational institutions of continental and diasporan Africans are concerned, Du Bois maintained that Africana education properly "begins with Negroes," "uses that variety of the English idiom which they understand," and, "above all, it is founded, or it should be founded on a knowledge of the history of their people in Africa and in the United States, and their present condition" (416). Hence, at first glance we could aver that Du Bois, similar to Frantz Fanon (1967), understood that speaking a language meant much more than using a certain syntax, learning the lexicon, and mastering the morphology, but it meant "above all to assume a culture, to support the weight of a civilization" (18).[2] Du Bois's emphasis on using "that variety of the English idiom which *they*"—meaning African Americans—"understand" also helps to highlight his concerns with and commitment to the production of practical knowledge expressed in language, whether written or spoken, that is accessible to Africana educators *across the disciplines*, as well as students and laypeople alike *across the wide spectrum of the African world*. He made it a point in both of the passages cited above to note that the language employed for critical pedagogical purposes is always and ever the *lingua franca*, or common language: Spanish in Spain, and French in France.[3]

Immediately after observing the importance of language in the learning process, Du Bois turns toward history. In each instance above it is the history of the particular people, in their specific geographical, social, and political setting that informs not only their pedagogical process(es), but also the very purpose and life principles of the people. Where Spanish education and educational institutions start "with Spanish history and [make] conditions in Spain the starting point of its teaching," and where French education "assumes a knowledge of French history" and makes the "present problems of the French people . . . its major problems," so then, Du Bois (1996a) decidedly declared:

> [S]tarting with present conditions and using the facts and the knowledge of the present situation of American Negroes, the Negro university expands toward the possession and the conquest of all knowledge. It seeks from a beginning of the history of the Negro in America and in Africa to interpret all history; from a beginning of social development among Negro slaves and freedmen in America and Negro tribes and kingdoms in Africa, to interpret and understand the social development of all mankind in all ages. It seeks to reach modern science of matter and life from the surroundings and habits and aptitudes of American Negroes and thus lead up to an understanding of life and matter in the universe. And this is a different program than a similar function would be in a white university, because it starts from a different point. It is a matter of beginnings and integrations of one group which sweep instinctive knowledge and inheritance and current reactions into a universal world of science, sociology, and art. In no other way can the American Negro college function. It cannot begin with history and lead to Negro history. It cannot start with sociology and end with Negro sociology. (418)

It is the history of continental and diasporan Africans that is at the heart of Du Bois's sociology of education, and it is the harsh realities of that history which demand a "different program" and require Africana education to "start . . . from a different point." As with contemporary Africana studies theory and research methods, Du Bois's prophetic pedagogy utilized Africana history and culture, Africana thought, spiritual traditions, and value systems to "interpret and understand" "all history" and "all mankind in all ages." For Du Bois (1897a)—and the same may be said of many Pan-Africanists, black nationalists, artists of the Harlem Renaissance and the black arts movement, Negritude theorists, black Marxists, and black feminists—Africana perspectives and points of view, Africana interpretations and explanations of the human experience (i.e., history) and the human condition (i.e., actuality) are viable and valid insofar as it is understood that "the Negro people, as a race, have a contribution to make to civilization and humanity, which no other race can make" (15).

Each human group has its philosophy, which is to say that each group of human beings harbors a certain "habit of reflection" that helps them "interpret and understand" the world in which they live. As the Ghanaian philosopher Kwasi Wiredu (1991) put it, "Any group of human beings will have to have some world outlook, that is, some general conceptions about the world in which they live and about themselves both as individuals and as members of society" (87). In Du Bois's critical social theory, it is Africana "world outlook[s]," Africana conceptions of history, society, politics, economics, religion, and art, among other important issues, that has afforded and continues to offer continental and diasporan Africa's "contributions" to human culture and civilization. Indeed, for Du Bois (1897a) Africana people have a "great message . . . for humanity," and it is only through careful, critical, and concerted study of their history and culture that they (and ethically committed anti-imperialist others) will be able to discover, as well as extend and expand not only what it means to be black in a white supremacist capitalist colonialist world, but also, and perhaps more importantly, what it means to be human and deeply devoted to the search for social justice in the neocolonial and/or (post)modern moment (10).

DU BOIS'S SOCIOLOGY OF CULTURE AND ITS IMPACT ON HIS CRITICAL EDUCATIONAL THEORY

Du Bois's sociology of education involves not only reclamation of Africana historical memory in the interest of radically reeducating critical educators and students about Africa's creation of, and contributions to, civilization, but also a struggle over the meaning of culture and cultural meanings. In order to resist the imperialist impulse, continental and diasporan Africans, along with other oppressed people, must to do more than merely rediscover their long-hidden history. They are obliged to also—as Amilcar Cabral (1973) succinctly put it—critically "return to the source" of their history, which is their culture, the distinct thought- and practice-traditions that they have developed to sustain and enhance their lifeworlds and lived experiences. For Du Bois, culture plays a special part in the critical consciousness-raising process (what Paulo Freire [1996, 41–58] calls "conscientização"), and its degradation helps to highlight the white supremacist and Eurocentric cultural hegemonic dimension of what is currently being variously called "globalization," "global capitalism," "transnational capitalism," and/or "corporate capitalism." Capitalism and racism, as with capitalism and sexism, are inextricable and constantly influencing and exacerbating each other. They are interlocking systems of exploitation, oppression, and violence that conceal a kind of cultural racism deeply embedded in the language(s) and logic(s), mores and twisted morals, institutions and individual imperialist expressions of the ruling race/gender/class/religion and its (neo)colonized "colored" lackeys. Concerning cultural racism and its ongoing effects on every aspect of the lives of the racially colonized, Du Bois (1973) revealingly wrote, "To kidnap a nation; to transplant it in a new land, to a new language, new climate, new economic organization, a new religion and new moral customs; to do this is a tremendous wrenching of social adjustments; and when society is wrenched and torn and revolutionized, then, whether the group be white or black, or of this race or that, the results are bound to be far reaching" (33).

Two of the many "far-reaching" results of the African holocaust, African enslavement, and racial colonization have been *historical amnesia* and *cultural dislocation*. In light of the fact that the preceding section was devoted to the role history plays in Du Bois's sociology of education, I will forego a discussion of historical amnesia here and focus instead on how Du Bois's sociology of culture informs his sociology of education. In the passage above, Du Bois observed that Africans were taken from Africa and coerced into a "new" culture and, in point of fact, their (classical or "precolonial") culture was "wrenched and torn and revolutionized." In the "new land," the diaspora—and often in the "old land," Africa—Africans (or "blacks," if you prefer) were "trained" only "grudgingly and suspiciously," and often without "reference to what we can be, but with sole reference to what somebody [else] wants us to be" (9). Two of the "far-reaching" results of this type of "training" was and continues to be *cultural degradation* and *cultural dislocation*.

Because continental and diasporan Africans' culture has been and continues to be "wrenched and torn and revolutionized" there is a decisive and dire need to break with and go beyond the borders and boundaries of the culture of the established imperialist order (i.e., the white supremacist-patriarchal-capitalist-colonialist world), and discover and recover those aspects of classical and traditional African culture which, in Wiredu's (1991) words, "may hold some lessons of moral significance for a more industrialized society" (98). Looking at this issue from the perspective of Du Bois's sociology of education, we are wont to ask a question that Du Bois (1973, 10) asked long ago: How can we use "the accumulated wisdom of the world for the development of full human power" and to "raise the black race to its full humanity"? What bothered Du Bois was the fact that Africana contributions to "the accumulated wisdom of the world" were often either utterly left out of, or claimed by whites (i.e., both Europeans and/or European Americans) in discussions of issues that he felt they had direct and practical bearing on. He was also perplexed by the fact that so many persons of African origin and descent knew few or "no norms" that were not "thoroughly shot through with [European imperialist] ideals," and relied so heavily on European thought traditions, religious conceptions, and cultural values. Du Bois's (1970e, vol. 2) critical comments are worth quoting at length:

> With few exceptions, we are all today "white folks' niggers." No, do not wince. I mean nothing insulting or derogatory, but this is a concrete designation which indicates that very very many colored folk: Japanese, Chinese, Indians, Negroes; and, of course, the vast majority of white folk; have been so enthused, oppressed, and suppressed by current white civilization that they think and judge everything by its terms. They have no norms that are not set in the nineteenth and twentieth centuries. They can conceive of no future world which is not dominated by present white nations and thoroughly shot through with their ideals, their method of government, their economic organization, their literature and their art; or in other words their throttling of democracy, their exploitation of labor, their industrial imperialism and their color hate. To broach before such persons any suggestion of radical change; any idea of intrusion, physical or spiritual, on the part of alien races is to bring down upon one's devoted head the most tremendous astonishment and contempt. (137)

When continental and diasporan Africans "think and judge everything by [their own] terms," they share the perspective or point of view of their particular people or cultural group with the wider world; they extend and expand what it means to be both African and human; they add to "the accumulated wisdom of the world"; and they take Du Bois (1897a) seriously when he said, "[I] believe that the Negro people, as a race, have a contribution to make to civilization and humanity, which no other race can make" (15). In order to contribute to "civilization and humanity," Africana and other oppressed and anti-imperialist people have to know not only *their* history, as was pointed out in the preceding section, but also *their* culture, which includes continental and diasporan traditions of critique, resistance, radical politics, and projects of multicultural, transethnic, and democratic social transformation. Without knowledge of cultural "norms" and "terms"—by which I take Du Bois to mean Africana views and values—prior to, and in defiance of, European imperial conquest and various forms of racial colonization, which continue well into the contemporary "postcolonial" period, black and other nonwhites are racistly rendered the very "cultural foundlings" and "social wards" that the acclaimed African

American philosopher Alain Locke (1983), and many members of the New Negro movement and Harlem Renaissance perceptively prophesied, unrepentantly resented, and warily warned against (247; see also Locke, 1968).

The "radical change" that Du Bois is intimating above is *radical sociocultural* and *politico-economic change*, which is one of the reasons he highlights not just "norms" and "terms," but also "ideals," "government," "economic organization," "literature," and "art." In the passage cited at the beginning of this section Du Bois noted that continental and diasporan Africans were not simply "kidnap[ped]" and "transplant[ed]" into a "new land," but that they were forced—which is why he used the term "kidnap[ped]"—to learn "a new language, new climate, new economic organization, a new religion and new moral customs." Though they were coerced into this "new" culture and various "new" societies, African Americans were still "separated and isolated" from the "new" established order (Du Bois, 1970e, vol. 2, 136). It is this separation and isolation, along with the explicit domination of, and discrimination against, Africans and other nonwhites in both their "new" and "old" lands, that compelled Du Bois to contend that blacks "form and long will form a perfectly definite group, not entirely segregated and isolated from our surroundings, but differentiated to such a degree that we have very largely a life and thought of our own. And it is this fact that we as scientists, and teachers and persons engaged in living, [and] earning a living, have got to take into account and make our major problem" (135).

For Du Bois, blacks have "very largely a life and thought of [their] own," which in other words is to say that continental and diasporan Africans, as Wiredu mentioned above, "have some world outlook . . . some general conceptions about the world in which they live and about themselves both as individuals and as members [or nonmembers] of society," even in the midst and often in spite of the machinations and manipulations of the culture of the established imperialist order. Du Bois (1996a) understood blacks to be bound together not by biology, but by psychology, stating, "Biologically we are mingled of all conceivable elements, but race is psychology, not biology; and psychologically we are a unified race with one history, one red memory, and one revolt" (421). In *Dusk of Dawn*, which was originally published in 1940, Du Bois (1968b) pointed out that it was blacks' collective experience of a "common disaster," their inheritance of the "social heritage of slavery," and their endurance of "discrimination and insult" that bound them together (117). In fact, "This heritage binds together not simply the children of Africa, but extends through yellow Asia and into the South Seas" (117).

Du Bois's sociology of culture, similar to his sociology of race, is primarily predicated on historical experience, not biology or geography, and this is one of the reasons he recurrently stresses psychology and discrimination (e.g., double-consciousness, the color-line, and racial colonization) in his overarching critical race theory. He cogently contended that "[t]here are certainly no biological races in the sense of people with large groups of unvarying inherited gifts and instincts thus set apart by nature as eternally separate," and "[w]e have seen the whole world reluctantly but surely approaching this truth" (Du Bois, 1973, 121). It was of miniscule consequence to Du Bois what one called this group who *experienced* and *endured* the "common disaster" of the African holocaust, enslavement, and collective racial "discrimination and insult" at almost every turn in both the "new" and "old" lands, which is also to say that Du Bois did not dive head first into semantics, and he did not care whether one referred to continental and diasporan Africans as a "race" or a "distinct and unique cultural" group, because "separated and isolated as we are so largely, we form in America an integral group, call it by any name you will, and this fact in itself has its meaning, its worth and its values" (122). It is the experience and endurance, then, of "the slave trade and slavery," "abolition," and "the struggle for emancipation"; of segregation, separation, and isolation; and of contemporary "discrimination and insult" that provided both the fuel and the fire for Du Bois's sociology of culture. Speaking directly to African Americans, again emphasizing both the psychology and sociology of the African American experience, Du Bois (1946) sternly stated:

> We American Negroes are not simply Americans, or simply Negroes. We form a minority group in a great vast conglomerated land and a minority group which by reason of its efforts during the last two generations has made extraordinary and gratifying progress. But in the making of this progress, in the working together of peoples belonging to this group, in the patterns of thinking which they have had to follow and the memories which they shared, they have built-up a distinct and unique culture, a body of habit, thought and adjustment which they cannot escape because it is in the marrow of their bones and which they ought not to ignore because it is the only path to a successful future. (235)

The lived experiences and lived endurances of African Americans have produced certain "patterns of thinking" and a "body of habit, thought and adjustment" that could and should be employed more frequently to address contemporary queries and crises, and not simply in the African world but in the world at large. How many contemporary questions could be answered if more people, those of African descent and otherwise, were willing to critically dialogue with African cultures and civilizations? To which contemporary problems might Du Bois's sociological discourse, and more generally the Africana tradition of critical theory, offer viable solutions?

To dialogue deeply with African cultures means, more than anything else, using them as a *resource* rather than as a mere *reference*. It means communicating critically and becoming conversant with continental and diasporan African thought- and practice-traditions that point to new passions and new possibilities. This is what Du Bois meant above when he said, "it"—meaning, understanding and grounding in Africana history and culture—"is the only path to a successful future" for African Americans. In so many words, he is intimating that African American and other progressive people should utilize the "patterns of thinking," "the memories they shared," the "distinct and unique culture," and the "body of habit, thought and adjustment" of classical and contemporary, continental and diasporan Africa as a resource rather than as a superficial, politically correct, or curt multicultural reference.

Where Hegel infamously argued that Africa has no history and no real relevance for "civilized" (read: European imperialist and bourgeois) history, countless white supremacists of almost every political persuasion have pygmyized Africana culture, contending that if indeed Africa (and its diaspora) does possess classical and contemporary culture it is "primitive" in comparison to, or, at the very least, derisively derived from European culture. Du Bois defiantly countered these claims by documenting Africana contributions to human culture and civilization, and by developing a sociology of continental and diasporan African culture—that is, a sociology of culture that is not only grounded in and grows out of continental and diasporan African conceptions of, and contributions to, the wider world of human culture but also an antiracist, countercultural, praxis-promoting sociology. This, then, brings us to a discussion of Du Bois's answer to the rhetorical question, "What is a culture?" His response reveals much about his sociology of culture:

> It is a careful Knowledge of the Past out of which the group as such has emerged: in our case a knowledge of African history and social development—one of the richest and most intriguing which the world has known. Our history in America, north, south and Caribbean, has been an extraordinary one which we must know to understand ourselves and our world. The experience through which our ancestors have gone for four hundred years is part of our bone and sinew whether we know it or not. The method which we evolved for opposing slavery and fighting prejudice are not to be forgotten, but learned for our own and others' instruction. We must understand the differences in social problems between Africa, the West Indies, South and Central America, not only among the Negroes but those affecting Indians and other minority groups. Plans for the future of our group must be built on a base of our problems, our dreams and frustrations; they cannot stem from empty air or successfully be based on the experiences of others alone. (235)

Beginning with "a careful Knowledge of the Past," both continental and diasporan African history, Du Bois's discursive definition of culture takes a hard turn toward "experience" and he states that the lived experiences of "our ancestors" are "part of our bone and sinew whether we know it or not." In fact, "we must know" "[o]ur history" in Africa, the Americas, and the Caribbean, in order to "understand ourselves and our world." Hence, besides being historically grounded in Africana lived experiences and lived endurances, Du Bois's sociology of culture gravitates and grows toward an experiential and existential exploration and explanation of past and present Africana lifeworlds and life struggles. In other words, if indeed culture has to do with "a careful Knowledge of the Past out of which the group as such has emerged," the "Past" in Du Bois's discourse was much more than history; it was also inextricably connected to culture.

Culture is the thought, belief, and value systems and traditions that a people create, extend, and expand to not only make sense of the world, but also to alter it in their own and other strugglers' anti-imperialist interests. That is why Du Bois asserted above, "The method which we evolved for opposing slavery and fighting prejudice are not to be forgotten, but learned for our own and others' instruction." Here he is suggesting that Africana liberation thought and practice in the face of, and in the fight against "slavery" (i.e., domination) and "prejudice" (i.e., discrimination) could and should be instructional for Africana and other people struggling against imperialism. It is these, and the other instructional elements of Africana liberation thought and practice, that have the greatest import for contemporary sociology of education and critical educational theory. Additionally, it is these same instructional elements that help to drive home Du Bois's unfailing contention that Africa and Africans have a "great message for the world."

The Malian philosopher Lansana Keita (1991) contends that "[p]hilosophical thought, like any human product, derives its value according to its perceived usefulness," and that "the theoreticians of philosophy in an African context must attempt to construct a modern African philosophy with the notion that its formulation would be geared toward helping in the development of a modern African civilization" (144, 147). Du Bois's sociology of education, like Africana educational thought in general, is defined by and demands historical and cultural grounding because it understands that Africana history and culture have been and remain under attack and threatened by both omission and erasure within the intellectual circles and educational centers of the white supremacist patriarchal capitalist colonialist world and, unfortunately, even in multicultural and critical pedagogical discourse. Without a "careful Knowledge of the Past out of which the group as such has emerged"—that is to say, without a careful and critical understanding of continental and diasporan African history and culture—Africana people at the dawn of, and well into, the twenty-first century will more than likely remain plagued by many of the "problems" of the twentieth century, problems that Lewis Gordon (1998) argues are "amazingly embodied in the thought of W. E. B. Du Bois in the North [meaning, North America] and Frantz Fanon in the Caribbean" (1).

For Gordon, Du Bois and Fanon help to highlight problems of identity, liberation, and "self-reflexive incompleteness." The problem of identity is compounded by the problem of the color-line, as Du Bois announced metaphorically at the dawn of the twentieth century in *The Souls of Black Folk*. But the color-line is not now and has never been simply about the social construction of race and the harsh realities of racism. Much more, it is also about racially categorizing and dividing human beings in adherence with white supremacist patriarchal capitalist colonialist social hierarchy. Indeed, the color-line at this point is an age-old imperial aggregate, a racist ruse created to conceal the constant construction and reconstruction of hegemonic borders based on denied humanity, dashed democratic dreams, bracketed identities, broken bodies, suppressed spirits, and grotesque global greed. As a metaphor, the color-line triggers and entraps all our anxieties about difference and deviance, and it exposes us to what the black feminist socialist-humanist Audre Lorde (1984) referred to as "the enemy's many faces," faces which are sometimes white and other times (oft-times) nonwhite (75). In our postmodern/postcolonial/post-Marxist/postfeminist twenty-first-century world, *who* we are is deeply bound up with *what* we are, or, at the least, what we are perceived to be. That is to say, at the heart of the problem of identity are not only existential but also ontological questions, crucial questions concerning essence and being.[4]

With regard to the problem of liberation, questions concerning decolonization and revolutionary social transformation arise. In terms of Africana philosophy of liberation, the Haitian revolution; the African American struggle against slavocracy, sharecropping, peonage, and Jim Crow segregation; and the continental and diasporan Pan-African movements serve as modern points of departure for those in pursuit of answers to questions such as, in Cabral's (1979, 75) words, "Against [what and] whom are our people struggling?" and, in Serequeberhan's (1991, 12) words, "What are the people of Africa trying to free themselves from and what are they trying to establish?"

Finally, the problem of incompleteness is posed on account of the very historical experiences and endurances that Du Bois argued Africana and other struggling people are not being exposed to, but should be critically and morally made aware of on account of their instructional import and contribution to "the accumulated wisdom of the world." Another way of putting it is this: The problem of incompleteness accents the fact that a bona fide philosophical anthropology is one that takes into consideration both the high points and horrors of human history, all the triumphs and tragedies of our transgressions, and based upon those events denies any essence, totality, or teleology outside of them. It engages our impulse to search and yearn for new modes and models of human existence and experience beyond ourselves and our societies as they currently exist.

Many of the problems of the past remain problems in the present, which is to say that, among other problems, problems of identity, liberation, and incompleteness continue to plague Africana and other oppressed people. Education in its best sense should expose continental and diasporan Africans not simply to their "distinct and unique" history and culture, but also to their problems and the historical circumstances and situations that imperially produced and neo-imperially perpetuate those problems. Also—and I should like to place special emphasis on this—education should expose Africana and other struggling people to ways in which they can solve their problems. As Du Bois put it above, "Plans for the future of our group must be built on a base of our problems, our dreams and frustrations; they cannot stem from empty air or successfully be based on the experiences of others alone." This means, then, that Du Bois's sociology of education is ultimately directed at rescuing and reclaiming the denied humanity of Africana and other oppressed people by critiquing and combating domination and discrimination and extending and expanding the prospects and promises of critical multicultural and radical democratic social transformation. However admirable Du Bois's educational intentions, though, it is extremely important for us to acknowledge the limitations and deficiencies of his educational discourse in the context of both his epoch and ours.

FROM "TALENTED TENTH" TO "GUIDING HUNDREDTH": A FEW OF THE LIMITATIONS AND DEFICIENCIES OF DU BOIS'S SOCIOLOGY OF EDUCATION

Du Bois's arguments for historical and cultural grounding in, and a different point of departure for, Africana education are penetrating and often brilliant. However, there is a sense in which certain aspects of his educational thought are severely underdeveloped and inadequate so far as concrete application is concerned. Put another way, Du Bois's educational thought is a virtual treasure trove in theoretical terms—meaning he engaged a multiplicity of educational issues over an extended period of time—but often gave few clues as to how and to whom his educational theory could and should be applied. This presents something of a paradox in Du Bois's educational thought, especially considering the fact that so much of it was decidedly geared toward the production of practical knowledge. Nevertheless, Du Bois's pedagogical weakness is also, I believe, a source of his critical theoretical strength and stamina, and this conceptual conundrum ultimately points to the profundity and durability of Du Bois's sociology of education in particular, and his sociological discourse in general.

It is precisely Du Bois's unrelenting refusal to offer concrete alternatives and solid solutions to pedagogical and pressing social problems that allows radical educators and critical social theorists from disparate disciplines and political organizations to deconstruct and reconstruct his theory in contemporary contexts, thereby deepening and developing his radical humanist, critical multiculturalist, and democratic socialist project(s) which have long traversed and transgressed the battery of borders built to protect imperial interests. He did not begin by bellowing against and aiming his critical theoretical weaponry at imperial educational practices, but believed in a form of liberal education that would eventually place social and political power in the hands of the black bourgeoisie. Du Bois's early educational thought, as we will soon see, was at best conservative and in direct and blatant contradiction to his later, more Marxist, and increasingly internationalist sociology of education. Instead of focusing on the seemingly schizophrenic nature of the history of his educational thought, a more meaningful and critical engagement of Du Bois's (1971b) constantly evolving pedagogy demands that we do precisely what he advised his students and critical readers to do in his "Last Message to the World," where he humbly and lovingly stated, "I have loved my work, I have loved people and my play, but always I have been uplifted by the thought that what I have done well will live long and justify my life; that what I have done ill or never finished can now be handed on to others for endless days to be finished, perhaps better than I could have done" (736). Here, with these extremely weighted words, a dying Du Bois openly asks us to learn from his mistakes and failures and build on and go beyond his intellectual and political contributions. In what follows I intend to honor his request and heed his last words by briefly discussing some of the limitations and deficiencies of his sociology of education and providing an alternate critical educational theory grounded in and growing out of his educational thought and contemporary Africana pedagogical theory and praxis.

At first issue is the fact that Du Bois's early educational thought, specifically with regard to essays such as "The Talented Tenth," "The Hampton Idea," and to a certain extent "Galileo Galilei," placed African American advancement squarely on the shoulders of the black intellectual elite (see Du Bois, 1903b, 1973, 2002). His thinking at this point did not in any way associate upward mobility with the black masses and black working classes. In fact, in his infamous 1903 essay "The Talented Tenth," he went so far as to query, "Was there ever a nation on God's fair earth civilized from the bottom upward?" Du Bois's (1986a) emphatic answer to his rhetorical question was, "Never; it is, ever was and ever will be from the top downward that culture filters. The Talented Tenth rises and pulls all that are worth saving up to their vantage ground" (847).

Besides exhibiting a virulent intellectual elitism that privileges black academics and professionals over the black masses and working classes, Du Bois's (1973) talented tenth theory proves impoverished and inadequate when one reflects on the fact that most people of African descent have few if any opportunities to do the very "cultural study" which he asserts is such an integral part of an authentic Africana pedagogical process (28). Du Bois is caught in a contradiction when one realizes, as he did much later, that his sociology of education is in no uncertain terms asking "teachers [to] teach that which they have learned in no American school" (98), which, in other words, is to say that Du Bois knew good and well—first, that his sociology of education was at loggerheads with Western European and European American educational thought and practice, and, second, that his sociology of education did not ask, but *demand* that Africana educators go above and beyond their training in Western European and European American history, culture, religion, politics, arts, and so forth, and reroot themselves and their constituencies in continental and diasporan African history and culture, as well as continental and diasporan African thought, belief, and value systems and traditions.

Recall, Du Bois stated above that people of African descent are often educated "grudgingly and suspiciously; trained not with reference to what we can be, but with sole reference to what somebody [else] wants us to be" (9). Even in "The Talented Tenth" he argues unequivocally for "culture training" for black "group leaders," the "leaders of thought among Negroes," and black "educated thinkers" (Du Bois, 1986a, 855). But here paradox presents itself immediately: If, indeed, the talented tenth "rises and pulls all that are worth saving up to their vantage ground," and if, as Du Bois intimated, the talented tenth are often educated "not with reference to what we can be, but with sole reference to what somebody [else] wants us to be," then, the question quickly becomes *which* or, more to the point, *whose* "vantage ground" will the talented tenth be pulling the black masses up to? We could throw a third critical query in here and ask: *How* will the talented tenth pull the black masses up to their "vantage ground" since, in Du Bois's own words, "they have no traditions to fall back upon, no long established customs, no strong family ties, [and] no well defined social classes" (852)?[5]

The "vantage ground" or worldview of the talented tenth is often that of the imperial agents who educate them "grudgingly and suspiciously." Hence, Du Bois unapologetically declared above that "very very many colored folk . . . can conceive of no future world which is not dominated by present white nations and thoroughly shot through with their ideals, their method of government, their economic organization, their literature and their art; or in other words their throttling of democracy, their exploitation of labor, their industrial imperialism and their color hate." It is the very "vantage ground" or worldview of the talented tenth that Du Bois would later argue is problematic and in need of radical reconstruction by the "human power" of much more than the black intelligentsia.

In 1948, forty-five years after his initial articulation of his talented tenth theory, Du Bois (1996c) delivered "The Talented Tenth Memorial Address," in which he sternly stated:

> When I came out of college into the world of work, I realized that it was quite possible that my plan of training a Talented Tenth might put in control and power, a group of selfish, self-indulgent, well-to-do men, whose basic interest in solving the Negro problem was personal; personal freedom and unhampered enjoyment and use of the world, without any real care, or certainly no arousing care, as to what became of the mass of American Negroes, or of the mass of any people. My Talented Tenth, I could see, might result in a sort of interracial free-for-all, with the devil taking the hindmost and the foremost taking anything they could lay hands on. (162)

Besides sounding like the penetrating pronouncements of Fanon in *The Wretched of the Earth* concerning the "national bourgeoisie" or the "national middle class" in their greed and intense identification with and imitation of the culture of the racial colonizers, Du Bois's assertions above help to highlight a shift in his liberation and leadership thought from the black elites to the black masses. In his revised and reformulated talented tenth thesis, Du Bois not only stresses *struggle, sacrifice,* and *service* as prerequisites for black and global human progress, but he ultimately abandons the talented tenth thesis for "the doctrine of the 'Guiding Hundredth.'" Here, as I observed in *Du Bois's Dialectics,* Du Bois is attempting to simultaneously democratize and internationalize his sociology of education and his black liberation and leadership theory.

It is not enough for the talented tenth to be talented, quipped Du Bois; they must also be willing and able to *struggle, sacrifice,* and *serve.* What black and other oppressed and poverty-stricken people need is "honest," "unselfish, far-seeing leadership." Du Bois (1996c) put it this way: "We cannot have perfection. We have few saints. But we must have honest men [and women] or we die. We must have unselfish, far-seeing leadership or we fail" (173). He learned from bitter experience that unless the talented tenth was composed of "men and women of character and almost fanatic devotion" to Africana and universal human liberation, then "mass misery" and "the poor [which] need not always be with us" will become permanent parts of the human experience (161–62).

In revising and reformulating his talented tenth thesis into a theory of "the Guiding Hundredth," Du Bois democratized and internationalized his black liberation and leadership thought, asserting that it must be based on "group-leadership, not simply educated and self-sacrificing, but with a clear vision of present world conditions and dangers, and conducting American Negroes to alliance with culture groups in Europe, America, Asia and Africa, and looking toward a new world culture" (168). Du Bois's theory of the "Guiding Hundredth," then, is predicated on a concept of collective leadership and participatory democracy which harbors an openness to coalitions and alliances with other "culture groups," and which is geared toward the creation of "a new world culture."

Where his early articulation of the talented tenth theory limited itself to both the African American intelligentsia and problems endemic to, and emanating from, African Americans' particular and peculiar existential and ontological experiences in the United States, Du Bois's evolving critical educational thought—and especially as embodied in his "Guiding Hundredth" thesis—took on a world-historical tone that found the greatest promise and potential for radical social and global change, not in the heads of intellectuals and academics, but in the hearts of "men and women of character"—regardless of their race, culture, class, and/or occupation. For Du Bois, character became the greatest gauge of radical political potential, and this is one of the reasons he repeatedly wrote of "great moral leaders," "prophets and reformers," "honest men," and "unselfish, far-seeing leadership" in "The Talented Tenth Memorial Address" (162, 173). In the face of his early black bourgeois pedagogical pronouncements, Du Bois now came to realize that education and ability were not panaceas for the problems plaguing people of African descent. In his own weighted words, "My Talented Tenth must be more than talented, and work not simply as individuals. Its passport to leadership was not alone learning but expert knowledge of modern economics as it affected American Negroes; and in addition to this and fundamental, would be its willingness to sacrifice and plan for such economic revolution in industry and just distribution of wealth, as would make the rise of our group possible" (163).

In the final analysis, education and ability must be coupled with character and radical democratic socialism, and in Du Bois's evolving critical social theory this involves not simply the black intelligentsia, but also the black masses' and the global working classes' "almost fanatic devotion" to cultural and "economic revolution"; "the ideal of plain living and high thinking, in defiance of American noise, waste and display"; "the rehabilitation of the indispensable family group"; and the eradication of the "wholesale neglect of invaluable human resources" (175, 177). The talented tenth, thus, was conceived and christened by Du Bois, long given his best blessings, and then, without a lot of brouhaha and brandishing of theoretical weaponry, laid to rest in an act of *intellectual infanticide*. There is a sense in which "The Talented Tenth Memorial Address" simultaneously serves as an epitaph for one of Du Bois's infamous theoretic failures and an exciting announcement that he was not afraid to conceptually begin again, revising and reconstructing his leadership and liberation thought in light of increasing African American professional and intellectual elitism, a growing black bourgeoisie shamelessly and pretentiously grounded in European imperial culture and, perhaps most importantly, his deep and abiding interests in coupling his sociology of education and critical race theory with Marxist critiques of capitalism, critical class theory, and radical democratic socialism.[6]

Education, liberation, and leadership are not the exclusive domain of the ruling race, gender, and/or class; they are vital human needs just as food, clothing, and shelter are human necessities. But, without critical education and authentic liberation thought that speaks to the specificities of Africana and other subjugated souls' lifeworlds and life struggles, ongoing hardships and unspeakable hurts, long-held utopian hopes and deep-seated radical democratic desires, then all oppressed and (neo)colonized people have are abstract and empty inquiries into Eurocentric notions of "justice," "freedom," "democracy," "liberation," "peace," and, perhaps most importantly, what it means to be "human." Capitalist, racial colonialist, and/or global imperialist "democracy" is a deformation of democracy that enables the ruling race, gender, and/or class to put the premium on *what* the oppressed are fighting for and *how* they should fight for what they are fighting for. Africana education must not simply expose and introduce us and tyrannized others to Africana history and culture, Africana thought, belief, and value systems and traditions, but it must also aid us in our efforts to engage, explore, and ethically alter the world in our own and other downtrodden and dispossessed peoples' anti-imperialist interests. What I am calling for here is nothing short of a critical multiculturalist, revolutionary humanist, and radical democratic socialist transgression and transcendence of Eurocentric-ideological-imperial education, socialization, and globalization.

CONCLUSION: DU BOIS, CRITICAL EDUCATIONAL THEORY, AND AFRICANA CRITICAL PEDAGOGY

Du Bois serves as an ideal point of departure for contemporary sociology of education when and where he asserts that continental and diasporan Africans "have a contribution to make to civilization and humanity, which no other race can make," and insofar as he stresses the necessity and importance of Africana education beginning with and being rooted in Africa—its people and problems, its history and culture, its thought, belief, and value systems and traditions—and ever expanding "toward the possession and the conquest of all knowledge." Du Bois also poses a paradigm for critical pedagogy, particularly in terms of recent efforts geared toward de-domesticating and reconstructing it to reflect constructive criticisms of its inattention to racism, sexism, radical politics, and revolutionary democratic socialist transformation. For example, critical pedagogues frequently reproach racism, but very rarely systematically analyze it and incorporate philosophy of race, sociology of race, and, especially, critical race theory into their educational theory (Dixson and Rousseau, 2006; Parker, Deyhle, and Villenas, 1999). Such a synthesis (i.e., one of critical pedagogy and critical race theory) has precedent in Du Bois's sociology of education in particular, and the history of Africana critical educational theory in general. What Du Bois's educational thought and Africana critical pedagogy urges conventional critical pedagogues to do is broaden their critical theoretical base by making it more multicultural and expanding the range of pedagogical (and social and political) problems to which they seek solutions.

Paulo Freire's philosophy of education has long served as the fountainhead and foundation for critical pedagogy, but the politics of postmodernism and/or postmodern politics have downplayed and diminished its inherent radical humanism and promotion of revolutionary democratic socialist projects. Postmodern pedagogues have pointed out that Freire's formulations often raise important issues but do not adequately provide the necessary philosophical foundation for putting forward more progressive and programmatic alternatives to the (mostly European, bourgeois, modernist, and masculinist) pedagogical perspectives he criticizes. For instance, Freire provides few concrete (as opposed to abstract) accounts of ways in which critical educators progress from critical thought to critical practice, self-consciously demanding that their critical pedagogical discourse constantly translate into and support radical politics and critical multicultural democratic socialist movements. However, I should obstinately observe, Freire's pedagogical pronouncements are often purposely universal, and this gives them their intellectual and political potency (much like Du Bois's critical educational thought) such that they can be conscripted by progressive educators to criticize and counterpoint imperial-ideological pedagogical practices worldwide.

Indeed, many of the postmodern pedagogues may have misread Freire's philosophy of education, but perhaps part of the confusion is due to the fact that there has been a mounting debate amongst Freirean critical pedagogues concerning how to best interpret and apply his radical pedagogy and radical politics. However, and this must be made clear, even before postmodernism taunted and tantalized pedagogues lost in the theoretical labyrinths of the last couple of decades, Freirean critical pedagogy failed to adequately engage race and racism, and the same should be said of its silence regarding gender and sexism (hooks, 1994b, 2003, 2009; Luke, 1996; Luke and Gore, 1992). Peter McLaren (2000b) makes the point: "The legacy of racism left by the New World European oppressor—that Blacks and Latino/as are simply a species of inferior invertebrates—was harshly condemned but never systematically analyzed by Freire. And while Freire was a vociferous critic of racism and sexism, he did not, as Kathleen Weiler points out, sufficiently problematize his conceptualization of liberation and the oppressed in terms of his own male experience" (14; see also Weiler, 1994, 2001).

Unfortunately, in all of the recent theoretical wrangling amongst Freireans, few have indexed the important deficiencies that could be developed were they to do as Freire admonished them to before the massive heart attack that claimed his life—"reinvent me," Freire said solemnly. In one of his last works he wrote, "The progressive educator must always be moving out on his or her own, continually reinventing me and reinventing what it means to be democratic in his or her own specific cultural and historical contexts" (quoted in McLaren, 2000b, 14). What I am advocating here is a "reinvention" and radical reconstruction of critical pedagogy, a return to its critical theoretical roots, if you will, and also a critical theoretical branching out that will bring it into dialogue with Du Bois's sociology, Fanon's philosophy, critical race theory, antiracist radical feminism, revolutionary democratic socialism, and the ongoing discourse on revolutionary decolonization.

Almost unanimously regarded as the preeminent sociologist of race of the twentieth century, Du Bois and his antiracist sociology of education helps to fill one of the major critical theoretical lacunae of Freire's philosophy of education and, therefore, a yawning intellectual chasm in contemporary critical pedagogy. Where Freire's work is weak when it comes to the critique of racism and sexism, Du Bois's educational discourse is particularly powerful and distinguished by its simultaneous emphasis on racial, gender, and economic justice. For instance, although many read him as an archetypal "race man," according to Joy James (1997) in *Transcending the Talented Tenth*, Du Bois actually practiced "a politics remarkably progressive for his time and ours" (36).[7] James further notes, "Du Bois confronted race, class, and gender oppression while maintaining conceptual and political linkages between the struggles to end racism, sexism, and war" (36–37). Both his social scientific and critical socio-theoretical discourses were dynamic and constantly integrated diverse components of African American liberation and critical race theory, anticolonial and decolonization theory, women's decolonization and women's liberation theory, peace and disarmament theory, and Marxist critiques of capitalism and revolutionary democratic socialist theory, among others.

Although complicated and brimming with contradictions, as we witnessed in chapter 3, Du Bois indeed does make several significant contributions to the sociology of gender and intersectional sociology. These contributions could aid both contemporary sociologists of education and critical pedagogues in their efforts to either develop or deepen their respective discursive formations' understanding of the interrelation between education and racism, and/or education and sexism. What is more, perhaps the most remarkable aspect of Du Bois's sociological discourse is that it offers an early example of intersectional sociology that seriously considers and is self-consciously connected to educational thought. Often in the rush to critique race, gender, and class, contemporary intersectional sociologists leave education (among other important issues, such as religion, social ecology, and state-sanctioned violence) out of the equation.

In terms of developing critical educational theory, and Africana critical pedagogy in particular, what I am most interested in here is how Du Bois maintained, as James put it above, "conceptual and political linkages" between various antiracist, antisexist, anticolonialist, and anticapitalist thought-traditions and sociopolitical movements. Unlike most of the critics in the Frankfurt School tradition of critical theory and Freirean critical pedagogues, Du Bois did not downplay racial and gender domination and discrimination. On the contrary, remarkably foreshadowing Fanon's critique of racial colonization, Du Bois's early insurgent intersectional sociology repeatedly placed the critique of sexism, colonialism, and racism right alongside Marxism and its critique of capitalism. In tune with the thinking of many Marxist feminists and socialist feminists, Du Bois was critical of both capitalism and patriarchy. He understood women, in general, to have great potential as agents of social transformation because of their simultaneous experience of, and resistance efforts against, capitalist and sexist oppression. However, similar to contemporary black feminist sociologists, Du Bois understood women of African descent, in particular, to have even greater potential as agents of radical social change on account of their simultaneous experience of and revolutionary praxis against racism, sexism, and economic exploitation, whether under capitalism or colonialism. Du Bois's social scientific and critical socio-theoretical discourses, therefore, have immense import for the discussion at hand so far as they provide contemporary sociology of education and Africana critical pedagogy with a paradigm and point of departure for developing a multiperspectival social theory that is simultaneously critical of racism, sexism, capitalism, and colonialism.

Although there is much more in Du Bois's educational thought that warrants our critical attention, I believe that the major issues—issues of historical and cultural grounding, intellectual elitism, pedagogical pitfalls, and the relationship between critical pedagogical theory and radical political praxis—have been adequately addressed. Therefore, despite the conundrums of, and contradictions in, his sociology of education, I believe that Du Bois was one of the most important critical pedagogues of the twentieth century, and that his lifework harbors an unrivaled relevance and crucial significance for Africana, critical multicultural, feminist, womanist, democratic socialist, and radical humanist sociologists of education attempting to grasp and grapple with the problems of the twenty-first century.

In conclusion, then, it could be said that as Du Bois came to see character, cultural grounding, anti-imperialist ethics, and radical resistance as the cornerstones of Africana education and leadership, he grew increasingly critical of bourgeois (both conservative and liberal) Africana educators and leaders, and, ironically, his own antecedent thought on Africana education and leadership. This was a consequence of his evolving critical consciousness and ultimate break with Eurocentric, elitist, and bourgeois conceptions of Africa and its diaspora. At the heart of Du Bois's sociology of education is an intense emphasis on continental and diasporan African history, culture, and struggle. Consequently, Derrick Alridge (2008) argues, Du Bois "believed that black intellectuals worldwide should take an active role in [both developing and] disseminating knowledge about Africa and African peoples" (130). Du Bois's sociology of education, like critical theory in its most general sense, critiques the ideology of the established imperial order. It provides contemporary sociologists of education with a paradigm to identify both the "problems" and "solutions" of Africana education. However, as intimated throughout this chapter, Du Bois's sociology of education is inextricable from the whole of his unique brand of sociology. It is with this in mind that we end where we began, returning to Alridge's work, which accents that "Du Bois believed firmly that education was the most effective strategy for correcting misinformation about Africa and for helping people of African descent around the world unite politically to overthrow outside oppression" (129). One of the many issues of "misinformation about Africa," and African Americans in particular, revolved around their *racial criminalization*. Just as Du Bois's sociology critiqued the racial colonization of gender, social classes, labor, religion, and education, the last major form of racial colonization that should be critically engaged before this book's close centers on black criminality. The final chapter, therefore, explores Du Bois's sociology of crime and reveals that he arguably developed the first social etiology and social ecology of African American crime and African Americans' receipt of differential justice.

NOTES

1. For critical investigations into Du Bois's educational thought in particular, and for examples of the types of texts I consulted in the construction of my arguments throughout this chapter, see Glascoe (1996), Goldstein (1972), Mielke (1977), Neal (1984), Nwankwo (1989), Oatts (2003, 2006), Okoro (1982), E. C. Smith (1975), Sumpter (1973), and Warren (1984). In terms of primary source material with regard to Du Bois's sociology of education, I have consulted and concentrated

on his articles and addresses collected in *The Education of Black People: Ten Critiques, 1906–1960*, edited by Herbert Aptheker, and *Du Bois on Education*, edited by Eugene F. Provenzo Jr., see Du Bois (1973, 2002).

2. Fanon's work, especially "The Negro and Language" in *Black Skin, White Masks*, helps to highlight the existential-linguistic dynamics and dimensions of the racially colonized being educated or, rather, *miseducated* in racial colonial languages. To begin, he noted that along with the racist-colonialist-capitalist church and its colonial missionary endeavors, the educational systems in colonial countries serve the interests of the racial colonizers and *not* the racially colonized. In the colonial school system, as they learn the language of the white colonizers, racially colonized black children are simultaneously indoctrinated into the Eurocentric-imperial-ideological world where various words impart the Eurocentric-imperial-ideological value judgments associated with the antonyms "black" and "white." Fanon (1967) prodded his readers to critically consider the matter: "Is not whiteness in symbols always ascribed in French [and in English, we might add] to Justice, Truth, Virginity? . . . The black man is the symbol of Evil and Ugliness. . . . *In Europe, the black man is the symbol of Evil*" (180, 188, emphasis in original). Notice Fanon's shift of tone and timbre here. He goes from critically questioning to unequivocally contending white supremacist constructions of blackness. Du Bois's emphasis on culture and language in his sociology of education, therefore, demonstrates that his dialectic, in several senses, prefigures Fanon's dialectical thought and, in addition, makes a major contribution to the discourse on decolonization. For further discussion of Fanon's contributions to the Africana tradition of critical theory, see Rabaka (2010a).

3. According to the African American feminist bell hooks (1984), radical pedagogues must develop the ability to "'translate' ideas to an audience that varies in age, sex, ethnicity, [and] degree of literacy" (111). Though she was writing directly to "feminist educators" and "feminist scholars" when she wrote this, I understand hooks's theory of "translation" techniques and textual practices to have great import for Africana, multicultural, and other educators and scholars as well, both female and male. For instance, she writes, "All too often educators, especially university professors, fear their work will not be valued by other academics if it is presented in a way that makes it accessible to a wider audience. If these educators thought of rendering their work in a number of different styles, 'translations,' they would be able to satisfy arbitrary academic standards while making their work available to masses of people" (111). This hits a chord that resonates profoundly with Du Bois's theory of the production of practical knowledge in particular, and his sociology of education in general. In advocating that Africana educators use "that variety of the English idiom which [their constituencies] understand," Du Bois is in no small way charging and challenging Africana educators and scholars to develop the ability to "'translate' ideas to an audience that varies in age, sex, ethnicity, [and] degree of literacy," and "render . . . their work in a number of different styles, 'translations.'" The production of practical knowledge, then, is predicated upon *the production of easily accessible knowledge*. Moreover, knowledge that has the ability to be accessed with ease often offers *attractive ethical and emancipatory alternatives* to both the oppressed and their oppressors (see Fanon, 1965, 1967, 1968, 1969; Freire, 1985, 1989, 1993, 1996, 1998). Also by bell hooks, and extremely informative with regard to the development of *Africana critical pedagogy* (see Rabaka, 2008a), are her books on con-

temporary teaching theory and pedagogical praxis: *Teaching to Transgress: Education as the Practice of Freedom* (1994b), *Teaching Communities: A Pedagogy of Hope* (2003), and *Teaching Critical Thinking: Practical Wisdom* (2009).

4. The Caribbean political philosopher Charles Mills offers an astute discussion of the ocularcentric and somatic syndrome in Western European and European American thought and behavior in his book, *The Racial Contract* (1997). Perception plays a big part in racial categorization and classification, and the way persons of African descent and other nonwhites are seen has curiously become—in the Eurocentric mindset—just as important as the way nonwhites actually are, or exist, or experience life and the world in which they live. In other words, I am hinting at the issue that Fanon (1967, 111–23) exposed in *Black Skins, White Masks* when he recollected how "the black body" is seen, or sometimes not seen because it is different from the white/Western European somatic norm—a norm, as Mills (1997, 53) points out, that is almost at every instance predicated on not simply the white body, but more specifically the *white male* body. For further discussion, see Rabaka (2010a).

5. In "W. E. B. Du Bois and 'The Talented Tenth,'" acclaimed African American literary theorist Henry Louis Gates Jr. (1996, 129) argues that Du Bois "overstates the case" when he writes "they"—meaning "the Talented Tenth"—"have no traditions to fall back upon, no long established customs, no strong family ties, [and] no well defined social classes," because he, Du Bois, is "attempting to persuade even the most skeptical or hostile racist, by appearing to accept the racist premise that the Negro people need social leadership more than most groups" on account of the African holocaust and African Americans' subsequent enslavement and experience and endurance of peonage, sharecropping, lynching, and Jim Crow segregation. Gates, I will concede, correctly contends that Du Bois's leadership thought at this point parallels many of the positions of the "pathological" sociological school of thought most evident in the thought and texts of Robert Park, a claim and/or connection which Jessica Marshall (1994) also makes in her doctoral dissertation "'Counsels of Despair': W. E. B. Du Bois, Robert E. Park, and the Establishment of American Race Sociology." However, there is a sense in which, I believe, Gates is too quick to call Du Bois's thought "pathological" without fully exploring, first, Du Bois's use of this part of his argument as a rhetorical device, and, second, the social, political, and intellectual context in which Du Bois's essay "The Talented Tenth" was written and published. At first issue, it could be said that Gates overlooks the fact that although *The Souls of Black Folk* was written for and directed at a broad public audience, both black and white, fairly knowledgeable of and sympathetic to "the plight of the Negro"—the essays collected in *The Souls of Black Folk*, according to David Levering Lewis (1993, 265–96), were culled from pieces Du Bois had published in the popular press, magazines and journals such as *The Independent, The Nation, The Southern Workman, Harper's Weekly, World's Work, The Outlook, The Missionary Review, The Literary Digest*, the *Annuals of the American Academy of Political and Social Science*, and *The Dial*. Du Bois's "The Talented Tenth" essay, on the other hand, was published the same year as *The Souls of Black Folk*, in 1903, in a volume entitled *The Negro Problem: A Series of Articles by Representative American Negroes of Today*, which Lewis (1993, 288) avers was compiled by "a now unidentifiable white editor," and which Gates (1996, 127) asserts is thought by many "to have been edited, or at least

endorsed, by Du Bois's nemesis, Booker T. Washington." By plodding momentarily down the "pathological" path, which was in and of itself a risky and rare thing for a writer of African descent in the United States at the dawn of the twentieth century, Du Bois was attempting to lure his readers into his overall argument, which was that, like it or not, both Southern white supremacists and Northern liberal white racists were continuing to pillage black potential by applauding Washington's accommodationism and incessant emphasis on industrial education. From the Du Boisian dialectical perspective, Washington's accommodationism, fully financed by anti-black racist and wealthy whites, was robbing African Americans of their right to choose between industrial or liberal arts education. For further discussion of Du Bois and Washington's intellectual history-making discourse on the optimal strategy for African American education, please see my extended analysis in "The Du Bois-Washington Debate: Social Leadership, Intellectual Legacy, and the Lingering Problematics of African American Politics" (Rabaka, 2008a, 43–118).

6. With regard to what I am referring to as Du Bois's "deep and abiding interests in coupling his sociology of education and critical race theory with Marxist critiques of capitalism, critical class theory, and radical democratic socialism," please see my extended exploration of Du Bois's inauguration of black Marxism in "Du Bois's Critique of Capitalism, Critical Marxism, and Discourse on Democratic Socialism" (Rabaka, 2007b, 101–36), as well as the aforementioned chapter of *Du Bois's Dialectics* (Rabaka, 2008a, 43–118).

7. On Du Bois and his "race man" reputation, see Alridge (2003), Carby (1998), and Lemons (2009).

significance for Africana, critical multicultural, feminist, womanist, democratic socialist, and radical humanist sociologists of education attempting to grasp and grapple with the problems of the twenty-first century.

In conclusion, then, it could be said that as Du Bois came to see character, cultural grounding, anti-imperialist ethics, and radical resistance as the cornerstones of Africana education and leadership, he grew increasingly critical of bourgeois (both conservative and liberal) Africana educators and leaders, and, ironically, his own antecedent thought on Africana education and leadership. This was a consequence of his evolving critical consciousness and ultimate break with Eurocentric, elitist, and bourgeois conceptions of Africa and its diaspora. At the heart of Du Bois's sociology of education is an intense emphasis on continental and diasporan African history, culture, and struggle. Consequently, Derrick Alridge (2008) argues, Du Bois "believed that black intellectuals worldwide should take an active role in [both developing and] disseminating knowledge about Africa and African peoples" (130). Du Bois's sociology of education, like critical theory in its most general sense, critiques the ideology of the established imperial order. It provides contemporary sociologists of education with a paradigm to identify both the "problems" and "solutions" of Africana education. However, as intimated throughout this chapter, Du Bois's sociology of education is inextricable from the whole of his unique brand of sociology. It is with this in mind that we end where we began, returning to Alridge's work, which accents that "Du Bois believed firmly that education was the most effective strategy for correcting misinformation about Africa and for helping people of African descent around the world unite politically to overthrow outside oppression" (129). One of the many issues of "misinformation about Africa," and African Americans in particular, revolved around their *racial criminalization*. Just as Du Bois's sociology critiqued the racial colonization of gender, social classes, labor, religion, and education, the last major form of racial colonization that should be critically engaged before this book's close centers on black criminality. The final chapter, therefore, explores Du Bois's sociology of crime and reveals that he arguably developed the first social etiology and social ecology of African American crime and African Americans' receipt of differential justice.

NOTES

1. For critical investigations into Du Bois's educational thought in particular, and for examples of the types of texts I consulted in the construction of my arguments throughout this chapter, see Glascoe (1996), Goldstein (1972), Mielke (1977), Neal (1984), Nwankwo (1989), Oatts (2003, 2006), Okoro (1982), E. C. Smith (1975), Sumpter (1973), and Warren (1984). In terms of primary source material with regard to Du Bois's sociology of education, I have consulted and concentrated

on his articles and addresses collected in *The Education of Black People: Ten Critiques, 1906–1960*, edited by Herbert Aptheker, and *Du Bois on Education*, edited by Eugene F. Provenzo Jr., see Du Bois (1973, 2002).

2. Fanon's work, especially "The Negro and Language" in *Black Skin, White Masks*, helps to highlight the existential-linguistic dynamics and dimensions of the racially colonized being educated or, rather, *miseducated* in racial colonial languages. To begin, he noted that along with the racist-colonialist-capitalist church and its colonial missionary endeavors, the educational systems in colonial countries serve the interests of the racial colonizers and *not* the racially colonized. In the colonial school system, as they learn the language of the white colonizers, racially colonized black children are simultaneously indoctrinated into the Eurocentric-imperial-ideological world where various words impart the Eurocentric-imperial-ideological value judgments associated with the antonyms "black" and "white." Fanon (1967) prodded his readers to critically consider the matter: "Is not whiteness in symbols always ascribed in French [and in English, we might add] to Justice, Truth, Virginity? . . . The black man is the symbol of Evil and Ugliness. . . . *In Europe, the black man is the symbol of Evil*" (180, 188, emphasis in original). Notice Fanon's shift of tone and timbre here. He goes from critically questioning to unequivocally contending white supremacist constructions of blackness. Du Bois's emphasis on culture and language in his sociology of education, therefore, demonstrates that his dialectic, in several senses, prefigures Fanon's dialectical thought and, in addition, makes a major contribution to the discourse on decolonization. For further discussion of Fanon's contributions to the Africana tradition of critical theory, see Rabaka (2010a).

3. According to the African American feminist bell hooks (1984), radical pedagogues must develop the ability to "'translate' ideas to an audience that varies in age, sex, ethnicity, [and] degree of literacy" (111). Though she was writing directly to "feminist educators" and "feminist scholars" when she wrote this, I understand hooks's theory of "translation" techniques and textual practices to have great import for Africana, multicultural, and other educators and scholars as well, both female and male. For instance, she writes, "All too often educators, especially university professors, fear their work will not be valued by other academics if it is presented in a way that makes it accessible to a wider audience. If these educators thought of rendering their work in a number of different styles, 'translations,' they would be able to satisfy arbitrary academic standards while making their work available to masses of people" (111). This hits a chord that resonates profoundly with Du Bois's theory of the production of practical knowledge in particular, and his sociology of education in general. In advocating that Africana educators use "that variety of the English idiom which [their constituencies] understand," Du Bois is in no small way charging and challenging Africana educators and scholars to develop the ability to "'translate' ideas to an audience that varies in age, sex, ethnicity, [and] degree of literacy,'" and "render . . . their work in a number of different styles, 'translations.'" The production of practical knowledge, then, is predicated upon *the production of easily accessible knowledge*. Moreover, knowledge that has the ability to be accessed with ease often offers *attractive ethical and emancipatory alternatives* to both the oppressed and their oppressors (see Fanon, 1965, 1967, 1968, 1969; Freire, 1985, 1989, 1993, 1996, 1998). Also by bell hooks, and extremely informative with regard to the development of *Africana critical pedagogy* (see Rabaka, 2008a), are her books on con-

6

Du Bois and the Sociology of Crime

Critiquing the Criminalization of Black (Among Other) Folk

> The Negro is not naturally criminal; he is usually patient and law-abiding. If slavery, the convict-lease system, the traffic in criminal labor, the lack of juvenile reformatories, together with the unfortunate discrimination and prejudice in other walks of life, have led to that sort of social protest and revolt which we call crime, then we must look for remedy in the sane reform of these wrong social conditions, and not in intimidation, savagery, or the legalized slavery of men.
>
> W. E. B. Du Bois, *Some Notes on Negro Crime*, 8–9

INTRODUCTION: DU BOIS'S CRIMINOLOGICAL CONTRIBUTIONS

As with many other disciplines in the American academy, American criminology has been almost universally understood to have Western European origins. Most histories of the disciplinary development of criminology acknowledge that: the Italian law professor Raffaele Garofalo coined the term "criminology" (*criminologia*, in Italian) in 1885; French anthropologist Paul Topinard utilized the term in French (i.e., *criminologie*) in the mid-1880s; and several utilitarian philosophers (e.g., Jeremy Bentham, John Stuart Mill, and Cesare Beccaria) laid the foundation for criminology's "classical school." Cesare Lombroso, widely known as "the father of criminology" and the founder of the Italian school of criminology in light of his scientific research methods and dogged insistence on empirical evidence in studying crime, ushered in the "positivist school" of criminology. Over time Western European criminologists began to move beyond Lombroso's early emphasis on biology-based causes of crime and criminal tendencies. Early criminologists, such as Enrico Ferri and Alexandre Lacassagne, eventually came to stress social and environmental factors, frequently synthesizing them with Lombroso's biological determinism and, therefore, they did not completely transcend Lombroso's biologism. Psychologists Hans Eysenck, Hervey Cleckley, and Robert Hare each emphasized various psychological factors, such as extraversion, neuroticism, and psychoticism as causes leading to criminal behavior and criminal acts. Thus, criminology is often discursively defined as an interdisciplinary field within the behavioral sciences that frequently draws from the disciplines of sociology and psychology, as well as law (e.g., criminal law, civil law, history of law, philosophy of law, and sociology of law) (Becker and Wetzell, 2004; Jones, 2006; Morris and Rothman, 1995; Wetzell, 2000).

Histories of criminology in the United States often began with the innovative work of the Chicago School (e.g., Robert Park, George Herbert Mead, Ernest Burgess, Edwin Sutherland, William Thomas, and Florian Znaniecki). However, several of W. E. B. Du Bois's U.S. Department of Labor commissioned studies decidedly demonstrate that his criminological contributions antedate those of the Chicago School. Recall in his previously discussed 1898 report "The Negroes of Farmville," he wrote of a black "criminal class," "loafers," "semi-criminals," and prostitutes. In his 1899 U.S. Department of Labor study "The Negro in the Black Belt," he again included a section on the "Unemployed and Criminal Classes." Du Bois undeniably contributed to the inception of American criminology with "The Negro Criminal" and "The Causes of Crime and Poverty" in *The Philadelphia Negro*. Furthermore, as my colleagues Earl Wright (2002a, 2002b, 2002c, 2005, 2008) and Shaun Gabbidon (1999) have more recently observed, the criminological contributions of the Atlanta School, under the auspices of Du Bois, predate those of the Chicago School. One need look no further than *Some Efforts of American Negroes for Their Own Social Betterment*, *Some Notes on Negro Crime*, and *Morals and Manners Among Negro Americans*, originally published in 1898, 1904, and 1914, respectively. If, indeed, Du Bois's sociology of crime preceded the criminological contributions of the Chicago School, why has it become common practice to begin histories of American criminology with the Chicago School? How can the historians of American criminology explain their longstanding omission of Du Bois's criminological discourse from the disciplinary development of criminology in the United States? Do we have here yet another instance of the insidious practices of *disciplinary decadence, intellectual historical amnesia,* and *epistemic apartheid*? Moreover, even if one is willing to concede Du Bois's criminological contributions, the question continues to beg: exactly what were his contributions to the inception of American criminology, and what, if any, is their continued relevance with respect to twenty-first-century criminology?

This chapter seeks to briefly, albeit critically, engage each of the foregoing questions. At the outset, however, it should be made clear that the intention here is not to offer an exhaustive analysis of each and every offering Du Bois made to criminology, but rather to introduce my readers (especially contemporary students of sociology, criminology, and Africana studies) to his seminal contributions to the sociology of crime, criminology, and criminal justice. Although often overlooked, Du Bois's early sociological discourse displays a recurring interest in criminology and criminal justice. In fact, his first publication in the *New York Globe* in 1883 at the age of fifteen helps to highlight his early interest in crime. He tellingly wrote, "The Citizens of the town are forming a Law and Order Society to enforce the laws against liquor selling which have been sadly neglected for the past year or two. It would be a good plan if some of the colored men should join it" (Du Bois, 1986b, p. 1). This prefiguring passage reveals several things of sociological significance. First, it accents Du Bois's acute awareness (at an extremely early age!) of the need for social organization and community action against the problem of alcoholism, which from his report we can gather was ravaging his hometown, Great Barrington. Second, the passage points to the fact that he earnestly believed that African Americans ought to actively participate in antialcoholism (and, it could easily be averred, other anticrime) campaigns. Finally, the young Du Bois's words here resonate with his later life emphasis on interracial cooperation, cultural working, and community caretaking, which ultimately became important cornerstones of his distinct vision and version of democracy.

David Levering Lewis's (1993, 4) research reveals that Du Bois's deep and abiding interest in criminal justice may have also grown out of his lived experience of being *racially criminalized—that is, hypercriminalized on the basis of one's race or, rather, the combined process(es) and/or predicament(s) of being simultaneously racialized and criminalized and the ongoing effects of simultaneous racialization and criminalization*. Although it was treated in a single paragraph in his autobiography, there is reason to believe that the incident surrounding Du Bois (1968a) and several other boys being caught "filch[ing] some choice and carefully tended grapes from a prominent citizen" had a deep and pervasive impact on him and his understanding of criminal justice (91). The county judge, Justin Dewey, was lenient with the white boys who were caught stealing grapes with Du Bois, but thought that a "poor, spirited black boy would be much improved learning a trade under lock and key." Were it not for his high school principal, Frank Hosmer, Du Bois would have more than likely spent his remaining teenage years languishing in a juvenile reformatory. Undoubtedly, this was a harrowing experience for the young Du Bois and it patently piqued his lifelong interest in criminal justice.

Through his lived experience he observed the *preferential* treatment whites, and *differential* treatment blacks were accorded with regard to crime and legal matters. It was a humiliating and bitter lesson to learn at such a young age but, in characteristic fashion, Du Bois (however clandestinely) used it to develop his distinct sociological discourse, always paying careful and critical attention to the ways in which race and racism played themselves out in local, national, and international communities, conventions, and institutions. Nearly eighty years after the incident, Du Bois noted in his autobiography that the harshness of the judge's initial ruling did not coincide with the crime committed: "During my ten years of boyhood life there was in the county one murder; once the bank was robbed of a small sum; there were minor cases of stealing and trespass and some drunkenness which called for arrest" (91). It is evident that Du Bois believed that the punishment (i.e., being sent to reform school) he would have been forced to endure were it not for principal Hosmer not only was not comparable to what his white friends received but, even more, simply was not proportional with the crime (i.e., stealing a bunch of grapes).

At the age of fifteen, therefore, Du Bois realized that even when whites and blacks commit the same crime, because of *racial criminalization* blacks usually receive disproportional punishments. In addition, he discovered that in order to receive something close to justice (although, it is likely, not authentic justice) blacks, in essence, need liberal and well-meaning white friends and fellow citizens who are willing to antiracistly oppose the injustice of blacks' constant *racial criminalization* both in and out of the criminal justice system. In other words, it seems that early in his life Du Bois was able to make connections between *racial criminalization* and the criminal justice system, as well as the omnipresent institutionalized racism of American culture, politics, and society at large. This brings us to several crucial questions: What if Du Bois had spent his remaining years as a teenager in a reformatory? Would he have gone to college: Fisk, Harvard, or Berlin? Would he have helped to inaugurate sociology in the United States? Would he have helped to found the Niagara movement and, ultimately, the NAACP? Would his intellectual absence have led to a delayed civil rights movement? Clearly the questions here are innumerable, and it will be important to bear them in mind as we explore Du Bois's criminological contributions.

In essence, this chapter is divided into three sections. This first section treats Du Bois's criminological contributions in "The Negro and Crime" and *The Philadelphia Negro*. The second section engages his contributions to criminology as they emerge from his Atlanta University studies, *Some Notes on Negro Crime* and *Morals and Manners Among Negro Americans*. The third and final section intensely explores the question of the continued relevance of Du Bois's criminological contributions for twenty-first-century sociology of crime and criminal justice. Throughout each of the sections Du Bois's miscellaneous musings (e.g., essays, articles, etc.) on criminal justice and *racial criminalization* will be identified and often briefly analyzed where appropriate.

DU BOIS'S SOCIOLOGY OF URBAN CRIME: "THE NEGRO AND CRIME," *THE PHILADELPHIA NEGRO*, AND THE RACIAL CRIMINALIZATION OF URBAN AFRICAN AMERICANS AT THE TURN OF THE TWENTIETH CENTURY

In many senses it could be said that Du Bois's sociology of crime began with a critical focus on the crimes of white folk. His early article, "The Enforcement of the Slave Trade Laws," which appeared in the *American Historical Association Annual Report, 1891*, took on the taboo topic of whites breaching laws put into place to suppress the enslavement of Africans in the United States (Du Bois, 1982b, 19–27). He, of course, resoundingly returned to this topic in his doctoral dissertation *The Suppression of the African Slave Trade to the United States of America, 1638–1870*. After completing his doctoral dissertation, Du Bois continued to deepen and develop his criminological discourse in the late 1890s with several publications which, although not exclusively devoted to crime and criminal justice, nonetheless do indeed speak to several criminological issues, including *racial criminalization*/social discrimination ("A Program of Social Reform" and "The Study of the Negro Problems," originally published in 1897 and 1898, respectively), recreation/crime prevention ("The Problem of Amusement" and "The Negro and Crime," originally published in 1897 and 1899, respectively), and criminal classes ("The Negroes of Farmville," "The Negro in the Black Belt," and *The Philadelphia Negro*, originally published in 1898, 1899, and 1899, respectively) (see Du Bois, 1899, 1980a, 5–65, 1982b, 32–39, 57–59, 67–69).

In "A Program of Social Reform," Du Bois (1982b) unapologetically announced, "Crime is an indication of social disorder, which may arise from misfortune, disease, carelessness, selfishness or vice, or from a combination of these causes. Ignorance is the greatest cause" (31). Although "social disorganization" is often associated with the work of Clifford Shaw and Henry McKay (1942) of the Chicago School, we witness here Du Bois's, however implicit and inchoate, early emphasis on the part that "social disorder" plays in criminality. In "The Negro and Crime," his first article explicitly focused on crime, Du Bois went even further to lay the foundation for many of his future criminological contributions. It is important to observe, first and foremost, his conception of a "Negro criminal class," which, it will be recalled, he also noted in his 1898 rural study, "The

Negroes of Farmville" (Du Bois, 1980a, 28–29). In "The Negro and Crime," Du Bois (1982b) revealing wrote:

> The development of a Negro criminal class after emancipation was to be expected. It is impossible for such a social revolution to take place without giving rise to a class of men, who, in the new stress of life, under new responsibilities, would lack the will and power to make a way, and would consequently sink into vagrancy, poverty and crime. Indeed it is astounding that a body of people whose family life had been so nearly destroyed, whose women had been forced into concubinage, whose labor had been enslaved and then set adrift penniless, that such a nation should in a single generation be able to point to so many pure homes, so many property-holders, so many striving law-abiding citizens. (57)

Du Bois thought it "astounding" that there was not more criminality among recently emancipated African Americans considering the criminal conditions they emerged from in the aftermath of the Civil War and the deep-seated anti-black racist resentment surrounding their progress during and after Reconstruction. Du Bois's early sociology of crime identified four major causes of black criminality at the turn of the twentieth century: first, the convict-lease or "chain gang" system; second, anti-black racism within the criminal justice system, especially among police officers, judges, and all-white juries; third, the anti-black racist vigilante violence of white mobs, which usually resulted in lynching; and finally, racial segregation or, rather, American apartheid. It should be emphasized that all four of the major causes of black criminality that Du Bois's early sociology of crime identified in one way or another stem from and revolve around the *racial criminalization* and racial segregation of black folk, which Du Bois understood to be not only a serious flaw within the criminal justice system, but one of the ongoing failures of American democracy.

With regard to the first of the four major causes of black criminality, the convict-lease system, Du Bois contended that many states "use their criminals as sources of revenue," most often placing "their criminals . . . in the hands of irresponsible speculators, who herd girls, boys, men and women promiscuously together without distinction or protection, who parade chained convicts in public, guarded by staves and pistols, and then plunged into this abyss of degradation the ignorant little black boy who steals a chicken or a handful of peanuts—what can such States expect but a harvest of criminals and prostitutes?" (58). Perhaps it need not be noted here, but above it was observed that Du Bois himself only narrowly escaped becoming one of those "ignorant little black boy[s] who [stole] a chicken or a handful of peanuts," and who, without the "blind justice" of the judge or jury, was to be "plunged into [an] abyss of degradation" (i.e., a "colored boys" reformatory). He seems to be surreptitiously writing here in a half-hidden autobiographical register and, as will be witnessed below, it gives his criminological contributions their own unique conceptual weight and gravity. Du Bois's sociology of crime is often inextricable from his sociology of class, and in this instance he concretely made the connection between the rich white landowners and former plantation "masters" and the black labor shortage in the wake of the Civil War and the Emancipation Proclamation. In other words, Du Bois early detected the political economy of racial segregation and *racial criminalization*, the racial injustice of the criminal justice system, and the convict-lease system, which, it would seem to me, patently prefigures the contemporary discourse on the political economy of the prison industrial complex.[1]

The second of the four causes of black criminality that Du Bois identified in "The Negro and Crime" was the anti-black racist "attitude of the courts." According to Du Bois's sociology of crime, "the courts erred in two ways." First, "in treating the crime of whites so leniently that red-handed murderers walk scot-free." Consequently, he boldly observed, the black "public has lost faith in [white] methods of justice." Second, "in treating the crimes and misdemeanors of Negroes with such severity," almost inevitably "the lesson of punishment is lost through pity for the punished." Taking this into critical consideration, Du Bois contended that criminologists would do well to approach black crime statistics with caution, going so far as to say, "Students must not forget this double standard of justice"—one for whites (especially wealthy whites), and one for blacks and other nonwhites (without regard to rank or social class) (58).[2]

The third cause of black criminality, Du Bois maintained, was a warranted psychosocial response to the "increasing lawlessness" and anti-black racist "barbarity of [white] mobs." Here Du Bois's sociology of crime not only accented the racial segregation and *racial criminalization* of black folk, but also the ways in which anti-black racist vigilante violence caused, as he stated above, blacks' to "los[e] faith in [white supremacist/Eurocentric] methods of justice" and "the lesson of punishment" to be "lost" because of African Americans' "pity for the [disproportionally and severely] punished." Du Bois deftly further developed this line of logic, almost as if attempting to make it accessible to liberal and well-meaning whites and, therefore, it is important to conceptually capture this intricate point in his own weighted words:

> Let a Negro be simply accused of any crime from barn-burning to rape and he is liable to be seized by a mob, given no chance to defend himself, given neither trial, judge nor jury, and killed. Passing over the acknowledged fact that many innocent Negroes have thus been murdered, the point that is of greater gravity is that lawlessness is a direct encouragement to crime. It shatters the faith of the mass of Negroes in justice; it leads them to shield criminals; it makes race hatred fiercer; it discourages honest effort; it transforms horror at

crime into sympathy for the tortured victim; and it binds the hands and lessens the influence of those race leaders who are striving to preach forbearance and patience and honest endeavor to their people. It teaches eight million wronged people to despise a civilization which is not civilized. (58–59)[3]

It would seem that one of the subtle leitmotifs of Du Bois's sociology of crime centers on the question of criminal justice for black folk within a white supremacist "civilization which is not civilized." In other words, in order for well-meaning liberal whites or authentic white antiracists to understand African Americans' approach to, or positions on various criminal justice issues, black folk's long, horror-filled history of racial segregation and *racial criminalization* must be seriously and sincerely taken into consideration. Prior to liberal and well-meaning whites weighing in on black criminality, they should first turn their attention to African Americans' history and incessant experience of anti-black racism *within* and *without* a criminal justice system that has allowed "many innocent Negroes" to be lynched (without a fair and unbiased trial by judge or jury) by white mobs (Dray, 2002; Madison, 2001; Pfeifer, 2004). In so many words, Du Bois was saying that it was anti-black racist vigilante violence, as opposed to some innate inclination toward criminality on the part of African Americans, which was the real culprit behind a great deal of black criminality. Hence, he unrepentantly reproached, the issue "that is of greater gravity is that [anti-black racist] lawlessness is a direct encouragement to [black] crime."

Racial segregation or, rather, American apartheid was the final cause of black criminality that Du Bois's early sociology of crime identified. He argued that it was the simultaneous racialization, colonization, and criminalization of blacks' lifeworlds and lived experiences that caused the "mass of whites to misinterpret the aims and aspirations of the Negroes" and "mistake self-reliance for insolence, and condemnation of lynch-law for [black] sympathy with crime." It was not that blacks "sympath[ized] with crime," according to Du Bois, as much as it was the case that they sought fair and unbiased judges and juries in their honest efforts to receive "blind justice." Notice here how Du Bois concretely made the connection between the ways in which the "social ecology" of a white supremacist society insidiously influenced the interpretation of the law and the criminal justice system, producing a situation where blacks justifiably believed that they were, in essence, "damned if they do, and damned if they don't" in light of the constant *racial criminalization* of all African Americans (without respect to rank or social class) within American apartheid. Du Bois (1982b) did not mince any words in expressing his disdain: "A drawing of the color-line, that extends to street-cars, elevators and cemeteries, which leaves no common ground of meeting, no medium of communication, no ties of sympathy between two races who live together and whose interests are at bottom one—such a discrimination is more than silly, it is dangerous" (59).

Du Bois concluded "The Negro and Crime" by reemphasizing African Americans' psychosocial response to racial segregation and *racial criminalization*, encouraging whites to epistemically open themselves to black lifeworlds and black life struggles, going so far as to suggest that what was really needed was "a calm Christian spirit." Racial segregation and racial criminalization, he asserted, "makes it possible for the Negroes to believe that the best people of the South hate and despise them. Such terrible misapprehensions are false, and the sooner some way is made by which the best elements of both races can sympathize with each other's struggles and in a calm Christian spirit discuss them together—the sooner . . . the lynch-law will disappear and crime be abated" (59). Although "The Negro and Crime" was researched and written as a riposte to "A Southern Woman's View" by Mrs. L. H. Harris, who insensitively said, "But the Negro is the mongrel of civilization. He has married its vices and he is incapable of imitating its virtues," it should not be conceptually quarantined to Du Bois's sociology of rural crime because it seminally sets the stage for his criminological corpus. As we witnessed above, "The Negro and Crime," much more than symbolizing Du Bois's first article exclusively devoted to crime, also prefigures and provides a paradigm for many of his criminological contributions, perhaps none more than those found in *The Philadelphia Negro*.

From a criminological perspective, *The Philadelphia Negro*'s overarching contribution is undoubtedly its unmitigated challenge to the then emerging criminal anthropological school. In chapter 1 of this book it was openly acknowledged that *The Philadelphia Negro* was the first empirically researched, social scientific study of African Americans, and it prefigured and provided paradigms for the Atlanta University studies carried out under Du Bois's auspices. Here, however, I would to like to suspend further discussion of *The Philadelphia Negro*'s other accomplishments in an effort to critically engage its criminological contributions. Although there are only two chapters solely dedicated to crime, when the volume is read with a critical criminological eye its offerings to the sociology of crime come rushing to the fore. Conceptually continuing the discourse he began in "The Negro and Crime," Du Bois divided *The Philadelphia Negro* into four parts: first, the history of African Americans in Philadelphia; second, their then current conditions; third, their social organization and social stratification (i.e., their social classes); and, finally, their physical and social environment. *The Philadelphia Negro*'s four-fold format was innovative from a criminological point of view because at the turn of the twentieth century most early criminologists did not take into consideration African Americans' distinct history, culture, and struggles, or if and when African Americans' peculiar history was acknowledged it was often to point to how their historical dehumanization, racial oppression, and economic exploitation caused their "cultural poverty" and racial criminality.

Du Bois (1899, 5–45) challenged the criminal anthropological school by observing that African Americans' ancestors (i.e., enslaved Africans) were murdered, robbed, and stolen away from Africa by white pirates, white enslavers and miscellaneous white miscreants, who where sponsored by Western European churches and the Western European bourgeoisie and, eventually, supported and sanctioned by the U.S. government, European American churches, and the emerging European American bourgeoisie. As was the case with his doctoral dissertation, *The Suppression of the African Slave Trade*, Du Bois reminded his white readers that the African holocaust and African American enslavement were, indeed, crimes against humanity. Although it may not be revelatory to my readers here in the twenty-first century, it should be strongly stressed that this contentious claim was completely innovative and, indeed, quite radical in 1899 when Du Bois published *The Philadelphia Negro*.

The first noteworthy discussion of crime in *The Philadelphia Negro* centers around the early influx of "freedmen, fugitives and foreigners" to Philadelphia and the resulting anti-black racist riots that rocked the city at the time. "These riots," Du Bois shared, "were occasioned by various incidents, but the underlying cause was the same: the simultaneous influx of freedmen, fugitives and foreigners into a large city, and the resulting prejudice, lawlessness, crime and poverty" (27). Note Du Bois's emphasis on "the simultaneous influx of freedmen, fugitives and foreigners," which, it would seem, loosely prefigures or, at the very least, has significant implications for contemporary criminological theories, such as social ecology, strain theory, and subcultural theory.[4] To reiterate, Du Bois's sociology of crime is inextricable from his sociology of class, and there is a sense in which the connections he made between the influx of "freedmen, fugitives and foreigners" and "lawlessness, crime and poverty" speaks in a special way to social structure theory and conflict theory within contemporary criminology, offering students of his criminology yet another early example of the ways in which racial segregation went hand in hand with *racial criminalization* and the political economy of anti-black racism at the turn of the twentieth century. If the "freedmen, fugitives and foreigners" of early Philadelphia are viewed as separate social classes, as they more or less perceived themselves, then Du Bois's emphatic focus on their conflicts with one another and their new urban environment is all the more innovative and awe-inspiring.[5]

Continuing with the "freedmen, fugitives and foreigners" influx theory in the section entitled "The City" in chapter 7 of *The Philadelphia Negro*, Du Bois once again contributed to social ecology or, more specifically, neighborhood ecology with his discussion of the inundation of European immigrants into the city. In the passage below he revealed that *anti-black racist criminalization* was nothing more than a white supremacist subterfuge insofar as European immigrants also suffered from the close proximity and prolonged mixing of "good and bad elements" in a confined geographic area (i.e., a single neighborhood). Du Bois disclosed:

> The new immigrants usually settle in pretty well-defined localities in or near the slums, and thus get the worst possible introduction to city life. . . . Today they are to be found partly in the slums and partly in those small streets with old houses, where there is a dangerous intermingling of good and bad elements fatal to growing children and unwholesome for adults. . . . This mingling swells the apparent size of many slum districts, and at the same time screens the real criminals. Investigators are often surprised in the worst districts to see red-handed criminals and good-hearted, hard-working, honest people living side by side in apparent harmony. Even when the new immigrants seek better districts, their low standard of living and careless appearance make them unwelcome to the better class of blacks and the great mass of whites. Thus they find themselves hemmed in between the slums and the decent sections, and they easily drift into the happy-go-lucky life of the lowest classes and rear young criminals for our jails. (81–82)

Another innovative aspect of the *The Philadelphia Negro* is that it made mention of early African American police officers. Du Bois thought it important enough to point out that "[t]here are about sixty colored policemen on the force at present." Initially, he reported, "there was violent opposition" to their presence. The "Negro policemen are put on duty mostly in or near the chief Negro settlements" and "the general impression seems to be that they make good average officers," although, he pointedly observed, "no one of them has yet been promoted from the ranks" (132). Two issues demand our attention here: first, the initial "violent [anti-black racist] opposition" to African American police officers and, second, the fact that they were repeatedly passed over with respect to promotions. This demonstrates the ways in which racial segregation not only influenced the interpretation of the law, but also who was or, rather, which persons were perceived to be best qualified to uphold and enforce the law—that is, whites only; hence, American apartheid.

It is also interesting to observe that *The Philadelphia Negro*, in essence, echoed Du Bois's earlier concern—for example, in "A Program of Social Reform" and "The Problem of Amusements"—about the paucity or complete lack of recreation for African American youth and the potential future ramifications, especially considering the pervasiveness of violent anti-black racism at the time. Du Bois sternly stated: "[T]here is in the city a grave and dangerous lack of proper places of amusement and recreation for young men. To fill this need a properly conducted Young Men's Christian Association, with books and newspapers, baths, bowling alleys and billiard tables, conversation rooms and short interesting religious services is demanded; it would cost far less than it now costs the courts to punish the petty misdemeanors of young men who do not know how to amuse themselves" (232). It was, indeed, prescient on Du Bois's part to propose precisely what most contemporary crime prevention specialists in the twenty-first century have come to conclude: it is more humane (i.e., in the spirit of community caretaking) and, in fact, cheaper to invest in preventive programs and measures instead of waiting until black youth enter into the criminal justice system and then doling out countless dollars to either see that justice is served or keep them incarcerated (Hawkins and Kempf-Leonard, 2005; Penn, Greene, and Gabbidon, 2006; Shelden, 2001; Sulton, 1996).

African American youth did not misbehave simply because they were "bad" or lacked "home-training" but, on a deeper, psychosocial or "double-conscious" level, Du Bois argued that anti-black racism, which directly impacted African American educational and employment opportunities, influenced their behavior, especially black criminality. In the only chapter devoted exclusively to crime in *The Philadelphia Negro*, "The Negro Criminal," Du Bois (1899) dramatically opened with the following declaration: "Crime is a phenomena of organized social life, and it is the open rebellion of an individual against his social environment. Naturally then, if men are suddenly transported from one environment to another, the result is lack of harmony with the new conditions; lack of harmony with the new physical surroundings leading to disease and death or modification of physique; lack of harmony with social surroundings leading to crime" (235). Corroborating his claims, Du Bois observed various historical events that helped to highlight social disorganization among African Americans as a result of their enslavement ("the disorder of the Negro slaves") and then their peculiar "emancipation" in an anti-black racist and white supremacist society. Asserting that "gambling, drunkenness and debauchery were widespread wherever Negroes settled," Du Bois provided a brief archaeology of several of the city ordinances and articles of legislation authorized to curb black criminality in Philadelphia.

Returning to his influx theory of "freedmen, fugitives and foreigners," Du Bois observed "the increased complexity of life, industrial competition, and the rush of great numbers to the large cities," as well as the Act of 1780, anti-black racist violence in the aftermath of Nat Turner's infamous insurrection in 1831, and "the disenfranchisement of the Negro in 1837, and the riots in the years 1830 to 1840" as key causes for the increase in black criminality. E. Franklin Frazier (1949), Shaun Gabbidon (1996), and Vernetta Young and Helen Greene (1995) have each observed the similarity of Du Bois's sociology of crime with more contemporary social disorganization discourse (see also Gabbidon, 2010; Gabbidon, Greene, and Young, 2002; Greene and Gabbidon, 2000). After offering a longitudinal analysis of crime statistics in Philadelphia, later in the chapter Du Bois noted an intense increase in black crime between 1830 and 1850. Systematically focusing on the available population and crime figures, he concluded that "the problem of Negro crime in Philadelphia from 1830 to 1850 arose from the fact that less than one-fourteenth of the population was responsible for nearly a third of the serious crimes committed. These figures however are apt to relate more especially to a criminal class" (238). Here Du Bois decidedly demonstrated his cogent comprehension of what contemporary criminologists often refer to as the concept of disproportionality (see Bhui, 2009; Cook and Hudson, 1993; V. D. Young, 1996).

Continuing his archaeology of African American criminality, Du Bois shifted his focus from anti-black crime city ordinances and articles of legislation to the racial composition of a particular criminal justice institution, Moyamensing prison in Philadelphia. After providing the pertinent facts and figures for Moyamensing prison, he quickly noted, "In 1896 the Negroes forming 4 per cent of the population furnish 9 per cent of the arrests, but in 1850 being 5 per cent of the population they furnished 32 per cent of the prisoners received at the county prison" (Du Bois, 1899, 239). In an effort to explain the disproportionality, specifically between the years 1836 and 1855, he stated, "Of course there are some considerations which must not be overlooked in interpreting these figures." Then, simultaneously critiquing the disproportionality, racial segregation, and *racial criminalization* of African Americans, he thundered: "It must be remembered that the discrimination against the Negro was much greater then than now: he was arrested for less cause and given longer sentences than whites. Great numbers of those arrested and committed for trial were never brought to trial so that their guilt could not be proven or disproven." Du Bois wrote further that "of the 737 Negroes committed for trial in six months of the year 1837, it is stated that only 123 were actually brought to trial; of the prisoners in the Eastern Penitentiary, 1829 to 1846, 14 per cent of the whites were pardoned and 2 per cent of the Negroes." This means, then, that "[a]ll these considerations increase the statistics to the disfavor of the Negro" (239). Examining Du Bois's analysis here from a contemporary criminological perspective unequivocally reveals the innovative nature of his early criminological contributions. In essence, prior to the turn of the twentieth century Du Bois concretized the historically tenuous connections between the differential justice dealt to blacks and whites, and the ensuing disproportional, overrepresentation of African Americans in prison population statistics in particular, and criminal justice statistics in general.

From Du Bois's view, the increase in black criminality after the Civil War had both historical and political economic implications. On the one hand, as was observed above, he argued that crime increased in the United States as a whole after the Civil War. He emphasized "the increased complexity of life, industrial competition, and the rush of great numbers to the large cities." On the other hand, he contended that African American and European immigrants' criminality developed along parallel paths, noting that although African Americans mainly moved to the big cities after 1880, their lived experiences and increased criminality were comparable to the experiences and increased criminality of white immigrants two to three decades prior. However, Du Bois was quick to quip, the most glaring difference between African American and European immigrant urban experiences had to do with the fact that African American social evolution had been historically "marked by some peculiarities" (240). In particular, Du Bois wrote, "in the case of the Negro there were special causes for the prevalence of crime: he had lately been freed from serfdom, he was the object of stinging oppression and ridicule, and paths of advancement open to many were closed to him. Consequently the class of the shiftless, aimless, idle, discouraged and disappointed was proportionately larger" (241).

The foregoing demonstrates that even though Du Bois openly acknowledged that his theory of African American criminality was in many instances applicable to whites as well, he also emphasized that consequent to their prior enslaved position and dehumanized status within U.S. society, African American educational and employment opportunities—indeed, their social acceptance in general—within the new world of urban American city life was profoundly racialized and much more problematic than it was for European immigrant groups—most of which, truth be told, were considered—in the candid but, for some, extremely controversial words of Thomas Guglielmo (2003)—"white on arrival" (see also R. Daniels, 2002; Ignatiev, 1995; Jacobson, 1998; Roediger, 2005, 2007). The increase of "bold and daring crimes committed by Negroes" in late nineteenth-century Philadelphia, Du Bois wrote, "has focused the attention of the city on this subject." In fact, he tersely said, "to the minds of many, this is the real Negro problem . . . crime is a difficult subject to study, more difficult to analyze into its sociological elements, and most difficult to cure or suppress. It is a phenomenon that stands not alone, but rather as a symptom of countless wrong social conditions" (241–42). In so many words, he was contending that African Americans were being collapsed into their criminal class, and that little or no distinction was being made between "good-hearted, hardworking, honest" African Americans and the "red-handed criminals" and the "Negro criminal class" that crowded in their midst. This, indeed, is what I have come to refer to as *the racial criminalization of African Americans* or, rather, *anti-black racist criminalization*.

Instead of heavy-handedly placing all of the blame on the black criminals, Du Bois again emphasized that crime "is a phenomenon that stands not alone, but rather as a symptom of countless wrong social conditions." In Du Bois's sociology of crime, the "countless wrong social conditions," indeed, did influence the interpretation and enforcement of the law. For instance, when he turned to the 541 blacks who were convicted for committing serious crimes, he wrote that although they were "all criminals convicted after trial for periods varying from six months to forty years," caution and critical interpretation must be employed in coming to conclusions based on the statistics. Why, we may earnestly ask? Because, he righteously roared,

> [t]his of course assumes that the convicts in the penitentiary represent with a fair degree of accuracy the crime committed. The assumption is not wholly true; in convictions by human courts the rich always are favored somewhat at the expense of the poor, the upper classes at the expense of the unfortunate classes, and whites at the expense of Negroes. We know for instance that certain crimes are not punished in Philadelphia because the public opinion is lenient, as for instance embezzlement, forgery, and certain sorts of stealing; on the other hand a commercial community is apt to punish with severity petty thieving, breaches of the peace, and personal assault or burglary. It happens, too, that the prevailing weakness of ex-slaves brought up in the communal life of the slave plantation, without acquaintanceship with the institution of private property, is to commit the very crimes which a great center of commerce like Philadelphia especially abhors. We must add to this the influences of social position and connections in procuring whites pardons and lighter sentences. It has been charged by some Negroes that color prejudice plays some part, but there is no tangible proof of this, save perhaps that there is apt to be a certain presumption of guilt when a Negro is accused, on the part of the police, public and judge. All these considerations modify somewhat our judgment of the moral status of the mass of Negroes. And yet, with all allowances, there remains a vast problem of crime. (249)

Both Dan Green (1973, 374) and Shaun Gabbidon (1996, 101) have observed that this passage, once again, demonstrates the prescient nature of Du Bois's sociological discourse insofar as he comes extremely close to conceptualizing what is currently being called "white-collar crimes." Even the most criminologically skeptical among us would have to concede, at the very least, that above Du Bois indeed does demonstrate his consciousness of the differential justice dealt to those who commit "blue-collar crimes" as opposed to those who commit "white-collar crimes" (i.e., "embezzlement, forgery, and certain sorts of stealing"). It is also important to note Du Bois's inchoate acknowledgement of what would be termed "racial profiling" today when he wrote, "It has been charged by some Negroes that color prejudice plays some part [i.e., in African Americans' receipt of differential justice], but there is no tangible proof of this, save perhaps that there is apt to be a certain presumption of guilt when a Negro is accused, on the part of the police, public and judge." As we come to the close of the first decade of the twenty-first century, contemporary criminologists may quickly conclude that there is much "tangible proof" of racial profiling "on the part of the police, public and judge[s]," although there remains a deep and pervasive white social unwillingness to acknowledge it. The wide range of contemporary criminological issues that Du Bois prophetically touched on and discursively prefigured is not only intellectually astounding, but speaks in a special way about the continued contemporary relevance of his criminological contributions in particular, and his sociological legacy in general.

It is important here to critically distinguish between my conception of *racial criminalization* and racial profiling (Pampel, 2004; Tator and Henry, 2006; Withrow, 2006). Where racial profiling usually indicates the inclusion of racial or ethnic characteristics in determining whether an individual could potentially commit a particular type of crime, an illegal act, or behave in a purportedly "predictable" (based on racial myths) manner, *racial criminalization* conceptually captures *the combined process(es) and/or predicament(s) of* an entire race or cultural group *being simultaneously racialized and criminalized and the ongoing effects of simultaneous racialization and criminalization* (e.g., double-consciousness, the Veil, the color-line, racial segregation, American apartheid, etc.). The difference between the two concepts is not simply that one seems to be more focused on individual experience (i.e., micrological) and the other on group experience (i.e., macrological), but has more to do with *racial criminalization*'s unflinching social scientific superstructural critique of the interrelation of the anti-black racism embedded within the criminal justice system and other seemingly neutral social institutions, such as religion, education, employment, entertainment, the medical industry, or the armed forces, among others. In other words, my conception of *racial criminalization* seeks to accent the interconnections and intersections of white supremacy within the criminal justice system and seemingly neutral social institutions. It also endeavors to highlight the ways in which the surreptitious white supremacism within the criminal justice system has been and remains informed and influenced by other seemingly neutral social institutions, and the ways in which other social institutions have been informed and influenced by it (i.e., something akin to a vulgar and vicious hermeneutic circle).

From the foregoing, we may conclude several things of criminological consequence with respect to *The Philadelphia Negro*. First, Du Bois's sociology of crime was much more than a mere catalogue of black criminality and, equally important, it certainly should not be interpreted as a defense of black criminality. He simply sought criminal justice (i.e., "blind justice") for African Americans. Second, he was undoubtedly one of the first to offer a history of the "Negro" criminal and a detailed description of "the Negro criminal class," which in many ways returns us to the discourse developed in chapter 1 of the present volume, where it was noted that Du Bois's sociology of class was distinguished from those of his contemporaries in light of the fact that he actually acknowledged African American social classes and, even more, the racialization of African American social classes. Finally, it is important to emphasize the ways in which Du Bois's criminological discourse prefigured contemporary criminological concepts, such as social disorganization, social ecology (neighborhood ecology), strain theory, disproportionality, differential justice, and racial profiling.

As previously mentioned, the Atlanta University studies under Du Bois's auspices have a special place in the history of African American sociology, as well as the history of American sociology more generally. The next section focuses exclusively on those Atlanta University volumes that expatiated Du Bois's criminological contributions and continue to contribute to the discourse and development of American criminology. In many senses, the succeeding section is proof-positive that "The Negro and Crime" and *The Philadelphia Negro* represent the first of several salvos that Du Bois discharged into the criminological discursive arena.

DU BOIS'S SOCIOLOGY OF RURAL CRIME: "THE PROBLEM OF NEGRO CRIME," *SOME NOTES ON NEGRO CRIME, MORALS AND MANNERS AMONG NEGRO AMERICANS*, AND THE RACIAL CRIMINALIZATION OF RURAL AFRICAN AMERICANS AT THE TURN OF THE TWENTIETH CENTURY

In many senses, Du Bois's Atlanta University studies could be said to be outgrowths or, at the least, indicative of the aftermath of his innovative research and analysis published prior to and in *The Philadelphia Negro*. His ambitious research program, simply said, was to "study systematically the greatest social problem that has ever faced a great modern nation" (Du Bois, 1904a, 88). The philosophical foundation of his research plan was presented at the 1897 annual conference of the American Academy of Political and Social Sciences in his essay "The Study of the Negro Problems." In this classic essay, Du Bois (1898b) detailed five areas of critical inquiry necessary in order to understand and effectively offer viable solutions to the "Negro Problem": first, the historical development of African American problems; second, the need for what we would today term "African American Studies"; third, critical review of social scientific studies of African Americans up to 1897 (of course, bearing in mind the scientific racism at the turn of the twentieth century); fourth, the creation and/or identification of theory and methodology that should be employed in African American Studies; and, finally, emphasis on which "scientific workers" are best qualified to undertake authentic African American studies (as opposed to Eurocentric studies of African American history, culture, and struggle). Du Bois based his Atlanta University studies on this research scheme, ultimately identifying ten subject areas to be systematically and critically studied annually, and then repeated over a period spanning a century. In his 1904 programmatic essay "The Atlanta Conferences," Du Bois (1904a) detailed his new research agenda with intellectual history-making words:

> The object of the Atlanta Conferences is to study the American Negro. The method employed is to divide the various aspects of his social condition into ten great subjects. To treat one of these subjects each year as carefully and exhaustively as means will allow until the cycle is completed. To begin then again on the same cycle for a second ten years. So that in the course of a century, if the work is well done we shall have a continuous record on the condition and development of a group of 10 to 20 millions of men—a body of sociological material unsurpassed in human annals. . . . [T]he sequence of the subjects studied has not been altogether logical but will in the end be exhaustive. In 1896 we studied the subject of health among Negroes; in 1897, the subject of homes; in 1898, the question of organization; in 1899, the economic development in business lines; in 1900 the higher education of Negroes; in 1901, the common schools and 1902, another phase of the economic developments—the Negro artisans. In 1903 we investigated the Negro church, and have still to take up the subjects of crime and the suffrage. We shall then begin the cycle again, studying in succession for the second decade, health, homes, occupations, organizations, religion, crime and suffrage. (88)

As observed earlier, Shaun Gabbidon (1999), Earl Wright (2002a, 2002b, 2002c, 2005, 2008), and Robert Wortham (2005b, 2005c) have each asserted that the Atlanta School was the first American school of sociology. In setting the agenda for this school of sociology, take special note of the fact that Du Bois thought that crime among, and crimes committed against, African Americans was significant enough to place it among the top "ten great subjects" within African American studies. Conceptually building on his earlier research on crime among urban African Americans in "The Negro and Crime" and *The Philadelphia Negro*, Du Bois's Atlanta University studies focused on crime among rural African Americans. However ironically, his first major contribution to the sociology of rural crime could be considered a serious misstep. In his often-overlooked 1900 essay "The Problem of Negro Crime," he contended that "the younger generation of American Negroes . . . drifted, and are still drifting, into crime and debauchery" because "[t]hey had not the severe training in social customs [i.e., African American enslavement and American apartheid] which their fathers had" (Du Bois, 1982b, 68). Absurdly advancing that the "inevitable" consequence of "the emancipation of the slaves . . . is crime," Du Bois seemed to backtrack from many of his more assertive positions on the causes of African American criminality put forward in *The Philadelphia Negro*.

The five preventive measures Du Bois outlined in the conclusion of "The Problem of Negro Crime" prefigured several of the preventive measures he would advance in his future crime-focused Atlanta University studies,

Some Notes on Negro Crime and *Morals and Manners Among Negro Americans*. Rhetorically asking "What can be done to prevent this [i.e., 'the younger generation of American Negroes' from 'drifting, into crime and debauchery']?," he initially directed his comments to whites, writing, "Certainly mob violence and torture will increase rather than decrease Negro crime. It spreads among the otherwise law-abiding masses deep-seated sympathy with crime and criminals because they honestly believe them to be largely martyrs to race prejudice."[6] Therefore, although Du Bois began this essay seemingly placing a great deal of the blame for black criminality on African Americans (e.g., "Emancipation is a great social revolution. The inevitable result of a social revolution is crime"), he ended the essay by emphasizing the social etiology and social ecology or, rather, the impact and effects antiblack racist violent vigilantism (i.e., lynching, "mob violence and torture") had on African American perceptions of both crime and criminal justice.

After briefly emphasizing the role that violent anti-black racism played in increasing black criminality at the turn of the twentieth century, Du Bois then offered five preventive measures to African Americans, many of which broadly resemble contemporary preventive measures (see Greene and Gabbidon, 2000, 2003; J. A. James, 2000; Sulton, 1996). First, Du Bois (1982b) stated, "[w]e can establish better homes," and then he went on to emphasize "cleanliness, order and discipline, where the training of children is a matter of thoughtful care." In light of the systematic destruction of the African American family during the period of enslavement and the racial colonization of the African American family in the aftermath of the Emancipation Proclamation and Reconstruction, Du Bois reminded his readers of the need for African Americans to create their own distinct conception of family and the need to practice good parenting. From Du Bois's sociological frame of reference, the connections between failing family life and poor parenting among African Americans and the increasing black criminality were clear. Beyond his sociology of crime, his contributions to the sociology of the African American family can be found in, as was discussed in chapter 1 of the present volume, *The Philadelphia Negro*, as well as his pioneering 1908 Atlanta University publication *The Negro American Family*. Second, he said, "[w]e can educate our children . . . education is the great preventive of crime." From the previous chapter, as well as the Atlanta University studies *The College-Bred Negro*, *The College-Bred Negro American*, and *The Common School and the American Negro*, we can gather that "education" for Du Bois was always and ever culturally grounded and historically rooted education that speaks to the special social, political, and cultural needs of African Americans and the wider world of multicultural America. His sociology of education incessantly emphasized the ways in which American apartheid restricted and racially colonized the educational opportunities of African Americans, thus distorting and deforming their lifeworlds and lived experiences, often causing many African Americans (especially black youth) to feel as though crime is the only viable response to the absurdity and agony of American apartheid. Third, he thundered, "[w]e must teach our children to work. . . . There is no kind of labor so menial, low and despicable as not to be infinitely better than idleness." In chapter 1 I hinted at Du Bois's contributions to industrial sociology. Here, then, we can make connections between his sociology of crime and his industrial sociology. The Atlanta University studies *The Negro in Business, The Negro Artisan,* and *The American Negro Artisan* each go far to demonstrate the ways in which American apartheid restricted or, at the least, racially colonized employment opportunities for African Americans, causing extremely high and chronic levels of unemployment and poverty. Fourth, he asserted, "[w]e must reform our social customs and build up social classes among ourselves." In *The Philadelphia Negro, Economic Cooperation Among Negro Americans,* and *Economic Cooperation Among the Negroes of Georgia,* Du Bois chronicled and critiqued both African American "social customs" and their increasing division into "social classes." Here, then, we are able to make connections between his sociology of crime and his sociology of racialized classes, particularly his contention that crime usually reflects "social wrongs" or poor social conditions. Finally, Du Bois advanced, "[w]e must unite in a movement to found in Georgia a reformatory for juvenile criminals who are now sent to the prison and chain gang" (68). This last point not only prefigured his critique of the convict-lease system and the chain gang in *Some Notes on Negro Crime* and *Morals and Manners Among Negro Americans,* but it also, in deep and profound ways, demonstrates that Du Bois helped to initiate the critique of what is currently being called "the prison industrial complex" as early as 1900. In fact, his 1899 article "The Negro and Crime" discussed above could be viewed as a prelude to his critique of the prison industrial complex with its, however brief, intense emphasis on the ills of the convict-lease system (Du Bois, 1982b, 58).

Perhaps the most startling chapter of *Some Notes on Negro Crime* is chapter 2, "Crime and Slavery," which was originally published in 1901 in *The Missionary Review of the World* as "The Spawn of Slavery: The Convict-Lease System in the South." In "Crime and Slavery," Du Bois connected the *racial criminalization* of African Americans with the political economy of anti-black racist capitalism. For instance, he opened the chapter by boldly asserting that "[t]wo systems of controlling human labor which still flourish in the South are the direct children of slavery. The crop-lien system and the convict-lease system" (Du Bois, 1904c, 2). Notice Du Bois's sociological sense of history as he opens "Crime and Slavery," referring to the crop-lien system and the convict-lease system as "the direct children of slavery." As with so many other aspects of his sociological legacy, one of the distinguishing characteristics of Du Bois's sociology of crime is its sonorous sense of history, and its profound predilection for African American history in particular. It would seem that his sociological discourse as a whole harbors a deep historical dimension that simultaneously enabled it to capture the social, political and cultural conditions and contradictions of the turn of the twentieth century and amazingly contribute to efforts to create critical sociologies of the social, political, and cultural conditions and contradictions of the twenty-first century.

If we understand "the prison industrial complex" to be a term created to conceptually capture all of the political economies and organizations involved in the construction, operation, and promotion of correctional facilities and the services they provide, there is a sense in which Du Bois's sociology of crime could be almost unequivocally said to prefigure and, consequently, contributes to contemporary critiques of the prison industrial complex. As a conglomerate of various groups—including private corrections companies, corporations that contract prison labor, construction companies, surveillance technology vendors, and lobbyists and their miscellaneous interest groups—it is important to take the term "prison industrial complex" to mean the entire network of agents and institutions whose interests and motivations are preoccupied with making a profit rather than punishing or rehabilitating criminals and reducing crime rates (Coyle, Campbell, and Neufeld, 2003; A. Y. Davis, 2003; Dyer, 2000; Logan, 1990; Sudbury, 2005). It is in taking this into consideration that we may now speak of "the prison industry" (Burton-Rose, Pens, and Wright, 1998; Shelden, 2001; Herivel and Wright, 2003). Du Bois's sociology of crime, as articulated in *Some Notes on Negro Crime*, demonstrates that if, indeed, the crop-lien system and the convict-lease system are "the direct children of slavery," then, here and now, in the twenty-first century a form of human enslavement and economic exploitation continues to exist in the United States. Even though most of the more vicious vestiges of the crop-lien system have disappeared, the existence of a contemporary, twenty-first-century form of the convict-lease system is irrefutable, and it is intellectually astounding to observe Du Bois's extremely early critique of the formation and institutionalization of the prison industrial complex.

After briefly explaining that the crop-lien system (i.e., "the peonage system," "debt bondage," "debt slavery," "indentured servitude," or "unfree labor") was "an arrangement of chattel mortgages, so fixed that the housing, labor, kind of agriculture and, to some extent, the personal liberty of the free black laborer is put into the hands of the landowner and merchant"—in other words, it was "absentee landlordism and the 'company store' united"—Du Bois (1904c) then provided a history of black criminality and what he referred to in "The Negro and Crime" as whites' "double standard of justice" (2; see also Daniel, 1990; Fierce, 1994; Mancini, 1996; Nieman, 1994). During African American enslavement the "punishment and trial of nearly all ordinary misdemeanors and crimes lay in the hands of the masters" (Du Bois, 1904c, 3). As a consequence, "so far as the state was concerned, there was no crime of any consequence among Negroes. The system of criminal jurisprudence had to do, therefore, with whites almost exclusively, and as is usual in a land of scattered population and aristocratic tendencies, the law was lenient in theory and lax in execution" (3). Detailing how the Klu Klux Klan emerged out of the "slave police" of the antebellum period, Du Bois contended that the "slave police" arose because immediately before the Civil War and the issuing of the Emancipation Proclamation the "fear of insurrection was ever before the South, and the ominous uprisings of Cato, Gabriel, Vesey, Turner, and Toussaint made this fear an ever-present nightmare." A "system of rural police" (i.e., the "slave police"), therefore, grew out of the "fear of insurrection," and it was "usually an effective organization," Du Bois wrote, "which terrorized the slaves, and to which all white men belonged, and were liable to active detailed duty at regular intervals" (3). With respect to "the ominous uprisings of Cato, Gabriel, Vesey, Turner, and Toussaint," Du Bois asserted, "[i]t will always be a nice question of ethics as to how far a conquered people can be expected to submit to the dictates of a victorious foe. Certainly the world must to a degree sympathize with resistance under such circumstances" (3). Here, then, in so many words Du Bois was etiologically arguing that a great deal of early black criminality was a response to white criminality (i.e., *antiblack racist violent vigilantism*: mass murdering, kidnapping, enslaving, raping, maiming and mauling, etc.). This, it seems to me, places a unique spin on African American social ecology in the sense that, etiologically speaking, black criminality historically emerged in the context of psychopathic and sadistic white supremacist and anti-black racist criminality and, even more egregious, crimes against humanity. Again, the deeply historical dimension of Du Bois's sociology of crime is distinctive and provides alternative understandings of the origins and certain ongoing aspects of black criminal causation.

During Reconstruction the "slave police" became "a lawless and illegal mob known to history as the Klu Klux Klan," and many of its members were police officers, judges, jurors, congressional officers, and other state and federal officials.[7] Therefore, anti-black racism was (re)embedded in post–Emancipation Proclamation legislation and surreptitiously (re)institutionalized under another name (Blackmon, 2008; Fierce, 1994). Because the white South "believed in slave labor, and was thoroughly convinced that free Negroes would not work steadily or effectively" they devised "[e]laborate and ingenious apprentice and vagrancy laws . . . designed to make the freedmen and their children work for their former masters at practically no wages" (Du Bois, 1904c, 3). We witness here, then, the inglorious inception of the prison industrial complex, and the ways in which

Du Bois's sociology of crime historically documented and sociologically demonstrated that at its origin it involved the reenslavement and the *racial criminalization* of African Americans. In essence, whites sought to remove the "new status of the freedmen" and return them to the "slave system." Du Bois's heartfelt words heed us here:

> It was perhaps as natural as it was unfortunate that amid this chaos the courts sought to do by judicial decisions what the legislatures had formerly sought to do by specific law—namely, reduce the freedmen to serfdom. As a result, the small peccadilloes of a careless, untrained class were made the excuse for severe sentences. The courts and jails became filled with the careless and ignorant, with those who sought to emphasize their new-found freedom, and too often with innocent victims of oppression. The testimony of a Negro counted for little or nothing in court, while the accusation of white witnesses was usually decisive. The result of this was a sudden large increase in the apparent criminal population of the Southern states—an increase so large that there was no way for the state to house it or watch it even had the state wished to. And the state did not wish to. Throughout the South laws were immediately passed authorizing public officials to lease the labor of convicts to the highest bidder. The lessee then took charge of the convicts—worked them as he wished under the nominal control of the state. Thus a new slavery and slave-trade was established. (4)

Over a century ago Du Bois's sociology of crime identified the earliest installation of the prison industrial complex as "a new slavery and slave-trade." According to the U.S. Department of Justice's *Bureau of Justice Statistics Report* for 2007, of the 7.3 million men and women under correctional supervision, African American males continue to constitute the largest group, being 5 percent of the total prison population, even though African Americans only constitute 12 percent of the national population. The *Bureau of Justice Statistics Report* also indicates that over the last several decades African American males have been incarcerated by the hundreds of thousands in disproportionate numbers. In fact, historically black males have experienced the highest rate of imprisonment—6.5 times that of white males and 2.5 that of Latino males—when the rate of imprisonment is compared. Further, black males have historically been executed at rates exponentially greater than those for the general population—approximately 4.5 times more than that of white prisoners and 17.5 times that of Latinos. Hence we may conclude, in real and concrete ways, Du Bois's sociology of crime has continued relevance for twenty-first-century sociology of crime insofar as African Americans, and African American males in particular, continue to endure what he perceived more than a century ago as an antiblack racist "double standard of justice."

In "Crime and Slavery" Du Bois focused his readers' attention on the ways in which whites cunningly continued "slavery" through the criminal justice system. In fact, he went so far as to question whether African Americans survived (as opposed to "lived") better during the era of enslavement, wryly writing that the convict-lease system was nothing other than "slavery without any of its redeeming features." Clearly it will be extremely difficult for most African Americans to come to terms with what Du Bois may have meant by invoking the allegedly "redeeming features" of the dehumanization and heightened horror of enslavement, but here, as I suspect was the case in "The Problem of Negro Crime" discussed above, he was doing some of his characteristic literary double-dealing—that is, double-consciously attempting to appeal to concerned blacks and liberal whites simultaneously. Notice here how he moved from appealing to liberal whites, then, to eloquently and poignantly expressing elements of the moral outrage of some of the more militant African Americans of his epoch:

> The abuses of this system have often been dwelt upon. It had the worst aspects of slavery without any of its redeeming features. The innocent, the guilty, and the depraved were herded together, children and adult, men and women, given into complete control of practically irresponsible men, whose sole object was to make the most money possible. The innocent were made bad, the bad worse; women were outraged and children tainted; whipping and torture were in vogue, and the death-rate from cruelty, exposure, and overwork rose to large percentages. The actual bosses over such leased prisoners were usually selected from the lowest classes of whites, and the camps were often far from settlements or public roads. The prisoners often had scarcely any clothing, they were fed on a scanty diet of corn bread and fat meat, and worked twelve or more hours a day. After work each must do his own cooking. There was insufficient shelter; in one Georgia camp, as late as 1896, sixty-one men slept in one room, seventeen by nineteen feet, and seven feet high. Sanitary condition were wretched, there was little or no medical attendance, and almost no care of the sick. Women were mingled indiscriminately with the men, both in working and in sleeping, and dressed often in men's clothes. A young girl at Camp Hardmont, Georgia, in 1896, was repeatedly outraged by several of her guards, and finally died in childbirth while in camp. (4–5)

In this passage Du Bois controversially claimed that black life was better during enslavement as compared with their sufferings under the convict-lease system. What he sought to highlight here was the frequently neglected fact that the physical, psychological, and sexual violence that blacks endured under the convict-lease system not only equaled, but most often unequivocally surpassed, the hell and horrors they endured during enslavement. This was both a bold and brilliant move on Du Bois's part, as he endeavored to turn the attention of both the white and black bourgeoisies to one of the most pressing social problems of his era. Similar to black lived endurances during enslavement, he contended, no distinctions were made between "the innocent, the guilty, and the depraved"; they were all "herded together, children and adult, men and women." Echoing the horrid history of the white overseers on the plantations of the antebellum period, convicted blacks, whether innocent or guilty, were "given into complete control of practically irresponsible men, whose sole object was to make the most money possible." Observe the way in which Du Bois, yet again, connected his sociology of crime with his sociology of class by emphasizing that because the white guards "were usually selected from the lowest classes of whites, and the camps were often far from settlements or public roads," in essence, the "innocent were made bad, the bad worse; women were outraged and children tainted; whipping and torture were in vogue, and the death-rate from cruelty, exposure, and overwork rose to large percentages."

Du Bois placed special emphasis on the ways in which the convict-lease system sexually exploited and violated African American women, stating that the "women were outraged"—"outraged," of course, meaning raped. Touching on the taboo topic of *the anti-black racist rape of African American women* by all manner of white men (i.e., bourgeois, proletarian, and lumpenproletarian), Du Bois concretized his critique of black women's sexual violation under the convict-lease system by relating to his readers a story of a young woman who was "repeatedly outraged by several of her guards" to the excruciating extent that she "finally died in childbirth while in camp." Here Du Bois's sociology of crime seems to dovetail with his sociology of gender with its intense emphasis on not only the racially gendered life struggles and lived endurances of African American women within the criminal justice system, but also their centuries-spanning lived experiences and lived endurances of *anti-black racist rape* or, rather, *white supremacist sexual violence*. In addition, emphasis should be placed on the fact that well into the twenty-first century African American women continue to experience higher rates of rape and other forms of sexual violence within the criminal justice system as compared to other female prisoners (Belknap, 1996; Girshick, 1999; P. C. Johnson, 2003; Pinar, 2001; Young and Reviere, 2006). Du Bois's sociology of crime, once again then, proves prescient in tackling tough issues and penal problems that stem from the historic and current clandestine criminality of U.S. social institutions and cultural conventions.

Bearing in mind what I referred to above as Du Bois's characteristic literary double-dealing—that is, double-consciously attempting to appeal to concerned blacks and liberal or progressive whites simultaneously—he concluded "Crime and Slavery" by critically exploring the impact of the convict-lease system on both blacks and whites, respectively. As if reemphasizing his innovative etiology of African American criminality, Du Bois

(1904c) detailed the effects of the convict-lease system on whites first, sternly stating:

> It is difficult to say whether the effect of such a system is worse on the whites or on the Negroes. So far as the whites are concerned, the convict-lease system lowered the respect for courts, increased lawlessness, and put the states into the clutches of penitentiary "rings." The courts were brought into politics, judgeships became elective for shorter and shorter terms, and there grew up a public sentiment which would not consent to considering the desert of a criminal apart from his color. If the criminal were white, public opinion refused to permit him to enter the chain gang save in the most extreme cases. The result is that even today it is difficult to enforce the criminal laws in the South against whites. On the other hand, so customary had it become to convict any Negro upon a mere accusation, that public opinion was loathe to allow a fair trial to black suspects, and was too often tempted to take the law into its own hands. Finally the state became a dealer in crime, profited by it so as to derive a net annual income from her prisoners. The lessees of the convicts made large profits also. Under such circumstances, it was almost impossible to remove the clutches of this vicious system from the state. Even as late as 1890, the Southern states were the only section of the Union where the income from prisons and reformatories exceeded the expense. Moreover, these figures do not include the county gangs where the lease system is today most prevalent and the net income largest. (5)

Based on the above it is virtually impossible to deny the contributions that Du Bois's sociology of crime makes to the contemporary discourse on, and critique of the prison industrial complex. By performing an archaeology of the interconnections and intersections of the clandestine continuation of African American enslavement, the crop-lien system, and the convict-lease system, Du Bois further expatiated his etiology of African American criminality. Where he focused on the severity and savagery of the convict-lease system with regard to black lifeworlds and black life struggles, in engaging its impact on whites he emphasized that state governments had become "dealer[s] in crime" and "profited by it so as to derive a net annual income from [their] prisoners." Further connecting the convict-lease system, and it would seem the entire U.S. criminal justice system, to the political economy of anti-black racist capitalism, Du Bois identified the convict-lease system as a comprador for both American apartheid and American capitalism. Speaking directly of the profit that states derived from this early incarnation of the prison industrial complex, Du Bois exclaimed, "Under such circumstances, it was almost impossible to remove the clutches of this vicious system from the state."

In some senses prefiguring the watershed work of David Theo Goldberg (1993, 1997, 2001, 2008) and Howard Winant (1994, 2001, 2004), Du Bois strongly stressed the interconnections and intersections of the "racial state," institutionalized racism, *racial criminalization*, and the political economy of anti-black racist capitalism. He developed his discourse on differential justice further by asserting that the white public unwittingly placed its *anti-black racist criminalization* of African Americans into bold relief because, almost as a rule, it "would not consent to considering the desert of a criminal apart from his color." Here we witness what I will call *anti-black racist differential justice*. For instance, on the one hand, if the criminal was white, then white "public opinion refused to permit him to enter the chain gang save in the most extreme cases." However, by the turn of the twentieth century anti-black racism had seeped into the criminal justice system to such an insidious extent that, Du Bois exasperatingly explained, it eventually became quite common to "convict any Negro upon a mere accusation." In essence, white "public opinion was loathe to allow a fair trial to black suspects" and, what is worse, it was "too often tempted to take the law into its own hands" (e.g., lynching, "race riots," and other forms of anti-black racist vigilante violence).

Shifting from the effects of the convict-lease system on whites to its impact on African Americans and their perception of crime and the criminal justice system, Du Bois declared:

> The effect of the convict-lease system on the Negroes was deplorable. First, it linked crime and slavery indissolubly in their minds as simply forms of the white man's oppression. Punishment, consequently, lost the most effective of its deterrent effects, and the criminal gained pity instead of disdain. The Negroes lost faith in the integrity of courts and the fairness of juries. Worse than all, the chain gangs became schools of crime which hastened the appearance of the confirmed Negro criminal upon the scene. That some crime and vagrancy should follow emancipation was inevitable. A nation cannot systematically degrade labor without in some degree debauching the laborer. But there can be no doubt but that the indiscriminate method by which Southern courts dealt with the freedmen after the war increased crime and vagabondage to an enormous extent. There are no reliable statistics to which one can safely appeal to measure exactly the growth of crime among the emancipated slaves. About seventy per cent of all prisoners in the South are black; this, however, is in part explained by the fact that accused Negroes are still easily convicted and get long sentences, while whites still continue to escape the penalty of many crimes even among themselves. And yet, allowing for all this, there can be no reasonable doubt but that there has arisen in the South since the war a class of black criminals, loafers and ne'er-do-wells who are a menace to their fellows, both black and white. (6)[8]

What stands out here is Du Bois's contention that African Americans "lost faith in the integrity of courts and the fairness of juries." The convict-lease system, and the same could be said of the U.S. criminal justice system as a whole at the turn of the twentieth century, had almost the exact opposite effect on African American criminality as it was supposed to—that is, the main interests and motivations of the convict-lease system, similar to the contemporary prison industrial complex, were preoccupied with making a profit rather than punishing or rehabilitating criminals and reducing crime rates (Hallett, 2006; Melossi and Payarini, 1981; Parenti, 1999). Hence, again expatiating his etiology of African American criminality and the obvious increase in black crime at the turn of the twentieth century, Du Bois wrote, "The chain gangs became schools of crime which hastened the appearance of the confirmed Negro criminal upon the scene."

It is important to emphasize that Du Bois did not deny the existence of "the confirmed Negro criminal" or "the real Negro criminal" as much as he historically and sociologically sought a critical etiological explanation for black criminality and its increase during the Reconstruction, post-Reconstruction, and turn-of-the-twentieth-century years. His sociology of crime discursively dovetailed with his sociology of race insofar as it incessantly accented the ways in which anti-black racism was, whether unwittingly or not, embedded within almost every aspect and activity of the criminal justice system. He unequivocally asserted, "[T]here is a long battle to be fought with prejudice and inertia before the South will realize that a black criminal is a human being, to be punished firmly but humanely, with the sole object of making him a safe member of society, and that a white criminal at large is a menace and a danger. The greatest difficulty today in the way of reform is this race question" (Du Bois, 1904c, 8).

It could, perhaps, go without saying that "the race question"—of course, along with the gender, class, and sexual orientation questions—continues to plague the U.S. criminal justice system (Barak, Leighton, and Flavin, 2007; Gregory, 1987; Schwartz and Milovanovic, 1996). One wonders what Du Bois would have to say about the uninterrupted and unbridled continuation of the convict-lease system of the turn of the twentieth century and its truculent transformation into the prison industrial complex of the turn of the twenty-first century. There are, indeed, bona fide reasons to believe that he probably would have despised the prison industrial complex as deeply as he did the convict-lease system that spawned it. In this sense, then, the weighted words Du Bois (1904c) concluded "Crime and Slavery" with must be borne in mind as we quickly conclude our exploration of his criminological contributions:

> Until the public opinion of the ruling masses of the South can see that the prevention of crime among Negroes is just as necessary, just as profitable, for the whites themselves, as prevention among whites, all true betterment in courts and prisons will be hindered. Above all, we must remember that crime is not normal; that the appearance of crime among Southern Negroes is a symptom of wrong social conditions—of a stress of life greater than a large part of the community can bear. The Negro is not naturally criminal; he is usually patient and law-abiding. If slavery, the convict-lease system, the traffic

in criminal labor, the lack of juvenile reformatories, together with the unfortunate discrimination and prejudice in other walks of life, have led to that sort of social protest and revolt which we call crime, then we must look for remedy in the sane reform of these wrong social conditions, and not in intimidation, savagery, or the legalized slavery of men. (8–9)

Soon after *Some Notes on Negro Crime* was published in 1904, as observed at the outset of this volume, Du Bois lost faith in an exclusively social scientific approach to social reform. As a result of the rising tidal wave of anti-black racist vigilante violence and ongoing black disenfranchisement, he began to increasingly and intensely turn his attention to radical politics and social activism.[9] His initial foray into this field remains best represented by his founding of the Niagara movement in 1905, which has the distinction of being the first organization exclusively devoted to civil rights in U.S. history. Four years after founding the fledgling Niagara movement, Du Bois joined with a wide range of blacks and whites, radicals and liberals to establish the NAACP in 1909. His embrace of radical politics and social activism, however, did not completely curtail or, rather, intellectually eclipse his commitments to social scientific scholarship, and he inaugurated and edited three journals consecutively: *The Moon*, *The Horizon*, and *The Crisis*. *The Horizon* was the mouthpiece of the Niagara movement, where *The Crisis* remains the official organ of the NAACP to the present day. Even after he moved to the NAACP headquarters in New York to helm *The Crisis* Du Bois continued to edit the Atlanta University studies with the assistance of one of his brightest graduate students, Augustus Dill. The 1914 volume *Morals and Manners Among Negro Americans*, therefore, should be examined for its sociological significance and criminological contributions right along with *Some Notes on Negro Crime*. In fact, it could be easily averred that in light of Du Bois's abrupt departure from the ivory towers and the *epistemic apartheid* of the American academy, his ongoing editorship of the Atlanta University studies represents his earnest effort to continue to contribute to, and critically dialogue with, the various discursive communities of American sociology in particular, and the American academy in general.

Several of the themes Du Bois discursively developed in *Some Notes on Negro Crime* reappeared in *Morals and Manners Among Negro Americans* a decade later. Within the decade that separated *Some Notes on Negro Crime* and *Morals and Manners Among Negro Americans*, Du Bois further expatiated his etiology of African American criminality and intensified his conception of certain elements of black crime as a "sort of social protest and revolt" which was a reflection or, rather, "a symptom of wrong social conditions." Unlike *Some Notes on Negro Crime*, *Morals and Manners* was not exclusively devoted to crime and, consequently, offers us a lot less in terms of our examination of Du Bois's criminological discourse. However, there are several noteworthy criminological contributions that should be briefly commented on.

First, in answering the question "How far has the moral condition of the Negroes shown itself in crime?," Du Bois (1914) critiqued the pseudo-methodology utilized to measure black crime. He was mostly miffed by what he understood to be the nonsensical and unprincipled practice of counting prisoners on a specific day. He argued that this practice could only lead to calculated conjectures and fallacious conclusions with regard to black crime (i.e., "exaggerated Negro crime") because blacks usually received longer sentences. He elaborated on his rationale, assuredly sharing with his readers:

> [A]ccording to the method of enumerating prisoners on a certain day every ten years, the Negro American forming one-eighth of the population seemed responsible for nearly one-third of the crime; and his criminal tendencies increase[d] rapidly from 1870 to 1880, enormously from 1880 to 1890, and perceptibly from 1890 to 1904. It was pointed out, however, in 1890 that this method of estimating crime was misleading and erroneous. Such a method furnish[ed] no basis for estimating the increase or decrease of crime; and without doubt it exaggerated Negro crime. For example: If in communities A and B five men a year are arrested but B punishes her men by twice as long terms as A, by the method of enumeration of prison population on a certain day community B appears on a given day with twice as many criminals as community A, when as a matter of fact there is no difference in the number of crimes committed. The better method is to count the number of prisoners committed within a certain time period. (37–38)

Keeping this example under consideration, Du Bois noted the census figures from 1890 to 1904, which demonstrated that when his preferred method is employed, African Americans actually account for 15.8 percent of the criminality, as opposed to more than 33 percent under the previously utilized pseudo-method (38). Explaining the extraordinary difference between his more critical criminological method and the pseudo-method of the census report, Du Bois seemed content to conclude, "In other words, one-eighth of the population furnish[ed] one sixth of the crime—a condition not unfavorable to the Negro, considering his past history" (38).

The second criminological contribution that *Morals and Manners* made revolves around Du Bois's return to the theme of *anti-black racist differential justice*—a subject, as we have witnessed, which was first taken up in *The Philadelphia Negro*, then further elaborated in *Some Notes on Negro Crime*. After accenting the pseudo-method employed, which in essence "exaggerated Negro crime," Du Bois then turned his attention to the more severe and "longer sentences" doled out to African Americans. For instance, critically focusing on the severity of black sentences, he went further: "In 1890 the average white prisoner had a sentence of three and one-half years, the average Negro of nearly five years. So, too, one-third of the white prisoners were in for less than a year; while only one-fifth of the Negroes were thus favored" (38). *Anti-black racist differential justice* is, therefore, clearly predicated on what the contemporary workers in critical race theory, and critical white studies in particular, have identified and discursively defined as "white privilege" (Jensen, 2005; Kendall, 2006; Rothenberg, 2002; L. F. Williams, 2003). If, indeed, the U.S. criminal justice system claimed to be delivering "blind" and "impartial" justice, then why were white prisoners receiving such blatant preferential treatment or, in Du Bois's (1904c) words, "[w]hy is it that Negroes were so severely punish[ed]?" (39) His extended answer to this question turned to the U.S. Census Bureau's 1904 report on *Prisoners and Juvenile Delinquents in Institutions*, where he gathered, "The editors of the census bulletin, while admitting the possibility of 'a somewhat greater severity in dealing with colored criminals than white' were disposed to think that a part of the cause is that the Negro is guilty of the more aggravated forms of crime. They divided all prisoners committed in 1904 into major and minor offenders and found that Negroes contributed thirty-one per cent of the graver and thirteen per cent of the minor offenses." Then, Du Bois accented the statistical fallacy and logical reductionism of the census report because its editors had not factored in *anti-black racist differential justice*. He ardently asserted that "[t]wo difficulties present themselves in this argument: 1. Length of sentence to some extent determines the classification into graver and minor offenses," and "2. Negroes are indicted often for the graver of two possible offenses: To strike a white woman is for a white man 'Assault'; for a Negro it may be 'Attempted Rape'" (39).

It would appear quite clear here that Du Bois was continuing the critical discourse on *anti-black racist differential justice* he developed in *The Philadelphia Negro* and *Some Notes on Negro Crime*. He went through great pains to highlight the ways in which the criminal justice system was initially, and caustically continued to be, informed by, and in turn influenced, white supremacist social institutions and cultural conventions. As with *The Philadelphia Negro* and *Some Notes on Negro Crime*, in *Morals and Manners* Du Bois's sociology of crime critiqued the political economy of black prison labor, which brings us to the third major criminological contribution emerging from *Morals and Manners*. Elaborating on his etiology of African American criminality and the increase in black crime documented and developed in *The Philadelphia Negro* and *Some Notes on Negro Crime*, among other miscellaneous articles, in *Morals and Manners* Du Bois (1914) reminded his readers that

1. Southern whites are not arrested and punish[ed] for smaller misdemeanors.
2. The number of foreigners in the South is very small.
3. The Negroes suffer from race discrimination.

The criminologist passes no judgment on the right or wrong of this discrimination. He simply recognizes it as a fact; but he knows:

(a) That many economic forces of the South depend largely on the courts for a supply of labor.
(b) That public opinion in the South exaggerates the guilt of Negroes in certain crimes and enforces itself thru [sic] police, jury, magistrate and judge.
(c) That southern public opinion over-looks and unduly minimizes certain other Negro misdemeanors, which lead to immorality and crime.

Of the truth of these statements there can be no reasonable doubt in the mind of any careful student. (41)

Here Du Bois returned to the hard-nosed historical sociology of *The Philadelphia Negro*, simultaneously emphasizing anti-black racism and whites' preferential treatment within the criminal justice system. Then, making overtures to social scientific "objectivity," he asserted that the "criminologist passes no judgment on the right or wrong of this discrimination . . . but he knows" several facts of sociological significance—perhaps one of the most important being that anti-black racist criminalization, differential justice, and prison labor were even more inextricable in 1914 than they were in 1904 when *Some Notes on Negro Crime* was published. Critiquing the continuation of the convict-lease system, Du Bois sternly stated:

[I]n the South road-building, mining, brick-making, lumbering and to some extent agriculture depend largely on convict labor. The demand for such labor is strong and increasing. The political power of the lessees is great and the income to the city and state is tempting. The glaring brutalities of the older lease system are disappearing but the fact still remains that the state is supplying a demand for degraded labor and especially for life and long term laborers and that almost irresistibly the police forces and sheriffs are push[ed] to find black criminals in suitable quantities. (42–43)

In so many words, or so it seems, Du Bois contended that the convict-lease system, in essence, created or, at the very least, exacerbated black criminality. If, indeed, there was an obvious increase in black criminality at the turn of the twentieth century, how much of it was a consequence of anti-black racist criminalization and differential justice, both of which were inextricable from the convict-lease system plaguing African Americans? This is a crucial question, and one to which Du Bois's sociology of crime astonishingly appears to offer several inchoate answers. First, we must bear in mind Du Bois's contention in *Some Notes on Negro Crime* that both the crop-lien system and the convict-lease system were "the direct children of slavery." Second, his sociology of crime understood the convict-lease system to be nothing other than "a new slavery and slave-trade," leading him ultimately to assert in *Some Notes on Negro Crime* that because the white

South "believed in slave labor, and was thoroughly convinced that free Negroes would not work steadily or effectively," they devised "[e]laborate and ingenious apprentice and vagrancy laws . . . designed to make the freedmen and their children work for their former masters at practically no wages." Finally, then, Du Bois's sociology of crime critically revealed the doubly diabolical nature of the convict-lease system: on the one hand, it was predicated on essentially *reenslaved black labor*—thus transforming it into *black prison labor*; and, on the other hand, in order to "find black criminals in suitable quantities" the criminal justice system, quite literally, employed the already anti-black racist social institutions and cultural conventions of the established order to crudely create and then malevolently manufacture "the confirmed Negro criminal" or "the real Negro criminal"—ipso facto, psychopathically putting into play the simultaneous racialization, colonization, segregation, and criminalization of African American lifeworlds and lived experiences post-Emancipation. Questions, therefore, concerning how authentically "free" African Americans historically have been, or are currently, are not simply mad meanderings spewed from the mouths of black militants, but most often heartfelt and profoundly humanist queries that should be both earnestly asked and answered.

Earlier it was observed that in *Some Notes on Negro Crime* Du Bois considered certain aspects of black crime to be a "sort of social protest and revolt" that was a reflection or, rather, "a symptom of wrong social conditions," which brings us to the fourth and final major criminological contribution emerging from *Morals and Manners*. Notice here how he continued this theme by connecting it to African Americans' "past economic history":

> In crimes against society (unchastity, perjury and violating United States laws) the Negro is less seldom committed than whites. This is because his crimes against chastity, when his own race are victims, are seldom punish[ed] properly in the South. His proportion of crimes against property are larger, due to his past economic history. His proportion of crimes against the person are greatest because right here, in his personal contact with his fellows, prejudice and discrimination, exasperation and revolt show themselves most frequently; and also because his masses are reaching the brawling stage of self-assertion. (41)

Having reached the "brawling stage of self-assertion," it seemed to Du Bois that almost every aspect of African Americans' embrace of their own unique human agency and distinct culture was an extreme offense to white supremacist social institutions and cultural conventions. For example, as illustrated in *The Philadelphia Negro*, the black bourgeoisie's ongoing prickly pretensions to openly assimilate European American middle-class culture and morality were mocked and frequently frowned upon by well-to-do whites, where white social scientists claimed that working-class blacks were caught within a world predicated on a "culture of poverty" or "cycle of poverty," supposedly doomed to illiteracy, illegitimacy, immorality, and increasing criminality (Gmelch and Zenner, 1980; Holloway, Fuller, Rambaud, and Eggers-Pierola, 1997; Leacock, 1971). The theme of American apartheid etiologically exacerbating black criminality was carried over from *Some Notes on Negro Crime* to *Morals and Manners*. However, where he emphasized elements of black crime as a "sort of social protest and revolt" against the white supremacist world in *Some Notes on Negro Crime*, in *Morals and Manners*, Du Bois turned his readers' attention to the ways in which black crime crippled African American communities. After outlining three particular kinds of crime African Americans frequently committed (i.e., "crimes against society," "crimes against property," and "crimes against the person"), observe here how Du Bois centered his discussion on "crimes against the person." With regard to "crimes against the person," Du Bois strongly stressed the almost inherent difficulty in interpreting the raw data and acute figures, starkly stating, "How much real guilt therefore lies back of the figures can only be conjectured."

Again emphasizing the conjectural nature of previous reports on black criminality, he then turned to a discussion of the patently taboo topic of black "crimes against the [white] person." Du Bois (1914) cautiously continued: "The really dangerous excess of Negro crime would appear to be in assault and homicide, fighting and killing." However, he insistently intoned, "Here again interpretation is difficult: How much of these are aggressions on whites, repelling of white aggressions on Negroes, and brawling among Negroes themselves? Undoubtedly the majority of cases belong to the last category, but a very large and growing number come under the other heads and must be set down to the debit of the race problem" (42).

On the one hand, Du Bois contended that black self-defensive "crimes" directed at the "repelling of white aggressions on Negroes . . . must be set down to the debit of the race problem." Some elements of black criminality, then, were etiologically interconnected with the rampant anti-black racism of the criminal justice system in particular, and U.S. social institutions and cultural conventions in general. In an effort to drive this point home, Du Bois returned to his discourse on *anti-black racist differential justice*, specifically the issue of sentencing disparity, asserting, "Any Negro tried for perjury, assault, robbery, rape, homicide, arson, burglary, larceny or fraud is going to get a severer penalty in the South than a white man similarly charged. This the white community judges to be necessary and its decisions are carried out by police forces, police magistrates and juries drawn from the white classes whose racial prejudices are strongest" (42).

On the other hand, Du Bois argued that most of the "assault and homicide, fighting and killing" attributable to African Americans was usually committed against other African Americans. Therefore, here we have, perhaps, the first etiology of intra-racial African American criminality (i.e., "black-on-black violence"), with Du Bois surmising that blacks' "proportion of crimes against the person are greatest because right here, in his personal contact with his fellows, prejudice and discrimination, exasperation and revolt show themselves most frequently." As chapter 2 of the present volume indicated, African Americans often intensely internalize anti-black racism—a process and predicament captured by Du Bois with his conception of "double-consciousness"—and very often, ultimately, they come to self-loathingly and psychotically despise "blackness" and anyone or anything associated with "blackness" or, even more egregiously, Africa and Africanity.

Du Bois's etiology and overall interpretation of African American criminality differed distinctly from those of his criminological contemporaries. This was so partly on account of his taking into critical consideration African Americans' unique historical and cultural evolution, and partly on account of his intense emphasis on anti-black racist criminalization, differential justice, and prolonged white privilege. Because Du Bois's historical sociology, industrial sociology, urban sociology, rural sociology, sociology of education, and sociology of race incessantly intersected with and directly informed his sociology of crime, he was able to make concrete connections between black criminality, black (un)employment, black (mis)education, and anti-black racism. Concluding his consideration of black crime in *Morals and Manners*, Du Bois asked, "What now is the remedy for Negro crime?" In essence echoing many of the positions and measures he put forward previously (e.g., in *The Philadelphia Negro* and *Some Notes on Negro Crime*) with regard to black crime prevention, Du Bois delineated the following:

1. Justice in Southern courts; Negroes on the police force and in the jury box.
2. Abolition of the economic demand for criminals in the South.
3. Better housing and free chance to work in the North.
4. National aid to Negro education.
5. Better wages.
6. Full civil and political rights for Negroes, on the same basis as they are granted to whites. (44)

It is interesting to compare and contrast the consistency of the remedies Du Bois advanced for African American crime, from *The Philadelphia Negro* to *Some Notes on Negro Crime*, to *Morals and Manners*. Above we have, in his own weighted words, empirical evidence of Du Bois's consistency and the sociological connections he innovatively made between anti-black racism, civil rights, education, employment, the political economy of the prison industrial complex, and the ongoing injustice of the criminal justice system. From the foregoing it would appear that Du Bois's sociology of crime can also be said to be a critique of Eurocentric criminological conjectures, grand theories, and pseudo-methodologies. This is truly amazing considering the well-documented clannishness of early American criminology (Gabbidon, Greene, and Wilder, 2004; Russell and Milovanovic, 2001; Young and Sulton, 1991). Whether his white criminological contemporaries would take his research seriously or not, Du Bois resolutely continued to contribute to American criminology, earnestly offering an alternative etiology and interpretation of African American criminality, as well as an intense interpretation of the ways in which anti-black racism and white privilege were making a mockery of the criminal justice system.

Ultimately, Du Bois's etiology of African American criminality and the increase of black crime at the turn of the twentieth century deftly demonstrated that black crime has historically been inextricable from anti-black racist criminalization, differential justice, and what criminologists are currently calling "the prison industrial complex." In fact, as was asserted above, it could be argued that Du Bois's sociology of crime doubles as an insurgent archaeology of the interconnections and intersections of the clandestine continuation of African American enslavement, the crop-lien system, and the convict-lease system, all of which, we may soberly surmise from Du Bois's sociology of crime, prove to be precursors of the prison industrial complex of the twenty-first century. Here it is, once again, important to highlight how the deeply historical dimension of Du Bois's sociological discourse distinguished his sociology of crime from those of his contemporaries. Ironically, it could be argued that the deeply historical dimension of Du Bois's sociological discourse is one of the reasons it remains relevant. Eschewing the free-floating grand theorizing of his intellectual age (especially within both criminological communities and sociological circles), Du Bois conducted or compiled empirical data on black criminality and African American perceptions of crime and the criminal justice system at a time when it appeared that few, if any, of their fellow white citizens cared about the ways in which crime was a reflection or, rather, "a symptom of wrong social conditions." Considering the above connections emphatically established between Du Bois's critique of the convict-lease system and the current critique of the prison industrial complex, as well as the critical connections made between *racial criminalization* and *anti-black racist differential justice*, we will quickly conclude this chapter with a discussion of the continued relevance of Du Bois's criminological contributions.

ON THE CONTINUED RELEVANCE OF DU BOIS'S CRIMINOLOGICAL CONTRIBUTIONS AT THE TURN OF THE TWENTY-FIRST CENTURY

In his watershed work *W. E. B. Du Bois on Crime and Justice*, renowned African American criminologist Shaun Gabbidon (2007) announced, "With his publication of *The Philadelphia Negro* in the last year of the nineteenth century, Du Bois was obviously one of the founders of the sociological approach in criminology. From 1897 until 1913, Du Bois's criminological writings primarily centered on the sociological approach" (65). Gabbidon continued: "During a period when the biological approach and the eugenics movement were picking up strength, Du Bois was leading the way with an alternative view that, along with its sociological underpinnings, invoked the role of prejudice and race discrimination in explaining the social problems of African Americans. While he was unsure of the magnitude of the influence of prejudice and race discrimination on crime, he recognized its role in the plight of African Americans" (65). Although my work above demonstrates that Du Bois came to increasingly believe that racial discrimination played a significant part in African Americans' racial criminalization and the differential justice they received, I am in complete agreement with Gabbidon with regard to his contention that "Du Bois was obviously one of the founders of the sociological approach in criminology." In other words, following Gabbidon, I am asserting that Du Bois should be considered one of the founders of American criminology.

Also in agreement with Gabbidon, I take issue with the work of Katheryn Russell (1992), Ihekobowa Onwudiwe and Michael Lynch (2000), and Everette Penn (2003), among others, when and where they call for the development of a "black criminology" all the while overlooking Du Bois's sociology of crime and the classical criminological contributions of other African Americans. As previously mentioned, because of the disciplinary decadence of most single subject–focused disciplines, many African American scholars, like their white counterparts, ignore or exclude contributions emerging from disciplines or fields of critical inquiry other than their own. As a consequence, *epistemic apartheid* is often put into play among black (and other nonwhite) scholars hyperpreoccupied, in the most negative and narrow-minded manner imaginable, with drawing from and contributing to specific monodisciplinary discursive formations and discursive practices. Thus, the arbitrary and artificial disciplinary borders and boundaries that have long wreaked havoc in the American academy have been frequently projected onto African American lifeworlds and life struggles—haunt ingly in the spurious spirit of the Berlin Conference of 1884–1885—by desperately double-conscious African Americans themselves, conceptually colonizing and intellectually segregating knowledge produced by or about African Americans. Emphasizing the ways in which many African American criminologists have missed an important opportunity to deconstruct and reconstruct, as well as diversify criminological curriculum, Gabbidon (2007) unapologetically advanced, "As an African American scholar, Du Bois's ideas particularly in *The Philadelphia Negro,* and his years at Atlanta University, paved the way for the research conducted later at the University of Chicago" (66). What is more, "With the development of the Chicago

School almost thirty years later, Du Bois's ideas were brought into the mainstream albeit with little credit given to him." Still further, Gabbidon adamantly intoned, "His other theoretical orientation now referred to as conflict theory, remains one of the primary approaches used by many white and African American criminologists to explain African American criminality" (67). Let us now, therefore, briefly look at the ways in which Du Bois's sociology of crime contributes to contemporary criminology.

Du Bois's criminological contributions remain relevant in light of the fact that much of his crime-related research proved to remarkably prefigure the theories and methodologies later discursively developed by several "pioneer" white criminologists. As discussed above, in *The Philadelphia Negro* Du Bois employed inchoate versions of what later came to be termed "social disorganization" and "strain" theory in his efforts to critically explain turn-of-the-twentieth-century African American criminality in Philadelphia in particular, and in Northern cities in general. Elaborating social disorganization theory nearly two decades prior to the establishment of the Chicago School, it is important to remind my readers that in *The Philadelphia Negro* Du Bois (1899) starkly stated: "Crime is a phenomena of organized social life, and it is the open rebellion of an individual against his social environment. Naturally then, if men are suddenly transported from one environment to another, the result is lack of harmony with the new conditions; lack of harmony with the new physical surroundings leading to disease and death or modification of physique; lack of harmony with social surroundings leading to crime" (235).

Prefiguring strain theory, it should be stressed that from his historical sociological perspective Du Bois asserted that African Americans' emancipation resulted, not simply in social disorganization in light of their increasing influx into urban environments, but also, because the opportunities they were led to believe, or on their own envisioned in urban environments were virtually nonexistent, the consequent psychological and social condition was "a strain upon the strength and resources of the Negro, moral, economic and physical, which drove many to the wall. For this reason the rise of the Negro in this city is a series of rushes and backslidings rather than a continuous growth" (283). Two things can be gathered from Du Bois's critique of black crime and the anti-black racism of the criminal justice system in *The Philadelphia Negro*: first, the intellectual origins of both social disorganization and strain theory can be traced back to Du Bois; and, second, Du Bois's sociology of crime demonstrated that both social disorganization and strain theory can be effectively employed to explain African American criminality in urban environments. Undoubtedly Durkheim (1933, 1963, 1972) is the major point of departure for strain theory. However, the longstanding custom within American criminology of going from Durkheim's discourse, and then skipping over or intellectually rendering invisible Du Bois's discourse, to eagerly expound on, for example, Merton (1938, 1968), Cohen (1955), Dubin (1959), and Cloward and Ohlin's (1960) discourses, seems to be almost unequivocally indicative of *epistemic apartheid*. Keep in mind, as detailed in chapter 1, that *The Philadelphia Negro* has long been hailed as a pioneering work within history, sociology, and African American studies; why, then, have its criminological contributions been consistently overlooked in favor of the work of the white sociologists and criminologists that followed in its wake (see Katz and Sugrue, 1998)? Once again, emphasis should be placed on the fact that viewing the discursive formations and discursive practices of the disciplinary development of criminology patently points to elements of intellectual erasure and exclusion that, I honestly believe, can be best conceptually captured by the critical theory of *epistemic apartheid*.

Even when critically engaged against the backdrop of strain theory's intellectual evolution into "anomie" theory, Du Bois's donations to the discourse on strain theory continue to resonate and ring true. In their discussion of anomie theory, for instance, critically acclaimed criminologists Marilyn McShane and Frank Williams (2009), however inadvertently, echo and offer what could otherwise be considered a Du Boisian definition of anomie theory:

> Because of social disorganization, the approved means to reach the success goals are not readily available to certain groups in society, even though the goals are said to apply equally to all. Certain groups of people, the lower social class and minorities . . . may be at a disadvantage in gaining business positions that would allow them to pursue the goal of financial success. When this inequality exists because of the way society is structured, Merton viewed the social structure as anomic. . . . The individuals caught in these anomic conditions (largely the lower classes) are then faced with the strain of being unable to reconcile their aspirations with their limited opportunities. (76–77)

Clearly Du Bois's discourse on strain theory conceptually coincides with McShane and Williams's work here. Du Bois's anomic analysis, although it centered on African Americans' migration from the South (i.e., rural regions) to the North (i.e., urban environments) at the turn of the twentieth century, should not be ghettoized to African American sociology and African American criminology only (i.e., the lifeworlds and lived experiences of "blacks only"). This should be strongly stressed because when Du Bois's contributions to strain theory are placed within their proper historical context, as well as the context of his corpus, then it becomes evident that his "strain" and/or "anomie" theory is virtually incomprehensible without taking into critical consideration the ways in which it simultaneously informed and, perhaps, was influenced by his previously noted influx theory of "freedmen, fugitives and foreigners" to Northern or, rather, more urban environments. With regard to African Americans in particular, Du Bois reported on the historical reality that in their migration from the South to the North, quite similar to the immigrants' migration from Europe to America, they had humble, all too human aspirations of achieving a better life (e.g., higher quality employment, education, community, etc.). Like many of the European immigrants, African Americans seemed to have jumped out of the frying pan into the fire, as it were, with truly feasible employment opportunities being few and far between, inadequate education, and poor social conditions abounding in the new urban environment. However, unlike most of the European immigrants, who were virtually and legally "white upon arrival" in U.S. cities, the anti-black racism and other unforeseen negative social factors African Americans experienced on their arrival in urban environments caused the "strain upon the strength and resources of the Negro, moral, economic and physical, which drove many to the wall"—that is, to "gambling, drunkenness and debauchery" and, ultimately, to crime. Du Bois's distinction, therefore, lies in his early and innovative emphasis on anti-black racism as an important variable in the etiology of African American criminality and the critical interpretation of black crime.

The connections made above between Du Bois's critique of the convict-lease system and contemporary criminological critiques of the prison industrial complex help to highlight the fact that Gabbidon (2007, 61–64) is on point when he claims that Du Bois can also be considered an early conflict theorist. As is well known, conflict theory has classical roots in both the critical social theory of Karl Marx and the interpretive sociology of Max Weber. In the United States, conflict theory is most often associated with the late Lewis Coser (1956, 1967) and the more contemporary Randall Collins (1971, 1975). Therefore, it would seem that *epistemic apartheid*, once again, has intellectually excluded Du Bois's discourse in general, and his contributions to conflict theory in particular. For instance, utilizing J. Robert Lilly, Francis Cullen, and Richard Ball's (2007) definition of conflict theory, Du Bois's contributions to this discourse become quite clear:

> Theories that focus attention on struggles between individuals and/or groups in terms of power differentials fall into the category of conflict theory. . . . Some conflict theories try to search for the sources of the apparent conflicts. Some seek to elucidate the basic principles by which conflict evolves. Others try to develop a theoretical foundation for eliminating the conflict. Some try to do all this and more. (132–33)

Obviously Du Bois's conflict theory, especially with regard to his critique of the convict-lease system, falls into the later category—that is, a more comprehensive conflict theory that unceasingly seeks to simultaneously "search for the sources of the apparent conflict," "elucidate the basic principles by which [the] conflict evolve[d]," and "develop a theoretical foundation for eliminating the conflict." In both *Some Notes on Negro Crime* and *Morals and Manners*, Du Bois argued that anti-black racist criminalization, differential justice, and the political economy of U.S. capitalism made the convict-lease system nothing other than "a new slavery and slave-trade." Hence, by invoking "slavery and slave-trade" in connection with the convict-lease system, a system which ironically developed after the issuing of the Emancipation Proclamation, Du Bois created an acute analogy between the criminal justice system and the continuation of African American enslavement, of course, via the convict-lease system and black prison labor. Returning to the deeply historical dimension of Du Bois's sociological discourse, it is important to point to the ways in which his criminological contributions double as an archaeology of the interconnections and intersections of the clandestine continuation of African American enslavement, the crop-lien system, and the convict-lease system through several city ordinances and articles of legislation authorized to reenslave and racially recolonize black labor. The whole range of the infamous "black codes," these city ordinances and articles of legislation, Du Bois clamorously exclaimed, were "designed to make the freedmen and their children work for their former masters at practically no wages" (see Foner, 1988; Litwack, 1979, 1998; Wilson, 1965).

Here, then, Du Bois's early and innovative challenge to the supposed neutrality of the U.S. criminal justice system takes us back to his discourse on *anti-black racist differential justice*, where he thundered, criminology "students must not forget this double standard of justice"—one for whites (especially wealthy whites), and one for blacks and other nonwhites (without regard to rank or social class). The disproportionality consequent to whites' preferential treatment and blacks' severe sentencing within the criminal justice system was virtually incontrovertible proof-positive of the *anti-black racist differential justice* doled out to African Americans. Taking the above into critical consideration it would appear that Du Bois can be uncontroversially characterized as a classical conflict theorist and, even more, a major pioneer with respect to the development of a macrological-historical-sociological approach in criminology. For instance, he was arguably the first criminologist to assert that a serious labor conflict emerged in the aftermath of African Americans' emancipation, which quickly led to the said city ordinances and articles of legislation (i.e., the "black codes") that, in essence, sanctioned the reenslavement and racial recolonization of black labor. Du Bois's sociology of crime, therefore, critically recognized that the crop-lien system and the convict-lease system were unequivocally "designed to make the freedmen and their children work for their former masters at practically no wages," which set into motion the hegemonic maneuvers of both anti-black racist criminalization and differential justice that remain unabated up to the present day.

In several senses this brings us full circle, back to the place where our critical exploration of Du Bois's sociological discourse began—that is, intensely accenting disciplinary decadence, intellectual historical amnesia, and, of course, *epistemic apartheid*. From the foregoing we may confidently conclude that Du Bois's sociology of crime was insurgently intersectional and discursively dovetailed with his historical sociology, industrial sociology, urban sociology, rural sociology, sociology of education, and sociology of race. Even with all of the intersectionality within Du Bois's sociological world, his sociology of crime, similar to each of the other areas of his sociology examined in this book, exhibits limitations and inadequacies. However, I honestly believe, when the dialectic is brought to bear on his criminological contributions, Du Bois's work continues to offer much to those scholars and students in criminology who seek alternative etiologies and interpretive paradigms in light of ongoing African American criminality in particular, and American criminality in general. In fact, something similar could be averred with regard to the contributions that Du Bois's overarching sociological discourse continues to make to African American sociology in particular, and contemporary sociology in general. The following conclusion continues this line of logic by emphasizing the continued relevance of Du Bois's sociological contributions with regard to sociology in the twenty-first century.

NOTES

1. It is interesting to compare and contrast George Cable's (1885) classic *Silent South: Together with the Freedman's Case in Equity and the Convict-Lease System* with more contemporary interpretations of the convict-lease system, such as Blackmon (2008), Curtin (2000), Fierce (1994), Mancini (1996), and Nieman (1994). Each of these works informed my interpretation of the convict-lease system here and throughout the remainder of this chapter. I offer a more detailed discussion of the implications of Du Bois's classic critique of the convict-lease system for contemporary criminology and critiques of the prison industrial complex below.

2. Du Bois's early critique of what is today termed "differential justice" has been echoed by several contemporary criminologists and critical race theorists, such as Bhui (2009), Browne-Marshall (2007), Cook and Hudson (1993), Hendricks and Byers (1994), and Weitzer and Tuch (2006).

3. Because an anti-black racist violence and lynching leitmotif runs throughout the remainder of this chapter, it will be important at the outset to acknowledge the noteworthy works that have informed my interpretation of *anti-black racist vigilante violence*; see Brundage (1993), Nevels (2007), Waldrep (1998, 2001, 2002, 2006, 2009), and A. L. Wood (2009).

4. For a few of the more noteworthy works in criminological theory which informed my interpretation of the discursive formations and discursive practices within the discipline of criminology, see Cote (2002), Lilly, Cullen, and Ball (2007),

Hagan (2008), Henry and Einstadter (1998), McShane and Williams (2009), Moyer (2001), and Sumner (2004). Special emphasis should be placed on the ways in which my work has been indelibly influenced by what is coming to be called "critical criminology" or, rather, "radical criminology"—for instance, Carrington and Hogg (2002), Inciardi (1980), Lynch and Michalowski (2006), J. I. Ross (2009), Swaaningen (1997), and Taylor, Walton, and Young (1975).

5. Further discussion of Du Bois as a "classical conflict theorist" is provided below.

6. Du Bois's assertion that anti-black racist violent vigilantism frequently creates among the black "masses deep-seated sympathy with crime and criminals because they honestly believe them to be largely martyrs to race prejudice" prefigures the etiological research and discourse on "legal cynicism" of contemporary African American and critical race criminologists. Please see, for example, Carr, Napolitano, and Keating (2007), Cook and Hudson (1993), Gabbidon (2007, 2010), S. L. Miller (2007), and Sulton (1996).

7. For further discussion of the ways in which the so-called slave police of the antebellum period evolved into the Klu Klux Klan of post-Emancipation, Reconstruction, post-Reconstruction, and on through to the civil rights movement era, see Chalmers (1987), Horn (1939), Ingalls (1979), K. T. Jackson (1992), Kennedy (1990), Sims (1996), Stanton (1991), Trelease (1995), and Wade (1987).

8. Du Bois's discourse here concerning the ways in which the injustice of the U.S. criminal justice system ironically "increased crime and vagabondage to an enormous extent" among recently emancipated African Americans was echoed at the turn of the twenty-first century by John May and Khalid Pitts in their pioneering *Building Violence: How America's Rush to Incarcerate Creates More Violence* (2000).

9. In his autobiographical writings, Du Bois (1968a, 222; 1968b, 67) revealed the gruesome culminating event that forever altered his understanding of the relationship between social science and social reform—the much-lamented lynching of Sam Hose. Hose was an African American farmer in Palmetto, just outside of Atlanta, who reportedly had fatally shot a white farmer after a brewing dispute over a debt. Anti-black racist vigilante violence instantaneously reared its ugly head, and the mounting mob of three thousand quickly formed itself into a merciless makeshift judge, jury, and executioner. Not content with brutally beating, lynching, and then burning Hose's lifeless body, historical records indicate that white men, white women, and white children fiercely fought over pieces of his charred flesh for souvenirs—that is, mementos of their murderous violation of his human and civil rights. For further discussion of the lynching of Sam Hose, see E. T. Arnold (2009).

Conclusion

On Ending Epistemic Apartheid

Continuing Du Bois's Transdisciplinary Transgressions

> Yet, for much of Du Bois's long and productive life he was an empirical social scientist. He pioneered in the conduct of comprehensive community social surveys, in the documentation of black community life, and in the theoretically grounded analysis of black-white relations. Were it not for the deeply entrenched racism in the United States during his early professional years, Du Bois would be recognized alongside the likes of Albion Small, Edward A. Ross, Robert E. Park, Lewis Wirth, and W. I. Thomas as one of the fountainheads of American sociology. Had not racism so thoroughly excluded him from placement in the center of the academy, he might arguably have come to rank with Max Weber or Emile Durkheim in stature. Today, urban anthropologists, historical economists, political scientists, social psychologists, and sociologists all attempt to claim a piece of the Du Boisian legacy.
>
> Lawrence Bobo, "Reclaiming a Du Boisian Perspective on Racial Attitudes," 187

EPILOGUE OF INTELLECTUAL SEGREGATION: ON THE TRAJECTORY OF DU BOIS'S TRANSDISCIPLINARY GRADUATE TRAINING AND THE CONTINUED RELEVANCE OF HIS SOCIOLOGICAL CONTRIBUTIONS

The previous chapters register as radical challenges to the conventional history of sociology. Freeing ourselves from the narrow conceptual confines of intellectual historical amnesia, disciplinary decadence, and *epistemic apartheid*, we may conclude that W. E. B. Du Bois made several seminal contributions to the disciplinary development and ongoing discourses of sociology in general, and American sociology in particular. When and where Du Bois's work has been acknowledged within the sociological world, his early volumes *The Philadelphia Negro* and *The Souls of Black Folk* usually have been looked at exclusively for the ways in which they contribute to the sociology of race, urban sociology, and ethnography. However, *Against Epistemic Apartheid* has demonstrated and deconstructed the longstanding logical reductionism which always and everywhere relegates Du Bois to the sociology of race, urban sociology, and ethnography. Undoubtedly, as advanced in chapter 2, Du Bois was one of the first (if not the first "great") sociologists of race in the history of sociology. But, as the remainder of the foregoing chapters revealed, he should also be considered a peerless and pioneering sociologist in several other subdisciplinary areas such as research methods, social problems, community studies, population studies, historical sociology, political sociology, rural sociology, industrial sociology, sociology of culture, sociology of family, sociology of class, sociology of gender, sociology of religion, sociology of education, and, sociology of crime.

Du Bois consistently went against the conventional currents of early sociology. For instance, when sociology seemed to be moving in a more deductive methodological direction, Du Bois's 1904 essays "Sociology Hesitant" and "The Atlanta Conferences" offered extremely convincing arguments for extending the inductive methodological approach. Moreover, in his 1898 classic, "The Study of the Negro Problems," he inaugurated authentic African American Studies by advocating for the utilization of an inductive, interdisciplinary social scientific approach in efforts to not only identify and understand, but also offer viable solutions to African American problems. As was witnessed in the preceding chapters, Du Bois employed the theories and methodologies emerging from a wide range of disciplines: from sociology and political economy to history and anthropology. Similar to Marx, Foucault, and Habermas, history held a particularly special place in Du Bois's discursive domain, where he developed the habit of undertaking interdisciplinary "archaeologies"—à la Foucault more than half a century later—of the evolution of certain social problems and social institutions. However, one of the many things that distinguishes Du Bois's early sociology from Foucault's philosophy was Du Bois's intense emphasis on inductive, empirical research, which several Du Bois scholars have argued can be traced back to his doctoral studies in the Department of Political Economy at the University of Berlin (see Barkin, 2000; Broderick, 1958b; Lemke, 2000; Schafer, 2001, 2008).

Even before Du Bois's "*Wanderjahre* in Europe" (1968a), the noted Harvard historian Albert Bushnell Hart had exposed Du Bois to the Rankean method while he was working on his master's degree (159). Leopold von Ranke, a professor of history at the University of Berlin from 1825 to 1871, made his most lasting contribution to the historical method with his ironclad adherence to research techniques, most importantly emphasizing the strict use and citation of primary sources (i.e., historical empiricism), the reconfiguration of collected evidence, critical analysis, and narrative history. By the time Du Bois arrived at Friedrich-Wilhelms Universität zu Berlin in the autumn of 1892 the German historical school of economics was recognized as a bona fide *Gesellschaftwissenschaft*—i.e., social science (Balabkins, 1988; Grimmer-Solem, 2003; Shionoya, 2001). He was undoubtedly intellectually elated to be entering the University of Berlin, which he well-knew boasted august alumni and associates, such as Bismarck, Fichte, Schopenhauer, Hegel, Marx, Engels, Dilthey, and, most recently, Weber. Indeed, these were those wonderful "*Wanderjahre* in Europe"! Working primarily with Gustav von Schmoller, Heinrich von Treitschke, and Adolf Wagner, according to Barrington S. Edwards (2006), "Du Bois's association with Schmoller, Treitschke, and Wagner steered him in a direction that allowed him to 'unite . . . economics and politics' for his research" (405; see also Du Bois, 1968a, 154–82; Lewis, 1993, 117–49).

At the University of Berlin, Du Bois (1968a) recollected, "I came in contact with several of the great leaders of the developing social sciences: in economic sociology and in social history" (162). Berlin presented an extremely different intellectual environment when compared with Harvard's academic world. Du Bois's two main graduate studies mentors, Hart and Schmoller, at Harvard and Berlin, respectively, offered him comparably different methodological approaches: on the one hand, empirical *historical* research at Harvard, while, on the other hand, empirical *social* research at Berlin. Having studied at Harvard, Paris, Berlin, and Freiburg, Hart was intellectually grounded in the Rankean tradition; therefore, he advanced historical-empirical inquiry independent of speculative philosophy, preferring a commitment to the method of observation, experimentation, and induction. Noticeably, then, the Rankean methodological orientation did not allow Du Bois the possibility of emphasizing the moral or ethical implications of certain social problems (e.g., the political economy of anti-black racism within the context of American capitalism and European imperialism).[1] The German historical school of economics method, however, enabled Du Bois to use empirical social research in the interest of inductively informing social policy and social reform—i.e., *social ethics* was at the heart of, and a logical element in the overall enterprise. According to Edwards (2006), "It was Schmoller, especially, who led Du Bois toward the empirical social research that linked, rather amorphously, economics, statistics, sociology, and history" (405). Perhaps the pioneering Du Bois scholar Francis Broderick (1958b) put it best when he opened his classic essay "German Influence on the Scholarship of W. E. B. Du Bois" by asserting that Du Bois "went to Europe in 1892 an historian; he returned two years later a sociologist" (367). During his Berlin years, therefore, Du Bois's transdisciplinary training decidedly transcended the Rankean method, and arguably much of Hart's wholly historical method, and eventually came to encompass coursework in statistics, economics, politics, sociology, history, philosophy, and labor studies (see Du Bois, 1997a, 20–21, 26). What is more, Edwards (2006) argues, after his graduate studies at Berlin Du Bois went on to shift and shape, challenge and change the methods of the German historical school of economics to speak to the special needs of African Americans in particular, and the United States in general:

> Du Bois remained committed to empirical social research and refounded affinities to Schmoller's vision of science, he was in search of his own voice as a credible social scientist within the American context. Over time, he carved out his "own sociology"—to quote him—in an effort to change the field's methodological approach to social questions. Neither endeavor was an easy feat. Although this was not always clear from his early writings, Du Bois held on to a persistent faith that scientific research could aid in the moral quest to bring about racial uplift. With regard to executing his research, Du Bois was at key moments wedged between two extremes: his craft (science) and his race (the Negro Problem). As an African American social scientist, his double-consciousness—his intellectual dubiety—caused him to vacillate between his two roles as scientist and race man. Few American sociologists recognized Du Bois as a colleague during his time. This is ironic considering that sociology in the United States did not have a strict disciplinary focus, but was amorphous. (409)

Admittedly, then, Du Bois innovatively modified the methods of the German historical school of economics in his pursuit of solutions to African American social problems.[2] Building on, and going beyond what he learned under the tutelage of William James, Josiah Royce, George Santayana, Charles Francis Dunbar, Frank William Taussig, and Albert Bushnell Hart at Harvard, and Gustav von Schmoller, Heinrich von Treitschke, Adolf Wagner, Wilhelm Dilthey, Rudolf von Gneist, Max Lenz, Karl Oldenberg, and Max Sering at Berlin, Du Bois (1997a) singularly synthesized history with economics, and philosophy with politics (20–21, 26). Taking into critical consideration the fact that Du Bois earned his undergraduate degrees in classics and philosophy, and his graduate degrees in history and political economy, African American economist Thomas Boston (1991) asserts that it is important not to overlook the fact that Du Bois actually earned his doctorate in both "history and political economy" (303). The W. E. B. Du Bois Papers at the University of Massachusetts reveal that Du Bois himself characterized his transdisciplinary graduate training as being, first and foremost, in the field of political science and secondarily in history. His 1891 letter to President Rutherford B. Hayes, which listed James, Hart, Taussig, and Peabody along with half a dozen other Harvard professors as well as the then-president of Harvard as references, read in part, "I have no money or property myself and am an orphan. My particular field in Political Science is the History of African Slavery from the economic and social standpoint" (Du Bois, 1997a, 11).

Although often overlooked, it is extremely important to emphasize Du Bois's graduate studies in history *and* political science prior to his doctoral coursework in the Department of Political Economy at the University of Berlin. Which is to say, based on his own weighted words, Du Bois's doctoral studies under the tutelage of Schmoller, Treitschke, Wagner, Dilthey, and the other members of the German historical school of economics extended and greatly expanded his prior graduate work in history and political science at Harvard. In other words, Du Bois had every intention of earning his doctorate in political economy from the University of Berlin, and his award of a doctorate in history and political science from Harvard ultimately and ironically boiled down to the simple fact that, in his own woeful words, "I have no money or property myself and am an orphan." David Levering Lewis (1993) helps to corroborate this claim by observing that the only reason Du Bois was not granted his doctorate in political economy from the University of Berlin was consequent to the fact that the Slater Fund refused to renew his scholarship (143-49). "Du Bois's failure to win the German doctorate resulted from a combination of the adventitious and the sinister," Lewis lamented (145). He went on to say, "Despite Schmoller's and Wagner's support and the dean's assurances, spirited objections from the senior professor of chemistry . . . precluded Du Bois's exemption from the requirement of four completed semesters before a student was permitted to stand for the doctoral examination" (145). The matter stubbornly did not stop there; apparently Du Bois's German professors felt strongly enough about his candidacy for the *Doktor der Philosophie* in political economy from the University of Berlin that "Wagner wrote a strong letter of support to the trustees, as did Schmoller, who pointed out that German universities required six semesters' work for the Ph.D., and that one semester was occasionally trimmed or, in Du Bois's case, even two ('because we were able to express so favorable an opinion'), but due to the chemistry-professor complication, unfortunately not three" (145-46).

As mentioned in the introduction, three months before he earned his second bachelor's degree—*cum laude*, in philosophy under the auspices of William James in 1890—Du Bois petitioned the Harvard Academic Council for scholarship assistance to pursue a PhD in social science. Even at this early age he was already clear on how he wanted to use his PhD in "the field of *social science* under *political science*," he unapologetically announced, "with a view to the ultimate application of its principles to the social and economic advancement of the Negro people" (Du Bois, 1997a, 7, all emphasis in original). In his autobiography Du Bois detailed his quandary as follows: "Then came the question as to whether I could continue my study in the graduate school. I had no resources in wealth or friends." Yet Du Bois (1968a) intoned, "I applied for a fellowship in the graduate school of Harvard and was appointed Henry Bromfield Rogers Fellow for a year and later the appointment was renewed; so that from 1890 to 1892 I was a fellow at Harvard University, studying history and political science and what would have been sociology if Harvard as yet recognized such a field" (148–49).[3]

This means, then, that even before he was exposed to the *Gesellschaftwissenschaft* and *Staatwissenschaften* of the German historical school of economics, Du Bois patently had plans to use his PhD in "the field of *social science* under *political science* . . . with a view to the ultimate application of its principles to the social and economic advancement of the Negro people." He candidly concluded, "Thus in my quest for basic knowledge with which to help guide the American Negro I came to the study of sociology, by way of philosophy and history rather than by physics and biology" (149). The most important point that I wish to emphasize here is that Du Bois had already undertaken interdisciplinary studies in philosophy, history, political science, economics, and "what would have been sociology if Harvard as yet recognized such a field" prior to his doctoral studies in the Department of Political Economy at the University of Berlin. He, consequently, was not a *Negro tabula rasa* or, rather, black blank slate upon arrival at the University of Berlin (see Du Bois, 1997a, 15–16).

Undeniably, let it be solemnly said, Du Bois's studies at Harvard and Berlin indelibly influenced his later development of an innovative *transdisciplinary* methodological orientation. However, his distinctive contributions to, and the ways in which his postdoctoral work went well beyond, the research methods and modes of analysis he was exposed to during his graduate studies should not be discursively diminished. Du Bois had a fierce sense of intellectual independence that only increased after he earned his doctorate in "history and political economy" from Harvard in 1895. He went on to become the first scholar to discursively develop an inductive, empirical social science "with a view to the ultimate application of its principles to the social and economic advancement of the Negro people." Without hyperbole or high-sounding words, then, it should be sincerely said that this intellectual history-making honor belongs to Du Bois, and Du Bois alone. Which is also to say, no matter what he may have giddily gathered from Hart, Schmoller, Treitschke, Wagner, or Dilthey, among others, Du Bois's distinction continues to revolve around the ways in which his work helped to inaugurate both American sociology and African American studies. On the one hand, it could be said that above all else this is precisely why Du Bois should be recognized, along with Marx, Weber, and Durkheim, as one of the founders of sociology. On the other hand, as this book has demonstrated, ironically it may very well be because of his intense focus on *American* social problems in general, and *African American* social problems in particular, that Du Bois's discourse has suffered from sociology's ongoing intellectual historical amnesia, disciplinary decadence, and *epistemic apartheid*.

Again, David Levering Lewis's (1993) words find their way into the fray, summing up Du Bois's decade of study at Fisk, Harvard, and Berlin. He stated, "This was his ego's learning decade, the ten or more years when the life and destiny of Africans in America merged inseparably with his own" (81). Then, he revealingly wrote, "But the transformation, though remarkably quick and thorough, proceeded unevenly, and, occasionally, even faltered. It took Du Bois time and considerable effort to become himself" (81). Indeed, Du Bois's coming into himself and his increasing intellectual independence began to show itself with greater and greater frequency and then increasing consistency after he earned his much-coveted doctorate. Hence, his postdoctoral publications, from "The Conservation of Races" in 1897 through to *The Philadelphia Negro* in 1899, reveal the remarkable acuity with which Du Bois doggedly approached the process of discursively developing "his own voice as a credible social scientist within the American context," to go back to Barrington Edwards's words. The Atlanta University Conference publications Du Bois edited between 1898 and 1914, therefore, should be considered the crowning achievements and proof-positive that he indeed did develop his own distinct intellectual identity. His work in philosophy, history, and political science at Harvard, coupled with his work in social history and political economy at Berlin, enabled Du Bois to chart the changing dynamics and dilemmas of African American social problems: from the era of enslavement through to the post-Emancipation period, from the Reconstruction and post-Reconstruction periods through to the first quarter of the twentieth century. In order to adequately trace the historical evolution of specific social issues, African American or otherwise, Du Bois discursively developed his sociological signature: *methodological triangulation*.

With regard to Du Bois's early research trademark *methodological triangulation*, in brief, he would identify a specific issue: say, for instance, black criminality. As discussed in the previous chapter, he would introduce current census data on black crime trends and then compare the census data with facts and figures gathered from small area studies and local surveys. These data would be further contrasted with ethnographic data collected personally by Du Bois or by his graduate students under his auspices. It is in this way that Du Bois's work discursively developed from a micrological to a macrological level; hence, his emphasis on an interdisciplinary inductive approach to African American social problems. Clearly, then, as discussed in chapter 1, *The Philadelphia Negro*, "The Negroes of Farmville," and "The Negro in the Black Belt" provide excellent examples of three comprehensive classic social studies that make use of his trademark *methodological triangulation*.

Similar to his contributions to research methods, Du Bois's donations to social problems discourse continue to be neglected within sociological circles. However, "The Study of the Negro Problems" was arguably one of the earliest and most provocative programmatic essays on the characteristics and consequences of absolutely "American" social problems presented in the United States during the last decade of the nineteenth century. Here, once again, we return to Du Bois's offerings to strain or anomie theory in light of the fact that, it will be recalled, in "The Study of the Negro Problems" he discursively defined "social problems" as a group's perception or outright recognition of the discrepancy between its concrete social conditions (i.e., what is) and its deeply desired social standing (i.e., what could or should be). Furthermore, with *The Philadelphia Negro* Du Bois's discourse on "social problems" can be said to have moved from the meta-theoretical and meta-methodological musings of "The Study of the Negro Problems" to actual application with regard to the social issues facing Philadelphia's African American community. What is more, each and every one of the Atlanta University Conference studies represents case studies of particular social problems.

Although the Chicago School is usually credited with pioneering more micrological or local surveys and community studies in the United States, the publication of *The Philadelphia Negro* preceded the formation of the said school by more than two decades. Moreover, as mentioned at the outset of *Against Epistemic Apartheid*, Earl Wright (2002a, 2002b, 2002c, 2005), Shaun Gabbidon (1999), and Robert Wortham (2005b, 2005c) have each put forward extremely convincing cases with respect to recognizing the sociology program at Atlanta University under Du Bois's auspices as the first school of sociology in the United States (see also Rabaka, 2010b; Rudwick, 1957c; R. A. Wortham, 2009b). As chapter 1 illustrated, Du Bois's local surveys and community studies (i.e., his micrological studies predicated on his trademark *methodological triangulation*) began in earnest with the 1898 publication of "The Negroes of Farmville," which symbolizes a significant contribution to rural sociology, rural ethnography, and rural ecology. Something very similar could be argued with regard to "The Negro in the Black Belt," "The Negro Landholder of Georgia," "The Negroes of Dougherty County, Georgia," "The Negro Farmer," and "The Sharecropping System in Lowndes County, Alabama," each of which, in one way or another, contributes to rural sociology, rural ethnography, and rural ecology. As aforementioned, Du Bois's Philadelphia study offers one of the first efforts in urban sociology, urban ecology, and urban ethnography published in the United States. The Atlanta University Conference publications he edited usually contained research based on local surveys and focused on local conditions. In fact, in his 1900 classic, "The Twelfth Census and the Negro Problems," Du Bois adamantly argued that micrological or local social studies frequently proved to provide both intricate and indispensable details about a specific social problem or social condition that census data and other macrological studies could not.

Du Bois made two of the earliest book-length contributions to population studies in the United States with *The Philadelphia Negro* and his 1906 Atlanta University Conference volume, *The Health and Physique of the Negro American*. Both volumes addressed the issues of population size, population dynamics (i.e., family, fertility, mortality, and migration), spatial distribution, and composition. As chapter 1 revealed, as early as "The Negroes of Farmville" and *The Philadelphia Negro* Du Bois detected a gender imbalance within the African American community (i.e., more women than men), making him one of the first sociologists to make such an observation. It is also important to note that Du Bois's discussion of African American migration from rural regions to urban environments—first, to ghettoes and, then, if financially feasible, into more affluent areas—prefigured the research of Robert Park, Ernest Burgess, and Roderick McKenzie's 1925 classic *The City*, among the work of other Chicago School sociologists, by more than a quarter of a century. Connecting capitalist political economy with the political economy of anti-black racism in the United States, Du Bois advanced that many of the distinct differences in black and white morality were a consequence of the majority of African Americans' lower class status and the poor quality of their lives. Deeply disturbed by the alarming number of African Americans plagued with "consumption," he argued that it was, in essence, a "social disease," which could be remedied with an adequate diet, regular exercise, access to better housing, and proper ventilation—hence, his work here also has implications for the sociology of disease (see also Reed, 1997, 27-34).

Although often interpreted as a "race man," chapter 3 accented the fallacy of single-mindedly focusing on Du Bois's contributions to the sociology of race without connecting them to his critical contributions to the sociology of gender. Undoubtedly, Du Bois's classical sociology of gender is distinctly different from contemporary sociology of gender. However, when viewed from the vantage point of black feminist sociology, Du Bois's "The Damnation of Women" and "The Freedom of Womanhood," among others, were shown to provide solutions to the "gender problem" and, even more, several of the most pressing social problems of working-class black women, which patently prefigured the emergence of intersectional sociology in the late twentieth and early twenty-first centuries. Amazingly, particularly when compared with the work of others (especially white male sociologists) of his era, Du Bois's discourse eventually evolved into an inchoate intersectional framework that, according to Susan Gillman and Alys Eve Weinbaum in *Next to the Color-Line: Gender, Sexuality, and W. E. B. Du Bois* (2007), "juxtaposed" race *with* gender *with* class to such an innovative extent that they audaciously announced "there could hardly be a more opportune time than the present to reengage his writings from the widest possible conceptual and historical vantage point" (1–2). In Du Bois studies there has been a long history of disrupting and disconnecting (as opposed to, à la Du Bois himself, transdisciplinarily *intersecting, interconnecting,* and *juxtaposing*) the various social problems he identified, critiqued, and sought solutions to, which in many ways erases or, at the least, renders intellectually invisible the implicit or veiled *racially gendered critical logic and language* at play in, and that is part and parcel of his renowned discourse on race and racism.

As observed in chapter 4, Du Bois contributed the first comprehensive and empirical sociological study of a religious institution in the United States with *The Negro Church*. Not only do the case studies contained in the volume document religious trends on the local level, but also the often-detailed descriptions of particular congregational practices foreshadowed what contemporary sociologists of religion have come to call "congregational studies." Long hailed as "the founder of the sociology of African American religion and black church studies," with *The Souls of Black Folk, The Negro Church,* and *Morals and Manners Among Negro Americans* Du Bois's research reverberated throughout the twentieth century and into the twenty-first century by providing a paradigm and point of departure for the noted studies of Mays and Nicholson (1933), Frazier (1974), Lincoln and Mamiya (1990), Billingsley (1999), and McRoberts (2003).

After exposing the reader to Du Bois's early intersectional sociology and sociology of religion in chapters 1–4, chapter 5 engaged the ways in which his historical and cultural sociology interconnected with and indelibly impacted his sociology of education. Along with his other sociological innovations, it was emphasized that upon its publication in 1900 Du Bois's *The College-Bred Negro* was the first social scientific study of African Americans in higher education. Yet again, Du Bois's sociological discourse proved unprecedented. Instead of the static and stoic aristocratic architect of the theory of the talented tenth, the fifth chapter revealed a Du Bois who was not afraid to fiercely dance with the dialectic and openly disagree with his own previous positions. The tired tendency to (mis)read Du Bois as a lifelong elitist and Eurocentrist was consistently called into question, and his sociology of education, similar to his sociological discourse in general, was shown to be ever-evolving, self-reflexive, and extremely relevant with regard to contemporary sociology of education, especially African American education. Indeed, Derrick Alridge's assertion that "[n]o other African American or other American scholar has ever offered as comprehensive a set of educational ideas for black people as did Du Bois" was shown to be squarely based on a body of work that has yet to be seriously engaged by contemporary sociologists of education.

As argued in the preceding chapter, Du Bois provided one of the earliest sociological inquiries concerning crime in the United States with the 1904 publication of *Some Notes on Negro Crime*. In employing a more contextual approach to crime by focusing on the interconnections between crime and race, crime and class, and crime and education, Du Bois early established the relationship between crime and social status, crime and social conditions, and crime and illiteracy. Du Bois's sociology of crime connected black criminality to several anti-black racist social institutions and cultural conventions, such as African American enslavement, post-Emancipation Proclamation white supremacist violent vigilantism, the crop-lien system, the convict-lease system, white privilege, planned black poverty, poor education (along with intentional miseducation), and the general lack of provisions for recreational and other amusement activities for black youth. There is a remarkable resemblance between Du Bois's sociology of crime and Robert Merton's "Social Structure and Anomie" (1938), where Merton initially advanced his strain theory. What is more, Du Bois's sociology of crime appears to also prefigure several other theories and discursive devices en vogue in contemporary criminological communities, such as critical race theory, social structure theory, social disorganization theory, subcultural theory, conflict theory, social ecology, disproportionality, differential justice, and racial profiling.

After taking all of this into consideration we seem to have come full circle, returning to the critical questions with which we began *Against Epistemic Apartheid*: Why has Du Bois's sociological legacy suffered sociological negation? Why have his contributions to the aforementioned sociological subdisciplines been excluded, ignored, or erased in the century since the founding of the American Sociological Association? In what ways does Du Bois's obvious absence from most classical, and very many contemporary histories of sociology's disciplinary development and discursive formations speak in special ways about American sociology's ongoing intellectual historical amnesia, disciplinary decadence, and, even more, its participation in *epistemic apartheid*? However, truth be told, sociology has not been alone in its negation of Du Bois's discourse. Indeed, there has been a longstanding intellectual eclipse hauntingly hovering over Du Bois's insurgent intellectual and radical political legacy—i.e., his oeuvre—in general when and where we come to the annals of the American academy throughout the twentieth century and well past the first decade of the twenty-first century.

AFRICANA STUDIES AND ANTIDISCIPLINARITY: LIFTING THE CONCEPTUAL QUARANTINE THAT DU BOIS'S DISCURSIVE FORMATIONS AND DISCURSIVE PRACTICES HAVE LONG LIVED IN

In truth, one of the reasons that there are so few serious studies of Du Bois's discourse involves the racial exclusionary discursive practices and the embedded institutionalized racism of many traditional academic disciplines—hence, my discursive development of a critical theory of *epistemic apartheid*.[4] Du Bois has never received his due recognition in disciplines, above and beyond sociology, he helped to establish or significantly contributed to—disciplines such as history, philosophy, religion, political science, economics, education, criminology, and anthropology, among others (see Anderson and Zuberi, 2000; Bell, Grosholz, and Stewart, 1996; Blackwell and Janowitz, 1974; Katz and Sugrue, 1998; Rabaka, 2010b; Zamir, 2008). His transdisciplinary discourse, consistently defying and redefining conventional academic culture, radical politics, and critical social theory, serves as heresy for many single subject–focused monodisciplinary scholars. Deeply connected to the American academy, state-sanctioned politics often point to academic anxieties over not simply radical social change, but also critical theoretical revolution(s). Furthermore, similar to academics (as opposed to *insurgent intellectual-activists*) in a repressed society, the politics of the established order repudiates transformations of consciousness that incite treasonous thoughts and/or seditious acts against the state. The highest treason, then, is that which lays hold of the hearts and minds of the masses and problematizes and destabilizes the "divine" authority and "democracy" of the government and their academic arm.

Undoubtedly, Du Bois's founding of the first civil rights organization in U.S. history, the NAACP, his pioneering leadership of the international Pan-African movement, and his eventual embrace of democratic socialism caused the U.S. government to perceive him as a real threat to "American democracy." His FBI file and his 1952 memoir *In Battle for Peace* concretely reveal as much (see Du Bois, 1952; Federal Bureau of Investigation, 1995, 2009). In other words, what began as an inductive, interdisciplinary, albeit purely academic association of social science with social reform (i.e., *Staatswissenschaften* à la Schmoller and the German historical school of economics) during his graduate studies in the Department of Political Economy at the University of Berlin ultimately translated itself into a treasonous transdisciplinary preoccupation with relating social science to radical democratic socialist transformation in light of the racist, sexist, and classist contradictions of U.S. social institutions and cultural conventions. Considering the bourgeois pretensions and general conservatism of the majority of American academics (black, white, or otherwise) throughout the twentieth century and well into the twenty-first century, the question begs: Is it any wonder, then, that Du Bois's discourse has not only suffered from "sociological negation" and "disciplinary decadence" within the world of the social sciences but, even more, from the constant conceptual quarantining of the ever illusive *epistemic apartheid* that has long plagued the American academy?

African American political economist James Stewart (1984) argues that another reason scholars have had a hard time with or simply do not engage Du Bois's oeuvre is because "Du Bois rejected the fragmentation of experience into disciplinary compartments, the attempt by the social sciences to use the natural sciences as a developmental model, because he believed that it was, in fact, man who causes 'movement and change'" (305).[5] Thus, it is Du Bois's trenchant transdisciplinarity in the interest of radically transforming the conditions of continental and diasporan Africa and Africans, along with other oppressed and struggling people, that challenges and, perhaps even more, dumbfounds traditional monodisciplinary theorists and at the same time accents the fact that he was, indeed, an undeniable architect of the transdisciplinary human science of Africana studies, as well as an authentic critical social theorist. But, again, critical sociologists and Africana studies scholars must do more than merely claim Du Bois as a transdisciplinary intellectual-activist ancestor; they must comprehensively and accessibly engage his corpus for its contribution to their respective insurgent intellectual arenas and radical political agendas. This means, then, critically engaging Du Bois's discourse as a *resource* rather than a mere *reference* or intellectual artifact. In other words, now that we are aware of his unprecedented and enormous offerings to sociology in particular, and the social sciences in general, how can we critically build on and go beyond his corpus in our earnest efforts to advance a critical theory of twenty-first-century society? Surely sincere sociologists and other social scientists will candidly concede that this is precisely what is currently happening with the work of Marx, Weber, and Durkheim, among other classical sociologists and social scientists, as we transition from the twentieth century into the twenty first century.

Another reason Du Bois has been and continues to be overlooked in the academy is because of his unorthodox appropriation and eclectic utilization of multiple methodologies (i.e., his trademark *methodological triangulation*), what Stewart (1984) dubbed "Du Bois's increasing belief in the complementarity of methodologies" (302). This issue is directly and deeply connected to Du Bois's transdisciplinarity and, again, helps to highlight his status as the doyen of Africana studies discourse and a major contributor to both critical methodological and critical theoretical discourse (see Rabaka, 2007b, 2008a, 2009a). His multi-methodological approach manifested itself most in groundbreaking scholarly studies, such as *The Philadelphia Negro, The Souls of Black Folk, The Negro, Darkwater, The Gift of Black Folk, Black Reconstruction, Black Folk, Then and Now, Color and Democracy,* and *The World and Africa,* among others; innumerable efforts at autobiography—for instance, *Darkwater, Dusk of Dawn, In Battle for Peace,* and *The Autobiography of W. E. B. Du Bois;* edited volumes, specifically the Atlanta University Conference studies; editorship of and publications in periodicals, such as *The Moon, The Horizon, The Crisis,* and *Phylon;* literally hundreds of critical essays and scholarly articles on a staggeringly wide range of topics; public intellectualism, political activism, and participation in national and international social movements, such as Pan-Africanism, the Niagara movement, the NAACP, the New Negro movement, the Harlem Renaissance, the civil rights movement, the women's liberation movement, and the peace movement, among others; and countless creative writings, which encompass novels, short stories, poetry, and plays. Stewart (1984) also stated that "Du Bois's early rejection of his socialization as a classically trained traditional Western scholar and the subsequent self-definition of an alternative program bear[s] strong similarities to Black Studies" (303). From this angle, then, Du Bois is not simply an architect of Africana studies, but a paradigmatic figure who could (and, I think, indeed *does*) provide many Africana studies scholars and critical social theorists lost in the labyrinth of the academy of the twenty-first century with intellectual guidance and political direction.

Du Bois's multi-methodological approach prefigures contemporary Africana studies' methodologies in that it was deeply dialectical, critical of traditional disciplines' omission of important intersectional (i.e., race, gender, class, and cultural) issues, and interested in drawing from and contributing to continental and diasporan African political-theoretical and social-activist traditions. His conception of the "complementarity of methodologies," along with his consistent focus on both continental and diasporan African social and political issues, simultaneously places him in the transdisciplinary intellectual arena now known as *Africana studies* and challenges those social scientists in traditional disciplines who would, in the most narrow-minded and monodisciplinary manner imaginable, claim Du Bois for their specific disciplines or disciplinary agendas. Commenting on Du Bois's conception of the "complementarity of methodologies," Stewart asserted that Du Bois's multi-methodological approach to the Africana experience was not simply theoretical eclecticism on his part, but a conscious effort to critically comprehend continental and diasporan African history, culture, and struggle in its totality and complexity. Stewart (1984) further stated that

> Du Bois perceived that certain methodologies of analysis and styles of presentation were more appropriate than others for capturing the complexity of the Black experience and for communicating that complexity in a manner that

generated new insights for non-Blacks and self-reflection among Blacks leading to social action. There is no doubt that Du Bois's methodological predilections violated traditional standards of historical research. . . . To understand Du Bois's methodology it is necessary to examine the connotation of the word "fact" as it relates to social science. What constitutes fact in social science is that which can be verified with respect to a particular paradigm. Throughout his career, Du Bois operated from a mind-set that posited the existence of systematic biases in the determination of what constituted "fact" with respect to the Black experience. Consequently, to seek substantial correspondence between his interpretation and the conventional wisdom was necessarily self-defeating. A more salient strategy was to construct alternative explanations and subject them to testing procedures that were indigenous to the alternative paradigm. This is what Du Bois did. At the same time, Du Bois was always concerned with preserving his reputation as a bona fide scholar among traditionalists. . . . Du Bois's increasing disenchantment with the methodology of the traditional social sciences took a variety of forms. (303–5)

Du Bois's emphasis on "alternative explanations," the development of an "alternative paradigm," and, as Stewart put it elsewhere, "a non-traditional program of instruction" does not simply resonate with contemporary Africana studies; it is the transdisciplinary human science's very conceptual core (307). Therefore, Du Bois's multi-methodological approach is inextricable from his transgressive transdisciplinarity, both of which place him well beyond the boundaries of traditional disciplines and their monodisciplinary maneuvers. As I have argued in chapter 5 of the present volume, Du Bois's sociology of education points to Africana studies' "non-traditional program of instruction," and it reveals Africana philosophy of education to be, in essence, a critical educational theory that is geared toward translating theory into progressive social praxis (Rabaka, 2003c, 2008a). However, the range and reach of Du Bois's discourse amazingly does not stop here.

Constantly cutting across disciplines and breaking through artificial academic boundaries, Du Bois's discourse is decidedly dialectical, meaning it does not simply challenge traditional disciplines, but it also offers an internal challenge to, and critique of, nontraditional disciplines or emerging fields of critical inquiry, such as—and I am thinking here most especially of—Africana studies. Du Bois challenges Africana studies scholars, and particularly the self-conscious discipline definers and developers, to beware of the pitfalls of disciplinary decadence and the poison of *intellectual esotericism*. If, indeed, Africana studies is a progressive social praxis-promoting transdisciplinary human science, then Africana studies scholars (and their authentic intellectual-activist allies) must constantly be concerned with critical consciousness-raising, radical politics, critical theoretical revolutions, and—I should strongly stress—world-historical, national and international, real-life social and political revolutions and movements geared toward not only black liberation, but also multiracial and transethnic human liberation, women's liberation and gender justice, revolutionary decolonization, revolutionary democratic socialist, and sexual orientation-sensitive (among other egalitarian) alternatives.

All of this brings to mind Arnold Rampersad's (1996) now legendary remarks concerning Du Bois's discursive challenge to disciplinary development and disciplinary decadence. He argues that there are aspects of Du Bois's work that are actually *antidisciplinary*, by which he means that Du Bois's corpus contains several texts that not only problematize but go utterly against the whole notion of an academic discipline. As Du Bois poignantly pointed out, particularly in his autobiographical writings, after he published his 1899 classic *The Philadelphia Negro* and then was unable to find funding to support his Atlanta University Conference studies, he lost faith in a purely social scientific or academic solution to African American and Pan-African social and political problems (see Du Bois, 1968a, 1968b; see also Lewis, 1993, chapter 9). Along with his loss of intellectual faith came an intense critique of the disciplinary decadence and *epistemic apartheid* of the academy and, more specifically, the arbitrariness and artificiality of academic disciplines. His intellectual soul-searching led him to develop scholastic and political positions that, Rampersad contends, parallel many of the critical social theories in vogue within "the volatile dynamic of American intellectual life today." Rampersad (1996) discursively detailed the following:

> If it would be difficult to relate Du Bois directly . . . to those intricacies of deconstruction and poststructuralism that have seized the attention of large sections of the American academy in the past dozen years or so, his life and career are connected nevertheless both to certain direct aspects of these intellectual forces and to certain germane trends and tensions. I refer both to the rise of relatively new and discrete disciplines and departments and to our vastly increased sense of the benefits of the interdisciplinary approach. I am thinking also about the growing tension between traditional humanistic discourse and the new antihumanist and posthumanist emphasis that has surfaced so strongly among the latest generation of scholars, and definitely among many of the brightest and most politically engaged among them. In Du Bois, I would suggest, one sees elements of this antihumanism and posthumanism peering out in spite of the deep commitment to humanism that Du Bois long cherished. I have referred to disciplinarity and interdisciplinarity; but I am also thinking of the increasing tendency of the cultural studies movement toward an anti-disciplinarity that is distinct from interdisciplinarity. In other words, I refer to important elements in the volatile dynamic of American intellectual life today, which is itself but a token of the volatile and sometimes ominous quality of contemporary American culture in general; and I see Du Bois, born almost 125 years ago and dead now almost 30 years, as having been intimately involved, in one way or another, in many of these questions I have mentioned. (290-91)

Building on Rampersad's bold assertions here, I would like to take this line of logic one step further by reiterating that Du Bois's discourse is indeed *antidisciplinary* and, even more, when situated within the worlds of traditional academic disciplines, it shows itself to be distinctly transdisciplinary—i.e., it, literally, transcends and transgresses the borders and boundaries of disciplines. Rampersad is right; Du Bois's discourse can be said to prefigure not only posthumanist, poststructuralist, postmodernist, and postcolonialist thought, but also several traditions of critical thought internal to, and emanating from contemporary Africana studies. For instance, Rampersad (1996) observed that Du Bois was instrumental in establishing the diasporan dimension of Africana studies with his seminal 1915 text, *The Negro*. Furthermore, in his magisterial *Black Marxism*, Cedric Robinson (2000) argued that Du Bois was one of the first persons of African descent to systematically and critically study Marxism, developing many of the first race-class theories and, consequently, he aided in inaugurating "black Marxism." Noted Du Bois scholar Elliott Rudwick (1982a) contentiously corroborated Robinson's claims when he observed that "Du Bois was both a pioneering advocate of black capitalism, and later was one of the country's most prominent black Marxists," although, Rudwick went on to assert, "his quasi-socialistic brand of economic nationalism was never widely accepted" (64, 78).

Du Bois's thought resists restriction to a single academic discipline and does, indeed, harbor aspects of what could be called an *antidisciplinary* approach to knowledge and phenomena. However, Du Bois's antidisciplinarity dovetails with Africana studies' current emphasis on interdisciplinarity, multidisciplinarity, transdisciplinarity, and supradisciplinarity.[6] In this sense, Du Bois was intellectually and politically prophetic, not necessarily in his ability to foresee the future, but in his ability to anticipate future political developments and discursive dilemmas. Du Bois's antidisciplinarity offers contemporary Africana studies scholars a caveat: We must be wary of those among us who would attempt to make Africana studies a discursively derivative black version of traditional white disciplines, severing the connection between blacks on the campus and the black community, creating an intellectual oasis in the academy that caters to the wishes and whims of whites and only speaks of and to the black community in condescending and acrimonious tones.

DU BOIS, SOCIAL SCIENCE, AND THE CRISES OF CRITICAL SOCIAL THEORY

Du Bois's work has previously been engaged and presented in one-dimensional ways that obscure its resilience and relevance for contemporary cultural critique, radical politics, and revolutionary social movements. One-sided biographical and intellectual-historical studies of Du Bois that read and render his thought and texts in arbitrary and artificial terms not only obfuscate Du Bois's intellectual past—and, therefore, much of modern continental and diasporan African intellectual history—but these studies also adumbrate (classical and contemporary) Africana studies' contributions to the quickly emerging interdisciplinary intellectual present. As I have endeavored to illustrate in the foregoing chapters of this book, Du Bois was an early transdisciplinarian whose history- and culture-centered theorizings consistently identified key sociopolitical problems and utilized a wide range of research spanning the entire spectrum of the disciplines in an effort to produce viable solutions to those problems. The "problems" that Du Bois's thought sought to grasp and grapple with went well beyond the realm of race and racism, and often encompassed other enigmatic issues, such as sexism, civil rights, capitalism, (neo)colonialism, religion, education, and crime, all of which remain on both liberal social reform and radical political movements' agendas.

Although his work is most frequently read for its contributions to the critique of racism, and white supremacy in particular, Du Bois actually understood racism to be one of many interlocking systems of oppression that threaten not only the souls of black folk, but also the heart and soul of all humanity. As Du Bois developed his discourse, various discursive themes and critical theories were either embraced or rejected contingent upon particular historical and cultural conditions, which, reiteratively, help to highlight the fact that his social science—geared toward, first, social reform and, later, social revolution—was deeply grounded in history and culture. The deep historical and cultural dimension in Du Bois's thought suggests that he took seriously the role of a critical social theorist as someone who is concerned with crises in human life and who is committed to constantly (re)conceptualizing what is essential to human liberation and creating a new, decidedly more democratic social(ist) world. As a critical social theorist, Du Bois's distinction is undoubtedly apparent when we note his ability to synthesize sociology, historical studies, cultural criticism, radical political theory, and economic analysis with social philosophy and public policy in an effort to 1) discover the fundamental features of contemporary society; 2) identify its most promising potentialities and paths to a liberated future; and 3) accessibly advance ways that the current society could be transformed to realize these newly identified egalitarian goals.[7]

As far back as his classic essay "The Study of the Negro Problems," Du Bois (1898b) declared, "Whenever any nation allows impulse, whim or hasty conjecture to usurp the place of conscious, normative, intelligent action, it is in grave danger. The sole aim of any society is to settle its problems in accordance with its highest ideals, and the only rational method of accomplishing this is to study those problems in the light of the best scientific research" (10). Sidestepping the scientism and quest for rationalism in the quote, Du Bois seems to suggest two things. First, just as society changes, so too must the social science that seeks not simply to chart those changes, but to have an emancipatory influence on them. And, second, social science must be much more *critical*, meaning it is imperative for it to constantly carry out ideological critique, as there are many imperial and neo-imperial "impulse[s], whim[s]," and "hasty conjecture[s]" that are blocking human beings from realizing their "higher ideals."[8]

Conventionally Du Bois's corpus has been categorized as falling into three distinct stages: first, there is his early elitist, empirical social scientist, and quasi-cultural nationalist stage, from 1896 to 1903; second, his Pan-African socialist or "black Marxist" middle stage, from 1904 to 1935; and, third, his revolutionary democratic socialist, radical humanist, insurgent internationalist, and peace activist final stage, from 1936 to the end of his life in 1963 (see Broderick, 1959; DeMarco, 1983; Moore, 1981; Rudwick, 1968; Wolters, 2001). Many problems, however, arise when Du Bois's discourse is periodized and interpreted in this way. At first issue is the simple fact that this scheme shrouds the complexity and trenchant transdisciplinarity of the first and second stages and, therefore, does not adequately prepare or equip social scientists of the present age with the intellectual history and conceptual tools necessary to critically interpret and understand Du Bois's later life ("third stage") ruptures with his early elitism and mid-period political radicalism. Earlier in this conclusion, I have demonstrated that Du Bois's thought does not fit into the nice and neat conceptual categories of traditional disciplines, but may best be interpreted by examining it as *transdisciplinary human science with emancipatory intent*. What appears to many Du Bois scholars and critics as three distinct stages in his oeuvre is actually a single, protracted, critical, and conjunctive thought process (i.e., the discursive development of a critical social theory) that—on careful and close reading—reveals recurring themes of *epistemic openness* and *radical political receptiveness*.

Throughout each of the "three stages," Du Bois's writings return again and again to the critique of domination and discrimination, human liberation, democratic political action, and radical social transformation. Although he began with bourgeois (and sometimes even Eurocentric imperialist) notions of social uplift, by the so-called second stage Du Bois was clearly collapsing conventional social scientific categories and exploring new social identities and programs of radical political action.[9] He incorporated a wide range of academic theory and grass roots political praxis into his burgeoning critical social theoretical framework; thus, his thought displays an unusual openness to, and critical engagement of black nationalism, black separatism, Ethiopianism, Pan-Africanism, African communalism, Marxism, Leninism,

Maoism, German romanticism, German nationalism, British socialism, American pragmatism, Third Worldism, multiculturalism, feminism, and womanism, among other thought traditions.

It would seem that the leitmotifs in Du Bois's thought would make his ideas more accessible and easier to interpret. However, it must be emphasized that although there are many recurring themes in his writings, he consistently revised his social theory and political analysis throughout each of the "three stages." Consequently, there are specific issues—usually race, gender, and class issues—that transgress the traditional "three stages" conceptualization of Du Bois's corpus, and which are persistently and, perhaps, perplexingly present at each stage. I argue, once more, that it is the *transdisciplinary* nature of his work that makes it so difficult to interpret in a one-dimensional or monodisciplinary (as opposed to multidisciplinary) manner. Also, Du Bois's transdisciplinarity, which is to say the way his work constantly transcends and transgresses the arbitrary and artificial borders and boundaries of traditional disciplines, coupled with his accent on inductive, empirical social science and radical political economy, and his consistent emphasis on race, gender, and class issues, make his work an ideal model for simultaneously reconceiving and recreating sociology, critical social theory, and Africana studies.

Interpretations of Du Bois based on the tripartite paradigm, then, are extremely problematic and often theoretically myopic, frequently displaying the disciplinary decadence and desires of the critics to fashion a Du Bois for their specific (postmodern) purposes. However, Du Bois will not be anyone's theoretical straw man (or "race man" either), if you will. His thought, like that of other provocative social scientific thinkers, must be approached from an angle that is sensitive to intellectual, historical and cultural context in order to be adequately, and one could say *correctly*, interpreted. For instance, as I argued in chapter 6 of the present study, Du Bois carried out one of the most devastating critiques of racial criminalization, differential justice, and the convict-lease system in the first half of the twentieth century. But one will hardly be able to fully appreciate the originality of his arguments, the radicalism of his political positions, and their relevance to critical theory of contemporary society unless his sociology of crime is linked to his historical sociology, industrial sociology, urban sociology, rural sociology, sociology of race, sociology of gender, and sociology of education.

By taking a conceptual (as opposed to the conventional chronological) approach to Du Bois's research and writings, I have been able to accent some of the significant developments of his social scientific thought that speak to ongoing and important issues revolving around race, gender, class, and the deconstruction and reconstruction of both sociology and critical social theory. Instead of viewing changes in his thought as signs of confusion, vacillation, or intellectual inertia, I have emphasized the subtle logic of the modifications Du Bois made in his thinking by placing it in the context of continental and diasporan African intellectual history, culture, and struggle, as well as the wider world of intellectual history, culture, and struggle. Additionally, engaging Du Bois's corpus conceptually has also enabled me to stress its strengths and weaknesses as a paradigm and point of departure for developing a more multicultural, transethnic, antiracist, antisexist, and sexual orientation–sensitive critical theory of contemporary society. Similar to several other critical social theorists, Du Bois oriented his political theory toward what he perceived as the most progressive political struggles (or lack thereof) of a particular moment and, thus, articulated possibilities and potentialities specific to *his* contemporary society and social reality, rather than putting forward a blueprint for future social change or an architecture for emancipation in an epoch to come. To put it plainly, this is the central task of contemporary critical theorists, Africana or otherwise.[10]

This means, then, that "we are on our own"—as the post-Marxists and postfeminists regularly remind us. However, it does not mean that we should abandon those aspects of Du Bois's social scientific thought that may aid us in our endeavors to develop a new, more multicultural, transethnic, transgender, transgenerational, transnational, sexual orientation–sensitive, and environmental justice–committed critical theory of contemporary society. Critical theory seeks to comprehend, critique, and offer alternatives to the contradictions of current culture and society. Therefore, it is always in need of revision and, literally, demands discursive development because its basic concepts and categories are time- and situation-sensitive. In other words, the basic concepts and categories of critical theory are historical; and history, to put it plainly, has never bowed to the wishes and whims of any human being or human group. Hence, history is always unfolding and playing itself out in new and unimagined ways. Critical theory, then, being a form of historical and cultural critique, must remain receptive to the various ways in which the world is changing if it is to truly transform contemporary culture and society.

THE TRAILS AND TRIBULATIONS OF TRANSDISCIPLINARITY: ON DU BOIS'S ONGOING EPISTEMIC OPENNESS, RADICAL POLITICAL RECEPTIVENESS, AND SOCIAL SCIENTIFIC SIGNIFICANCE

In summary, it must be openly admitted that the social scientific and critical theoretic tensions noted in the previous paragraphs point to and produce an extremely uneasy combination of criticisms and interpretations that defy simple synopsis or conventional conceptual rules. Consequently, most of Du Bois's critics have heretofore downplayed and diminished the real brilliance and brawn of his work by failing to grasp its antinomies. They have, therefore, put forward a divided and distorted Du Bois, who is either, for example, a Pan-Africanist *or* Europhile; a black nationalist *or* radical humanist; a social scientist *or* propagandist; a race man *or* radical women's rights man; or a bourgeois elitist *or* dogmatic Marxist. Each of the aforementioned superficial ascriptions falls shamefully short of capturing the complex and chameleonic character of Du Bois's discourse and the difficulties involved in interpreting it employing the one-sided, single-subject-focused, and monodisciplinary discursive devices that his research, writings, and radicalism consistently transgressed, transcended, and transversed—hence, my characterization of Du Bois as a *transdisciplinary human scientist* and *critical social theorist*.

Many dismiss Du Bois and charge his work with being dense because it employs a wide range of theory and methodology from several different disciplines, while others, such as myself, are attracted to his work because it is methodologically monumental and theoretically thick, rich in both radicality and originality, and boldly crosses so many academic and political boundaries. No matter what one's ultimate attitude toward Du Bois, I believe the fact that his thought and texts continue to cause contemporary controversies, and that it has been discussed and debated *across the disciplines* for more than a century, in some degree points to the multidimensionality and transdisciplinarity of his ideas, which offer enigmatic insights for everyone either to embrace enthusiastically or demur definitively. Hence, the dialectic of attraction and repulsion in Du Bois studies can partly be attributed to the ambiguities inherent in his thought and the monodisciplinary anxieties of many of the interpreters of his work. Suffice it to say this is the case, then, several previous studies of his thought are seriously flawed because they have sought to grasp and grapple with Du Bois's oeuvre using a monodisciplinary instead of a multidisciplinary model or, even more, a transdisciplinary trajectory critical of *epistemic apartheid*.

Whatever the deficiencies of his thought and the problems with his approach to critical issues confronting the souls of black folk and humanity as a whole, Du Bois forces his readers to think deeply, to criticize thoroughly, and to move beyond the *epistemic apartheid* of the academy and the imperial impulses of the established order. Many critics have made solid criticisms of some aspects of Du Bois's discourse but, when analyzed objectively, his lifework and intellectual legacy is impressive and inspiring, as is his loyalty to the most radical and revolutionary thought- and practice-traditions in Africana and world history. His impact and influence has been widespread, not only cutting across academic disciplines, but also setting aglow several revolutionary social movements and radical political programs.

Where some sociologists dogmatically hold views simply because they are academically fashionable or politically popular, Du Bois's work draws from a diverse array of often eclectic and enigmatic sources and, therefore, offers no closed system or absolute truths. His thought was constantly open and routinely responsive to changing historical and cultural conditions, both nationally and internationally. There are several, sometimes stunning, transformations in his critical social theory that are in most instances attempts to answer conundrums created by changing sociopolitical, historical, and cultural conditions. In conclusion, then, I want to suggest that it is the epistemic openness and consistently nondogmatic radicalism of Du Bois's project, the richness and wide range and reach of his ideas, and the absence of any finished system or closed body of clearly defined truths that can be accepted or rejected at ease, which constitute both the contemporary social scientific significance and continuing critical importance of W. E. B. Du Bois and his discourse.

NOTES

1. Those Du Bois scholars and students with access to the W. E. B. Du Bois Papers, housed in the W. E. B. Du Bois Library in the Department of Special Collections and University Archives at the University of Massachusetts at Amherst, are urged to consult the Harvard graduate school papers Du Bois researched and wrote prior to his doctoral studies in the Department of Political Economy at the University of Berlin. For example, please see "A Constructive Critique of Wage-Theory," "Contributions to the Negro Problem," "Harvard and the South," and his intellectual history-making 1891 American Historical Association conference paper "The Enforcement of the Slave Trade Laws." It is extremely interesting to compare and contrast Du Bois's master's thesis, "The Enforcement of the Slave Trade Laws," with his Berlin doctoral dissertation, "*Der Gross und Klein Betrieb des Ackerbaus, in den Sudstaaten der Vereinigten Staaten, 1840–1890*" or "The Large and Small-Scale System of Agriculture in the Southern United States, 1840–1890," and then with his Harvard doctoral dissertation, *The Suppression of the African Slave Trade to the United States of America, 1638–1870*. It should be emphasized that although Du Bois was awarded his PhD under the guise of history at Harvard in 1895, his completion of his doctoral coursework and dissertation in political economy at Berlin prior to his return to Harvard in 1894 gives us grounds to suggest that he actually earned his doctorate in political economy *and* history, which is a contention at the heart of Thomas Boston's (1991) Du Bois scholarship. For further discussion, please see Du Bois (1968a, 154–82; 1968b, 25–49; 1997a, 10–29).

2. Where Edwards asserts that "Du Bois held on to a persistent faith that scientific research could aid in the moral quest to bring about racial uplift," Adolph Reed (1997) argues that Du Bois maintained a belief that the presentation of social scientific facts could also possibly foment critique of capitalist political economy, writing

that "for Du Bois scholarly pursuit always was linked directly and consciously with some purpose of social reform" (49). Then, he quickly quipped, "Not so much a self-contained activity directed toward a community of scholars concerned first of all with the expansion of knowledge, research's fundamental purpose was to Du Bois the correction of popular misconceptions in the interest of social improvement. To that extent Du Bois shares a basic view of the role of scholarship—if explicitly political differences were held constant—with policy-oriented social scientists, the practical inheritors of the liberal tradition in the United States." Interestingly enough, Reed continued, "At the same time, just as Du Bois defined the purpose of scholarly activity in relation to a notion of social intervention for the realization of progress, the activism to which he adhered was more didactic than militant. Even after he became more trenchantly critical of capitalism, his strategy for opposition was ultimately the same—informing people of the facts" (49). From my understanding Du Bois's activism was the inverse of Reed's interpretation here (i.e., actually more militant than didactic). The W. E. B. Du Bois Papers reveal that Du Bois spoke out against lynching, led civil rights marches, brandished a shotgun in self-defense, pioneered Pan-Africanism, founded both the Niagara movement and the NAACP, touted the Russian Revolution of 1917, intermittently embraced black nationalism, even advocated for black separatism, and was jailed at eighty-two years of age during the height of McCarthyism because the U.S. government considered him to be one of the most militant "Negroes" in America. Therefore, it is difficult to understand what on earth Reed could mean with his statement that "the activism to which [Du Bois] adhered was more didactic than militant," unless he is completely disregarding the historical context in which Du Bois undertook his activism. It is a historical fact that Du Bois was considered quite militant at the turn of the twentieth century and for much of his adult life. Now, he may not have been Malcolm X–militant, that much must be conceded, but, I reiterate, for his epoch, especially when compared with both his black and white contemporaries, he grew increasingly more radical as most of his peers (if not all of them) backslid from bourgeois liberalism to quaint conservatism. However subtly, Du Bois modified the methodological orientation of the German historical school of economics and, ultimately, deconstructed and reconstructed it in his pursuit of solutions to African American social and political problems in particular, and American social and political problems in general. This must be borne in mind, whether we understand his intellectual-activism to be militant or not, in order to comprehend Du Bois's significance with regard to the intellectual history and discursive development of American sociology.

3. It may also interest Du Bois studies scholars and students to know that the bulk of Du Bois's Harvard education was funded through his receipt of various scholarships, although he also had to secure loans: the Price-Greenleaf Grant (1888–1890); the Mathews Scholarship (1888–1890); the Henry Bromfield Rogers Fellowship in Political Science (1890–1892); and the John L. Slater Fund (1892–1894). See Du Bois (1997a, 11–17).

4. For critical discussions of the racial exclusionary practices and/or the institutionalized racism of traditional academic disciplines, see Goldberg (1993, 2001, 2008), Gordon (2006a, 2006b, 2006c), Gordon and Gordon (2006a, 2006b), and Rabaka (2008a, 2009a).

5. Stewart's assertion that "Du Bois rejected the fragmentation of experience into disciplinary compartments, the attempt by the social sciences to use the natural sciences as a developmental model," seems to patently prefigure Lewis Gordon's (2006b) conception of disciplinary decadence. Where Gordon does not engage Stewart's work, he limits his discussion of Du Bois's contributions to the discourse on disciplinary decadence to "The Conservation of Races" and *The Souls of Black Folk* (see also J. B. Stewart, 2004). One wonders how Gordon's admittedly innovative conception of disciplinary decadence might be less meta-philosophical and meta-methodological, and more historical, sociological, or political (i.e., more social scientific) if Du Bois's *The Philadelphia Negro*, rural sociological studies, and Atlanta University Conference publications had been taken into careful and critical consideration in his discursive development of disciplinary decadence. I humbly and earnestly offer *Against Epistemic Apartheid* as an initial answer to this critical question—an initial answer, I profoundly pray, which will lead Africana studies and social science in particular, and the American academy in general, in new discursive directions that utterly and unapologetically go *against epistemic apartheid*.

6. For critical discussions of Africana studies' interdisciplinarity, multidisciplinarity, transdisciplinarity, and/or supradisciplinarity, see Aldridge and James (2007), Aldridge and Young (2000), Anderson and Stewart (2007), Asante and Karenga (2006), Bobo and Michel (2000), Bobo, Hudley, and Michel (2004), and Gordon and Gordon (2006a, 2006b).

7. With regard to the last three points, which provide a basic outline for my conception of critical theory, I have generously drawn from the work of Joy James (1996, 1997, 1999), whose texts have consistently raised the issue of connecting theory to praxis; the realities of the "ugliness" of antiracist, antisexist and anti-imperial struggle (both inside and outside "radical" thought-traditions and movements); and the need for progressive intellectual-activists to move "beyond literary insurgency or rhetorical resistance to bring the element of the fight into our daily lives with the specificity of political struggles around economic, sexual, and racial violence" (James, 1996, 23). Here I am also borrowing, however loosely, from the theoretical orientations and methodological work of Marcuse (2001, 2004, 2007b), Habermas (1984, 1987a, 1988, 1989b), Harding (1987, 1993, 1998, 2004), and Foucault (1971, 1974, 1984, 1996). As discussed in the introduction to this volume, Foucault's conception of and contributions to critical theory, in particular, helped me to hone a critical methodological perspective that transcends and transgresses not only the borders and boundaries of traditional social science and academic disciplines, but also the Frankfurt School critical theorists' obsession with Marx and Marxism as the major theoretical thread that connects one version of critical theory to another. Where Foucault turned to Nietzsche and other counter- or post-Marxian thinkers to develop his distinct critical theoretical discourse, I have labored with Du Bois, Fanon, Cabral, and several other Africana social and political theorists (see Rabaka, 2007b, 2008a, 2009a, 2010a).

8. For a series of critical discussions commemorating the centennial of Du Bois's classic essay, "The Study of the Negro Problems," and its relevance for contemporary Africana and global radical politics, sociology, progressive social movements, philosophy, economic analysis, cultural criticism, feminism, and radical humanism,

see Anderson and Zuberi (2000). The influence of this essay on my conception of critical theory, Africana critical theory, cannot be overemphasized.

9. Wilson Moses (1978, 1996, 1998) and Paul Gilroy (1993) have demonstrated that the "Eurocentric imperialist" aspect of Du Bois's early social uplift theory was derived, in part, from his affinity with German nationalism, which he admired, arguably, since his undergraduate days at Fisk. For further discussion, see also Barkin (1998, 2000), Beck (1996), Broderick (1958b), Schafer (2001), and Zamir (1995, 2008).

10. In terms of the time sensitivity and theoretical specificity of critical theory, Herbert Marcuse made an excellent statement regarding the critical theorists' primary task of wrestling with the most pressing issues of their epoch, as opposed to pointing to or pointing out the future "forces of transformation." In his own words:

> If Marx saw in the proletariat the revolutionary class, he did so also, and maybe even primarily, because the proletariat was free from the repressive needs of capitalist society, because the new needs for freedom could develop in the proletariat and were not suffocated by the old, dominant ones. Today [in 1967] in large parts of the most highly developed capitalist countries that is no longer the case. The working-class no longer represents the negation of existing needs. That is one of the most serious facts with which we have to deal. As far as the forces of transformation themselves are concerned, I grant you without further discussion that today nobody is in a position to give a prescription for them in the sense of being able to point and say, "Here you have your revolutionary forces, this is their strength, this and this must be done." The only thing I can do is point out what forces potentially make for a radical transformation of the system. (Marcuse, 1970, 70)

This means, then, that critical theorists need not feel compelled to accept the call of the prophet, although, it should be duly noted, Du Bois has regularly been interpreted from this angle (see Blum, 2007; Blum and Young, 2009; West, 1989, 1996). Critical theory is, or, rather, at its best *should be*, deeply rooted in empirical and historical research, and its theoretical positions *should be* linked to concrete social and political struggles. Therefore, although a part of its focus is on the future, critical theory is ultimately a theory of the present whose philosophical foundation rests on and revolves around classical and contemporary radical/revolutionary thought and practices.

Bibliography

Alcoff, Linda, and Potter, Elizabeth. (Eds.). (1993). *Feminist Epistemologies.* New York: Routledge.

Aldridge, Delores P. (2008). *Imagine a World: Pioneering Black Women Sociologists.* Lanham, MD: University Press of America.

Aldridge, Delores P., and James, E. Lincoln. (Eds.). (2007). *Africana Studies: Philosophical Perspectives and Theoretical Paradigms.* Pullman: Washington State University Press.

Aldridge, Delores P., and Young, Carlene. (Eds.). (2000). *Out of the Revolution: An Africana Studies Anthology.* Lanham, MD: Lexington Books.

Aldridge, Derrick P. (2003). "W. E. B. Du Bois: Race Man, Teacher, and Scholar." In Sherry Field and Michael Bergson (Eds.), *They Led by Teaching: Influential Educators* (102–14). Indianapolis: Phi Delta Pi Publications.

———. (2008). *The Educational Thought of W. E. B. Du Bois: An Intellectual History.* New York: Teachers College Press.

Alexander, M. Jacqui, and Mohanty, Chandra Talpade. (Eds.). (1997). *Feminist Genealogies, Colonia Legacies, Democratic Futures.* New York: Routledge.

Allen, Theodore W. (1994). *The Invention of the White Race* (Volume 1). New York: Verso.

———. (1997). *The Invention of the White Race* (Volume 2). New York: Verso.

Almaguer, Tomás. (1994). *Racial Fault Lines: The Historical Origins of White Supremacy in California.* Berkeley: University of California Press.

Anderson, Elijah. (1996). "Introduction to the 1996 Edition of *The Philadelphia Negro.*" In W. E. B. Du Bois, *The Philadelphia Negro: A Social Study* (viiii–xxxvi). Philadelphia: University of Pennsylvania Press.

———. (2000). "The Emerging Philadelphia African American Class Structure." *Annals of the American Academy of Political and Social Science* 568, 41–53.

Anderson, Elijah, and Massey, Douglas S. (Eds.). (2001). *The Problem of the Century: Racial Stratification in the United States.* New York: Russell Sage Foundation.

Anderson, Elijah, and Zuberi, Tukufu. (Eds.). (2000). *The Study of African American Problems: W. E. B. Du Bois's Agenda, Then and Now.* Thousand Oaks, CA: Sage.

Anderson, Talmadge, and Stewart, James B. (2007). *Introduction to African American Studies: Transdisciplinary Approaches and Implications.* Baltimore: Black Classic Press.

Anderson, Victor. (1995). *Beyond Ontological Blackness: An Essay on African American Religious and Cultural Criticism.* New York: Continuum.

Andrews, William L. (Ed.). (1985). *Critical Essays on W. E. B. Du Bois.* Boston: G. K. Hall.

Apel, Dora. (2004). *Imagery of Lynching: Black Men, White Women, and the Mob.* New Brunswick, NJ: Rutgers University Press.

Appiah, Kwame Anthony. (1985). "The Uncompleted Argument: Du Bois and the Illusion of Race." *Critical Inquiry* 12 (1), 21–37.

———. (1990). "Racisms." In David Theo Goldberg (Ed.), *Anatomy of Racism* (3–17). Minneapolis: University of Minnesota Press.

———. (1992). *In My Father's House: Africa in the Philosophy of Culture.* New York: Oxford University Press.

———. (1996). "Race, Culture, Identity." In Kwame Anthony Appiah and Amy Gutman, *Color Conscious: The Political Morality of Race* (3–75). Princeton: Princeton University Press.

———. (1997). "'But Would That Still Be Me?' Notes on Gender, 'Race,' Ethnicity as a Source of Identity." In Naomi Zack (Ed.), *Race/Sex: Their Sameness, Difference, and Interplay* (75–82). New York: Routledge.

Aptheker, Herbert. (1980a). "Introduction." In W. E. B. Du Bois, *Contributions of W. E. B. Du Bois in Government Publications and Proceedings* (1–3). Millwood, NY: Kraus-Thomson.

———. (1980b). "Introduction to *Prayers for Dark People.*" In W. E. B. Du Bois, *Prayers for Dark People* (iv–xi). Amherst: University of Massachusetts.

———. (1982). "W. E. B. Du Bois and Religion: A Brief Reassessment." *Journal of Religious Thought* 59, 5–11.

Arnesen, Eric. (2002). *Black Protest and the Great Migration: A Brief History with Documents.* Boston: Bedford/St. Martin's Press.

Arnold, Edwin T. (2009). *What Virtue There is in Fire: Cultural Memory and the Lynching of Sam Hose.* Athens: University of Georgia Press.

Asante, Molefi K., and Karenga, Maulana. (Eds.). (2006). *The Handbook of Black Studies.* Thousand Oaks, CA: Sage.

Baer, Hans A. (1984). *Black Spiritual Movement: A Religious Response to Racism.* Knoxville: University of Tennessee.

Baer, Hans A., and Singer, Merrill. (2002). *African American Religion: Varieties of Protest and Accommodation.* Knoxville: University of Tennessee Press.

Bailey, Leon. (1994). *Critical Theory and the Sociology of Knowledge: A Comparative Study in the Theory of Ideology.* New York: Peter Lang Publishing.

Balabkins, Nicholas W. (1988). *Not by Theory Alone . . . : The Economics of Gustav Von Schmoller and Its Legacy to America.* Berlin: Duncker & Humblot.

Banks, William M. (1996). *Black Intellectuals: Race and Responsibility in American Life.* New York: W. W. Norton.

Banner-Haley, Charles Pete T. (1993). *To Do Good and To Do Well: Middle Class Blacks and the Depression, Philadelphia, 1929–1941*. New York: Garland Publishers.

———. (1994). *The Fruits of Integration: Black Middle-Class Ideology and Culture, 1960–1990*. Jackson: University Press of Mississippi.

Bannister, Robert C. (1979). *Social Darwinism: Science and Myth in Anglo-American Social Thought*. Philadelphia: Temple University Press.

Barak, Gregg, Leighton, Paul, and Flavin, Jeanne. (2007). *Class, Race, Gender, and Crime: The Social Realities of Justice in America*. Lanham, MD: Rowman & Littlefield.

Barkin, Kenneth. (1998). "W. E. B. Du Bois and the Kaiserreich Articles: An Introduction to Du Bois's Manuscripts on Germany." *Central European History* 31 (3), 155–71.

———. (2000). "'Berlin Days,' 1892–1894: W. E. B. Du Bois and German Political Economy." *Boundary 2* 27 (3), 79–101.

Barrett, Leonard E. (1974). *Soul-Force: African Heritage in Afro-American Religion*. Garden City, NY: Anchor.

Bascom, William R. (1980). *Sixteen Cowries: Yoruba Divination from Africa to the New World*. Bloomington: Indiana University Press.

Bass, Amy. (2009). *Those About Him Remained Silent: The Battle Over W. E. B. Du Bois*. Minneapolis: University of Minnesota Press.

Bastide, Roger. (1971). *African Civilization in the New World*. New York: Harper and Row.

———. (1978). *The African Religions of Brazil: Toward a Sociology of the Interpretation of Civilization*. Baltimore: Johns Hopkins University Press.

Bauerlin, Mark. (2001). *Negrophobia: A Race Riot in Atlanta, 1906*. San Francisco: Encounter Books.

Bay, Mia. (1998). "'The World Was Thinking Wrong About Race': The Philadelphia Negro and Nineteenth-Century Science." In Michael B. Katz and Thomas J. Sugrue (Eds.), *W. E. B. Du Bois, Race, and the City: The Philadelphia Negro and Its Legacy* (41–60). Philadelphia: University of Pennsylvania Press.

Beauman, Katherine Bentley. (1996). *Women and the Settlement Movement*. New York: St. Martin's Press.

Beck, Hamilton. (1996). "W. E. B. Du Bois as a Study Abroad Student in Germany, 1892–1894." *Frontiers: The Interdisciplinary Journal of Study Abroad* 2 (1), 45–63.

Becker, Peter, and Wetzell, Richard F. (Eds.). (2004). *Criminals and Their Scientists: The History of Criminology in International Perspective*. New York: Cambridge University Press.

Belknap, Joanne. (1996). *Invisible Woman: Gender, Crime, and Justice*. Belmont, CA: Wadsworth Publishing.

Bell, Bernard W., Grosholz, Emily R., and Stewart, James B. (Eds.). (1996). *W. E. B. Du Bois: On Race and Culture*. New York: Routledge.

Bernal, John D. (1970). *Science and Industry in the Nineteenth Century*. Bloomington: Indiana University Press.

Bernasconi, Robert. (1996). "Casting the Slough: Fanon's New Humanism for a New Humanity." In Lewis R. Gordon, T. Denean Sharpley-Whiting, and Renee T. White (Eds.), *Fanon: A Critical Reader* (113–21). Cambridge: Blackwell.

Bernstein, Patricia. (2005). *The First Waco Horror: The Lynching of Jesse Washington and the Rise of the NAACP*. College Station: Texas A&M University Press.

Berryman, Phillip. (1987). *Liberation Theology: Essential Facts about the Revolutionary Movement in Latin America and Beyond*. Philadelphia: Temple University Press.

Bhui, Hindpal Singh. (Ed.). (2009). *Race and Criminal Justice*. Los Angeles: Sage.

Billingsley, Andrew. (1988). *Black Families in White America*. New York: Simon & Schuster.

———. (1992). *Climbing Jacob's Ladder: The Enduring Legacy of African American Families*. New York: Simon & Schuster.

———. (1999). *Mighty Like a River: The Black Church and Social Reform*. New York: Oxford University Press.

Blackmon, Douglas A. (2008). *Slavery by Another Name: The Re-Enslavement of Black People in America, From the Civil War to World War II*. New York: Doubleday.

Blackwell, James E., and Janowitz, Morris. (Eds.). (1974). *Black Sociologists: Historical and Contemporary Perspectives*. Chicago: University of Chicago Press.

Blaut, James M. (1987). *The Colonial Question: Decolonizing the Theory of Nationalism*. London: Zed Books.

———. (1993). *The Colonizer's Model of the World: Geographical Diffusionism and Eurocentric History*. New York: Guilford Press.

———. (2000). *Eight Eurocentric Historians*. New York: Guilford Press.

Bloom, Harold. (2001). *W. E. B. Du Bois*. New York: Chelsea House Publishers.

Blum, Edward J. (2004). "The Soul of W. E. B. Du Bois." *Philosophia Africana* 7 (2), 1-16.

———. (2005a). "Religion and the Sociological Imagination of W. E. B. Du Bois." *Sociation Today* 3 (1). Online at www.ncsociology.org/sociationtoday/v31/blum.htm [Accessed 23 February 2005].

———. (2005b). "'There Won't Be Any Rich People in Heaven': The Black Christ, White Hypocrisy, and the Gospel According to W. E. B. Du Bois." *Journal of African American History* 90 (4), 368-86.

———. (2007). *W. E. B. Du Bois: American Prophet*. Philadelphia: University of Pennsylvania Press.

Blum, Edward J., and Young, Jason R. (Eds.). (2009). *The Souls of W. E. B. Du Bois: New Essays and Reflections*. Macon, GA: Mercer University Press.

Blyden, Edward W. (1994). *Christianity, Islam, and the Negro Race*. Baltimore: Black Classic Press.

Bobo, Jacqueline, and Michel, Claudine. (Eds.). (2000). *Black Studies: Current Issues, Enduring Questions*. Dubuque, IA: Kendall/Hunt.

Bobo, Jacqueline, Hudley, Cynthia, and Michel, Claudine. (Eds.). (2004). *The Black Studies Reader*. New York: Routledge.

Bobo, Lawrence D. (2000). "Reclaiming a Du Boisian Perspective on Racial Attitudes." *Annals of the American Academy of Political and Social Science* 568, 186-202.

Boff, Clodovis. (1987). *Theology and Praxis: Epistemological Foundations*. Maryknoll, NY: Orbis.

Boff, Leonardo, and Boff, Clodovis. (1987). *Introducing Liberation Theology*. Maryknoll, NY: Orbis.

Bogues, Anthony. (2003). *Black Heretics, Black Prophets: Radical Political Intellectuals*. New York: Routledge.

Bologh, Roslyn W. (1990). *Love or Greatness: Max Weber and Masculine Thinking, A Feminist Inquiry*. London: Unwin Hayman.

Bonilla-Silva, Eduardo. (2001). *White Supremacy and Racism in the Post-Civil Rights Era*. Boulder, CO: Lynne Rienner.

———. (2003). *Racism Without Racists: Color-Blind Racism and the Persistence of Racial Inequality in the United States*. Lanham, MD: Rowman and Littlefield.

Bonilla-Silva, Eduardo, and Doane, Ashley. (Eds.). (2003). *White Out: The Continuing Significance of Racism*. New York: Routledge.

Bonilla-Silva, Eduardo, and Zuberi, Tukufu. (Eds.). (2008). *White Logic, White Methods: Racism and Methodology*. Lanham, MD: Rowman & Littlefield.

Boone, Elizabeth, and Mignolo, Walter. (Eds.). (1994). *Writing Without Words: Alternative Literacies in Mesoamerica and the Andes*. Durham, NC: Duke University Press.

Boston, Thomas D. (1991). "W. E. B. Du Bois and the Historical School of Economics." *American Economic Review* 81 (2), 303–6.

Bowser, Benjamin P. (2007). *The Black Middle Class: Social Mobility and Vulnerability*. Boulder, CO: Lynne Rienner.

Broderick, Francis L. (1955). "W. E. B. Du Bois: The Trail of His Ideas." PhD dissertation, Harvard University.

———. (1958a). "The Academic Training of W. E. B. Du Bois." *Journal of Negro Education* 27, 10–16.

———. (1958b). "German Influence on the Scholarship of W. E. B. Du Bois." *Phylon* 19, 367–71.

———. (1958c). "The Tragedy of W. E. B. Du Bois." *Progressive* 22, 29–32.

———. (1959). *W. E. B. Du Bois: Negro Leader in a Time of Crisis*. Palo Alto, CA: Stanford University Press.

———. (1974). "W. E. B. Du Bois: History of an Intellectual." In James E. Blackwell and Morris Janowitz (Eds.), *Black Sociologists: Historical and Contemporary Perspectives* (3–24). Chicago: University of Chicago Press.

Browne-Marshall, Gloria J. (2007). *Race, Law, and American Society: 1607 to Present*. New York: Routledge.

Brundage, W. Fitzhugh. (1993). *Lynching in the New South: Georgia and Virginia, 1880–1930*. Urbana: University of Illinois Press.

———. (Ed.). (1997). *Under Sentence of Death: Lynching in the South*. Chapel Hill: University of North Carolina Press.

Bullard, Robert D., Grigsby, J. Eugene, III, and Lee, Charles. (Eds.). (1994). *Residential Apartheid: The American Legacy*. Los Angeles: CAAS Publications.

Bulmer, Martin. (1984). *The Chicago School of Sociology: Institutionalization, Diversity, and the Rise of Sociological Research*. Chicago: University of Chicago Press.

———. (1991). "W. E. B. Du Bois as a Social Investigator: *The Philadelphia Negro*, 1899." In Martin Bulmer, Kevin Bales, and Kathryn Kish Sklar (Eds.), *The Social Survey in Historical Perspective, 1880–1940* (170–88). Cambridge: Cambridge University Press.

Bulmer, Martin, and Solomos, John. (Eds.). (2004). *Researching Race and Racism:* New York: Routledge.

Burns, Rebecca. (2006). *Rage in the Gate City: The Story of the 1906 Atlanta Race Riot*. Cincinnati, OH: Emmis.

Burton-Rose, Daniel, Pens, Dan, and Wright, Paul. (Eds.). (1998). *The Celling of America: An Inside Look at the U. S. Prison Industry*. Monroe, ME: Common Courage Press.

Cabral, Amilcar. (1972). *Revolution in Guinea: Selected Texts*. New York: Monthly Review Press.

———. (1973). *Return to the Source: Selected Speeches of Amilcar Cabral*. New York: Monthly Review Press.

———. (1979). *Unity and Struggle: Speeches and Writings of Amilcar Cabral*. New York: Monthly Review Press.

Cantor, Milton. (1969). *Black Labor in America*. Westport, CT: Negro Universities Press.

Carby, Hazel V. (1998). *Race Men*. Cambridge, MA: Harvard University Press.

Carr, Patrick J., Napolitano, Laura, and Keating, Jessica. (2007). "We Never Call the Cops and Here is Why: A Qualitative Examination of Legal Cynicism in Three Philadelphia Neighborhoods." *Criminology* 45 (2), 445–80.

Carrington, Kerry, and Hogg, Russell. (Eds.). (2002). *Critical Criminology: Issues, Debates, Challenges*. Portland, OR: Willan Publishing.

Carroll, Ann Elizabeth. (2005). *Word, Image, and the New Negro: Representation and Identity in the Harlem Renaissance*. Bloomington: Indiana University Press.

Carroll, Rebecca. (Eds.). (2003). *Saving the Race: Conversations on Du Bois from a Collective Memoir of* The Souls of Black Folk. New York: Harlem Moon.

Carson, Mina Julia. (1990). *Settlement Folk: Social Thought and the American Settlement Movement, 1885–1930*. Chicago: University of Chicago Press.

Carter, J. Kameron. (2008). *Race: A Theological Account*. New York: Oxford University Press.

Chalmers, David M. (1987). *Hooded Americanism: The History of the Ku Klux Klan*. Durham, NC: Duke University Press.

Chapman, Mark L. (1996). *Christianity on Trial: African American Religious Thought Before and After Black Power*. Maryknoll, NY: Orbis Books.

Chandler, Nahum D. (2006). "The Figure of W. E. B. Du Bois as a Problem for Thought." *CR: The New Centennial Review* 6 (3), 29–55.

———. (2007). "The Possible Forum of an Interlocution: W. E. B. Du Bois and Max Weber in Correspondence, 1904–1905." *CR: The New Centennial Review* 7 (1), 213–72.

Cloward, Richard A., and Ohlin, Lloyd E. (1960). *Delinquency and Opportunity: A Theory of Delinquent Gangs*. Glencoe, IL: Free Press.

Cohen, Albert K. (1955). *Delinquent Boys: The Culture of the Gang*. Glencoe, IL: Free Press.

Collins, Chuck, and Yeskel, Felice. (2005). *Economic Apartheid in America: A Primer on Economic Inequality and Insecurity*. New York: New Press.

Collins, Patricia Hill. (1990). *Black Feminist Thought: Knowledge, Consciousness, and the Politics of Empowerment*. New York: Routledge.

———. (1998). *Fighting Words: Black Women and the Search for Social Justice*. Minneapolis: University of Minnesota Press.

———. (2000a). *Black Feminist Thought: Knowledge, Consciousness, and the Politics of Empowerment* (second edition). New York: Routledge.

——. (2000b). "Gender, Black Feminism, and Black Political Economy." *Annals of the American Academy of Political and Social Science* 568, 41–53.

——. (2003). "Some Group Matters: Intersectionality, Situated Standpoints, and Black Feminist Thought." In Tommy L. Lott and John P. Pittman (Eds.), *A Companion to African American Philosophy* (205–30). Malden: Blackwell.

——. (2005). *Black Sexual Politics: African Americans, Gender, and the New Racism.* New York: Routledge.

——. (2006). *From Black Power to Hip Hop: Racism, Nationalism, and Feminism.* Philadelphia: Temple University Press.

——. (2007). "Pushing Boundaries or Business as Usual? Race, Class, and Gender Studies and Sociological Inquiry." In Craig J. Calhoun (Ed.), *Sociology in America: A History* (572–604). Chicago: University of Chicago Press.

Collins, Randall. (1971). "Functional and Conflict Theories of Educational Stratification." *American Sociological Review* 36 (6), 1002–19.

——. (1975). *Conflict Sociology: Toward an Explanatory Science.* New York: Academic.

Cone, James H. (1969). *Black Theology and Black Power.* New York: Seabury Press.

——. (1970). *A Black Theology of Liberation.* Philadelphia: Lippincott.

——. (1975). *God of the Oppressed.* New York: Seabury Press.

Cone, James H., and Wilmore, Gayraud S. (Eds.). (1993). *Black Theology: A Documentary History* (2 volumes). Maryknoll, NY: Orbis.

Conyers, James L., and Barnett, Alva P. (Eds.). (1999). *African American Sociology: A Social Study of the Pan-African Diaspora.* Chicago: Nelson-Hall Publishers.

Cook, Dee, and Hudson, Barbara. (Eds.). (1993). *Racism and Criminology.* Thousand Oaks, CA: Sage.

Cooper, Anna Julia. (1998). *The Voice of Anna Julia Cooper: Including* A Voice From the South *and Other Important Essays, Papers, and Letters* (Charles Lemert and Esme Bhan, Eds.). Lanham, MD: Rowman & Littlefield.

Coser, Lewis A. (1956). *Functions of Social Conflict.* Glencoe, IL: Free Press.

——. (1967). *Continuities in the Study of Social Conflict.* New York: Free Press.

Cote, Suzette. (Ed.). (2002). *Criminological Theories: Bridging the Past to the Future.* Thousand Oaks, CA: Sage.

Cowan, Rosemary. (2003). *Cornel West: The Politics of Redemption.* Cambridge: Polity.

Cox, Oliver C. (1948). *Caste, Class, and Race: A Study in Social Dynamics.* New York: Monthly Review Press.

——. (1976). *Race Relations: Elements of Social Dynamics.* Detroit: Wayne State University Press.

——. (1987). *Race, Class, and the World System* (Herbert M. Hunter and Sameer Y. Abraham, Eds.). New York: Monthly Review Press.

——. (2000). *Race: A Study in Social Dynamics.* New York: Monthly Review Press.

Coyle, Andrew, Campbell, Allison, and Neufeld, Rodney. (Eds.). (2003). *Capitalist Punishment: Prison Privatization & Human Rights.* London: Zed Books.

Crenshaw, Kimberle, Gotanda, Neil, Peller, Gary, and Thomas, Kendall. (Eds.). (1995). *Critical Race Theory: The Key Writings That Formed the Movement.* New York: New Press.

Crocker, Ruth. (1992). *Social Work and Social Order: The Settlement Movement in Two Industrial Cities, 1889–1930.* Urbana: University of Illinois Press.

Cross, Malcolm. (Ed.). (2000). *The Sociology of Race and Ethnicity* (3 volumes). Cheltenham, UK; Northampton, MA: E. Elgar Publishing.

Crouch, Stanley, and Benjamin, Playthell. (2002). *Reconsidering The Souls of Black Folk: Thoughts on the Groundbreaking Classic Work of W. E. B. Du Bois.* Philadelphia: Running Press.

Cruse, Harold. (1967). *The Crisis of the Negro Intellectual.* New York: Morrow.

Curtin, Mary Ellen. (2000). *Black Prisoners and Their World, Alabama, 1865–1900.* Charlottesville: University Press of Virginia.

Dabashi, Hamid. (2008). *Islamic Liberation Theology: Resisting the Empire.* New York: Routledge.

Daniel, Pete (1990). *The Shadow of Slavery: Peonage in the South, 1901–1969.* New York: Oxford University Press.

Daniels, Roger. (2002). *Coming to America: A History of Immigration and Ethnicity in American Life.* New York: Perennial.

Davis, Allen F., and Haller, Mark H. (Eds). (1973). *The Peoples of Philadelphia: A History of Ethnic Groups and Lower-Class Life, 1790–1940.* Philadelphia: Temple University Press.

Davis, Allison. (1983). *Leadership, Love, and Aggression.* San Diego, CA: Harcourt Brace Jovanovich.

Davis, Angela Y. (1995). "Reflections on the Black Woman's Role in the Community of Slaves." In Beverly Guy-Sheftall (Ed.), *Words of Fire: An Anthology of African American Feminist Thought* (200–218). New York: The Free Press.

———. (2003). *Are Prisons Obsolete?* New York: Seven Stories Press.

Davis, Arthur Paul. (1975). *The New Negro Renaissance: An Anthology.* New York: Holt, Rinehart, and Winston.

Delamont, Sara. (2003). *Feminist Sociology.* Thousand Oaks, CA: Sage.

Delgado, Richard. (Ed.). (1995). *Critical Race Theory: The Cutting Edge.* Philadelphia: Temple University Press.

Delgado, Richard, and Stefancic, Jean. (Eds.). (1997). *Critical White Studies: Looking Behind the Mirror.* Philadelphia: Temple University Press.

———. (2001). *Critical Race Theory: An Introduction.* New York: New York University Press.

DeMarco, Joseph P. (1983). *The Social Thought of W. E. B. Du Bois.* Lanham, MD: University Press of America.

Dennis, Rutledge M. (1972). "W. E. B. Du Bois as Sociologist." *Journal of African American Studies* 2, 6279.

———. (1975). "The Sociology of W. E. B. Du Bois." PhD dissertation, Washington State University.

———. (1977). "Du Bois and the Role of the Educated Elite." *Journal of Negro Education* 46 (4), 388–402.

———. (1979). "Race, Structured Inequality, and the Consequences of Racial Domination: The Political Sociology of W. E. B. Du Bois." In Vivian Gordon (Ed.), *Black Scholars on Black Issues* (54–83). Washington, D.C.: University of America Press.

———. (1996a). "Continuities and Discontinuities in the Social and Political Thought of W. E. B. Du Bois." *Research in Race & Ethnic Relations* 9, 3–23.

———. (1996b). "Du Bois's Concept of Double Consciousness: Myth and Reality." *Research in Race & Ethnic Relations* 9, 69–90.

———. (Ed.). (1996c). *W. E. B. Du Bois: The Scholar as Activist*. Greenwich, CT: JAI Press.

———. (1997). "Introduction: W. E. B. Du Bois and the Tradition of Radical Intellectual Thought." *Research in Race & Ethnic Relations* 10, xi–xxiv.

———. (2003). "W. E. B. Du Bois's Concept of Double-Consciousness." In John Stone and Rutledge M. Dennis (Eds.), *Race and Ethnicity: Comparative and Theoretical Approaches* (23–47). Malden, MA: Blackwell.

Di Stephano, Christine. (1991). "Masculine Marx." In Mary Lyndon Shanley and Carole Pateman (Eds.), *Feminist Interpretations and Political Theory* (146–64). University Park: Penn State University Press.

Dickens, Peter. (2000). *Social Darwinism: Linking Evolutionary Thought to Social Theory*. Buckingham, UK: Open University Press.

Dixson, Adrienne D., and Rousseau, Celia K. (Eds.). (2006). *Critical Race Theory in Education: All God's Children Got a Song*. New York: Routledge.

Douglass, Frederick. (1992). *Frederick Douglass on Women's Rights* (Philip S. Foner, Ed.). New York: Da Capo Press.

———. (1994). *Autobiographies: Narrative of the Life, My Bondage and My Freedom, Life and Times*. New York: Library of America.

Dray, Philip (2002). *At the Hands of Persons Unknown: The Lynching of Black America*. New York: Random House.

Dred Scott vs. Sanford 1857: 60 US (19 How.).

Du Bois, W. E. B. (1897a). "The Conservation of Races." *The American Negro Academy Occasional Papers* 2, 1–15.

———. (1897b). "A Program for a Sociological Society." [Unpublished manuscript]. W. E. B. Du Bois Papers, Department of Special Collections and University Archives, W. E. B. Du Bois Library, University of Massachusetts at Amherst.

———. (1898a). "The Negroes of Farmville, Virginia: A Social Study." *Bulletin of the Department of Labor* 3 (14), 1–38.

———. (1898b). "The Study of the Negro Problems." *Annals of the American Academy of Political and the Social Science* 11, 1–23.

———. (1899). *The Philadelphia Negro: A Social Study*. Philadelphia: University of Pennsylvania Press.

———. (1900). "Post-Graduate Work in Sociology at Atlanta University." [Unpublished manuscript]. W. E. B. Du Bois Papers, Department of Special Collections and University Archives, W. E. B. Du Bois Library, University of Massachusetts at Amherst.

———. (1901a). "The Negroes of Dougherty County, Georgia." In Industrial Commission (Ed.), *Report of the Industrial Commission on Education* 15 (159–75). Washington, D.C.: United States Industrial Commission Reports.

———. (1901b). "The Relation of the Negroes to the Whites of the South." *Annals of the American Academy of Political and the Social Science* 18, 121–40.

———. (1901c). "The Spawn of Slavery: The Convict Lease-System in the South." *Missionary Review of the World* 24, 727–45.

———. (Ed.). (1903a). *The Negro Church*. Atlanta: Atlanta University Press.

———. (1903b). "Sociology Hesitant." [Unpublished manuscript]. W. E. B. Du Bois Papers, Department of Special Collections and University Archives, W. E. B. Du Bois Library, University of Massachusetts at Amherst.

———. (1903c). *The Souls of Black Folk: Essays and Sketches.* Chicago: A. C. McClurg.

———. (1904a). "The Atlanta Conference." *Voice of the Negro* 1 (3), 85–90.

———. (1904b). "The Development of a People." *International Journal of Ethics* 14, 291–311.

———. (1904c). *Some Notes on Negro Crime, Particularly in Georgia.* Atlanta: Atlanta University Press.

———. (1905). "The Negro South and North." *Biblioteca Sacra* 62, 500–513.

———. (1906a). "Die Negerfrage in den Vereingten Staaten." *Archiv für Sozialwissenschaft und Sozialpolitik* 22, 31–79.

———. (1906b). *The Health and Physique of the Negro American.* Atlanta: Atlanta University Press.

———. (1906c). "The Minister." *Hampton Negro Conference Annual Report* 2, 91–92.

———. (1906d). "The Sharecropping System in Lowndes County, Alabama." U.S. Bureau of Census (Subsequently "destroyed" by the U.S. Bureau of Census and, therefore, "lost").

———. (1907). "Sociology and Industry in Southern Education." *Voice of the Negro* 4, 170–75.

———. (Ed.). (1908). *The Negro American Family.* Atlanta: Atlanta University Press.

———. (1910). "Post-Graduate Work in Sociology at Atlanta University." [Unpublished manuscript]. W. E. B. Du Bois Papers, Department of Special Collections and University Archives, W. E. B. Du Bois Library, University of Massachusetts at Amherst.

———. (1911a). *The Quest of the Silver Fleece: A Novel.* Chicago: McClurg.

———. (1911b). "The Social Evolution of the Black South." *American Negro Monographs* 1, 3–12.

———. (1911c). "Writers." *Crisis* 1 (6), 20–21.

———. (1912a). "The Rural South." *American Statistical Association Publications,* 80–84.

———. (1912b). "The Upbuilding of Black Durham." *World's Work* 23, 334–38.

———. (Ed.). (1914). *Morals and Manners Among Negro Americans.* Atlanta: Atlanta University Press.

———. (1920). *Darkwater: Voices From Within the Veil.* New York: Harcourt, Brace and Howe.

———. (1924). *The Gift of Black Folk: The Negroes in the Making of America.* Boston: Stratford.

———. (1928). *Dark Princess: A Romance.* New York: Harcourt, Brace & Co.

———. (1930a). *Africa, Its Geography People and Products.* Girard, KS: Haldeman-Julius.

———. (1930b). *Africa, Its Place in Modern History.* Girard, KS: Haldemen-Julius.

———. (1938). *A Pageant in Seven Decades, 1868–1938.* Atlanta: Atlanta University Press.

———. (1939). *Black Folk Then and Now: An Essay in the History and Sociology of the Negro Race.* New York: Henry Holt.

———. (1940). "The Atlanta University Studies of the Social Conditions Among Negroes, 1896–1913" [Unpublished manuscript]. W. E. B. Du Bois Papers, Department of Special Collections and University Archives, W. E. B. Du Bois Library, University of Massachusetts at Amherst.

———. (1941). "The Future of the Negro State University." *Wilberforce University Quarterly* 2, 53–60.

———. (1942). "Review of Robert Austin Warner's *New Haven Negroes: A Social Study*." *American Historical Review* 47 (2), 376–77.

———. (1945). *Color and Democracy: Colonies and Peace*. New York: Harcourt Brace.

———. (1946). "The Future and Function of the Negro Private College." *Crisis* 53, 234–46, 253–54.

———. (1952). *In Battle for Peace: The Story of My 83rd Birthday*. New York: Masses & Mainstream.

———. (1954). *The Suppression of the African Slave Trade to the United States of America, 1638–1870*. New York: The Social Science Press.

———. (1957). *The Ordeal of Mansart*. New York: Mainstream.

———. (1958). *Pan-Africa, 1919–1958*. Accra, Ghana: Bureau of African Affairs.

———. (1959). *Mansart Builds a School*. New York: Mainstream.

———. (1960a). *Africa in Battle Against Colonialism, Racism, and Imperialism*. Chicago: Afro-American Heritage Association.

———. (1960b). "A Negro Student at Harvard at the End of the Nineteenth Century." *Massachusetts Review* 1, 439–58.

———. (1960c). *W. E. B. Du Bois: A Recorded Autobiography* [Compact Disc]. Washington, D.C.: Folkways

———. (1960d). *W. E. B. Du Bois: Socialism and the American Negro* [Compact Disc]. Washington, D.C.: Folkways.

———. (1961a). *Africa: An Essay Toward a History of the Continent of Africa and Its Inhabitants*. Moscow: Soviet Institute of African Studies.

———. (1961b). *Worlds of Color*. New York: Mainstream.

———. (1962). *John Brown*. New York: International Publishers.

———. (1963). *Colonial and Colored Unity: A Program of Action* (George Padmore, Ed.). London: Hammersmith.

———. (1964). *The Selected Poems of W. E. B. Du Bois*. Accra, Ghana: University of Ghana Press.

———. (1965). *The World and Africa: An inquiry into the part which Africa has played in world history*. New York: International Publishers.

———. (1968a). *The Autobiography of W. E. B. Du Bois: A Soliloquy on Viewing My Life from the Last Decade of Its First Century*. New York: International Publishers.

———. (1968b). *Dusk of Dawn: An Essay Toward an Autobiography of a Race Concept*. New York: Schocken.

———. (1969a). *An ABC of Color: Selections from over a Half Century of the Writings of W. E. B. Du Bois*. New York: International Publishers.

———. (Ed.). (1969b). *Atlanta University Publications, 1896–1916, Nos. 1–20* (2 volumes). New York: Arno Press.

———. (Ed.). (1969c). *Atlanta University Publications, Nos. 12–15*. New York: Russell and Russell.

———. (1970a). *The Gift of Black Folk: The Negro in the Making of America.* New York: Simon & Schuster.
———. (1970b). *The Negro.* New York: Oxford University Press.
———. (1970c). *The Selected Writings of W. E. B. Du Bois* (Walter Wilson, Ed.). New York: Mentor Books.
———. (1970d). *W. E. B. Du Bois: A Reader* (Meyer Weinberg, Ed.). New York: Harper and Row.
———. (1970e). *W. E. B. Du Bois Speaks: Speeches and Addresses, 1899–1963* (2 volumes, Philip S. Foner, Ed.). New York: Pathfinder Press.
———. (1971a). *The Seventh Son: The Thought and Writings of W. E. B. Du Bois* (Volume 1, Julius Lester, Ed.). New York: Vintage Books.
———. (1971b). *The Seventh Son: The Thought and Writings of W. E. B. Du Bois* (Volume 2, Julius Lester, Ed.). New York: Vintage Books.
———. (1971c). *W. E. B. Du Bois: A Reader* (Andrew Paschal, Ed.). New York: Collier Books.
———. (1972a). *The Emerging Thought of W. E. B. Du Bois* (Henry Lee Moon, Ed.). New York: Simon & Schuster.
———. (1972b). *The Reminiscences of W. E. B. Du Bois: An Oral History.* New York: Columbia University Libraries.
———. (1972c). *W. E. B. Du Bois: The Crisis Writings* (Daniel Walden, Ed.). Greenwich, CT: Fawcett.
———. (1973). *The Education of Black People: Ten Critiques, 1906–1960* (Herbert Aptheker, Ed.). New York: Monthly Review Press.
———. (1975). *The Gift of Black Folk: The Negroes in the Making of America.* Millwood, NY: Kraus-Thomson.
———. (1977). *Book Reviews by W. E. B. Du Bois* (Herbert Aptheker, Ed.). Millwood, NY: Kraus-Thomson.
———. (1978). *W. E. B. Du Bois on Sociology and the Black Community* (Dan S. Green and Edwin D. Driver, Eds.). Chicago: University of Chicago Press.
———. (1980a). *Contributions of W. E. B. Du Bois in Government Publications and Proceedings* (Herbert Aptheker, Ed.). Millwood, NY: Kraus-Thomson.
———. (1980b). *The Papers of W. E. B. Du Bois, 1877–1963* (89 reels of microfilm; Herbert Aptheker, Ed.). Sanford, NC: Microfilming Corporation of America.
———. (1980c). *Prayers for Dark People* (Herbert Aptheker, Ed.). Amherst: University of Massachusetts Press.
———. (1980d). *Selections from the Brownies Book* (Herbert Aptheker, Ed.). Millwood, NY: Kraus-Thomson.
———. (1980e). *Selections from Phylon* (Herbert Aptheker, Ed.). Millwood, NY: Kraus-Thomson.
———. (1982a). *Writings in Non-Periodical Literature Edited by Others* (Herbert Aptheker, Ed.). Millwood, NY: Kraus-Thomson.
———. (1982b). *Writings in Periodicals Edited by Others* (Volume 1, Herbert Aptheker, Ed.). Millwood, NY: Kraus-Thomson.
———. (1982c). *Writings in Periodicals Edited by Others* (Volume 2, Herbert Aptheker, Ed.). Millwood, NY: Kraus-Thomson.
———. (1982d). *Writings in Periodicals Edited by Others* (Volume 3, Herbert Aptheker, Ed.). Millwood, NY: Kraus-Thomson.

———. (1982e). *Writings in Periodicals Edited by Others* (Volume 4, Herbert Aptheker, Ed.). Millwood, NY: Kraus-Thomson.

———. (1983a). *Selections from The Crisis,* (Volume 1, Herbert Aptheker, Ed.). Millwood, NY: Kraus-Thomson.

———. (1983b). *Selections from The Crisis,* (Volume 2, Herbert Aptheker, Ed.). Millwood, NY: Kraus-Thomson.

———. (1985a). *Against Racism: Unpublished Essays, Papers, Addresses, 1887–1961* (Herbert Aptheker, Ed.). Amherst: University of Massachusetts Press.

———. (1985b). *Creative Writings by W. E. B. Du Bois: A Pageant, Poems, Short Stories and Playlets* (Herbert Aptheker, Ed.). Millwood, NY: Kraus-Thomson.

———. (1985c). *Selections from Horizon* (Herbert Aptheker, Ed.). White Plains, NY: Kraus-Thomson.

———. (1986a). *Du Bois: Writings* (Nathan Irvin Huggins, Ed.). New York: Library of America Press.

———. (1986b). *Newspaper Columns by W. E. B. Du Bois* (Volume 1, Herbert Aptheker, Ed.). White Plains, NY: Kraus-Thomson.

———. (1986c). *Newspaper Columns by W. E. B. Du Bois* (Volume 2, Herbert Aptheker, Ed.). White Plains, NY: Kraus-Thomson.

———. (1986d). *Pamphlets and Leaflets* (Herbert Aptheker, Ed.). New York: Kraus-Thomson.

———. (1989). *The Souls of Black Folk.* New York: Bantam-Doubleday.

———. (1992). *The World of W. E. B. Du Bois* (Meyer Weinberg, Ed.). Westport, CT: Greenwood.

———. (1995a). *Black Reconstruction in America, 1860–1880.* New York: Touchstone.

———. (1995b). *W. E. B. Du Bois Reader* (David Levering Lewis, Ed.). New York: Henry Holt.

———. (1996a). *The Oxford W. E. B. Du Bois Reader* (Eric Sundquist, Ed.). New York: Oxford University Press.

———. (1996b). *The Philadelphia Negro: A Social Study.* Philadelphia: University of Pennsylvania Press.

———. (1996c). "The Talented Tenth Memorial Address." In Henry Louis Gates Jr. and Cornel West, *The Future of the Race* (159–79). New York: Alfred A. Knopf.

———. (1997a). *The Correspondence of W. E. B. Du Bois: Volume I—Selections, 1877–1934* (Herbert Aptheker, Ed.). Amherst: University of Massachusetts Press.

———. (1997b). *The Correspondence of W. E. B. Du Bois: Volume II—Selections, 1934–1944* (Herbert Aptheker, Ed.). Amherst: University of Massachusetts Press.

———. (1997c). *The Correspondence of W. E. B. Du Bois: Volume III—Selections, 1944–1963* (Herbert Aptheker, Ed.). Amherst: University of Massachusetts Press.

———. (1997d). *The Souls of Black Folk* (Robert Gooding-Williams and David W. Blight, Eds.). Boston: Bedford Books.

———. (1998a). "The Present Condition of German Politics—1893." *Central European History* 31 (3), 171–89 [Special Issue on "W. E. B. Du Bois and the Kaiserreich Articles"].

———. (1998b). "The Socialism of the German Socialists." *Central European History* 31 (3), 189–225 [Special Issue on "W. E. B. Du Bois and the Kaiserreich Articles"].

———. (1999). *Darkwater: Voices from within the Veil*. Mineola, NY: Dover.

———. (2000a). *Du Bois on Religion* (Phil Zuckerman, Ed.). Walnut Creek, CA: AltaMira.

———. (2000b). *W. E. B. Du Bois's Historic Lecture: "The Sufferings of Black Americans, Socialism, and the Arrogance of U. S. Capitalism"* [Compact Disc]. Durham, NC: Black Historic CD Series.

———. (2001). *The Negro*. Mineola, NY: Dover.

———. (2002). *Du Bois on Education* (Eugene F. Provenzo Jr., Ed.). Walnut Creek, CA: AltaMira.

———. (2004). *The Social Theory of W. E. B. Du Bois* (Phil Zuckerman, Ed.). Thousand Oaks, CA: Sage.

———. (2005a). *Du Bois on Reform: Periodical-Based Leadership for African Americans* (Brian Johnson, Ed.). Lanham, MD: AltaMira Press.

———. (2005b). *The Illustrated Souls of Black Folk* (Eugene F. Provenzo Jr., Ed.). Boulder, CO: Paradigm Publishers.

———. (2005c). *W. E. B. Du Bois on Asia: Crossing the World Color Line* (Bill Mullen and Cathryn Watson, Eds.). Jackson: University Press of Mississippi.

———. (2006). "Die Negerfrage in den Vereinigten Staaten (The Negro Question in the United States)." *CR: The New Centennial Review* 6 (3), 241–90.

———. (2009). *W. E. B. Du Bois and the Sociological Imagination: A Reader, 1897–1914* (Robert A. Wortham, Ed.). Waco, TX: Baylor University Press.

Du Bois, W. E. B., and Washington, Booker T. (1970). *The Negro in the South*. New York: University Books.

Dubin, Robert. (1959). "Deviant Behavior and Social Structure: Continuities in Social Theory." *American Sociological Review* 24, 147–63.

Dunaway, Wilma A. (2003). *The African American Family in Slavery and Emancipation*. New York: Cambridge University Press.

Duran, Jane. (1991). *Toward a Feminist Epistemology*. Savage, MD: Rowman & Littlefield.

Durkheim, Emile. (1933). *The Division of Labor in Society*. New York: The Free Press.

———. (1963). *Emile Durkheim: Selections From His Work* (George Simpson, Ed.). New York: Thomas Y. Crowell Company.

———. (1972). *Emile Durkheim: Selected Writings* (Anthony Giddens, Ed.). Cambridge: Cambridge University Press.

Dyer, Joel. (2000). *Perpetual Prisoner Machine: How America Profits from Crime*. Boulder, CO: Westview Press.

Edelin, Ramona Hoage. (1981). "The Philosophical Foundations and Implications of William Edward Burghardt Du Bois's Social Ethic." PhD dissertation, Boston University.

Edwards, Barrington Steven. (2001). "W. E. B. Du Bois: Empirical Social Research and the Challenge to Race, 1868–1910." PhD dissertation, Harvard University.

———. (2006). "W. E. B. Du Bois Between Worlds: Berlin, Empirical Social Research, and the Race Question." *Du Bois Review: Social Science Research on Race* 3 (2), 395–424.

Ellison, Ralph. (1980). *Invisible Man*. New York: Vintage Books.

Engineer, Asgharali. (1990). *Islam and Liberation Theology: Essays on Liberative Elements in Islam*. New Delhi, India: Sterling Publishers.

Erickson, Victoria L. (1993). *Where Silence Speaks: Feminism, Social Theory, and Religion*. Minneapolis: Fortress Press.

Essed, Philomena, and Goldberg, David Theo. (Eds.). (2001). *Race Critical Theories: Texts and Contexts*. Malden, MA: Blackwell.

Evans, Curtis. (2007). "W. E. B. Du Bois: Interpreting Religion and the Problem of *The Negro Church*." *Journal of the American Academy of Religion* 75 (2), 268–97.

Eze, Emmanuel Chukwudi. (Ed.). (1997a). *African Philosophy: An Anthology*. Malden, MA: Blackwell.

———. (Ed.). (1997b). *(Post) Colonial African Philosophy: A Critical Reader*. Malden, MA: Blackwell.

Fanon, Frantz. (1965). *A Dying Colonialism* New York: Grove.

———. (1967). *Black Skin, White Masks*. New York: Grove.

———. (1968). *The Wretched of the Earth*. New York: Grove.

———. (1969). *Toward the African Revolution*. New York: Grove.

Fay, Brian. (1996). *Contemporary Philosophy of Social Science: A Multicultural Approach*. Cambridge, MA: Blackwell.

Feagin, Joe R. (1994). *Living with Racism: The Black Middle Class Experience*. Boston: Beacon Press.

Federal Bureau of Investigation. (1995). *The FBI File on W. E. B. Du Bois* (One microfilm reel). Wilmington, DE: Scholarly Resources.

———. (2009). *W. E. B. Du Bois: The FBI Files*. Washington, D.C.: Department of Justice/Government Printing Office.

Felder, Cain Hope. (2002). *Race, Racism, and the Biblical Narratives*. Minneapolis: Fortress Press.

Fierce, Milfred C. (1994). *Slavery Revisited: Blacks and the Southern Convict-Lease System, 1865–1933*. New York: City University of New York Press.

Flynn, Charles L. (1983). *White Land, Black Labor: Caste and Class in the Late Nineteenth-Century*. Baton Rouge: Louisiana State University Press.

Flynt, J. Wayne. (1979). *Dixie's Forgotten People: The South's Poor Whites*. Bloomington: Indiana University Press.

Foley, Barbara. (2003). *Spectres of 1919: Class and Nation in the Making of the New Negro*. Urbana: University of Illinois Press.

Foner, Eric. (1988). *Reconstruction: America's Unfinished Revolution, 1863–1877*. New York: Harper & Row.

Foner, Philip Sheldon. (1982). *Organized Labor and the Black Worker, 1619–1981*. New York: International Publishers.

Fong, Timothy P. (Ed.). (2008). *Ethnic Studies Research: Approaches and Perspectives*. Lanham, MD: AltaMira Press.

Fontenot, Chester J., Jr. (Ed.). (2001). *W. E. B. Du Bois & Race: Essays Celebrating the Centennial Publication of The Souls of Black Folk*. Macon, GA: Mercer University.

Fontenot, Chester J., Jr., and Keller, Mary. (Eds.). (2007). *Re-Cognizing W. E. B. Du Bois in the Twenty-First Century: Essay on W. E. B. Du Bois*. Macon, GA: Mercer University Press.

Forney, Craig Allen. (2002). "W. E. B. Du Bois: The Spirituality of a Weary Traveler." PhD dissertation, University of Chicago.

Forret, Jeff. (2006). *Race Relations at the Margins: Slaves and Poor Whites in the Antebellum Southern Countryside*. Baton Rouge: Louisiana State University Press.

Foucault, Michel. (1971). *The Order of Things: An Archaeology of the Human Sciences.* New York: Pantheon.
———. (1973). *Madness and Civilization: A History of Insanity in the Age of Reason.* New York: Vintage.
———. (1974). *The Archaeology of Knowledge and the Discourse on Language.* New York: Pantheon.
———. (1977a). *Language, Counter-Memory, Practice: Selected Essays and Interviews by Michel Foucault* (Donald F. Bouchard, Ed.). Ithaca, NY: Cornell University Press.
———. (1977b). *Power/Knowledge: Selected Interviews and Other Writings, 1972–1977* (Colin Gordon, Ed.). New York: Pantheon.
———. (1979). *Discipline and Punish: The Birth of the Prison.* New York: Vintage.
———. (1984). *The Foucault Reader* (Paul Rabinow, Ed.). New York: Pantheon.
———. (1988). *Politics, Philosophy, Culture: Interviews and Other Writings, 1977–1984* (Lawrence D. Kritzman, Ed.). New York: Routledge.
———. (1990a). *The History of Sexuality, Volume 1: The Will to Knowledge.* New York: Vintage.
———. (1990b). *The History of Sexuality, Volume 2: The Use of Pleasure.* New York: Vintage.
———. (1990c). *The History of Sexuality, Volume 3: The Care of the Self.* New York: Vintage.
———. (1994). *The Birth of the Clinic: An Archaeology of Medical Perception.* New York: Vintage.
———. (1996). *Foucault Live: Interviews, 1961–1984* (Sylvère Lotringer, Ed.). New York: Semiotext(e).
———. (2003). *Society Must Be Defended: Lectures at the College de France, 1975–76.* New York: St. Martin's Press.
———. (2009). *The History of Madness in the Classical Age.* New York: Routledge.
Franklin, Donna L. (1997). *Ensuring Inequality: The Structural Transformation of the African American Family.* New York: Oxford University Press.
Franklin, Robert Michael. (1990). *Liberating Visions: Human Fulfillment and Social Justice in African American Thought.* Minneapolis, MN: Fortress Press.
Frazier, E. Franklin. (1939). *The Negro Family in the United States.* Chicago: University of Chicago Press.
———. (1949). *The Negro in the United States.* New York: Macmillan.
———. (1951). *The Integration of the Negro into American Society.* Washington, D.C.: Howard University Press.
———. (1957). *Race and Culture Contacts in the Modern World.* New York: Knopf.
———. (1962). *The Black Bourgeoisie: The Rise of a New Middle Class in the United States.* New York: Collier.
———. (1968). *On Race Relations: Selected Writings* (G. Franklin Edwards, Ed.). Chicago: University of Chicago Press.
———. (1974). *The Negro Church in America.* New York: Schocken.
Freire, Paulo. (1985). *The Politics of Education: Culture, Power, and Liberation.* South Hadley, MA: Bergin and Garvey Publishers.
———. (1989). *Learning to Question: A Pedagogy of Liberation.* New York: Continuum.
———. (1993). *Pedagogy of the Oppressed.* New York: Continuum.

———. (1996). *Education for Critical Consciousness*. New York: Continuum.
———. (1998). *The Paulo Freire Reader* (Ana Maria Araujo Freire and Donaldo Macedo, Eds). New York: Continuum.
Fuhrman, Ellsworth R. (1980). *The Sociology of Knowledge in America, 1883–1915*. Charlottesville: University Press of Virginia.
Gabbidon, Shaun L. (1996). "The Criminological Writings of W. E. B. Du Bois: A Historical Analysis." PhD dissertation, Indiana University of Pennsylvania.
———. (1999). "W. E. B. Du Bois and the 'Atlanta School' of Social Scientific Research, 1897–1913." *Journal of Criminal Justice Education* 10 (1), 21–38.
———. (2000). "An Early American Crime Poll by W. E. B. Du Bois." *Western Journal of Black Studies* 24 (3), 167–74.
———. (2001). "W. E. B. Du Bois: Pioneering American Criminologist." *Journal of Black Studies* 31 (5), 581–99.
———. (2007). *W. E. B. Du Bois on Crime and Justice: Laying the Foundations of Sociological Criminology*. Burlington, VT: Ashgate.
———. (2010). *Race, Ethnicity, Crime, and Justice: An International Dilemma*. Los Angeles: Sage.
Gabbidon, Shaun L., Greene, Helen Taylor, and Wilder, Kideste. (2004). "Still Excluded: An Update on the Status of African American Scholars in the Discipline of Criminology and Criminal Justice." *Journal of Research in Crime and Delinquency* 41 (4), 384–406.
Gabbidon, Shaun L., Greene, Helen Taylor, and Young, Vernetta D. (Eds). (2002). *African American Classics in Criminology & Criminal Justice*. Thousand Oaks, CA: Sage.
Gaines, Kevin K. (1996). *Uplifting the Race: Black Leadership, Politics, and Culture in the Twentieth Century*. Chapel Hill: University of North Carolina Press.
Gaines, Stanley O., Jr. (1996). "Perspectives of Du Bois and Fanon on the Psychology of Oppression." In Lewis R. Gordon, T. Denean Sharley-Whiting, and Renee T. White (Eds.), *Fanon: A Critical Reader* (24–34). Cambridge, MA: Blackwell.
Gaines, Stanley O., Jr., and Reed, Edward S. (1994). "Two Social Psychologies of Prejudice: Gordon W. Allport, W. E. B. Du Bois, and the Legacy of Booker T. Washington." *Journal of Black Psychology* 20 (1), 8–28.
Garvey, Marcus. (1966). *Aims and Objects of Movement for Solution of Negro Problem Outlined: Asks White Race to Be Considerate and Sympathetic; Help Negroes to Have a Nation of Their Own in Africa; Friendly Appeal of Negro for His Race*. New York: Universal Negro Improvement Association.
Gates, Henry Louis, Jr. (1996). "W. E. B. Du Bois and 'The Talented Tenth.'" In Henry Louis Gates Jr. and Cornel West, *The Future of the Race* (115–32). New York: Alfred A. Knopf.
Gates, Henry Louis, Jr., and Jarrett, Gene Andrew. (Eds.). (2007). *The New Negro: Readings on Race, Representation, and African American Culture, 1892–1938*. Princeton, NJ: Princeton University Press.
Giddens, Anthony. (1971). *Capitalism and Modern Social Theory: An Analysis of the Writings of Marx, Durkheim and Max Weber*. Cambridge: Cambridge University Press.
Gilkes, Cheryl Townsend. (1996). "The Margin as the Center of a Theory of History: African American Women, Social Change, and the Sociology of W. E. B. Du Bois."

In Bernard W. Bell, Emily R. Grosholz, and James B. Stewart (Eds.), *W. E. B. Du Bois: On Race and Culture* (111–41). New York: Routledge.

Gillman, Susan, and Weinbaum, Alys E. (Eds.). (2007). *Next to the Color-Line: Gender, Sexuality, and W. E. B. Du Bois*. Minneapolis: University of Minnesota Press.

Gilroy, Paul. (1993). *The Black Atlantic: Modernity and Double-Consciousness*. Cambridge, MA: Harvard University Press.

Gilyard, Keith. (2008). *Composition and Cornel West: Notes Toward a Deep Democracy*. Carbondale: Southern Illinois University Press.

Girshick, Lori B. (1999). *No Safe Haven: Stories of Women in Prison*. Boston: Northeastern University Press.

Glascoe, Myrtle G. (1996). "W. E. B. Du Bois: His Evolving Theory of Education." *Research in Race & Ethnic Relations* 9, 171–88.

Gmelch, George, and Zenner, Walter P. (Eds.). (1980). *Urban Life: Readings in Urban Anthropology*. New York: St. Martin's Press.

Goetting, Ann, and Fenstermaker, Sarah. (Eds.). (1995). *Individual Voices, Collective Visions: Fifty Years of Women in Sociology*. Philadelphia: Temple University Press.

Godshalk, David F. (2005). *Veiled Visions: The 1906 Atlanta Race Riot and the Reshaping of American Race Relations*. Chapel Hill: University of North Carolina Press.

Goldberg, David Theo. (Ed.). (1990). *Anatomy of Racism*. Minneapolis: University of Minnesota Press.

———. (1993). *Racist Culture: Philosophy and the Politics of Meaning*. Cambridge: Blackwell.

———. (Ed.). (1994). *Multiculturalism: A Critical Reader*. Cambridge: Blackwell.

———. (1997). *Racial Subjects: Writing on Race in America*. New York: Routledge.

———. (2001). *The Racial State*. Malden, MA: Blackwell.

———. (2008). *The Threat of Race: Reflections on Racial Neoliberalism*. Malden, MA: Blackwell-Wiley.

Goldberg, David Theo, and Solomos, John. (Eds.). (2002). *A Companion to Racial and Ethnic Studies*. Malden, MA: Blackwell.

Goldenberg, David M. (2003). *Curse of Ham: Race and Slavery in Early Judaism, Christianity, and Islam*. Princeton, NJ: Princeton University Press.

Goldstein, Stanley L. (1972). "The Influence of Marxism on the Educational Philosophy of W. E. B. Du Bois." PhD dissertation, University of Texas, Austin.

Gonzales-Day, Ken. (2006). *Lynching in the West, 1850–1935*. Durham, NC: Duke University Press.

Goodin, Patrick. (2002). "Du Bois and Appiah: The Politics of Race and Racial Identity." In Robert E. Birt (Ed.), *The Quest for Community and Identity: Critical Essays in Africana Social Philosophy* (73–83). Lanham, MD: Rowman & Littlefield.

Gooding-Williams, Robert. (1987). "Philosophy of History and Social Critique in *The Souls of Black Folk*." *Social Science Information* 26, 99–114.

———. (1994). "Du Bois's Counter-Sublime." *Massachusetts Review* 35, 203–24.

———. (1996). "Outlaw, Appiah, and Du Bois's 'The Conservation of Races.'" In Bernard W. Bell, Emily R. Grosholz, and James B. Stewart (Eds.), *W. E. B. Du Bois: On Race and Culture* (39–56). New York: Routledge.

———. (2009). *In the Shadow of Du Bois: Afro-Modern Political Thought in America*. Cambridge, MA: Harvard University Press.

Gordon, Lewis R. (1995a). *Bad Faith and Anti-Black Racism*. Atlantic Highlands, NJ: Humanities Press.

———. (1995b). *Fanon and the Crisis of the European Man: An Essay on Philosophy and the Human Sciences*. New York: Routledge.

———. (1995c). "Sartrean Bad Faith and Anti-Black Racism." In Steven Crowell (Ed.), *The Prism of the Self: Essays in Honor of Maurice Natanson* (107–29). Dordrecht, the Netherlands: Kluwer Academic Publishers.

———. (Ed.). (1997a). *Existence in Black: An Anthology of Black Existential Philosophy*. New York: Routledge.

———. (1997b). *Her Majesty's Other Children: Sketches of Racism from a Neocolonial Age*. Lanham, MD: Rowman & Littlefield.

———. (1998). "African American Philosophy: Theory, Politics, and Pedagogy." *Philosophy of Education Yearbook: 1998* [Online article]. Available at www.ed.uiuc.edu/EPS/PES-Yearbook/1998/gordon.htm [17 October 2001].

———. (2000a). "Du Bois's Humanistic Philosophy of Human Sciences." *Annals of the American Academy of Political and Social Science* 568, 265–80.

———. (2000b). *Existentia Africana: Understanding Africana Existential Thought*. New York: Routledge.

———. (2000c). "What Does It Mean to Be a Problem?: W. E. B. Du Bois on the Study of Black Folk." In Lewis R. Gordon, *Existentia Africana: Understanding Africana Existential Thought* (62–95). New York: Routledge.

———. (2006a). "African American Philosophy, Race, and the Geography of Reason." In Lewis R. Gordon and Jane Anna Gordon (Eds.), *Not Only the Master's Tools: African American Studies in Theory and Practice* (3–50). Boulder, CO: Paradigm.

———. (2006b). *Disciplinary Decadence: Living Thought in Trying Times*. Boulder, CO: Paradigm Publishers.

———. (2006c). "Theorizing Race and Racism in an Age of Disciplinary Decadence." *Shibboleths: Journal of Comparative Theory* 1 (1), 20–36.

———. (2008). *An Introduction to Africana Philosophy*. Cambridge: Cambridge University Press.

Gordon, Lewis R., and Gordon, Jane Anna. (Eds). (2006a). *A Companion to African American Studies*. Malden, MA: Blackwell.

———. (2006b). *Not Only the Master's Tools: African American Studies in Theory and Practice*. Boulder, CO: Paradigm.

Grady-Willis, Winston A. (2006). *Challenging U. S. Apartheid: Atlanta and Black Struggles for Human Rights, 1960–1977*. Durham, NC: Duke University Press.

Gramsci, Antonio. (1971). *Selections from the Prison Notebooks of Antonio Gramsci* (Quintin Hoare and Geoffrey Nowell-Smith, Eds.). New York: International.

———. (1977). *Selections from the Political Writings, 1910–1920* (Quintin Hoare, Ed.). New York: International.

———. (1978). *Selections from the Political Writings, 1921–1926* (Quintin Hoare, Ed.). New York: International.

———. (1985). *Selections from the Cultural Writings*. (David Forgacs and Geoffrey Nowell-Smith, Eds.). Cambridge, MA: Harvard University Press.

———. (1992). *Prison Notebooks, Volume 1* (Joseph A. Buttigieg, Ed.). New York: Columbia University Press.

———. (1995). *Antonio Gramsci: Further Selections from the Prison Notebooks* (Derek Boothman, Ed.). Minneapolis: University of Minnesota Press.

———. (1996). *Prison Notebooks, Volume 2* (Joseph A. Buttigieg, Ed.). New York: Columbia University Press.

———. (2000). *The Antonio Gramsci Reader: Selected Writings, 1916–1935* (David, Forgacs, Ed.). New York: New York University Press.

Grant, Jacquelyn. (1989). *White Women's Christ and Black Women's Jesus: Feminist Christology and Womanist Response*. Atlanta: Scholars Press.

Green, Danforth Stuart. (1973). "The Truth Shall Make Ye Free: The Sociology of W. E. B. Du Bois." PhD dissertation, University of Massachusetts at Amherst.

Green, Dan S., and Driver, Edwin D. (1976). "W. E. B. Du Bois: A Case in the Sociology of Sociological Negation." *Phylon* 37 (4), 308–33.

Green, Dan S., and Smith, Earl. (1983). "W. E. B. Du Bois and the Concepts of Race and Class." *Phylon* 44, 262–72.

Greene, Helen Taylor, and Gabbidon, Shaun L. (2000). *African American Criminological Thought*. Albany: State University of New York Press.

———. (2003). "African American Scholarship in Criminological Research Published in the 1990s: A Content Analysis." *Journal of Criminal Justice Education* 14 (1), 1–15, 182.

Greer, Margaret R., Mignolo, Walter D., and Quilligan, Maureen. (Eds.). (2007). *Rereading the Black Legend: The Discourse of Religious and Racial Difference in the Renaissance Empires*. Chicago: University of Chicago Press.

Gregg, Robert. (1998). "Giant Steps: W. E. B. Du Bois and the Historical Enterprise." In Michael B. Katz and Thomas J. Sugrue (Eds.), *W. E. B. Du Bois, Race, and the City: The Philadelphia Negro and Its Legacy* (41–60). Philadelphia: University of Pennsylvania Press.

Gregory, Jeanne. (1987). *Sex, Race, and the Law: Legislating for Equality*. Newberry Park, CA: Sage.

Griggs, Sutton E. (1969). *Imperium in Imperio: A Study of the Negro Race Problem, A Novel*. New York: Ayer Co. Pubs.

Grimmer-Solem, Erik. (2003). *The Rise of Historical Economics and Social Reform in Germany, 1864–1894*. Oxford: Oxford University Press.

Grossman, James R. (1991). *Land of Hope: Chicago, Black Southerners, and the Great Migration*. Chicago: University of Chicago Press.

Guglielmo, Thomas A. (2003). *White on Arrival: Italians, Race, Color, and Power in Chicago, 1890–1945*. New York: Oxford University Press.

Gunaratnam, Yasmin. (2003). *Researching Race and Ethnicity: Methods, Knowledge, and Power*. Thousand Oaks, CA: Sage.

Gutiérrez, Gustavo. (1983). *The Power of the Poor in History: Selected Writings of Gustavo Gutiérrez*. Maryknoll, NY: Orbis.

———. (1988). *A Theology of Liberation: History, Politics, and Salvation*. Maryknoll, NY: Orbis.

———. (1994). *Las Casas: In Search of the Poor of Jesus Christ*. Maryknoll, NY: Orbis.

———. (1996). *Essential Writings of Gustavo Gutiérrez* (James B. Nickoloff, Ed.). Maryknoll, NY: Orbis.

———. (1999). "The Task and Content of Liberation Theology." In Christopher Rowland (Ed.), *The Cambridge Companion to Liberation Theology* (19–38). New York: Cambridge University Press.

Gutman, Herbert George. (1976). *The Black Family in Slavery and Freedom, 1750–1925*. New York: Pantheon Books.

Guy-Sheftall, Beverly. (1990). *Daughters of Sorrow: Attitudes Toward Black Women, 1880–1920*. New York: Carlson.

———. (Ed.). (1995). *Words of Fire: An Anthology of African American Feminist Thought*. New York: The Free Press.

Gyekye, Kwame. (1995). *An Essay on African Philosophical Thought: The Akan Conceptual Scheme*. Philadelphia: Temple University Press.

———. (1997). *Tradition and Modernity: Philosophical Reflections on the African Experience*. New York: Oxford University Press.

Habermas, Jurgen. (1984). *Theory of Communicative Action* (Volume 1). Boston: Beacon.

———. (1986a). *Knowledge and Human Interests*. Cambridge: Polity Press.

———. (1986b). *Theory and Practice*. Cambridge: Polity Press.

———. (1986c). *Toward a Rational Society*. Cambridge: Polity Press.

———. (1987a). *The Philosophical Discourse on Modernity*. Cambridge, MA: MIT Press.

———. (1987b). *Theory of Communicative Action* (Volume 2). Boston: Beacon.

———. (1988). *On the Logic of the Social Sciences*. Cambridge, MA: MIT Press.

———. (1989a). *On Society and Politics: A Reader* (Steven Seidman, Ed.). Boston: Beacon.

———. (1989b.) *The Structural Transformation of the Public Sphere*. Cambridge, MA: MIT Press.

Hagan, Frank E. (2008). *Introduction to Criminology: Theories, Methods, and Criminal Behavior*. Thousand Oaks, CA: Sage.

Hall, Stuart. (1996). *Stuart Hall: Critical Dialogues in Cultural Studies* (David Morley and Kuan-Hsing Chen, Eds.). New York: Routledge.

Hallett, Michael A. (2006). *Private Prisons in America: A Critical Race Perspective*. Urbana: University of Illinois Press.

Hammond, Evelynn M. (1997). "Toward A Genealogy of Black Female Sexuality: The Problematic of Silence." In M. Jacqui Alexander and Chandra Talpade Mohanty (Eds.), *Feminist Genealogies, Colonial Legacies, Democratic Futures* (170–81). New York: Routledge.

Haraway, Donna J. (1989). *Primate Visions: Gender, Race, and Nature in the World of Modern Science*. New York: Routledge.

———. (1997). *Modest Witness@SecondMillenium. FemaleMan Meets OncoMouse: Feminism and Technoscience*. New York: Routledge.

———. (2004). *The Haraway Reader*. New York: Routledge.

Harding, Sandra G. (1976). *Can Theories Be Refuted?: Essays on the Duhem-Quine Thesis*. Dordrecht, the Netherlands; Boston: D. Reidel Pub. Co.

———. (1986). *The Science Question in Feminism*. Ithaca, NY: Cornell University Press.

———. (Ed.). (1987). *Feminism and Methodology: Social Science Issues*. Bloomington: Indiana University Press.

———. (1991). *Whose Science? Whose Knowledge?: Thinking of Women's Lives*. Ithaca, NY: Cornell University Press.

———. (Ed.). (1993). *The "Racial" Economy of Science: Toward a Democratic Future*. Bloomington: Indiana University Press.

———. (1994). "Is Science Multicultural?: Challenges, Resources, Opportunities, Uncertainties." In David Theo Goldberg (Ed.), (1994). *Multiculturalism: A Critical Reader* (344–70). Cambridge: Blackwell.

———. (1997). "Is Modern Science an Ethno-science?: Rethinking Epistemological Assumptions." In Emmanuel C. Eze (Ed.), *(Post)Colonial African Philosophy: A Critical Reader* (45–70). Malden, MA: Blackwell.

———. (1998). *Is Science Multicultural?: Postcolonialisms, Feminisms, and Epistemologies*. Bloomington: Indiana University Press.

———. (Ed.). (2004). *The Feminist Standpoint Theory Reader: Intellectual and Political Controversies.* New York: Routledge.

———. (2006). *Science and Social Inequality: Feminist and Postcolonial Issues.* Urbana: University of Illinois Press.

———. (2008). *Sciences from Below: Feminisms, Postcolonialities, and Modernities.* Durham, NC: Duke University Press.

Harding, Sandra G., and Figueroa, Robert. (Eds). (2003). *Science and Other Cultures: Issues in Philosophies of Science and Technology.* New York: Routledge.

Harding, Sandra G., and Hintikka, Merrill B. (Eds.). (1983). *Discovering Reality: Feminist Perspectives on Epistemology, Metaphysics, Methodology, and Philosophy of Science.* Boston: Kluwer.

Harding, Sandra G., and Narayan, Uma. (Eds). (2000). *Decentering the Center: Philosophy for a Multicultural, Postcolonial, and Feminist World.* Bloomington: Indiana University Press.

Harding, Sandra G., and O'Barr, Jean F. (Eds). (1987). *Sex and Scientific Inquiry.* Chicago: University of Chicago Press.

Hare, Bruce R. (Ed.). (2002). *2001 Race Odyssey: African Americans and Sociology.* Syracuse, NY: Syracuse University Press.

Harris, Cheryl I. (1993). "Whiteness as Property." *Harvard Law Review* 106 (8), 1707–91.

Harrison, Alferdteen. (Ed.). (1991). *Black Exodus: The Great Migration from the American South.* Jackson: University Press of Mississippi.

Hartsock, Nancy C. M. (1998). *The Feminist Standpoint Revisited and Other Essays.* Boulder, CO: Westview Press.

Hattery, Angela J., and Smith, Earl. (2005). "William Edward Burghardt Du Bois and the Concepts of Race, Class, and Gender." *Sociation Today* 3 (1). Online at www.ncsociology.org/sociationtoday/v31/smith.htm.

Hattery, Angela J., and Smith, Earl. (2007). *African American Families.* Thousand Oaks, CA: Sage Publications.

Hawkesworth, M. E. (1990). *Beyond Oppression: Feminist Theory and Political Strategy.* New York: Continuum.

———. (2006a). *Feminist Inquiry: From Political Conviction to Methodological Innovation.* New Brunswick, NJ: Rutgers University Press.

———. (2006b). *Globalization and Feminist Activism.* Lanham, MD: Rowman & Littlefield.

Hawkins, Mike. (1997). *Social Darwinism in European and American Thought, 1860–1945: Nature as Model and Nature as Threat.* Cambridge: Cambridge University Press.

Hawkins, Darnell F., and Kempt-Leonard, Kimberly. (Eds.). (2005). *Our Children, Their Children: Confronting Racial and Ethnic Differences in American Juvenile Justice*. Chicago: University of Chicago Press.

Haynes, Stephen R. (2002). *Noah's Curse: The Biblical Justification of American Slavery*. Oxford: Oxford University Press.

Hearn, Jeff. (1987). *The Gender of Oppression: Men, Masculinity, and the Critique of Marxism*. New York: St. Martin's Press.

———. (1991). "Gender: Biology, Nature, and Capitalism." In Terrell Carver (Ed.), *The Cambridge Companion to Marx* (222–45). New York: Cambridge University Press.

Held, David. (1980). *Introduction to Critical Theory: Horkheimer to Habermas*. Berkeley: University of California Press.

Hendricks, James E., and Byers, Bryan. (Eds.). (1994). *Multicultural Perspectives in Criminal Justice and Criminology*. Springfield, IL: Charles C. Thomas.

Hennelly, Alfred T. (1995). *Liberation Theologies: The Global Pursuit of Justice*. Mystic, CT: Twenty-Third Publications.

Henry, Ronda C. (2009). "Buddha and Christ in *Darkwater* and *Dark Princess*: The Gendered Politics of Pan-Africanism." In Edward J. Blum and Jason R. Young (Eds.). *The Souls of W. E. B. Du Bois: New Essays and Reflections* (254–76). Macon, GA: Mercer University Press.

Henry, Stuart, and Einstadter, Werner. (Eds.). (1998). *Criminology Theory Reader*. New York: New York University Press.

Herivel, Tara, and Wright, Paul. (Eds.). (2003). *Prison Nation: The Warehousing of America's Poor*. New York: Routledge.

Hershberg, Theodore. (Ed.). (1981). *Philadelphia: Work, Space, Family, and Group Experience in the 19th Century: Essays Toward an Interdisciplinary History of the City*. New York: Oxford University Press.

Hesse-Biber, Sharlene N. (Ed.). (2007). *Handbook of Feminist Research: Theory and Praxis*. Thousand Oaks, CA: Sage.

Hesse-Biber, Sharlene, Gilmartin, Christina, and Lydenberg, Robin. (Eds.). (1999). *Feminist Approaches to Theory and Methodology: An Interdisciplinary Reader*. New York: Oxford University Press.

Hindley, Geoffrey. (2003). *Crusades: A History of Armed Pilgrimage and Holy War*. New York: Carroll & Graf Publishers.

Hine, Darlene Clark, and Jenkins, Earnestine. (Eds.). (1999). *A Question of Manhood: A Reader in U. S. Black Men's History and Masculinity* (Volume 1). Bloomington: Indiana University Press.

———. (Eds.). (2001). *A Question of Manhood: A Reader in U. S. Black Men's History and Masculinity* (Volume 2). Bloomington: Indiana University Press.

Hine, Darlene Clark, and Thompson, Kathleen. (1998). *A Shining Thread of Hope: The History of Black Women in America*. New York: Broadway Books.

Hofstadter, Richard. (1944). *Social Darwinism in American Thought, 1860–1915*. Philadelphia: University of Pennsylvania Press.

Holloway, Joseph E. (Ed.). (1991). *Africanisms in American Culture*. Bloomington: Indiana University Press.

Holloway, Jonathan Scott, and Keppel, Ben. (Eds). (2007). *Black Scholars on the Line: Race, Social Science, and American Thought in the Twentieth Century*. Notre Dame, IN: University of Notre Dame Press.

Holloway, Susan, Fuller, Bruce, Rambaud, Marylee F., and Eggers-Pierola, Costanza. (1997). *Through My Own Eyes: Single Mothers and the Cultures of Poverty*. Cambridge, MA: Harvard University Press.

Hood, Robert E. (1990). *Must God Remain Greek?: Afro-Cultures and God-Talk*. Minneapolis: Fortress Press.

hooks, bell. (1981). *Ain't I A Woman: Black Women and Feminism*. Boston: South End.

———. (1984). *Feminist Theory: From Margin to Center*. Boston: South End.

———. (1989). *Talking Back: Thinking Feminist, Thinking Black*. Boston: South End.

———. (1990). *Yearning: Race, Gender, and Cultural Politics*. Boston: South End.

———. (1991). *Black Looks: Race and Representation*. Boston: South End.

———. (1994a). *Outlaw Culture: Resisting Representation*. New York: Routledge.

———. (1994b). *Teaching to Transgress: Education as the Practice of Freedom*. New York: Routledge.

———. (1995). *Killing Rage: Ending Racism*. New York: Henry Holt.

———. (2003). *Teaching Community: A Pedagogy of Hope*. New York: Routledge.

———. (2009). *Teaching Critical Thinking: Practical Wisdom*. New York: Routledge.

Hopkins, Dwight N. (Ed.). (1999a). *Black Faith and Public Talk: Critical Essays on James H. Cone's Black Theology and Black Power*. Maryknoll, NY: Orbis.

———. (1999b). *Introducing Black Theology of Liberation*. Maryknoll, NY: Orbis.

Horn, Stanley F. (1939). *Invisible Empire: The Story of the Ku Klux Klan, 1866–1871*. Montclair, NJ: Patterson Smith Publishing Corporation.

Horne, Gerald. (1986). *Black and Red: W. E. B. Du Bois and the Afro-American Response to the Cold War, 1944–1963*. Albany: State University of New York Press.

———. (2009). *W. E. B. Du Bois: A Biography*. Westport, CT: Greenwood Press.

Howard-Pitney, David. (2005). *African American Jeremiad: Appeals for Justice in America*. Philadelphia: Temple University Press.

Hubbard, Dolan. (Ed.). (2003). *The Souls of Black Folk: One Hundred Years Later*. Columbia: University of Missouri Press.

Hudson, Kenneth. (1983). *The Archaeology of the Consumer Society: The Second Industrial Revolution in Britain*. Rutherford, NJ: Fairleigh Dickinson University Press.

Hutchinson, George. (1995). *The Harlem Renaissance in Black and White*. Cambridge, MA: Harvard University Press.

———. (2007). (Ed.). *The Cambridge Companion to the Harlem Renaissance*. Cambridge: Cambridge University Press.

Ifill, Sherrilyn A. (2007). *On the Courthouse Lawn: Confronting the Legacy of Lynching in the Twenty-First Century*. Boston: Beacon Press.

Ignatiev, Noel. (1995). *How the Irish Became White*. New York: Routledge.

Inciardi, James A. (Ed.). (1980). *Racial Criminology: The Coming Crises*. Beverly Hills: Sage.

Ingalls, Robert P. (1979). *Hoods: The Story of the Ku Klux Klan*. New York: G. P. Putnam's Sons.

Jackson, Kenneth T. (1992). *The Ku Klux Klan in the City, 1915–1930*. New York: Oxford University Press.

Jackson, John P., Jr. (2001). *Social Scientists for Justice: Making the Case for Segregation*. New York: New York University Press.
——. (Ed.). (2002). *Science, Race, and Ethnicity: Readings from Isis and Osiris*. Chicago: University of Chicago Press.
——. (2005). *Science for Segregation: Race, Law, and the Case Against Brown v. Board of Education*. New York: New York University Press.
Jackson, John P., Jr., and Weidman, Nadine M. (2004). *Race, Racism, and Science: Social Impact and Interaction*. Santa Barbara, CA: ABC-CLIO.
Jacobson, Matthew Frye. (1998). *Whiteness of a Different Color: European Immigrants and the Alchemy of Race*. Cambridge, MA: Harvard University Press.
James, C. L. R. (1994). *C. L. R. James and Revolutionary Marxism: Selected Writings of C. L. R. James, 1939–1949* (Scott McLemee and Paul Le Blanc, Eds.). Atlantic Highlands, NJ: Humanities Press.
——. (1996). *C. L. R. James on the "Negro Question"* (Scott McLemee, Ed.). Jackson: University of Mississippi Press.
——. (1999). *Marxism for Our Times: C. L. R. James on Revolutionary Organization* (Martin Glaberman, Ed.). Jackson: University of Mississippi Press.
James, Joy A. (1996). *Resisting State Violence: Radicalism, Gender, and Race in U. S. Culture*. Minneapolis: University of Minnesota Press.
——. (1997). *Transcending the Talented Tenth: Black Leaders and American Intellectuals*. New York: Routledge.
——. (1999). *Shadow Boxing: Representations of Black Feminist Politics*. New York: St. Martin's Press.
——. (Ed.). (2000). *States of Confinement: Policing, Detention, and Prisons*. New York: St. Martin's Press.
James, Joy A., and Sharpley-Whiting, T. Denean. (Eds.). (2000). *The Black Feminist Reader*. Malden, MA: Blackwell.
JanMohamed, Abdul R. (1985). "The Economy of Manichean Allegory: The Function of Racial Difference in Colonialist Literature." *Critical Inquiry* 12, 59–87.
——. (1988). *Aesthetics: The Politics of Literature in Colonial Africa* (second edition). Amherst: University of Massachusetts Press.
Jay, Martin. (1996). *The Dialectical Imagination: A History of the Frankfurt School and the Institute of Social Research, 1923–1950*. Berkeley: University of California Press.
Jennings, Patricia K. (1998). "The Lions and the Canon: The Formative Contributions of W. E. B. Du Bois and Frantz Fanon to Social Theory." *American Sociological Association*.
Jensen, Robert. (2005). *The Heart of Whiteness: Confronting Race, Racism, and White Privilege*. San Francisco: City Lights.
Johnson, Brain L. (2008). *W. E. B. Du Bois: Toward Agnosticism, 1868–1934*. Lanham, MD: Rowman & Littlefield.
Johnson, Paula C. (2003). *Inner Lives: Voices of African American Women in Prison*. New York: New York University Press.
Jones, Stephen P. (2006). *Criminology*. New York: Oxford University Press.
Jordan, Winthrop D. (1968). *White Over Black: American Attitudes Toward the Negro, 1550–1812*. Chapel Hill: University of North Carolina Press.

Kahn, Jonathon S. (2004). "Religion and the Binding of *The Souls of Black Folk*." *Philosophia Africana* 7 (2), 17–31.

———. (2009). *The Divine Discontent: The Religious Imagination of W. E. B. Du Bois*. New York: Oxford University Press.

Katz, Michael B., and Sugrue, Thomas J. (Eds.). (1998). *W. E. B. Du Bois, Race, and the City: The Philadelphia Negro and Its Legacy*. Philadelphia: University of Pennsylvania Press.

Keita, Lansana. (1991). "Contemporary African Philosophy: The Search for a Method." In Tsenay Serequeberhan (Ed.), *African Philosophy: The Essential Readings* (132–55). New York: Paragon House.

Kellner, Douglas. (1989). *Critical Theory, Marxism, and Modernity*. Baltimore: Johns Hopkins University Press.

Kendall, Frances E. (2006). *Understanding White Privilege: Creating Pathways to Authentic Relationships Across Race*. New York: Routledge.

Kennedy, Stetson. (1990). *The Klan Unmasked*. Gainesville: University Press of Florida.

Key, R. Charles. (1978). "Society and Sociology: The Dynamics of Black Sociological Negation." *Phylon* 39, 35–48.

Khatri, Daryao S., and Hughes, Anne O. (2002). *America Education Apartheid—Again?* Lanham, MD: Scarecrow Press.

Kincaid, Harold, Dupré, John, and Wylie, Alison. (Eds.). (2007). *Value-Free Science? Ideals and Illusions*. Oxford: Oxford University Press.

King, Deborah K. (1995). "Multiple Jeopardy, Multiple Consciousness: The Contest of Black Feminist Ideology." In Beverly Guy-Sheftall (Ed.), *Words of Fire: AnAnthology of African American Feminist Thought* (294–318). New York: The Free Press.

King, William M. (1990). "Challenges Across the Curriculum: Broadening the Bases of How Knowledge is Produced." *American Behavioral Scientist* 34 (2), 165–80.

———. (1995). "Triumphs of Tribalism: The American University as a Reflection of Eurocentric Culture." In Benjamin P. Bowser, Terry Jones, and Gale S. Aulletta (Eds.), *Toward the Multicultural University* (21–39). Westport, CT: Greenwood.

———. (2009). "Dr. William M. King Interviewed: National Council for Black Studies Founding Member." *Journal of Pan-African Studies* 3 (1), 23–53.

Kirschkle, Amy Helene. (2007). *Art in Crisis: W. E. B. Du Bois and the Struggle for African American Identity and Memory*. Bloomington: Indiana University Press.

Kozol, Jonathan. (2005). *The Shame of the Nation: The Restoration of Apartheid Schooling in America*. New York: Crown Publishing.

Kunnie, Julian. (1994). *Models of Black Theology: Issues in Class, Culture, and Gender*. Valley Forge, PA: Trinity Press.

Kushner, James A. (1980). *Apartheid in America: An Historical and Legal Analysis of Contemporary Racial Segregation in the United States*. Arlington, VA: Carrollton Press.

Lacy, Karyn R. (2007). *Blue-Chip Black: Race, Class, and Status in the New Black Middle Class*. Berkeley: University of California Press.

Ladner, Joyce A. (Ed.). (1998). *The Death of White Sociology: Essays on Race and Culture*. Baltimore: Black Classic Press.

Landry, Bart. (1987). *The New Black Middle Class*. Berkeley: University of California Press.

Lasch-Quinn, Elizabeth. (1993). *Black Neighbors: Race and the Limits of Reform in the American Settlement House Movement, 1890–1945*. Chapel Hill: University of North Carolina Press.

Leacock, Eleanor Burke. (Ed.). (1971). *The Culture of Poverty: A Critique*. New York: Simon & Schuster.

Lehmann, Jennifer M. (1994). *Durkheim and Women*. Lincoln: University of Nebraska Press.

Lemann, Nicholas. (1991). *The Promised Land: The Great Black Migration and How it Changed America*. New York: Vintage Books.

Lemert, Charles C. (1994). "A Classic from the Veil: Du Bois's *Souls of Black Folk*." *Sociological Quarterly* 35 (3), 383–96.

———. (2000a). "The Race of Time: Du Bois and Reconstruction." *Boundary 2* 27 (3), 215–48.

———. (2000b). "W. E. B. Du Bois." In George Ritzer (Ed.), *The Blackwell Companion to Major Social Theorists* (345–67). Malden, MA: Blackwell.

Lemire, Elise Virginia. (2002). *"Miscegenation": Making Race In America*. Philadelphia: University of Pennsylvania Press.

Lemke, Sieglinde. (2000). "Berlin and Boundaries: Sollen Versus Geschehen." *Boundary 2*, 27 (3), 45–78.

Lemons, Gary L. (2001). "'When and Where [We] Enter': In Search of a Feminist Forefather—Reclaiming the Womanist Legacy of W. E. B. Du Bois." In Rudolph P. Byrd and Beverly Guy-Sheftall (Eds.), *Traps: African American Men on Gender and Sexuality* (71–89). Indianapolis: Indiana University Press.

———. (2009). *Womanist Forefathers: Frederick Douglass and W. E. B. Du Bois*. Albany: State University of New York Press.

Lengermann, Patricia M., and Niebrugge-Brantley, Jill. (1998). *The Women Founders: Sociology and Social Theory, 1830–1930*. Boston: McGraw-Hill.

Levinson, David. (2006). *Sewing Circles, Dime Suppers, and W. E. B. Du Bois: A History of the A. M. E. Zion Church*. Great Barrington, MA: Berkshire Publishing Group.

Lewis, David Levering. (1989). *When Harlem Was in Vogue*. New York: Oxford University Press.

———. (1993). *W. E. B. Du Bois: Biography of a Race, 1868–1919*. New York: Henry Holt.

———. (2000). *W. E. B. Du Bois: The Fight for Equality and the American Century, 1919–1963*. New York: Henry Holt.

Licht, Walter. (1992). *Getting Work: Philadelphia, 1840–1950*. Cambridge, MA: Harvard University Press.

Lilly, J. Robert, Cullen, Francis T., and Ball, Richard A. (2007). *Criminological Theory: Context and Consequences*. Thousand Oaks, CA: Sage.

Lincoln, Eric C., and Mamiya, Lawrence H. (1990). *The Black Church in the African American Experience*. Durham, NC: Duke University Press.

Litwack, Leon F. (1979). *Been in the Storm So Long: The Aftermath of Slavery*. New York: Vintage Books.

———. (1998). *Trouble in Mind: Black Southerners in the Age of Jim Crow.* New York: Alfred A. Knopf.

Locke, Alain L. (Ed.). (1968). *The New Negro.* New York: Arno Press.

———. (1983). "The New Negro." In Leonard Harris (Ed.), *Philosophy Born of Struggle: An Anthology of Afro-American Philosophy from 1917* (242–51). Dubuque, IA: Kendall/Hunt.

Logan, Charles H. (1990). *Private Prisons: Cons and Pros.* New York: Oxford University Press.

Logan, Rayford W. (1954). *The Negro in American Life and Thought: The Nadir, 1877–1901.* New York: Dial Press.

Lorde, Audre. (1984). *Sister Outsider: Essays and Speeches by Audre Lorde.* Freedom, CA: The Crossing Press Feminist Series.

Lott, Tommy L. (1997). "Du Bois on the Invention of Race." In John P. Pittman (Ed.), *African American Perspectives and Philosophical Traditions* (166–87). New York: Routledge.

———. (1999). *The Invention of Race: Black Culture and the Politics of Representation.* Malden, MA: Blackwell.

———. (2000). "Du Bois and Locke on the Scientific Study of the Negro." *Boundary 2* 27 (3), 135–52.

———. (2001). "Du Bois's Anthropological Notion of Race." In Robert Bernasconi (Ed.), *Race* (59–83). Malden, MA: Blackwell.

Lott, Tommy L., and Pittman, John P. (Eds.). (2003). *A Companion to African American Philosophy.* Malden, MA: Blackwell.

Lucal, Betsy. (1996). "Race, Class, and Gender in the Work of W. E. B. Du Bois: An Exploratory Study." *Research in Race & Ethnic Relations* 9, 191–210.

Luke, Carmen. (Eds.). (1996). *Feminisms and Pedagogies of Everyday Life.* Albany: State University of New York Press.

Luke, Carmen, and Gore, Jennifer. (Eds.). (1992). *Feminisms and Critical Pedagogy.* New York: Routledge.

Lynch, Michael J., and Michalowski, Raymond. (2006). *Primer in Radical Criminology: Critical Perspectives on Crime, Power, and Identity.* Monsey, NY: Willow Tree Press.

MacEvitt, Christopher Hatch. (2008). *Crusades and the Christian World of the East: Rough Tolerance.* Philadelphia: University of Pennsylvania Press.

Madison, James H. (2001). *Lynching in the Heartland: Race and Memory in America.* New York: Palgrave.

Mancini, Matthew J. (1996). *One Dies, Get Another: Convict-Leasing in the American South, 1866–1928.* Columbia: University of South Carolina Press.

Mannheim, Karl. (1972). *Essays on the Sociology of Knowledge* (Paul Kecskemeti, Ed.). London: Routledge and Kegan Paul.

Marable, Manning. (1983). *How Capitalism Underdeveloped Black America.* Boston: South End.

———. (1986). *W. E. B. Du Bois: Black Radical Democrat.* Boston: Twayne.

———. (1998). *Black Leadership.* New York: Columbia University Press.

———. (Ed.). (2000). *Dispatches from the Ebony Towers: Intellectuals Confront the African American Experience.* New York: Columbia University Press.

———. (Ed). (2005). *The New Black Renaissance: The Souls Anthology of Critical African American Studies*. Boulder, CO: Paradigm Publishers.

Marcuse, Herbert. (1970). *Five Lectures: Psychoanalysis, Politics, and Utopia*. Boston: Beacon.

———. (2001). *Towards a Critical Theory of Society: The Collected Papers of Herbert Marcuse* (Volume 2, Douglas Kellner, Ed.). New York: Routledge.

———. (2004). *The New Left and the 1960's: The Collected Papers of Herbert Marcuse* (Volume 3, Douglass Kellner, Ed.). New York: Routledge.

———. (2005). *Heideggerian Marxism*. (Richard Wolin and John Abromeit, Eds.). Lincoln: University of Nebraska Press.

———. (2007a). *Art and Liberation: The Collected Papers of Herbert Marcuse* (Volume 4, Douglass Kellner, Ed.). New York: Routledge.

———. (2007b). *The Essential Marcuse: Selected Writings of Philosopher and Social Critic Herbert Marcuse* (Andrew Feenberg and William Leiss, Eds.). Boston: Beacon.

Markovitz, Jonathan. (2004). *Legacies of Lynching: Racial Violence and Memory*. Minneapolis: University of Minnesota Press.

Marks, Carole. (1989). *Farewell, We're Good and Gone: The Great Black Migration*. Bloomington: Indiana University Press.

Marshall, Jessica. (1994). "'Counsels of Despair': W. E. B. Du Bois, Robert E. Park, and the Establishment of American Race Sociology." PhD dissertation, Harvard University.

Massey, Douglas S., and Denton, Nancy A. (1993). *American Apartheid: Segregation and the Making of the Underclass*. Cambridge, MA: Harvard University Press.

Mastnak, Tomaz. (2002). *Crusading Peace: Christendom, the Muslim World, and Western Political Order*. Berkeley: University of California Press.

May, John P., and Pitts, Khalid R. (Eds.). (2000). *Building Violence: How America's Rush to Incarcerate Creates More Violence*. Thousand Oaks, CA: Sage.

Mays, Benjamin E., and Nicholson, Joseph W. (1933). *Negro's Church*. New York: Institute of Social and Religious Research.

Mazrui, Ali A. (1986). *The Africans: A Triple Heritage*. Boston: Little Brown.

McAdoo, Harriette Pipes. (Ed.). (2006). *Black Families*. Thousand Oaks, CA: Sage Publications.

McCarthy, E. Doyle. (1996). *Knowledge as Culture: The New Sociology of Knowledge*. New York: Routledge.

McGovern, Arthur. (1989). *Liberation Theology and Its Critics: Toward an Assessment*. Maryknoll, NY: Orbis.

McKay, Nellie Y. (1985). "W. E. B. Du Bois: The Black Woman in His Writings—Selected Fictional and Autobiographical Portraits." In William L. Andrews (Ed.), *Critical Essays on W. E. B. Du Bois* (230–52). Boston: G. K. Hall.

———. (1990). "The Souls of Black Women Folk in the Writings of W. E. B. Du Bois." In Henry Louis Gates Jr. (Ed.), *Reading Black/Reading Feminist: A Critical Anthology* (227–43). New York: Meridian.

McKee, James B. (1993). *Sociology and the Race Problem: The Failure of a Perspective*. Urbana: University of Illinois Press.

McLaren, Peter. (2000a). *Che Guevara, Paulo Freire, and the Pedagogy of Revolution*. Lanham, MD: Rowman & Littlefield.

———. (2000b). "Paulo Freire's Pedagogy of Possibility." In Peter McLaren, Robert Bahruth, Stan Steiner, and Mark Krank (Eds.), *Freirean Pedagogy, Praxis, and Possibilities: Projects for the New Millennium* (1–22). New York: Falmer Press.

McRoberts, Omar M. (2003). *Streets of Glory: Church and Community in a Black Urban Neighborhood*. Chicago: University of Chicago Press.

McShane, Marilyn D., and Williams, Frank P., III. (2009). *Criminological Theory*. Englewood Cliffs, NJ: Prentice Hall.

Meier, August. (1959). "From 'Conservative' to 'Radical': The Ideological Development of W. E. B. Du Bois, 1885–1905." *Crisis* 75, 527–36.

———. (1963). *Negro Thought in America, 1880–1915: Racial Ideologies in the Age of Booker T. Washington*. Ann Arbor: University of Michigan Press.

Melossi, Dario, and Pavarini, Massimo. (1981). *Prison and the Factory: Origins of the Penitentiary System*. London: Macmillan.

Merton, Robert K. (1938). "Social Structure and Anomie." *American Sociological Review* 3, 672–82.

———. (1968). *Social Theory and Social Structure*. New York: Free Press.

———. (1972). "Insiders and Outsiders: A Chapter in the Sociology of Knowledge." *American Journal of Sociology* 77, 9–47.

———. (1975). *Conflict Sociology: Toward an Explanatory Science*. New York: Academic.

Mielke, David Nathaniel. (1977). "W. E. B. Du Bois: An Educational Critique." PhD dissertation, University of Tennessee, Knoxville.

Mignolo, Walter. (2000). *Local Histories/Global Designs: Coloniality, Subaltern Knowledges, and Border Thinking*. Princeton, NJ: Princeton University Press.

———. (2003). *The Darker Side of the Renaissance: Literacy, Territoriality, and Colonization*. Ann Arbor: University of Michigan Press.

———. (2005). *The Idea of Latin America*. Malden, MA: Blackwell.

Milbank, John. (1990). *Theology and Social Theory: Beyond Secular Reason*. Cambridge: Blackwell.

Miller, Susan L. (Ed.). (2007). *Criminal Justice Research and Practice: Diverse Voices from the Field*. Boston: Northeastern University Press.

Mills, Charles W. (1997). *The Racial Contract*. Ithaca, NY: Cornell University Press.

———. (1998). *Blackness Visible: Essays on Philosophy and Race*. Ithaca, NY: Cornell University Press.

———. (1999). "The Racial Polity." In Susan E. Babbitt and Susan Campbell (Eds.), *Racism and Philosophy* (13–31, [endnotes] 255–57). Ithaca, NY: Cornell University Press.

———. (2003a). *From Class to Race: Essays in White Marxism and Black Radicalism*. Lanham, MD: Rowman & Littlefield.

———. (2003b). "White Supremacy." In Tommy L. Lott and John P. Pittman (Eds.), *A Companion to African American Philosophy* (269–84). Malden, MA: Blackwell.

Mirecki, Paul and BeDuhn, Jason. (Eds.). (2001). *The Light and the Darkness: Studies in Manichaeism and its World*. Boston: Brill.

Mixon, Gregory. (2005). *The Atlanta Riot: Race, Class, and Violence in a New South City*. Gainsville: University Press of Florida.

Mocombe, Paul C. (2008). *The Soul-less Souls of Black Folk: A Sociological Reconsideration of Black Consciousness as Du Boisian Double-Consciousness*. Lanham, MD: University Press of America.

Mohanty, Chandra Talpade. (2003). *Feminism Without Borders: Decolonizing Theory, Practicing Solidarity.* Durham, NC: Duke University Press.
Moore, Jack B. (1981). *W. E. B. Du Bois.* Boston: Twayne.
Morris, Aldon D. (2007). "Sociology of Race and W. E. B. Du Bois." In Craig J. Calhoun (Ed.), *Sociology in America: A History* (503-34). Chicago: University of Chicago Press.
Morris, Norval, and Rothman, David J. (Eds). (1995). *Oxford History of the Prison: The Practice of Punishment in Western Society.* Oxford: Oxford University Press.
Morrison, Toni. (1990). *Playing in the Dark: Whiteness and the Literary Imagination.* Cambridge, MA: Harvard University Press.
Moses, Wilson Jeremiah. (1978). *The Golden Age of Black Nationalism, 1850-1925.* New York: Oxford University Press.
———. (1993). "W. E. B. Du Bois's 'The Conservation of Races' and Its Context: Idealism, Conservatism, and Hero Worship." *Massachusetts Review* 34, 275-94.
———. (1996). "Culture, Civilization, and the Decline of the West: The Afrocentricism of W. E. B. Du Bois." In Bernard W. Bell, Emily R. Grosholz, and James B. Stewart (Eds.), *W. E. B. Du Bois: On Race and Culture* (243-60). New York: Routledge.
———. (1998). *Afrotopia: The Roots of African American Popular History.* Cambridge: Cambridge University Press.
Moss, Kirby. (2003). *The Color of Class: Poor Whites and the Paradox of Privilege.* Philadelphia: University of Pennsylvania Press.
Moyer, Imogene L. (2001). *Criminological Theories: Traditional and Non-Traditional Voices and Themes.* Thousand Oaks, CA: Sage.
Murphy, Joseph M. (1994). *Working the Spirit: Ceremonies of the African Diaspora.* Boston: Beacon.
Myers, Kristen A., Anderson, Cynthia D., and Risman, Barbara J. (Eds.). (1998). *Feminist foundations: Toward Transforming Sociology.* Thousand Oaks, CA: Sage.
Myrdal, Gunnar. (1944). *An American Dilemma: The Negro Problem and Modern Democracy.* New York: Harper & Brothers.
Naples, Nancy A. (2003). *Feminism and Method: Ethnography, Discourse Analysis, and Activist Research.* New York: Routledge.
Narayan, Uma. (1997). *Dislocating Cultures: Identities, Traditions, and Third World Feminism.* New York: Routledge.
Naseef, Omar. (2007). *Liberation Theology: Islam and the Feminist Agenda in the Qur'an.* Bloomington, IN: AuthorHouse.
Neal, Terry Ray. (1984). "W. E. B. Du Bois's Contributions to the Sociology of Education." PhD dissertation, University of Cincinnati.
Nevels, Cynthia Skove. (2007). *Lynching to Belong: Claiming Whiteness Through Racial Violence.* College Station: Texas A&M University Press.
Nielsen, Joyce McCarl. (Ed.). (1990). *Feminist Research Methods: Exemplary Readings in the Social Sciences.* Boulder, CO: Westview Press.
Nieman, Donald G. (Ed.). (1994a). *African Americans and Non-Agricultural Labor in the South, 1865-1900.* New York: Garland.
———. (Ed.). (1994b). *The African American Family in the South, 1861-1900.* New York: Garland.
———. (Ed.). (1994c). *Black Southerners and the Law, 1865-1900.* New York: Garland.

Novak, Daniel A. (1978). *The Wheel of Servitude: Black Forced Labor After Slavery.* Lexington: University Press of Kentucky.

Nwankwo, Henry C. (1989). "The Educational Philosophy of W. E. B. Du Bois: A Nigerian Interpretation." PhD dissertation, East Texas State University.

Oatts, Terry O'Neal. (2003). "W. E. B. Du Bois and Critical Race Theory: Toward a Du Boisian Philosophy of Education." EdD dissertation, Georgia Southern University.

———. (2006). *W. E. B. Du Bois and Critical Race Theory: Toward a Du Boisian Philosophy of Education.* Sydney: Exceptional Publications.

Okoro, Martin Umachi. (1982). "W. E. B. Du Bois's Ideas on Education: Implications for Nigerian Education." PhD dissertation, Loyola University of Chicago.

Olaniyan, Tejumola. (1992). "Narrativing Postcoloniality: Responsibilities." *Public Culture* 5 (1), 47–55.

———. (2000). "Africa: Varied Colonial Legacies." In Henry Schwarz and Sangeeta Ray (Eds.), *A Companion to Postcolonial Studies* (269–81). Malden, MA: Blackwell.

Olson, Joel. (2004). *The Abolition of White Democracy.* Minneapolis: University of Minnesota Press.

———. (2005). "W. E. B. Du Bois and the Race Concept." *SOULS: A Critical Journal of Black Politics, Culture, and Society* 7 (3–4), 118–28.

Olupona, Jacob K., and Gemignani, Regina. (Eds.). (2007). *African Immigrant Religions in America.* New York: New York University Press.

Omi, Michael, and Winant, Howard. (1994). *Racial Formation in United States: From the 1960's to the 1990's.* New York: Routledge.

Onwudiew, Ihekobowa, and Lynch, Michael J. (2000). "Reopening the Debate: Reconsidering a Black Criminology." *Social Pathology* 6 (3), 182–98.

Outlaw, Lucius T., Jr. (1990). "Toward a Critical Theory of 'Race.'" In David Theo Goldberg (Ed.), *Anatomy of Racism* (58–82). Minneapolis: University of Minnesota Press.

———. (1995). "On W. E. B. Du Bois's 'The Conservation of Races.'" In Linda A. Bell and David Blumenfeld (Eds.), *Overcoming Racism and Sexism* (79–102). Lanham, MD: Rowman & Littlefield.

———. (1996a). "'Conserve' Races?: In Defense of W. E. B. Du Bois." In Bernard W. Bell, Emily R. Grosholz, and James B. Stewart (Eds.), *W. E. B. Du Bois: On Race and Culture* (15–38). New York: Routledge.

———. (1996b). *On Race and Philosophy.* New York: Routledge.

———. (1997a). "African, African American, Africana Philosophy." In John P. Pittman (Ed.), *African American Perspectives and Philosophical Traditions* (63–93). New York: Routledge.

———. (1997b). "Is There a Distinctive African American Philosophy?" *Academic Questions* 10 (2), 29–46.

———. (2000). "W. E. B. Du Bois on the Study of Social Problems." *Annals of the American Academy of Political and Social Science* 568, 281–97.

———. (2005). *Critical Social Theory in the Interests of Black Folk.* Lanham, MD: Rowman & Littlefield.

Painter, Nell Irvin. (1996). *Sojourner Truth: A Life, A Symbol.* New York: Norton.

Palmié, Stephan. (Ed.). (2008). *Africas of the Americas: Beyond the Search for Origins in the Study of Afro-Atlantic Religions*. Boston: Brill.

Pampel, Fred C. (2004). *Racial Profiling*. New York: Facts on File.

Parenti, Christian. (1999). *Lockdown America: Police and Prisons in the Age of Crisis*. New York: Verso.

Parker, Laurence, Deyhle, Donna, and Villenas, Sofia. (Eds.). (1999). *Race Is, Race Isn't: Critical Race Theory and Qualitative Studies in Education*. Boulder, CO: Westview.

Pascoe, Peggy. (2009). *What Comes Naturally: Miscegenation Law and the Making of Race in America*. New York: Oxford University Press.

Pateman, Carole. (1988). *The Sexual Contract*. Palo Alto, CA: Stanford University Press.

Pattillo, Mary E. (2000). *Black Picket Fences: Privilege and Peril Among the Black Middle Class*. Chicago: University of Chicago Press.

Penn, Everette B. (2003). "On Black Criminology: Past, Present, and Future." *Criminal Justice Studies: A Critical Journal of Crime, Law, and Society* 16 (4), 317–27.

Penn, Everette B., Greene, Helen Taylor, and Gabbidon, Shaun L. (Eds). (2006). *Race and Juvenile Justice*. Durham, NC: Carolina Academic Press.

Pettigrew, Thomas F. (Ed.). (1980). *The Sociology of Race Relations: Reflection and Reform*. New York: Free Press.

Pfiefer, Michael J. (2004). *Rough Justice: Lynching and American Society, 1874–1947*. Urbana: University of Illinois Press.

Phillips, Layli. (Ed.). (2006). *The Womanist Reader*. New York: Routledge.

Pieterse, Jan Nederveen. (1992). *White on Black: Images of Africa and Blacks in Western Popular Culture*. New Haven, CT: Yale University Press.

Pinar, William F. (2001). *Gender of Racial Politics and Violence in America: Lynching, Prison Rape, and the Crisis of Masculinity*. New York: P. Lang.

Pinn, Anthony B. (2003). *Terror and Triumph: The Nature of Black Religion*. Minneapolis: Fortress Press.

Pinn, Anthony B. (Ed.). (2009). *Black Religion and Aesthetics: Religious Thought and Life in Africa and the African Diaspora*. New York: Palgrave-Macmillan.

Pinsky, Valerie, and Wylie, Alison. (Eds.). (1989). *Critical Traditions in Contemporary Archaeology: Essays in the Philosophy, History, and Socio-Politics of Archaeology*. Cambridge: Cambridge University Press.

Poliakov, Leon. (1974). *The Aryan Myth*. New York: Basic Books.

Prentiss, Craig R. (Ed.). (2003). *Religion and the Creation of Race and Ethnicity: An Introduction*. New York: New York University Press.

Quayson, Ato. (2000a). *Postcolonialism: Theory, Practice or Process?* Malden, MA: Polity.

———. (2000b). "Postcolonialism and Postmodernism." In Henry Schwarz and Sangeeta Ray (Eds.), *A Companion to Postcolonial Studies* (87–111). Malden, MA: Blackwell.

Rabaka, Reiland. (2003a). "'Deliberately Using the Word *Colonial* in a Much Broader Sense': W. E. B. Du Bois's Concept of 'Semi-Colonialism' as Critique of and Contribution to Postcolonialism." *Jouvert: A Journal of Postcolonial Studies* 7 (2), 1–32. Available online at social.chass.ncsu.edu/jouvert/index.htm [Accessed on 23 February 2003].

———. (2003b). "W. E. B. Du Bois and 'The Damnation of Women': An Essay on Africana Anti-Sexist Critical Social Theory." *Journal of African American Studies* 7 (2), 39–62.

———. (2003c). "W. E. B. Du Bois's Evolving Africana Philosophy of Education." *Journal of Black Studies* 33 (4), 399–449.

———. (2004). "The Souls of Black Female Folk: W. E. B. Du Bois and Africana Anti-Sexist Critical Social Theory." *Africalogical Perspectives* 1 (2), 100–141.

———. (2005). "W. E. B. Du Bois and Decolonization: Pan-Africanism, Postcolonialism, and Radical Politics." In James L. Conyers (Ed.), *W. E. B. Du Bois, Marcus Garvey, and Pan-Africanism* (123–54). Lewistown, NY: Mellen Press.

———. (2006a). "Africana Critical Theory of Contemporary Society: Ruminations on Radical Politics, Social Theory, and Africana Philosophy." In Molefi K. Asante and Maulana Karenga (Eds.), *The Handbook of Black Studies* (130–52). Thousand Oaks, CA: Sage.

———. (2006b). "The Souls of Black Radical Folk: W. E. B. Du Bois, Critical Social Theory, and the State of Africana Studies." *Journal of Black Studies* 36 (5), 732–63.

———. (2006c). "The Souls of White Folk: W. E. B. Du Bois's Critique of White Supremacy and Contributions to Critical White Studies (Part I)." *Ethnic Studies Review: Journal of the National Association for Ethnic Studies* 29 (2), 1–19.

———. (2006d). "W. E. B. Du Bois's 'The Comet' and Contributions to Critical Race Theory: An Essay on Black Radical Politics and Anti-Racist Social Ethics." *Ethnic Studies Review: Journal of the National Association of Ethnic Studies* 29 (1), 34–57.

———. (2007a). "The Souls of White Folk: W. E. B. Du Bois's Critique of White Supremacy and Contributions to Critical White Studies (Part II)." *Journal of African American Studies* 11 (1), 1–15.

———. (2007b). *W. E. B. Du Bois and the Problems of the Twenty-First Century: An Essay on Africana Critical Theory.* Lanham, MD: Lexington Books.

———. (2008a). *Du Bois's Dialectics: Black Radical Politics and the Reconstruction of Critical Social Theory.* Lanham, MD: Lexington Books.

———. (2008b). "Malcolm X and Africana Critical Theory: Rethinking Revolutionary Black Nationalism, Black Radicalism, and Black Marxism." In James L. Conyers and Andrew P. Smallwood (Eds.), *Malcolm X: A Historical Reader* (281–98). Durham, NC: Carolina Academic Press.

———. (2008c). "The Prophet of Problems: W. E. B. Du Bois, Philosophy of Religion, Sociology of Religion, and Black Liberation Theology—A Critical Review of Edward J. Blum's *W. E. B. Du Bois: American Prophet.*" *Journal of Southern Religion* 11. Available online at jsr.fsu.edu/Volume11/Rabaka.htm [Accessed on 23 February 2009].

———. (2009a). *Africana Critical Theory: Reconstructing the Black Radical Tradition, from W. E. B. Du Bois and C. L. R. James to Frantz Fanon and Amilcar Cabral.* Lanham, MD: Lexington Books.

———. (2009b). "Teoria Crítica Africana." In Elisa L. Nascimento (Ed.), *Afrocentricidade: Uma abordagem epistemológica inovadora* (129–46). São Paulo, Brazil: Selo Negro Edições. [In Portugese.]

———. (2009c). "W. E. B. Du Bois, Reparations, Radical Politics, and Critical Race Theory." In James L. Conyers (Ed.), *Racial Structure and Radical Politics in the African Diaspora* (81–113). New Brunswick, NJ: Transaction.

———. (2010a). *Forms of Fanonism: Frantz Fanon's Critical Theory and the Dialectics of Decolonization*. Lanham, MD: Lexington Books.

———. (Ed.). (2010b). *W. E. B. Du Bois: A Critical Reader*. Fanham, Surrey, UK: Ashgate Publishing.

———. (forthcoming). *The Souls of White Folk: W. E. B. Du Bois and Critical White Studies*. Lanham, MD: Lexington Books.

Raboteau, Albert J. (1978). *Slave Religion: The "Invisible Institution" in the Antebellum South*. New York: Oxford University Press.

Ramji, Hasmita. (2009). *Researching Race: Theory, Methods, and Analysis*. Maidenhead, UK: Open University Press.

Rampersad, Arnold. (1990). *The Art and Imagination of W. E. B. Du Bois*. New York: Schocken.

———. (1996). "W. E. B. Du Bois, Race, and the Making of American Studies." In Bernard W. Bell, Emily R. Grosholz, and James B. Stewart (Eds.), *W. E. B. Du Bois: On Race and Culture* (289–305). New York: Routledge.

Rawls, Anne Warfield. (2000). "'Race' as an Interaction Order Phenomenon: W. E. B. Du Bois's 'Double-Consciousness' Thesis Revisited." *Sociological Theory* 18 (2), 241–74.

Reed, Adolph L., Jr. (1997). *W. E. B. Du Bois and American Political Thought: Fabianism and the Color Line*. New York: Oxford University Press.

Rege, Sharmila. (Ed.). (2003). *Sociology of Gender: The Challenge of Feminist Sociological Knowledge*. Thousand Oaks, CA: Sage.

Riley-Smith, Jonathan. (2008). *Crusades, Christianity, and Islam*. New York: Columbia University Press.

Ritzer, George. (Ed.). (2000). *The Blackwell Companion to Major Social Theorists*. Malden, MA: Blackwell.

———. (Ed.). (2004). *Handbook of Social Problems: A Comparative International Perspective*. Thousand Oaks, CA: Sage.

———. (2006). *Contemporary Sociological Theory and Its Classical Roots: The Basics*. Boston: McGraw-Hill.

———. (2008a). *Classical Sociological Theory*. Boston: McGraw-Hill.

———. (2008b). *Modern Sociological Theory*. Boston: McGraw-Hill.

Roberts, J. Deotis. (2003). *Black Religion, Black Theology: The Collected Essays of J. Deotis Roberts* (David Emmanuel Goatley, Ed.). Harrisburg, PA: Trinity Press.

Robinson, Cedric J. (2000). *Black Marxism: The Making of the Black Radical Tradition*. Chapel Hill: University of North Carolina.

Roediger, David R. (1994). *Towards the Abolition of Whiteness: Essays on Race, Politics, and Working Class History*. New York: Verso.

———. (Ed.). (1998). *Black on White: Black Writers on What It Means To Be White*. New York: Schocken.

———. (2002). *Colored White: Transcending the Racial Past*. Berkeley: University of California Press.

———. (2005). *Working Toward Whiteness: How America's Immigrants Became White—The Strange Journey from Ellis Island to the Suburbs*. New York: Basic Books.

———. (2007). *The Wages of Whiteness: Race and the Making of the American Working Class*. New York: Verso.

———. (2008). *How Race Survived U.S. History: From Settlement and Slavery to the Obama Phenomenon*. New York: Verso.
Rojas, Fabio. (2007). *From Black Power to Black Studies: How a Radical Social Movement Became an Academic Discipline*. Baltimore: Johns Hopkins University Press.
Rooks, Noliwe M. (2006). *White Money/Black Power: The Surprising History of African American Studies and the Crisis of Race in Higher Education*. Boston: Beacon Press.
Ross, Jeffrey Ian. (Ed.). (2009). *Cutting the Edge: Current Perspectives in Radical/Critical Criminology and Criminal Justice*. New Brunswick, NJ: Transaction Publishers.
Ross, Marlon Bryan. (2004). *Manning the Race: Reforming Black Men in the Jim Crow Era*. New York: New York University Press.
Rothenberg, Paula S. (Ed.). (2002). *White Privilege: Essential Readings on the Other Side of Racism*. New York: Worth Publishers.
Rowland, Christopher. (Ed.). (1999). *The Cambridge Companion to Liberation Theology*. Cambridge: Cambridge University Press.
Rudwick, Elliot M. (1956). "W. E. B. Du Bois: A Study in Minority Group Leadership." PhD dissertation, University of Pennsylvania.
———. (1957a). "The National Negro Committee Conference of 1909." *Phylon* 18 (4), 413–19.
———. (1957b). "The Niagara Movement." *Journal of Negro History* 42, 177–200.
———. (1957c). "W. E. B. Du Bois and the Atlanta University Studies on the Negro." *Journal of Negro Education* 26 (4), 466–76.
———. (1958a). "Du Bois's Last Year as *Crisis* Editor." *Journal of Negro Education* 27 (4), 426–33.
———. (1958b). "W. E. B. Du Bois: In the Role of *Crisis* Editor." *Journal of Negro History* 18 (July), 214–40.
———. (1959a). "Du Bois versus Garvey: Race Propagandists at War." *Journal of Negro Education* 28 (Fall), 421–29.
———. (1959b). "W. E. B. Du Bois and the Universal Races Congress of 1911." *Phylon* 20 (4), 372–78.
———. (1960a). "Booker T. Washington's Relations with the National Association for the Advancement of Colored People." *Journal of Negro Education* 29 (2), 134–44.
———. (1960b). *W. E. B. Du Bois: A Study in Minority Group Leadership*. Philadelphia: University of Pennsylvania.
———. (1968). *W. E. B. Du Bois: Propagandists of the Negro Protest*. New York: Antheneum.
———. (1969). "Notes on a Forgotten Black Sociologists: W. E. B. Du Bois and the Sociological Profession." *American Sociologist* 4 (4), 303–36.
———. (1974). "W. E. B. Du Bois as Sociologists." In James E. Blackwell and Morris Janowitz (Eds.), *Black Sociologists: Historical and Contemporary Perspectives* (25–55). Chicago: University of Chicago Press.
———. (1982a). "W. E. B. Du Bois: Protagonist of the Afro-American Protest." In John Hope Franklin and August Meier (Eds.), *Black Leaders of the Twentieth Century* (63–84). Chicago: University of Illinois Press.
———. (1982b). *W. E. B. Du Bois: Voice of the Black Movement*. Urbana: University of Illinois Press.

Ruffin, Josephine St. Pierre. (1895). "Address to the First National Conference of Colored Women." *The Woman's Era* 2 (5), 13–15.

Rumney, Jay. (1966). *Herbert Spencer's Sociology: A Study in the History of Social Theory.* New York: Atherton Press.

Runciman, Steven. (1982). *The Medieval Manichee: A Study of the Christian Dualist Heresy.* Cambridge: Cambridge University Press.

Ruse, Michael, and Richards, Robert J. (Eds). (2009). *The Cambridge Companion to the "Origins of Species."* Cambridge: Cambridge University Press.

Russell, Katheryn K. (1992). "Development of a Black Criminology and the Role of the Black Criminologist." *Justice Quarterly* 9 (4), 667–83.

Russell, Katheryn K., and Milovanovic, Dragan. (Eds.). (2001). *Petit-Apartheid in the U. S. Criminal Justice System.* Durham, NC: Carolina Academic Press.

Rutledge, John. (1989). *Rust to Riches: The Coming of the Second Industrial Revolution.* New York: Harper & Row.

Saint-Arnaud, Pierre. (2009). *African American Pioneers of Sociology: A Critical History.* Toronto: University of Toronto Press.

Sandoval, Chela. (2000). *Methodology of the Oppressed.* Minneapolis: University of Minnesota Press.

Sargent, Lydia. (Ed.). (1981). *Women and Revolution: A Discussion of the Unhappy Marriage of Marxism and Feminism.* Boston: South End.

Savage, Barbara Dianne. (2000). "W. E. B. Du Bois and 'The Negro Church.'" *Annals of the American Academy of Political and Social Science* 568, 253–49.

Sawyer, Mary R. (1994). *Black Ecumenism: Implementing the Demands of Justice.* Valley Forge, PA: Trinity Press International.

Schafer, Axel R. (2001). "W. E. B. Du Bois, German Social Thought, and the Racial Divide in American Progressivism, 1892–1909." *Journal of American History* 88 (3), 925–50.

———. (2008). "Du Bois on Race: Economic and Cultural Perspectives." In Shamoon Zamir (Ed.), *The Cambridge Companion to W. E. B. Du Bois* (102–16). Cambridge: Cambridge University Press.

Schmidt, Bettina E. (2008). *Caribbean Diaspora in the USA: Diversity of Caribbean Religions in New York City.* Aldershot, UK: Ashgate.

Schwartz, Martin D., and Milovanovic, Dragan. (Eds.). (1996). *Race, Gender, and Class in Criminology: The Intersection.* New York: Garland Publishing.

Scranton, Philip. (1986). *Work Sights: Industrial Philadelphia, 1890–1950.* Philadelphia: Temple University Press.

Sefa Dei, George J., and Singh Johal, Gurpreet. (Eds.). (2005). *Critical Issues in Anti-Racist Research Methodologies.* New York: P. Lang.

Segundo, Juan Luis. (1976). *Liberation of Theology.* Maryknoll, NY: Orbis Books.

Serequeberhan, Tsenay. (Ed.). (1991). *African Philosophy: The Essential Readings.* New York: Paragon House.

———. (1994). *The Hermeneutics of African Philosophy: Horizon and Discourse.* New York: Routledge.

Sernett, Milton C. (Ed). (1999). *African American Religious History: A Documentary Witness.* Durham, NC: Duke University Press.

Sevitch, Benjamin. (2002). "W. E. B. Du Bois and Jews: A Lifetime of Opposing Anti-Semitism." *Journal of African American History* 87, 323–38.

———. (2009). "W. E. B. Du Bois as America's Foremost Black Zionist." In Edward J. Blum and Jason R. Young (Eds.), *The Souls of W. E. B. Du Bois: New Essays and Reflections* (233–53). Macon, GA: Mercer University Press.

Shapiro, Herbert. (1988). *White Violence and Black Response: From Reconstruction to Montgomery.* Amherst: University of Massachusetts Press.

Shaw, Clifford R., and McKay, Henry D. (1942). *Juvenile Delinquency and Urban Areas.* Chicago: University of Chicago Press.

Shelden, Randall G. (2001). *Controlling the Dangerous Classes: A Critical Introduction to the History of Criminal Justice.* Boston: Allyn and Bacon.

Shimkin, Demitri B., Shimkin, Edith M., and Frate, Dennis A. (Eds.). (1978). *The Extended Family in Black Societies.* Chicago: Aldine.

Shionoya, Yuichi. (Ed.). (2001). *The German Historical School: The Historical and Ethical Approach to Economics.* New York: Routledge.

Simpson, George E. (1978). *Black Religions in the New World.* New York: Columbia University Press.

Sims, Edward. (1978). *Black Nomads in the Urban Centers: The Effects of Racism and Urbanism on the Black Family.* Washington, D.C.: University Press of America.

Sims, Patsy. (1996). *The Klan.* Lexington: University Press of Kentucky.

Smith, Christian. (1991). *The Emergence of Liberation Theology: Radical Religion and Social Movement Theory.* Chicago: University of Chicago Press.

Smith, Dorothy E. (1990). *The Conceptual Practices of Power: A Feminist Sociology of Knowledge.* Boston: Northeastern University Press.

———. (1993). *Texts, Facts, and Femininity: Exploring the Relations of Ruling.* New York: Routledge.

———. (1999). *Writing the Social: Critique, Theory, and Investigations.* Toronto: University of Toronto Press.

Smith, Eddie Calvin. (1975). "Educational Themes in the Published Work of W. E. B. Du Bois, 1883–1960: Implications for African American Educators." PhD dissertation, University of Wisconsin–Milwaukee.

Smith, John David. (Ed.). (1993a). *Anti-Abolition Tracts and Anti-Black Stereotypes: General Statements of "The Negro Problem," Part I.* New York: Garland.

———. (Ed.). (1993b). *The "Ariel" Controversy: Religion and "The Negro Problem," Part I.* New York: Garland.

———. (Ed.). (1993c). *The Biblical and "Scientific" Defense of Slavery: Religion and "The Negro Problem," Part II.* New York: Garland.

———. (Ed.). (1993d). *Racial Determinism and the Fear of Miscegenation Pre-1900: Race and "The Negro Problem," Part I.* New York: Garland.

———. (Ed.). (1993e). *Racial Determinism and the Fear of Miscegenation Pre-1900: Race and "The Negro Problem," Part II.* New York: Garland.

———. (Ed.). (1993f). *Racist Southern Paternalism: General Statements of "The Negro Problem," Part II.* New York: Garland.

Smith, Linda Tuhiwai. (1999). *Decolonizing Methodologies: Research and Indigenous Peoples.* Dunedin: University of Otago Press.

Stanley, Liz. (Ed). (1990). *Feminist Praxis: Research, Theory, and Epistemology in Feminist Sociology.* New York: Routledge.

Stanton, Bill. (1991). *Klanwatch: Bringing the Ku Klux Klan to Justice.* New York: Grove Weidenfeld.

Staples, Robert. (1975). *Introduction to Black Sociology*. New York: McGraw-Hill.
——. (1999). *The Black Family: Essays and Studies*. Belmont, CA: Wadsworth.
Stehr, Nico, and Meja, Volker. (Eds.). (2005). *Society & Knowledge: Contemporary Perspectives in the Sociology of Knowledge & Science*. New Brunswick, NJ: Transaction Publishers.
Stephan, Nancy Leys. (1982). *The Idea of Race in Science: Great Britain, 1800–1960*. New York: MacMillan.
Stewart, James B. (1984). "The Legacy of W. E. B. Du Bois for Contemporary Black Studies." *Journal of Negro Education* 53 (3), 296–311.
——. (2004). *Flight: In Search of Vision*. Trenton, NJ: Africa World Press.
Stewart, Maria W. (1987). *Maria W. Stewart, America's First Black Woman Political Writer: Essays and Speeches* (Marilyn Richardson, Ed.). Indianapolis: Indiana University Press.
Street, Paul Louis. (2005). *Segregated Schools: Educational Apartheid in Post-Civil Rights America*. New York: Routledge.
Stuckey, Sterling. (1987). *Slave Culture: Nationalist Theory and the Foundations of Black America*. New York: Oxford University Press.
Sudbury, Julia. (Ed.). (2005). *Global Lockdown: Race, Gender, and the Prison-Industrial Complex*. New York: Routledge.
Sulton, Anne T. (Ed.). (1996). *African American Perspectives on Crime Causation, Criminal Justice Administration, and Crime Prevention*. Boston: Butterworth Heinemann.
Sumpter, Richard David. (1973). "A Critical Study of the Educational Thought of W. E. B. Du Bois." PhD dissertation, Peabody College for Teacher of Vanderbilt University.
Summers, Martin Anthony. (2004). *Manliness and its Discontents: The Black Middle Class and The Transformation of Masculinity, 1900–1930*. Chapel Hill: University of North Carolina Press.
Sumner, Colin. (Ed.). (2004). *Blackwell Companion to Criminology*. Malden, MA: Blackwell Publishing.
Sundquist, Eric J. (1993). *To Wake the Nations: Race in the Making of American Literature*. Cambridge, MA: Harvard University Press.
——. (1996). "W. E. B. Du Bois and the Autobiography of Race." In W. E. B. Du Bois, *The Oxford W. E. B. Du Bois Reader* (Eric Sundquist, Ed., 3–36). New York: Oxford University Press.
Swaaningen, René van. (1997). *Critical Criminology: Visions from Europe*. Thousand Oaks, CA: Sage.
Sydie, Rosalind A. (1987). *Natural Women, Cultured Men: A Feminist Perspective on Sociological Theory*. New York: New York University Press.
Tardieu, Michel. (2008). *Manichaeism*. Urbana: University of Illinois Press.
Tator, Carol, and Henry, Frances. (2006). *Racial Profiling in Canada: Challenging the Myth of "A Few Bad Apples."* Toronto: University of Toronto Press.
Taylor, Ian, Walton, Paul, and Young, Jock. (Eds.). (1975). *Critical Criminology*. Boston: Routledge and Kegan Paul.
Taylor, Paul C. (2000). "Appiah's Uncompleted Argument: W. E. B. Du Bois and the Reality of Race." *Social Theory and Practice* 26 (1), 103–28.
——. (2004). *Race: A Philosophical Introduction*. Malden, MA: Blackwell.

Taylor, Robert Joseph, Jackson, James Scott, and Chatters, Linda M. (Eds). (1997). *Family Life in Black America*. Thousand Oaks, CA: Sage Publications.

Teele, James E. (Ed.). (2002). *E. Franklin Frazier and Black Bourgeoisie*. Columbia: University of Missouri Press.

Thomas, Brook. (Ed.). (1997). *Plessy v. Ferguson: A Brief History With Documents*. Boston: Bedford Books.

Thorpe, Earl E. (1961). *The Mind of the Negro: An Intellectual History of Afro-Americans*. Baton Rouge, LA: Ortlieb Press.

Tomisawa, Rieko. (2003). "The Crisis of Democracy in a Pluralistic Society: A Genealogy of W. E. B. Du Bois's Double-Consciousness." PhD dissertation, Michigan State University.

Towns, Saundra. (1974). "The Black Woman as Whore: Genesis of the Myth." *The Black Position* 3, 39–59.

Travis, Toni Michelle C. (1996). "Double-Consciousness and the Politics of the Elite." *Research in Race and Ethnic Relations* 9, 91–123.

Trelease, Allen W. (1995). *White Terror: The Ku Klux Klan Conspiracy and Southern Reconstruction*. Baton Rouge: Louisiana State University Press.

Trolander, Judith Ann. (1987). *Professionalism and Social Change: From the Settlement House Movement to Neighborhood Centers, 1886 to the Present*. New York: Columbia University Press.

Trost, Theodore Louis. (Ed.). (2007). *African Diaspora and the Study of Religion*. New York: Palgrave-Macmillan.

Twine, France Winddance and Warren, Jonathan W. (Eds.). (2000). *Racing Research, Researching Race: Methodological Dilemmas in Critical Race Studies*. New York: New York University Press.

Wacker, R. Fred. (1983). *Ethnicity, Pluralism, and Race: Race Relations Theory in America Before Myrdal*. Westport, CT: Greenwood Press.

Wade, Wyn Craig. (1987). *The Fiery Cross: The Ku Klux Klan in America*. New York: Simon & Schuster.

Waldrep, Christopher. (1998). *Roots of Disorder: Race and Criminal Justice in the American South, 1817–80*. Urbana: University of Illinois Press.

———. (2001). *Racial Violence on Trial: A Handbook with Cases, Laws, and Documents*. Santa Barbara, CA: ABC-CLIO.

———. (2002). *Many Faces of Judge Lynch: Extralegal Violence and Punishment in America*. New York: Palgrave-Macmillan.

———. (Ed.). (2006). *Lynching in America: A History in Documents*. New York: New York University Press.

———. (2009). *African Americans Confront Lynching: Strategies of Resistance from the Civil War to the Civil Rights Era*. Lanham, MD: Rowman & Littlefield.

Waldrep, Christopher, and Nieman, Donald G. (Eds.). (2001). *Local Matters: Race, Crime, and Justice in the Nineteenth-Century South*. Athens: University of Georgia Press.

Walker, David. (1993). *David Walker's Appeal in Four Articles*. Baltimore: Black Classic Press.

Wallace, Michele. (1990a). *Black Macho and the Myth of the Superwoman*. New York: Verso.

———. (1990b). *Invisibility Blues: From Pop to Theory*. New York: Verso.

Wallace, Ruth A. (Ed.). (1989). *Feminism and Sociological Theory*. Newbury Park, CA: Sage.
Ward, Julie K., and Lott, Tommy L. (Eds). (2002). *Philosophers on Race: Critical Essays*. Malden, MA: Blackwell.
Warner, Sam Bass, Jr. (1984). *Urban Growth in America: Philadelphia, 1774–1930*. Ann Arbor: University of Michigan Press.
Warren, Nagueyalti. (1984). "The Contributions of W. E. B. Du Bois to Afro-American Studies in Higher Education." PhD dissertation, University of Mississippi.
Washington, Booker T. (1900). *A New Negro For A New Century: An Accurate and Up to-Date Record of the Upward Struggles of the Negro Race. The Spanish American War, Causes of it; Vivid Descriptions of Fierce Battles; Superb Heroism and Daring Deeds of the Negro Soldier . . . Education, Industrial Schools, Colleges, Universities and Their Relationship to the Race Problem*. Chicago: American Publishing House.
Washington, Harriet A. (2006). *Medical Apartheid: The Dark History of Medical Experimentation on Black Americans from Colonial Times to the Present*. New York: Doubleday.
Washington, Joseph R., Jr. (1984). *Anti-Blackness in English Religion, 1500–1800*. New York: E. Mellen Press.
Washington, Robert E., and Cunnigen, Donald. (Eds.). (2002). *Confronting the American Dilemma of Race: The Second Generation of Black American Sociologists*. Lanham, MD: University of America Press.
Waters, Kristin, and Conaway, Carol B. (Eds.). (2007). *Black Women's Intellectual Traditions: Speaking Their Minds*. Burlington, VT: University of Vermont Press.
Watts, Jerry. (Ed.). (2004). *Harold Cruse's The Crisis of the Negro Intellectual Reconsidered*. New York: Routledge.
Weiler, Kathleen. (1994). "Freire and Feminist Pedagogy of Difference." In Peter McLaren and Colin Lankshear (Eds.), *Politics of Liberation: Paths from Freire* (12–40). New York: Routledge.
———. (Ed.). (2001). *Feminist Engagements: Reading, Resisting, and Revisioning Male Theorists in Education and Cultural Studies*. New York: Routledge.
Weitzer, Ronald, and Tuch, Steven A. (2006). *Race and Policing in America: Conflict and Reform*. Cambridge: Cambridge University Press.
West, Cornel. (1982). *Prophesy Deliverance!: An Afro-American Revolutionary Christianity*. Philadelphia: Westminster.
———. (1988). "Marxist Theory and the Specificity of Afro-American Oppression." In Cary Nelson and Lawrence Grossberg (Eds.), *Marxism and the Interpretation of Culture* (17–34). Chicago: University of Illinois Press.
———. (1989). "W. E. B. Du Bois: The Jamesian Organic Intellectual." In *The American Evasion of Philosophy: A Genealogy of Pragmatism* (138–50). Madison: University of Wisconsin Press.
———. (1993a). *Keeping Faith: Philosophy and Race in America*. New York: Routledge.
———. (1993b). *Race Matters*. New York: Random House.
———. (1996). "Black Strivings in a Twilight Civilization." In Henry Louis Gates Jr. and Cornel West, *The Future of the Race* (53–114). New York: Alfred A. Knopf.
———. (Ed.). (1999). *The Cornel West Reader*. New York: Civitas.
Wetzell, Richard F. (2000). *Inventing the Criminal: A History of German Criminology, 1880–1945*. Chapel Hill: University of North Carolina Press.

Whitehead, John W. (1994). *Religious Apartheid*. Chicago: Moody Press.
Wiggerhaus, Rolf. (1995). *The Frankfurt School: Its History, Theories, and Political Significance*. Cambridge, MA: MIT Press.
Wilcox, Walter Francis. (1904). *Negroes in the United States*. Washington, D.C.: Department of Commerce and Labor/Government Printing Office.
Wilder, Craig S. (2001). *In the Company of Black Men: The African Influence on African American Culture in New York City*. New York: New York University.
Williams, Linda Faye. (2003). *The Constraint of Race: Legacies of White Skin Privilege in America*. University Park: Pennsylvania State University Press.
Williams, Robert W. (2003). "W. E. B. Du Bois and the Socio-Political Structures of Education." *The Negro Educational Review* 55 (1), 9-26.
———. (2006). "The Early Social Science of W. E. B. Du Bois." *Du Bois Review: Social Science Research on Race* 3 (2), 365-94.
Williamson, Joel. (1984). *South Since Emancipation*. New York: Oxford University Press.
———. (1986). *A Rage for Order: Black/White Relations in the American South Since Emancipation*. New York: Oxford University Press.
———. (1995). *New People: Miscegenation and Mulattoes in the United States*. Baton Rouge: Louisiana State University Press.
Wilmore, Gayraud S. (1983). *Black Religion and Black Radicalism: An Interpretation of the Religious History of Afro-American People*. Maryknoll, NY: Orbis.
———. (Ed.). (1989). *African American Religious Studies: An Interdisciplinary Anthology*. Durham, NC: Duke University Press.
Wilson, Theodore B. (1965). *The Black Codes of the South*. Tuscaloosa: University of Alabama Press.
Winant, Howard. (1994). *Racial Conditions: Politics, Theory, Comparisons*. Minneapolis: University of Minnesota Press.
———. (2001). *The World is a Ghetto: Race and Democracy Since World War II*. New York: Basic Books.
———. (2004). *The New Politics of Race: Globalism, Difference, Justice*. Minneapolis: University of Minnesota Press.
———. (2007). "The Dark Side of the Force: One Hundred Years of the Sociology of Race." In Craig J. Calhoun (Ed.), *Sociology in America: A History* (535-71). Chicago: University of Chicago Press.
Wintz, Cary D. (Ed.). (1996). *The Politics and Aesthetics of "New Negro" Literature*. New York: Garland.
Wiredu, Kwasi. (1991). "On Defining African Philosophy." In Tsenay Serequeberhan (Ed.), *African Philosophy: The Essential Readings* (87-110). New York: Paragon House.
———. (Ed.). (2004). *A Companion to African Philosophy*. Malden, MA: Blackwell.
Withrow, Brian L. (2006). *Racial Profiling: From Rhetoric to Reason*. Upper Saddle River, NJ: Pearson/Prentice Hall.
Wolfenstein, E. Victor. (2007). *A Gift of the Spirit: Reading The Souls of Black Folk*. Ithaca, NY: Cornell University Press.
Wolters, Raymond. (2001). *Du Bois and His Rivals*. Columbia: University of Missouri Press.

Wood, Amy Louise. (2009). *Lynching and Spectacle: Witnessing Racial Violence in America, 1890–1940*. Chapel Hill: University of North Carolina Press.

Wood, David. (2000). *Cornel West and the Politics of Prophetic Pragmatism*. Urbana: University of Illinois Press.

Wortham, Robert A. (2005a). "Du Bois and the Sociology of Religion: Rediscovering a Founding Figure." *Sociological Inquiry* 75 (4), 433–52.

———. (2005b). "The Early Sociological Legacy of W. E. B. Du Bois." In Anthony J. Blasi (Ed.), *Diverse Histories of American Sociology* (74–95). Boston: Brill.

———. (2005c). "Introduction to the Sociology of W. E. B. Du Bois." *Sociation Today* 3 (1). Online at www.ncsociology.org/sociationtoday/v31/atlanta.htm [Accessed on 23 February 2005].

———. (2008). "W. E. B. Du Bois's Urban Sociology: Reflections on African American Quality of Life in Philadelphia." *Sociation Today* 6 (1), www.ncsociology.org/sociationtoday/v61/dubois2.htm.

———. (2009a). "W. E. B. Du Bois, the Black Church, and the Sociological Study of Religion." *Sociological Spectrum* 29 (2), 144–72.

———. (2009b). "W. E. B. Du Bois and the Scientific Study of Society: 1897–1914." In Robert A. Wortham (Ed.), *W. E. B. Du Bois and the Sociological Imagination: A Reader, 1897–1914* (1–20). Waco, TX: Baylor University Press.

Wray, Matt. (2006). *Not Quite White: White Trash and the Boundaries of Whiteness*. Durham, NC: Duke University Press.

Wray, Matt, and Newitz, Annalee. (Eds). (1997). *White Trash: Race and Class in America*. New York: Routledge.

Wright, Earl, II. (2002a). "The Atlanta Sociological Laboratory, 1896–1924: A Historical Account of the First American School of Sociology." *Western Journal of Black Studies* 23 (3), 165–74.

———. (2002b). "Using the Master's Tools: The Atlanta Sociological Laboratory and American Sociology, 1896–1924." *Sociological Spectrum* 22, 15–39.

———. (2002c). "Why Black People Tend To Shout!: An Earnest Attempt to Explain the Sociological Negation of the Atlanta Sociological Laboratory Despite Its Possible Unpleasantness." *Sociological Spectrum* 22, 335–61.

———. (2005). "W. E. B. Du Bois and the Atlanta Sociological Laboratory." *Sociation Today* 3 (1). Online at www.ncsociology.org/sociationtoday/v31/wright.htm.

———. (2008). "Deferred Legacy!: The Continued Marginalization of the Atlanta Sociological Laboratory." *Sociological Compass* 2 (1), 195–207.

Wright, Earl, II, and Calhoun, Thomas C. (2006). "Jim Crow Sociology: Toward an Understanding of the Origin and Principles of Black Sociology Via the Atlanta Sociological Laboratory." *Sociological Focus* 39 (1), 1–18.

Wylie, Alison. (2002). *Thinking from Things: Essays in the Philosophy of Archaeology*. Berkley: University of California Press.

Yancy, George. (Ed.). (2001). *Cornel West: A Critical Reader*. Malden, MA: Blackwell.

Yee, Shirley J. (1992). *Black Women Abolitionists: A Study in Activism, 1828–1860*. Knoxville: University of Tennessee Press.

Young, Alford A., Jr. (1993). "The 'Negro Problem' and the Social Character of Black Community: Charles S. Johnson, E. Franklin Frazier, and the Constitution of a Black Sociological Tradition, 1920–1935." *National Journal of Sociology* 7 (1), 95–133.

Young, Alford A., Jr., and Deskins, Donald R., Jr. (2001). "Early Traditions of African American Sociological Thought." *Annual Review of Sociology* 27, 445–77.

Young, Jason R. (2009). "Between the Crescent and the Cross: W. E. B. Du Bois on Christianity and Islam." In Edward J. Blum and Jason R. Young (Eds.), *The Souls of W. E. B. Du Bois: New Essays and Reflections* (211–32). Macon, GA: Mercer University Press.

Young, Joseph, and Braziel, Jane Evans. (Eds.). (2006). *Race and the Foundations of Knowledge*. Champaign: University of Illinois Press.

Young, Robert Alexander. (1996). "The Ethiopian Manifesto." In Wilson Jeremiah Moses (Ed.), *Classical Black Nationalism: From the American Revolution to Marcus Garvey*. New York: New York University Press.

Young, Vernetta D. (1996). "The Politics of Disproportionality." In Anne T. Sulton (Ed.), *African American Perspectives on Crime Causation, Criminal Justice Administration, and Crime Prevention* (69–81). Boston: Butterworth-Heinemann.

Young, Vernetta D., and Greene, Helen T. (1995). "Pedagogical Reconstruction: Incorporating African American Perspectives into the Curriculum." *Journal of Criminal Justice Education* 6 (1), 85–104.

Young, Vernetta D., and Reviere, Rebecca. (2006). *Women Behind Bars: Gender and Race in U. S. Prisons*. Boulder, CO: Lynne Rienner Publishers.

Young, Vernetta D., and Sulton, Anne Thomas. (1991). "Excluded: The Current Status of African American Scholars in the Field of Criminology and Criminal Justice." *Journal of Research in Crime and Delinquency* 28, 101–16.

Zamir, Shamoon. (1995). *Dark Voices: W. E. B. Du Bois and American Thought, 1888–1903*. Chicago: University of Chicago Press.

———. (Ed.). (2008). *The Cambridge Companion to W. E. B. Du Bois*. Cambridge: Cambridge University Press.

Zangrando, Robert L. (1980). *The NAACP Crusade Against Lynching, 1909–1950*. Philadelphia: Temple University Press.

Zuberi, Tufuku [a.k.a. Antonio McDaniel]. (1998). "The 'Philadelphia Negro' Then and Now: Implications for Empirical Research." In Michael B. Katz and Thomas J. Sugrue (Eds.), *W. E. B. Du Bois, Race, and the City: The Philadelphia Negro and Its Legacy* (155–94). Philadelphia: University of Pennsylvania Press.

———. (2004). "W. E. B. Du Bois's Sociology: *The Philadelphia Negro* and Social Science." *Annals of the American Academy of Political and Social Science* 595, 146–56.

Zuckerman, Phil. (2002). "The Sociology of Religion of W. E. B. Du Bois." *Sociology of Religion* 63 (2), 239–53.

———. (2004). "Introduction to the Social Theory of W. E. B. Du Bois." In Phil Zuckerman (Ed.), *The Social Theory of W. E. B. Du Bois* (1–17). Thousand Oaks, CA: Sage.

———. (2009). "The Irreligiosity of W. E. B. Du Bois." In Edward J. Blum and Jason R. Young (Eds.), *The Souls of W. E. B. Du Bois: New Essays and Reflections* (3–17). Macon, GA: Mercer University Press.

Zuckerman, Phil, Barnes, Sandra L., and Cady, Daniel. (2003). "*The Negro Church*: An Introduction." In W. E. B. Du Bois (Ed.), *The Negro Church* (vii–xxvi). Walnut Creek: AltaMira.

Index

Abbot, Edith, 14
Abbot, Grace, 14
academic ghettoization, 206
J'accuse (Zola), 261n5
Addams, Jane, 14, 69–70, 83, 95, 104n10
Adorno, Theodor, 19
The Advance, 126
Africa: An Essay Toward a History of the Continent of Africa and Its Inhabitants (Du Bois), 163
Africa, Its Geography, People and Products (Du Bois), 163
Africa—Its Place in Modern History (Du Bois), 163
Africana academia, 132
Africana critical pedagogy, 268, 285–89
Africana critical theory, 2, 18–22, 27–30, 33, 43n3, 76–77, 84, 97–98, 101, 131, 249
African American family, 55–60, 88–94, 101n5, 102n6
African American sociology, 67, 71–72, 75–76, 98, 206, 309, 331
Africana philosophy, 17–22, 254, 351
Africana studies, 11–15, 28–29, 44n8, 66, 80, 271–72, 348–53
Afrotopia (Moses), 262n9

agapē, 244, 257
agency, 82, 118, 133–34, 154, 158, 160, 214
Ain't I A Woman (hooks), 220n7
Aldridge, Delores, 201
Alridge, Derrick, 265, 289
Alexander, Virginia, 221n8
Allen, Theodore, 146
American Academy of Political and Social Sciences, 126, 209
American Birth Control League, 219n3
American Economic Association, 3
American Historical Association Annual Report, 1891, 297
American Historical Review, 126, 197
American Journal of Sociology, 4
American Negro Academy, 109, 120
The American Negro Artisan (Du Bois), 312
The American Negro Family (Du Bois), 101n5
American Sociological Association, 347
American Sociological Society, 3
An Appeal in Four Articles (Walker), 225
Anderson, Elijah, 9, 68–70, 73, 104n11

Annals of the American Academy of Political and Social Sciences, 126
anomie theory, 331, 344, 347
anti-black racism, 24, 128–68
anti-black racist alchemy, 157–59
anti-black racist criminalization, 306, 319, 324, 327
anti-black racist differential justice, 319, 323–24, 326, 328–29, 333
anti-black racist misogyny, 194
anti-black racist rape, 317
anti-black racist vigilante violence, 298–300, 319, 321, 335n6, 335n9
antidisciplinary, 132, 348–53
anti-sociology, 71–72
Anzaldúa, Gloria, 201
apartheid (American), 17, 23–24, 34–35, 44n6, 59, 60, 62, 63–64, 65, 70, 71, 78, 79, 97–99, 99, 133, 142, 144, 146, 298, 299, 300, 311–12, 326
Appiah, Anthony, 108, 168n1
appropriation, 22, 120, 158, 160
Aptheker, Herbert, 50, 227, 229, 241, 257
archaeology, 11, 25–27, 41–43, 304–5, 318, 333
The Archaeology of Knowledge (Foucault), 25
Archiv für Sozialwissenschaft und Sozialpolitik, 8
arrival time (of African Americans in urban environments), 81, 332
The Art and Imagination of W. E. B. Du Bois (Rampersad), 132, 189
Athenian democracy, 153
"The Atlanta Conferences" (Du Bois), 1, 310, 338
"Atlanta Exposition Address" (Washington), 102n7
Atlanta Race Riot of 1906, 228
Atlanta University, 3, 8, 12, 38, 50, 53, 226, 234, 266–67, 296, 301, 309–12, 321, 344–45
"Atlanta University" (Du Bois), 266
The Atlantic Monthly, 126

The Autobiography of W. E. B. Du Bois, 78, 182, 199, 218n2, 227, 230, 350

bad faith, 34
Baer, Hans, 247
Baldwin, James, 81
Ball, Richard, 332
Banks, William, 75
Bay, Mia, 97–98, 100n1
Bearden, Romare, 129
Beccaria, Cesare, 293
Benjamin, Walter, 19
Bentham, Jeremy, 293
Berlin Conference of 1884–1885, 329
The Birth of the Clinic: An Archaeology of Medical Perception (Foucault), 25
black anonymity, 81, 135
black bourgeoisie, 61–62, 83, 86–94
The Black Bourgeoisie (Frazier), 61
black codes, 10, 66, 133, 145, 151, 159, 333
black criminology, 329–30
"Black Folk and Birth Control" (Du Bois), 219n3
Black Folk, Then and Now (Du Bois), 109, 163–64, 172, 208, 252, 350
black hyperinvisibility, 134
black invisibility, 81, 135
"The Black Man Brings His Gifts" (Du Bois), 109
Black Marxism (Robinson), 353
"The Black Mother" (Du Bois), 188, 190, 202, 215
black prison labor, 323, 325, 333
Black Reconstruction (Du Bois), 109, 159–62, 169n5
Black Skin, White Masks (Fanon), 290n2, 291n4
black sociology, 74–75, 98, 206
A Black Theology of Liberation (Cone), 257
blond beast, 153
Blum, Edward, 223, 251, 262n7
Blumenbach, Johann Friedrich, 116
Blyden, Edward, 225
Boas, Franz, 164

Bobo, Lawrence, 337
Bogues, Anthony, 75
Booklover's Magazine, 126
Booth, Charles, 69–70, 83, 95–96
Boston, Thomas, 340, 359n1
Breckinridge, Sophonisba, 14
Brewer, Rose, 201
Broderick, Francis, 261n6, 339–40
Brown, John, 238
Building Violence: How America's Rush to Incarcerate Creates More Violence (May and Pitts), 335n8
Bulmer, Martin, 96
"The Burden of Black Women" (Du Bois), 215
burden of black women's sexuality, 88–94
"The Burden of Negro Schooling" (Du Bois), 266
Bureau of Justice Statistics Report, 315
Burgess, Ernest, 294, 345

Cable, George, 334n1
Cabral, Amilcar, 21, 172, 272, 279
Calvinism, 227, 235
canonization, 4, 14, 36–37, 39
capitalism, 158–66, 173n12, 332–33
Carby, Hazel, 217n1, 218n2
"Careers Open to College-Bred Negroes" (Du Bois), 48, 266
Catt, Carrie Chapman, 176
"The Causes of Crime and Poverty" (Du Bois), 294
Census of Religious Bodies, 226
Cesaire, Aime, 81
Chapman, Mark, 247
Charities, 126
Chicago School, 3–5, 95, 127, 294, 297, 344–45
The Chicago Tribune, 126
Chicago Women's School, 14
child labor, 60
children, 58–64, 82, 89–90, 93, 102n6, 219n3
Christian Crusades, 245
Christianity, 225, 227–30, 235–36, 248, 251–58, 262n7

Christianity, Islam, and the Negro Race (Blyden), 225
"The Church and the Color-Line" (Du Bois), 246
"The Church and the Negro" (Du Bois), 247, 256
The City (Park, Burgess, and McKenzie), 345
The City Wilderness (Woods), 70
civil rights movement, 133, 350
Civil War, 63, 151, 298–99, 305, 314
class, 50–68, 77–94, 111–16, 170n7
Cleckley, Hervey, 294
The College-Bred Negro, 266, 311, 346
The College-Bred Negro American (Du Bois), 266, 311
College-Bred Negro Communities (Du Bois), 266
College de France, 170n6
College Settlement Association, 68
Collins, Patricia Hill, 184, 185, 201, 209, 220n7
Collins, Randall, 332
colonial capitalism, 165
color blindness, 162
Color and Democracy (Du Bois), 163, 215, 208, 215
"The Color-Line and the Church" (Du Bois), 247
The Common School (Du Bois), 266
The Common School and the Negro American (Du Bois), 266, 311
communism, 109
Comte, Auguste, 13, 70–71
"The Concept of Race" (Du Bois), 114–15
conceptual colonization, 34
conceptual conservatism, 94, 99
conceptual coup d'état, 77, 82
conceptual decolonization, 66
conceptual incarceration, 11–22, 30, 170n6
conceptual quarantine, 206, 348–53
Cone, James, 256–58
Congregationalism, 227
conscientização, 273

"The Conservation of Races" (Du Bois), 40, 47, 113–20, 122, 151, 153, 162–63
Conway, Carol, 75
Cooke, Anne, 221n8
Cooke, Marvel Jackson, 221n8
Cooley, Charles Horton, 74
Cooper, Anna Julia, 14, 83, 85, 189, 193, 209, 213–14
The Correspondence of W. E. B. Du Bois, 234
Coser, Lewis, 332
counter-identities, 33
counter-sciences, 33
counter-sociology, 71–72, 76
Courant, 180, 182
Cox, Oliver C., 112
The Creative Writings of W. E. B. Du Bois (Du Bois), 234
"Credo" (Du Bois), 228, 260n5
crime, 293–334
"Crime and Slavery" (Du Bois), 312, 315, 317, 320
The Crisis, 2–3, 155, 191, 208–9, 241, 255, 321, 350
critical Africana consciousness, 135–36
critical black consciousness, 135, 172
critical race theory, 120–68
critical theory, 19–38
critical theory of the human sciences, 18
critical white studies, 145–68
Crummell, Alexander, 83, 130, 131, 186, 239
Cruse, Harold, 75
Cullen, Francis, 332
cultural banditry, 113, 158–63
cultural racism, 149, 159–62
cultural theft, 149, 155, 158–63

"The Damnation of Women" (Du Bois), 179, 186, 188–212
Les damnés de la terre (Fanon), 133
Dark Princess (Du Bois), 208
Darkwater (Du Bois), 109, 146, 150, 155, 163, 175, 183, 186, 202, 208, 230, 237, 238

Darwin, Charles, 116
Daughters of Sorrow: Attitudes Toward Black Women, 1880–1920 (Guy-Sheftall), 176
Davis, Angela, 85
Dearborn Independent, 151
Delany, Martin, 130
De Mortie, Louise, 184
Department of Labor, 50–51, 57–58, 294
"Depoliticizing Representations: Sexual-Racial Stereotypes" (James), 220n7
Dessalines, Jean Jacques, 192
"The Development of a People" (Du Bois), 50
Dewey, Justin, 295
The Dial, 126
Diggs, Ellen Irene, 221n8
Dill, Augustus, 321
Dill, Bonnie Thornton, 201
Dilthey, Wilhelm, 339–42
disciplinary decadence, 11–22
Discipline and Punish: The Birth of the Prison (Foucault), 26, 31
divide and conquer, 23, 45n11
The Divine Discontent: The Religious Imagination of W. E. B. Du Bois (Kahn), 223
"Does the Negro Need Separate Schools?" (Du Bois), 266
domestic servants, 63–64
Douglass, Frederick, 83, 125, 126, 130, 152, 176, 183, 186, 190, 193, 216, 225, 238
Dred Scott v. Emerson, 160
Dred Scott v. Sandford, 160
Driver, Edwin, 2
Du Bois, Mary Silvina Burghardt, 180, 189, 227
Du Bois, Rachel Davis, 221n8
Du Bois, W. E. B.: activism of, 360n2; on anti-black racist rape, 317; aristocratic interpretations of, 50–100; assimilationism of, 52, 66–73, 76, 86, 89, 90, 94, 98–100; on birth control, 219n3; black

bourgeoisie, critique of, 77–94; on the black church, 233–48; on black folk as "beasts of burden," 165; on black folk as "half-devil and half-child," 165; on the black mammy, 188; on black mothers, 183–90; on blacks as property, 157–61, 166–67; on black women, 175–217; on the burden of black women's sexuality, 88–94; on the chain gang, 298, 312, 318–20; child labor, critique of, 60–61; Christianity, critique of, 227–60; on class formation, 60, 66, 77–78, 83–84, 87, 105n13; on the color-line, 128–45, 156–59, 167–68; on the complementarity of methodologies, 349–51; conceptual conservatism of, 94, 99; and conflict theory, 302, 330–33, 347; and congregational studies, 346; on the conjugal conditions of African Americans, 54–59, 68, 89–90; on consciousness, 135–36, 139–45; contributions to, 120–45; on the convict-lease system, 293, 298–99, 312–25, 328, 332–33; critical optimism of, 156–57; critical pessimism of, 157; critical race theory, critical white studies, contributions to, 145–68; on the crop-lien system, 65–66, 159, 312–13, 318, 324–25, 328, 333, 347; on democracy, 150–56, 160–63, 202–4, 208–10, 242–43, 246, 274–75, 282–301; on differential justice, 305–9, 319, 323–24, 326, 328–29, 334n2; on disproportionality, 305, 333, 347; on domestic servants, 63–64, 87–88, 188–89, 210–11; double-consciousness, concept of, 128–45; on the double standard of justice, 299, 315, 333; and economic sociology, 339; elitism of, 54, 58, 62, 68–69, 73, 76–77, 86–89, 93–95, 98–99, 126, 197; empirical sociology of, 51, 69–70, 74–76, 96; Eurocentrism of, 29, 31, 54, 58, 62, 68–69, 73–76, 86, 98–99, 126, 197; extramarital affairs of, 221n8; Fisk University, experiences and studies at, 7, 230–31, 260n3; and the German historical school of economics, 339–42, 348, 360n2; and German nationalism, 356, 362n9; and *Gesellschaftwissenschaft*, 339; gift theory of, 109, 128–45, 150–53, 163–64, 167; the Guiding Hundredth, conception of, 280–85; Harvard University, experiences and studies at, 7–9, 70, 95, 231, 339–43, 359n1, 360n3; and historical empiricism, 339; and the historical method, 339–40; historical sociology of, 48–49, 77–88, 110, 162, 168n1, 206, 267–72, 324, 334; humanism of, 109, 123, 135, 140, 165, 241–42, 261, 286, 352–53; and industrial sociology, 9, 49, 98, 312, 327, 356; interpretive elitism of, 77–100, 97; interpretive radicalism of, 69, 77–100; intersectional sociology, contributions to, 175–217; on Islam, 252–53; on Jesus Christ, 228–30, 241–43, 247, 251–57; on Jonah, 227–28; on the Klu Klux Klan, 140, 314; on language, 270–71, 290n2; on legal cynicism, 335n6; liberation sociology of, 74; methodological triangulation, inauguration of, 37, 226, 343–44, 349–50; on miscegenation, 57–59, 116; on "the monogamic ideal," 90–92; on the "mother-idea," 184; on Obe Worship, 235; on Pan-Africanism, 96, 355; on Pan-Negroism, 120; on Paul, 231; the prison industrial complex, early critiques of, 312–15, 318–20, 327–28; and psychology of race, 275–76; public intellectualism of, 127; public sociology, as pioneer of, 127; on race, 107–68; on race-based antiracism, 120–28; on racial class(es), 77–88; on racial intermingling, 115–16; on racial profiling, 307–9; on racial real estate, 157–61; and the Rankean method, 338–39; religious hypocrisy, critique of, 245–46; research methods of, 94–100; on rural education, 59–61; and rural sociology, 50–68; scholarships and fellowships awarded to, 341–42, 360n3; second-sight, concept of, 128–45; on sexual deviance, 90; on the "slave police," 314; on social disorganization, 297, 304, 330–31; social ethics of, 122, 125, 339; and social science, 7–8, 13–14, 18, 68–75, 97–98, 100n1, 136–37, 199–200, 335n9, 339–42, 348–57; sociological empiricism of, 48–49, 98–99; sociological insensitivity of, 65–66; sociological negation of, 3–6, 15, 22, 32–34, 53–55, 84, 113, 207, 226, 349; sociological sensitivity of, 65; and sociology of class, 77–88; and sociology of crime, 293–334; and sociology of culture, 272–80; and sociology of deviance, 88–100; and sociology of disease, 345; and sociology of economics, 90–100; and sociology of education, 265–89; and sociology of the family, 50–68, 88–100; and sociology of gender, 175–217; and sociology of race, 107–68; and sociology of religion, 223–60; on sociology as a science, 1, 7–8, 69–76; and sociology of work, 50–68, 77–100; on soul, 135; on *The Souls of Black Folk*, 129–31; Spencerian sociology, critique of, 48, 51, 70–72, 232; on the "submerged tenth," 77–88, 101n4, 105n13; on the "talented few," 73, 77–88, 94, 106n14; "The Talented Tenth," 42, 88, 214, 266, 268, 280–85; on traditional African religions, 251–52; University of Berlin, experiences and studies at, 8–9, 38–40, 95, 100n1, 338–43, 348–49, 359n1; University of Pennsylvania, experiences and research at, 4–5; and urban sociology, 68–100; the Veil, concept of, 128–45; on Voodooism, 235; on welfare queens, 89; on welfarism, 88–89; on white blindness, 138–42, 150, 155–58, 161, 168; on white-collar crimes, 307; on white forgetfulness, 156–61; on white indebtedness, 144–58; on whiteness, 145–68; on white supremacist sexual violence, 210, 316–17; white supremacy, critique of, 145–68; on the working class, 50–68, 77–88

Du Bois's Dialectics (Rabaka), 15, 283
Dunbar, Charles Francis, 340
Durkheim, Emile, 10, 13, 38, 100n1, 204, 207, 226, 251, 330–31, 337, 343, 349
Dusk of Dawn (Du Bois), 12, 109, 112, 114–15, 122, 124, 199, 215, 230–31, 275, 350
A Dying Colonialism (Fanon), 31

Economic Cooperation Among Negro Americans (Du Bois), 312
Economic Cooperation Among the Negroes of Georgia (Du Bois), 312
"The Economics of the Family" (Du Bois), 62
economic sociology, 339
"The Economy of Manichean Allegory: The Function of Racial Difference in Colonialist Literature" (JanMohamed), 44n11
Edelin, Ramona, 169n4
The Educational Thought of W. E. B. Du Bois (Alridge), 265
"Education in Africa" (Du Bois), 266
"Education and Work" (Du Bois), 266
Edwards, Barrington S., 339, 340, 343, 359n2
Egypt, 164, 252
Ellington, Duke, 129

Ellison, Ralph, 81, 135, 262n6
Ellwood, Charles, 48
Emancipation Proclamation, 6, 66, 77, 81, 146, 151, 236
emancipatory epistemology, 254
"The Enforcement of the Slave Trade Laws" (Du Bois), 297
Enlightenment (European), 25, 169n2
episteme, 17, 29, 30, 44n7
epistemic apartheid, 5, 11-38, 83-84, 97-98, 108, 128, 131, 133, 170n6, 177, 206-7, 226, 254, 259, 321, 329, 331-32, 337-47
epistemic closure, 13, 132, 196, 254
epistemic elasticity, 18
epistemic openness, 28, 254, 355
epistemic reductionism, 36
epistemic unreceptiveness, 196
An Essay on African Philosophical Thought (Gyekye), 169n2
essentialism, 33-34, 125
The Ethiopian Manifesto (Young), 225
ethnocentrism, 125, 148
eugenicist movement, 151
European modernity, 21, 25, 111-12, 118, 146, 148, 167, 169n2, 251
European supremacy, 137
Evolution of the United States (Wright), 51
existentialism, 27
expropriation, 160
extended family, 62, 219n3
Eysenck, Hans, 293

family, 101n5
Fanon, Frantz, 16, 18, 21, 27-28, 31, 43n3, 44n11, 59, 81, 85, 119, 123, 133, 141, 166, 171n9, 192, 270-71, 279, 283, 287-88, 290n2, 291n4
Fauset, Jessie, 221n8
Felder, Cain, 247
feminism, 175-217
Ferguson, Kate, 238-39
Ferri, Enrico, 294
The Field and Function of a Negro College (Du Bois), 266

First Congregational Church of Great Barrington, 227
First National Conference of Colored Women, 181
Fisk Herald, 180
Fisk University, 7, 38, 39, 104n9, 230-31, 234, 243, 260n3, 343
Ford, Henry, 151
"The Forethought" (Du Bois), 134
Foucault, Michel, 18, 25-28, 31, 33, 44n7, 121, 139, 170n6, 209, 338, 361n7
Foucault Live, 44n7
Frankenstein, 153
Frankfurt School, 19, 27, 288, 361n7
Frazier, E. Franklin, 3, 61, 105n14, 304, 346
"The Freedmen's Bureau" (Du Bois), 266
"The Freedom to Learn" (Du Bois), 266
"The Freedom of Womanhood" (Du Bois), 41, 193-94, 209-10, 212, 215, 345
Freiburg University, 8, 339
Freire, Paulo, 273, 286-88
Freud, Sigmund, 19
Friedrich-Wilhelm III Universität, 8
Frobenius, Leo, 164
Fromm, Erich, 19

Gabbidon, Shaun, 294, 304, 307, 310, 328-30, 332, 344
"Galileo Galilei" (Du Bois), 281
Gandhi, Mohandas, 242
Garnet, Henry Highland, 130
Garofalo, Raffaele, 293
Garvey, Marcus, 104n9, 186
Gates, Henry Louis, 56, 57, 291n5
genealogy, 26-27, 37
generic racism, 164
German historical school of economics, 339-42, 348, 360
"German Influence on the Scholarship of W. E. B. Du Bois" (Broderick), 339-40
Gesellschaftwissenschaft, 339
Giddens, Anthony, 204

Giddings, Franklin Henry, 74
The Gift of Black Folk (Du Bois), 109, 113, 150–58, 162, 193, 208, 233, 238, 350
gift of remembering, 156
gift theory, 109, 128–45, 150–53, 163–64, 167
Gilkes, Cheryl, 180–81, 182, 195, 202–5, 208–10
Gillman, Susan, 111, 177–78
Gilman, Charlotte Perkins, 14
Gilroy, Paul, 362n9
global racism, 146–47
Gneist, Rudolph von, 340
Goldberg, David Theo, 119, 121, 123–24, 318
Goldenberg, David, 247
Gordon, Lewis, 13–14, 16–18, 24, 31–33, 135, 219n4, 278–80, 361n5
Gramsci, Antonio, 170n7
Grant, Jacquelyn, 234
Great Barrington, Massachusetts, 6, 189, 227, 230, 295
Green, Dan, 2–3, 55, 307
Greene, Helen, 304
Gregg, Robert, 79
Griggs, Sutton, 104n9
Grimké, Archibald, 106n15
"Grounding with My Sisters: Patriarchy and the Exploitation of Black Women" (Marable), 211
Guglielmo, Thomas, 306
"Guiding Hundredth," 88, 268, 280–85
Gutierrez, Gustavo, 255, 258
Guy-Sheftall, Beverly, 176, 217n1, 219n3
Gyekye, Kwame, 169n2

Habermas, Jürgen, 19, 338, 361n7
"Hail Columbia!" (Du Bois), 202, 215
Haiti, 119, 192, 279
Hall, Stuart, 267
"The Hampton Idea" (Du Bois), 242, 266, 281
Harding, Sandra, 29–32, 195–96
Hare, Bruce, 75
Hare, Robert, 294

Harlem Renaissance, 103, 150, 186, 272, 275
Harper, Frances, 189, 209
Harper's Weekly, 126, 291
Harris, Cheryl, 33, 157
Hart, Albert Bushnell, 8, 39, 338, 340
Harvard Academic Council, 7, 341
"Harvard Daily Themes" (Du Bois), 180, 182
Harvard Historical Monograph Series, 9
Harvard University, 7–9, 38–39, 70, 95, 100n1, 231, 296, 338–43, 359n1, 360n3
Hattery, Angela, 206, 207
Hayes, Rutherford B., 341
Haynes, Stephen, 247
The Health and Physique of the Negro American (Du Bois), 116, 345
Hegel, Georg Wilhelm Friedrich, 19, 277, 339
hegemony, 170n7
Henry Street Settlement, 104n10
hermeneutics, 27, 254
herrenrasse demokratie, 153, 203
"The Higher Education of the Negro" (Du Bois), 266
Hill, Mozell, 3
historical empiricism, 339
historical method, 339, 340
The History of Madness in the Classical Age (Foucault), 25
The History of Sexuality, Vol. 1: The Will to Knowledge (Foucault), 26
The History of Sexuality, Vol. 2: The Use of Pleasure (Foucault), 26
The History of Sexuality, Vol. 3: The Care of the Self (Foucault), 26
Holloway, Jonathan, 75
Hood, Robert, 247
hooks, bell, 82, 204, 220n7, 290n3
The Horizon, 208, 321, 350
Horkheimer, Max, 19
Horne, Gerald, 79
Hoses, Sam, 137, 335n9
Hosmer, Frank Alvin, 7, 295, 296
Howard-Pitney, David, 247
Howard University, 191

Hull House, 96, 104n10
Hull House Maps and Papers (Addams), 69
Huxley, Thomas Henry, 116

ideological hegemony, 170n7
ideological warfare, 171n7
ideologies of gender, 218n2
In Battle for Peace (Du Bois), 230, 348, 350
The Independent, 126, 146
Industrial Revolution, 63, 81
"Insiders and Outsiders: A Chapter in the Sociology of Knowledge" (Merton), 196
institutional racism, 16
instrumental interpretation, 132–33
intellectual desegregation, 24
intellectual esotericism, 351
intellectual historical amnesia, 11–22, 24, 84, 161, 226, 273, 294, 337, 343, 347
intellectual infanticide, 284
intellectual niggerification, 206
intellectual segregation, 23, 27–38
interpretive elitism, 87–100, 197
interpretive radicalism, 69, 77, 86
The Invention of the White Race (Allen), 146
"The Irreligiosity of W. E. B. Du Bois" (Zuckerman), 233
Islam, 30, 251–53

James, C. L. R., 112
James, Joy, 75, 175, 178, 202, 214, 217n1, 220n7, 287–88, 361n7
James, William, 7–9, 39, 340–41
JanMohamed, Abdul, 44n11
John Brown (Du Bois), 233
Johnson, Brian, 223, 260n2
Johnson, Georgia Douglas, 221n8
Johnson, James Weldon, 186
Johnston, Harry, 164
Jones, Mildred Bryant, 221n8

Kahn, Jonathan, 223
Kant, Immanuel, 44n7

Kearney, Belle, 176
Keita, Lansana, 278
Kelley, Florence, 14, 96, 106n15
Kellor, Frances, 14
Keppel, Ben, 75
King, Deborah, 201, 208
King, Martin Luther, 242
King, William, 27
Knights of the White Camelia, 151
Ku Klux Klan, 140, 151, 314, 335n7

Lacassagne, Alexandre, 294
Ladner, Joyce, 75
language, 270–71, 290n2
"The Large and Small-Scale System of Agriculture in the Southern United States, 1840-1890" (Du Bois), 359n1
"Last Message to the World" (Du Bois), 281
Lathrop, Julia, 14
legal cynicism, 335n6
Lemons, Gary, 183, 188, 217n1
Lenz, Max, 340
Lewis, David Levering, 6–7, 52–53, 68–72, 75, 79–81, 136–37, 143, 172, 180, 189, 221n8, 230, 261n5, 291n5, 295, 341, 343
liberation sociology, 74
liberation theology, 248–60
Liberian Order of African Redemption, 253
Life and Labor of the People in London (Booth), 69
Lilly, J. Robert, 332
"A Litany of Atlanta" (Du Bois), 228
The Literary Digest, 126, 291
Locke, Alain, 186, 275
Logan, Rayford, 103n7
Lombroso, Cesare, 293–94
Lorde, Audre, 97, 123, 195, 279
Lott, Tommy, 113, 120
L'Ouveture, Toussaint, 119
Lucal, Betsy, 200
lumpenproletariat, 61, 78, 81, 83, 84, 101n4
Lynch, Michael, 329

lynching, 103n7, 137, 145, 151, 159, 166, 251, 257, 298, 311, 319, 335n9

MacLean, Anne Marion, 14
Malcolm X, 360n2
"Mammies, Matriarchs, and Other Controlling Images" (Collins), 185, 220n7
Manichaeanism, 31, 44n11
Manichean Aesthetics: The Politics of Literature in Colonial Africa (JanMohamed), 44n11
Marable, Manning, 7, 75, 79, 176, 211–12, 227
Marcuse, Herbert, 19, 361n7, 362n10
Martineau, Harriet, 14
Marx, Karl, 10, 12, 13, 19, 38–39, 61, 70–71, 77–78, 82–84, 86, 100n1, 101n4, 204, 207, 332, 338–39, 343, 349, 361n7, 362n10
Marxism, 27, 42, 61, 78, 105, 110, 148, 155, 158, 161, 168, 173n12, 175, 178, 183, 212, 214, 250, 262, 268, 272, 281, 285–88, 353, 355
May, John, 335n8
Mazrui, Ali, 251
McCarthyism, 360n2
McKay, Henry, 297
McKay, Nellie, 176, 183, 217n1, 218n2
McKenzie, Roderick, 345
McLaren, Peter, 286–87
McShane, Marilyn, 331
Mead, George Herbert, 13, 294
Meditations From the Pen of Mrs. Maria Stewart (Stewart), 225
Meier, August, 261n6
Memorial to the Legislature of Georgia on Negro Common Schools (Du Bois), 266
Merton, Robert, 196–98, 331, 347
methodological triangulation, 37–38, 226, 343–45, 349
Middle Passage, 78, 156
Mill, John Stuart, 293
Miller, Kelly, 191–92
Mills, Charles, 147, 149, 167, 291n4

"The Minister" (Du Bois), 242
minstrelism, 103n7
miscegenation, 57–59
"Miscegenation" (Du Bois), 116
The Missionary Review of the World, 126, 312
modernity (European), 21, 25, 111–12, 118, 146, 148, 167, 169n2, 251
Monk, Thelonious, 137
The Moon, 208, 321, 350
Morals and Manners Among Negro Americans (Du Bois), 294, 296, 311–12, 321–28, 346
"The More Things Change, the More They Stay the Same: African American Women and the New Politics of Containment" (Collins), 220n7
Morgan, J. P. (John Pierpont), 242
Morris, Aldon, 127, 130, 210
Morrison, Toni, 135
Moscowitz, Henry, 106n15
Moses, Wilson Jeremiah, 262n9, 362n9
Moyamensing prison, 305

Nashville, Tennessee, 7
The Nation, 126
National American Woman Suffrage Association, 176
National Association for the Advancement of Colored People (NAACP), 105n11, 106n15, 150, 182, 210, 238, 321, 348, 350, 360n2
National Association of Colored Women, 181, 237–38
National Council of Negro Women, 181
National Federation of Afro-American Women, 180
The National Guardian, 209
National League of Colored Women, 102n7
"To the Nations of the World" (Du Bois), 183
"Die Negerfrage in den Vereinigten Staaten" ("The Negro Question in the United States") (Du Bois), 8

The Negro (Du Bois), 116, 163, 350, 353
The Negro American Family (Du Bois), 102, 311
The Negro Artisan (Du Bois), 312
"The Negro in the Black Belt" (Du Bois), 50-51, 101n4, 102n6, 294, 297, 344
The Negro in Business (Du Bois), 312
The Negro Church (Du Bois), 226, 233-38, 252, 346
"The Negro and Crime" (Du Bois), 42, 297-301, 309-10, 312-13
"The Negro Criminal" (Du Bois), 294
"Negro Education" (Du Bois), 266
"The Negroes of Dougherty County, Georgia" (Du Bois), 50, 344
"The Negroes of Farmville, Virginia" (Du Bois), 40, 48-68, 77, 91, 101n2, 102n6, 108, 199, 214, 294, 297-98, 344-45
Negroes in the United States (Wilcox), 48
"The Negro Farmer" (Du Bois), 50, 344
Negroization, 78
"The Negro Landholder of Georgia" (Du Bois), 50, 344
the "Negro Problem," 48, 51, 71-72, 78-80, 102n6, 103n9, 107, 133, 152, 197-98, 246, 283, 309, 340
The Negro Problem: A Series of Articles by Representative American Negroes of Today, 291n5
"The Negro Question in the United States" (Du Bois), 8
The Negro in the South (Du Bois and Washington), 233
"The Negro South and North" (Du Bois), 50
Negro tabula rasa, 342
New Europe, 25
New Haven Negroes: A Social History (Warner), 197
New Negro movement, 63, 91, 102n7, 104n10, 186, 350
The New World, 126
New York Globe, 180, 295
The New York Times Magazine Supplement, 126

Next to the Color-Line: Gender, Sexuality, and W. E. B. Du Bois (Gilman and Weinbaum), 111, 177, 346
Niagara movement, 150, 182, 210, 296, 321, 350, 360
Nietzsche, Friedrich, 153, 361

Odum, Howard, 3
"Of Alexander Crummell" (Du Bois), 131
"Of the Black Belt" (Du Bois), 131
"Of the Culture of White Folk" (Du Bois), 110, 163
"Of the Dawn of Freedom" (Du Bois), 131
"Of the Faith of the Fathers" (Du Bois), 131, 239, 263n9
"Of the Meaning of Progress" (Du Bois), 131
"Of Mr. Booker T. Washington and Others" (Du Bois), 131
"Of the Passing of the First-Born" (Du Bois), 131
"Of the Quest of the Golden Fleece" (Du Bois), 131
"Of the Ruling of Men" (Du Bois), 202-3
"Of the Sons of Master and Man" (Du Bois), 131
"Of the Training of Black Men" (Du Bois), 131
"Of the Wings of Atalanta" (Du Bois), 131
Oldenberg, Karl, 340
Olson, Joel, 173n12
Omi, Michael, 119
ontology, 141, 200
Onwudiwe, Ihekobowa, 329
The Order of Things: An Archaeology of the Human Sciences (Foucault), 25
Outlaw, Lucius, 20, 101n2
Outline of Practical Sociology (Wright), 51
The Outlook, 126
Ovington, Mary White, 106n15

Page, Thomas Nelson, 188
A Pageant of Seven Decades (Du Bois), 172n10

Pan-Africanism, 27, 96, 108–9, 120, 122, 163–65, 172n10, 215, 261, 279, 348, 350, 352
Pan-Negroism, 120
Pareto, Vilfredo, 13
Park, Robert, 4, 127, 291n5, 294, 337, 345
Parsons, Elsie Clews, 14
Pateman, Carole, 195
Penn, Everette, 329
"The People of Peoples and Their Gifts to Men" (Du Bois), 109
phenomenology, 27
The Philadelphia Negro (Du Bois), 2, 47–50, 68–100, 155–57, 191, 297–309
"The 'Philadelphia Negro' Then and Now" (Zuberi), 4
Philadelphia Settlement, 96
"The Philosophical Foundations and Implications of William Edward Burghardt Du Bois's Social Ethic" (Edelin), 169n4
Phylon: A Review of Race and Culture, 3, 208, 350
Pitts, Khalid, 335n8
Plessy v. Ferguson, 24, 103n7
Political Science Quarterly, 126
postmodernism, 12, 16, 19, 133, 148, 169n2, 250, 254, 267, 279, 286, 353, 356
Prayers for Dark People (Du Bois), 231, 234
prime property, 161
Prisoners and Juvenile Delinquents in Institutions, 323
prison industrial complex, 299, 312–15, 318–20, 328
prison industry, 313
Prison Notebooks (Gramsci), 171n7
"The Problem of Amusement" (Du Bois), 239, 243, 297, 303
"The Problem of Negro Crime" (Du Bois), 309–28
"A Program for Land-Grant Colleges" (Du Bois), 266
"A Program of Social Reform" (Du Bois), 297
"A Program for a Sociological Society" (Du Bois), 47–48
Progressive Era/Progressivism, 104n10
proletariat, 78, 81, 83–84, 110, 155, 162, 362n10
Prophet, Elizabeth, 221n8
psychology, 20, 31, 128, 141, 275–76, 294
public intellectualism, 41, 127, 179–80, 208–9, 350
public sociology, 127
Puritan ethics, 227

Raboteau, Albert, 234
race, 107–68
race-based antiracism, 120–28
"Race, Culture, Identity: Misunderstood Connections" (Appiah), 168n1
"Race Friction Between Black and White" (Du Bois), 110, 163
Race Men (Carby), 219n2
racial class, 77–88
racial colonization, 10, 16, 64, 78, 95, 136, 141–42, 234, 240–48, 273–75, 288–89
The Racial Contract (Mills), 167, 291n4
racial criminalization, 295, 297–328
racial essentialism, 33–34, 125
racial intermingling, 115
racial polity, 148–49
racial profiling, 307–9
racial state, 119
The Racial State (Goldberg), 124
racial theft, 113, 151, 155, 158–62
racism, 107–68
Racist Culture (Goldberg), 121
racist science, 113
radical humanism, 109, 123, 135, 140, 165, 173n13, 261, 286
Rampersad, Arnold, 101n2, 131–33, 189, 227–28, 232, 352–53
Ranke, Leopold von, 339
Rankean method, 338–39
rape, 210, 299–300, 316–17, 323, 326

Ratzel, Friedrich, 116
Ray, Ethel, 221n8
"Reclaiming a Du Boisian Perspective on Racial Attitudes" (Bobo), 337
Reconstruction, 134, 145, 146, 151–53, 298, 311, 314, 320, 343
Reed, Adolph, 104n10, 359n2
Reid, Ira De Augustine, 3
"The Relation of the Negroes to the Whites of the South" (Du Bois), 50
"Religion in the South" (Du Bois), 244
religious apartheid, 246–47
religious economy, 224, 236
Remond, Charles Lenox, 152, 190, 216
researcher bias, 196
"The Revelation of Saint Orgne the Damned" (Du Bois), 243
reverse racism, 114
revolutionary decolonization, 123, 143, 351–52
revolutionary humanism, 123, 352
revolving-door community/culture, 54
Ritzer, George, 14
Roberts, Deotis, 256
Robinson, Cedric, 353
Rosetta Stone, 50, 68
Ross, Edward Alsworth, 74, 337
Rowland, Christopher, 249
Royce, Josiah, 7, 39, 340
Rudwick, Elliott, 4, 262n6, 353
Ruffin, Josephine St. Pierre, 41, 178–82, 189, 209
rural education, 59–61
Russell, Katheryn, 329
Russian Revolution, 229, 359n2

Saint-Arnaud, Pierre, 69–76, 83
Santayana, George, 7, 39, 340
Sartre, Jean-Paul, 34
Schmoller, Gustav von, 8, 39, 83, 339–42, 348
Scudder, Evarts, 227
Second Industrial Revolution, 63
segregation, 23–25, 33, 35, 132–33, 141–42, 145–46, 246–47, 265, 276, 298–305, 337–47

semiotics, 27
separate but equal, 24, 66, 103
Serequeberhan, Tsenay, 269, 279
Sering, Max, 340
settlement movement, 104n10
"Sex, Race, and the Matrices of Desire in an Anti-Black World" (Gordon), 195
"Sex and Racism" (Du Bois), 202, 215
"Sexism and the Black Female Slave Experience" (hooks), 220n7
The Sexual Contract (Pateman), 195
Shadd, Mary Ann, 192
"The Sharecropping System in Lowndes County, Alabama" (Du Bois), 50, 344
Shaw, Clifford, 297
Shelley, Mary, 153
Shivery, Louie, 221n8
Silent South: Together with the Freedman's Case in Equity and the Convict-Lease System (Cable), 334n1
Simmel, Georg, 13, 226, 251
Sketches of the Higher Classes of Colored Society in Philadelphia (Willson), 105n13
Slave Culture (Stuckey), 240
Slave Religion (Raboteau), 234
Small, Albion, 337
Smith, Earl, 206
Smith, John David, 247
Social Darwinism, 71–72, 76, 101n1
social disorganization theory, 330, 347
socialism, 109, 155, 165, 284–87, 348
"Social Planning for the Negro, Past and Present" (Du Bois), 109
"Social Structure and Anomie" (Merton), 347
sociological negation, 3–6, 15, 22, 32–34, 53–55, 84, 113, 207, 226, 349
"Sociology Hesitant" (Du Bois), 338
"Sociology and Industry in Southern Education" (Du Bois), 50
sociology of sociology, 6, 10

Some Efforts of American Negroes for Their Own Social Betterment (Du Bois), 48, 294
Some Notes on Negro Crime (Du Bois), 293, 309–28
"The Sorrow Songs" (Du Bois), 131, 143
soul-lives, 130, 134
The Souls of Black Folk (Du Bois), 8, 24, 40, 58, 107, 109, 113, 127–45, 150–55, 171n7, 197–98, 266
"The Souls of Black Men" (Carby), 218n2
"The Souls of Black Women Folk in the Writings of W. E. B. Du Bois" (McKay), 176
The Souls of W. E. B. Du Bois (Blum and Young), 223
"The Souls of White Folk" (Du Bois), 40, 110, 113, 145–68
South Africa, 146
The Southern Workman, 126
Soviet Union, 229
"The Spawn of Slavery: The Convict Lease-System in the South" (Du Bois), 50, 312
The Spelman Messenger, 126
Spencer, Herbert, 13, 48, 51, 71–72, 101n1, 232
Staatwissenschaften, 342
standpoint epistemology, 195–96, 200, 201, 205
standpoint theory, 29–31, 37, 183, 195
Starr, Ellen Gates, 104n10
Stewart, James, 349–51, 361n5
Stewart, Maria, 209, 225
Still, Mary, 238
Stowe, Harriet Beecher, 193
strain theory, 309, 330–31
"The Strivings of the Negro People" (Du Bois), 48
strong objectivity, 29
Stuckey, Sterling, 240
"The Study of the Negro Problems" (Du Bois), 40, 48, 109, 297, 309, 338, 344, 354

"subjugated knowledge," 139, 170n6, 183, 196, 209
"submerged tenth," 77–88, 101n4, 105n13
"Suffering Suffragettes" (Du Bois), 215
Sundquist, Eric, 187
"The Superior Race" (Du Bois), 163
The Suppression of the African Slave Trade to the United States of America, 1638–1870 (Du Bois), 8–9, 297, 302, 359n1
Sutherland, Edwin, 294

Talbot, Marion, 14
"talented few," 73, 77–88, 94, 106n14
"The Talented Tenth" (Du Bois), 42, 88, 214, 266, 268, 280–85
"The Talented Tenth Memorial Address" (Du Bois), 283–84
Taussig, Frank, 7, 340, 341
Terrell, Mary Church, 182, 209, 238
theodicean openness, 250–51
Thomas, William, 294, 337
Thorpe, Earl, 75
Tom Brown at Fisk (Du Bois), 180
Tönnies, Ferdinand, 13
Topinard, Paul, 293
To Wake the Nations: Race in the Making of American Literature (Sundquist), 187
Toward the African Revolution (Fanon), 31
Tradition and Modernity: Philosophical Reflections of the African Experience (Gyekye), 169n2
Transcending the Talented Tenth (James), 175, 287
transdisciplinarity, 6–23, 27–29, 37–38, 97–98, 131–32, 176–78, 337–57
"The Transubstantiation of the White Poor" (Du Bois), 155
Treitschke, Heinrich von, 8, 39, 339–42
Truth, Sojourner, 152, 184, 192–93, 209, 237, 238
Tubman, Harriet, 152, 184, 192, 237, 238

Turner, Nat, 304, 314
Tuskegee Machine, 126
"The Twelfth Census and the Negro Problems" (Du Bois), 345

ugly beauty, 137
"The Uncompleted Argument: Du Bois and the Illusion of Race" (Appiah), 168n1
University of Berlin, 8, 38–39, 70, 100n1, 231, 338–42, 348, 359n1
University of Chicago, 4, 38–39, 329
University of Massachusetts, 340
University of Pennsylvania, 4, 9, 12
Up From Slavery (Washington), 261n5

Veblen, Thorstein, 13
Villard, Oswald Garrison, 106n15

W. E. B. Du Bois and American Political Thought (Reed), 104n10
W. E. B. Du Bois: American Prophet (Blum), 223, 262n7
W. E. B. Du Bois: Biography of a Race, 1868–1919 (Lewis), 189, 212n8
W. E. B. Du Bois: Black Radical Democrat (Marable), 176
"W. E. B. Du Bois: A Case in the Sociology of Sociological Negation" (Green and Driver), 2–3
W. E. B. Du Bois on Crime and Justice (Gabbidon), 328–30
W. E. B. Du Bois: The Fight for Equality and the American Century, 1919–1963 (Lewis), 221n8
W. E. B. Du Bois Papers, 360n2
"W. E. B. Du Bois and Religion" (Aptheker), 227
"W. E. B. Du Bois and 'The Talented Tenth'" (Gates), 291n5
W. E. B. Du Bois: Toward Agnosticism, 1868–1934 (Johnson), 223, 260n2
"W. E. B. Du Bois's Urban Sociology: Reflections on African American Quality of Life in Philadelphia" (Wortham), 37
Wagner, Adolf, 8, 39, 339, 341–42

Wald, Lillian, 104n10
Walker, David, 130, 225
Wallace, Michelle, 184
Walling, William English, 106n15
Ward, Lester Frank, 48, 74
Waring, Nora, 221n8
Warner, Robert Austin, 197–99
Washington, Booker T., 83, 104n9, 126, 131, 150, 186, 261n5, 266, 292n5
Washington, Joseph, 247
Waters, Kristin, 75
Watts, Jerry, 75
Webb, Beatrice Potter, 14
Weber, Marianne, 14
Weber, Max, 8, 10, 13–14, 19, 38–39, 66, 77–84, 100n1, 204, 207, 226, 251, 332, 337, 339, 343, 349
Weiler, Kathleen, 287
Weinbaum, Alys Eve, 111, 177–78
welfare queens, 89
welfarism, 89
Wells, Ida B., 14, 83, 106n15, 180, 182, 189, 193, 209, 238
West, Cornel, 21, 125
"What Intellectual Training Is Doing for the Negro" (Du Bois), 266
Wheatley, Phillis, 184
"'When and Where [We] Enter': In Search of a Feminist Forefather—Reclaiming the Womanist Legacy of W. E. B. Du Bois" (Lemons), 218n2
white blindness, 138–42, 150, 155–58, 161, 168
White Citizen's Party, 151
"White Co-Workers" (Du Bois), 110, 163
"The White Folk Have a Right to Be Ashamed" (Du Bois), 163
white guilt, 161
Whitehead, John, 246–47
white hypervisibility, 134
white indebtedness, 144, 152, 156–58
white middle class, 49, 52–58, 64, 68, 72–73, 87–94, 99
white privilege, 136, 146, 323, 327–28, 347

"The White Proletariat in Alabama, Georgia, and Florida" (Du Bois), 163
white supremacist sexual violence, 316–17
white supremacist sorcery, 157–58
white supremacy, 4, 145–68
White Women's Christ and Black Women's Jesus (Grant), 234
"The White Worker" (Du Bois), 110, 155, 163
"The White World" (Du Bois), 110, 163
"Whither Now and Why?" (Du Bois), 265
Wilberforce University, 9, 12
Wilcox, Walter Francis, 48
Williams, Frank, 331
Willson, Joseph, 105n13
"Will the Church Remove the Color-Line?" (Du Bois), 223, 246
Wilmore, Gayraud, 253
Winant, Howard, 119, 128, 318–19
Wiredu, Kwasi, 272, 273, 275
Wirth, Lewis, 337
womanism, 27, 188, 355–56
"Woman Suffrage" (Du Bois), 184, 191, 202, 209
Women's Era, 180
Women's Era Club, 102n7, 180

Woods, Robert, 70
"The Work of Negro Women in Society" (Du Bois), 202, 215, 221n9
The World and Africa (Du Bois), 109, 164, 208, 215, 252, 350
World War I, 4
"'The World Was Thinking Wrong About Race': *The Philadelphia Negro* and Nineteenth Century Science" (Bay), 97–98, 100n1
The World's Work, 126
Wortham, Robert, 37, 226, 236, 310, 344
The Wretched of the Earth (Fanon), 31, 166, 171n9, 283
Wright, Carroll Davidson, 51
Wright, Earl, 3, 294, 310, 344
Wright, Richard, 81

Young, Jason, 223, 251
Young, Robert Alexander, 130, 225
Young, Vernetta, 304

Zinn, Maxine Baca, 201
Znaniecki, Florian, 294
Zola, Émile François, 261n5
Zuberi, Tufuku, 4
Zuckerman, Phil, 3–5, 95–96, 225–26, 233

About the Author

Reiland Rabaka is an associate professor of Africana studies in the Department of Ethnic Studies at the University of Colorado at Boulder, where he is also an affiliate professor in the Women and Gender Studies Program and a research fellow at the Center for Studies of Ethnicity and Race in America (CSERA). His ongoing research interests include history, philosophy, and methodology of the human sciences; Africana intellectual and cultural history; history of race; politics of race; sociology of race; psychology of race; anthropology of race; philosophy of race; critical race theory; critical white studies; feminist theory; sociology of gender; postcolonial studies; radical politics; critical social theory; critical pedagogy; sociology of education; sociology of religion; and liberation theology. Included among his regular teaching topics are black abolitionism, the black women's club movement, the New Negro movement, the Harlem Renaissance, Pan-Africanism, negritude, black Nationalism, black Marxism, the civil rights movement, the black power movement, the black women's liberation movement, black liberation theology, Du Bois studies, Fanon studies, critical race theory, critical white studies, hip hop studies, and intersectional critical social theory (race, gender, class, and sexuality studies). His research has been published in *Journal of African American Studies, Journal of Black Studies, Western Journal of Black Studies, Africana Studies Annual Review, Africalogical Perspectives, Handbook of Black Studies, Ethnic Studies Review, Jouvert: A Journal of Postcolonial Studies,* and *Journal of Southern Religion,* among others. Professor Rabaka is the author of *W. E. B. Du Bois and the Problems of the Twenty-First Century* (2007); *Du Bois's Dialectics: Black Radical Politics and the Reconstruction of Critical Social Theory* (2008); *Africana Critical Theory: Reconstructing the Black Radical Tradition, from W. E. B. Du Bois and C. L. R. James to Frantz Fanon* and *Amilcar Cabral* (2009); *Forms of Fanonism: Frantz Fanon's Critical Theory and the Dialectics of Decolonization* (2010); and *The Souls of White Folk: W. E. B. Du Bois and Critical White Studies* (forthcoming). He is, in addition, the editor of *W. E. B. Du Bois: A Critical Reader* (2010), which is the first volume of critical commentary exclusively devoted to scholarship on Du Bois's pioneering contributions to the discourse and development of sociology. Also, he is the coeditor (along with Arturo Aldama, Elisa Facio, and Daryl Maeda) of *Enduring Legacies: Ethnic Histories and Cultures of Colorado* (forthcoming), which is the first anthology of critical commentary exclusively devoted to the discourse and development of race, gender, and class studies in Colorado and the wider American West. His research has been recognized with several awards, including the W. E. B. Du Bois-Anna Julia Cooper Award and the Cheikh Anta Diop Award. He has collected data, conducted archival research, and lectured extensively both nationally and internationally, and has been the recipient of numerous community service citations, teaching awards, and research fellowships.

E 185.97 .D73 R322 2010
Rabaka, Reiland, 1972-
Against epistemic apartheid

JUL 2 0 2010